Revenge Tragedies

THE SPANISH TRAGEDY	by Thomas Kyd
HAMLET	by William Shakespeare
THE REVENGER'S TRAGEDY	by Cyril Tourneur
THE MAID'S TRAGEDY	by Francis Beaumont and John Fletcher

Renaissance titles from College Publishing

Sir Philip Sidney's An Apology for Poetry
and Astrophil and Stella: *Texts and Contexts*
edited by Peter C. Herman of San Diego State University

Revenge Tragedies

Edited by
Bente A. Videbæk
The State University of New York at Stony Brook

College Publishing
Glen Allen, Virginia

College Publishing books
are printed on acid-free paper

ISBN: 0967912156
Library of Congress Card Number: 2003100165

College Publishing
12309 Lynwood Drive, Glen Allen, VA 23059
T (804) 364-8410 F (804) 364-8408
collegepub@mindspring.com

And if *any* mischief follow, then thou shalt give life for life, Eye for eye, tooth for tooth, hand for hand, foot for foot, Burning for burning, wound for wound, stripe for stripe.

(King James Bible, Exodus 21.23-25)

To me belongeth vengeance, and recompense; their foot shall slide in due time . . .

(King James Bible, Deuteronomy 32.35)

Dearly beloved, avenge not yourselves, but rather give place unto wrath: for it is written, VENGEANCE IS MINE; I WILL REPAY, saith the Lord.

(King James Bible, Romans 12.19)

Wise sir, do not grieve. It is always better
to avenge dear ones than to indulge in mourning.

(Beowulf, ll. 1383-84, trans. S. Heaney)

'Tis done, and now my soul shall sleep in rest.
Sons that revenge their father's blood are blest.

(Marston, *Antonio's Revenge*, V.iii.114-15)

Melina: Greek women, like Elektra, always avenge their loved ones.

(007 — For Your Eyes Only, 1981)

Grail Knight: He chose poorly . . .

(Indiana Jones and The Last Crusade, 1989)

Commodus: Slave! You will remove your helmet and tell me your name!
Maximus: My name is Maximus Desmus Meridius, Commander of the Armies of the North, General of the Felix Legions; loyal servant to the true emperor, Marcus Aurelius; father to a murdered son, husband to a murdered wife, and I will have my vengeance in this life or the next.

(Gladiator, 2000)

El Lupo/The Wolf: Well, it seems we're both willing to kill for a cause, so what's the difference between you and I?
Gordy Brewer: The difference is — I'm just gonna kill *you*.

(Collateral Damage, 2002)

In Memoriam
J. L. Styan, dear friend and mentor,
who passed away July 1, 2002.

I will always keep you with me.

Revenge Tragedies

List of Illustrations

To Students and Colleagues

It has always been my hope to see a series of Renaissance drama textbooks featuring "Shakespeare in Context." Shakespeare has always been the love of my working life. However, the more Renaissance courses I have taught, the more I have felt the need to see The Bard presented in the context of others than himself. After all, Shakespeare wrote in the same developing cultural environment as his fellow dramatists, and many values and themes are shared among playwrights who can conveniently illuminate each other's interpretations of their culture. I decided to teach "revenge tragedy" one semester quite some time ago, and though I could easily find many single editions of the plays I wanted, I had trouble finding a textbook spanning sufficient time to demonstrate what I had in mind; I had no luck at all finding Shakespeare in any company but his own. I have long wished to help create such a textbook, and finally here it is, spanning from Kyd to Beaumont and Fletcher, from Elizabeth I to James I, from the beginnings of English revenge tragedy to the point where revenge and domestic tragedy begin to merge.

I have edited and annotated with the classroom in mind. All notes are footnotes rather than endnotes, and I have possibly sinned on the side of glossing more than strictly necessary in the hopes of avoiding student frustration; also, I have tried to keep my introductory remarks short. At the same time I have attempted to keep my own critical inclinations as neutral as possible; as instructors, we all have our critical preferences, and I myself like to meet my students presenting things my way. But I find it is impossible to introduce the plays without some interpretation. I have also tried to keep the balance between excessive faithfulness to the text and excessive "doctoring" of it. When faced with the choice, I have chosen the longer variation of the text. There is no such thing as *the* final text of any Renaissance playwright's work, as the plays went through many stages and many hands before they reached publication. Additions in later editions may reflect the playwrights' intentions or a variation in taste. However, I would like the students using this volume to have the fullest text possible.

Spelling and punctuation have been modernized to make the reading experience more pleasant. This may sometimes yield an extra "foot" in the line of blank verse; please consider the ending "-ed," for example, as either a syllable in its own right or not, as fits the meter. Tourneur, for one, is creative with the word "duke," which fluctuates between one and two syllables within the same speech. I have mixed and matched a large variety of Quarto and Folio editions, creating the text I find most readable, comprehensive, and interesting. Other editors of more scholarly volumes should be consulted for thoughts about the merit of various early editions of the plays; I have seen no reason to duplicate their work. Stage directions have been kept as close to the original as possible, but as they are few and far between, I have sometimes taken the liberty of adding to them, again to help the reader. Still, most stage directions are obvious and embedded in the text — nobody would talk about being on his or her knees if not actually kneeling! The "aside," though, is a Renaissance convention which may be unfamiliar to twenty-first century playgoers and readers, and so I have added stage directions for these.

I hope the glossary and context section will be of help. I would welcome suggestions for additions to the glossary, more texts-in-context, and especially websites any reader has found helpful, to add to this book.

Bente Videbæk

Introduction

> *Every station bookstall shows our fascination with revenge. In the crime section,* Vendetta *rubs shoulders with* A Suitable Vengeance. *Providing more in the way of action is a thriller called* Wild Justice. *Over on the newspaper rack, the theme is equally prominent. Vicious reciprocations are meat and drink to the tabloids, while upmarket broadsheets run pieces headed 'Revenge is for losers', 'Getting your own back can hurt'. One purpose of* Revenge Tragedy *is to show that there is nothing new in all this.*
>
> — John Kerrigan, *Revenge Tragedy*, 1996

Revenge and Revenge Tragedy

We first find instances of revenge tragedy in the plays of ancient Greece and Rome. In the English Renaissance, interested as people were in these ancient cultures, revenge tragedy once more came into *vogue*. The Roman philosopher and playwright Seneca was first to be translated into English, and his revenge plays were an inspiration for Thomas Kyd, whose *The Spanish Tragedy* in turn became influential.

Seneca's *Thyestes*[1] is possibly his most influential revenge tragedy upon the English tradition. It features the ghost of Tantalus, who is horribly punished in the Underworld[2] for killing his son Pelops and serving his flesh to the gods. Fury, either rage personi-

---

[1] An highly readable and excellent new translation can be found in *Seneca: The Tragedies*, ed. and trans. David R. Slavitt.

[2] Tantalus is punished with immense thirst which he cannot slake, standing up to his chin in a pool of water which recedes when he tries to drink, and perpetual hunger which he cannot satisfy, because the fruits on the branches above him shrink from his hand.

fied or an avenging Fury, forces him back to earth to goad his family to further outrage; Tantalus complies:

> Whatever space
> is not yet filled in the land of the damned, whatever
> cell is unassigned by the terrible judges,
> my children and their children shall lay claim to
> with the right of terrible wrongs, so long as my house,
> Pelop's damnable house, stains the light
> that assaults my vision.

(17-23)

Fury elaborates:

> Your grandson Atreus sits
> brooding now the cloudy thoughts that will stain
> the ground with blood . . .
>   . . . Goad them on:
> in hatred and in lust, they finger the hilts of their swords,
> warming their passions, savage, blind, and mad—
> a terrible thing in rulers.

(59-61; 82-85)

Tantalus claims to be incapable of carrying out what Fury dictates after all:

> I have learned
> to be torture's victim, not its henchman. I cannot
> bear it that I have become a visitation,
> a pestilence infecting my grandchildren
> and then through them the city at large . . .
>   . . . I shall defy
> the Fates and Furies, will warn them myself, speak out
> to keep their hands from such an evil thing.

(85-94)

But of course Fury wins out, and a bloodbath ensues.

Atreus, Pelop's son and king of Argos, is planning spectacular revenge on his brother Thyestes. He believes a king has absolute right to do anything he wants, marking himself as a tyrant: "The point of being a king / is exactly this: that whatever the people cannot / praise in your actions, they have to endure" (207-209). His brother has seduced his wife, and stolen the golden fleece,[3] and Atreus is not certain who his children's father is in his rage. He plans to make Thyestes the "weapon" of his revenge (259); remembering how Procne slaughtered her son as revenge for the rape of her sister Philomela and served him to her rapist husband, he decides to put a similar scheme into place:

> . . . I will fill
>
> Thyestes' belly full. Let the father tear
> the flesh from his sons' bodies and let him drink
> the blood of his blood and gnaw the bone of his bone.
> . . . Then he will hate himself
> with something like my own hot hatred.

(279-85)

He sends his own children to invite Thyestes' three to a reconciliation of the family, and to use the children's pleas to persuade their father. When asked by the Attendant if he would let his children take part in such schemes, he answers that the throne corrupts anyway, so why not learn young; and at any rate they are "born evil, heirs of an evil house,/ whether they're his or mine" (316-318).

---

[3] The ram's skin Jason was sent to fetch from Colchis; there he was set more tests, which he finally accomplished with the help of Medea, enchantress and daughter of the King of Colchis. According to Atreus in *Thyestes*, this fleece is a symbol of "all our power" and will "keep us secure on the throne" (228-230).

Thyestes is eager to be reconciled and arrives with his children; deviously, his brother offers to share the throne and power, and Thyestes believes him. The people are delighted at this *rapprochement*, but in the midst of their celebrating they are told that Atreus has sacrificed Thyestes' children with all due ritual, then butchered and roasted them, and served them to their father. He now feels all-powerful, like a god (910-913). When Thyestes asks for his real treasure in life, his sons, Atreus brings him their heads on a platter (1003-1004). When asked why he went to this extreme, he answers, "Because they were yours" (1109); a vengeful mind needs no other excuse. The play ends with them mutually laying curses on each other's house.

One Chorus member, however, sees revenge as a necessary cleansing that the gods must have:

> Perhaps the gods are only preparing
> that dreadful cleansing they have it in mind
> to visit upon us. One learns to long
> for such a conclusion, when every blade
> of grass is an outrage, a green affront.
> One wants the satisfaction of seeing
> justice done. However oppressive
> the penalties are, the world deserves
> more and worse. The life we hate
> wants some extravagant extirpation.
>
>   (862-871)

Seneca shows us a violence that strikes modern readers as gratuitous and disturbing, even inundated as we are with violence in films and literature. It is not the actual killing that wrenches us, however; it is the dismemberment and violation of innocence, the violation of family ties, the moral abasement of the avenger, and, not least, the absence of intervention from any deity. Seneca forces us to ask ourselves whether there are any gods, or whether they are of our own making, sprung from our need to create sense of our lives and our world. For if there were gods, would they not feel a need to intervene in a situation like this? Would they not be good? Should they not care about us? And the question of the gods aside, is there a bar to man's cruelty and drive to satisfy his own urges at any cost? The moral universe of *Thyestes* is questionable to put it mildly. Possibly this should not surprise us; Seneca was tutor to the emperor Nero and saw much random cruelty in his time, culminating in an order to commit suicide, with which he immediately complied. His plays may well to some extent be a commentary on his own world.

Of course Christian morality and ethics in the Renaissance must see revenge in a different light than the ancient Romans did. Seneca's Atreus, like Saxo's pagan Viking, Amlet,[4] has no qualms about the concept of blood revenge; Amlet is even socially and culturally obliged to seek compensation, preferably a life, for his father's murder. In Renaissance society, a strong, Christian message as well as obedience to the law of the land have altered the picture. If individual citizens of a highly structured society take the law into their own hands and administer "justice" as they see fit, chaos will ensue. If a crime such as theft, assault, or murder has been committed, the correct approach is to take one's case to court and let the law of the land prevail. Should the decision of the court go against the plaintiff, the Bible advises us to turn the other cheek and let the Lord judge the miscreant.

Public revenge by way of the courts was seen as an acceptable way to obtain justice for injuries suffered;[5] however, public revenge was not always to be had. Where tyranny can be defined as "law without justice," private revenge can be defined as "justice without law." All four tragedies in this volume present us with an

---

[4] The Danish source for *Hamlet*.

[5] For contemporary views of revenge, public and private, see the "Texts in Context" section of this book.

injustice committed by somebody unreachable by the law. In *The Spanish Tragedy*, Hieronimo, himself a staunch upholder of publicly obtained justice, finds that a prince and a nephew to the King have murdered his son and now bar his access to the King, the one who embodies and administers the law. He is thus forced to take private revenge, devising his own plot and acting himself. He has a witness to the murder in Bel-imperia, who joins her quest for revenge with his; as a woman and facing the same obstacles as Hieronimo, she has no other option but obtaining assistance with private revenge. Hamlet never contemplates public revenge. His father's Ghost demands revenge, and Hamlet promises to carry this out. His deliberation and hesitation is caused by his basic human decency, and moreover he has only the Ghost's word and his own feelings to support the claim that Claudius is indeed a murderer. Vindice of *The Revenger's Tragedy* also has a murder to avenge, and again this murder is committed by a corrupt, reigning duke. And though the King in *The Maid's Tragedy* commits no murder in the accepted sense, he plans, cuckoo fashion, to plant his bastards as Amintor's sons, effectively ending his bloodline and inheritance, and has no qualms about "murdering" Evadne's honor and Aspatia's future in pursuit of his own lust. Again, public revenge is unobtainable.

All four avengers are or have been admirable people, but thoughts of revenge, let alone the deed itself, have a corroding effect on morals. We are allowed to witness Hieronimo's every step as he deserts the sober principles he has lived by his entire life, and we suffer with him as he is reduced to embracing senseless bloodshed. Vindice's corruption is already well advanced when we meet him, but close contact with the greater corruption of the court accelerates his descent. Melantius is convinced of the justice of his actions to the last, but the cost of his revenge is so great that he sees death as the sole path he can take. Hamlet is the only one who leaves the audience with a sense that his moral universe could be salvaged, but his personality has been severely altered in his quest for revenge.

It is interesting to trace the development of the revenge tragedy genre from Thomas Kyd's Elizabethan world, which is highly moral with heroic ideals, and which sees the avenger's moral plight as a test of his spirit, to Beaumont and Fletcher's Jacobean society and its deep fascination with romance, gratuitous violence, sensationalism, and psychological twists. Though the theater reflects a changing society and delivers to the public what the public wants, still certain basic traits remain stable. From the Renaissance to the present day, revenge has captured the interest of readers, theater audiences, and now moviegoers. Much of our fascination with revenge probably stems from our ability to empathize. After all, who among us has never felt the urge to retaliate? And who has better cause to avenge than a son whose father was murdered, or a friend and brother who sees his friend's and sister's honor dragged through the dirt because of a corrupt leader? We easily identify with a quest for justice in a corrupt universe that makes a mockery of law and decency. Still, witnessing the deterioration of the avenger, often to a point where he becomes morally identical with the target of his revenge, makes us pause and reflect. Private revenge satisfies some deep urge in us all, but it may be better not to indulge in it if moral corruption is the price to be exacted.

The Development of Revenge Tragedy

Many Senecan elements, or "ingredients" as it were, find their way into Renaissance revenge tragedy, where the demands of changing times reshape them to become meaningful in their new setting. One of these is the presence of a ghost. Tantalus' ghost is the first character to enter in *Thyestes*. He seems belched up from the Underworld to witness the havoc his own wrongdoings wreak upon his world, for in Seneca's plays transgression is a spreading stain, tainting not only the guilty one, but his family and community as well. "The ghost watching" became one of the staples in Renaissance revenge tragedy, but it developed and changed during its journey.

The Spanish Tragedy by Kyd opens on the Ghost of Andrea, a man killed in battle, who has been returned from the Underworld by Proserpina, accompanied by Revenge, to witness the cleansing of the corrupt world he inhabited. Kyd lets the Ghost become a frame; Andrea and Revenge remain on stage, a "double audience" along with the spectators and a constant reminder that we know the promised end. Like Tantalus, Andrea's ghost is more a catalyst than a participant; he needs to find his fitting place in the Underworld, and only a setting to rights of his own world will accomplish this. At play's end he is given the disposal of friend and foe alike, and devises exquisite, eternal torture for his enemies, finally obtaining the justice he has sought. In *The Spanish Tragedy*, the tie to the classical Underworld is clear.

Shakespeare's *Hamlet* also has a Ghost, but one of a different stamp. This ghost also has returned from an underworld, but this time one with Christian connotations. His description of his days closely resembles Catholic Purgatory, and no wonder. There was only about half a century between Henry VIII's reformation of the English church and the writing of *Hamlet*, and ideas such as the torments of Purgatory and the existence of ghosts coming back to admonish the living capture the imagination wonderfully; ghosts also make for excellent "special effects" on stage. Unlike Andrea's, this ghost boldly thrusts himself into the world of the living to demand revenge of his son. He is no mere figment of Hamlet's imagination, for three other people, a scholar and two sober watchmen, see him, and Horatio recognizes him as Hamlet of Denmark. Still, young Hamlet is the only one the ghost actively interacts with; he is an entity much different from Andrea's passively observing ghost. Another, very dissimilar reminder from the world beyond reaches out to Hamlet; in V.i he becomes reconciled to death and decay through the skull of his childhood companion, Yorick the Jester. Where his father's Ghost creates a turmoil of uncertainty within Hamlet (Is the Ghost a true ghost or a demon? If I do what the Ghost demands, will my actions damn my soul?),

Yorick's passive, undemanding skull allows Hamlet to not only confront the fact of change and decay, but also to realize that memory of the living can make the horrible reality of death easier to bear.

The Revenger's Tragedy by Tourneur caters to an audience whose tastes have begun changing. The focus, from Elizabethan to Jacobean times, is shifting. Where Elizabethan revenge tragedy is highly moral in nature, that of Jacobean times moves towards the contemplation of a morally questionable universe and becomes increasingly interested in the more lurid aspects of human nature. The ghost is no longer a spiritual entity; it has been turned into a concrete, tangible, visible object; but to those who understand it, its "ghost" is present and cries out for revenge. Vindice meets us holding the skull of Gloriana, his betrothed wife, whose purity caused the old Duke to have her killed when she resisted his sexual advances. The avenger here sets out to cleanse society of moral taint, and Gloriana is with him, playing an active part, when the Duke meets his end.

The Maid's Tragedy has no ghost, unless we count the ghost of morality and decency, which definitely cries out for revenge. This play centers on the spread of moral corruption bred when tyrants succeed in breaking social and moral rules and convince women to follow suit. So revenge here is taken as a result of the tainting of a kinswoman and a friend's honor rather than an actual murder. However, foisting another man's bastard unto one's husband, as Evadne clearly intends to do, can be seen as a form of murder. An ideal wife is the preserver of her husband's bloodline, assuring that his inheritance remains within his family. [6] Evadne and the King have planned effectively to put an end to Amintor's bloodline. The King's transgression transcends actual murder. His ac-

---

[6] See Shakespeare's *King John*. Here, too, the Bastard is of royal blood, but he is not of his mother's husband's blood, and his inheritance as eldest son is violently contested. See glossary: Primogeniture.

tions reach into the nucleus of the community, the family unit, and brings corrosion to the very fabric of society.

Another staple from Seneca is the avenger's motivation: revenge for the murder or violation of a kinsman. Seneca's Atreus wants revenge for his violated wife and honor, and for the fact that his children may not be his by blood. Kyd's Hieronimo avenges his son's murder, Bel-imperia her lover's; Hamlet's father was murdered, as was Vindice's beloved. For Melantius, a soldier, honor is paramount, and so his revenge is for his friend's and family's honor. Where Atreus is infuriated, the Renaissance avengers are melancholy men,[7] but the Elizabethan protagonist is slower to kindle and more morally troubled than his Jacobean counterpart. Hieronimo and Hamlet spend much of their stage time alone with the audience, pondering the ramifications of their revenge. Vindice has contemplated revenge for several years, but once the opportunity is offered, he throws himself gleefully and enthusiastically into action with no moral scruples whatsoever. Melantius examines the case Amintor puts before him, believes his friend is truthful, and immediately, honor-driven as he is, decides on action, creates a plan, and carries it out.

All four Renaissance avengers are created by circumstances. None of them is evil by nature or inherently a murderer, like some of their victims certainly are; all live in a corrupt society and become aware of and disgusted by this corruption. An ideal society has a legitimate ruler who is just and who can and will punish and reward according to what is the subject's due, but no such ideal is to be found in revenge tragedy. In Kyd's universe, the evil element is small, as it is in Shakespeare's Denmark; only one person is truly responsible for the tragedy. The Spanish King is blissfully unaware of his Machiavellian nephew's crimes, and Claudius, an effective ruler, gives us the reason for having murdered, and does not seem likely to murder again until he feels cornered by Hamlet. Still, his

---

[7] See glossary: Melancholia; Four Temperaments.

rule is based on an evil deed, and more evil will follow. In Tourneur's play, the entire society is tainted by the morally fallen court, and the only way to avoid the stain is to remain aloof and in isolation; only Vindice's sister truly succeeds in this, while other innocent ladies are corrupted, raped, and murdered. Beaumont and Fletcher's society, in turn, seems most noxious of them all. Here the King has made willing, often eager, participants of many of his subjects, and even those who recognize his evil are emasculated by his claim to absolute power. Only Melantius, the honorable outsider, is capable of cutting through to the source of corruption and eliminating it.

Once he is given the external impetus to action, the decline of the avengers begins. Much of the reason why revenge plays affect their audiences so deeply is the slow tainting and moral decline of an originally decent man[8] who is only too aware of what is happening to him. We all prefer to believe that we are living in a society where we all play by the same rules, and having the scales forcefully peeled from our eyes is a painful experience, which we share with the avenger as he is created. Elizabethan revenge tragedy's Hieronimo and Hamlet show us that we may not be too different from them, and that we ourselves, given similar circumstances, might slide into similar corruption. Jacobean revenge tragedy makes us distance ourselves more, but also realize that we may be the objects of moral corruption, that our society and our rulers may affect us horribly, and that we may not even realize this before it is too late.

In order to achieve justice, the avenger must become inundated with the evil he seeks to eradicate, and in the process, people not involved in the revenge scheme in any way, often women, will be made to suffer, run mad, and die. The avenger, self-absorbed and permeated with his own moral dilemma, himself becomes a contaminant as he pursues revenge, making casualties of the inno-

---

[8] Vindice is in part an exception.

cent, adding to his own moral decay. Hieronimo uses Bel-imperia in his play-within as a tool for revenge and neglects to console his grieving wife who stabs herself to death in her madness; Hamlet sacrifices Ophelia and her feelings; Vindice sweeps his brother into his killing-spree of a revenge — still, nobody except Castiza is pure in this society and remains alive, and most of the "victims" richly deserve their fate; Evadne, after having been the King's victim, becomes her brother's victim as he makes her a tool for his revenge, and Aspatia, the innocent title character of *The Maid's Tragedy*, sacrifices herself in the hopelessness of her love. Again, Jacobean society is presented as less pure and more complicated than Elizabethan, and the line between good and evil, pure and tainted, just and unjust, often blurs.

Contamination affects the avenger so deeply that he must die in order for his society to have an opportunity to heal itself. Fortinbras, supported by Hamlet's "dying voice," may well heal the Kingdom of Denmark, and Lysippus may have learned enough from witnessing the results of his brother's crimes to make Rhodes a good and just realm. But Spain has no heir to its throne, as the King of Spain and Viceroy of Portugal have lost all their children and close kinsmen and exit the stage in deep mourning, and *The Revenger's Tragedy*'s duchy is left in the hands of an old man with no wife and no son; the prospects for the healing of these two countries is tenuous at best. Private revenge is indeed shown to be a dangerous thing.

While the focus of revenge tragedy changes with the changing society the theater caters to, it always gives its audience chilling images of horror. In *The Spanish Tragedy,* as in *Thyestes,* we are presented with concrete, bloody spectacle. The mental image of Thyestes' murdered children and the real image of slain and hanged Horatio are crass, visual inducements to revenge; and Pedringano is a trusting if not innocent servant, who is publicly executed to silence him. The focus of *Hamlet* changes to depict the avenger's development from a young prince not much different from other young men of his society into a scheming Machiavellian capable of murder. We have only the Ghost as a visual reminder of the crime committed, and the vivid verbal image of the killing and its spiritual consequences that he paints. Much of the horror in *Hamlet* is created through Hamlet's words rather than visual impact, but we do see the stabbing of Polonius and the carnage at the end. In *The Revenger's Tragedy,* we have not only Gloriana's skull, but also the excesses which Vindice is willing to commit. We have an engineered execution not meant to have happened, slow death by poison administered by the skull's "lips," on-stage desecration of a corpse, and joyous taunting during the slow death of a victim of stabbing, all in the name of morality and revenge! It is difficult for an audience to lament Vindice's looming death at play's end, but then the entire moral fabric of this society is corrupt to a degree that only allows a spectator distanced analysis, no identification. Finally, in *The Maid's Tragedy*, we are allowed to witness the corruption as it spreads. We are lulled by the ceremony of Amintor's wedding into believing that this society is sound, only to have our illusion shattered. A bride refuses to share her husband's bed and sees him only as a front to cover up her adulterous relationship with the King and provide a name for the resulting children. This same woman, once convinced of the error of her ways, binds her lover's hands to the bedpost in what he sees as an exciting new sex game, then stabs him to death in an act of "reverse penetration." The horror of this tragedy is tightly connected to women and the evils they bring on their family if they become corrupted. The nature of the horror presented has shifted from a motivation to revenge, easily understood and identified with by the audience, and its bloody aftermath, to an invisible evil that insinuates itself into our very homes. The Elizabethan protagonists are larger than we could ever be, and the horror of their deed and its aftermath serve as a moral lesson. In Jacobean revenge tragedy the spectators are much closer to the action personally, and especially in *The Maid's Tragedy* one can imagine the horror of finding oneself in

Amintor's or Aspatia's situation. Jacobean revenge tragedy has become almost voyeuristic, catering as it often does to a coterie audience of the same social class as the protagonists.

The Playhouses, Players, and Plays

The Renaissance was an age of extravagance and spectacle, remarkably theatrical in many aspects. The monarch was on display, "on stage" as it were, during his or her progresses of state through England; Elizabeth especially is known for her lavish progresses. Spectacle was also involved in the elaborate public executions of the period, especially in the traitor's punishment,[9] where the spectators not only had a visual, gruesome warning against committing the awful crime of treason and the edification of the condemned's last words on the scaffold, but also had an opportunity to admire the craftsmanship of a truly skilled executioner. The theater, of course, was another arena that specialized in display and spectacle.

In 1580, public performances of drama for profit and the idea of playgoing as a pastime were relatively new. There had been performances before, to be sure, in connection with church festivals sponsored by the guilds, in the Tudor hall as entertainment, and in inn-yards, but playhouses erected solely for the purpose of providing the paying public with entertainment were a novelty.

Players did not fit easily into the categories of organized society. They were regarded as vagrants and "masterless men" along with other suspicious characters such as peddlers and tinkers who moved about in an otherwise static society, taking advantage of people, stealing and conniving. Only when a group of players had obtained the patronage of nobility or royalty as "servants" could they perform without fear of interference by the authorities. Shakespeare, for example, became one of a newly formed company under the Lord Chamberlain's protection in 1594, and after

[9] See glossary.

James I ascended the English throne his company became "The King's Men."

When we stop to think about the long list of plays that we still have preserved and the even longer list of lost plays,[10] the numbers are impressive; a comparison is possible between the number of movies produced in a given period and the few that will survive into the future. Which Renaissance plays would survive, however, was much less predictable than the movie comparison may suggest. One reason that we have as many Shakespearean plays as we do is the dedication of members of Shakespeare's acting company that saw to the publication of the First Folio after his death. A play was usually not printed until it was no longer profitable for the company, and a printed edition might create a small extra profit. Thomas Kyd's *The Spanish Tragedy* is an instance in point; it was first published long after its first run, then revived on stage with additions, then printed again in its new form.

The reason for the staggering number of plays was the large number of playgoers and the relatively few theaters. We have documentation enough to figure that the Admiral's Men of the Rose Theatre put on roughly forty plays in one year, and there is little reason to doubt that the same was true for the other theaters.[11] The plays had very short runs, and one play was never performed on consecutive days in order not to lose audience support. It is difficult to imagine the pressure on a leading actor who would have had to memorize some 40,000 lines per year. Renaissance theater had its "stars" like we have ours, and the public would often pay to see Burbage, Shakespeare's leading man, or Kemp, Shakespeare's early company clown, perform, and would demand to see their favorites. Though prestige might follow noble and royal patronage, the money to be made in order to stabilize a shareholding player's social position came from the admission fee

[10] See e.g. Alfred Harbage's *Annals of English Drama 975-1700*.

[11] See map of playhouses in Steven Mullaney, *The Place of the Stage* 28-29.

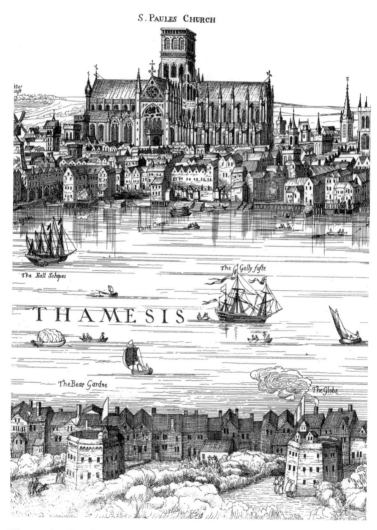

Figure 1. *Londinum Florentissima Britanniae Urbs*, which shows the location of the Globe Theatre. Map L85c no. 7 copy 1, detail of section 2. By permission of the Folger Shakespeare Library.

to the public theaters, so the companies strove to give its public what it wanted.

Playhouses were located in "the liberties," areas not under the control of London's Lord Mayor. Few of these could be found within the city walls, all relics of former monasteries. Theaters were generally situated well outside the city walls in the suburbs with a concentration in Southwark on the south bank of the Thames River where the Globe stood. An assembled motley crowd such as a playhouse attracted was regarded as not only noisy and unpleasant, but it also drew unsavory elements:

> . . . At plaies, the Nip standeth there leaning like some manerly gentleman against the doore as men go in, and there finding talke with some of his companions, spieth what everie man hath in his purse, and where, in what place, and in which sleeve or pocket he puts the boung and according to that so he worketh either where the thrust is great within, or else as they come out at the doors.
> (Robert Greene, *The second Part of Conny Catching*, 1591)[12]

> . . . the quality of such as frequent the sayed places, beeing the ordinary places of meetings for all vagrant persons & maisterles men that hang about the Citie, theeves, horsestealers, whoremongers, coozeners, connycatching persons, practizers of treason, & other such lyke . . .
> (Lord Mayor to Lord Burghley, 3 November 1594 (repeated in petition for abolition of playhouses 28 July 1597 to the Privy Council))[13]

A large crowd was also seen as a suspicious and potentially riotous lot, not welcome in good neighborhoods; no wonder perfor-

---

[12] Qtd. in Gurr, *Playgoing in Shakespeare's London*, Appendix 2, entry 13.
[13] Ibid. entry 21.

Figure 2. *The White Hart Inn.* In such an inn-yard actors would perform plays. Art File L847h2 no. 3. By permission of the Folger Shakespeare Library.

mances such as those put on at inns were banned within the city in 1594. To compensate, the public playhouses were licensed, thus situating drama and performance outside the city limits.

Having a playhouse with an entrance where admission could be taken was a great improvement over passing the hat after a performance at an inn-yard; people paid in advance and could not enter without payment. The playhouses were constructed on two models, the square inn-yard and the multi-sided polygon of an animal baiting arena. Both models had galleries with benches, usually three levels, each level protruding over the level beneath and the upmost one thatched;[14] in case of rain, some shelter could be provided here for the people standing around the stage itself. Admission for standing room was the cheapest, a seat on a gallery bench more expensive, and the price rose again for admission to a "Gentleman's Box" on the first gallery, immediately above and to the sides of the stage, and the "Lord's Rooms" on the balcony above the stage, seats making sure that the occupant was seen and remarked upon! The Globe galleries could seat some 2,000 people, and, when a popular play was offered, about 1,000 groundlings could be squeezed into the yard. All performances in the public playhouses took place in the afternoon by natural light, which seems foreign to a twenty-first century playgoer who is accustomed to sitting in darkness, hushed and silent, expecting theater of illusion. The Renaissance audiences were lively lots, buying and consuming food and drink, sometimes fighting, sometimes negotiating with a prostitute for services, and always commenting loudly about the business on stage, whether favorably or the opposite. The audience surrounded the stage area on all sides, and nobody was really far from the stage. Being surrounded by spectators put very different demands on the actors from what we are used to in our

---

[14] See sketches for the rebuilding of the New Globe in Mulryne and Shewring's *Shakespeare's Globe Rebuilt*, 118-119. http://www.reading.ac.uk/globe/ is another excellent visual resource.

contemporary theaters. They would unavoidably have their backs turned to part of the audience, and the spectators would see a "different play" depending on their position in the auditorium.

The stage itself was a platform about five feet tall and about 1,180 square feet in size. It had a trapdoor in the middle to give access to the "hell" beneath from which devils could ascend, sinners could descend, and ghosts could emerge; *Hamlet*'s gravedigging clown is also well accommodated here. Above the stage was a gallery with a balcony which was used both as boxes for spectators and as a secondary staging area for scenes such as *Romeo and Juliet*'s balcony scene and for Richard the Second's entry when challenged by Bolingbrook at Flint Castle; possibly the musicians so many plays call for also found room here. This gallery and the stage itself were covered by "the heavens," supported by sturdy pillars, from which a trapdoor allowed such figures as Jove to descend to the stage and be elevated again. The Renaissance public playhouse thus resembles the Mediaeval stage, only where the religiously inspired plays had a horizontal arrangement of heaven-earth-hell, the amphitheater's is vertical. The back of the stage was a wall, the *frons scenae*, with three openings, two doors on either side for regular entrances and exits, and a middle aperture, the "discovery space," which could be covered by a painted tapestry or curtain. This was a convenient space from which to "discover" Juliet in her tomb, a tableau like Ferdinand and Miranda's chess game in *The Winter's Tale*, or the fake corpses of the Duchess' family in Webster's *The Duchess of Malfi*. We assume that both "the heavens" and the *frons scenae* were richly decorated; The New Globe certainly has followed this assumption with beautiful result.[15] Behind this wall was the "tiring house" where the actors readied themselves for performance and awaited their cue to enter.

A stage like the Globe's could, of course, not be curtained off like our "picture frame" stages can. This meant no elaborate

---

[15] See http://www.reading.ac.uk/globe/

scene changes were possible. A Renaissance play in a public playhouse would be performed in one continuous action with no act divisions and no intermissions, making for a speedier experience than we are used to in the twenty-first century. Scenery was minimal, and most of it was painted by the playwright's words. When two people are standing five feet from one another (*Hamlet* I.i) and say that they are unable to see each other, the audience smoothly infers that the time is night. When we are told, "[T]his is the forest of Arden" in *As You Like It* (II.iv), we accept that trees surround the actors and are unsurprised when a lover pins poems onto a convenient tree/support pillar. Those of us who have experienced "theater in the round" will agree that we adapt to the bare stage, the minimal use of props, and the set painted by the dramatist in words with greater ease than might be expected from more modern generations used to spectacular special effects, movies, and theater of illusion.

Props were present, to be sure, and Mr. Henslowe's papers have given us extensive lists of what was to be had. We find few large properties, which were unwieldy and difficult to remove without interrupting the action. Beds, for example, could be presented from the discovery space, but if a character was ill and needed to be closer to the audience to speak, he would be rolled in in a chair. Most props were handheld and left the stage with the actor. Often small props identified the bearer (a "scenic emblem"): a king, of course, needs his crown, his scepter, and his sphere; a jester would carry a bauble; only gentlemen wore swords; Hieronimo's dagger and rope (*Spanish Tragedy* IV.v) marked him as contemplating suicide. But small props could take on large significance. Yorick's skull (*Hamlet* V.i) becomes Hamlet's teacher; the Page's box (*The Spanish Tragedy* III.v) takes on a life of its own; and Evadne's dagger (*The Maid's Tragedy* V.i) takes on sexual connotations. Every time an original stage direction specifies use of a handprop, it is a good idea to open one's imagination to the symbolic possibilities of that prop.

On the bare, open stage there were only the pillars supporting "the heavens," and so no place for an actor to hide when spying or eavesdropping. The playwright's words often suffice to "hide" the actor—nobody but the audience will be aware of his presence. This leads to a discussion of the conventions that were taken for granted in the Renaissance. One convention we hardly think about and readily accept while experiencing theater in the round is that of place. The bare stage comfortably and seamlessly changes from castle to marketplace to bedchamber by means of the playwright's words. We know we are in a theater watching a play, not truly in the Duke's chamber or a Danish graveyard, but part of the contract we sign when buying our ticket is that we will choose not to credit this knowledge; we allow ourselves to be transported wherever the play takes us. By the same token we accept that when an actor turns from another to deliver "an aside," only we can hear it; and when an actor declares himself hidden, or in some cases invisible, we believe, but we relish being "in the know." We also readily accept a few soldiers as representatives of an entire army, and a few skirmishes as an entire battle.

What the stage lacked in properties and scenery, it made up for by its lavish use of costumes. Again from Henslowe's papers we have knowledge of the extensive wardrobe available to the actors, and presumably all performance took place in contemporary dress. The actors probably supplied their own costumes when nothing out of the ordinary was needed, but theater management had outfits to accommodate what the play needed, notably several suits of armor and padding, which were necessary for the actors to remain unhurt during the frequent bouts of enthusiastic swordplay so loved by the audience. Clothing assists in setting the stage: an actor appears in a cloak and boots, and so we know that we are out-of-doors and probably traveling; we see a nightcap and a nightshirt, and we know we are in the presence of a roused sleeper; Hamlet's black garb signals mourning. Social status is defined by dress: a velvet garment signals a lady, but if she adds cloth of gold or gold lace, she is of the high nobility. Indeed, the Sumptuary Laws[16] set down rules for what fabrics were acceptable for each social class. Only the nobility could wear silk and taffeta, for instance, so such garments were supplied by the theater. Members of different trades were readily identifiable by their garb and accessories; Shakespeare's *Julius Caesar* specifies an "apron and rule" for a carpenter (I.i).

The plays produced on the public stages were significantly different from the Mediaeval performances in themes and topics.[17] Miracle and Morality plays concern themselves with religious instruction, the salvation of the human soul, our realization of our susceptibility to succumb to committing sins and the consequences thereof, and with our awareness of our place in the greater scheme of things. Many passages were rich in comedic elements, but the main focus of even slapstick comedy was the religiously motivated moral message to be sent. Once theatergoing became a commercial enterprise, there was a clear shift in the themes and topics presented. English history plays became a vehicle for patriotism and often glorified the past of the reigning dynasty.[18] Moreover, history plays lent themselves to such attractions as battles, spectacle, and military music. As the period progressed, the concept of "kingship" and "government" were frequently debated issues, which were problematized on stage not only in the history plays, but also in other, more abstract contexts such as we find it in Beaumont and Fletcher's *The Maid's Tragedy* and Shakespeare's *King*

[16] "A law regulating expenditure, especially with view to restraining excess in food, dress, equipage, etc." (O.E.D.)

[17] There is much more to be said on this topic than this introduction has room for. For a brilliant and thorough treatment, see Glynne Wickham's *A History of the Theatre*.

[18] Shakespeare's *Richard the Third* is an instance in point. The man who saves England from the bloody tyranny of Richard's rule is Elizabeth's grandfather!

Lear and *Macbeth*. Other popular topics were the moral ramifications of private versus public revenge and, in both comedies and tragedies, the issues connected with love and marriage; in most cases room could be found for swordplay or duels with rapiers, and the actors' skills with their weapons did not go unnoticed or uncheered.

Parallel to the adult companies of actors, and giving them strong competition, there existed groups of boy actors, for instance "The Children of the Chapel Royal," who performed once or twice a week. Boy companies had been known since the fourteenth century and were much favored by both Henry VIII and Elizabeth. These boys were connected to a church or school where they were receiving a gentleman's education, which among other things included rhetoric. Performing plays as part of higher education was defensible because the boys learned to

> . . . try their voices and confirm [strengthen] their memories; to frame [control] their speech; to conform them to convenient action [suitable behaviour]; to try what metal is in every one, and of what disposition they are of; whereby never any one amongst us, that I know was made the worse, many have been much the better.
>
> (William Gager, qtd. in Styan, *The English Stage*)

Besides acting, the boys received training in singing, dancing, and music, and their training made them so versatile that they attracted the attention of several major playwrights who wrote, sometimes exclusively, for the boy companies; their major strength was light comedy. A skilled boy actor was also in high demand from the adult companies, who needed him to play female parts.[19]

The boys performed indoors, notably at The Blackfriars The-

---

[19] All roles were played by male actors during the Renaissance; not until the Restoration did an English actress set foot on stage.

atre, which in the 1580s was regarded as a fashionable place to go and attracted an audience of gentlemen. Once the hall playhouses again were permitted within London city limits in 1599, the boy companies resumed public performance, but adult companies were still barred from performance in the city until 1608, when Burbage and Shakespeare's company took over Blackfriars.[20]

The popularity of the children's companies may seem strange to us, but they had a long history of royal favor, there was an aura of the genteel about them not found with adult companies, and once indoor performance was again established, such a theater gave protection against the weather and offered an intimate and sophisticated atmosphere in a small setting. The popularity of playwrights such as Ben Jonson, who favored the boys, certainly added to the attraction, and competition between adults and boys was sometimes fierce.[21] Admission to an indoor or "private" playhouse was higher than to a public one, which also served to create a more sophisticated, coterie audience.

Like the outdoor, the indoor playhouse had galleries flanking the stage, but the space in front of it had benches to sit on. The seats nearest to the stage were the most expensive, quite the opposite of the public playhouses, and the auditorium could seat only about 700 if three galleries were available, 600 if two. The balcony above the stage no longer had seating, but it had space for musicians, who played during the interludes necessary to trim the wicks of the candles used for illumination[22] and to lend mood throughout the play. The stage itself was considerably smaller than

---

[20] James Burbage adapted Blackfriars to accommodate adult performance and probably to get winter quarters for his company in 1596, but he was not permitted to bring the adult company in, and so Blackfriars was leased to the boys.

[21] See *Hamlet* II.ii.330 ff.

[22] Usually four trimmings during a performance, splitting the play into five "acts."

that of an outdoor theater, about 400 square feet to about 1200 square feet, and this space was further limited by the practice of having a few extra-paying gallants sit on stools on the stage itself. The trapdoor to "hell" could be found in the stage floor, but from above more and more machinery made more and more elaborate special effects possible, such as "flying."

The plays written for the private playhouses differ somewhat from those designed for the public ones. The smaller stage and the confined space did not lend themselves well to battle scenes because of their sheer magnitude and noise; now battles of wit took precedence over actual skirmish. Because the daylight convention no longer was necessary, as lighting to a great degree could be controlled, the verbal painting of time of day was no longer necessary. Control over light and darkness made it possible to create eerie spectacles and dumb shows, such as we see in Webster's *The Duchess of Malfi*, and elaborate masques such as Beaumont and Fletcher's wedding masque in *The Maid's Tragedy*, which takes place in the dark of night with only the moon for illumination. The private playhouses offered spectacle, sophisticated dialogue, music, and song, all suitable to the intimate space. But of course many popular plays found themselves transposed from one setting to the other after the adult companies gained access to both types of playhouses and moved favorite plays to the arena they occupied.

But how have these plays been preserved for us? And in what form?[23]

The playwright's words were most closely represented in the so-called "foul papers," which are a challenge for a modern reader as they are in flowing, contemporary handwriting, "the secretary hand," and the spelling is idiosyncratic. This version would have strike-outs, additions, marginal comments, and would generally

---

[23] Good readings on the preserving and printing of the plays can be found in Gurr and Ichikawa's *Staging in Shakespeare's Theatres* and McDonald's *The Bedford Companion*.

look like what we consider "a draft." In *Much Ado About Nothing*, for example, we sometimes find the actor's name substituted for the character's name in the speech headings; sometimes, "Clown" is substituted for a character's name. These "errors" might easily find their way into print. Furthermore, many of the changes brought about by performance will not be found in the "foul papers."

It is easier to read the next stage, the "fair copy," but it could be made by a copyist as well as the playwright, and so might perpetuate mistakes and even add more. And whoever copied the "foul papers" would add his own idiosyncratic spelling conceptions to those already present, and sometimes punctuation became an issue as well.

"The book of the play" is the final version, treasured by the company, which contains enough information for the bookkeeper—the stage manager—to make performance go smoothly. He marked up this copy to make sure everybody knew what props were needed when, when entrances were to take place, and from which door. Once an actor was on stage, there was no way to help him, except from fellow actors, should he forget his lines. After 1570, when censorship began, the "book of the play," or the "prompt copy," had to be approved by the Master of the Revels, who signed the book for the company as proof that nothing in it was offensive. A shorter version than the approved one was in order, but nothing could be added. If the London theaters were closed, for example during outbreaks of the plague, the company might take three or four plays and their respective costumes and props on tour; in such a situation the play might well be abbreviated, but the Master of the Revels' signature guaranteed the acceptability of the text.

Once the actors thought the play had lost its audience appeal as a performed text, they might sell it—and so give up all rights—to a printer. The government controlled the Stationers' Company or Register, which regulated all the printers in London; the printer would pay a fee to register his printed copy with this company, after which he could print and reprint as the market dictated. Many title pages of the time, such as the one for *Arden of Feversham* which mentions no author, make this ownership known: "Imprinted at London for Edward White, dwelling at the lyttle north dore of Paules Church at the signe of the Gun. 1592." The printer would use one or more of the copies mentioned above, "foul papers," "fair copy," "book of the play," as a basis for his text.

Printing was a relatively new thing in the Renaissance, and type setting and actual printing was executed by hand and open to variation, as spelling was by no means standardized at the time; especially the setting of type introduced idiosyncratic spelling and punctuation. It is possible through Shakespeare's *Folio* to ascertain which composer[24] set a given page because of his preferred spelling or, say, love of the parenthesis or the colon. Because production could be furthered by it, several composers were setting type for the same sheet, and they were doing it in an atmosphere of deafening noise from the hand-operated machinery, ink stains everywhere, and the stench from the leather balls used for applying the ink, which were soaking in human urine to keep them supple.

Many of the variations and errors introduced during all these steps in preserving the text for us have scholars puzzled to this day, and we find this puzzlement reflected in "the war of the footnotes." If we ask ourselves whether we will ever be able to reconstruct the actual text used in the actual playhouse in Renaissance times, the answer must be no; *the* text is a phantom.[25]

---

[24] The one who placed the metal letters in the wooden frame for printing.
[25] See Rosenbaum's "Shakespeare in Rewrite" for an illuminating discussion of this topic.

Figure 3. Exterior of the Globe Theatre, London. 2002. By permission of Flemming Videbæk.

An Expression of Gratitude

As every editor must, I feel a great debt to the many people who have helped me with this task; who have taught me throughout my career as a student; who as colleagues have discussed Renaissance drama with me; who have been my interesting and interested students. Still, most of all, I acknowledge my debt to those editors whose works I have consulted for this volume.

For *The Spanish Tragedy:*

> Frederick S. Boas, *The Works of Thomas Kyd*, Clarendon Press, 1901; 1955.
>
> Andrew S. Cairncross, Regents Renaissance Drama Series, University of Nebraska Press, 1967.
>
> Philip Edwards, The Revels Plays, 1959.
>
> J. R. Mulryne, New Mermaid Series, 1970.
>
> William Tydeman, *Two Tudor Tragedies*, Penguin Classics, 1992.

For *Hamlet*

> Philip Edwards, The New Cambridge Shakespeare, 1985.
>
> Stephen Greenblatt, The Norton Shakespeare, 1997.
>
> J. R. Hibbard, The Oxford Shakespeare, 1987.
>
> Harold Jenkins, The Arden Shakespeare, 1984.
>
> John Dover Wilson, The Works of Shakespeare, Cambridge U. P., 1971.

For *The Revenger's Tragedy*

> R. A. Foakes, The Revels Plays, 1966.
>
> Brian Gibbons, New Mermaid Series, 1967.
>
> George Parfitt, *The Plays of Cyril Tourneur*, Cambridge U.P., 1978.
>
> Lawrence J. Ross, Regents Renaissance Drama Series, University of Nebraska Press, 1966.

For *The Maid's Tragedy*

    Andrew Gurr, University of California Press, 1969.

    Howard B. Norland, Regents Renaissance Drama Series, University of Nebraska Press, 1968.

    Martin Wiggins, *Four Jacobean Sex Tragedies*, Oxford English Drama Series, 1998.

THE SPANISH TRAGEDY

by

THOMAS KYD

Introductory Remarks

Thomas Kyd

Kyd was born in 1558 into a comfortably well-off middle-class family. His father was a scrivener, a copier of documents, who via his profession had close connection to the legal system. The few preserved pieces of Kyd's handwriting suggest that he may have followed his father's profession, at least for a while; his writing is extremely neat and elegant.

He was educated at the Merchant Tailor's School, beginning at the age of seven, and was there most probably instructed in French and Italian, Latin, and maybe some Greek. Kyd was exposed to the theater and performance at a young age. As part of the boys' training in rhetoric, plays were performed at this school, and we know that the students acted at court, entertaining Queen Elizabeth.

We have no evidence of Kyd's life as a young man until around 1585, close to the assumed date for *The Spanish Tragedy*, when we know that he was writing plays for the Queen's Company. Unfortunately, most of these plays are lost, and only through Thomas Heywood's *Apology for Actors* (1612) do we know for a fact that Kyd was the author of *The Spanish Tragedy*, as no copy of the play in contemporary printing bears his name on the title page.

Most of our knowledge of Kyd's later life stems from his arrest on May 12, 1593. He was detained and possibly tortured during the Privy Council's attempt to discover who was responsible for "certain libels," probably directed against foreigners living in London. During the search of his chambers were found papers considered to be "vile hereticall Conceiptes denyinge the deity of Jhesus Christe o^r Savio^r,"[1] which ensured Kyd's arrest for blasphemy. After fellow playwright Christopher Marlowe's death

---

[1] Quoted in Freeman, *Thomas Kyd: Facts and Problems*.

in a barroom brawl, Kyd claimed that the papers were Marlowe's and had been left among Kyd's things by him at a time when they had both been "wrytinge in one chamber" while in service with an unidentified lord. Marlowe was known for harboring sentiments that could be seen as vile and heretical. It is not known whether Kyd suspected that Marlowe had informed on him—Marlowe himself was imprisoned May 20th to May 30th that same year—or whether he accused Marlowe to escape prison and torture once the latter was known to be dead.

Kyd died in 1594, just over a year after his release, at the age of thirty-six; most probably his demise was hastened by his prison experience.

The Play

Senecan Elements and Revenge Tragedy

The Spanish Tragedy introduced revenge tragedy to the English stage. The revenge theme has its roots in the tragedies of Seneca, the first classical writer of tragedies to be translated into English, whose main interest is the effect of revenge over multiple generations of a family. Also, Seneca's protagonists often display those character traits the "civilized" human is ashamed of, such as vengefulness, pride, greed, and spite. According to David Slavitt,[2] there are

> . . . two questions that the tragedies of Seneca generally pose . . . first whether there is any divine justice. Are there any gods, or more particularly, does their mere existence matter to us if they do not occupy themselves with rewarding virtue and punishing wickedness? And then, as a corollary question, Seneca's plays test our assumptions about the limits of the cruelty men and women can visit upon one another. Or worse, he asks whether there are any such limits . . . Seneca [demonstrates] that we live in a

[2] Editor of *Seneca, The Tragedies*, vol. 1 and 2.

morally indifferent universe. . .

[Preface, viii-ix]

Kyd does not take human cruelty to the extremes of Seneca, but he does take a bleak view of human justice and debates the morality thereof.

In *The Spanish Tragedy*, Kyd quotes Seneca directly and uses many of his rhetorical techniques, one such being stichomythia, verse dialogue in single lines; another, highly polished, rhetorically elegant speeches. But where Seneca's tragedies seem static and not very appealing from the point of view of staging, Kyd's tragedy is definitely for and of the stage. The Senecan elements were an inspiration for Kyd, not something to be imitated completely.

The Spanish Tragedy has all the elements we associate with revenge tragedy. First of all, the on-stage audience present throughout the play are the Ghost of Don Andrea and Revenge.[3] The restless ghost that must be avenged has his roots in Senecan tragedy, but Kyd uses this presence as a tool to guide the perceptions of his audience. After the Introduction, the spectators know the outcome of the play; Revenge assures Don Andrea that Balthazar, who slew him in battle, will be killed by Bel-imperia, Andrea's love. Armed with this knowledge, the audience can concentrate, not on what is going to happen, but on how the result is brought about.

The traditional reason for revenge, a murder, usually of a kinsman, is not present for Don Andrea, who was killed in battle, and who cannot, of course, avenge his own death; his end, as presented by Horatio (I.iii.6-29), shows Balthazar in a less than flattering light. However, one act of revenge sets another in motion. Bel-imperia wants revenge on Balthazar for her lover's death;

---

[3] The present editor has decided to leave Revenge and Andrea on stage throughout the play and only have them exit at the end, thus creating a frame for the play which constantly reminds the audience of the expected outcome.

Lorenzo and Balthazar want revenge on Horatio for winning Belimperia's love and thwarting a politically motivated marriage plan; Hieronimo wants revenge on his son's murderers. Each of these intrigues has a different motivation and explores different aspects of how human beings interact. Revenge amplifies human actions and reactions and makes us ponder why we undertake certain tasks and react in certain ways, and so it becomes a splendid tool for examining the conflicts between protagonists that make Elizabethan tragedy so fascinating.

Kyd shows us that the path to obtaining revenge is long, twisted, and tortuous, and that the revenger, notably Hieronimo, becomes tainted because of the revenge process. As Knight Marshal of Spain, essentially a judge, Hieronimo's life has been centered on meting out justice to others. Now, incapable of finding justice for his murdered son through the courts, he is faced with a dilemma. He can either turn the other cheek, and like a good Christian let God mete out justice, or he can break the law he holds in such high esteem in the pursuit of private revenge. The opening of IV.v displays this dilemma eloquently. The book Hieronimo carries must be by Seneca, as the Latin quotations show, but his first words, "*Vindicta mihi!*" refer to the Lord's right to vengeance (Romans xii.19). Still, Seneca, who is for revenge, wins out in Hieronimo's tortured debate with himself. The transition is difficult, but once the decision is made, Hieronimo is a changed man, capable of extreme deeds.

As always in revenge tragedy, the innocent suffer along with the guilty; in fact, at the end of a revenge tragedy, the "wild justice" the law ought to weed out[4] has dire consequences for everyone involved. Part of the cost is often madness and suicide, here visited most movingly upon Isabella, Horatio's mother. Isabella is completely innocent of any wrong, but her emotional suffering is

[4] Bacon; see his "Essay on Revenge" among the Texts in Context in this volume.

tremendous. The Spanish King, his brother, and the Portuguese Viceroy are not directly involved in the revenge plot either, but they, too, suffer loss and grief, even loss of life.

The quest for justice is further complicated by the rashness of judgment shown by the Viceroy of Portugal, who condemns the wrong man to death for supposedly killing his son, and Lorenzo's coldly sending Pedringano to the scaffold, seduced into believing that he will be saved at the last moment. Juxtaposed with these injustices we see Hieronimo's care when rendering judgment, all the while lamenting the lack of justice in his own son's murder.[5] He even questions whether a higher power is concerned with justice on earth at all.

Throughout the play, the spectators are more knowledgeable about the play's complications than any of the characters on stage, and know from the start that Revenge will have what is his due. This enables the audience members to appreciate the twists and turns of Kyd's well-crafted plot and allows them to fully appreciate the ironies of fate and human nature so pervasive in *The Spanish Tragedy*.

The Characters

Like many Renaissance dramatists, Kyd sets his play in a foreign country, which allows him to express himself more freely; no Englishman could be offended as the rash and inconsistent Viceroy is of Portugal and the aloof and proud King is of Spain. There seems to be no historical background for the recently fought battle in the play. Kyd needed a warlike situation, and this, too, could be more easily created if the setting of his fiction was removed from England itself.

The Spanish King is inordinately proud, reveling in his power, and creating opportunities for the spectacle and pomp so beloved by a Renaissance audience. In I.i he causes his victorious army to "enter and pass by" in great display twice in the same scene; he

[5] See especially III.vi.1-10 and III.vii.10-18.

welcomes Balthazar to the court with a banquet and a dumb show in I.iii; and he encourages the play-within[6] in the final scene. All these displays of pomp and pride become ironic to the audience, who are privy to Hieronimo's plan. Before the play opens, the Portuguese Viceroy was proud enough to have rebelled against mighty Spain, but he is now humbled both by the loss of the war and the presumed loss of his son. Fallen pride is shown as less than regal, unreasonable in the face of loss, and prone to be self-indulgent. Both rulers are humbled by the close of the play.

Prince Balthazar is shown as susceptible to flattery and as one easily led, neither of which is a desired quality in a prince or a leader. When convinced that he is in love, his stilted Petrarchan language and his mood swings further distance the audience from him. His status as prisoner in the Spanish court is an honorable one as he is held for ransom, and he is therefore at all times treated as a prince rather than a captured enemy. Lorenzo, son of the King's brother, is an early version of the popular stage Machiavel, a scheming, plotting character who claims to know his fellow man, freely shares his plans with the audience, and thoroughly enjoys his own evil. Ironically, his demise is brought about because he does not truly know his own sister.

Bel-imperia, whose name implies both beauty (Bel) and proud royalty (imperia), is not the traditional chaste, silent, and obedient Renaissance woman. Don Andrea's "In secret I possessed a worthy dame / Which hight sweet Bel-imperia by name" (Intro. 10-11) strongly suggests a sexual relationship between the two, and we are also told that her choice of lover was highly unacceptable to her family. Despite this she herself chooses Horatio for her second lover, though he is of a lower social standing than she and there are plans for her arranged marriage to Balthazar. Bel-imperia is a headstrong young woman, who takes her fate into her own hands. A modern-day audience can be puzzled by the ease with

[6] See glossary.

which she changes her allegiance from Don Andrea to Horatio. This often gives rise to speculations about her morality and character, but Kyd needs this new love interest to further his plot, and it is neither the first nor the last time practicality takes precedence over psychological probability in Renaissance Drama. Besides, Horatio is worthy; even Don Andrea seems to approve.

Horatio is an almost impossibly perfect young man. He is courageous and well-spoken, and his love scene with Bel-imperia serves as a strong contrast to Balthazar's fumbling attempts at love poetry. The problems he faces are his social standing, something the court never lets us forget, and the fact that Lorenzo has plans to further his own interest through Balthazar's marriage to his sister. In reality, Bel-imperia has no control over whom she is to marry; her social standing dictates what her family deems a suitable marriage, which most probably would be arranged in any case. It is interesting to note how Bel-imperia is the only one in the court to see Horatio for what he is and not as a function of his social class.

Hieronimo is by far the most complicated and interesting character of the play. He is the epitome of an honorable, upright citizen and judge, whose life up to the point of his son's murder has been circumscribed by the law. He is a good father and husband, a poet, a courtier. His struggles with his conscience as he gives himself over to the chaos that follows in the wake of revenge, and the quality of his inner debates display the depths of revenge tragedy. Through Hieronimo, the audience sees that though anybody can feel sympathy for a man who seeks private revenge, even understand the motivation on a personal level and in some way applaud the resulting "justice," the price the revenger pays is high; the process that leads to the actual revenge taints Hieronimo and lowers him to the level of his prey. The rhetorical elements of his speeches may take a reader some getting used to, but once we overcome our tendency to see Kyd's language as "overdone," the beauty of the language emerges.

The Stage and the Text

Kyd uses all the possibilities of his stage in truly professional fashion. Where Senecan tragedy tells, he shows. He makes room in his play for spectacle and procession. He makes use of the balcony for Lorenzo and Balthazar's eavesdropping, and for Bel-imperia to drop her letter written in blood so the audience can see the red writing as it flutters down. The presence of Revenge and Don Andrea's Ghost throughout, quiet, static, hovering, creates a contrast to the violently propelled, bloody revenge plot of the play proper.

Kyd makes use of props, large and small, from arbor to letter. The arbor, as can be seen from the title page to the revised edition of *The Spanish Tragedy*, is quite a sizable set piece, as it must be sturdy enough to support Horatio's body. A piece as elaborate as this must see some use to justify its presence, and indeed the arbor does. First it serves to provide an intimate and seemingly secure trysting place for Bel-imperia and Horatio, bringing home the irony of the illusion of safety. Then it serves as a scaffold for Horatio, and, again ironically, when Hieronimo enters to help the woman he heard cry out his name, what he expected to find is much different from actual reality. The "stake" Alexandro is tied to in III.i is probably the arbor, and placing him there will bring the audience to compare Viluppo's and Lorenzo's plans and actions. Hieronimo's soliloquy in III.ii is made more moving when delivered close to the arbor, and the set piece can serve as scaffold for Pedringano's execution. Finally, in V.ii, Isabella destroys the arbor in her madness before taking her own life. A suitable place to position this large piece might be close to the discovery space,[7] where it can be ignored when not needed for action or poignant reminders.

Smaller props are equally well employed by Kyd. The Viceroy's crown in I.ii serves to underscore his distress, and Bel-imperia's scarf, once given to Andrea, now to Horatio in I.iii, and her dropped

---

[7] See glossary under "Playhouse."

glove later in the same scene can both be wonderful vehicles for demonstrating her love for Horatio, while the glove reveals that love to Lorenzo and Balthazar. The page's box, which allegedly contains Pedringano's pardon, takes on a delightful life of its own in III.iv, v, and vi. Pedringano's letter, clutched in III.vi and found in III.vii, stresses Lorenzo's casual cruelty, and the letter written in blood adds graphic visual emphasis to Hieronimo's discovery of the identity of his son's murderers in III.ii. The rope and dagger with which Hieronimo enters in IV.v immediately mark him as a suicide, and there must, of course, be something resembling a tongue thudding to the stage in the final scene, probably a piece of raw liver. Blood from the multiple stab wounds could be stored in small containers such as bladders to be pierced with a weapon.

Revenge tragedy was in vogue in the Renaissance. The violent plot, the attraction of the theme, and Kyd's use of language and stage ensured the popularity of *The Spanish Tragedy*. It was revived several times, printed, and printed again with several additions, which the present editor has decided to place at the end of the play.

We know that the play was written before February 23rd, 1592, when we have evidence of a performance. The actual date of composition is unknown, and speculations range from as early as 1582 to as late as 1591, but there is no evidence extant to enable us to decisively date the play. The additions printed in the 1602 edition reflect the change in taste between the play's first run and its revival. Whether the play was ever performed in its long version, or whether the additions were written to replace part of Kyd's text which had become old-fashioned or unappealing to a new audience, is unclear. The additions expand Hieronimo's part and give the actor much opportunity to portray a madness only briefly suggested in the 1592 printing, indicating that madscenes had become fashionable.

The author of the additions is unknown, but their existence is proof of the long-lasting popularity of *The Spanish Tragedy*.

The Spanish Tragedie:

OR,

Hieronimo is mad againe.

Containing the lamentable end of *Don Horatio*, and
Belimperia; with the pittifull death of *Hieronimo*.

Newly corrected, amended, and enlarged with new
Additions of the *Painters* part, and others, as
it hath of late been diuers times acted.

LONDON,
Printed by W. White, for I. White and T. Langley,
and are to be sold at their Shop ouer againſt the
Sarazens head without New-gate. 1615.

Figure 4. STC 15091a, the 1615 title page for *The Spanish Tragedy*.
This image gives us valuable clues about staging and costumes of
the time. By permission of the Folger Shakespeare Library.

Dramatis Personae

Chorus:

> The Ghost of Andrea
> Revenge

The King of Spain
Cyprian, Duke of Castile, the King's brother
Lorenzo, son of the Duke
Bel-imperia, daughter of the Duke
Spanish General

Hieronimo, Marshal of Spain
Isabella, his wife
Horatio, their son

The Viceroy of Portugal
Don Pedro, his brother
Balthazar, his son
Alexandro, a Portuguese nobleman
Villuppo, a Portuguese nobleman
The Ambassador of Portugal

Pedringano, Bel-imperia's servant
Serberine, Balthazar's servant
Christophil, Lorenzo's servant
Bazulto, an old man; Senex in speech headings

First Dumb Show:

> Three knights
> Three kings
> A drummer

Second Dumb Show:
>Hymen
>Two torch bearers

Characters in Hieronimo's play:
>Balthazar as Soliman, Sultan of Turkey
>Lorenzo as Erastus, Knight of Rhodes
>Hieronimo as The Bashaw
>Bel-imperia as Perseda, a Christian captive

Soldiers, Officers, Nobles, Attendants, Halberdiers, Watchmen, Messenger, Page, Deputy, Hangman, Citizens, Servants, Maid

The Spanish Tragedy

Act I
Introduction

Enter the Ghost of Andrea, and with him Revenge

Andrea's Ghost
>   When this eternal substance of my soul
>   Did live imprisoned in my wanton flesh,
>   Each in their function serving other's need,
>   I was a courtier in the Spanish court.
>   My name was Don Andrea, my descent   5
>   Though not ignoble, yet inferior far
>   To gracious fortunes of my tender youth.
>   For there in prime[8] and pride[9] of all my years,
>   By duteous service and deserving love,
>   In secret I possessed[10] a worthy dame,   10
>   Which hight[11] sweet Bel-imperia by name.
>   But in the harvest of my summer joys
>   Death's winter nipped the blossom of my bliss,
>   Forcing divorce[12] betwixt my love and me.
>   For in the late conflict with Portingale[13]   15
>   My valor drew me into danger's mouth
>   Till life to death made passage through my wounds.

---

[8] Early time, springtime.
[9] Optimal condition.
[10] Made love to.
[11] Was called.
[12] Separation.
[13] Portugal.

When I was slain, my soul descended straight
To pass the flowing stream of Acheron.[14]
But churlish Charon,[15] only boatman there,   20
Said that, my rites of burial not performed,
I might not sit amongst his passengers.
Ere Sol[16] had slept three nights in Thetis'[17] lap,
And slaked[18] his smoking chariot in her flood,
By Don Horatio, our Knight Marshal's[19] son,   25
My funerals and obsequies were done.
Then was the ferryman of hell content
To pass me over to the slimy strand
That leads to fell Avernus'[20] ugly waves.
There, pleasing Cerberus[21] with honeyed speech,   30
I passed the perils of the foremost porch.[22]
Not far from hence, amidst ten thousand souls,
Sat Minos, Aeacus, and Radamanth,[23]
To whom no sooner 'gan I make approach,
To crave a passport for my wand'ring ghost,   35
But Minos, in graven leaves of lottery,
Drew forth the manner of my life and death.[24]

[14] River in the Underworld. Kyd apparently identifies it here with the River Styx.

[15] The ferryman of the underworld.

[16] The sun.

[17] Homer's goddess of the sea, here used for "the sea."

[18] Extinguished.

[19] In England, a legal official of the King's household. Here, already, Hieronimo is associated with the law and justice.

[20] Volcanic lake near Puzzuoli (north of Naples, Italy), where the entrance to the Underworld was thought to be.

[21] The three-headed dog that guards the entrance to the Underworld.

[22] Entry.

[23] Judges of the Underworld.

[24] Minos is acquainted with Andrea's life, death, and deeds.

"This knight," quoth[25] he, "both lived and died in love,
And for his love tried fortune of the wars,
And by war's fortune lost both love and life."   40
"Why then," said Aeacus, "convey him hence,
To walk with lovers in our fields of love,
And spend the course of everlasting time
Under green myrtle trees and cypress shades."
"No, no," said Radamanth, "it were not well   45
With loving souls to place a martialist.[26]
He died in war and must to martial fields,
Where wounded Hector[27] lives in lasting pain,
And Achilles' Myrmidons[28] do scour[29] the plain."
Then Minos, mildest censor of the three,   50
Made this device to end the difference:
"Send him," quoth he, "to our infernal king,
To doom him as best seems his majesty."
To this effect my passport straight was drawn.
In keeping on my way to Pluto's[30] court,   55
Through dreadful shades of ever-glooming night,[31]
I saw more sights than thousand tongues can tell,
Or pens can write, or mortal hearts can think.
Three ways there were: that on the right-hand side
Was ready way unto the 'foresaid fields   60
Where lovers live and bloody martialists,
But either sort contained within his bounds.
The left-hand path, declining fearfully,

---

[25] Said.

[26] Warrior, soldier.

[27] Foremost Trojan hero in the war with the Greeks, son of Priam.

[28] The killers of Hector, followers of Achilles, the foremost Greek hero in the same war.

[29] Race across.

[30] King of the Underworld, the "infernal world."

[31] Always dark and dangerous.

Was ready downfall to the deepest hell,
Where bloody Furies[32] shake their whips of steel,　　　65
And poor Ixion[33] turns an endless wheel;
Where usurers are choked with melting gold,
And wantons are embraced with ugly snakes,
And murderers groan with never-killing wounds,
And perjured wights[34] scalded in boiling lead,　　　70
And all foul sins with torments overwhelmed.
'Twixt these two ways I trod the middle path,
Which brought me to the fair Elysian green,[35]
In midst whereof there stands a stately tower,
The walls of brass, the gates of adamant.[36]　　　75
Here finding Pluto with his Proserpine,[37]
I showed my passport, humbled on my knee,
Whereat fair Proserpine began to smile,
And begged that only she might give my doom.
Pluto was pleased and sealed it with a kiss.　　　80
Forthwith, Revenge, she rounded thee in th'ear,[38]
And bade thee lead me through the gates of horn,[39]
Where dreams have passage in the silent night.
No sooner had she spoke but we were here,
I wot[40] not how, in twinkling of an eye.　　　85

Revenge

　　　Then know, Andrea, that thou art arrived

---

[32] Mythical deities avenging wrongs and blood-guilt.

[33] The world's first parricide and would-be rapist of Hera, Zeus' wife; as punishment he was crucified on a fiery wheel, turning for all eternity.

[34] Beings.

[35] Where the shades of the blessed dwell.

[36] Stone of impenetrable hardness.

[37] Queen of the Underworld, Pluto's wife.

[38] Whispered in your ear.

[39] The gate of *true* dreams. False dreams go through the ivory gate.

[40] Know.

Where thou shalt see the author of thy death,
Don Balthazar, the prince of Portingale,
Deprived of life by Bel-imperia.
Here sit we down to see the mystery,   90
And serve for Chorus in this tragedy.

Act I, Scene i

Enter Spanish King, General, Duke of Castile, and Hieronimo

King

Now say, Lord General, how fares our camp?
General

All well, my sovereign liege, except some few
That are deceased by fortune of the war.
King

But what portends thy cheerful countenance,
And posting[41] to our presence thus in haste?   5
Speak, man, hath fortune given us victory?
General

Victory, my liege, and that with little loss.
King

Our Portingals[42] will pay us tribute then?
General

Tribute and wonted homage therewithal.
King

Then blest be heaven and guider of the heavens,   10
From whose fair influence such justice flows.
Duke of Castile

O multum dilecte Deo, tibi militat aether,

---

[41] Hurrying with all speed.
[42] Portuguese.

Et conjuratae curvato poplite gentes
Succumbunt: recti soror est victoria juris.[43]

King

    Thanks to my loving brother of Castile.   15

    But General, unfold[44] in brief discourse

    Your form of battle and your war's success,

    That, adding all the pleasure of thy news

    Unto the height of former happiness,

    With deeper wage and greater dignity   20

    We may reward thy blissful chivalry.[45]

General

    Where Spain and Portingale do jointly knit

    Their frontiers, leaning on each other's bound,

    There met our armies in their proud array,[46]

    Both furnished well, both full of hope and fear,   25

    Both menacing alike with daring shows,

    Both vaunting sundry colours of device,[47]

    Both cheerly sounding trumpets, drums and fifes,[48]

    Both raising dreadful clamours to the sky,

    That valleys, hills and rivers made rebound,   30

    And heaven itself was frighted with the sound.

    Our battles both were pitched in squadron form[49]

    Each corner strongly fenced with wings of shot.[50]

    But ere we joined and came to push of pike,[51]

---

[43] "O, muchfavored of God, Heaven fights for thee and the conspiring people fall down on bended knee; victory is the sister of just law."

[44] Make clear.

[45] Prowess; military skill.

[46] Full splendor.

[47] Both proudly flaunting their coats of arms.

[48] Small, shrill sounding flutes.

[49] Square formation.

[50] Firearms at the edge of the formation.

[51] Hand-to-hand combat; pike = long wooden shaft with pointed metal head.

I brought a squadron of our readiest shot   35
From out our rearward to begin the fight.
They brought another wing to encounter us.
Meanwhile our ordinance[52] played on either side,
And captains strove to have their valours tried.
Don Pedro, their chief horseman's colonel,   40
Did with his cornet[53] bravely make attempt
To break the order of our battle ranks,
But Don Rogero, worthy man of war,
Marched forth against him with our musketeers,
And stopped the malice of his fell approach.   45
While they maintain hot skirmish to and fro,
Both battles join and fall to handy blows,[54]
Their violent shot resembling th'ocean's rage,
When, roaring loud, and with a swelling tide,
It beats upon the rampiers[55] of huge rocks   50
And gapes to swallow neighbour-bounding lands.
Now while Bellona[56] rageth here and there,
Thick storms of bullets rain like winter's hail,
And shivered[57] lances dark[58] the troubled air.
> *Pede pes et cuspide cuspis;*   55
> *Arma sonant armis, vir petiturque viro.*[59]
On every side drop captains to the ground,
And soldiers, some ill maimed, some slain outright:
Here falls a body sundered from his head,

[52] Heavy artillery.

[53] Troop.

[54] Close combat.

[55] Ramparts.

[56] The goddess of war.

[57] Splintered.

[58] Darken.

[59] "Foot against foot, and blade against blade; arms clash on arms, and man attacks man."

There legs and arms lie bleeding on the grass,   60
Mingled with weapons and unbowelled steeds,
That scattering overspread the purple[60] plain.
In all this turmoil, three long hours and more,
The victory to neither part inclined,
Till Don Andrea with his brave lanciers[61]   65
In their main battle made so great a breach
That, half dismayed, the multitude retired.
But Balthazar, the Portingales' young prince,
Brought rescue and encouraged them to stay.
Here-hence[62] the fight was eagerly renewed,   70
And in that conflict was Andrea slain,
Brave man at arms, but weak to Balthazar.
Yet while the prince, insulting[63] over him,
Breached out proud vaunts,[64] sounding to our reproach,
Friendship and hardy valour, joined in one,   75
Pricked forth[65] Horatio, our Knight Marshal's son
To challenge forth that prince in single fight.
Not long between these twain the fight endured,
But straight the prince was beaten from his horse,
And forced to yield him prisoner to his foe.   80
When he was taken, all the rest they fled,
And our carbines[66] pursued them to the death,
Till, Phoebus[67] waning to the western deep,
Our trumpeters were charged to sound retreat.

---

[60] The color of blood.
[61] Lancers.
[62] Therefore, because of this.
[63] In triumph.
[64] Boasts.
[65] Spurred.
[66] Probably soldiers armed with carbines.
[67] The sun.

King

    Thanks, good Lord General, for these good news.   85

    And for some argument[68] of more to come,

    Take this and wear it for thy sovereign's sake.

                                    Gives him his gold chain

    But tell me now, hast thou confirmed a peace?

General

    No peace, my liege, but peace conditional,

    That if with homage tribute be well paid,   90

    The fury of your forces will be stayed;

    And to this peace their viceroy hath subscribed,

                               Gives the king a paper

    And made a solemn vow that during life

    His tribute shall be truly paid to Spain.

King

    These words, these deeds, become thy person well.   95

    But now, Knight Marshal, frolic[69] with thy King,

    For 'tis thy son that wins this battle's prize.

Hieronimo

    Long may he live to serve my sovereign liege,

    And soon decay unless he serve my liege.

                          A tucket [70] *afar off*

King

    Nor thou, nor he, shall die without reward.   100

    What means the warning of this trumpet's sound?

General

    This tells me that your grace's men of war,

    Such as war's fortune hath reserved from death,

    Come marching on towards your royal seat

    To show themselves before your majesty,   105

[68] Sign.

[69] Celebrate.

[70] Trumpet fanfare.

For so I gave in charge at my depart.
Whereby by demonstration shall appear
That all (except three hundred or few more)
Are safe returned, and by their foes enriched.

The army enters; Balthazar, between Lorenzo and Horatio, captive

King

    A gladsome sight! I long to see them here.   110
                                 They enter and pass by

    Was that the warlike prince of Portingale,
    That by our nephew was in triumph led?
General

    It was, my liege, the prince of Portingale.
King

    But what was he that on the other side
    Held him by th'arm, as partner of the prize?   115
Hieronimo

    That was my son, my gracious sovereign,
    Of whom, though from his tender infancy
    My loving thoughts did never hope but well,
    He never pleased his father's eye till now,
    Nor filled my heart with overcloying[71] joys.   120
King

    Go let them march once more about these walls,
    That, staying them, we may confer and talk
    With our brave prisoner and his double guard.
    Hieronimo, it greatly pleaseth us
    That in our victory thou have a share   125
    By virtue of thy worthy son's exploit.
                            Enter the army again

    Bring hither the young prince of Portingale.

---

[71] Almost too satisfying.

The rest march on, but ere they be dismissed
We will bestow on every soldier
Two ducats, and on every leader ten,   130
That they may know our largess welcomes them.
      Exeunt all the army but Balthazar, Lorenzo, and Horatio
Welcome, Don Balthazar, welcome, nephew,
And thou, Horatio, thou art welcome too.
Young prince, although thy father's hard misdeeds,
In keeping back the tribute that he owes,   135
Deserve but evil measure at our hands,
Yet shalt thou know that Spain is honourable.

Balthazar

The trespass that my father made in peace
Is now controlled by fortune of the wars,
And cards once dealt, it boots[72] not ask, "Why so?"   140
His men are slain, a weakening to his realm,
His colours seized, a blot unto his name,
His son distressed, a corsive[73] to his heart.
Those punishments may clear his late offense.

King

Ay, Balthazar, if he observe this truce,   145
Our peace will grow the stronger for these wars.
Meanwhile live thou, though not in liberty,
Yet free from bearing any servile yoke,
For in our hearing thy deserts were great,
And in our sight thyself art gracious.   150

Balthazar

And I shall study to deserve this grace.

King

But tell me (for their holding[74] makes me doubt)
To which of these twain art thou prisoner?

---

[72] Is no use.

[73] A substance that corrodes.

[74] The way the two of them restrain you.

Lorenzo

   To me, my liege.

Horatio   To me, my sovereign.

Lorenzo

   This hand first took his courser[75] by the reins.   155

Horatio

   But first my lance did put him from his horse.

Lorenzo

   I seized his weapon and enjoyed it first.

Horatio

   But first I forced him lay his weapons down.

King

   Let go his arm, upon our privilege.[76]   *They let him go*

   Say, worthy prince, to whether[77] didst thou yield?   160

Balthazar

   To him in courtesy, to this perforce.

   He spake me fair, this other gave me strokes.

   He promised life, this other threatened death.

   He won my love, this other conquered me,

   And truth to say I yield myself to both.   165

Hieronimo

   But that I know your grace for just and wise,

   And might seem partial in this difference,

   Enforced by nature and by law of arms

   My tongue should plead for young Horatio's right.

   He hunted well that was a lion's death,   170

   Not he that in a garment wore his skin;

   So hares may pull dead lions by the beard.

King

   Content thee, Marshal, thou shalt have no wrong,

   And for thy sake thy son shall want no right.

[75] War horse.

[76] Right as King.

[77] To which of them.

Will both abide the censure of my doom?[78]   175

Lorenzo

    I crave no better than your grace awards.

Horatio

    Nor I, although I sit beside my right.

King

    Then by my judgment thus your strife shall end:

    You both deserve, and both shall have reward.

    Nephew, thou took'st his weapon and his horse,   180

    His weapons and his horse are thy reward.

    Horatio, thou didst force him first to yield,

    His ransom therefore is thy valor's fee,

    Appoint the sum as you shall both agree.

    But nephew, thou shalt have the prince in guard   185

    For thine estate best fitteth such a guest;

    Horatio's house were small for all his train.

    Yet in regard thy substance passeth his,

    And that just guerdon[79] may befall desert,

    To him we yield the armour of the prince.   190

    How likes Don Balthazar of this device?

Balthazar

    Right well my liege, if this proviso were,

    That Don Horatio bear us company,

    Whom I admire and love for chivalry.

King

    Horatio, leave him not that loves thee so.   195

    Now let us hence to see our soldiers paid,

    And feast our prisoner as our friendly guest.   *Exeunt*

---

[78] The judgment I shall render.

[79] Remuneration, reward.

Act I, Scene ii

Enter Viceroy, Alexandro, Villuppo and Attendants

Viceroy

    Is our ambassador despatched for Spain?

Alexandro

    Two days, my liege, are passed since his depart.

Viceroy

    And tribute payment gone along with him?

Alexandro

    Ay, my good lord.

Viceroy

    Then rest we here awhile in our unrest,   5

    And feed our sorrows with some inward sighs,

    For deepest cares break never into tears.

    But wherefore sit I in a regal throne?

                    Falls to the ground and takes off his crown

    This better fits a wretch's endless moan.

    Yet this is higher than my fortunes reach,   10

    And therefore better than my state deserves.[80]

    Ay, ay, this earth, image of melancholy,[81]

    Seeks him whom fates adjudge to misery.

    Here let me lie, now am I at the lowest.

    Qui jacet in terra, non habet unde cadat.   15

    In me consumpsit vires fortuna nocendo,

    Nil superest ut jam possit obesse magis.[82]

---

[80] Situation merits.

[81] See word list under "the four humors."

[82] "He who lies upon the ground cannot fall any further. Fortune has spent all her power to hurt me. Nothing is left that can harm me any more."

Yes, Fortune[83] may bereave me of my crown,
Here, take it now, let Fortune do her worst,
She will not rob me of this sable weed.[84]   20
O no, she envies none but pleasant things.
Such is the folly of despiteful chance.
Fortune is blind and sees not my deserts,
So is she deaf and hears not my laments;
And could she hear, yet is she wilful mad,[85]   25
And therefore will not pity my distress.
Suppose that she could pity me, what then?
What help can be expected at her hands
Whose foot is standing on a rolling stone
And mind more mutable than fickle winds?   30
Why wail I then, where's hope of no redress?
Oh yes, complaining makes my grief seem less.
My late ambition hath distained[86] my faith,
My breach of faith occasioned bloody wars,
Those bloody wars have spent my treasure,   35
And with my treasure my people's blood,
And with their blood, my joy and best beloved,
My best beloved, my sweet and only son.
O wherefore went I not to war myself?
The cause was mine, I might have died for both.   40
My years were mellow, his but young and green,
My death were natural, but his was forced.

Alexandro

No doubt, my liege, but still the prince survives.

---

[83] Fortune is usually depicted as unstable and changeable. She is blind and/or deaf, or she may stand on a sphere. Her wheel will turn randomly and irrationally; man has no control over her.

[84] Black clothes for mourning.

[85] Purposefully unreasonable.

[86] Tainted.

Viceroy

    Survives! Ay, where?

Alexandro

    In Spain, a prisoner by mischance of war.   45

Viceroy

    Then they have slain him for his father's fault.

Alexandro

    That were a breach to common law of arms.

Viceroy

    They reck[87] no laws that meditate revenge.

Alexandro

    His ransom's worth will stay from[88] foul revenge.

Viceroy

    No, if he lived the news would soon be here.   50

Alexandro

    Nay, evil news fly faster still than good.

Viceroy

    Tell me no more of news, for he is dead.

Villuppo

    My sovereign, pardon the author[89] of ill news,

    And I'll bewray[90] the fortune of thy son.

Viceroy

    Speak on, I'll guerdon[91] thee whate'er it be.   55

    Mine ear is ready to receive ill news,

    My heart grown hard 'gainst mischief's battery.[92]

    Stand up, I say, and tell thy tale at large.

Villuppo

    Then hear that truth which these mine eyes have seen.

[87] Obey.
[88] Hinder.
[89] Bringer.
[90] Reveal.
[91] Reward.
[92] The assault of ill fortune.

When both the armies were in battle joined,   60
Don Balthazar, amidst the thickest troops,
To win renown did wondrous feats of arms.
Amongst the rest I saw him hand to hand
In single fight with their Lord General,
Till Alexandro, that here counterfeits   65
Under the colour[93] of a duteous friend,
Discharged his pistol at the prince's back,
As though he would have slain their general.
But therewithal Don Balthazar fell down,
And when he fell, then we began to fly.   70
But had he lived, the day had sure been ours.

Alexandro

O wicked forgery! O Traitorous miscreant!

Viceroy

Hold thou thy peace! But now, Villuppo, say
Where then became the carcass of my son?

Villuppo

I saw them drag it to the Spanish tents.   75

Viceroy

Ay, ay, my nightly dreams have told me this.
Thou false, unkind, unthankful, traitorous beast,
Wherein had Balthazar offended thee
That thou shouldst thus betray him to our foes?
Was't Spanish gold that bleared so thine eyes   80
That thou couldst see no part of our deserts?
Perchance, because thou art Terceira's[94] lord,
Thou hast some hope to wear this diadem,
If first my son and then myself were slain,
But thy ambitious thought shall break thy neck.   85
Ay, this was it that made thee spill his blood.

---

[93] Semblance.
[94] One of the islands of the Azores.

Takes the crown and puts it on again

But I'll now wear it till thy blood be spilt.

Alexandro

Vouchsafe, dread sovereign, to hear me speak.

Viceroy

Away with him, his sight[95] is second hell.

Keep him till we determine of his death.   90

Alexandro is led away

If Balthazar be dead, he shall not live.

Villuppo, follow us for thy reward.   *Exit Viceroy*

Villuppo

Thus have I with an envious, forged tale

Deceived the king, betrayed mine enemy,

And hope for guerdon of my villainy.   *Exit* 95

Act I, Scene iii

Enter Horatio and Bel-imperia

Bel-imperia

Signior Horatio, this is the place and hour

Wherein I must entreat thee to relate

The circumstance of Don Andrea's death,

Who, living, was my garland's sweetest flower,

And in his death hath buried my delights.   5

Horatio

For love of him and service to yourself,

I nil[96] refuse this heavy doleful charge.

Your tears and sighs, I fear, will hinder me.

When both our armies were enjoined in fight,

---

[95] The sight of him.
[96] Will not.

Your worthy chevalier[97] amidst the thick'st,   10
For glorious cause still aiming at the fairest,[98]
Was at the last by young Don Balthazar
Encountered hand to hand. Their fight was long,
Their hearts were great, their clamours menacing,
Their strength alike, their strokes both dangerous.   15
But wrathful Nemesis[99] that wicked power,
Envying at Andrea's praise and worth,
Cut short his life to end his praise and worth,
She, she herself, disguised in armour's mask,
(As Pallas[100] was before proud Pergamus)[101]   20
Brought in a fresh supply of halberdiers.[102]
Which paunched[103] his horse, and dinged[104] him to the ground.
Then young Don Balthazar with ruthless rage
Taking advantage of his foe's distress
Did finish what his halberdiers begun,   25
And left not till Andrea's life was done.
Then, though too late, incensed with just remorse,[105]
I with my band set forth against the prince,
And brought him prisoner from his halberdiers,

Bel-imperia

Would thou hadst slain him that so slew my love.   30
But then was Don Andrea's carcass lost?

Horatio

No, that was it for which I chiefly strove,

---

[97] Knight in a lady's service.
[98] Striving for his best in a most worthy cause (here: love of Bel-imperia).
[99] Goddess of retribution, "relentless Fate."
[100] The goddess Athena, on the Greek side in the Trojan War.
[101] Troy.
[102] Soldiers armed with halberds, a combination spear and battle ax.
[103] Stabbed in the belly.
[104] Hurled.
[105] Justly enraged and pitying.

    Nor stepped I back till I recovered him.
    I took him up and wound[106] him in mine arms,
    And wielding[107] him unto my private tent   35
    There laid him down and dewed him with my tears
    And sighed and sorrowed as became a friend.
    But neither friendly sorrow, sighs nor tears
    Could win pale Death from his usurped right.
    Yet this I did, and less I could not do,   40
    I saw him honoured with due funeral.
    This scarf[108] I plucked from off his lifeless arm,
    And wear it in remembrance of my friend.

Bel-imperia

    I know the scarf, would he had kept it still.
    For had he lived he would have kept it still   45
    And worn it for his Bel-imperia's sake,
    For 'twas my favour[109] at his last depart.
    But now wear thou it both for him and me,
    For after him thou hast deserved it best.
    But for thy kindness in his life and death,   50
    Be sure while Bel-imperia's life endures
    She will be Don Horatio's thankful friend.

Horatio

    And madam, Don Horatio will not slack
    Humbly to serve fair Bel-imperia.
    But now, if your good liking stand thereto,   55
    I'll crave your pardon to go seek the prince,
    For so the duke your father gave me charge.   *Exit*

Bel-imperia

    Ay, go, Horatio, leave me here alone,

[106] Held.

[107] Carrying.

[108] Scarves, gloves, handkerchiefs, even sleeves were often given by a lady for her love to wear as a love token.

[109] Gift given as a love token.

For solitude best fits my cheerless mood.
Yet what avails to wail Andrea's death,   60
From whence Horatio proves my second love?
Had he not loved Andrea as he did,
He could not sit in Bel-imperia's thoughts.
But how can love find harbour in my breast
Till I revenge the death of my beloved?   65
Yes, second love shall further my revenge.
I'll love Horatio, my Andrea's friend,
The more to spite the prince that wrought his end.
And where Don Balthazar that slew my love
Himself now pleads for favour at my hands,   70
He shall in rigour of my just disdain[110]
Reap long repentance for his murderous deed.
For what was't else but murderous cowardice,
So many to oppress one valiant knight
Without respect of honour in the fight?   75
And here he comes that murdered my delight.

Enter Lorenzo and Balthazar

Lorenzo
    Sister, what means this melancholy walk?
Bel-imperia
    That for a while I wish no company.
Lorenzo
    But here the prince is come to visit you.
Bel-imperia
    That argues that he lives in liberty.   80
Balthazar
    No madam, but in pleasing servitude.

---

[110] Indignation.

Bel-imperia

    Your prison then, belike, is your conceit.[111]

Balthazar

    Ay, by conceit my freedom is enthralled.

Bel-imperia

    Then with conceit enlarge yourself[112] again.

Balthazar

    What if conceit have laid my heart to gage?[113]   85

Bel-imperia

    Pay that you borrowed and recover it.

Balthazar

    I die if it return from whence it lies.

Bel-imperia

    A heartless man and live? A miracle!

Balthazar

    Ay, lady, love can work such miracles.

Lorenzo

    Tush. tush, my lord, let go these ambages,[114]   90

    And in plain terms acquaint her with your love.

Bel-imperia

    What boots[115] complaint, when there's no remedy?

Balthazar

    Yes, to your gracious self must I complain,

    In whose fair answer lies my remedy,

    On whose perfection all my thoughts attend,   95

    On whose aspect mine eyes find beauty's bower,

    In whose translucent breast my heart is lodged.[116]

---

[111] Is of your imagination.

[112] Free yourself.

[113] Pawned my heart.

[114] Circumlocutions.

[115] Helps; serves.

[116] True lovers often see themselves as having exchanged hearts.

Bel-imperia
> Alas, my lord, these are but words of course,[117]
> And but device to drive me from this place.

She, in going in, lets fall her glove, which Horatio, coming out, takes up

Horatio
> Madam, your glove.   100
Bel-imperia
> Thanks, good Horatio, take it for thy pains.
Balthazar
> Signior Horatio stooped in happy time.
Horatio
> I reaped more grace than I deserved or hoped.
Lorenzo
> My lord, be not dismayed for what is passed,
> You know that women oft are humorous;[118]   105
> These clouds will overblow with little wind.
> Let me alone, I'll scatter them myself.
> Meanwhile, let us devise to spend the time
> In some delightful sports and revelling.
Horatio
> The king, my lord, is coming hither straight   110
> To feast the Portingale ambassador.
> Things were in readiness before I came.
Balthazar
> Then here it fits us to attend the King,
> To welcome hither our ambassador,
> And learn my father and my country's health.   115

Enter the banquet,[119]   trumpets, the King, and ambassador

---

[117] Stale phrases.

[118] Changeable, capricious.

[119] Banquets were usually carried in, spectacularly arranged, to be set on a table.

King

    See, Lord Ambassador, how Spain entreats

    Their prisoner Balthazar, thy viceroy's son.

    We pleasure more in kindness than in wars.

Ambassador

    Sad is our King, and Portingale laments,

    Supposing that Don Balthazar is slain.   120

Balthazar (*aside*)

    So am I slain by beauty's tyranny.

    (*aloud*) You see, my lord, how Balthazar is slain!

    I frolic with the Duke of Castile's son,

    Wrapped every hour in pleasures of the court,

    And graced with favours of his majesty.   125

King

    Put off your greetings till our feast be done.

    Now come and sit with us and taste our cheer.

                           They sit to the banquet

    Sit down, young prince, you are our second guest.

    Brother, sit down, and nephew, take your place.

    Signior Horatio, wait thou upon our cup,   130

    For well thou hast deserved to be honoured.

    Now, lordings, fall to; Spain is Portugal,

    And Portugal is Spain, we both are friends,

    Tribute is paid, and we enjoy our right.

    But where is old Hieronimo, our marshal?   135

    He promised us, in honour of our guest,

    To grace our banquet with some pompous jest.[120]

Enter Hieronimo with a drummer, three knights, each with his scutcheon,[121] *then he fetches three kings. The knights take their crowns and them captive* [122]

[120] Entertainment fit for the court.

[121] Shield, bearing coat of arms.

[122] Kyd makes several historical errors in Hieronimo's explanation of this dumb show.

Hieronimo, this masque contents mine eye,
Although I sound not well the mystery.[123]

Hieronimo

The first armed knight that hung his scutcheon up   140

He takes the scutcheon and gives it to the King

Was English Robert, Earl of Glouchester,
Who, when King Stephen bore sway in Albion,[124]
Arrived with five and twenty thousand men
In Portingale, and by success of war
Enforced the King, then but a Saracen,   145
To bear the yoke of th'English monarchy.[125]

King

My lord of Portingale, by this you see
That which may comfort both your King and you,
And make your late discomfort seem the less.
But say, Hieronimo, what was the next?   150

Hieronimo

The second knight that hung his scutcheon up

He doth as he did before

Was Edmund, Earl of Kent[126] in Albion,
When English Richard wore the diadem.[127]
He came likewise and razed Lisbon walls,
And took the King of Portingale in fight,   155
For which, and other suchlike service done,
He after was created Duke of York.

King

This is another special argument
That Portingale may deign to bear our yoke,
When it by little England hath been yoked.   160

---

[123] Do not quite understand the hidden meaning.
[124] England.
[125] This refers to the capture of Lisbon in 1147; the earl was not present.
[126] Led expedition against Portugal in 1381 with no result.
[127] Crown.

But now, Hieronimo, what were the last?

Hieronimo

The third and last, not least in our account,

Doing as before

Was as the rest a valiant Englishman,
Brave John of Gaunt, the Duke of Lancaster,[128]
As by his scutcheon plainly may appear.   165
He with a puissant[129] army came to Spain,
And took our King of Castile prisoner.

Ambassador

This is an argument for our Viceroy
That Spain may not insult for her success,
Since English warriors likewise conquered Spain,   170
And made them bow their knees to Albion.

King

Hieronimo, I drink to thee for this device,
Which hath pleased both the ambassador and me.
Pledge me, Hieronimo, if you love the King.

Takes the cup of[130] *Horatio*

My Lord, I fear we sit but overlong,   175
Unless our dainties were more delicate,
But welcome are you to the best we have
Now let us in, that you may be despatched;
I think our council is already set.   *Exeunt omnes*

Chorus

Andrea

Come we for this from depth of underground,   180
To see him feast that gave me my death's wound?

[128] Forced to retreat from Spain in 1385.
[129] Strong.
[130] From.

These pleasant sights are sorrow to my soul,
Nothing but league,[131] and love, and banqueting.
Revenge
Be still, Andrea. Ere we go from hence,
I'll turn their friendship into fell despite,[132]   185
Their love to mortal hate, their day to night,
Their hope into despair, their peace to war,
Their joys to pain, their bliss to misery.

---

[131] Alliance.
[132] Cruel hatred.

Act II, Scene i

Enter Lorenzo and Balthazar

Lorenzo

    My lord, though Bel-imperia seem thus coy,

    Let reason hold you in your wonted joy.

    In time the savage bull sustains the yoke.

    In time all haggard hawks will stoop to lure,[133]

    In time small wedges cleave the hardest oak,   5

    In time the flint is pierced with softest shower.

    And she in time will fall from her disdain,

    And rue the sufferance of your friendly pain.[134]

Balthazar

    No, she is wilder and more hard withal,

    Than beast, or bird, or tree, or stony wall.   10

    But wherefore blot I Bel-imperia's name

    It is my fault, not she, that merits blame.

    My feature[135] is not to content her sight,

    My words are rude and work her no delight.

    The lines I send her are but harsh and ill,   15

    Such as to drop from Pan and Marsyas'[136] quill.[137]

    My presents are not of sufficient cost,

    And, being worthless, all my labour's lost.

    Yet might she love me for my valiancy,[138]

    Ay, but that's slandered by captivity.   20

---

[133] Untrained hawks will learn to come to the lure, a device used in training.

[134] Take pity on your patient suffering.

[135] Not only the face, but the whole person.

[136] Pan, "guardian of flocks," a god of shepherds, and Marsyas, a satyr. Both challenged Apollo to a contest of music, and both lost.

[137] Means both pen and flute-like instrument.

[138] Bravery, valor.

Yet might she love me to content her sire,
Ay, but her reason masters her desire.
Yet might she love me as her brother's friend,
Ay, but her hopes aim at some other end.
Yet might she love me to uprear her state,[139]   25
Ay, but perhaps she hopes some nobler mate.
Yet might she love me as her beauty's thrall,
Ay, but I fear she cannot love at all.

Lorenzo

My lord, for my sake leave these ecstasies,[140]
And doubt not but we'll find some remedy.   30
Some cause there is that lets you not be loved;
First that must needs be known, and then removed.
What if my sister love some other knight?

Balthazar

My summer's day will turn to winter's night.

Lorenzo

I have already found a stratagem   35
To sound the bottom of this doubtful theme.
My lord, for once you shall be ruled by me,
Hinder me not whate'er you hear or see.
By force or fair means will I cast about
To find the truth of all this question out.   40
Ho, Pedringano!

Pedringano (*within*)

        Signior!

Lorenzo

              Vien qui presto![141]

Enter Pedringano

---

[139] To gain a better social position.
[140] Violent passions.
[141] "Come here at once" (Italian).

Pedringano

    Hath your lordship any service to command me?

Lorenzo

    Ay, Pedringano, service of import.

    And not to spend the time in trifling words,

    Thus stands the case. It is not long, thou know'st,   45

    Since I did shield thee from my father's wrath

    For thy conveyance[142] in Andrea's love,

    For which thou wert adjudged to punishment.

    I stood betwixt thee and thy punishment,

    And since, thou know'st how I have favoured thee.   50

    Now to these favours will I add reward,

    Not with fair words, but store of golden coin,

    And lands and living joined with dignities,

    If thou but satisfy my just demand.

    Tell truth, and have me for thy lasting friend.   55

Pedringano

    Whate'er it be your lordship shall demand,

    My bounden duty bids me tell the truth,

    If case it lie in me[143] to tell the truth.

Lorenzo

    Then, Pedringano, this is my demand:

    Whom loves my sister, Bel-imperia?   60

    For she reposeth all her trust in thee.

    Speak, man, and gain both friendship and reward,

    I mean, whom loves she in Andrea's place?

Pedringano

    Alas, my lord, since Don Andrea's death

    I have no credit with her as before,   65

    And therefore know not if she love or no.

---

[142] Acting as go-between.
[143] If I can.

Lorenzo

>Nay, if thou dally, then I am thy foe,   *Draws his sword*
>And fear shall force what friendship cannot win.
>Thy death shall bury what thy life conceals.
>Thou diest for more esteeming her than me.   70

Pedringano

>O stay, my lord!

Lorenzo

>Yet speak the truth, and I will guerdon[144] thee,
>And shield thee from whatever can ensue,
>And will conceal whate'er proceeds from thee.
>But if thou dally once again, thou diest.   75

Pedringano

>If Madam Bel-imperia be in love—

Lorenzo

>What, villain! Ifs and ands!   *Offers to kill him*

Pedringano

>O stay, my lord, she loves Horatio.   *Balthazar starts back*

Lorenzo

>What, Don Horatio, our Knight Marshal's son?

Pedringano

>Even him, my lord.   80

Lorenzo

>Now say but how know'st thou he is her love,
>And thou shalt find me kind and liberal.
>Stand up, I say, and fearless tell the truth.

Pedringano

>She sent him letters, which myself perused,
>Full-fraught[145] with lines and arguments of love,   85
>Preferring him before Prince Balthazar.

---

[144] Reward.
[145] Loaded to capacity.

Lorenzo

    Swear on this cross[146] that what thou say'st is true

    And that thou wilt conceal what thou hast told.

Pedringano

    I swear to both by him that made us all.

Lorenzo

    In hope thine oath is true, here's thy reward.   90

    But if I prove thee perjured and unjust,[147]

    This very sword whereon thou took'st thine oath

    Shall be the worker of thy tragedy.

Pedringano

    What I have said is true, and shall, for me

    Be still concealed from Bel-imperia.   95

    Besides, your honour's liberality

    Deserves my duteous service even till death.

Lorenzo

    Let this be all that thou shalt do for me:

    Be watchful when and where these lovers meet,

    And give me notice in some secret sort.   100

Pedringano

    I will, my lord.

Lorenzo

    Then shalt thou find that I am liberal.

    Thou know'st that I can more advance thy state[148]

    Than she, be therefore wise and fail me not.

    Go and attend her as thy custom is,   105

    Lest absence make her think thou dost amiss.[149]

                             Exit Pedringano

    Why so! *Tam armis quam ingenio.*[150]

---

[146] The sword-hilt is shaped like a cross.

[147] Dishonest.

[148] Better your position.

[149] You are into mischief.

[150] "By force and skill equally."

Where words prevail not, violence prevails,
But gold doth more than either of them both.
How likes Prince Balthazar this stratagem?   110

Balthazar

Both well and ill, it makes me glad and sad:
Glad, that I know the hinderer of my love,
Sad, that I fear she hates me whom I love.
Glad, that I know on whom to be revenged,
Sad, that she'll fly me if I take revenge.   115
Yet must I take revenge or die myself,
For love resisted grows impatient.
I think Horatio be my destined plague:
First, in his hand he brandished a sword,
And with that sword he fiercely waged war,   120
And in that war, he gave me dangerous wounds,
And by those wounds he forced me to yield,
And by my yielding I became his slave.
Now in his mouth he carries pleasing words,
Which pleasing words do harbour sweet conceits,[151]   125
Which sweet conceits are limed with[152] sly deceits,
Which sly deceits smooth[153] Bel-imperia's ears,
And through her ears dive down into her heart,
And in her heart set him where I should stand.
Thus hath he ta'en my body by his force,   130
And now by sleight[154] would captivate my soul.
But in his fall I'll tempt the destinies,
And either lose my life or win my love.

Lorenzo

Let's go, my lord, your staying stays revenge.

---

[151] Charming figures of speech.
[152] Are made into traps; from "bird lime," a glue-like substance smeared onto branches to make birds stick.
[153] Gentle; flatter.
[154] On the sly.

Do you but follow me and gain your love.   135
Her favour must be won by his remove.[155]   *Exeunt*

Act II, Scene ii

Enter Horatio and Bel-imperia

Horatio

Now, madam, since by favour of your love
Our hidden smoke is turned to open flame,
And that with looks and words we feed our thoughts,
Two chief contents[156] where more cannot be had,
Thus in the midst of love's fair blandishments,   5
Why show you sign of inward languishments?

Pedringano showeth all to the Prince and Lorenzo placing them in secret [157]

Bel-imperia

My heart, sweet friend,[158] is like a ship at sea:
She wisheth port, where, riding all at ease
She may repair what stormy times have worn,
And leaning on the shore may sing with joy   10
That pleasure follows pain, and bliss annoy.[159]
Possession of thy love's the only port
Wherein my heart, with fears and hopes long tossed,
Each hour doth wish and long to make resort,
There to repair the joys that it hath lost,   15

[155] Removing him.

[156] Means of being content.

[157] The eavesdropping takes place on the balcony.

[158] "Friend," in Elizabethan times, often used to address a lover.

[159] Trouble.

And, sitting safe, to sing in Cupid's choir
That sweetest bliss is crown of love's desire.

Balthazar (*above*)

O sleep, mine eyes, see not my love profaned;
Be deaf, my ears, hear not my discontent;
Die, heart, another joys[160] what thou deservest.   20

Lorenzo

Watch still, mine eyes, to see this love disjoined;
Hear still, mine ears, to hear them both lament;
Live, heart, to joy at fond[161] Horatio's fall.

Bel-imperia

Why stands Horatio speechless all this while?

Horatio

The less I speak, the more I meditate.   25

Bel-imperia

But whereon dost thou chiefly meditate?

Horatio

On dangers past, and pleasures to ensue.

Balthazar

On pleasures past, and dangers to ensue.

Bel-imperia

What dangers and what pleasures dost thou mean?

Horatio

Dangers of war, and pleasures of our love.   30

Lorenzo

Dangers of death, but pleasures none at all.

Bel-imperia

Let dangers go, thy war shall be with me,
But such a war as breaks no bond of peace.
Speak thou fair words, I'll cross them with fair words.
Send thou sweet looks, I'll meet them with sweet looks.   35

---

[160] Enjoys.
[161] Foolish; too enamored.

Write loving lines, I'll answer loving lines.
Give me a kiss, I'll countercheck[162] thy kiss!
Be this our warring peace, or peaceful war.

Horatio

But, gracious madam, then appoint the field
Where trial of this war shall first be made. 40

Balthazar

Ambitious villain, how his boldness grows!

Bel-imperia

Then be thy father's pleasant bower[163] the field,
Where first we vowed a mutual amity.
The court were dangerous, that place is safe.
Our hour shall be when Vesper[164] 'gins to rise, 45
That summons home distressful travellers.
There none shall hear us but the harmless birds.
Happily[165] the gentle nightingale
Shall carol us asleep ere we be 'ware,
And, singing with the prickle at her breast,[166] 50
Tell our delight and mirthful dalliance.
Till then each hour will seem a year and more.

Horatio

But, honey sweet, and honourable love,
Return we now into your father's sight;
Dangerous suspicion waits on our delight. 55

Lorenzo

Ay, danger mixed with jealous[167] despite
Shall send thy soul into eternal night. *Exeunt*

---

[162] Take action against.

[163] Arbor; seat enclosed with trellises, branches, or the like.

[164] The evening star.

[165] Maybe.

[166] Nightingales were supposed to sing with a thorn against their breast.

[167] Suspicious.

Act II, Scene iii

Enter King of Spain, Portingale, Ambassador, Don Cyprian, etc.

King

    Brother of Castile, to the prince's love

    What says your daughter Bel-imperia?

Duke of Castile

    Although she coy it[168] as becomes her kind,[169]

    And yet dissemble that she loves the prince,

    I doubt not, I, but she will stoop[170] in time.   5

    And were she froward,[171] which she will not be,

    Yet herein shall she follow my advice,

    Which is to love him or forego my love.

King

    Then, Lord Ambassador of Portingale,

    Advise thy King to make this marriage up,   10

    For strengthening of our late-confirmed league;

    I know no better means to make us friends.

    Her dowry shall be large and liberal.

    Besides that she is daughter and half-heir

    Unto our brother here, Don Cyprian,   15

    And shall enjoy the moiety[172] of his land

    I'll grace her marriage with an uncle's gift,

    And this it is: In case the match go forward,

    The tribute which you pay shall be released,

    And if by Balthazar she have a son,   20

    He shall enjoy the kingdom after us.

---

[168] Pretends coyness.

[169] As women will do.

[170] Obey; a hawk "stoops to the lure" when trained.

[171] Not obedient, rebellious.

[172] Half.

Ambassador

    I'll make the motion to my sovereign liege,

    And work it if my counsel may prevail.

King

    Do so, my lord, and if he give consent,

    I hope his presence here will honour us   25

    In celebration of the nuptial day;

    And let himself determine of the time.

Ambassador

    Will't please your grace command me aught beside?

King

    Commend me to the King, and so farewell.

    But where's Prince Balthazar to take his leave?   30

Ambassador

    That is performed already, my good lord.

King

    Amongst the rest of what you have in charge,

    The prince's ransom must not be forgot.

    That's none of mine, but his that took him prisoner,

    And well his forwardness[173] deserves reward.   35

    That was Horatio, our Knight Marshal's son.

Ambassador

    Between us there's a price already pitched,[174]

    And shall be sent with all convenient speed.

King

    Then once again farewell, my lord.

Ambassador

    Farewell, my Lord of Castile and the rest.   *Exit* 40

King

    Now, brother, you must take some little pains

    To win fair Bel-imperia from her will.

[173] Skill.

[174] Agreed upon.

Young virgins must be ruled by their friends.
The prince is amiable and loves her well.
If she neglect him and forego his love,   45
She both will wrong her own estate and ours.
Therefore, whiles I do entertain the prince
With greatest pleasure that our court affords,
Endeavour you to win your daughter's thought.
If she give back,[175] all this will come to naught.   *Exeunt*

Act II, Scene iv

Enter Horatio, Bel-imperia, and Pedringano

Horatio

    Now that the night begins with sable[176] wings
    To overcloud the brightness of the sun,
    And that in darkness pleasures may be done,
    Come, Bel-imperia, let us to the bower,
    And there in safety pass a pleasant hour.   5

Bel-imperia

    I follow thee, my love, and will not back,
    Although my fainting heart controls my soul.[177]

Horatio

    Why, make you doubt of Pedringano's faith?

Bel-imperia

    No, he is as trusty as my second self.
    Go, Pedringano, watch without[178] the gate,   10
    And let us know if any make approach.

---

[175] Turns away from us.
[176] Black.
[177] Her heart (fearful) is in conflict with her soul (amorous).
[178] Outside.

Pedringano (*aside*)

    Instead of watching, I'll deserve more gold

    By fetching Don Lorenzo to this match.   *Exit Pendrango*

Horatio

    What means my love?

Bel-imperia   I know not what myself

    And yet my heart foretells me some mischance.   15

Horatio

    Sweet, say not so, fair fortune is our friend,

    And heavens have shut up day to pleasure us.

    The stars, thou see'st, hold back their twinkling shine,

    And Luna[179] hides herself to pleasure us.

Bel-imperia

    Thou hast prevailed, I'll conquer my misdoubt,   20

    And in thy love and counsel drown my fear.

    I fear no more, love now is all my thoughts.

    Why sit we not? For pleasure asketh ease.

Horatio

    The more thou sit'st within these leafy bowers,

    The more will Flora[180] deck it with her flowers.   25

Bel-imperia

    Ay, but if Flora spy Horatio here,

    Her jealous eye will think I sit too near.

Horatio

    Hark, madam, how the birds record[181] by night,

    For joy that Bel-imperia sits in sight.

Bel-imperia

    No, Cupid counterfeits the nightingale,   30

    To frame sweet music to Horatio's tale.

---

[179] The moon.

[180] The goddess of blossoming plants.

[181] Sing.

Horatio

If Cupid sing, then Venus[182] is not far;

Ay thou art Venus or some fairer star.

Bel-imperia

If I be Venus, thou must needs be Mars,[183]

And where Mars reigneth, there must needs be wars.   35

Horatio

Then thus begin our wars! Put forth thy hand,

That it may combat with my ruder[184] hand.

Bel-imperia

Set forth thy foot to try the push of mine.

Horatio

But first my looks shall combat against thine.

Bel-imperia

Then ward[185] thyself! I dart this kiss at thee.   40

Horatio

Thus I retort the dart thou threw'st at me.

Bel-imperia

Nay then, to gain the glory of the field,

My twining arms shall yoke and make thee yield.

Horatio

Nay then, my arms are large and strong withal;

Thus elms by vines are compassed till they fall.   45

Bel-imperia

O let me go, for in my troubled eyes

Now mayst thou read that life in passion dies.[186]

---

[182] The goddess of passionate love.

[183] The god of war. Venus (in Greek mythology Aphrodite) betrayed her husband Hephaestus with Mars (Ares).

[184] Rougher.

[185] Guard.

[186] This "die," as well as others in this scene, plays on the common Elizabethan double meaning of actual death and sexual orgasm.

Horatio

O stay a while, and I will die with thee,

So shalt thou yield and yet have conquered me.

Bel-imperia

Who's there? Pedringano? We are betrayed!   50

Enter Lorenzo, Balthazar, Serberine, Pedringano, disguised

Lorenzo

My lord, away with her, take her aside.

O sir, forbear, your valour is already tried.

Quickly despatch, my masters.   *They hang him in the arbour*

Horatio

What, will you murder me?

Lorenzo

Ay, thus, and thus! These are the fruits of love.   55

They stab him

Bel-imperia

O save his life, and let me die for him!

O save him, brother, save him, Balthazar!

I loved Horatio, but he loved not me.

Balthazar

But Balthazar loves Bel-imperia.

Lorenzo

Although his life was still ambitious proud,[187]   60

Yet is he at the highest now he is dead.

Bel-imperia

Murder! Murder! Help, Hieronimo, help!

Lorenzo

Come, stop her mouth, away with her.

Exeunt, leaving Horatio's body

---

[187] Out for a position to satisfy his pride.

Act II, Scene v

Enter Hieronimo in his shirt[188]

Hieronimo

What outcries pluck me from my naked bed,
And chill my throbbing heart with trembling fear,
Which never danger yet could daunt before?
Who calls Hieronimo? Speak, here I am.
I did not slumber, therefore 'twas no dream.   5
No, no, it was some woman cried for help
And here within this garden did she cry,
And in this garden must I rescue her.
But stay, what murderous spectacle is this?
A man hanged up and all the murderers gone,   10
And in my bower to lay the guilt on me.
This place was made for pleasure, not for death.

He cuts him down

Those garments that he wears I oft have seen—
Alas, it is Horatio, my sweet son!
O no, but he that whilom[189] was my son.   15
O was it thou that calledst me from my bed?
O speak, if any spark of life remain!
I am thy father. Who hath slain my son?
What savage monster, not of human kind,
Hath here been glutted with thy harmless blood,   20
And left thy bloody corpse dishonoured here,
For me, amidst these dark and deathful shades,
To drown thee with an ocean of my tears?
O heavens, why made you night to cover sin?
By day this deed of darkness had not been.   25

---

[188] Nightshirt.
[189] Until now.

O earth, why didst thou not in time devour
The vild[190] profaner of this sacred bower?
O poor Horatio, what hadst thou misdone,
To lose thy life ere life was new begun?[191]
O wicked butcher, whatsoe'er thou wert,   30
How could thou strangle virtue and desert?
Ay me most wretched, that have lost my joy,
In losing my Horatio, my sweet boy!

Enter Isabella

Isabella

My husband's absence makes my heart to throb.
Hieronimo!   35
Hieronimo

Here, Isabella, help me to lament,
For sighs are stopped and all my tears are spent.
Isabella

What world of grief! My son Horatio!
O where's the author[192] of this endless woe?
Hieronimo

To know the author were some ease of grief,   40
For in revenge my heart would find relief.
Isabella

Then is he gone? And is my son gone too?
O, gush out, tears, fountains and floods of tears;
Blow, sighs, and raise an everlasting storm,
For outrage[193] fits our cursed wretchedness. [Ψ]   45

---

[190] Vile.

[191] Had begun a new phase.

[192] The responsible one.

[193] Great passion.

[Ψ] See Appendix for the first 1602 addition, placed here.

Hieronimo

    Sweet lovely rose, ill plucked before thy time,

    Fair worthy son, not conquered, but betrayed,

    I'll kiss thee now, for words with tears are stayed.

Isabella

    And I'll close up the glasses of his sight,[194]

    For once these eyes were only my delight.   50

Hieronimo

    Seest thou this handkercher besmeared with blood?

    It shall not from me till I take revenge.

    Seest thou those wounds that yet are bleeding fresh?

    I'll not entomb them till I have revenged.

    Then will I joy amidst my discontent,   55

    Till then my sorrow never shall be spent.

Isabella

    The heavens are just, murder cannot be hid;

    Time is the author both of truth and right,

    And time will bring this treachery to light.

Hieronimo

    Meanwhile, good Isabella, cease thy plaints,[195]   60

    Or at the least dissemble them awhile;

    So shall we sooner find this practice out,

    And learn by whom all this was brought about.

    Come, Isabel, now let us take him up,   *They take him up*

    And bear him in from out this cursed place.   65

    I'll say his dirge,[196] singing fits not this case.

    O aliquis mihi pulchrum ver educat herbas

                         Hieronimo sets his breast unto his sword

    Misceat, et nostro detur medicina dolori;

    Aut, si qui faciunt animis oblivia, succos

---

[194] His eyes.

[195] Complaints.

[196] Funeral song.

Praebeat; ipse metam magnum quaecunque per orbem   70
Gramina Sol pulchras effert in luminis oras;
Ipse bibam quicquid mediatur saga veneni,
Quicquid et herbarum vi caeca nenia nectit:
Omnia perpetiar, lethum quoque, dum semel omnis
Noster in extincto moriatur pectore sensus.   75
Ergo tuos oculos nunquam, mea vita, videbo,
Et tua perpetuus sepelivit lumina somnus?
Emoriar tecum: sic, sic juvat ire sub umbras.
At tamen absistam properato cedere letho,
Ne mortem vindicta tuam tum nulla sequatur.[197]   80

     Here he throws the sword from him and bears the body away

Chorus

Andrea

    Brought'st thou me hither to increase my pain?
    I looked[198] that Balthazar should have been slain;
    But 'tis my friend Horatio that is slain,
    And they abuse fair Bel-imperia,
    On whom I doted[199] more than all the world,   85
    Because she loved me more than all the world.

---

[197] "O, let someone mix me herbs brought forth by the beautiful spring, and let there be balm for our grief; or let him offer potions if any be that bring forgetfulness. I shall myself gather any fair plants the sun brings forth into light in this great world; I'll drink whatever potion the wise-woman shall brew and whatever herbs her spells unite in secret force. I will endure all things, even death, until all our feelings die in this already dead breast. And so, my life, I shall never see your eyes again, and has everlasting sleep buried your lights (i.e., eyes)? Let me die with you, so would I happily go into the shadows. Nonetheless I will avoid yielding to a hasty death, for then no vengeance should follow your death."

[198] Expected.

[199] Whom I loved inordinately.

Revenge

    Thou talk'st of harvest when the corn is green:

    The end is crown of every work well done;

    The sickle comes not till the corn be ripe.

    Be still, and ere I lead thee from this place,   90

    I'll show thee Balthazar in heavy case.[200]

[200] In a tight spot.

Act III, Scene i

Enter the Viceroy of Portingale, Nobles, Villuppo

Viceroy

    Unfortunate condition of kings,
    Seated amidst so many helpless doubts!
    First we are placed upon extremest height,
    And oft supplanted with exceeding heat,
    But ever subject to the wheel of chance;   5
    And at our highest never joy we so
    As we both doubt and dread our overthrow.
    So striveth not the waves with sundry winds
    As Fortune toileth in the affairs of kings,
    That would be feared, yet fear to be beloved,   10
    Sith fear or love to kings is flattery.[201]
    For instance, lordings,[202] look upon your King,
    By hate deprived of his dearest son,
    The only hope of our successive line.

First Nobleman

    I had not thought that Alexandro's heart   15
    Had been envenomed with such extreme hate,
    But now I see that words have several works,[203]
    And there's no credit in the countenance.[204]

Villuppo

    No, for, my lord, had you beheld the train[205]

---

[201] Kings, too, are subjected to the vagaries of Fortune; her wheel will plunge one from the utmost heights to the low point of defeat and death at random.

[202] Lords.

[203] A man's action and speech do not always match.

[204] You cannot judge a man by his face.

[205] Deceit.

That feigned love has coloured in his looks,   20
When he in camp consorted[206] Balthazar,
Far more inconstant had you thought the sun,
That hourly[207] coasts[208] the centre of the earth,[209]
Than Alexandro's purpose to[210] the prince.

Viceroy

No more, Villuppo, thou hast said enough,   25
And with thy words thou slay'st our wounded thoughts,
Nor shall I longer dally with the world,
Procrastinating Alexandro's death.
Go, some of you, and fetch the traitor forth.
That as he is condemned he may die.   30

Enter Alexandro with a nobleman and Halberts[211]

Second Nobleman

In such extremes will naught but patience serve.

Alexandro

But in extremes what patience shall I use?
Nor discontents it me to leave the world
With whom there nothing can prevail but wrong.[212]

Second Nobleman

Yet hope the best.

Alexandro   'Tis Heaven is my hope.   35
As for the earth, it is too much infect
To yield me hope of any of her mould.[213]

---

[206] Was in company with.

[207] Regularly; within a given number of hours.

[208] Circles.

[209] Here, the old cosmology still applies. The earth is the center around which the sun, with constancy, revolves.

[210] Relationship with.

[211] Halberdiers.

[212] All I receive is injustice.

[213] Anyone created on earth.

Viceroy

    Why linger ye? Bring forth that daring fiend,

    And let him die for his accursed deed.

Alexandro

    Not that I fear the extremity of death,   40

    For nobles cannot stoop to servile fear,

    Do I, O King, thus discontented live.

    But this, O this, torments my labouring soul,

    That thus I die suspected of a sin

    Whereof, as heavens have known my secret thoughts,   45

    So am I free from this suggestion.[214]

Viceroy

    No more, I say! To the tortures! When!

    Bind him and burn his body in those flames

                         They bind him to the stake

    That shall prefigure those unquenched fires

    Of Phlegethon[215] prepared for his soul.   50

Alexandro

    My guiltless death will be avenged on thee,

    On thee, Villuppo, that hath maliced[216] thus,

    Or for thy meed[217] hast falsely me accused.

Villuppo

    Nay Alexandro, if thou menace me,

    I'll lend a hand to send thee to the lake[218]   55

    Where those thy words shall perish with thy works.

    Injurious traitor, monstrous homicide!

Enter Ambassador

[214] Wrongful accusation.

[215] Fiery river in the Underworld.

[216] Intended harm.

[217] Gain.

[218] Acheron, river or lake in the Underworld.

Ambassador

 Stay, hold a while,

 And here, with pardon of his majesty,

 Lay hands upon Villuppo.

Viceroy   Ambassador,   60

 What news hath urged this sudden entrance?

Ambassador

 Know, sovereign lord, that Balthazar doth live.

Viceroy

 What say'st thou? Liveth Balthazar, our son?

Ambassador

 Your highness' son, Lord Balthazar, doth live;

 And, well entreated in the court of Spain,   65

 Humbly commends him to your majesty.

 These eyes beheld, and these my followers;

 With these, the letters of the King's commends,[219]

             Gives him letters

 Are happy witnesses of his Highness' health.

     The Viceroy looks on the letters, and proceeds

Viceroy (*reads*)

 "Thy son doth live, your tribute is received,   70

 Thy peace is made, and we are satisfied.

 The rest resolve upon[220] as things proposed

 For both our honours and thy benefit."

Ambassador

 These are his highness' farther articles.

          He gives him more letters

Viceroy

 Accursed wretch, to intimate[221] these ills   75

 Against the life and reputation

 Of noble Alexandro! Come, my lord,

---

[219] Greetings.

[220] Decide.

[221] Proclaim.

Let him unbind thee that is bound to death,
To make a quital[222] for thy discontent.   *They unbind him*

Alexandro

Dread lord, in kindness[223] you could do no less   80
Upon report of such a damned fact.
But thus we see our innocence hath saved
The hopeless life which thou, Villuppo, sought
By thy suggestions to have massacred.

Viceroy

Say, false Villuppo, wherefore didst thou thus   85
Falsely betray Lord Alexandro's life?
Him, whom thou knowest that no unkindness else
But even the slaughter of our dearest son
Could once have moved us to have misconceived.[224]

Alexandro

Say, treacherous Villuppo, tell the King   90
Wherein hath Alexandro used thee ill?

Villuppo

Rent with remembrance of so foul a deed,
My guilty soul submits me to thy doom,
For not for Alexandro's injuries,
But for reward and hope to be preferred,   95
Thus have I shamelessly hazarded his life.

Viceroy

Which, villain, shall be ransomed with thy death,
And not so mean a torment as we here
Devised for him who thou said'st slew our son,
But with the bitterest torments and extremes   100
That may be yet invented for thine end.

Alexandro seems to entreat

---

[222] Requital.
[223] As king ("being of the king kind").
[224] Thought badly of.

Entreat me not, go, take the traitor hence.

Exit Villuppo and Guard

And, Alexandro, let us honour thee
With public notice of thy loyalty.
To end those things articulated[225] here   105
By our great lord, the mighty King of Spain,
We with our council will deliberate.
Come, Alexandro, keep us company.   *Exeunt*

Act III, Scene ii

Enter Hieronimo

Hieronimo

O eyes, no eyes, but fountains fraught[226] with tears.
O life, no life, but lively form of death.
O world, no world, but mass of public wrongs,
Confused and filled with murder and misdeeds!
O sacred heavens! If this unhallowed deed,   5
If this inhuman and barbarous attempt,
If this incomparable murder thus
Of mine, but now no more my son,
Shall unrevealed and unrevenged pass,
How should we term your dealings to be just,   10
If you unjustly deal with those that in your justice trust?
The night, sad secretary to my moans,
With direful visions wake my vexed soul,
And with the wounds of my distressful[227] son
Solicit me for notice of his death.   15

---

[225] Set down.
[226] Filled.
[227] Distressed.

The ugly fiends do sally forth of hell,
And frame my steps to unfrequented paths,
And fear[228] my heart with fierce inflamed thoughts.
The cloudy day my discontents records,
Early begins to register my dreams   20
And drive me forth to seek the murderer.
Eyes, life, world, heavens, hell, night and day,
See, search, show, send some man, some mean, that may—

A letter falleth

What's here? a letter? Tush, it is not so!
A letter written to Hieronimo!   *Red ink*[229] 25
(*Reads*[230]) "For want of ink, receive this bloody writ.
Me hath my hapless[231] brother hid from thee.
Revenge thyself on Balthazar and him,
For these were they that murdered thy son.
Hieronimo, revenge Horatio's death,   30
And better fare than Bel-imperia doth."
What means this unexpected miracle?
My son slain by Lorenzo and the prince!
What cause had they Horatio to malign?[232]
Or what might move thee, Bel-imperia,   35
To accuse thy brother, had he been the mean?
Hieronimo, beware, thou art betrayed,
And to entrap thy life this train[233] is laid.
Advise thee therefore, be not credulous:
This is devised to endanger thee   40
That thou, by this, Lorenzo shouldst accuse,

---

[228] Make fearful.
[229] This stage direction indicates that the letter is meant to be seen by the audience.
[230] The 1592 edition of the play has Bel-imperia speak the text of the letter.
[231] Luckless.
[232] Seek to harm.
[233] Trap, plot.

And he, for thy dishonour done, should draw
Thy life in question, and thy name in hate.
Dear was the life of my beloved son,
And of his death behoves me be revenged.   45
Then hazard not thine own, Hieronimo,
But live t'effect thy resolution.[234]
I therefore will by circumstances[235] try
What I can gather to confirm this writ,
And, hearkening near the Duke of Castile's house,   50
Close[236] if I can with Bel-imperia,
To listen more, but nothing to bewray.[237]

Enter Pedringano

   Now, Pedringano!
Pedringano   Now, Hieronimo!
Hieronimo
   Where's thy lady?
Pedringano   I know not; here's my lord.

Enter Lorenzo

Lorenzo
   How now, who's this? Hieronimo?
Hieronimo   My lord.   55
Pedringano
   He asketh for my lady Bel-imperia.
Lorenzo
   What to do, Hieronimo? The duke, my father, hath

---

[234] To carry out what you have decided to do.
[235] In a roundabout way.
[236] Meet.
[237] Betray, give away.

Upon some disgrace awhile removed her hence
But if it be aught I may inform her of,
Tell me, Hieronimo, and I'll let her know it.   60

Hieronimo

Nay, nay, my lord, I thank you, it shall not need.
I had a suit unto her, but too late,
And her disgrace makes me unfortunate.

Lorenzo

Why so, Hieronimo? Use me.^Ψ

Hieronimo

O no, my lord, I dare not, it must not be,   65
I humbly thank your lordship.

Lorenzo   Why then, farewell.

Hieronimo

My grief no heart, my thoughts no tongue can tell.   *Exit*

Lorenzo

Come hither, Pedringano, see'st thou this?

Pedringano

My lord, I see it, and suspect it too.

Lorenzo

This is that damned villain, Serberine,   70
That hath, I fear, revealed Horatio's death.

Pedringano

My lord, he could not, 'twas so lately done,
And since, he hath not left my company.

Lorenzo

Admit he have not, his condition²³⁸'s such
As fear or flattering words may make him false.   75
I know his humour,²³⁹ and therewith repent
That e'er I used him in this enterprise.

---

^Ψ See appendix for 1602 addition beginning here, replacing ll. 65-66.

²³⁸ Nature.

²³⁹ Disposition.

But, Pedringano, to prevent the worst,
And 'cause I know thee secret as my soul,
Here, for thy further satisfaction, take thou this,   80

Gives him more gold

And hearken to me. Thus it is devised.
This night thou must, and prithee so resolve
Meet Serberine at Saint Luigi's Park—
Thou know'st 'tis here hard by behind the house—
There take thy stand, and see thou strike him sure,   85
For die he must, if we do mean to live.

Pedringano

But how shall Serberine be there, my lord?

Lorenzo

Let me alone,[240] I'll send to him to meet
The prince and me, where thou must do this deed.

Pedringano

It shall be done, my lord, it shall be done,   90
And I'll go arm myself to meet him there.

Lorenzo

When things shall alter, as I hope they will,
Then shalt thou mount[241] for this; thou know'st my mind.

Exit Pedringano

Che le Ieron![242]

Enter Page

Page   My lord?
Lorenzo   Go, sirrah, to Serberine,
And bid him forthwith meet the prince and me   95
At Saint Luigi's Park, behind the house,
This evening, boy.

---

[240] Leave that to me.
[241] Rise (but later Pedringano "mounts" the gallows).
[242] Unexplained, but seems to be a summons for the page.

Page   I go, my lord.

Lorenzo

But, sirrah, let the hour be eight o'clock.
Bid him not fail.

Page   I fly, my lord.   *Exit*

Lorenzo

Now to confirm the complot[243] thou hast cast[244]   100
Of all these practices,[245] I'll spread the watch,[246]
Upon precise commandment from the King,
Strongly to guard the place where Pedringano
This night shall murder hapless Serberine.
Thus must we work that will avoid distrust,   105
Thus must we practise to prevent mishap,
And thus one ill another must expulse.[247]
This sly enquiry of Hieronimo
For Bel-imperia breeds suspicion,
And this suspicion bodes a further ill.   110
As for myself, I know my secret fault,
And so do they, but I have dealt for them.
They that for coin their souls endangered,
To save my life for coin shall venture theirs.
And better it's that base[248] companions die,   115
Than by their life to hazard our good haps.[249]
Nor shall they live, for me to fear their faith.
I'll trust myself, myself shall be my friend,
For die they shall, slaves[250] are ordained to no other end

                                                        Exit

[243] Plot.
[244] Planned.
[245] Schemes.
[246] Position the constables.
[247] Remove.
[248] Of low class.
[249] Fortune.
[250] Lowly fellows, knaves.

Act III, Scene iii

Enter Pedringano with a pistol

Pedringano

    Now, Pedringano, bid thy pistol hold![251]

    And hold on, Fortune, once more favour me!

    Give but success to mine attempting spirit,

    And let me shift[252] for taking of mine aim!

    Here is the gold, this is the gold proposed,   5

    It is no dream that I adventure for,

    But Pedringano is possessed thereof.

    And he that would not strain his conscience

    For him that thus his liberal purse hath stretched,

    Unworthy such a favour, may he fail.   10

    And wishing, want, when such as I prevail,

    As for the fear of apprehension,

    I know, if need should be, my noble lord

    Will stand between me and ensuing harms.

    Besides, this place is free from all suspect.[253]   15

    Here therefore will I stay and take my stand.

Enter the Watch

First Watch

    I wonder much for what intent it is

    That we are thus expressly charged to watch.

Second Watch

    'Tis by commandment in the King's own name.

---

[251] Work properly.
[252] Let it be up to me.
[253] Suspicion.

Third Watch

> But we were never wont to watch and ward[254]   20
> So near the duke his brother's house before.

Second Watch

> Content yourself, stand close,[255] there's somewhat in't.

Enter Serberine

Serberine

> Here, Serberine, attend and stay thy pace,[256]
> For here did Don Lorenzo's page appoint
> That thou by his command shouldst meet with him.   25
> How fit a place, if one were so disposed,
> Methinks this corner is, to close with[257] one.

Pedringano

> Here comes the bird that I must seize upon.
> Now, Pedringano, or never play the man!

Serberine

> I wonder that his lordship stays so long,   30
> Or wherefore should he send for me so late?

Pedringano

> For this, Serberine, and thou shalt ha't.   *Shoots the dag*[258]
> So, there he lies, my promise is performed.

The Watch come forward

First Watch

> Hark, gentlemen, this is a pistol shot.

[254] Keep guard.
[255] Hidden.
[256] Stop walking.
[257] Meet secretly.
[258] Pistol.

Second Watch

And here's one slain! Stay[259] the murderer! 35

Pedringano

Now by the sorrows of the souls in hell,

He strives with the Watch

Who first lays hand on me, I'll be his priest.

Third Watch

Sirrah, confess, and therein play the priest.

Why hast thou thus unkindly[260] killed this man?

Pedringano

Why? Because he walked abroad so late. 40

Third Watch

Come sir, you had been better kept your bed

Than have committed this misdeed so late.

Second Watch

Come, to the marshal's with the murderer!

First Watch

On to Hieronimo's. Help me here

To bring the murdered body with us too. 45

Pedringano

Hieronimo? Carry me before whom you will,

Whate'er he be, I'll answer him and you.

And do your worst, for I defy you all. *Exeunt*

Act III, Scene iv

Enter Lorenzo and Balthazar

Balthazar

How now, my lord, what makes you rise so soon?

---

[259] Stop.
[260] Unnaturally.

Lorenzo

    Fear of preventing our mishaps too late.

Balthazar

    What mischief is it that we not mistrust?[261]

Lorenzo

    Our greatest ills we least mistrust, my lord,

    And inexpected harms do hurt us most.   5

Balthazar

    Why, tell me, Don Lorenzo, tell me, man,

    If ought concerns our honour and your own.

Lorenzo

    Nor you, nor me, my lord, but both in one.

    For I suspect, and the presumption's great,

    That by those base confederates in our fault[262]   10

    Touching the death of Don Horatio,

    We are betrayed to old Hieronimo.

Balthazar

    Betrayed, Lorenzo? Tush, it cannot be.

Lorenzo

    A guilty conscience, urged with the thought

    Of former evils, easily cannot err.   15

    I am persuaded, and dissuade me not,

    That all's revealed to Hieronimo.

    And therefore know that I have cast it thus[263]—

Enter Page

    But here's the page. How now, what news with thee?

Page

    My lord, Serberine is slain.   20

[261] Suspect.

[262] Our partners in crime.

[263] Planned it like this.

Balthazar

    Who? Serberine, my man?

Page

    Your highness' man, my lord.

Lorenzo

    Speak, page, who murdered him?

Page

    He that is apprehended for the fact.

Lorenzo

    Who?   25

Page

    Pedringano.

Balthazar

    Is Serberine slain that loved his lord so well?

    Injurious villain, murderer of his friend!

Lorenzo

    Hath Pedringano murdered Serberine?

    My lord, let me entreat you to take the pains   30

    To exasperate[264] and hasten his revenge

    With your complaints unto my lord the King.

    This their dissension breeds a greater doubt.

Balthazar

    Assure thee, Don Lorenzo, he shall die,

    Or else his highness hardly shall deny.[265]   35

    Meanwhile, I'll haste[266] the Marshal sessions,

    For die he shall for this his damned deed.   *Exit Balthazar*

Lorenzo

    Why so, this fits our former policy,

    And thus experience bids the wise to deal.

    I lay the plot, he prosecutes the point.   40

[264] Make harsher.
[265] Will be hard on me, denying me.
[266] Speed up.

I set the trap, he breaks the worthless twigs,
And sees not that wherewith the bird was limed.[267]
Thus hopeful men that mean to hold their own
Must look like fowlers to their dearest friends.
He runs to kill whom I have holpe[268] to catch,   45
And no man knows it was my reaching fatch.[269]
'Tis hard to trust unto a multitude,
Or anyone, in mine opinion,
When men themselves their secrets will reveal.

Enter a Messenger with a letter

Boy!		50

Page
   My lord?
Lorenzo
   What's he?
Messenger   I have a letter to your lordship,
Lorenzo
   From whence?
Messenger   From Pedringano that's imprisoned.
Lorenzo
   So he's in prison?
Messenger   Ay, my good lord.
Lorenzo
   What would he with us? He writes us here   55
   To stand good lord[270] and help him in distress.
   Tell him I have his letters, know his mind,
   And what we may, let him assure him of.[271]

---

[267] Caught in bird lime.
[268] Helped.
[269] Carefully devised plan.
[270] Be his lordly protector.
[271] Let him be sure I'll do all I may.

Fellow, be gone; my boy shall follow thee.   *Exit Messenger*
This works like wax;[272] yet once more try thy wits.   60
Boy, go, convey this purse to Pedringano,
Thou knowest the prison, closely[273] give it him,
And be advised that none be thereabout.
Bid him be merry still, but secret;
And though the marshal sessions be today,   65
Bid him not doubt of his delivery.
Tell him his pardon is already signed,
And thereon bid him boldly be resolved.[274]
For, were he ready to be turned off,[275]
As 'tis my will the uttermost be tried,   70
Thou with his pardon shalt attend him still.
Show him this box, tell him his pardon's in't,
But open't not and if[276] thou lovest thy life,
But let him wisely keep his hopes unknown.
He shall not want while Don Lorenzo lives.   75
Away!

Page   I go, my lord, I run.

Lorenzo

But sirrah, see that this be cleanly done.   *Exit Page*
Now stands our fortune on a tickle[277] point,
And now or never ends Lorenzo's doubts.
One only thing is uneffected yet,   80
And that's to see the executioner.
But to what end? I list not[278] trust the air

---

[272] I.e., easily; wax is extremely malleable.
[273] In secret.
[274] Assured.
[275] Hanged.
[276] "And if" = if.
[277] Unsteady.
[278] Do not wish to.

With utterance of our pretence[279] therein,
For fear the privy whispering of the wind
Convey our words amongst unfriendly ears,   85
That lie too open to advantages.
E quel che voglio io, nessun lo sa;
Intendo io: quel mi basterá.[280]   *Exit*

Act III, Scene v

Enter Boy with the box

Page

My master hath forbidden me to look in this box, and by
my troth 'tis likely, if he had not warned me, I should not
have had so much idle time. For we men's-kind in our mi-
nority[281] are like women in their uncertainty; that they are
most forbidden, they will soonest attempt. So I now. By   5
my bare honesty, here's nothing but the bare, empty box.
Were it not sin against secrecy, I would say it were a piece
of gentlemanlike knavery. I must go to Pedringano and tell
him his pardon is in this box. Nay, I would have sworn it,
had I not seen the contrary. I cannot choose but smile to   10
think how the villain will flout[282] the gallows, scorn the audience, and descant on[283] the hangman, and all presuming
of his pardon from hence. Will't not be an odd jest, for me
to stand and grace every jest he makes, pointing my finger

---

[279] Plot.

[280] "And what I wish no one knows; I know, and that is enough for me"
(Italian).

[281] While still children.

[282] Mock.

[283] Carry on about.

at this box, as who would say, "Mock on, here's thy war- 15
rant." Is't not a scurvy[284] jest that a man should jest himself
to death? Alas, poor Pedringano, I am in a sort sorry for
thee, but if I should be hanged with thee, I cannot weep.

Exit

Act III, Scene vi

Enter Hieronimo and the Deputy

Hieronimo
    Thus must we toil in other men's extremes,
    That know not how to remedy our own,
    And do them justice, when unjustly we,
    For all our wrongs can compass no redress.
    But shall I never live to see the day 5
    That I may come by justice of the heavens,
    To know the cause that[285] may my cares allay?
    This toils[286] my body, this consumeth age,[287]
    That only I to all men just must be,
    And neither gods nor men be just to me. 10
Deputy
    Worthy Hieronimo, your office asks
    A care to punish such as do transgress.
Hieronimo
    So is't my duty to regard his death
    Who, when he lived, deserved my dearest blood.
    But come, for that we came for, let's begin, 15

---

[284] Low.

[285] Experience that which.

[286] Burdens.

[287] Makes me old before my time.

For here lies that[288] which bids me to be gone.

Enter Officers, Hangman, Boy, and Pedringano, with a letter in his hand, bound

Deputy

Bring forth the prisoner, for the court is set.

Pedringano

Gramercy,[289] boy, but it was time to come,

For I had written to my lord anew,

A nearer matter that concerneth him,   20

For fear his lordship had forgotten me.

But sith he hath remembered me so well,

Come, come, come on, when shall we to this gear?[290]

Hieronimo

Stand forth, thou monster, murderer of men,

And here, for satisfaction of the world,   25

Confess thy folly and repent thy fault,

For there's thy place of execution.

Pedringano

This is short work. Well, to your Marshalship

First I confess, nor fear I death therefore,

I am the man, 'twas I slew Serberine.   30

But sir, then you think this shall be the place

Where we shall satisfy you for this gear?

Deputy

Ay, Pedringano.

Pedringano   Now I think not so.

Hieronimo

Peace, impudent, for thou shalt find it so;

---

[288] This may refer to the bloody handkerchief, or maybe to Hieronimo's heart.

[289] Exclamation to signify Pedringano's relief.

[290] Business.

For blood with blood shall, while I sit as judge,   35
Be satisfied, and the law discharged.
And though myself cannot receive the like,
Yet will I see that others have their right.
Dispatch, the fault's approved[291] and confessed,
And by our law he is condemned to die.   40

Hangman

Come on, sir, are you ready?

Pedringano

To do what, my fine officious knave?

Hangman

To go to this gear.[292]

Pedringano

O sir, you are too forward; thou wouldst fain furnish me
with a halter, to disfurnish me of my habit.[293] So I should   45
go out of this gear, my raiment, into that gear, the rope.
But, hangman, now I spy your knavery, I'll not change
without boot,[294] that's flat.

Hangman

Come, sir.

Pedringano

So then, I must up?   50

Hangman

No remedy.

Pedringano

Yes, but there shall be for my coming down.

Hangman

Indeed, here's a remedy for that.

---

[291] Demonstrated.

[292] Business, here the hanging.

[293] Clothes; part of the hangman's fee is the executed man's clothes.

[294] Without further payment.

Pedringano

How? Be turned off?[295]

Hangman

Ay, truly! Come, are you ready? I pray sir, dispatch, the   55
day goes away.

Pedringano

What, do you hang by the hour? If you do, I may chance
to break your old custom.

Hangman

Faith, you have reason, for I am like to break your young
neck.   60

Pedringano

Dost thou mock me, hangman? Pray God I be not preserved to break your knave's pate for this.

Hangman

Alas, sir, you are a foot too low to reach it, and I hope
you will never grow so high while I am in the office.

Pedringano

Sirrah, dost see yonder boy with the box in his hand?   65

Hangman

What, he that points to it with his finger?

Pedringano

Ay, that companion.[296]

Hangman

I know him not, but what of him?

Pedringano

Dost thou think to live till his old doublet will make thee
a new truss?[297]   70

[295] Pushed off the platform, hanged.
[296] Fellow.
[297] Jacket.

Hangman

> Ay, and many a fair year after, to truss up[298] many an
> honester man that either thou or he.

Pedringano

> What hath he in his box as thou think'st?

Hangman

> Faith, I cannot tell, nor I care not greatly. Methinks you
> should rather hearken to[299] your soul's health.   75

Pedringano

> Why, sirrah hangman, I take it that that is good for the
> body is likewise good for the soul, and it may be, in that
> box is balm for both.

Hangman

> Well, thou art even the merriest piece of man's flesh that
> e'er groaned at my office door.   80

Pedringano

> Is your roguery become an office with a knave's name?

Hangman

> Ay, and that shall all they witness that see you seal it with a
> thief's name.

Pedringano

> I prithee, request this good company to pray with me.

Hangman

> Ay marry, sir, this is a good motion. My masters, you see   85
> here's a good fellow.

Pedringano

> Nay, nay, now I remember me, let them alone till some
> other time, for now I have no great need.

Hieronimo

> I have not seen a wretch so impudent!
> O monstrous times, where murder's set so light,   90

---

[298] Hang.
[299] Take care of.

And where the soul that should be shrined in heaven
Solely delights in interdicted things,
Still wandering in the thorny passages
That intercepts itself of happiness.
Murder, O bloody monster, God forbid   95
A fault so foul should 'scape unpunished.
Despatch and see this execution done.
This makes me to remember thee, my son.   *Exit Hieronimo*

Pedringano

Nay soft,[300] no haste.

Deputy

Why, wherefore stay you? Have you hope of life?   100

Pedringano

Why, ay.

Hangman

As how?

Pedringano

Why, rascal, by my pardon from the King.

Hangman

Stand you on that?[301] Then you shall off with this.

He turns him off

Deputy

So, executioner. Convey him hence,   105
But let his body be unburied:
Let not the earth be choked or infect
With that which heaven contemns, and men neglect.   *Exeunt*

[300] Easy, now.
[301] Do you rely on that?

Act III, Scene vii

Enter Hieronimo

Hieronimo

    Where shall I run to breathe abroad[302] my woes,
    My woes whose weight hath wearied the earth?
    Or mine exclaims,[303] that have surcharged the air
    With ceaseless plaints for my deceased son?
    The blustering winds, conspiring with my words,   5
    At my lament have moved the leafless trees,
    Disrobed the meadows of their flowered green,
    Made mountains marsh with spring tides of my tears,
    And broken through the brazen gates of hell.
    Yet still tormented is my tortured soul   10
    With broken sighs and restless passions,
    That winged mount,[304] and hovering in the air,
    Beat at the windows of the brightest heavens,
    Soliciting for justice and revenge.
    But they are placed in those empyreal[305] heights,   15
    Where, countermured[306] with walls of diamond,
    I find the place impregnable, and they
    Resist my woes, and give my words no way.

Enter Hangman with a letter

Hangman

    O lord, sir, God bless you, sir, the man, sir,

---

[302] Express.
[303] Cries.
[304] That rise into the air, born on wings.
[305] Celestial.
[306] With double walls.

Petergade,[307] sir, he that was so full of merry conceits[308]   20

Hieronimo

Well, what of him?

Hangman

O Lord, sir, he went the wrong way, the fellow had a fair
commission to the contrary. Sir, here is his passport. I
pray you, sir, we have done him wrong.

Hieronimo

I warrant thee,[309] give it me.   25

Hangman

You will stand between the gallows and me?

Hieronimo

Ay, ay.

Hangman

I thank your lord worship.   *Exit Hangman*

Hieronimo

And yet, though somewhat nearer me concerns,
I will, to ease the grief that I sustain,   30
Take truce with sorrow while I read on this.
"My lord, I writ as mine extremes[310] required,
That you would labour my delivery.
If you neglect, my life is desperate,
And in my death I shall reveal the troth.[311]   35
You know, my lord, I slew him for your sake,
And was confederate with the prince and you.
Won by rewards and hopeful promises,
I holp to murder Don Horatio too."
Holp he to murder mine Horatio?   40
And actors in th'accursed tragedy

---

[307] Hangman's "take" on Pedringano's name.

[308] Jests.

[309] I tell you.

[310] Predicament.

[311] 1) The loyalty I pledged to you; 2) the truth.

Wast thou, Lorenzo, Balthazar and thou?
Of whom my son, my son, deserved so well?
What have I heard, what have mine eyes beheld?
O sacred heavens, may it come to pass   45
That such a monstrous and detested deed,
So closely smothered[312] and so long concealed,
Shall thus by this be vengéd[313] or revealed!
Now see I what I durst not then suspect,
That Bel-imperia's letter was not feigned.   50
Nor feigned she, though falsely they have wronged
Both her, myself, Horatio and themselves.
Now may I make compare 'twixt hers and this,
Of every accident[314] I ne'er could find[315]
Till now, and now I feelingly[316] perceive   55
They did what Heaven unpunished would not leave.
O false Lorenzo, are these thy flattering looks?
Is this the honour that thou didst my son?
And Balthazar, bane[317] to my soul and me,
Was this the ransom he reserved thee[318] for?   60
Woe to the cause of these constrained wars!
Woe to thy baseness and captivity,
Woe to thy birth, thy body, and thy soul,
Thy cursed father, and thy conquered self!
And banned[319] with bitter execrations be   65
The day and place where he did pity thee!
But wherefore waste I mine unfruitful words,

---

[312] Kept so very secret.
[313] Revenged.
[314] Event.
[315] Understand.
[316] Clearly; with feeling.
[317] Death.
[318] Preserved you; let you live.
[319] Accursed.

When naught but blood will satisfy my woes?
I will go plain me[320] to my lord the King,
And cry aloud for justice through the court,   70
Wearing the flints with these my withered feet,
And either purchase justice by entreats
Or tire them all with my revenging threats.   *Exit*

---

[320] Complain.

Act IV, Scene i

Enter Isabella and her Maid

Isabella

So that, you say, this herb will purge the eye,
And this the head?
Ah, but none of them will purge the heart.
No, there's no medicine left for my disease,
Nor any physic to recure[321] the dead.   *She runs lunatic* 5
Horatio! O, where's Horatio?

Maid

Good madam, affright not thus yourself
With outrage[322] for your son Horatio.
He sleeps in quiet in Elysian[323] fields.

Isabella

Why, did I not give you gowns and goodly things,   10
Bought you a whistle and a whipstalk[324] too,
To be revenged on their villainies?

Maid

Madam, these humours[325] do torment my soul.

Isabella

"My soul," poor soul, thou talks of things
Thou know'st not what; my soul hath silver wings,   15
That mounts me up unto the highest heavens.
To heaven, ay, there sits my Horatio,
Backed with a troop of fiery cherubins

---

[321] Return to life.
[322] Passionate behavior.
[323] Where the blessed go in the afterlife.
[324] Whip handle.
[325] Fancies.

Dancing about his newly healed wounds,
Singing sweet hymns and chanting heavenly notes,   20
Rare harmony to greet his innocence,
That died, ay died a mirror[326] in our days.
But say, where shall I find the men, the murderers,
That slew Horatio? Whither shall I run
To find them out that murdered my son?   *Exeunt* 25

Act IV, Scene ii

Bel-imperia at a window[327]

Bel-imperia

What means this outrage that is offered me?
Why am I thus sequestered[328] from the court?
No notice?[329] Shall I not know the cause
Of this my secret and suspicious ills?
Accursed brother, unkind[330] murderer,   5
Why bends thou thus my mind to martyr me?
Hieronimo, why writ I of thy wrongs,
Or why art thou so slack in thy revenge?
Andrea, O Andrea, that thou sawest
Me for thy friend Horatio handled thus,   10
And him for me thus causeless murdered.
Well, force perforce,[331] I must constrain myself
To patience, and apply me[332] to the time,

---

[326] Example of excellence.
[327] Entrance, probably, on the balcony.
[328] Hidden away.
[329] Kept uninformed.
[330] Unnatural.
[331] Of necessity.
[332] Conform.

Till heaven, as I have hoped, shall set me free.   14

Enter Christophil

Christophil
    Come, Madam Bel-imperia, this may not be.   *Exeunt*

Act IV, Scene iii

Enter Lorenzo, Balthazar, and the Page

Lorenzo
    Boy, talk no further, thus far things go well.
    Thou art assured that thou sawst him dead?
Page
    Or else, my lord, I live not.
Lorenzo   That's enough.
    As for his resolution[333] in the end
    Leave that to him with whom he sojourns now.   5
    Here, take my ring and give it Christophil,
    And bid him let my sister be enlarged,[334]
    And bring her hither straight.   *Exit Page*
    This that I did was for a policy[335]
    To smooth and keep the murder secret,   10
    Which as a nine-days' wonder, being o'erblown,[336]
    My gentle sister will I now enlarge.
Balthazar
    And time, Lorenzo, for my lord the Duke,

[333] Courage.
[334] Set free.
[335] Ingenious purpose.
[336] The murder is no longer fresh news.

You heard, enquired for her yesternight.

Lorenzo

    Why, and, my lord, I hope you heard me say   15

    Sufficient reason why she kept away.

    But that's all one. My lord, you love her?

Balthazar   Ay.

Lorenzo

    Then in your love beware, deal cunningly,

    Salve[337] all suspicions; only soothe me up.[338]

    And if she hap to stand on terms[339] with us   20

    As for her sweetheart and concealment so,

    Jest with her gently; under feigned jest

    Are things concealed that else would breed unrest.

    But here she comes.

Enter Bel-imperia

                Now, sister—

Bel-imperia   Sister? No!

    Thou art no brother but an enemy,   25

    Else wouldst thou not have used thy sister so:

    First, to affright me with thy weapons drawn,

    And with extremes[340] abuse my company[341]

    And then to hurry me, like whirlwind's rage,

    Amidst a crew of thy confederates,   30

    And clap me up[342] where none might come at me,

    Nor I at any, to reveal my wrongs.

    What madding fury did possess thy wits?

---

[337] Gentle; stop.

[338] Agree with me, say what I say.

[339] Gainsay us; argue.

[340] Violent actions.

[341] Companion, i.e., Horatio.

[342] Hide me.

Or wherein is't that I offended thee?

Lorenzo

Advise you better, Bel-imperia, 35

For I have done you no disparagement;[343]

Unless, by more discretion than deserved,

I sought to save your honour and mine own.

Bel-imperia

Mine honour? Why, Lorenzo, wherein is't

That I neglect my reputation so, 40

As you, or any, need to rescue it?

Lorenzo

His highness and my father were resolved

To come confer with old Hieronimo

Concerning certain matters of estate[344]

That by the viceroy was determined. 45

Bel-imperia

And wherein was mine honour touched in that?

Balthazar

Have patience, Bel-imperia; hear the rest.

Lorenzo

Me, next in sight,[345] as messenger they sent

To give him notice that they were so neigh.

Now when I came, consorted with[346] the prince, 50

And unexpected in an arbour there

Found Bel-imperia with Horatio—

Bel-imperia

How then?

Lorenzo

Why then, remembering that old disgrace,

[343] Disgrace.

[344] State matters.

[345] Being near them; being in sight.

[346] In the company of.

Which you for Don Andrea had endured,   55
And now were likely longer to sustain
By being found so meanly accompanied,[347]
Thought rather, for I knew no readier mean,
To thrust Horatio forth my father's way.

Balthazar

And carry you obscurely somewhere else,   60
Lest that his highness should have found you there.

Bel-imperia

Even so, my lord? And you are witness
That this is true which he entreateth of?
You, gentle brother, forged this for my sake,
And you, my lord, were made his instrument.   65
A work of worth, worthy the noting too.
But what's the cause that you concealed me since?

Lorenzo

Your melancholy, sister, since the news
Of your first favourite Don Andrea's death,
My father's old wrath hath exasperate.[348]   70

Balthazar

And better was't for you, being in disgrace,
To absent yourself and give his fury place.

Bel-imperia

But why had I no notice of his ire?

Lorenzo

That were to add more fuel to your fire,
Who burnt like Aetna[349] for Andrea's loss.   75

Bel-imperia

Hath not my father then enquired for me?

Lorenzo

Sister, he hath, and thus excused I thee.

---

[347] Being found in the company of a person of lower social standing.
[348] Made worse.
[349] Volcano in Sicily.

He whispereth in her ear

    But, Bel-imperia, see the gentle prince!
    Look on thy love, behold young Balthazar,
    Whose passions by thy presence are increased,   80
    And in whose melancholy thou may'st see
    Thy hate, his love; thy flight, his following thee.

Bel-imperia

    Brother, you are become an orator—
    I know not, I, by what experience—
    Too politic[350] for me, past all compare,   85
    Since last I saw you; but content yourself,
    The prince is meditating higher things.

Balthazar

    'Tis of thy beauty, then, that conquers kings;
    Of those thy tresses, Ariadne's twines,[351]
    Wherewith my liberty thou hast surprised;[352]   90
    Of that thine ivory front,[353] my sorrow's map,
    Wherein I see no haven to rest my hope.

Bel-imperia

    To love and fear, and both at once, my lord,
    In my conceit,[354] are things of more import
    Than women's wits are to be busied with.   95

Balthazar

    'Tis I that love.

Bel-imperia   Whom?

Balthazar   Bel-imperia.

Bel-imperia

    But I that fear.

---

[350] Cunning.
[351] Ariadne, daughter of Minos, King of Crete, used thread to guide Theseus through her father's labyrinth in return for a promise of marriage.
[352] Captured.
[353] Forehead.
[354] In my opinion.

| Balthazar | Whom? |
| Bel-imperia | Bel-imperia. |

Lorenzo

    Fear yourself?

Bel-imperia	Ay, brother.
Lorenzo	How?
Bel-imperia	As those

    That what they love are loath and fear to lose.

Balthazar

    Then, fair, let Balthazar your keeper be.   100

Bel-imperia

    No, Balthazar doth fear as well as we:

    Et tremulo metui pavidum junxere timorem,

    Et vanum stolidae proditionis opus.[355]   *Exit*

Lorenzo

    Nay, and you argue things so cunningly,

    We'll go continue this discourse at court.   105

Balthazar

    Led by the loadstar[356] of her heavenly looks,

    Wends[357] poor oppressed Balthazar,

    As o'er the mountain walks the wanderer,

    Incertain to effect[358] his pilgrimage.   *Exeunt*

Act IV, Scene iv

Enter two Portingales, and Hieronimo meets them

---

[355] "Fearful fear was yoked to fearful man; the workings of total treachery are vain."

[356] Star to steer by.

[357] Walks.

[358] Not certain whether he may complete.

First Portingale

    By your leave, sir.[Ψ]

Hieronimo

    Good leave have you; nay, I pray you go,

    For I'll leave you; if you can leave me, so.

Second Portingale

    Pray you, which is the next[359] way to my lord the Duke's?

Hieronimo

    The next way from me.

First Portingale   To his house, we mean.   5

Hieronimo

    O, hard by, 'tis yon house that you see.

Second Portingale

    You could not tell us if his son were there?

Hieronimo

    Who, my lord Lorenzo?

First Portingale   Ay, sir.

He goeth in at one door and comes out at another

Hieronimo   O, forbear,

    For other talk for us far fitter were.

    But if you be importunate to know[360]   10

    The way to him, and where to find him out,

    Then list to me, and I'll resolve your doubt.

    There is a path upon your left-hand side

    That leadeth from a guilty conscience

    Unto a forest of distrust and fear,   15

    A darksome place, and dangerous to pass.

    There shall you meet with melancholy thoughts,

[Ψ] See appendix for third 1602 addition.

[359] Nearest.

[360] Insist on knowing.

Whose baleful humours if you but uphold,[361]
It will conduct you to despair and death;
Whose rocky cliffs when you have once beheld,   20
Within a hugy[362] dale of lasting night,
That, kindled with the world's iniquities,
Doth cast up filthy and detested fumes.
Not far from thence, where murderers have built
A habitation for their cursed souls,   25
There, in a brazen cauldron, fixed by Jove
In his fell[363] wrath upon a sulphur flame,
Yourselves shall find Lorenzo bathing him
In boiling lead and blood of innocents.

First Portingale

Ha, ha, ha!

Hieronimo   Ha, ha, ha!   30
Why, ha, ha, ha! Farewell, good, ha, ha, ha!   *Exit*

Second Portingale

Doubtless this man is passing[364] lunatic,
Or imperfection of his age[365] doth make him dote.
Come, let's away to seek my lord the Duke.   *Exeunt*

Act IV, Scene v

Enter Hieronimo, with a poniard in one hand, and a rope in the other[366]

[361] Persist.
[362] Huge.
[363] Cruel.
[364] Extremely.
[365] Senility.
[366] These are stock hand props for a would-be suicide on the Elizabethan stage.

Hieronimo

> Now sir, perhaps I come and see the King,
> The King sees me, and fain would hear my suit.
> Why, is not this a strange and seld-seen[367] thing,
> That standers-by with toys[368] should strike me mute?
> Go to, I see their shifts,[369] and say no more.   5
> Hieronimo, 'tis time for thee to trudge.
> Down by the dale that flows with purple[370] gore
> Standeth a fiery tower; there sits a judge
> Upon a seat of steel and molten brass,
> And 'twixt his teeth he holds a firebrand,   10
> That leads unto the lake where hell doth stand.
> Away, Hieronimo, to him be gone,
> He'll do thee justice for Horatio's death.
> Turn down this path,[371] thou shalt be with him straight;
> Or this, and then thou need'st not take thy breath.   15
> This way or that way? Soft and fair, not so.
> For if I hang or kill myself, let's know
> Who will revenge Horatio's murder then?
> No, no! Fie, no! Pardon me, I'll none of that.
>
>   *He flings away the dagger and halter*
>
> This way I'll take, and this way comes the King   20
>
>   *He takes them up again*
>
> And here I'll have a fling at him, that's flat.[372]
> And, Balthazar, I'll be with thee to bring,[373]
> And thee, Lorenzo! Here's the King—nay, stay

[367] Rarely seen.
[368] Trifling things.
[369] Tricks.
[370] Blood red.
[371] The "paths" referred to are the two means of suicide available here.
[372] That is for certain.
[373] Bring to punishment.

And here, ay here—there goes the hare away.[374]

Enter King, Ambassador, Duke of Castile, and Lorenzo

King

    Now show, Ambassador, what our Viceroy saith.   25

    Hath he received the articles we sent?

Hieronimo

    Justice, O, justice to Hieronimo.

Lorenzo

    Back, see'st thou not the King is busy?

Hieronimo

    O, is he so?

King

    Who is he that interrupts our business?   30

Hieronimo

    Not I. Hieronimo, beware, go by, go by.

Ambassador

    Renowned King, he hath received and read

    Thy kingly proffers and thy promised league,

    And, as a man extremely overjoyed

    To hear his son so princely entertained,   35

    Whose death he had so solemnly bewailed,

    This for thy further satisfaction

    And kingly love, he kindly lets thee know:

    First, for the marriage of his princely son

    With Bel-imperia, thy beloved niece,   40

    The news are more delightful to his soul

    Than myrrh or incense to the offended heavens.

    In person, therefore, will he come himself,

    To see the marriage rites solemnized,

    And, in the presence of the court of Spain,   45

---

[374] "There I lost my chance."

To knit a sure, inexecrable[375] band
Of kingly love and everlasting league
Betwixt the crowns of Spain and Portingale.
There will he give his crown to Balthazar,
And make a queen of Bel-imperia.   50

King

Brother, how like you this our viceroy's love?

Duke of Castile

No doubt, my lord, it is an argument[376]
Of honourable care to keep his friend,
And wondrous zeal to Balthazar his son,
Nor am I least indebted to his grace,   55
That bends his liking to my daughter thus.

Ambassador

Now last, dread lord, here hath his highness sent,
Although he sent not that his son return,
His ransom due to Don Horatio.

Hieronimo

Horatio! Who calls Horatio?   60

King

And well remembered, thank his majesty.
Here, see it given to Horatio.

Hieronimo

Justice, O justice, justice, gentle King!

King

What is that? Hieronimo?

Hieronimo

Justice, O justice! O my son, my son,   65
My son, whom naught can ransom or redeem!

Lorenzo

Hieronimo, you are not well advised.

---

[375] Sacred; not to be execrated.
[376] Proof.

Hieronimo

> Away, Lorenzo, hinder me no more,
>
> For thou hast made me bankrupt of my bliss.
>
> Give me my son, you shall not ransom him!   70
>
> Away, I'll rip the bowels of the earth,
>
> > *He diggeth with his dagger*
>
> And ferry over to th'Elysian plains,[377]
>
> And bring my son to show his deadly wounds.
>
> Stand from about me!
>
> I'll make a pickax of my poniard,   75
>
> And here surrender up my marshalship;
>
> For I'll go marshal up the fiends in hell,
>
> To be avenged on you all for this.

King

> What means this outrage?[378]
>
> Will none of you restrain his fury?   80

Hieronimo

> Nay, soft and fair; you shall not need to strive,
>
> Needs must he go that the devils drive.   *Exit*

King

> What accident hath happed[379] Hieronimo?
>
> I have not seen him to demean him[380] so.

Lorenzo

> My gracious lord, he is with extreme pride   85
>
> Conceived of young Horatio, his son,
>
> And covetous of having to himself
>
> The ransom of the young prince Balthazar,
>
> Distract, and in a manner lunatic.

King

> Believe me, nephew, we are sorry for't.   90

---

[377] The place for the blessed dead in the afterlife.

[378] Outcry.

[379] Happened to.

[380] Behave.

This is the love that fathers bear their sons.
But, gentle brother, go give him this gold,
The prince's ransom, let him have his due.
For what he hath Horatio shall not want,
Haply[381] Hieronimo hath need thereof.   95

Lorenzo

But if he be thus helplessly distract,
'Tis requisite his office be resigned
And given to one of more discretion.

King

We shall increase his melancholy so.
'Tis best that we see further in it first,   100
Till when, ourself will exempt the place.[382]
And, brother, now bring in the Ambassador,
That he may be a witness of the match
'Twixt Balthazar and Bel-imperia,
And that we may prefix a certain time   105
Wherein the marriage shall be solemnized,
That we may have thy lord, the Viceroy, here.

Ambassador

Therein your highness highly shall content
His majesty, that longs to hear from hence.

King

On, then, and hear you, Lord Ambassador.   *Exeunt* [ψ] 110

Act IV, Scene vi

Enter Hieronimo, with a book in his hand

[381] Perhaps.
[382] We will continue business without an acting Knight Marshal.
[ψ] See appendix for the fourth 1602 addition, a scene between IV.v and IV.vi.

Hieronimo

> *Vindicta mihi!*[383]
>
> Ay, heaven will be revenged of every ill,
>
> Nor will they suffer murder unrepaid.
>
> Then stay, Hieronimo, attend their will,
>
> For mortal men may not appoint their time.   5
>
> *Per scelus semper tutum est sceleribus iter.*[384]
>
> Strike, and strike home, where wrong is offered thee!
>
> For evils unto ills conductors be,
>
> And death's the worst of resolution.[385]
>
> For he that thinks with patience to contend   10
>
> To quiet life, his life shall easily end.
>
> *Fata si miseros juvant, habes salutem;*
>
> *Fata si vitam negant, habes sepulchrum.*[386]
>
> If destiny thy miseries do ease,
>
> Then hast thou health, and happy shalt thou be.   15
>
> If misery deny thee life, Hieronimo,
>
> Yet shall thou be assured of a tomb.
>
> If neither, yet let this thy comfort be,
>
> Heaven covereth him that hath no burial.
>
> And to conclude, I will revenge his death!   20
>
> But how? not as the vulgar[387] wits of men,
>
> With open, but inevitable ills,
>
> As by a secret, yet a certain mean,[388]
>
> Which under kindship will be cloaked best.[389]
>
> Wise men will take their opportunity,   25
>
> Closely[390] and safely fitting things to time,

[383] "Vengeance is mine" (Romans xii.19).

[384] "The safe path is always from crime to crimes."

[385] Death is the worst outcome of decisive action.

[386] The next four lines translate this adequately.

[387] Base.

[388] Instrument.

[389] Which kindness best hides.

[390] Subtly.

But in extremes advantage hath no time,
And therefore all times fit not for revenge.
Thus, therefore, will I rest me in unrest.
Dissembling quiet in unquietness,   30
Not seeming that I know their villainies,
That my simplicity may make them think
That ignorantly I will let all slip.
For ignorance, I wot,[391] and well they know,
Remedium malorum iners est,[392]   35
Nor aught avails it me to menace them,
Who, as a wintry storm upon a plain,
Will bear me down with their nobility.[393]
No, no, Hieronimo, thou must enjoin
Thine eyes to observation, and thy tongue   40
To milder speeches than thy spirit affords,
Thy heart to patience, and thy hands to rest,
Thy cap to courtesy, and thy knee to bow,
Till to revenge thou know, when, where, and how.

A noise within

How now, what noise? What coil is that you keep?[394]   45

Enter a Servant

Servant
　　Here are a sort[395] of poor petitioners,
　　That are importunate,[396] and[397] it shall please you, sir,
　　That you should plead their cases to the King.

[391] I know.
[392] "An ineffective remedy for evils."
[393] Rank as noblemen.
[394] What is this disturbance you're making?
[395] Group.
[396] Solicit urgently.
[397] If.

Hieronimo

 That I should plead their several actions?[398]

 Why, let them enter, and let me see them.   50

Enter Three Citizens and an Old Man

First Citizen

 So, I tell you this, for learning and for law,

 There is not any advocate in Spain

 That can prevail, or will take half the pain

 That he will in pursuit of equity.

Hieronimo

 Come near, you men, that thus importune me.   55

 Now must I bear a face of gravity,

 For thus I used, before my marshalship,

 To plead in causes as corregidor.[399]

 Come on, sirs, what's the matter?

Second Citizen   Sir, an action.

Hieronimo

 Of battery?

First Citizen   Mine of debt.

Hieronimo   Give place.   60

Second Citizen

 No, sir, mine is an action of the case.[400]

Third Citizen

 Mine an *ejectione firmae*[401] by a lease.

Hieronimo

 Content you, sirs, are you determined

 That I should plead your several actions?

---

[398] Law cases.

[399] Advocate (here; literally the word means "magistrate").

[400] An action needing a special writ to cover it.

[401] Writ ejecting a tenant.

First Citizen

    Ay, sir, and here's my declaration.[402]   65

Second Citizen

    And here is my band.[403]

Third Citizen   And here is my lease.

                        They give him papers

Hieronimo

    But wherefore stands yon silly[404] man so mute,

    With mournful eyes and hands to heaven upreared?

    Come hither, father, let me know thy cause.

Senex

    O, worthy sir, my cause, but slightly known,   70

    May move the hearts of warlike Myrmidons,[405]

    And melt the Corsic[406] rocks with ruthful tears.

Hieronimo

    Say, father, tell me, what's thy suit?

Senex

    No, sir, could my woes

    Give way unto my most distressful words,   75

    Then should I not in paper, as you see,

    With ink bewray what blood began in me.

Hieronimo

    What's here? "The humble supplication

    Of Don Bazulto for his murdered son."

Senex

    Ay, sir.

Hieronimo   No, sir, it was my murdered son.   80

    O my son, my son, O my son Horatio!

---

[402] Plaintiff's statement of claim.

[403] Bond.

[404] Simple.

[405] Achilles' followers, known for their fierceness.

[406] Corsican.

But mine, or thine, Bazulto, be content.
Here, take my handkercher and wipe thine eyes,
Whiles wretched I in thy mishap may see
The lively[407] portrait of my dying self.   85

He draweth out a bloody napkin

O no, not this! Horatio, this was thine,
And when I dyed it in thy dearest blood,
This was a token 'twixt thy soul and me
That of thy death revenged I should be.
But here, take this,[408] and this—what, my purse?—   90
Ay, this, and that, and all of them are thine,
For all as one are our extremities.[409]

First Citizen

O see the kindness of Hieronimo!

Second Citizen

This gentleness shows him a gentleman.

Hieronimo

See, see, O see thy shame, Hieronimo,   95
See here a loving father to his son!
Behold the sorrows and the sad laments
That he delivereth for his son's decease.
If love's effects so strive in lesser things,
If love enforce such moods in meaner[410] wits,   100
If love express such power in poor estates,
Hieronimo, when as a raging sea
Tossed with the wind and tide, o'erturneth then
The upper billows, course of waves to keep,
Whiles lesser waters labour in the deep,   105
Then sham'st thou not, Hieronimo, to neglect

---

[407] Living.
[408] (Probably) this coin.
[409] Great suffering.
[410] Socially lower.

The sweet revenge of thy Horatio?[411]
Though on this earth justice will not be found,
I'll down to hell, and in this passion
Knock at the dismal gates of Pluto's court,   110
Getting by force, as once Alcides[412] did,
A troop of Furies and tormenting hags
To torture Don Lorenzo and the rest.
Yet, lest the triple-headed porter should
Deny my passage to the slimy strond,   115
The Thracian poet[413] thou shalt counterfeit.
Come on, old father, be my Orpheus,
And if thou canst no notes upon the harp,
Then sound the burden[414] of thy sore heart's grief,
Till we do gain that Proserpine may grant   120
Revenge on them that murdered my son.
Then will I rent and tear them thus and thus,
Shivering their limbs in pieces with my teeth.   *Tear the paper*

First Citizen

    O sir, my declaration!   *Exit Hieronimo and they after*

Second Citizen

    Save my bond!   125

Enter Hieronimo

---

[411] This passage compares Hieronimo (upper billows) and Bazulto (lesser waters); Bazulto, socially inferior, seeks recourse in the law as his situation demands; Hieronimo does not do what he thinks he ought to do, and therefore should be ashamed.

[412] Hercules, whose twelfth labor was to capture Cerberus, the three-headed dog guarding the entrance to the Underworld, Pluto's kingdom.

[413] Orpheus, who went to win his wife Eurydice from the Underworld by means of his music. Pluto's wife, Proserpine, gave her to him.

[414] Refrain.

Second Citizen

    Save my bond!

Third Citizen

    Alas, my lease! It cost me ten pound,

    And you, my lord, have torn the same.

Hieronimo

    That cannot be, I gave it never a wound;

    Show me one drop of blood fall from the same.   130

    How is it possible I should slay it then?

    Tush, no; run after, catch me if you can.

                        Exeunt all but the Old Man

Bazulto remains till Hieronimo enters again, who, staring him in the face, speaks

Hieronimo

    And art thou come, Horatio, from the depth,

    To ask for justice in this upper earth?

    To tell thy father thou art unrevenged,   135

    To wring more tears from Isabella's eyes,

    Whose lights[415] are dimmed with overlong laments?

    Go back, my son, complain to Aeacus,[416]

    For here's no justice; gentle boy, be gone,

    For justice is exiled from the earth.   140

    Hieronimo will bear thee company,

    Thy mother cries on righteous Radamanth

    For just revenge against the murderers.

Senex

    Alas, my lord, whence springs this troubled speech?

---

[415] Eyes.

[416] Judge of the Underworld (see Introduction), as are Radamanth and Minos.

Hieronimo

    But let me look on my Horatio.   145

    Sweet boy, how art thou changed in death's black shade!

    Had Proserpine no pity on thy youth,

    But suffered thy fair crimson-coloured spring

    With withered winter to be blasted thus?

    Horatio, thou art older than thy father.   150

    Ah, ruthless fate, that favour[417] thus transforms!

Senex

    Ah my good lord, I am not your young son.

Hieronimo

    What, not my son? Thou then a Fury art,

    Sent from the empty kingdom of black night

    To summon me to make appearance   155

    Before grim Minos and just Radamanth,

    To plague Hieronimo that is remiss,

    And seeks not vengeance for Horatio's death.

Senex

    I am a grieved man, and not a ghost,

    That came for justice for my murdered son.   160

Hieronimo

    Ay, now I know thee, now thou nam'st thy son.

    Thou are the lively[418] image of my grief.

    Within thy face my sorrows I may see.

    Thy eyes are gummed with tears, thy cheeks are wan,

    Thy forehead troubled, and thy muttering lips   165

    Murmur sad words abruptly broken off

    By force of windy sighs thy spirit breathes,

    And all this sorrow riseth for thy son.

    And selfsame sorrow feel I for my son.

    Come in, old man, thou shalt to Isabel.   170

[417] Appearance.
[418] Living.

Lean on my arm; I thee, thou me shalt stay,[419]
And thou, and I, and she will sing a song,
Three parts in one, but all of discords framed.
Talk not of cords,[420] but let us now be gone,
For with a cord Horatio was slain.   *Exeunt* 175

Act IV, Scene vii

Enter King of Spain, The Duke of Castile, Viceroy, and Lorenzo, Balthazar, Don Pedro, and Bel-imperia[421]

King

    Go, brother, it is the Duke of Castile's cause,

    Salute the Viceroy in our name.

Duke of Castile   I go.

Viceroy

    Go forth, Don Pedro, for thy nephew's sake,

    And greet the Duke of Castile.

Don Pedro   It shall be so.

King

    And now to meet these Portuguese;   5

    For as we now are, so sometimes were these,

    Kings and commanders of the western Indies.

    Welcome, brave Viceroy, to the court of Spain,

    And welcome all his honourable train.[422]

    'Tis not unknown to us for why you come,   10

    Or have so kingly crossed the seas.

---

[419] Support.

[420] Pun on 1) musical chord; 2) rope.

[421] They enter as two groups, one from each door.

[422] Company.

Sufficeth it, in this we note the troth[423]
And more than common love you lend to us.
So is it that mine honourable niece,
For it beseems us now that it be known,   15
Already is betrothed to Balthazar,
And by appointment and our condescent[424]
Tomorrow are they to be married.
To this intent we entertain thyself,
Thy followers, their pleasure and our peace,   20
Speak, men of Portingale, shall it be so?
If ay, say so; if not, say flatly no.

Viceroy

Renowned King, I come not as thou think'st
With doubtful followers, unresolved men,
But such as have upon thine articles   25
Confirmed thy motion and contented me.
Know, Sovereign, I come to solemnise
The marriage of thy beloved niece,
Fair Bel-imperia, with my Balthazar,
With thee, my son, whom, sith I live to see,   30
Here take my crown, I give it her and thee;
And let me live a solitary life.
In ceaseless prayers,
To think how strangely heaven hath thee preserved.

King

See, brother, see how nature strives in him![425]   35
Come, worthy Viceroy, and accompany
Thy friend with thine extremities,[426]
A place more private fits this princely mood.

---

[423] Loyalty.

[424] Consent.

[425] He is weeping.

[426] Emotional outbursts.

Viceroy

    Or here, or where your highness thinks it good.

                Exeunt all but the Duke of Castile and Lorenzo

Duke of Castile

    Nay, stay, Lorenzo, let me talk with you.   40

    See'st thou this entertainment[427] of these Kings?

Lorenzo

    I do, my lord, and joy to see the same.

Duke of Castile

    And knowest thou why this meeting is?

Lorenzo

    For her, my lord, whom Balthazar doth love,

    And to confirm their promised marriage.   45

Duke of Castile

    She is thy sister?

Lorenzo   Who, Bel-imperia?

    Ay, my gracious lord, and this is the day

    That I have longed so happily to see.

Duke of Castile

    Thou wouldst be loath that any fault of thine

    Should intercept her in her happiness?   50

Lorenzo

    Heavens will not let Lorenzo err so much.

Duke of Castile

    Why, then, Lorenzo, listen to my words:

    It is suspected and reported too,

    That thou, Lorenzo, wrong'st Hieronimo,

    And in his suits towards his Majesty   55

    Still keep'st him back and seeks to cross[428] his suit.

Lorenzo

    That I, my lord?

---

[427] Greetings.
[428] Prevent.

Duke of Castile

    I tell thee, son, myself have heard it said,

    When, to my sorrow, I have been ashamed

    To answer for thee, though thou art my son.   60

    Lorenzo, knowest thou not the common[429] love

    And kindness that Hieronimo hath won

    By his deserts within the court of Spain?

    Or seest thou not the King my brother's care

    In his behalf, and to procure his health?   65

    Lorenzo, shouldst thou thwart his passions,[430]

    And he exclaim against thee to the King,

    What honour were't in this assembly,

    And what a scandal were't among the Kings

    To hear Hieronimo exclaim on thee?   70

    Tell me, and look thou tell me truly too,

    Whence grows the ground of this report in court?

Lorenzo

    My lord, it lies not in Lorenzo's power

    To stop the vulgar,[431] liberal of their tongues.

    A small advantage makes a water-breach,[432]   75

    And no man lives that long contenteth all.

Duke of Castile

    Myself have seen thee busy to keep back

    Him and his supplications from the King.

Lorenzo

    Yourself, my lord, hath seen his passions,

    That ill beseemed the presence of a King.   80

    And for I pitied him in his distress,

    I held him thence with kind and courteous words

    As free from malice to Hieronimo

---

[429] General.

[430] Complaints.

[431] The common folk.

[432] A little weakness grows into a broken-down dike.

As to my soul, my lord.

Duke of Castile

Hieronimo, my son, mistakes thee then.   85

Lorenzo

My gracious father, believe me, so he doth.
But what's a silly[433] man, distract in mind,
To think upon the murder of his son?
Alas, how easy is it for him to err!
But for his satisfaction and the world's,   90
'Twere good, my lord, that Hieronimo and I
Were reconciled, if he misconster[434] me.

Duke of Castile

Lorenzo, thou hast said, it shall be so,
Go, one of you, and call Hieronimo.

Enter Balthazar and Bel-imperia

Balthazar

Come, Bel-imperia, Balthazar's content,   95
My sorrow's ease and sovereign of my bliss,
Sith heaven hath ordained thee to be mine.
Disperse those clouds and melancholy looks,
And clear them up with those thy sun-bright eyes,
Wherein my hope and heaven's fair beauty lies.   100

Bel-imperia

My looks, my lord, are fitting for my love,
Which, new begun, can show no brighter yet.

Balthazar

New-kindled flame should burn as morning sun.

Bel-imperia

But not too fast, lest heat and all be done.

---

[433] Poor.
[434] Willfully makes wrong assumptions of.

I see my lord my father.

Balthazar   Truce, my love,   105
   I will go salute him.

Duke of Castile   Welcome, Balthazar,
   Welcome, brave prince, the pledge of Castile's peace;
   And welcome, Bel-imperia. How now, girl?
   Why com'st thou sadly to salute us thus?
   Content thyself, for I am satisfied.   110
   It is not now as when Andrea lived,
   We have forgotten and forgiven that,
   And thou art graced with a happier love.
   But, Balthazar, here comes Hieronimo,
   I'll have a word with him.   115

Enter Hieronimo and Servant

Hieronimo
   And where's the Duke?
Servant   Yonder.
Hieronimo   Even so.
   What new device[435] have they devised, trow?[436]
   Pocas palabras![437] Mild as the lamb,
   Is't I will be revenged? No, I am not the man.
Duke of Castile
   Welcome, Hieronimo.   120
Lorenzo
   Welcome, Hieronimo.
Balthazar
   Welcome, Hieronimo.

---

[435] Plot.
[436] Do you think.
[437] Few words.

Hieronimo

    My lords, I thank you for Horatio.

Duke of Castile

    Hieronimo, the reason that I sent

    To speak with you is this.

Hieronimo   What, so short?   125

    Then I'll be gone, I thank you for't.

Duke of Castile

    Nay, stay, Hieronimo—go, call him, son.

Lorenzo

    Hieronimo, my father craves a word with you.

Hieronimo

    With me, sir? Why, my lord, I thought you had done.

Lorenzo

    No. Would he had!

Duke of Castile   Hieronimo, I hear   130

    You find yourself aggrieved at my son

    Because you have not access unto the King,

    And say 'tis he that intercepts your suits.

Hieronimo

    Why, is not this a miserable thing, my lord?

Duke of Castile

    Hieronimo, I hope you have no cause,   135

    And would be loath that one of your deserts

    Should once have reason to suspect my son,

    Considering how I think of you myself.

Hieronimo

    Your son Lorenzo? Whom, my noble lord?

    The hope of Spain, mine honourable friend?   140

    Grant me the combat of them,[438] if they dare.

                                 Draws out his sword

    I'll meet him face to face to tell me so.

---

[438] Let me fight with them.

These be the scandalous reports of such
As love not me and hate my lord too much.
Should I suspect Lorenzo would prevent   145
Or cross[439] my suit, that loved my son so well?
My lord, I am ashamed it should be said.

Lorenzo

Hieronimo, I never gave you cause.

Hieronimo

My good lord, I know you did not.

Duke of Castile   There then, pause,
And for the satisfaction of the world,   150
Hieronimo, frequent my homely[440] house,
The Duke of Castile, Cyprian's ancient seat,
And when thou wilt, use me, my son, and it.
But here, before Prince Balthazar and me,
Embrace each other, and be perfect friends.   155

Hieronimo

Ay, marry, my lord, and shall.
Friends, quoth he? See, I'll be friends with you all,
Specially with you, my lovely lord;
For diverse causes it is fit for us
That we be friends. The world is suspicious,   160
And men may think what we imagine not.

Balthazar

Why, this is friendly done, Hieronimo.

Lorenzo

And thus I hope old grudges are forgot.

Hieronimo

What else? It were a shame it should not be so.

Duke of Castile

Come on, Hieronimo, at my request.   165

---

[439] Hinder.
[440] Home-like.

Let us entreat your company today.

Exeunt all but Hieronimo

Hieronimo

Your lordship's to command. Pha![441] keep your way.

Chi mi fa più carezze che non suole,

Tradito mi ha, o tradir vuole.[442]   *Exit*

Chorus: Ghost of Andrea and Revenge

Andrea

Awake, Erichtho![443] Cerberus, awake!   170

Solicit Pluto, gentle Proserpine!

To combat, Acheron[444] and Erebus![445]

For ne'er by Styx and Phlegethon[446] in Hell

Nor ferried Charon[447] to the fiery lakes

Such fearful sights, as poor Andrea sees!   175

Revenge, awake!

Revenge

Awake? For why?

Andrea

Awake, Revenge, for thou art ill-advised

To sleep away what thou art warned to watch!

Revenge

Content thyself, and do not trouble me.   180

---

[441] Exclamation of disgust.

[442] "He who caresses me more than usually has betrayed me or is going to betray me" (Italian).

[443] A witch.

[444] River or lake in the Underworld.

[445] Son of Chaos, name for the dark spaces through which the shades must travel on their way to the Underworld.

[446] Two rivers in the Underworld.

[447] The ferryman of the dead.

Andrea

> Awake, Revenge, if love, as love hath had,
> Have yet the power or prevalence in hell!
> Hieronimo with Lorenzo is joined in league,
> And intercepts our passage to revenge!
> Awake, Revenge, or we are woebegone!   185

Revenge

> Thus worldlings ground, what they have dreamed, upon.[448]
> Content thyself, Andrea; though I sleep,
> Yet is my mood soliciting their souls.
> Sufficeth thee that poor Hieronimo
> Cannot forget his son Horatio.   190
> Nor dies Revenge although he sleep awhile,
> For in unquiet, quietness is feigned,
> And slumbering is a common worldly wile.
> Behold, Andrea, for an instance how
> Revenge hath slept, and then imagine thou   195
> What 'tis to be subject to destiny.

Enter a dumb show,[449] act, and exeunt

Andrea

> Awake, Revenge, reveal this mystery.

Revenge

> The two first the nuptial torches bore,
> As brightly burning as the midday's sun.
> But after them doth Hymen[450] hie as fast,   200
> Clothed in sable[451] and a saffron[452] robe,

---

[448] Mortals take their dreams for facts and believe them.
[449] For contents, see Revenge's next speech.
[450] God of marriages.
[451] Black.
[452] Yellow.

And blows them out, and quencheth them with blood,
As discontent that things continue so.

Andrea

Sufficeth me; thy meaning's understood,
And thanks to thee and those infernal powers   205
That will not tolerate a lover's woe.
Rest thee, for I will sit to see the rest.

Revenge

Then argue not, for thou hast thy request.

Act V, Scene i

Enter Bel-imperia and Hieronimo

Bel-imperia

    Is this the love thou bear'st Horatio?

    Is this the kindness that thou counterfeits?

    Are these the fruits of thy incessant tears?

    Hieronimo, are these thy passions,[453]

    Thy protestations and thy deep laments   5

    That thou wert wont to weary men withal?

    O unkind father, O deceitful world!

    With what excuses canst thou show thyself?

    From this dishonour and the hate of men,

    Thus to neglect the loss and life of him,   10

    Whom both my letters and thine own belief

    Assures thee to be causeless slaughtered?

    Hieronimo, for shame, Hieronimo,

    Be not a history[454] to after times

    Of such ingratitude unto thy son.   15

    Unhappy mothers of such children then,

    But monstrous fathers to forget so soon

    The death of those, whom they with care and cost

    Have tendered so, thus careless should be lost.

    Myself, a stranger in respect of[455] thee,   20

    So loved his life as still I wish their deaths.

    Nor shall his death be unrevenged by me,

    Although I bear it out for fashion's sake.[456]

    For here I swear in sight of heaven and earth,

---

[453] Passionate outcries.

[454] Example.

[455] Compared to.

[456] Pretend to accept for appearance's sake.

> Shouldst thou neglect the love thou shouldst retain   25
> And give it over and devise[457] no more,
> Myself should send their hateful souls to hell
> That wrought his downfall with extremest death.

Hieronimo

> But may it be that Bel-imperia
> Vows such revenge as she hath deigned to say?   30
> Why then, I see that heaven applies our drift[458]
> And all the saints do sit soliciting
> For vengeance on those cursed murderers.
> Madam, 'tis true, and now I find it so.
> I found a letter, written in your name,   35
> And in that letter how Horatio died.
> Pardon, O pardon, Bel-imperia,
> My fear and care in not believing it,
> Nor think I thoughtless[459] think upon a mean
> To let his death be unrevenged at full   40
> And here I vow, so you but give consent,
> And will conceal my resolution,
> I will ere long determine of their deaths
> That causeless thus have murdered my son.

Bel-imperia

> Hieronimo, I will consent, conceal,   45
> And aught that may effect for thine avail.[460]
> Join with thee to avenge Horatio's death.

Hieronimo

> On then; whatsoever I devise,
> Let me entreat you, grace[461] my practices.
> For why, the plot's already in mine head.   50

---

[457] Scheme.
[458] Approves what we are driving at.
[459] Without care.
[460] In your support.
[461] Support.

Here they are.

Enter Balthazar and Lorenzo

Balthazar

            How now, Hieronimo?
   What, courting Bel-imperia?
Hieronimo   Ay, my lord.
   Such courting as, I promise you,
   She hath my heart, but you, my lord, have hers.

Lorenzo

   But now, Hieronimo, or never, we   55
   Are to entreat your help.
Hieronimo   My help?
   Why, my good lords, assure yourselves of me,
   For you have given me cause, ay, by my faith, have you.
Balthazar
   It pleased you, to the entertainment of the Ambassador,
   To grace the King so much as with a show.   60
   Now were your study so well furnished[462]
   As, for the passing of the first night's sport,
   To entertain my father with the like,
   Or any suchlike pleasing motion,[463]
   Assure yourself it would content them well.   65
Hieronimo
   Is this all?
Balthazar
   Ay, this is all.
Hieronimo
   Why then, I'll fit you,[464] say no more.

---

[462] Equipped.
[463] Production.
[464] I will give you what you need.

When I was young I gave my mind
And plied myself to fruitless poetry,   70
Which, though it profit the professor[465] naught,
Yet is it passing pleasing to the world.

Lorenzo

And how for that?

Hieronimo   Marry, my good lord, thus—
And yet, methinks, you are too quick with us[466] —
When in Toledo there I studied,   75
It was my chance to write a tragedy,
See here, my lords,   *He shows them a book*
Which, long forgot, I found this other day.
Now, would your lordship favour me so much
As but to grace me with your acting it,   80
I mean each one of you to play a part,
Assure you it will prove most passing strange
And wondrous plausible[467] to that assembly.

Balthazar

What, would you have us play a tragedy?

Hieronimo

Why, Nero[468] thought it no disparagement,[469]   85
And kings and emperors have ta'en delight
To make experience of their wits in plays.

Lorenzo

Nay, be not angry, good Hieronimo,
The prince but asked a question.

---

[465] Practitioner.

[466] Unclear. The line can be seen as Hieronimo straining to control anger, or as conveying that Lorenzo is too importunate.

[467] Pleasing.

[468] Roman emperor, who did take part in theatrical productions, but who is remembered more for his fierce cruelty.

[469] Baseness.

Balthazar

In faith, Hieronimo, and you be in earnest,   90
I'll make one.

Lorenzo   And I another.

Hieronimo

Now my good lord, could you entreat
Your sister Bel-imperia to make one?
For what's a play without a woman in it?

Bel-imperia

Little entreaty shall serve me, Hieronimo,   95
For I must needs be employed in your play.

Hieronimo

Why, this is well. I tell you, lordings,
It was determined to have been acted
By gentlemen and scholars too
Such as could tell[470] what to speak.   100

Balthazar

And now it shall be played by princes and courtiers,
Such as can tell how to speak,
If, as it is our country manners,
You will but let us know the argument.[471]

Hieronimo

That shall I roundly.[472] The chronicles of Spain   105
Record this written of a knight of Rhodes:
He was betrothed, and wedded at the length,
To one Perseda, an Italian dame,
Whose beauty ravished all that her beheld,
Especially the soul of Soliman,   110
Who at the marriage was the chiefest guest.
By sundry means sought Soliman to win

---

[470] Knew well.

[471] Apparently Hieronimo provides the plotline and the actors improvise the speeches.

[472] In plain terms.

Perseda's love, and could not gain the same.
Then gan he break[473] his passions to a friend,
One of his bashaws,[474] whom he held full dear.   115
Her had this bashaw long solicited,
And saw she was not otherwise to be won
But by her husband's death, this Knight of Rhodes,
Whom presently by treachery he slew.
She, stirred with an exceeding hate therefore   120
As cause of this slew Soliman;
And to escape the bashaw's tyranny
Did stab herself, and this the tragedy.

Lorenzo

O, excellent!

Bel-imperia   But say, Hieronimo,
What then became of him that was the bashaw?   125

Hieronimo

Marry, thus: moved with remorse of his misdeeds,
Ran to a mountain top, and hung himself.

Balthazar

But which of us is to perform that part?

Hieronimo

O, that will I, my lords, make no doubt of it.
I'll play the murderer, I warrant you,   130
For I already have conceited[475] that.

Balthazar

And what shall I?

Hieronimo   Great Soliman, the Turkish emperor.

Lorenzo

And I?

Hieronimo   Erastus, the knight of Rhodes.

[473] Tell.
[474] Courtiers; Pashas.
[475] Decided.

Bel-imperia

    And I?

Hieronimo   Perseda, chaste and resolute.   135

    And here, my lords, are several abstracts[476] drawn,

    For each of you to note your parts,

    And act it as occasion offered you.

    You must provide a Turkish cap,

    A black mustachio, and a fauchion.[477]   140

                         Gives a paper to Balthazar

    You with a cross like to a knight of Rhodes.

                         Gives another to Lorenzo

    And madam, you must attire yourself

                        He giveth Bel-imperia another

    Like Phoebe,[478] Flora,[479] or the Huntress,[480]

    Which to your discretion shall seem best.

    And as for me, my lords, I'll look to[481] one,   145

    And with the ransom that the Viceroy sent

    So furnish and perform this tragedy

    As all the world shall say Hieronimo

    Was liberal in gracing of it[482] so.

Balthazar

    Hieronimo, methinks a comedy were better.   150

Hieronimo

    A comedy?

    Fie, comedies are fit for common wits!

    But to present a kingly troop withal,

    Give me a stately-written tragedy,

---

[476] Outlines of plot.

[477] Curved broadsword.

[478] Artemis, moon goddess.

[479] Goddess of flowers and spring.

[480] Diana, goddess of the hunt.

[481] Make ready.

[482] Making much of it.

Tragedia cothurnata,[483] fitting kings,   155
Containing matter,[484] and not common things.
My lords, all this must be performed.
As fitting for the first night's revelling.
The Italian tragedians[485] were so sharp of wit
That in one hour's meditation   160
They would perform anything in action.

Lorenzo

And well it may, for I have seen the like
In Paris, 'mongst the French tragedians.

Hieronimo

In Paris? Mass,[486] and well remembered!
There's one thing more that rests[487] for us to do.   165

Balthazar

What's that, Hieronimo? Forget not anything.

Hieronimo

Each one of us
Must act his part in unknown[488] languages,
That it may breed the more variety.[489]
As you, my lord, in Latin, I in Greek,   170
You in Italian. And for because I know
That Bel-imperia hath practised the French,
In courtly French shall all her phrases be.

Bel-imperia

You mean to try my cunning,[490] then, Hieronimo.

---

[483] Tragedy of the most serious kind.
[484] Weighty material.
[485] *Commedia dell' arte* performers.
[486] By the mass (oath).
[487] Is left.
[488] Foreign.
[489] The audience knows the argument, so possibly the playlet was acted in several languages.
[490] Ability.

Balthazar

    But this will be a mere confusion,   175

    And hardly shall we all be understood.

Hieronimo

    It must be so, for the conclusion

    Shall prove the invention and all was good.

    And I myself in an oration,

    And with a strange and wondrous show besides,   180

    That I will have there behind a curtain,

    Assure yourself shall make the matter known.

    And all shall be concluded in one scene,

    For there's no pleasure ta'en in tediousness.

Balthazar (*to Lorenzo*)

    How like you this?

Lorenzo   Why, thus, my lord,   185

    We must resolve to soothe his humours up.[491]

Balthazar

    On then, Hieronimo, farewell till soon.

Hieronimo

    You'll ply this gear?[492]

Lorenzo   I warrant you.   *Exeunt all by Hieronimo*

Hieronimo   Why so.

    Now shall I see the fall of Babylon,

    Wrought by the heavens in this confusion.   190

    And if the world like not this tragedy,

    Hard is the hap of old Hieronimo.   *Exit*

[491] Go along with this.
[492] Perform this.

Act V, Scene ii

Enter Isabella with a weapon

Isabella

> Tell me no more! O monstrous homicides!
> Since neither piety nor pity moves
> The King to justice or compassion
> I will revenge myself upon this place
> Where thus they murdered my beloved son.   5

She cuts down the arbour

> Down with these branches and these loathsome boughs
> Of this unfortunate and fatal pine.
> Down with them, Isabella, rent them up
> And burn the roots from whence the rest is sprung.
> I will not leave a root, a stalk, a tree,   10
> A bough, a branch, a blossom, nor a leaf,
> No, not an herb within this garden plot.
> Accursed complot[493] of my misery,
> Fruitless for ever may this garden be!
> Barren the earth, and blissless whosoever   15
> Imagines not to keep it unmanured!
> An eastern wind commixed with noisome[494] airs
> Shall blast the plants and the young saplings.
> The earth with serpents shall be pestered,
> And passengers,[495] for fear to be infect,   20
> Shall stand aloof, and, looking at it, tell,
> "There, murdered, died the son of Isabel."
> Ay, here he died, and here I him embrace.
> See where his ghost solicits with his wounds

[493] Plot; place.
[494] Noxious.
[495] Passers-by.

Revenge on her that should revenge his death.   25
Hieronimo, make haste to see thy son,
For sorrow and despair hath cited[496] me
To hear Horatio plead with Radamanth,[497]
Make haste, Hieronimo, to hold excused
Thy negligence in pursuit of their deaths,   30
Whose hateful wrath bereaved him of his breath.
Ah nay, thou dost delay their deaths
Forgives the murderers of thy noble son,
And none but I bestir me—to no end.
And as I curse this tree from further fruit,   35
So shall my womb be cursed for his sake.
And with this weapon will I wound the breast,
The hapless breast that gave Horatio suck.

She stabs herself and exit

Act V, Scene iii

Enter Hieronimo; he knocks up the curtain.[498] *Enter the Duke of Castile*

Duke of Castile
    How now, Hieronimo, where's your fellows,[499]
    That you take all this pain?
Hieronimo
    O sir, it is for the author's credit
    To look that all things may go well.
    But, good my lord, let me entreat your grace   5

---

[496] Called.
[497] One of the three judges of the Underworld.
[498] Hieronimo hangs a curtain, either before an entrance door or the discovery space.
[499] Co-actors.

To give the King the copy of the play.
This is the argument of what we show.

Duke of Castile

I will, Hieronimo.

Hieronimo

One thing more, my good lord.

Duke of Castile

What's that?   10

Hieronimo

Let me entreat your grace
That, when the train are passed into the gallery,
You would vouchsafe to throw me down the key.

Duke of Castile

I will, Hieronimo.   *Exit Duke of Castile*

Hieronimo

What, are you ready, Balthazar?   15
Bring a chair and a cushion for the King.

Enter Balthazar with a chair

Well done, Balthazar. Hang up the title.
Our scene is Rhodes. What, is your beard on?

Balthazar

Half on, the other is in my hand.

Hieronimo

Despatch,[500] for shame, are you so long?   *Exit Balthazar*
Bethink thyself, Hieronimo,   21
Recall thy wits, recompt[501] thy former wrongs
Thou hast received by murder of thy son.
And lastly, not least, how Isabel,
Once his mother and thy dearest wife,   25

---

[500] Hurry up.
[501] Remember.

All woebegone for him hath slain herself.
Behoves thee then, Hieronimo, to be revenged.
The plot is laid of dire revenge.
On then, Hieronimo, pursue revenge,
For nothing wants but acting of revenge.   *Exit Hieronimo*   30

Act V, Scene iv

Enter Spanish King, Viceroy, the Duke of Castile, and their train

King

Now, Viceroy, shall we see the tragedy
Of Soliman the Turkish emperor,
Performed of pleasure by your son the Prince,
My nephew Don Lorenzo, and my niece.

Viceroy

Who, Bel-imperia?   5

King

Ay, and Hieronimo, our marshal,
At whose request they deign to do't themselves.
These be our pastimes in the court of Spain.
Here, brother, you shall be the bookkeeper.[502]
This is the argument of that they show.   10

He giveth him a book

Gentlemen, this play of Hieronimo, in sundry languages, was thought good to be set down in English more largely, for the easier understanding to every public reader[503]

---

[502] Prompter.

[503] As noted earlier, the play may well have been performed in "sundry languages"; however, for the printed text a translation is provided.

Enter Balthazar, Bel-imperia, and Hieronimo

Balthazar

> *Bashaw, that Rhodes is ours, yield heavens the honour,*
> *And holy Mahomet, our sacred prophet;*
> *And be thou graced with every excellence*
> *That Soliman can give, or thou desire.*
> *But thy deserts in conquering Rhodes is less*   15
> *Than in reserving this fair Christian nymph,*
> *Perseda, blissful lamp of excellence,*
> *Whose eyes compel like powerful adamant,*[504]
> *The warlike heart of Soliman to wait.*

King

> See, Viceroy, that is Balthazar, your son,   20
> That represents the emperor Soliman!
> How well he acts his amorous passion.

Viceroy

> Ay, Bel-imperia hath taught him that.

Duke of Castile

> That's because his mind runs all on Bel-imperia.

Hieronimo

> *Whatever joy earth yields betide your majesty.*   25

Balthazar

> *Earth yields no joy without Perseda's love.*

Hieronimo

> *Let then Perseda on your grace attend.*

Balthazar

> *She shall not wait on me, but I on her.*
> *Drawn by the influence of her lights,*[505] *I yield.*
> *But let my friend, the Rhodian knight, come forth,*   30
> *Erasto, dearer than my life to me,*

---

[504] The lodestone, which is magnetic.
[505] Eyes.

That he may see Perseda, my beloved.

Enter Lorenzo as Erasto

King

Here comes Lorenzo; look upon the plot,
And tell me, brother, what part plays he?

Bel-imperia

Ah, my Erasto, welcome to Perseda.   35

Lorenzo

Thrice happy is Erasto that thou liv'st!
Rhodes' loss is nothing to Erasto's joy,
Sith his Perseda lives, his life survives.

Balthazar

Ah, bashaw, here is love between Erasto
And fair Perseda, sovereign of my soul.   40

Hieronimo

Remove Erasto, mighty Soliman,
And then Perseda will be quickly won.

Balthazar

Erasto is my friend, and while he lives
Perseda never will remove her love.

Hieronimo

Let not Erasto live to grieve great Soliman.   45

Balthazar

Dear is Erasto in our princely eye.

Hieronimo

But if he be your rival, let him die.

Balthazar

Why, let him die, so love commandeth me.
Yet grieve I that Erasto should so die.

Hieronimo

Erasto, Soliman saluteth thee,   50
And lets thee wit by me his highness' will

Which is, thou shouldst be thus employed.　　　*Stab him*

Bel-imperia

Ay me, Erasto! See, Soliman, Erasto's slain!

Balthazar

Yet liveth Soliman to comfort thee.

Fair queen of beauty, let not favour die,　　　55

But with a gracious eye behold his grief

That with Perseda's beauty is increased,

If by Perseda his grief be not released.

Bel-imperia

Tyrant, desist soliciting vain suits!

Relentless are mine ears to thy laments,　　　60

As thy butcher is pitiless and base,

Which seized on my Erasto, harmless knight,

Yet by thy power thou thinkest to command,

And to thy power Perseda doth obey.

But were she able, thus she would revenge　　　65

Thy treacheries on thee, ignoble prince!　　　*Stab him*

And on herself she would be thus revenged.　　*Stab herself*

King

Well said,[506] old Marshal, this was bravely done!

Hieronimo

But Bel-imperia plays Perseda well.

Viceroy

Were this in earnest, Bel-imperia　　　70

You would be better to my son than so.

King

But now what follows for Hieronimo?

Hieronimo

Marry, this follows for Hieronimo:

Here break we off our sundry languages

And thus conclude I in our vulgar tongue.[507]　　75

---

[506] Well done.

[507] Ordinary language.

Haply[508] you think, but bootless[509] are your thoughts,
That this is fabulously counterfeit,
And that we do as all tragedians do:
To die today, for fashioning our scene,
The death of Ajax,[510] or some Roman peer,   80
And in a minute starting up again,
Revive to please tomorrow's audience.
No, princes, know I am Hieronimo,
The hopeless father of a hapless son,
Whose tongue is tuned to tell his latest[511] tale,   85
Not to excuse gross errors in the play.
I see your looks urge instance[512] of these words;
Behold the reason urging me to this: *Shows his dead son*[513]
See here my show,[514] look on this spectacle.
Here lay my hope, and here my hope hath end;   90
Here lay my heart, and here my heart was slain;
Here lay my treasure, here my treasure lost;
Here lay my bliss, and here my bliss bereft;
But hope, heart, treasure, joy, and bliss, *Asyndeton*
All fled, failed, died, yea, all decayed with this.   95
From forth these wounds came breath that gave me life.
They murdered me that made these fatal marks.
The cause was love, whence grew this mortal hate,
The hate, Lorenzo and young Balthazar,
The love, my son to Bel-imperia.   100
But night, the coverer of accursed crimes,

[508] Maybe.

[509] To no avail.

[510] Greek warrior in the Trojan war.

[511] Last.

[512] Explanation.

[513] The body may be in the discovery space or behind the door which Hieronimo curtained off at the preparation for the play-within.

[514] Display.

With pitchy[515] silence hushed these traitors' harms
And lent them leave, for they had sorted[516] leisure
To take advantage in my garden plot
Upon my son, my dear Horatio.   105
There merciless they butchered up my boy,
In black dark night, to pale dim cruel death.
He shrieks, I heard, and yet methinks I hear
His dismal outcry echo in the air.
With soonest speed I hasted to the noise,   110
Where, hanging on a tree, I found my son,
Through-girt[517] with wounds, and slaughtered as you see.
And grieved I, think you, at this spectacle?
Speak, Portuguese, whose loss resembles mine,
If thou canst weep upon thy Balthazar,   115
'Tis like I wailed for my Horatio.
And you, my lord, whose reconciled[518] son
Marched in a net and thought himself unseen[519]
And rated me for brainsick lunacy,
With "God amend that mad Hieronimo!"   120
How can you brook our play's catastrophe?
And here behold this bloody handkercher,
Which at Horatio's death I weeping dipped
Within the river of his bleeding wounds.
It as propitious,[520] see, I have reserved,   125
And never hath it left my bloody heart,
Soliciting remembrance of my vow
With these, O these accursed murderers.
Which now, performed, my heart is satisfied.

---

[515] Pitch black.

[516] Found.

[517] Pierced; run through.

[518] Probably reconciled with Hieronimo.

[519] Thought his deceit was well concealed (proverbial).

[520] A token of good omens.

And to this end the bashaw I became   130
That might revenge me on Lorenzo's life,
Who therefore was appointed to the part
And was to represent the knight of Rhodes
That I might kill him more conveniently.
So, Viceroy, was this Balthazar, thy son,   135
That Soliman which Bel-imperia
In person of Perseda murdered,
Solely appointed to that tragic part
That she might slay him that offended her.
Poor Bel-imperia missed her part[521] in this,   140
For though the story saith she should have died,
Yet I of kindness, and of care to her,
Did otherwise determine of her end,
But love of him whom they did hate too much
Did urge her resolution to be such.   145
And princes, now behold Hieronimo,
Author and actor in this tragedy,
Bearing his latest fortune in his fist,
And will as resolute conclude his part
As any of the actors gone before.   150
And, gentles, thus I end my play.
Urge no more words, I have no more to say.

He runs to hang himself

King

O hearken, Viceroy! Hold, Hieronimo!
Brother, my nephew and thy son are slain!

Viceroy

We are betrayed! My Balthazar is slain!   155
Break ope the doors, run, save Hieronimo.

They break in and hold Hieronimo

Hieronimo, do but inform the King of these events.

---

[521] Did not perform her part as intended.

Upon mine honour, thou shalt have no harm.

Hieronimo

    Viceroy, I will not trust thee with my life,

    Which I this day have offered to my son.   160

    Accursed wretch!

    Why stayest thou him that was resolved to die?

King

    Speak, traitor! Damned, bloody murderer, speak!

    For now I have thee I will make thee speak.

    Why hast thou done this undeserving deed?   165

Viceroy

    Why hast thou murdered my Balthazar?

Duke of Castile

    Why hast thou butchered both my children thus?[ψ]

Hieronimo

    O! Good words!

    As dear to me was my Horatio

    As yours, or yours, or yours, my lord, to you.   170

    My guiltless son was by Lorenzo slain,

    And by Lorenzo and that Balthazar

    Am I at last revenged thoroughly,

    Upon whose souls may heavens be yet avenged

    With greater far than these afflictions.   175

Duke of Castile

    But who were thy confederates in this?

Viceroy

    That was thy daughter, Bel-imperia,

    For by her hand my Balthazar was slain.

    I saw her stab him.

King   Why speak'st thou not?

Hieronimo

    What lesser liberty can kings afford   180

[ψ] See appendix for the fifth 1602 addition, replacing ll.167–191.

Than harmless silence? Then afford it me.

Sufficeth I may not, nor I will not tell thee.

King

Fetch forth the tortures.

Traitor as thou art, I'll make thee tell.

Hieronimo   Indeed,

Thou may'st torment me, as his wretched son   185

Hath done in murdering my Horatio,

But never shalt thou force me to reveal

The thing which I have vowed inviolate.

And therefore, in despite of all thy threats,

Pleased with their deaths, and eased with their revenge,   190

First take my tongue, and afterwards my heart.

He bites out his tongue

King

O monstrous resolution of a wretch!

See, Viceroy, he hath bitten forth his tongue

Rather than to reveal what we required.

Duke of Castile

Yet can he write.   195

King

And if in this he satisfy us not,

We will devise th'extremest kind of death

That ever was invented for a wretch.

Then Hieronimo makes signs for a knife to mend his pen

Duke of Castile

O, he would have a knife to mend his pen.

Viceroy

Here. And advice thee[522] that thou write the troth.   200

King

Look to my brother! Save Hieronimo!

Hieronimo with a knife stabs the Duke and himself

[522] Take care.

What age hath ever heard such monstrous deeds?
My brother, and the whole succeeding hope
That Spain expected after my decease!
Go bear his body hence, that we may mourn   205
The loss of our beloved brother's death,
That he may be entombed, whate'er befall.
I am the next, the nearest, last of all.

Viceroy

And thou, Don Pedro, do the like for us.
Take up our hapless son, untimely slain.   210
Set me with him, and he with woeful me,
Upon the mainmast of a ship unmanned,
And let the wind and tide haul me along
To Scylla's[523] barking and untamed gulf,
Or to the loathsome pool of Acheron,[524]   215
To weep my want for my sweet Balthazar.
Spain hath no refuge for a Portingale.

The trumpets sound a dead march, the King of Spain mourning after his brother's body, and the Viceroy of Portingale bearing the body of his son.

Chorus: Ghost of Andrea and Revenge

Andrea

Ay, now my hopes have end in their effects,
When blood and sorrow finish my desires:
Horatio murdered in his father's bower,   220
Vild[525] Serberine by Pedringano slain,

---

[523] Scylla and Charybdis were a pair of dangerous rocks between Italy and Sicily, upon which ships frequently were said to founder.
[524] Lake or river in the Underworld.
[525] Vile.

False Pedringano hanged by quaint device,
Fair Isabella by herself misdone,[526]
Prince Balthazar by Bel-imperia stabbed,
The Duke of Castile and his wicked son   225
Both done to death by old Hieronimo,
My Bel-imperia fallen as Dido[527] fell,
And good Hieronimo slain by himself.
Ay, these were spectacles to please my soul.
Now will I beg at lovely Proserpine   230
That, by the virtue of her princely doom,[528]
I may consort[529] my friends in pleasing sort,
And on my foes work just and sharp revenge.
I'll lead my friend Horatio through those fields
Where never-dying wars are still inured.[530]   235
I'll lead fair Isabella to that train
Where pity weeps but never feeleth pain.
I'll lead my Bel-imperia to those joys
That vestal virgins[531] and fair queens possess.
I'll lead Hieronimo where Orpheus plays,   240
Adding sweet pleasures to eternal days.
But say, Revenge, for thou must help, or none,
Against the rest how shall my hate be shown?

Revenge

This hand shall hale[532] them down to deepest hell
Where none but furies, bugs[533] and tortures dwell.   245

---

[526] Killed.
[527] Dido, Queen of Carthage, killed herself when abandoned by Aeneas.
[528] Judgment.
[529] Accompany.
[530] Waged.
[531] The goddess Vesta's chaste servants.
[532] Drag.
[533] Bugbears.

Andrea

    Then, sweet Revenge, do this at my request:
    Let me be judge and doom them to unrest.
    Let loose poor Tityus[534] from the vulture's gripe,
    and let Don Cyprian supply his room;[535]
    Place Don Lorenzo on Ixion's wheel,[536]   250
    And let the lover's endless pain surcease—
    Juno[537] forgets old wrath and grants him ease.
    Hang Balthazar about Chimera's[538] neck,
    And let him there bewail his bloody love,
    Repining at our joys that are above.   255
    Let Serberine go roll the fatal stone
    And take from Sisyphus[539] his endless moan.
    False Pedringano for his treachery,
    Let him be dragged through boiling Acheron,
    And there live, dying still in endless flames,   260
    Blaspheming gods and all their holy names.

Revenge

    Then haste we down to meet thy friends and foes:
    To place thy friends in ease, the rest in woes.
    For here, though death hath end their misery,
    I'll there begin their endless tragedy.   *Exeunt* 265

---

[534] Giant punished for assault by having two vultures eternally tear his liver, the seat of passion.

[535] Take his place.

[536] For sexually assaulting Hera, wife of Zeus, Ixion was chained to a fiery wheel, revolving in eternity.

[537] Hera's Roman equivalent.

[538] Chimera has a lion's front, a serpent's or dragon's tail, and is a goat in the middle; sometimes it is equipped with a fire-breathing head.

[539] Founder and king of Corinth, condemned to roll a huge stone uphill as punishment for cheating death; when the stone reaches the top of the hill, it rolls back down.

Appendix

Additions to *The Spanish Tragedy* printed in the 1602 edition

Added *DRAMATIS PERSONAE*
>Pedro, servant to Hieronimo
>Jaques, servant to Hieronimo
>Bazardo, a Painter

First addition, between II.v.45 and 46

[Isabella
>For outrage fits our cursed wretchedness.   45]
>Ay me, Hieronimo, sweet husband, speak.
Hieronimo
>He supped with us tonight, frolic[540] and merry,
>And said he would go visit Balthazar
>At the Duke's palace; there the prince doth lodge.
>He had no custom to stay out so late,   5
>He may be in his chamber. Some go see.
>Roderigo, ho!

Enter Pedro and Jaques

Isabella
>Ay me, he raves. Sweet Hieronimo!

---

[540] Happy.

Hieronimo

> True, all Spain takes note of it.
>
> Besides, he is so generally beloved   10
>
> His majesty the other day did grace him
>
> With waiting on his cup. These be favours
>
> Which do assure he cannot be short-lived.

Isabella

> Sweet Hieronimo!

Hieronimo

> I wonder how this fellow got his clothes?   15
>
> Sirrah, sirrah, I'll know the truth of all.
>
> Jaques, run to the Duke of Castile's presently[541]
>
> And bid my son Horatio to come home.
>
> I and his mother have had strange dreams tonight.
>
> Do you hear me, sir?

Jaques   Ay, sir.

Hieronimo   Well sir, begone.   20

> Pedro, come hither, knowest thou who this is?

Pedro

> Too well, sir.

Hieronimo

> Too well? Who is it? Peace, Isabella.
>
> Nay, blush not, man.

Pedro   It is my lord Horatio.

Hieronimo

> Ha, ha! Saint James, but this doth make me laugh,   25
>
> That there are more deluded than myself.

Pedro

> Deluded?

Hieronimo

> Ay, I would have sworn myself within this hour
>
> That this had been my son Horatio,

---

[541] At once.

His garments are so like.   30
    Ha! are they not great persuasions?
Isabella
    O, would to God it were not so!
Hieronimo
    Were not, Isabella? Dost thou dream it is?
    Can thy soft bosom entertain a thought
    That such a black deed of mischief should be done   35
    On one so pure and spotless as our son?
    Away! I am ashamed.
Isabella   Dear Hieronimo,
    Cast a more serious eye upon thy grief.
    Weak apprehension[542] gives but weak belief.
Hieronimo
    It was a man, sure, that was hanged up here,   40
    A youth, as I remember. I cut him down.
    If it should prove my son, now, after all?
    Say you, say you, light! Lend me a taper,
    Let me look again. O God!
    Confusion, mischief, torment, death, and hell,   45
    Drop all your stings at once in my cold bosom,
    That now is stiff with horror, kill me quickly.
    Be gracious to me, thou infective[543] night,
    And drop this deed of murder down on me;
    Gird in[544] my waste of grief with thy large darkness,   50
    And let me not survive; to see the light
    May put me in the mind I had a son.
Isabella
    O sweet Horatio, O, my dearest son!

---

[542] Understanding.
[543] Carrying infection.
[544] Limit.

Hieronimo   46]

> How strangely had I lost my way to grief!
> [Sweet lovely rose, ill plucked before thy time,

Second addition, replacing III.ii.65-66

[Lorenzo

> Why so, Hieronimo. Use me.   64]

Hieronimo

> Who, you, my lord?
> I reserve your favour for a greater honour;
> This is a very toy,[545] my lord, a toy.

Lorenzo

> All's one, Hieronimo, acquaint me with it.

Hieronimo

> I'faith, my lord, 'tis an idle thing.   5
> I must confess I ha' been too slack, too tardy.
> Too remiss unto your honour.

Lorenzo   How now, Hieronimo?

Hieronimo

> In troth, my lord, it is a thing of nothing,
> The murder of a son, or so,
> A thing of nothing, my lord.   10

[Lorenzo   Why then, farewell.   66]

Third addition, between IV.iv.1-2

[First Portingale

> By your leave, sir.   1]

---

[545] A nothing.

Hieronimo

 'Tis neither as you think, nor as you think,

 Nor as you think; you're wide[546] all.

 These slippers are not mine, they were my son Horatio's.

 My son, and what is a son? A thing begot

 Within a pair of minutes, thereabout;   5

 A lump bred up in darkness, and doth serve

 To ballace[547] these light creatures we call women,

 And, at nine moneths' end, creeps forth to light.

 What is there yet in a son

 To make a father dote, rave, or run mad?   10

 Being born, it pouts, cries, and breeds teeth.[548]

 What is there yet in a son? He must be fed,

 Be taught to go[549] and speak. Ay, or yet?

 Why might not a man love a calf as well?

 Or melt in passion o'er a frisking kid,   15

 As for a son? Methinks a young bacon[550]

 Or a fine little smooth horse-colt

 Should move a man as much as doth a son.

 For one of these in very little time

 Will grow to some good use, whereas a son,   20

 The more he grows in stature and in years,

 The more unsquared, unbevelled[551] he appears,

 Reckons his parents among the rank of fools,

 Strikes care upon their heads with his mad riots,

 Makes them look old before they meet with age. 25

 This is a son. And what a loss were this,

---

[546] Off the mark.

[547] Be ballast to.

[548] Teethes.

[549] Walk.

[550] Pig.

[551] Two terms of carpentry; both refine the wood and make it ready for use. Adolescent boys are not seen as easily refined here.

Considered truly? Oh, but my Horatio
Grew out of reach of these insatiate humors:[552]
He loved his loving parents,
He was my comfort and his mother's joy,   30
The very arm that did hold up our house.
Our hopes were stored up in him,
None but a damned murderer could hate him.
He had not seen the back of nineteen year,[553]
When his strong arm unhorsed   35
The proud Prince Balthazar, and his great mind,
Too full of honour, took him unto mercy,
That valiant but ignoble Portingale.
Well, heaven is heaven still,
And there is Nemesis[554] and Furies,   40
And things called whips,
And they sometimes do meet with murderers;
They do not always 'scape, that's some comfort.
Ay, ay, ay, and then time steals on,
And steals and steals, till violence leaps forth   45
Like thunder wrapped in a ball of fire,
And so doth bring confusion[555] to them all.
[Good leave have you, nay, I pray you go,   2]

Fourth addition, between IV.v and IV.vi

Enter Jaques and Pedro

Jaques
    I wonder, Pedro, why our master thus

---

[552] Childlike behavior.
[553] He was still only nineteen years old.
[554] Goddess of retribution.
[555] Destruction.

At midnight sends us with our torches light,
When man and bird and beast are all at rest,
Save those that watch for rape and bloody murder?

Pedro

    O Jaques, know thou that our master's mind   5
    Is much distraught since his Horatio died,
    And—now his aged years should sleep in rest,
    His heart in quiet—like a desperate man,
    Grows lunatic and childish for his son.
    Sometimes, as he doth at his table sit,   10
    He speaks as if Horatio stood by him;
    Then starting in a rage, falls on the earth,
    Cries out, "Horatio, where is my Horatio?"
    So that with extreme grief and cutting sorrow
    There is not left in him one inch of man.   15
    See where he comes.

Enter Hieronimo

Hieronimo

    I pry through every crevice of each wall,
    Look on each tree, and search through every brake,[556]
    Beat at the bushes, stamp our grandam earth,
    Dive in the water, and stare up to heaven,   20
    Yet cannot I behold my son Horatio.
    How now, who's there, sprites, sprites?[557]

Pedro

    We are your servants that attend you, sir.

Hieronimo

    What make you with your torches in the dark?

[556] Thicket.
[557] Spirits; demons.

Pedro

> You bid us light them and attend you here.   25

Hieronimo

> No, no, you are deceived, not I, you are deceived!
> Was I so mad to bid you light your torches now?
> Light me your torches at the mid of noon,
> Whenas[558] the sun god rides in all his glory;
> Light me your torches then?

Pedro   Then we burn daylight.   30

Hieronimo

> Let it be burnt! Night is a murderous slut,
> That would not have her treasons to be seen.
> And yonder pale-faced Hecate[559] there, the moon,
> Doth give consent to that is done in darkness,
> And all those stars that gaze upon her face,   35
> Are aglets[560] on her sleeve, pins on her train.
> And those that should be powerful and divine,
> Do sleep in darkness when they most should shine.

Pedro

> Provoke them not, fair sir, with tempting words.
> The heavens are gracious, and your miseries   40
> And sorrow makes you speak you know not what.

Hieronimo

> Villain, thou liest, and thou doest naught
> But tell me I am mad. Thou liest, I am not mad.
> I know thee to be Pedro, and he Jaques.
> I'll prove it to thee, and were I mad, how could I?   45
> Where was she that same night when my Horatio
> Was murdered? She should have shone; search thou the
>   book.[561]

---

558 When.

559 Goddess associated with magic, witchcraft, and the moon.

560 Ornaments or pendants.

561 Almanac.

Had the moon shone, in my boy's face there was a kind of
grace,
That I know—nay, I do know—had the murderer seen him,
His weapon would have fallen and cut the earth,   50
Had he been framed of naught but blood and death.
Alack, when mischief doth it knows not what,
What shall we say to mischief?

Enter Isabella

Isabella
Dear Hieronimo, come in a-doors,
O seek not means so to increase thy sorrow.   55
Hieronimo
Indeed, Isabella, we do nothing here,
I do not cry. Ask Pedro and ask Jaques.
Not I, indeed, we are very merry, very merry.
Isabella
How? Be merry here, be merry here?
Is not this the place, and this the very tree,   60
Where my Horatio died, where he was murdered?
Hieronimo
Was—do not say what. Let her weep it out.
This was the tree, I set it of a kernel,[562]
And when our hot Spain could not let it grow,
But that the infant and the human sap   65
Began to wither, duly twice a morning
Would I be sprinkling it with fountain water.
At last it grew and grew, and bore and bore,
Till at length
It grew a gallows, and did bear our son.   70
It bore thy fruit and mine. O wicked, wicked plant.

---

[562] Planted it from seed.

One knocks within at the door

    See who knocks there.

Pedro   It is a painter, sir.

Hieronimo

    Bid him come in and paint some comfort,

    For surely there's none lives but painted[563] comfort.

    Let him come in. One knows not what may chance.   75

    God's will that I should set this tree—but even so

    Masters ungrateful servants rear from naught,

    And then they hate them that did bring them up.

Enter the Painter

Painter

    God bless you, sir.

Hieronimo

    Wherefore? Why, thou scornful villain,   80

    How, where, or by what means should I be blessed?

Isabella

    What wouldst thou have, good fellow?

Painter   Justice, madam.

Hieronimo

    O, ambitious beggar, wouldst thou have that

    That lives not in the world?

    Why, all the undelved mines[564] cannot buy   85

    An ounce of justice, 'tis a jewel so inestimable.

    I tell thee,

    God hath engrossed all justice in his hands,[565]

    And there is none but what comes from him.

---

[563] Artificial.

[564] Mines yet to be dug.

[565] Taken all justice into his own hands.

Painter

    O, then I see   90

    That God must right me for my murdered son.

Hieronimo

    How, was thy son murdered?

Painter

    Ay, sir, no man did hold a son so dear.

Hieronimo

    What, not as thine? That's a lie

    As massy[566] as the earth. I had a son,   95

    Whose least unvalued hair did weigh

    A thousand of thy sons; and he was murdered.

Painter

    Alas, sir, I had no more but he.

Hieronimo

    Nor I, nor I, but this same one of mine

    Was worth a legion. But all is one.   100

    Pedro, Jaques, go in a-doors, Isabella, go,

    And this good fellow here and I

    Will range this hideous orchard up and down,

    Like to two lions reaved[567] of their young,

    Go in a-doors, I say.   *Exeunt. The Painter and he sit down*

                  Come, let's talk wisely now.   105

    Was thy son murdered?

Painter   Ay, sir.

Hieronimo   So was mine.

    How dost take it? Art thou not sometimes mad?

    Is there no tricks that comes before thine eyes?

Painter

    O Lord, yes sir.

---

[566] Heavy.
[567] Bereft.

Hieronimo

> Art a painter? Canst paint me a tear, or a wound, a groan, 110
> or a sigh? Canst paint me such a tree as this?

Painter

> Sir, I am sure you have heard of my painting. My name is
> Bazardo.

Hieronimo

> Bazardo! Afore God, an excellent fellow! Look you sir,
> do you see, I'd have you paint me in my gallery, in your oil 115
> colours matted, and draw me five years younger than I
> am. Do you see sir, let five years go, let them go, like the
> Marshal of Spain. My wife Isabella standing by me, with
> a speaking look to my son Horatio, which should intend
> to this or some such like purpose: "God bless thee, my 120
> sweet son," and my hand leaning upon his head, thus, sir,
> do you see? May it be done?

Painter

> Very well sir.

Hieronimo

> Nay, I pray mark me sir. Then, sir, would I have you paint
> me this tree, this very tree. Canst paint a doleful cry?   125

Painter

> Seemingly,[568] sir.

Hieronimo

> Nay, it should cry; but all is one. Well sir, paint me a youth
> run through and through with villains' swords, hanging
> upon this tree. Canst thou draw a murderer?

Painter

> I'll warrant you, sir, I have the pattern[569] of the most no- 130
> torious villains that ever lived in all Spain.

[568] Believably.
[569] Model.

Hieronimo

O, let them be worse, worse! Stretch thine art, and let
their beards be of Judas his own colour,[570] and let their
eyebrows jutty over, in any case observe that. Then sir,
after some violent noise, bring me forth in my shirt, and 135
my gown under mine arm, with my torch in my hand,
and my sword reared up thus, and with these words: *What
noise is this? Who calls Hieronimo?* May it be done?

Painter

Yea sir.

Hieronimo

Well sir, then bring me forth, bring me through alley and 140
alley, still with a distracted countenance going along, and
let my hair heave up my nightcap. Let the clouds scowl,
make the moon dark, the stars extinct, the winds blowing, the bells tolling, the owl shrieking, the toads croaking,
the minutes jarring, and the clock striking twelve. And 145
then, at last sir, starting, behold a man hanging, and tottering,[571] and tottering as you know the wind will weave a
man, and I with a trice[572] to cut him down. And looking
upon him by the advantage of my torch, find it to be my
son Horatio. There you may show a passion, there you 150
may show a passion. Draw me like old Priam of Troy,
crying, "The house is afire, the house is afire as the torch
over my head!" Make me curse, make me rave, make me
cry, make me mad, make me well again, make me curse
hell, invocate heaven, and in the end leave me in a trance— 155
and so forth.

Painter

And is this the end?

---

[570] Red; in Renaissance times Judas Iscariot was shown as a redhead.
[571] Swinging.
[572] All at once.

Hieronimo

O no, there is no end! The end is death and madness! As
I am never better than when I am mad, then methinks I
am a brave fellow, then I do wonders; but reason abuseth[573] 160
me, and there's the torment, there's the hell. At the last, sir,
bring me to one of the murderers. Were he as strong as
Hector, thus would I tear and drag him up and down.

He beats the Painter in, then comes out again with a book in his hand

Fifth addition, replacing V.iv.167-190   167]

[Duke of Castile

Why hast thou butchered both my children thus?

Hieronimo

But are you sure they are dead?

Duke of Castile   Ay, slave, too sure.

Hieronimo

What, and yours too?

Viceroy

Ay, all are dead, not one of them survive.

Hieronimo

Nay, then, I care not, come, and we shall be friends,
Let us lay our heads together.   5

See, here's a goodly noose will hold them all.

Viceroy

O damned devil, how secure[574] he is.

Hieronimo

Secure? Why dost thou wonder at it?
I tell thee, Viceroy, this day I have seen revenge,

[573] Deceives.
[574] Assured.

And in that sight am grown a prouder monarch   10
Than ever sat under the crown of Spain.
Had I as many lives as there be stars,
As many heavens to go to as those lives,
I'd give them all, ay, and my soul to boot,[575]
But I would see thee ride in this red pool.   15

Duke of Castile

Speak, who were thy confederates in this?

Viceroy

That was thy daughter Bel-imperia,
For by her hand my Balthazar was slain.
I saw her stab him.

Hieronimo   O good words!

As dear to me was my Horatio   20
As yours, or yours, or yours, my lord, to you.
My guiltless son was by Lorenzo slain,
And by Lorenzo and that Balthazar
Am I at last revenged thoroughly.
Upon whose souls may heavens yet be revenged   25
With greater far than these afflictions.
Methinks since I grew inward with revenge,
I cannot look with scorn enough on death.

King

What, dost thou mock us, slave? Bring tortures[576] forth.

Hieronimo

Do, do, do, and meantime I'll torture you.   30
You had a son, as I take it, and your son
Should ha' been married to your daughter,
Ha, was't not so? You had a son too,
He was my liege's nephew. He was proud
And politic. Had he lived, he might ha' come   35

---

[575] In addition.
[576] Instruments of torture.

To wear the crown of Spain, I think 'twas so.
'Twas I that killed him. Look you, this same hand,
'Twas it that stabbed his heart. Do you see this hand?
For one Horatio, if you ever knew him, a youth,
One that they hanged up in his father's garden,   40
One that did force your valiant son to yield,
While your more valiant son did take him prisoner.

Viceroy

Be deaf, my senses, I can hear no more.

King

Fall, heaven, and cover us with thy sad ruins.

Duke of Castile

Roll all the world within thy pitchy cloud.   45

Hieronimo

Now do I applaud what I have acted
Nunc iners cadat manus.[577]
Now to express the rupture[578] of my part,
[First take my tongue, and afterwards my heart.   190]

[577] "Now let the hand fall idle."
[578] Breaking off.

THE TRAGEDY OF HAMLET, PRINCE OF DENMARK

by

WILLIAM SHAKESPEARE

Introductory Remarks

William Shakespeare

Shakespeare was born in April of 1564 in Stratford-upon-Avon, first son to John Shakespeare, a glove-maker and worker of leather goods. Shakespeare Senior quickly rose in society through holding public office, the highest of which was as "bailiff," equivalent to a mayor of a small town. We have little hard knowledge about Shakespeare's youth, but Stratford had a grammar school created for sons of prominent citizens, such as William was. Here he would have studied Latin and Roman history and literature.

After 1576, Shakespeare's father fell into debt, sold off parts of his property, lost his position as alderman, was fined for not coming to church regularly, and for not appearing at a court hearing. Near the end of his life, though, his fortunes picked up again. His son had petitioned for and been granted a family coat of arms on his father's behalf, and at his death John Shakespeare again had a place in the town council. There is some speculation whether the Shakespeare family entertained Catholic sympathies; after all, Henry VIII's break with Rome was only about half a century old. But there is no evidence that they did not follow the law and attend Anglican church, except for the fine given Shakespeare's father, who may have avoided church in order to escape his creditors. Either way, the plays themselves are rich in evidence that Shakespeare knew his Bible well.

At eighteen, Shakespeare married the pregnant, eight-years-older Anne Hathaway and eventually had three children by her. Apart from the children's christenings, we have no record of our dramatist until Shakespeare made his mark in London in 1592. He probably had arrived a few years earlier in order to be sufficiently established to attract the attention of Robert Greene, educated rake and playwright, who called him an "upstart crow." There are legends about the time between, such as his escaping Stratford because of being charged with poaching, being a schoolmaster, and joining a group of players, but as of now we have no documented knowledge to support any of these suppositions.

Also in 1592, Thomas Nashe, fellow writer, noted the great success of the *Henry VI* plays, and Shakespeare published his long poem *Venus and Adonis*. He wrote *The Rape of Lucrece* the following year, and was composing his 154 sonnets. It seems that Shakespeare wrote poetry when the theaters were closed due to an outbreak of the plague, when there was no immediate demand for new plays. As soon as the playhouses reopened, he returned to playwriting. Many speculations have been made about the nature of Shakespeare's relationship with the third Earl of Southampton, to whom the two long poems were dedicated, as well as about the identity of the "dark lady" and the "fair youth" of the sonnets; but again, we have no hard evidence.

How Shakespeare became involved with acting and/or writing for the stage or what group he first joined we do not know, but he did form a group with Richard Burbage, a gifted actor, and six other players as The Lord Chamberlain's Men in 1594, finding a home at The Theatre, a building north of London's walls. They performed at court that same Christmas and soon became successful, probably due at least in part to Shakespeare's talents as a playwright. In 1596 their lease of The Theatre became problematic, which eventually led to the construction of The Globe Theatre, in which ten members, Shakespeare included, owned a share, and later to the lease of the indoor Blackfriars stage.

In May 1603 King James granted them royal license

> . . . to use and exercise the art and faculty of playing comedies, tragedies, histories, interludes, morals, pastorals, stageplays, and such other like as they have already studied or hereafter shall use or study as well for the recreation of our loving subjects as for our solace and pleasure when we shall think good to see

them during our pleasure.[1]

They now were The King's Men with status as his majesty's servants, a position they held long after Shakespeare's death. And a profitable business it became indeed. Shakespeare was able to buy both land and a large cottage in Stratford, a house in London (bought 1612), as well as making other substantial investments. It seems that the gifted playwright had a keen nose for business as well as a sense for what would draw the crowds to his theater.

Throughout his career, Shakespeare kept experimenting with different genres and topics, probably capitalizing on public taste; around 1600 he left histories and "happy comedies" for the darker aspects of human nature, and explored the dark side of comedy as well as the darker side that is tragedy; around 1608 another shift in interest happened, this time to romance, and late in his career he collaborated with Fletcher on *The Two Noble Kinsmen*, a tragi-comedy. Why he retired from the stage when he did remains a mystery, but at the end of his career he was able to return to Stratford as a wealthy and famous man.

Again, we have little factual information about Shakespeare's last years beyond official documents, and we do not know the cause of his death in 1616. He did change his will shortly before his death in order to protect his daughter's marriage portion from exploitation by her shady husband. The other daughter and her husband inherited the house in Stratford and probably had Shakespeare's widow stay with them, using "the second-best bed" bequeathed to her. There is no mention of his plays in his will; they belonged not to him, but to the company that performed them. His fellow actors received money to buy rings to remember him by. He lies buried in Holy Trinity Church in Stratford.

Seven years after his death, his fellow actors Heminges and Condell had his collected plays published in The First Folio of

---

[1] Qtd. in *The Bedford Companion*, p. 33.

thirty-six plays, called *Mr. William Shakespeares Comedies, Histories, & Tragedies.*

The Play
Setting and Characters

Hamlet's earliest known source is to be found in Saxo Grammaticus' *Gesta Danorum*,[2] written at the end of the twelfth to the beginning of the thirteenth century. Amlet, like Hamlet, finds himself the revenger of his father's death, and he, too, decides to feign madness in order to survive until he can effectuate his revenge. The mother of each man marries the murderer, her first husband's brother, incestuously; both men are tempted by a woman sent for that purpose, Amlet sexually, Hamlet mentally; both confront their mother in her private room, with a planted listener in place whom they murder; both are brilliant orators; and both are sent to England to die, but alter the message and get the bearers killed. Here the similarities end. Amlet marries the daughter of the King of England, and has no compunctions about the revenge task at hand, and no hesitation once the time is ripe and the opportunity presents itself; after all, Viking morality includes the concept of *wergeld*, the price that must be paid for taking a life, which often takes the form of accepted blood revenge. He also survives his revenge to become King of Denmark and go on with his life, the doer of spectacular deeds. Shakespeare's source is set in Denmark, and so he follows suit, but *Hamlet*'s Denmark feels much closer to Renaissance England than to its Viking past.

According to Ophelia, Hamlet was a Renaissance man before his father's death:

> The courtier's, soldier's, scholar's, eye, tongue, sword,
> The expectancy and rose of the fair state,
> The glass of fashion and the mould of form,

[2] Latin: The Deeds of the Danes.

> The observed of all observers, quite, quite down!
>
> (III.i.154-157)

The text allows us many glimpses of the Hamlet that was, such as the friendliness with which he greets the soldiers of the watch and the way he receives his old friends. That Hamlet appears to have been like any other high-born nobleman, interested in his world and in women, in educating himself as a gentleman, in forming friendships, and aware, but not overly proud, of his social position and that of his family. He was clearly keen to be accepted as the young man-about-town as can be seen in his interaction with the players and his eagerness to be esteemed by them as being a cultured man of taste. His father's death and meeting his father's revenge-craving ghost shatters this well-known, safe world. Suddenly Hamlet, already grieving and stricken by his mother's incestuous marriage, has to face the fact that public revenge cannot be had; he must choose between exacting private revenge, potentially damning his own soul, and turning the other cheek to let the Lord mete out justice in His own time. When the ghost demands revenge, Hamlet immediately and eagerly complies; but once he is away from the ghost's presence, doubt sets in. A melancholy man[3] is particularly susceptible to the blandishments of devils and evil spirits, and Hamlet is only too aware of his own mood. The putting on of the "antic disposition"[4] can free him to both gain time to investigate and a freedom of speech much needed for such investigation.

In the course of the play, as Hamlet gains knowledge about the workings of the court and the mind of his Machiavellian uncle, the young courtier develops into a Machiavellian in his own right. As always in revenge plays, the evil prompting the revenge reaches out to taint the avenger, and Hamlet gradually becomes more like

---

[3] See glossary.
[4] I.v.163-167.

Claudius. The killing of Polonius, the first time Hamlet demonstrates his ability to act quickly and decisively when not given time to ponder, becomes a means to an end to explore Claudius' mind. But cold-bloodedly and calculatingly sending Rosencrantz and Guildenstern to the block in his stead is quite a different thing from killing Polonius; rash manslaughter[5] progresses to plotted murder. Still, the public practice bout with Laertes that ends both their lives leaves Hamlet unsuspecting of attack. He yet has a way to go before he is capable of Claudius' underhandedness. He avenges his father, but not coldly and calculatedly, rather in another rush of unpremeditated action. But the Hamlet dying in V.ii has come a very long way during the play, especially through his conversation with the Gravedigger in V.i. Here, finally, he has matured sufficiently to see that everything in life is mutable, not static, that "all that lives must die" (I.ii.72), be he Alexander the Great, a syphilis-ridden "pocky corpse," or even Prince Hamlet himself. The audience must agree with Fortinbras' pronouncement:

> Let four captains
> Bear Hamlet, like a soldier, to the stage,
> For he was likely, had he been put on,
> To have proved most royally; and for his passage,
> The soldiers' music and the rites of war
> Speak loudly for him.
>
> (V.ii.385-390)

Hamlet has, indeed, been at war throughout the play, and has not been tainted as much or gone nearly as far in his revenge as does Hieronimo of *The Spanish Tragedy*, Vindice of *The Revenger's Tragedy*, or Melantius of *The Maid's Tragedy*. Still, like Vindice feels, the atmo-

---

[5] I use the word in the modern, not the Renaissance, sense of the word. Then manslaughter was immediate, unpremeditated retaliation to an injury.

sphere of the court is morally corrupting, all the more so because the corruption is covered with a layer of seeming accord and excellence. In the audience's eyes, Fortinbras honors both the Hamlet that was and the struggle that created the Hamlet dying at his feet.

Claudius, the murderer of Hamlet Senior, is a more complicated villain than any other revenge target. He is highly intelligent, a consummate politician, and, if the audience had not received information from both the Ghost and Claudius himself that he is a murderer, it would be easy to see him as an effective ruler. He deals efficiently with domestic matters and foreign politics in I.ii, and seemingly supports Gertrude's wish to have Hamlet remain at the Danish court; still, it is wise to keep potential enemies close where they can be watched. In the manner of Polonius, he sets spies on Hamlet in a practical fashion, and he is not above spying himself or using Ophelia and Hamlet's mother to gather information. In III.iii.54 he reveals the reasons for the murder; he coveted "[his] crown, [his] own ambition, and [his] Queen," and it is impossible for him to truly repent because he wants to continue enjoying the fruits of his sin. Interestingly, he is a revenge play villain who acknowledges the moral consequences of his sin. Once convinced that Hamlet is not mad and that he knows too much, Claudius sets about getting rid of him in typically Machiavellian fashion, never associating himself directly with the tools of his schemes. When Hamlet escapes the England trap, he seizes upon the manipulable Laertes, and in a brilliant maneuver recruits him as his tool, arranging for poison as a back-up measure. Only Laertes' essentially good nature makes the plan backfire.

Horatio is Hamlet's friend in true Renaissance fashion.[6] Hamlet sees his strengths clearly in III.ii.50-70; he is no flatterer, not "passion's slave," and takes what fortune dishes out to him stoically. Unlike Rosencrantz and Guildenstern, Horatio cannot be used as a tool against Hamlet; he is Hamlet's anchor, pulling him

---

[6] See glossary: "male friendship."

back from the brink of exaggerated feelings more than once.[7] This friendship illuminates the Hamlet that was, the man capable of inspiring such friendship. In Horatio's presence, Hamlet is able to be "himself" to the greatest degree. He is the one who knows that Hamlet has misgivings about the King's wager with Laertes, and he is finally persuaded to remain in this world by Hamlet's impassioned plea, discharging the last duty friendship has laid upon him: telling Hamlet's story from Hamlet's point of view. So much more than a dramatic device, a "foil" to Hamlet, Horatio's is a brilliant instance of Renaissance male friendship, that intimate sharing of feeling and experience between two worthy equals.

Gertrude and Ophelia can both be seen as casualties of men's choices. Gertrude is on Claudius' list of why he committed murder, but she is also "[t]he imperial jointress to this warlike state" (I.ii.9). The *Oxford English Dictionary* defines "jointress" as a widow holding a jointure, a dowager who has inherited an estate, which in this case would be Denmark, and cites *Hamlet*, 1602, as first usage. We know from I.i that the country is preparing for war, and that the tension among the watchmen is great; part of the reason for the marriage could be placing a king rather than a female ruler at the helm in times of trouble.[8] Claudius cannot have Denmark without Gertrude and *vice versa*. Claudius is also careful to implicate his entire council in his incestuous[9] marriage in I.ii.14-

---

[7] Such as I.v when Hamlet is reeling from his meeting with the Ghost; III.ii when Hamlet's glee almost resembles hysterics after "The Mousetrap" play; and twice V.i, when Hamlet revels in his wit to an unpleasant degree after having seen Yorick's skull, and later, calming him during the fight with Laertes in Ophelia's grave. Hamlet's pretended madness teeters on the brink of real disturbance from time to time, maybe more than Hamlet himself is aware of, and Horatio is invaluable in such instances. He is not, however, present in the "closet scene" in III.iv, where Hamlet may be seen to go overboard with his mother.

[8] In Renaissance times, despite the astute government of Elizabeth, "female ruler" was somewhat of an oxymoron.

16, politically a wise move. Gertrude seems to genuinely care for her son, but her second marriage is a hard blow to Hamlet; he saw his parents' relationship as ideally close and loving,[10] but this exchange makes him devalue romantic love and attribute human relationships to lust only, as he so clearly demonstrates to Gertrude in III.iv. Despite what her father and brother think of the matter, Ophelia seems to be Gertrude's choice for Hamlet's bride, and Ophelia herself is convinced that Hamlet loved her.[11] Polonius and Laertes both imply that Hamlet's interest in her is dishonorably lustful,[12] and Hamlet backs this interpretation up in III.i.102-142.

Mature, widowed women who remarried were traditionally seen as yearning for the sexual relationship they had come to crave, branding themselves as lustful creatures; Hamlet berates Gertrude for having just these motives in III.iv, claiming that, at her age, such thoughts should be far behind her. Ophelia, being young, is seen as an object of lust by the men around her, and while she claims Hamlet wooed her with honorable intentions, Polonius sees their relationship in commercial terms. Ophelia can be bought and sold, her value kept up or diminished according to her behavior and reputation. According to her father, young men will promise anything in order to get what they want, then leave the girl ruined. Ophelia herself becomes persuaded that she is no more than an object for lust, as is borne out by her St. Valentine's Day song, IV.v.47-64.

Major Themes

In *Hamlet* we meet four children of three fathers who have met a violent death, and we are given a brilliantly constructed op-

---

[9] See glossary, "incest."

[10] See Greenblatt's *Hamlet in Purgatory* for a wonderful analysis of Hamlet's parents' relationship seen through Hamlet's eyes.

[11] III.i.37-42; V.i.238-41.

[12] Laertes in I.iii.5-44; Polonius somewhat more forcefully and directly in I.iii.90-135.

portunity to examine how they are affected by their fathers' fate. The comparison is clear and unavoidable, both in the theater[13] and in the study.

Fortinbras, Prince of Norway, lost his father through single combat with Hamlet Senior. Determined to get even, Fortinbras chooses a form of public revenge, mustering an army which he intends to lead against Denmark. Once his purpose is discovered and he has been forced to abandon it, he decides to pursue honor and glory for their own sake, pointing his army towards an insignificant site in Poland. Fortinbras, according to Hamlet, does what a prince ought to do:

> Witness this army of such mass and charge
> Led by a delicate and tender prince . . .
>   . . . Rightly to be great
> Is not to stir without great argument,
> But greatly to find quarrel in a straw
> When honour's at the stake.
>
> (IV.iv.47-56)

At play's end, Fortinbras is King of Denmark, supported by Hamlet's dying breath.

Laertes, who begins the play as a carefree young noble, probably not unlike what Hamlet used to be, reacts very differently to the news of his father's murder and unceremonious interment. He determines to execute private revenge immediately, and in a treasonous act rouses a mob of Danish rebels to seek revenge on Claudius. Because he is rash and his acts lack premeditation, he is relatively easily persuaded by Claudius that Hamlet should be the object of his revenge, Claudius all the while believing that Hamlet has been safely executed in England. When news of Hamlet's re-

---

[13] The present editor is always upset when a *Hamlet* production cuts Fortinbras.

turn reaches him, he quickly converts Laertes' need for an elder to guide and advise him, like his own father used to do so wordily, into yet another treasonous act,[14] setting up the practice match with the unblunted foil, the point of which Laertes decides to anoint with poison for good measure. But Claudius realizes the practicality of backing this plan up with a poisoned cup of his own. Laertes is volatile, and when he rushes off stage after Gertrude's report of Ophelia's death, Claudius is by no means certain where his loyalties lie. Once he is scratched with his own blade during the duel, Laertes does the morally right thing at last; he tells Hamlet the source of this last act of treason and allows Hamlet to have his revenge.

Ophelia has no recourse to action. She has been raised as the perfect Renaissance woman and is passive, chaste, silent, and obedient; in fact, the only glimpse of rebellion comes in I.iii, where she reiterates that Hamlet has honest intentions, but Polonius' retorts soon stop her voice, and the scene's last line is, "I shall obey, my lord." She knows that the family is a microcosm of the kingdom, and that her father is her absolute ruler. Only when she marries does she emerge from under his dominion, now to be governed by her husband, who, according to the Bible, is the woman's head.[15] She obediently reports Hamlet's advances in her closet to her father, and without protest lets herself be used in the eavesdropping scene, III.i. With her brother in France and her father killed by Hamlet, she has no definition of herself, and her grief drives her insane. Where the young men turn their sorrow and anger outward and act, she turns her sorrow inwards and breaks. She, like Aspatia of *The Maid's Tragedy*, is yet another example of the chaos private revenge and treason bring upon the innocent.

---

[14] IV.vii.

[15] Ephesians 5:22-23: "Wives, submit yourselves unto your own husbands, as unto the Lord. For the husband is the head of the wife, even as Christ is the head of the church. . ."

Madness with its ensuing suicide was a staple of revenge tragedy for much of its *vogue*; Ophelia delivers both, drowning in a swan song off stage. Her madness alters her behavior and speech patterns completely. One cannot help but speculate that this serves to cast light on Hamlet's "antic disposition," which in speech, mood, and behavior can be reminiscent of the antics of the court jesters of Shakespeare's comedies, complete with a jig!

Hamlet's reaction to his father's murder shares elements from all three other bereft children. He has Fortinbras' sense of honor, but does not always act on it; Laertes' rashness, but not to the extremes Laertes shows; and Ophelia's introverted brooding. The reality and quality of *his* madness, however, is something each audience member and reader is left to ponder and decide.

One theme pervading *Hamlet* is that of "poison through the ear." The first instance is relayed by the Ghost, who describes his poisoning. Claudius stole up

> With juice of cursed hebenon in a vial,
> And in the porches of my ears did pour
> The leperous distilment, whose effect
> Holds such an enmity with blood of man
> That swift as quicksilver it courses through
> The natural gates and alleys of the body,
> And with a sudden vigour doth posset
> And curd, like eager droppings into milk,
> The thin and wholesome blood. So did it mine,
> And a most instant tetter barked about,
> Most lazar-like, with vile and loathsome crust,
> All my smooth body.

(I.v.62-73)

But this is not Claudius' only attempt. His approaches to Hamlet to persuade him to become his "son" and exchange his dead father for his living uncle in I.ii is an attempt at poisoning, only this time the poison is verbal. Rosencrantz and Guildenstern are "poisoned" into betraying Hamlet in obedience to their King, and Claudius and Polonius may be said to poison Ophelia through the ear, first by persuading her that Hamlet's intentions are lustful, and then into being their pawn in the eavesdropping scene (III.i). Laertes is another victim of such poisoning when Claudius seemingly makes him his confidant in IV.vii and then persuades him to betray Hamlet. His final attempt at poisoning Hamlet with the drink reaches out to encompass both himself and the Queen. Hamlet himself makes one attempt at poisoning through both eyes and especially ears. "The Mousetrap," the play-within that is directed and partly written, we are led to believe, by Hamlet, is intended to confront Claudius with Hamlet's knowledge of his deed as a test of the Ghost's veracity. All Hamlet's "antic disposition" speeches have some degree of deception embedded in them, but though especially the scene with Ophelia in III.i can be seen as an attempt to poison through the ear, another interpretation springs to mind. Ophelia unwittingly gives away the fact that she is her father's— and so the King's—willing pawn, and so she becomes the second woman to have betrayed Hamlet's trust. In this scene, all thoughts of romantic love are banished and replaced with a view of love-as-lust, and therefore filthy.

Hamlet centers on the theme of maturation, of growing acceptance of the inevitable death that ends all our lives, be we beggars or kings. When the play opens, he rejects his mother's and Claudius' admonition to accept death of fathers as "common" to the human condition, and much of the play is taken up with his brooding over his father. With each instance of Hamlet Senior as a topic of conversation, it becomes increasingly clear that Hamlet, in the process of forgetting our dead that we all must go through, is idealizing his father's memory and his parents' relationship. In the closet scene with Gertrude, the father has become a conglomerate of gods and creatures of mythology.[16] Once returned from England, confronted with the Gravedigger's nonchalant attitude to his work, and having had to face the skull of his childhood friend, Yorick the Jester, Hamlet begins to change. Over Ophelia's corpse, sparring with the excessively grieving Laertes, Hamlet is capable of criticizing another's exaggerated grief:

> 'Swounds, show me what thou'lt do!
> Woo't weep? Woo't fight? Woo't fast? Woo't tear
> thyself?
>
> Woo't drink up eisel? Eat a crocodile?
> I'll do't. Dost thou come here to whine?
> To outface me with leaping in her grave?
> Be buried quick with her, and so will I.
> And, if thou prate of mountains, let them throw
> Millions of acres on us, till our ground,
> Singeing his pate against the burning zone,
> Make Ossa like a wart! Nay, an thou'lt mouth,
> I'll rant as well as thou.
>
> (v.i.271-281)

In I.ii Hamlet was the object of criticism for immoderate grief. Here his hyperbolical words point the same finger at Laertes, though Gertrude wishes to pass his remarks off as madness. And in V.ii, finally, Hamlet is capable of saying:

> There's a special providence in the fall of a sparrow. If it be now, 'tis not to come. If it be not to come, it will be now. If it be not now, yet it will come. The readiness is all. Since no man has aught of what he leaves, what is't to leave betimes?
>
> (V.ii.205-210)

---

[16] See Greenblatt's *Hamlet in Purgatory* for a thorough analysis.

He has finally accepted the common fate of man. Mutability is the natural way of things. We shall all be reduced to bone in God's own time, and so we will do well to stand prepared for our final reckoning.

Hamlet is a play open to innumerable interpretations and approaches; it can be staged in more ways and with more different intentions than possibly any other Renaissance play. As a revenge tragedy, it is the richest of its genre.

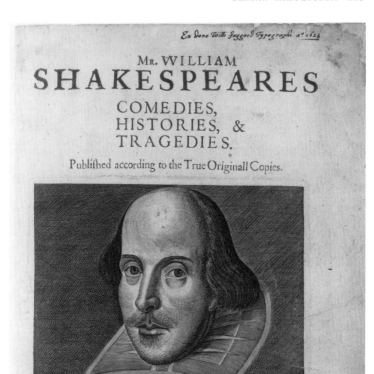

Figure 5. STC 22273, the 1623 *First Folio* title page; "Hamlet" is included among the Tragedies. By permission of the Folger Shakespeare Library.

Dramatis Personae

Hamlet, Prince of Denmark
Claudius, King of Denmark, Hamlet's uncle
The Ghost of the late King, Hamlet's father
Gertrude, the Queen, Hamlet's mother and Claudius' wife
Voltemand, councillor and ambassdaor to Norway
Cornelius, councillor and ambassador to Norway
Marcellus, member of the King's Guard
Bernardo, member of the King's Guard
Francisco, member of the King's Guard
Osric, a courtier
A Gentleman of the Court

Polonius, Councillor of State
Laertes, Polonius' son
Ophelia, Polonius' daughter
Reynaldo, servant to Polonius

Horatio, friend and confidant of Hamlet
Rosencrantz, courtier and schoolfellow of Hamlet
Guildenstern, courtier and schoolfellow of Hamlet

Fortinbras, Prince of Norway
A Captain in Fortinbras' Army

Players
A Priest
First Clown, a Gravedigger
Second Clown, the Gravedigger's Companion
English Ambassadors
Lords, Ladies, Soldiers, Sailors, Messengers, and Attendants

Act I, Scene i

Francisco, a sentinel, at his post. Enter to him Bernardo

Bernardo

    Who's there?

Francisco

    Nay, answer me. Stand, and unfold[17] yourself.

Bernardo

    Long live the King!

Francisco

    Bernardo?

Bernardo

    He.   5

Francisco

    You come most carefully upon your hour.[18]

Bernardo

    'Tis now struck twelve. Get thee to bed, Francisco.

Francisco

    For this relief much thanks. 'Tis bitter cold,

    And I am sick at heart.

Bernardo

    Have you had quiet guard?   10

Francisco

    Not a mouse stirring.

Bernardo

    Well, good night.

    If you do meet Horatio and Marcellus,

    The rivals of my watch,[19] bid them make haste.

---

[17] Declare.

[18] On time.

[19] Fellow watchmen.

Francisco

    I think I hear them. Stand, ho! Who's there?   15

Enter Horatio and Marcellus

Horatio

    Friends to this ground.

Marcellus   And liegemen[20] to the Dane.[21]

Francisco

    Give you good night.

Marcellus

    O, farewell, honest soldier. Who hath relieved you?

Francisco

    Bernardo has my place. Give you good night.   *Exit*

Marcellus

    Holla! Bernardo!   20

Bernardo

    Say, what, is Horatio there?

Horatio

    A piece of him.[22]

Bernardo

    Welcome, Horatio. Welcome, good Marcellus.

Marcellus

    What, has this thing appeared again to-night?

Bernardo

    I have seen nothing.   25

Marcellus

    Horatio says 'tis but our fantasy,[23]

    And will not let belief take hold of him

---

[20] Retainers; servants.

[21] The King of Denmark.

[22] Probably his extended hand, the only part visible in the darkness.

[23] Imagination.

Touching this dreaded sight, twice seen of us.
Therefore I have entreated him along
With us to watch the minutes of this night,   30
That if again this apparition come,
He may approve our eyes[24] and speak to it.[25]

Horatio

Tush, tush, 'twill not appear.

Bernardo   Sit down a while,
And let us once again assail your ears
That are so fortified against our story   35
What we have two nights seen.

Horatio   Well, sit we down,
And let us hear Bernardo speak of this.

Bernardo

Last night of all,
When yond same star that's westward from the pole[26]
Had made his course to illume that part of heaven   40
Where now it burns, Marcellus and myself,
The bell then beating[27] one,—

Enter Ghost

Marcellus

Peace, break thee off! Look, where it comes again!

Bernardo

In the same figure, like the King that's dead.

Marcellus (*to Horatio*)

Thou art a scholar, speak to it, Horatio.   45

[24] Confirm what we saw.
[25] Horatio, a scholar, knows Latin, the language appropriate for an
exorcism; also, ghosts do not speak until addressed.
[26] Probably Capella, that appears west of the Pole-Star in winter.
[27] Striking.

Bernardo

    Looks it not like the King? Mark it, Horatio.

Horatio

    Most like. It harrows me with fear and wonder.

Bernardo

    It would be spoke to.

Marcellus   Question it, Horatio.

Horatio

    What art thou that usurp'st[28] this time of night,

    Together with that fair and warlike form   50

    In which the majesty of buried Denmark

    Did sometimes march? By heaven I charge thee, speak!

Marcellus

    It is offended.

Bernardo   See, it stalks away!

Horatio

    Stay! Speak, speak! I charge thee, speak!   *Exit Ghost*

Marcellus

    'Tis gone, and will not answer.   55

Bernardo

    How now, Horatio! You tremble and look pale.

    Is not this something more than fantasy?

    What think you on't?

Horatio

    Before my God, I might not this believe

    Without the sensible and true avouch[29]   60

    Of mine own eyes.

Marcellus

    Is it not like the King?

---

[28] Takes unjust possession of.

[29] Proof through the senses.

Horatio

    As thou art to thyself.

    Such was the very armour he had on

    When he the ambitious Norway[30] combated.   65

    So frowned he once, when, in an angry parle,[31]

    He smote the sledded Polacks[32] on the ice.

    'Tis strange.

Marcellus

    Thus twice before, and jump[33] at this dead hour,

    With martial stalk hath he gone by our watch.   70

Horatio

    In what particular thought to work I know not.[34]

    But in the gross and scope[35] of my opinion,

    This bodes some strange eruption[36] to our state.

Marcellus

    Good[37] now, sit down, and tell me, he that knows,

    Why this same strict and most observant watch   75

    So nightly toils the subject of the land,[38]

    And why such daily cast[39] of brazen cannon,

    And foreign mart[40] for implements of war,

    Why such impress[41] of shipwrights, whose sore task

    Does not divide the Sunday from the week.   80

---

[30] The King of Norway.

[31] Parley; encounter.

[32] Poles traveling on sleds.

[33] Exactly.

[34] I do not know what thought pattern to follow.

[35] The general drift.

[36] Disturbance.

[37] Good friend; good fellow.

[38] Makes the country's subjects work

[39] Casting (in brass, here).

[40] Trading.

[41] Impressment into forced service.

What might be toward,[42] that this sweaty haste
Doth make the night joint-labourer with the day?
Who is't that can inform me?

Horatio   That can I.

At least, the whisper goes so. Our last King,
Whose image even but now appeared to us,   85
Was, as you know, by Fortinbras of Norway,
Thereto pricked on[43] by a most emulate[44] pride,
Dared to the combat; in which our valiant Hamlet,
For so this side of our known world esteemed him,
Did slay this Fortinbras, who by a sealed compact[45]   90
Well ratified by law and heraldry,[46]
Did forfeit, with his life, all those his lands
Which he stood seized of,[47] to the conqueror,
Against the which, a moiety competent[48]
Was gaged[49] by our King; which had returned   95
To the inheritance of Fortinbras,
Had he been vanquisher, as, by the same covenant,
And carriage of the article designed,[50]
His fell to Hamlet. Now, sir, young Fortinbras,
Of unimproved mettle[51] hot and full,   100
Hath in the skirts[52] of Norway here and there

[42] Be imminent.
[43] Spurred.
[44] Striving to excel; "jealous."
[45] Mutual agreement.
[46] Ratified according to the rules of chivalry, where heralds were moderators.
[47] Held sway over.
[48] A part of acceptable size.
[49] Set.
[50] According to contract.
[51] Untested courage.
[52] Outlying areas.

Sharked up a list[53] of lawless resolutes,
For food and diet, to some enterprise
That hath a stomach[54] in't, which is no other,
As it doth well appear unto our state,   105
But to recover of us, by strong hand
And terms compulsatory, those foresaid lands
So by his father lost. And this, I take it,
Is the main motive of our preparations,
The source of this our watch and the chief head[55]   110
Of this post-haste and rummage[56] in the land.

Bernardo

I think it be no other but e'en so.
Well may it sort[57] that this portentous[58] figure
Comes armed through our watch so like the King
That was and is the question[59] of these wars.   115

Horatio

A mote it is to trouble the mind's eye.[60]
In the most high and palmy[61] state of Rome,
A little ere the mightiest Julius fell,
The graves stood tenantless and the sheeted dead[62]
Did squeak and gibber in the Roman streets;   120
As stars with trains of fire[63] and dews of blood,

[53] Ravenously—like a shark—gathered a number.

[54] Challenge (the stomach is the seat of courage).

[55] Origin.

[56] Bustling activity.

[57] Tally.

[58] That is a portent, an omen.

[59] Cause.

[60] Like a grain of dust in the eye, insignificant in size, but enough to irritate tremendously.

[61] Thriving; flourishing. The palm is a symbol of victory.

[62] Corpses in winding sheets.

[63] Comets, usually considered an ill omen.

Disasters in the sun; and the moist star[64]
Upon whose influence Neptune's empire[65] stands
Was sick almost to doomsday[66] with eclipse.
And even the like precurse[67] of feared events,   125
As harbingers[68] preceding still[69] the fates
And prologue to the omen[70] coming on,
Have heaven and earth together demonstrated
Unto our climatures[71] and countrymen.
But soft,[72] behold! Lo, where it comes again!   130

Re-enter Ghost

I'll cross it, though it blast me.[73] Stay, illusion!
If thou hast any sound, or use of voice,
Speak to me!
If there be any good thing to be done,
That may to thee do ease and grace to me,   135
Speak to me!
If thou art privy to thy country's fate,
Which, happily,[74] foreknowing may avoid,
O, speak!
Or if thou hast uphoarded in thy life   140

[64] The moon.

[65] The sea, subject to the tidal pull of the moon.

[66] Matthew xxiv.29, Revelation vi.12; total darkness is expected before the second coming of Christ.

[67] Forerunner.

[68] Messengers.

[69] Always.

[70] Here not warning of a disastrous event, but the event itself.

[71] Climate; regional area.

[72] Be still.

[73] Cross its path and confront it, thus exposing himself to its malicious influence.

[74] Perhaps; possibly.

Extorted treasure in the womb of earth,
For which, they say, you spirits oft walk in death,
Speak of it! Stay, and speak!   *Cock crows*
                Stop it, Marcellus.

Marcellus
    Shall I strike at it with my partisan?[75]
Horatio
    Do, if it will not stand.   145
Bernardo
    'Tis here!   *Exit Ghost*
Horatio
    'Tis here!
Marcellus
    'Tis gone!
    We do it wrong, being so majestical,
    To offer it the show of violence;   150
    For it is, as the air, invulnerable,
    And our vain blows malicious mockery.[76]
Bernardo
    It was about to speak when the cock crew.
Horatio
    And then it started like a guilty thing
    Upon a fearful summons. I have heard,   155
    The cock, that is the trumpet to the morn,
    Doth with his lofty and shrill-sounding throat
    Awake the god of day,[77] and, at his warning,
    Whether in sea or fire, in earth or air,
    The extravagant and erring[78] spirit hies[79]   160

[75] Long-handled spear.
[76] Only resembling malice.
[77] Apollo, the sun god.
[78] Straying beyond its boundaries.
[79] Hurries.

To his confine;[80] and of the truth herein
This present object made probation.[81]

Marcellus

It faded on the crowing of the cock.
Some say that ever 'gainst[82] that season comes
Wherein our Saviour's birth is celebrated   165
The bird of dawning singeth all night long,
And then, they say, no spirit dares stir abroad.
The nights are wholesome; then no planets strike,[83]
No fairy takes,[84] nor witch hath power to charm,
So hallowed and so gracious is the time.   170

Horatio

So have I heard and do in part believe it.
But, look, the morn, in russet mantle clad,
Walks o'er the dew of yon high eastward hill.
Break we our watch up, and, by my advice,
Let us impart what we have seen to-night   175
Unto young Hamlet; for, upon my life,
This spirit, dumb to us, will speak to him.
Do you consent we shall acquaint him with it,
As needful in our loves, fitting our duty?

Marcellus

Let's do't, I pray, and I this morning know   180
Where we shall find him most conveniently.

Exeunt

---

[80] Place of confinement.
[81] "The example we just saw was proof of this."
[82] In expectation of.
[83] There is no malicious influence from the stars and planets.
[84] Casts a spell.

Act I, Scene ii

Flourish. Enter King Claudius, Queen Gertrude, Hamlet, Lord Polonius,
Laertes, Voltimand, Cornelius, Lords, and Attendants, with others

King Claudius

    Though yet of Hamlet our[85] dear brother's death

    The memory be green, and that it us befitted

    To bear our hearts in grief and our whole kingdom

    To be contracted in one brow of woe,[86]

    Yet so far hath discretion fought with nature[87]   5

    That we with wisest sorrow think on him,

    Together with remembrance of ourselves.

    Therefore our sometime[88] sister, now our Queen,

    The imperial jointress[89] to this warlike state,

    Have we, as 'twere with a defeated joy,   10

    With an auspicious and a dropping eye,[90]

    With mirth in funeral and with dirge in marriage,

    In equal scale weighing delight and dole,[91]

    Taken to wife. Nor have we herein barred

    Your better wisdoms,[92] which have freely gone   15

    With this affair along. For all, our thanks.

    Now follows that you know, young Fortinbras,

    Holding a weak suppose[93] of our worth,

---

[85] Claudius uses "the royal we" in referring to himself (see glossary).

[86] Simultaneously suggests the unity of the kingdom and the grief and sorrow over King Hamlet's demise.

[87] Natural impulse; see glossary.

[88] Former.

[89] A woman whose husband's estate passes on to her after his death.

[90] One hopeful, one weeping eye.

[91] Grief.

[92] Acted without your wise consent.

[93] Low opinion.

Or thinking by our late dear brother's death
Our state to be disjoint and out of frame,[94]   20
Colleagued with the dream of his advantage,[95]
He hath not failed to pester us with message,
Importing[96] the surrender of those lands
Lost by his father, with all bonds of law,
To our most valiant brother. So much for him.   25
Now for ourselves and for this time of meeting,
Thus much the business is: we have here writ
To Norway, uncle of young Fortinbras,
Who, impotent and bed-rid, scarcely hears
Of this his nephew's purpose, to suppress   30
His further gait[97] herein, in that the levies,
The lists, and full proportions are all made
Out of his subject;[98] and we here dispatch
You, good Cornelius, and you, Voltimand,
For bearers of this greeting to old Norway,   35
Giving to you no further personal power
To business with the King, more than the scope
Of these dilated[99] articles allow.
Farewell, and let your haste commend your duty.[100]

Cornelius and Voltimand

In that and all things will we show our duty.   40

King Claudius

We doubt it nothing.[101] Heartily farewell.

                                    Exeunt Voltimand and Cornelius

---

[94] Disturbed; out of proper order.
[95] Supported by his own visions of success.
[96] Concerning.
[97] Proceeding.
[98] He is only making use of Norwegian resources.
[99] Written down in detail.
[100] "Hurry and do your errand without parting formalities."
[101] "I do not doubt it."

And now, Laertes, what's the news with you?
You told us of some suit. What is't, Laertes?
You cannot speak of reason to the Dane,[102]
And loose your voice. What wouldst thou beg, Laertes,   45
That shall not be my offer, not thy asking?
The head is not more native[103] to the heart,
The hand more instrumental to the mouth,
Than is the throne of Denmark to thy father.
What wouldst thou have, Laertes?

Laertes   My dread[104] lord,   50
Your leave and favour[105] to return to France,
From whence though willingly I came to Denmark
To show my duty in your coronation,
Yet now I must confess, that duty done,
My thoughts and wishes bend again toward France   55
And bow them to your gracious leave and pardon.[106]

King Claudius
He hath, my lord, wrung from me my slow leave
Have you your father's leave? What says Polonius?

Lord Polonius
He hath, my lord, wrung from me my slow leave
By laboursome petition, and at last
Upon his will I sealed my hard[107] consent.   60
I do beseech you, give him leave to go.

King Claudius
Take thy fair hour,[108] Laertes. Time be thine,
And thy best graces[109] spend it at thy will!

[102] King of Denmark.
[103] The king is his country's head (see glossary: King's Two Bodies).
[104] Respected.
[105] Your permission and sanction.
[106] And as humbly beg your permission to leave.
[107] Hard-won.
[108] Seize the day.
[109] Your most favorable qualities (ensuring that time will be well spent).

But now, my cousin Hamlet, and my son—

Hamlet (*aside*)

A little more than kin, and less than kind.[110]   65

King Claudius

How is it that the clouds still hang on you?

Hamlet

Not so, my lord, I am too much i' the sun.[111]

Queen Gertrude

Good Hamlet, cast thy nighted colour[112] off,

And let thine eye look like a friend on Denmark.

Do not for ever with thy vailed[113] lids   70

Seek for thy noble father in the dust:

Thou know'st 'tis common; all that lives must die,

Passing through nature to eternity.

Hamlet

Ay, madam, it is common.[114]

Queen Gertrude   If it be,

Why seems it so particular with thee?   75

Hamlet

Seems, madam! Nay it is! I know not 'seems.'

'Tis not alone my inky cloak, good mother,

Nor customary suits of solemn black,

Nor windy suspiration of forced breath,[115]

No, nor the fruitful[116] river in the eye,   80

Nor the dejected 'havior[117] of the visage,

---

[110] See glossary.

[111] A pun on son/sun; see glossary.

[112] Black for mourning; and the color of melancholy is black (see glossary: Four Humors).

[113] Lowered.

[114] Ordinary; but also crude.

[115] Deep sighs.

[116] Which yields much.

[117] Demeanor.

Together with all forms, moods, shapes of grief
That can denote me truly. These indeed seem,
For they are actions that a man might play.
But I have that within which passeth show,   85
These but the trappings and the suits of woe.

King Claudius

'Tis sweet and commendable in your nature, Hamlet,
To give these mourning duties to your father;
But, you must know, your father lost a father,
That father lost, lost his, and the survivor bound   90
In filial obligation for some term
To do obsequious sorrow.[118] But to persever
In obstinate condolement[119] is a course
Of impious stubbornness, 'tis unmanly grief;
It shows a will most incorrect[120] to heaven,   95
A heart unfortified, a mind impatient,
An understanding simple[121] and unschooled.
For what we know must be and is as common
As any the most vulgar thing to sense,[122]
Why should we in our peevish opposition   100
Take it to heart? Fie! 'Tis a fault to heaven,
A fault against the dead, a fault to nature,
To reason most absurd, whose common theme
Is death of fathers, and who still[123] hath cried,
From the first corse[124] till he that died to-day,   105
'This must be so.' We pray you, throw to earth

---

[118] To mourn suitably.

[119] Grief.

[120] Not submissive.

[121] Ignorant.

[122] As anything our senses may perceive.

[123] Constantly.

[124] Abel's; Cain murdered his brother, so the allusion easily springs to Claudius' mind.

This unprevailing[125] woe, and think of us
As of a father. For let the world take note,
You are the most immediate[126] to our throne;
And with no less nobility[127] of love   110
Than that which dearest father bears his son,
Do I impart toward you. For your intent
In going back to school in Wittenberg, [128]
It is most retrograde to our desire,
And we beseech you, bend you to remain   115
Here, in the cheer and comfort of our eye,
Our chiefest courtier, cousin, and our son.

Queen Gertrude

Let not thy mother lose her prayers, Hamlet!
I pray thee, stay with us; go not to Wittenberg.

Hamlet

I shall in all my best obey you, madam.   120

King Claudius

Why, 'tis a loving and a fair reply!
Be as ourself in Denmark. Madam, come.
This gentle and unforced accord of Hamlet
Sits smiling to my heart, in grace[129] whereof,
No jocund health that Denmark[130] drinks to-day,   125
But the great cannon to the clouds shall tell,
And the King's rouse[131] the heavens all bruit again,[132]
Re-speaking earthly thunder. Come away.

Flourish. Exeunt all but Hamlet

---

[125] Unavailing.
[126] Nearest.
[127] Depth.
[128] German university town, the place of study of Luther and Melanchton.
[129] Thanksgiving.
[130] The King of Denmark.
[131] Toast.
[132] Send back echo.

Hamlet

    O, that this too too solid flesh would melt

    Thaw and resolve[133] itself into a dew!   130

    Or that the Everlasting had not fixed

    His canon[134] 'gainst self-slaughter! O God! God!

    How weary, stale, flat, and unprofitable

    Seem to me all the uses[135] of this world!

    Fie on't! Ah fie! 'Tis an unweeded garden,   135

    That grows to seed. Things rank and gross in nature

    Possess it merely.[136] That it should come to this!

    But two months dead, nay, not so much, not two!

    So excellent a King; that was, to this,

    Hyperion[137] to a satyr,[138] so loving to my mother   140

    That he might not beteem[139] the winds of heaven

    Visit her face too roughly. Heaven and earth!

    Must I remember? Why, she would hang on him,

    As if increase of appetite had grown

    By what it fed on, and yet, within a month—   145

    Let me not think on't! Frailty, thy name is woman!—

    A little month, or ere[140] those shoes were old

    With which she followed my poor father's body,

    Like Niobe,[141] all tears, why she, even she!

[133] Dissolve.

[134] Law.

[135] Business.

[136] Completely.

[137] Here: the sun-god; Hyperion, a Titan and husband of his sister Theia, fathered the sun, the moon, and dawn.

[138] Mythological creature, half man, half goat.

[139] Allow.

[140] Before.

[141] Niobe's fourteen children were killed by Apollo and Artemis because she bragged about them; even after she was turned into stone, she still wept.

O, God! A beast that wants discourse of reason[142]   150
Would have mourn'd longer — married with my uncle,
My father's brother, but no more like my father
Than I to Hercules. Within a month,
Ere yet the salt of most unrighteous tears
Had left the flushing in her galled eyes,[143]   155
She married. O, most wicked speed, to post[144]
With such dexterity to incestuous[145] sheets!
It is not nor it cannot come to good.
But break, my heart, for I must hold my tongue.

Enter Horatio, Marcellus, and Bernardo

Horatio

  Hail to your lordship!

Hamlet   I am glad to see you well: 160
  Horatio, or I do forget myself.

Horatio

  The same, my lord, and your poor servant ever.

Hamlet

  Sir, my good friend. I'll change that name with you:
  And what make you from[146] Wittenberg, Horatio?
  Marcellus?

Marcellus   My good lord.   165

Hamlet

  I am very glad to see you. *(To Bernardo)* Good even, sir.
  But what, in faith, make you from Wittenberg?

---

[142] An animal without the power of rational thinking; the ability to reason separated men from beasts.

[143] Swollen, tear-reddened eyes.

[144] Rush.

[145] Marrying a sibling's widow/widower was considered incest; see glossary.

[146] Away from.

Horatio

    A truant disposition, good my lord.

Hamlet

    I would not hear your enemy say so,

    Nor shall you do mine ear that violence   170

    To make it truster of your own report

    Against yourself. I know you are no truant.

    But what is your affair in Elsinore?[147]

    We'll teach you to drink deep ere you depart.

Horatio

    My lord, I came to see your father's funeral.   175

Hamlet

    I pray thee, do not mock me, fellow-student!

    I think it was to see my mother's wedding.

Horatio

    Indeed, my lord, it followed hard upon.

Hamlet

    Thrift, thrift, Horatio! The funeral baked meats[148]

    Did coldly[149] furnish forth the marriage tables.   180

    Would I had met my dearest[150] foe in heaven

    Or ever I had seen that day, Horatio!

    My father! Methinks I see my father.

Horatio

    Where, my lord?

Hamlet   In my mind's eye, Horatio.

Horatio

    I saw him once. A[151] was a goodly King.   185

---

[147] Helsingør, a well-known city in Denmark with a strongly fortified castle; members of Shakespeare's troupe had performed there.

[148] Meat baked in pastry.

[149] As cold left-overs.

[150] Worst.

[151] He.

Hamlet

    He was a man, take him for all in all,

    I shall not look upon his like again.

Horatio

    My lord, I think I saw him yesternight.

Hamlet

    Saw? Who?

Horatio   My lord, the King your father.

Hamlet

    The King my father!   190

Horatio

    Season your admiration[152] for awhile

    With an attent[153] ear, till I may deliver,

    Upon the witness of these gentlemen,

    This marvel to you.

Hamlet   For God's love, let me hear!

Horatio

    Two nights together had these gentlemen,   195

    Marcellus and Bernardo, on their watch,

    In the dead waste[154] and middle of the night,

    Been thus encountered. A figure like your father,

    Armed at point[155] exactly, cap-à-pie,[156]

    Appears before them, and with solemn march   200

    Goes slow and stately by them. Thrice he walked

    By their oppressed and fear-surprised eyes,

    Within his truncheon's[157] length, whilst they, distilled[158]

[152] Hold your astonishment in check.

[153] Attentive.

[154] Emptiness.

[155] Correctly.

[156] From head to foot.

[157] Staff of command such as an officer might carry.

[158] Reduced.

Almost to jelly with the act[159] of fear,
Stand dumb and speak not to him. This to me   205
In dreadful secrecy impart they did,
And I with them the third night kept the watch,
Where, as they had delivered, both in time,
Form of the thing, each word made true and good,
The apparition comes. I knew your father;   210
These hands are not more like.[160]

Hamlet

But where was this?

Marcellus

My lord, upon the platform where we watched.

Hamlet

Did you not speak to it?

Horatio   My lord, I did,
But answer made it none. Yet once methought   215
It lifted up its head and did address
Itself to motion,[161] like as it would speak,
But even[162] then the morning cock crew loud,
And at the sound it shrunk in haste away,
And vanished from our sight.

Hamlet   'Tis very strange.   220

Horatio

As I do live, my honoured lord, 'tis true;
And we did think it writ down in our duty
To let you know of it.

Hamlet

Indeed, indeed, sirs, but this troubles me.
Hold you the watch to-night?

---

[159] Effect.
[160] The ghost was as like the King as Horatio's two hands are like each other.
[161] Began to move.
[162] Just.

Marcellus and Bernardo   We do, my lord.   225

Hamlet

    Armed, say you?

Marcellus and Bernardo Armed, my lord.

Hamlet   From top to toe?

Marcellus and Bernardo

    My lord, from head to foot.

Hamlet   Then saw you not his face?

Horatio

    O yes, my lord, he wore his beaver[163] up.

Hamlet

    What[164] looked he, frowningly?

Horatio

    A countenance more in sorrow than in anger.   230

Hamlet

    Pale or red?

Horatio

    Nay, very pale.

Hamlet   And fixed his eyes upon you?

Horatio

    Most constantly.

Hamlet   I would I had been there.

Horatio

    It would have much amazed you.

Hamlet

    Very like, very like. Stayed it long?   235

Horatio

    While one with moderate haste might tell[165] a hundred.

Marcellus and Bernardo

    Longer, longer.

---

[163] Faceguard of the helmet.

[164] How.

[165] Count to.

Horatio

Not when I saw't.

Hamlet

His beard was grizzled,[166] no?

Horatio

It was, as I have seen it in his life,   240

A sable[167] silvered.

Hamlet   I will watch tonight.

Perchance 'twill walk again.

Horatio   I warrant[168] it will.

Hamlet

If it assume my noble father's person,

I'll speak to it, though hell itself should gape

And bid me hold my peace. I pray you all,   245

If you have hitherto concealed this sight,

Let it be tenable in your silence still,

And whatsoever else shall hap[169] to-night,

Give it an understanding, but no tongue.

I will requite your loves. So, fare you well.   250

Upon the platform, 'twixt eleven and twelve,

I'll visit you.

All   Our duty to your honour.

Hamlet

Your loves, as mine to you. Farewell.   *Exeunt all but Hamlet*

My father's spirit in arms! All is not well.

I doubt[170] some foul play. Would the night were come   255

Till then, sit still, my soul. Foul deeds will rise,

Though all the earth o'erwhelm them, to men's eyes.   *Exit*

---

[166] Turning gray.

[167] The heraldic color black.

[168] Guarantee.

[169] Happen; chance.

[170] Fear; suspect.

Act I, Scene iii

Enter Laertes and Ophelia

Laertes

> My necessaries are embarked.[171] Farewell.
> And, sister, as the winds give benefit
> And convoy is assistant,[172] do not sleep,
> But let me hear from you.

Ophelia   Do you doubt that?

Laertes

> For Hamlet and the trifling of his favour,   5
> Hold it a fashion and a toy in blood,[173]
> A violet in the youth of primy[174] nature,
> Forward,[175] not permanent, sweet, not lasting,
> The perfume and suppliance[176] of a minute,
> No more.

Ophelia   No more but so?

Laertes   Think it no more.   10

> For nature, crescent,[177] does not grow alone
> In thews and bulk,[178] but, as this temple[179] waxes,
> The inward service[180] of the mind and soul
> Grows wide withal. Perhaps he loves you now,

---

[171] On shipboard.
[172] Means of conveyance is available.
[173] A young man's sexual whim.
[174] In its spring, the time when youth "blooms."
[175] Speedy in action.
[176] Pastime.
[177] As it grows.
[178] Strength and size.
[179] The body is the soul's temple.
[180] Duty.

And now no soil[181] nor cautel[182] doth besmirch   15
The virtue of his will,[183] but you must fear,
His greatness weighed,[184] his will is not his own,
For he himself is subject to his birth.
He may not, as unvalued persons[185] do,
Carve for himself,[186] for on his choice depends   20
The sanity[187] and health of this whole state;
And therefore must his choice be circumscribed
Unto the voice[188] and yielding[189] of that body[190]
Whereof he is the head. Then if he says he loves you,
It fits[191] your wisdom so far to believe it   25
As he in his particular act and place[192]
May give his saying deed[193], which is no further
Than the main voice[194] of Denmark goes withal.
Then weigh what loss your honour may sustain,
If with too credent[195] ear you list[196] his songs,   30
Or lose your heart, or your chaste treasure[197] open
To his unmastered importunity.

---

[181] Spot.

[182] Craftiness.

[183] Desires; see glossary.

[184] When his social position is taken into account.

[185] Commoners.

[186] Make his own choice; "go for the best piece of the roast."

[187] Well-being.

[188] Election.

[189] Consent.

[190] The body politic; the nation. See glossary.

[191] Befits.

[192] Social position and what goes along with it.

[193] May let action follow word.

[194] Collective opinion; vote.

[195] Believing.

[196] Listen to.

[197] Virginity.

Fear it, Ophelia, fear it, my dear sister,
And keep you in the rear[198] of your affection,
Out of the shot and danger of desire.   35
The chariest[199] maid is prodigal enough,
If she unmask her beauty to the moon.
Virtue itself 'scapes[200] not calumnious strokes.
The canker[201] galls[202] the infants[203] of the spring,
Too oft before their buttons be disclosed,[204]   40
And in the morn and liquid dew of youth
Contagious blastments[205] are most imminent.
Be wary then; best safety lies in fear.
Youth to itself rebels, though none else near.[206]

Ophelia

I shall the effect of this good lesson keep.   45
As watchman to my heart. But, good my brother,
Do not, as some ungracious[207] pastors do,
Show me the steep and thorny way to heaven
Whiles, like a puffed[208] and reckless libertine,
Himself the primrose path of dalliance treads,   50
And recks not his own rede.[209]

Laertes   O, fear me not.
I stay too long. But here my father comes.

---

[198] Military metaphor; Ophelia's affection may run on ahead towards danger, but she herself stays behind the lines where she is protected.
[199] Most virtuous and modest.
[200] Escapes.
[201] Cankerworm.
[202] Harms.
[203] The buds.
[204] Before the buds open.
[205] Blights.
[206] Youth, in and of itself, is rebellious.
[207] Ungodly.
[208] Swollen (with pride).
[209] Does not take his own advice.

Enter Polonius

    A double blessing is a double grace,
    Occasion smiles upon [210] a second leave.
Lord Polonius
    Yet here, Laertes! Aboard, aboard, for shame!   55
    The wind sits in the shoulder of your sail,
    And you are stayed[211] for. There, my blessing with thee!
    And these few precepts in thy memory
    See thou character.[212] Give thy thoughts no tongue,
    Nor any unproportioned[213] thought his act.   60
    Be thou familiar,[214] but by no means vulgar.
    Those friends thou hast, and their adoption tried,[215]
    Grapple them to thy soul with hoops of steel,
    But do not dull thy palm with entertainment[216]
    Of each new-hatched, unfledged comrade. Beware   65
    Of entrance to a quarrel, but being in,
    Bear't[217] that the opposed may beware of thee.
    Give every man thy ear, but few thy voice.
    Take each man's censure,[218] but reserve thy judgment.
    Costly thy habit[219] as thy purse can buy,   70
    But not expressed in fancy,[220] rich, not gaudy;

[210] Happy circumstance gives the opportunity for.
[211] Waited.
[212] Engrave; make note of.
[213] Unprincipled.
[214] Friendly.
[215] Having made certain that your friends can be trusted.
[216] Greeting, handshakes.
[217] Carry it out.
[218] Opinion.
[219] Clothing.
[220] Overly ornamental.

For the apparel oft proclaims the man,
And they in France of the best rank and station
Are of a most select and generous chief in that.[221]
Neither a borrower nor a lender be,   75
For loan oft loses both itself and friend,
And borrowing dulls the edge of husbandry.[222]
This above all: to thine own self be true,
And it must follow, as the night the day,
Thou canst not then be false to any man.   80
Farewell, my blessing season[223] this in thee!

Laertes

Most humbly do I take my leave, my lord.

Lord Polonius

The time invites you, go. Your servants tend.[224]

Laertes

Farewell, Ophelia, and remember well
What I have said to you.

Ophelia   'Tis in my memory locked,   85
And you yourself shall keep the key of it.

Laertes

Farewell.   *Exit*

Lord Polonius

What is't, Ophelia, he hath said to you?

Ophelia

So please you, something touching the Lord Hamlet.

Lord Polonius

Marry,[225] well bethought.   90

---

[221] French nobility excel at displaying rank through dressing richly but unostentatiously.
[222] Saving; sensible use of money.
[223] Ripen.
[224] Attend; wait.
[225] Mild oath, "by the Virgin Mary."

'Tis told me, he hath very oft of late
Given private time to you, and you yourself
Have of your audience[226] been most free and bounteous,
If it be so, as so 'tis put on me,
And that in way of caution—I must tell you,   95
You do not understand yourself so clearly
As it behoves my daughter and your honour.
What is between you? Give me up the truth.

Ophelia

He hath, my lord, of late made many tenders[227]
Of his affection to me.   100

Lord Polonius

Affection! Pooh! You speak like a green[228] girl,
Unsifted[229] in such perilous circumstance.
Do you believe his tenders, as you call them?

Ophelia

I do not know, my lord, what I should think.

Lord Polonius

Marry, I'll teach you! Think yourself a baby   105
That you have ta'en these tenders for true pay,
Which are not sterling.[230] Tender yourself more dearly,
Or—not to crack the wind[231] of the poor phrase,
Running it thus—you'll tender me a fool.[232]

Ophelia

My lord, he hath importuned me with love   110

[226] Company.
[227] Offers; see glossary for the full range of meaning explored in the following lines.
[228] Immature.
[229] Inexperienced.
[230] Genuine money.
[231] The image conveyed is that of "a broken-winded horse."
[232] The pun works on several levels: Ophelia could be a fool; she could cause Polonius to look like one; the word "fool" also means baby.

In honourable fashion.

Lord Polonius

Ay, fashion you may call it. Go to, go to.[233]

Ophelia

And hath given countenance[234] to his speech, my lord,
With almost all the holy vows of heaven.

Lord Polonius

Ay, springes to catch woodcocks.[235] I do know,   115
When the blood burns, how prodigal the soul
Lends the tongue vows. These blazes, daughter,
Giving more light than heat, extinct in both,
Even in their promise, as it is a-making,
You must not take for fire. From this time   120
Be somewhat scanter of your maiden presence.
Set your entreatments[236] at a higher rate
Than a command to parley. For Lord Hamlet,
Believe so much in[237] him, that he is young
And with a larger tether may he walk   125
Than may be given you. In few,[238] Ophelia,
Do not believe his vows; for they are brokers,[239]
Not of that dye which their investments[240] show,
But mere implorators[241] of unholy suits,
Breathing like sanctified and pious bawds,   130
The better to beguile. This is for all.
I would not, in plain terms, from this time forth,

[233] "Enough of this!"
[234] Confirmation.
[235] Traps to catch woodcocks, notoriously unintelligent birds.
[236] Negotiations (military term).
[237] About.
[238] In short.
[239] Middlemen.
[240] Garb; clothes.
[241] Entreaters.

Have you so slander[242] any moment leisure
As to give words or talk with the Lord Hamlet.
Look to't, I charge you. Come your ways.[243]   135
Ophelia
I shall obey, my lord.   *Exeunt*

Act I, Scene iv

Enter Hamlet, Horatio, and Marcellus

Hamlet
The air bites shrewdly,[244] it is very cold.
Horatio
It is a nipping and an eager[245] air.
Hamlet
What hour now?
Horatio   I think it lacks of twelve.
Hamlet
No, it is struck.
Horatio   Indeed?
I heard it not. Then it draws near the season[246]   5
Wherein the spirit held his wont to[247] walk.

A flourish of trumpets, and ordnance[248] shot off within[249]

---

[242] Abuse.
[243] Come along.
[244] Keenly.
[245] Sharp.
[246] Time.
[247] Was used to.
[248] Cannon.
[249] Off-stage; behind the scenes.

What does this mean, my lord?

Hamlet

The King doth wake tonight and takes his rouse,[250]
Keeps wassail, and the swaggering upspring reels.[251]
And, as he drains his draughts of Rhenish[252] down,   10
The kettle-drum and trumpet thus bray out
The triumph[253] of his pledge.

Horatio   Is it a custom?

Hamlet

Ay, marry, is't,
But to my mind, though I am native here
And to the manner[254] born, it is a custom   15
More honoured in the breach than the observance.[255]
This heavy-headed revel east and west
Makes us traduced and taxed of other nations.
They clepe[256] us drunkards, and with swinish phrase
Soil our addition[257] and indeed it takes   20
From our achievements, though performed at height,
The pith[258] and marrow of our attribute.[259]
So, oft it chances in particular men,
That for some vicious mole of nature[260] in them,
As, in their birth,[261] wherein they are not guilty,   25

---

[250] Carouses

[251] Dances a wild dance (upspring).

[252] German wine; Rhine wine.

[253] Festive celebration.

[254] Custom.

[255] Lines 16 to 38 were omitted in the Folio text; King James' Queen was Anne of Denmark, who might have taken offense.

[256] Call.

[257] Reputation.

[258] Vital part.

[259] Achievement; fame gained from the achievement.

[260] Natural flaw.

[261] Stemming from their parents.

Since nature cannot choose his origin,
By the o'ergrowth of some complexion,[262]
Oft breaking down the pales and forts[263] of reason,
Or by some habit that too much o'erleavens[264]
The form of plausive[265] manners, that these men,   30
Carrying, I say, the stamp of one defect,
Being nature's livery, or fortune's star,[266]
His virtues else, be they as pure as grace,
As infinite as man may undergo,[267]
Shall in the general censure[268] take corruption   35
From that particular fault. The dram[269] of evil
Doth all the noble substance[270] often dout[271]
To his own scandal.

Horatio   Look, my lord, it comes!

Enter Ghost

Hamlet
Angels and ministers of grace defend us!
Be thou a spirit of health or goblin damned,   40
Bring with thee airs[272] from heaven or blasts from hell,
Be thy intents wicked or charitable,
Thou com'st in such a questionable shape[273]

---

[262] See glossary: The Four Humors.

[263] Fences and fortifications.

[264] Spoils, as bread is spoilt when too much yeast is used.

[265] Pleasing.

[266] Either given in birth (natural) or later by ill luck (fortune).

[267] Sustain.

[268] The people's opinion.

[269] A tiny amount; "drop."

[270] What is inherent, essential.

[271] Extinguish.

[272] Breezes.

[273] A form that invites questions.

That I will speak to thee. I'll call thee Hamlet,
King, father, royal Dane! O, answer me!   45
Let me not burst in ignorance, but tell
Why thy canonized[274] bones, hearsed[275] in death,
Have burst their cerements,[276] why the sepulchre,
Wherein we saw thee quietly inurned,[277]
Hath oped his ponderous and marble jaws,   50
To cast thee up again. What may this mean,
That thou, dead corse, again in complete steel[278]
Revisitst thus the glimpses of the moon,
Making night hideous, and we fools of nature[279]
So horridly to shake our disposition[280]   55
With thoughts beyond the reaches of our souls?
Say, why is this? Wherefore? What should we do?

Ghost beckons Hamlet

Horatio
    It beckons you to go away with it,
    As if it some impartment[281] did desire
    To you alone.
Marcellus   Look, with what courteous action   60
    It waves you to a more removed ground.
    But do not go with it.
Horatio   No, by no means.

---

[274] Consecrated.
[275] Coffined.
[276] Winding sheets treated with wax.
[277] Interred.
[278] Full armor.
[279] We who are nature's creatures (ghosts are not "natural").
[280] Mental foundation.
[281] Communication.

Hamlet
>It will not speak. Then I will follow it.

Horatio
>Do not, my lord.

Hamlet   Why, what should be the fear?
>I do not set my life in a pin's fee,[282]   65
>And for my soul, what can it do to that,
>Being a thing immortal as itself?
>It waves me forth again. I'll follow it.

Horatio
>What if it tempt you toward the flood, my lord,
>Or to the dreadful summit of the cliff   70
>That beetles[283] o'er his base into the sea,
>And there assume some other horrible form,
>Which might deprive your sovereignty of reason
>And draw you into madness? Think of it.
>The very place puts toys of desperation,[284]   75
>Without more motive, into every brain
>That looks so many fathoms to the sea
>And hears it roar beneath.

Hamlet   It waves me still.
>Go on, I'll follow thee.

Marcellus
>You shall not go, my lord.

Hamlet   Hold off your hands.   80

Horatio
>Be ruled, you shall not go.

Hamlet   My fate cries out,
>And makes each petty artery in this body
>As hardy as the Nemean lion's[285] nerve.

---

[282] At the value of a pin.

[283] Hangs.

[284] Desperate thoughts; freaks of fancy.

[285] Killing this beast was the first labor of Hercules.

Still am I called. Unhand me, gentlemen.
By heaven, I'll make a ghost of him that lets[286] me!   85
I say, away! Go on! I'll follow thee.

Exeunt Ghost and Hamlet

Horatio

He waxes desperate with imagination.

Marcellus

Let's follow. 'Tis not fit thus to obey him.

Horatio

Have after.[287] To what issue will this come?

Marcellus

Something is rotten in the state of Denmark.   90

Horatio

Heaven will direct it.[288]

Marcellus   Nay, let's follow him.   *Exeunt*

Act I, Scene v

Enter Ghost and Hamlet

Hamlet

Whither wilt thou lead me? Speak! I'll go no further.

Ghost

Mark me.

Hamlet   I will.

Ghost   My hour[289] is almost come,
When I to sulphurous and tormenting flames
Must render up myself.

---

[286] Hinders.

[287] Let us go after him.

[288] The issue, that which is rotten.

[289] Daybreak, when ghosts must return to their designated places.

Hamlet   Alas, poor ghost!

Ghost

    Pity me not, but lend thy serious hearing   5
    To what I shall unfold.

Hamlet   Speak, I am bound to hear.

Ghost

    So art thou to revenge, when thou shalt hear.

Hamlet

    What?

Ghost

    I am thy father's spirit,
    Doomed for a certain term to walk the night,   10
    And for the day confined to fast in fires,
    Till the foul crimes done in my days of nature[290]
    Are burnt and purged away. But that I am forbid
    To tell the secrets of my prison-house,
    I could a tale unfold whose lightest word   15
    Would harrow up thy soul, freeze thy young blood,
    Make thy two eyes, like stars, start from their spheres,
    Thy knotted and combined locks to part
    And each particular hair to stand on end,
    Like quills upon the fretful porpentine.[291]   20
    But this eternal blazon[292] must not be
    To ears of flesh and blood. List,[293] list, O, list!
    If thou didst ever thy dear father love—

Hamlet

    O God!

Ghost

    Revenge his foul and most unnatural murder.   25

---

[290] My nature-given lifespan.

[291] Porcupine.

[292] Picture of the afterlife eternal.

[293] Listen.

Hamlet
>Murder!

Ghost
>Murder most foul, as in the best it is,
>But this most foul, strange and unnatural.

Hamlet
>Haste me to know't, that I, with wings as swift
>As meditation or the thoughts of love,   30
>May sweep to my revenge.

Ghost   I find thee apt,
>And duller shouldst thou be than the fat weed
>That roots itself in ease on Lethe[294] wharf,
>Wouldst thou not stir in this. Now, Hamlet, hear!
>'Tis given out that, sleeping in my orchard,   35
>A serpent stung me. So the whole ear of Denmark
>Is by a forged process[295] of my death
>Rankly abused. But know, thou noble youth,
>The serpent that did sting thy father's life
>Now wears his crown.   40

Hamlet
>O my prophetic soul! My uncle!

Ghost
>Ay, that incestuous, that adulterate[296] beast,
>With witchcraft of his wit, with traitorous gifts—
>O wicked wit and gifts, that have the power
>So to seduce!—won to his shameful lust   45
>The will[297] of my most seeming-virtuous Queen:
>O Hamlet, what a falling-off was there!
>From me, whose love was of that dignity

---

[294] Lethe is the river of forgetfulness in classical mythology.
[295] Falsified account.
[296] Adulterous.
[297] Love; see glossary.

That it went hand in hand even with the vow
I made to her in marriage, and to decline   50
Upon a wretch whose natural gifts were poor
To those of mine!
But virtue, as it never will be moved,
Though lewdness court it in a shape of heaven,
So lust, though to a radiant angel linked,   55
Will sate itself[298] in a celestial bed,
And prey on garbage.
But, soft! Methinks I scent the morning air.
Brief let me be. Sleeping within my orchard,
My custom always of the afternoon,   60
Upon my secure hour thy uncle stole,
With juice of cursed hebenon[299] in a vial,
And in the porches[300] of my ears did pour
The leperous distilment,[301] whose effect
Holds such an enmity with blood of man   65
That swift as quicksilver it courses through
The natural gates and alleys of the body,
And with a sudden vigour doth posset[302]
And curd, like eager[303] droppings into milk,
The thin and wholesome blood. So did it mine,   70
And a most instant tetter[304] barked about,
Most lazar-like,[305] with vile and loathsome crust,

[298] Satisfy itself.

[299] A poison. No one has yet identified the plant or source, though critical conjecture is plentiful. My suggestion is that the unknown is more horrific than the known—hence a "newfangled" name.

[300] Openings.

[301] Liquid which makes the skin scaly as found in victims of leprosy.

[302] Curdle like milk when an acidic liquid is added.

[303] Acidic liquid.

[304] Scaly rash, looking like bark.

[305] Like a leper.

All my smooth body.
Thus was I, sleeping, by a brother's hand
Of life, of crown, of Queen at once dispatched,[306]   75
Cut off even in the blossoms of my sin,[307]
Unhouseled, disappointed, unaneled,[308]
No reckoning made, but sent to my account
With all my imperfections on my head.
O, horrible! Horrible! Most horrible!   80
If thou hast nature[309] in thee, bear it not;
Let not the royal bed of Denmark be
A couch for luxury[310] and damned incest.
But, howsoever thou pursuest this act,
Taint not thy mind, nor let thy soul contrive   85
Against thy mother aught. Leave her to heaven
And to those thorns that in her bosom lodge,
To prick and sting her. Fare thee well at once!
The glow-worm shows the matin[311] to be near,
And gins[312] to pale his uneffectual fire.   90
Adieu, adieu! Hamlet, remember me.   *Exit*

Hamlet

O all you host of heaven! O earth! What else?
And shall I couple[313] hell? O, fie! Hold, hold, my heart,
And you, my sinews, grow not instant old,
But bear me stiffly up. Remember thee!   95

---

[306] Deprived by death.

[307] With my sins unforgiven, "blooming."

[308] Deprived of all last rites. Unhousel = deprived of the Eucharist; disappointed = deprived of all other rites, e.g., confession/absolution; unaneled = deprived of extreme unction.

[309] Natural feeling.

[310] Lust.

[311] Morning.

[312] Begins.

[313] Add.

Ay, thou poor ghost, while memory holds a seat
In this distracted globe.[314] Remember thee!
Yea, from the table[315] of my memory
I'll wipe away all trivial fond[316] records,
All saws of books,[317] all forms,[318] all pressures[319] past,   100
That youth and observation copied there,
And thy commandment all alone shall live
Within the book and volume of my brain
Unmixed with baser matter. Yes, by heaven!
O most pernicious woman!   105
O villain, villain, smiling, damned villain!
My tables. Meet it is I set it down,
That one may smile, and smile, and be a villain.
At least I'm sure it may be so in Denmark.   *Writing*
So, uncle, there you are. Now to my word.[320]   110
It is 'Adieu, adieu! Remember me.'
I have sworn 't.

Enter Horatio and Marcellus, calling

Marcellus and Horatio
    My lord, my lord—
Marcellus
    Lord Hamlet—
Horatio   Heaven secure him!

---

[314] Head; also world; also, maybe, a pun on The Globe Theatre where *Hamlet* was performed.
[315] Tablet; students and scholars might carry two, linked together to form a book (see l. 107).
[316] Foolish.
[317] Memorable quotations from books.
[318] Shapes drawn or written.
[319] Impressions.
[320] Motto.

Hamlet (*aside*)   So be it!

Horatio

    Hillo, ho, ho, my lord!   115

Hamlet

    Hillo, ho, ho, boy! Come, bird, come.

Marcellus

    How is't, my noble lord?

Horatio   What news, my lord?

Hamlet

    O, wonderful!

Horatio

    Good my lord, tell it.

Hamlet   No, you'll reveal it.

Horatio

    Not I, my lord, by heaven.

Marcellus   Nor I, my lord.   120

Hamlet

    How say you, then, would heart of man once think it?

    But you'll be secret?

Horatio and Marcellus   Ay, by heaven, my lord.

Hamlet

    There's ne'er a villain dwelling in all Denmark

    But he's an arrant[321] knave.

Horatio

    There needs no ghost, my lord, come from the grave   125

    To tell us this.

Hamlet   Why, right, you are i'the right;

    And so, without more circumstance[322] at all,

    I hold it fit that we shake hands and part:

    You, as your business and desire shall point you;

    For every man has business and desire,   130

---

[321] Utter.

[322] Further ceremony.

Such as it is—and for mine own poor part,

Look you, I'll go pray.

Horatio

These are but wild and whirling words, my lord.

Hamlet

I'm sorry they offend you, heartily,

Yes, faith heartily.

Horatio   There's no offence, my lord.   135

Hamlet

Yes, by Saint Patrick,[323] but there is, Horatio,

And much offence too. Touching this vision here,

It is an honest[324] ghost, that let me tell you.

For your desire to know what is between us,

O'ermaster't as you may. And now, good friends,   140

As you are friends, scholars, and soldiers,

Give me one poor request.

Horatio   What is't, my lord? We will.

Hamlet

Never make known what you have seen tonight.

Horatio and Marcellus

My lord, we will not.

Hamlet   Nay, but swear't.

Horatio

In faith, my lord, not I.[325]

Marcellus   Nor I, my lord, in faith.   145

Hamlet

Upon my sword.[326]

Marcellus   We have sworn, my lord, already.

---

[323] Saint Patrick is the keeper of Purgatory.

[324] Genuine, not an evil spirit.

[325] I will reveal nothing.

[326] A sword's cruciform hilt is an excellent substitute for a cross to swear an oath upon.

Hamlet

    Indeed, upon my sword, indeed.

Ghost (*cries under the stage*[327])   Swear!

Hamlet

    Ah, ha, boy! say'st thou so? Art thou there, truepenny?[328]

    Come on! You hear this fellow in the cellarage.

    Consent to swear.

Horatio   Propose the oath, my lord.   150

Hamlet

    Never to speak of this that you have seen,

    Swear by my sword.

Ghost   Swear!   *They swear on his sword*

Hamlet

    Hic et ubique?[329] Then we'll shift our ground.

    Come hither, gentlemen,

    And lay your hands again upon my sword.   155

    Never to speak of this that you have heard,

    Swear by my sword.

Ghost   Swear!   *They swear*

Hamlet

    Well said, old mole! Canst work i'the earth so fast?

    A worthy pioneer![330] Once more remove,[331] good friends.

Horatio

    O day and night, but this is wondrous strange!   160

Hamlet

    And therefore as a stranger give it welcome.

    There are more things in heaven and earth, Horatio,

---

[327] The area under the stage, accessible through a trapdoor, was known as "hell."

[328] Honest one.

[329] "Here and everywhere."

[330] Foot-soldier, who usually preceded the army to dig trenches; also, miner.

[331] Move.

Than are dreamt of in your philosophy.[332] But come.
Here, as before, never, so help you mercy,
How strange or odd soe'er I bear myself,   165
As I perchance hereafter shall think meet
To put an antic disposition on,[333]
That you, at such times seeing me, never shall,
With arms encumbered[334] thus, or this headshake,
Or by pronouncing of some doubtful phrase,[335]   170
As 'Well, we know,' or 'We could, an if[336] we would,'
Or 'If we list to[337] speak,' or 'There be, an if they might;[338]'
Or such ambiguous giving out, to note
That you know aught[339] of me: this not to do,
So grace and mercy at your most need help you,   175
Swear.

Ghost   Swear.   *They swear*

Hamlet

Rest, rest, perturbed spirit! So, gentlemen,
With all my love I do commend me to you,
And what so poor a man as Hamlet is
May do, to express his love and friending[340] to you,   180
God willing, shall not lack.[341] Let us go in together;
And still[342] your fingers on your lips, I pray.

---

[332] Not Horatio's in particular, but human knowledge in general ("your" = our).
[333] To pretend madness (antic = odd, strange).
[334] Folded.
[335] Phrase with double meaning.
[336] An if = if.
[337] Wanted to.
[338] "There are people who could tell, if allowed."
[339] Anything.
[340] Friendship.
[341] Be found wanting.
[342] Always.

The time is out of joint.[343] O cursed spite,
That ever I was born to set it right!
Nay, come, let's go together.[344]   *Exit* 185

---

[343] In deep disorder.
[344] Though Hamlet is the prince, he does not expect anybody to give him precedence.

Act II, Scene i

Enter Polonius and Reynaldo, his man

Lord Polonius

    Give him this money and these notes, Reynaldo.

Reynaldo

    I will, my lord.

Lord Polonius

    You shall do marvellous wisely, good Reynaldo,

    Before you visit him, to make inquire

    Of his behavior.

Reynaldo   My lord, I did intend it.   5

Lord Polonius

    Marry, well said, very well said. Look you, sir,

    Inquire me first what Danskers[345] are in Paris,

    And how, and who, what means,[346] and where they keep,[347]

    What company, at what expense; and finding

    By this encompassment[348] and drift of question   10

    That they do know my son, come you more nearer[349]

    Than your particular demands[350] will touch it.

    Take[351] you, as 'twere, some distant knowledge of him,

    As thus, 'I know his father and his friends,

    And in part him.' Do you mark this, Reynaldo?   15

Reynaldo

    Ay, very well, my lord.

---

[345] Danes.

[346] Their wealth.

[347] Lodge.

[348] Roundabout.

[349] You will get further.

[350] Direct questioning.

[351] Assume.

Lord Polonius

 'And in part him, but' you may say 'not well,

 But, if't be he I mean, he's very wild,

 Addicted so and so.' And there put on him[352]

 What forgeries[353] you please—marry, none so rank[354] 20

 As may dishonour him, take heed of that—

 But, sir, such wanton,[355] wild and usual slips

 As are companions noted and most known

 To youth and liberty.

Reynaldo

 As gaming, my lord?   25

Lord Polonius

 Ay, or drinking, fencing, swearing, quarrelling,

 Drabbing[356]—you may go so far.

Reynaldo

 My lord, that would dishonour him.

Lord Polonius

 'Faith, no, as you may season it in the charge.[357]

 You must not put another scandal on him,   30

 That he is open to incontinency,[358]

 That's not my meaning. But breathe his faults so quaintly[359]

 That they may seem the taints of liberty,[360]

 The flash and outbreak of a fiery mind,

---

[352] Bestow on him.

[353] Fabrications.

[354] Foul.

[355] Wayward.

[356] Whoring.

[357] "You can make it sound not too serious."

[358] Prone to excess sexually.

[359] With such art.

[360] Faults resulting from freedom (e.g., the freedom of being away from home).

    A savageness[361] in unreclaimed[362] blood,   35

    Of general assault.[363]

Reynaldo   But, my good lord,—

Lord Polonius

    Wherefore[364] should you do this?

Reynaldo   Ay, my lord,

    I would know that.

Lord Polonius   Marry, sir, here's my drift,

    And I believe, it is a fetch of warrant.[365]

    You laying these slight sullies on my son,   40

    As 'twere a thing a little soiled i'the working,[366]

    Mark you,

    Your party in converse,[367] him you would sound,

    Having ever seen in the prenominate crimes

    The youth you breathe of guilty,[368] be assured   45

    He closes with you in this consequence.[369]

    'Good sir,' or so, or 'friend,' or 'gentleman,'

    According to the phrase or the addition[370]

    Of man and country.

Reynaldo   Very good, my lord.

Lord Polonius

    And then, sir, does he this—he does—what was I about 50

    to say? By the mass, I was about to say something: where

    did I leave?

---

[361] Wildness.

[362] Uncontrolled (for "blood" in this connection, see glossary).

[363] "Which all young men suffer from."

[364] Why.

[365] Justifiable trick; "the ends justify the means.

[366] Something soiled by being handled; "shopworn."

[367] Your conversation partner.

[368] Examine to see if he ever heard of such faults as you mentioned in the young man you talk of as guilty.

[369] He will confide in you about this.

[370] Form of address; that which is added to the name.

Reynaldo

 At 'closes in the consequence,' at 'friend

 Or so,' and 'gentleman.'

Lord Polonius

 At 'closes in the consequence,' ay, marry,   55

 He closes thus: 'I know the gentleman,

 I saw him yesterday, or t' other day,

 Or then, or then, with such or such; and, as you say,

 There was a[371] gaming, there o'ertook in's rouse,[372]

 There falling out[373] at tennis.' Or perchance,   60

 'I saw him enter such a house of sale,'

 Videlicet,[374] a brothel, or so forth.

 See you now?

 Your bait of falsehood takes this carp of truth:

 And thus do we of wisdom and of reach,[375]   65

 With windlasses[376] and with assays of bias,[377]

 By indirections find directions out.

 So by my former lecture[378] and advice

 Shall you my son. You have me,[379] have you not?

Reynaldo

 My lord, I have.

Lord Polonius   God b'wi'you. Fare you well.   70

Reynaldo

 Good my lord!

---

[371] He.

[372] Overcome by drinking.

[373] Quarreling.

[374] That is.

[375] Worldly experience.

[376] Roundabout routes.

[377] Devious probing.

[378] Lesson.

[379] You understand me.

Lord Polonius

    Observe his inclination in[380] yourself.

Reynaldo

    I shall, my lord.

Lord Polonius   And let him ply[381] his music.

Reynaldo

    Well, my lord.

Lord Polonius

    Farewell!   *Exit Reynaldo*

Enter Ophelia

            How now, Ophelia! what's the matter?   75

Ophelia

    O, my lord, my lord, I have been so affrighted!

Lord Polonius

    With what, i' the name of God?

Ophelia

    My lord, as I was sewing in my closet,[382]

    Lord Hamlet, with his doublet[383] all unbraced[384]

    No hat upon his head, his stockings fouled,   80

    Ungartered, and down-gyved[385] to his ancle,

    Pale as his shirt, his knees knocking each other,

    And with a look so piteous in purport

    As if he had been loosed out of hell

    To speak of horrors, he comes before me.   85

Lord Polonius

    Mad for thy love?

---

[380] For.

[381] Study.

[382] Chamber.

[383] Jacket.

[384] Unfastened.

[385] Fallen around his ankles, now resembling a prisoner's fetters (gyves).

Ophelia   My lord, I do not know,
 But truly, I do fear it.
Lord Polonius   What said he?
Ophelia
 He took me by the wrist and held me hard.
 Then goes he to the length of all his arm,
 And, with his other hand thus o'er his brow,   90
 He falls to such perusal of my face
 As he would draw it. Long stayed he so.
 At last, a little shaking of mine arm,
 And thrice his head thus waving up and down,
 He raised a sigh so piteous and profound   95
 As it did seem to shatter all his bulk
 And end his being. That done, he lets me go,
 And, with his head over his shoulder turned,
 He seemed to find his way without his eyes.
 For out o'doors he went without their helps,   100
 And, to the last, bended their light[386] on me.
Lord Polonius
 Come, go with me, I will go seek the King.
 This is the very ecstasy[387] of love,
 Whose violent property fordoes itself[388]
 And leads the will to desperate undertakings   105
 As oft as any passion under heaven
 That does afflict our natures. I am sorry.
 What, have you given him any hard words of late?
Ophelia
 No, my good lord, but, as you did command,

---

[386] It was believed that light went out from and entered eyes, thus enabling us to see.

[387] "Madness" resulting from the faculty of reason being "suspended" temporarily.

[388] So violent that it self-destructs.

I did repel his letters and denied   110
His access to me.
Lord Polonius   That hath made him mad.
I am sorry that with better heed and judgment
I had not quoted[389] him. I feared he did but trifle
And meant to wreck thee.[390] But, beshrew[391] my jealousy![392]
By heaven, it is as proper to our age   115
To cast beyond ourselves[393] in our opinions
As it is common for the younger sort
To lack discretion. Come, go we to the King.
This must be known, which, being kept close,[394] might move
More grief to hide than hate to utter love.[395]   *Exeunt* 120

Act II, Scene ii

Enter King Claudius, Queen Gertrude, Rosencrantz, Guildenstern, and Attendants

King Claudius
Welcome, dear Rosencrantz and Guildenstern!
Moreover[396] that we much did long to see you,

---

[389] Observed.

[390] Ruin (through seduction).

[391] Curse.

[392] Suspicion.

[393] "Cast" = what a hunting dog does when seeking scent; here: old men are prone to be overly careful.

[394] Secret.

[395] I.e., telling the King of Hamlet's love may cause anger, but not telling would possibly cause grief.

[396] Besides.

The need we have to use you did provoke
Our hasty sending.[397] Something have you heard
Of Hamlet's transformation—so I call it,   5
Sith[398] nor the exterior nor the inward man
Resembles that it was. What it should be,
More than his father's death, that thus hath put him
So much from the understanding of himself,
I cannot dream of. I entreat you both,   10
That, being of so young days[399] brought up with him,
And sith so neighboured to[400] his youth and havior,[401]
That you vouchsafe your rest[402] here in our court
Some little time, so by your companies
To draw him on to pleasures, and to gather,   15
So much as from occasion[403] you may glean,
Whether aught to us unknown afflicts him thus,
That, opened,[404] lies within our remedy.

Queen Gertrude

Good gentlemen, he hath much talked of you,
And sure I am two men there are not living   20
To whom he more adheres.[405] If it will please you
To show us so much gentry[406] and good will
As to expend your time with us awhile,
For the supply and profit of our hope,[407]

---

[397] Sending for you.
[398] Since.
[399] From childhood.
[400] Intimate with.
[401] Behavior; manner.
[402] Agree to stay.
[403] Opportunity.
[404] Revealed.
[405] Is attached.
[406] Courtesy.
[407] In order to support and further what we hope.

Your visitation shall receive such thanks   25
    As fits a king's remembrance.

Rosencrantz   Both your majesties
    Might, by the sovereign power you have of us,
    Put your dread[408] pleasures more into command
    Than to entreaty.

Guildenstern   But we both obey,
    And here give up ourselves, in the full bent[409]   30
    To lay our service freely at your feet
    To be commanded.

King Claudius
    Thanks, Rosencrantz and gentle Guildenstern.

Queen Gertrude
    Thanks, Guildenstern and gentle Rosencrantz.
    And I beseech you instantly to visit   35
    My too much changed son. Go, some of you,
    And bring these gentlemen where Hamlet is.

Guildenstern
    Heavens make our presence and our practices
    Pleasant and helpful to him!

Queen Gertrude   Ay, amen!

    Exeunt Rosencrantz, Guildenstern, and some Attendants

Enter Polonius

Lord Polonius
    The ambassadors from Norway, my good lord,   40
    Are joyfully returned.

King Claudius
    Thou still[410] hast been the father of good news.

[408] Deeply respected.
[409] To our limit.
[410] Always.

Lord Polonius

    Have I, my lord? I assure my good liege,

    I hold my duty, as I hold my soul,

    Both to my God and to my gracious King.   45

    And I do think—or else this brain of mine

    Hunts not the trail of policy[411] so sure

    As it hath used to do — that I have found

    The very cause of Hamlet's lunacy.

King Claudius

    O, speak of that, that do I long to hear.   50

Lord Polonius

    Give first admittance to the ambassadors.

    My news shall be the fruit[412] to that great feast.

King Claudius

    Thyself do grace to them, and bring them in.   *Exit Polonius*

    He tells me, my dear Gertrude, he hath found

    The head[413] and source of all your son's distemper.   55

Queen Gertrude

    I doubt[414] it is no other but the main[415]—

    His father's death, and our o'erhasty marriage.

King Claudius

    Well, we shall sift him.[416]

Re-enter Polonius, with Voltimand and Cornelius

                    Welcome, my good friends!

    Say, Voltimand, what from our brother[417] Norway?

[411] Statecraft.

[412] Dessert.

[413] Origin.

[414] Fear.

[415] Chief point.

[416] Subject Polonius to serious interrogation.

[417] Fellow in kingship.

Voltimand

 Most fair return of greetings and desires.[418]   60
 Upon our first,[419] he sent out to suppress
 His nephew's levies, which to him appeared
 To be a preparation 'gainst the Polack;[420]
 But, better looked into, he truly found
 It was against your highness, whereat grieved   65
 That so his sickness, age, and impotence
 Was falsely borne in hand,[421] sends out arrests[422]
 On Fortinbras; which he, in brief, obeys,
 Receives rebuke from Norway, and in fine[423]
 Makes vow before his uncle never more   70
 To give the assay of arms[424] against your majesty.
 Whereon old Norway, overcome with joy,
 Gives him three thousand crowns in annual fee
 And his commission to employ those soldiers,
 So levied as before, against the Polack,   75
 With an entreaty, herein further shown,   *Giving a paper*
 That it might please you to give quiet pass
 Through your dominions for this enterprise,
 On such regards of safety and allowance[425]
 As therein are set down.

King Claudius   It likes[426] us well,   80
 And at our more considered time[427] we'll read,

---

[418] Well-wishing.

[419] When first we mentioned the matter.

[420] The King of Poland.

[421] Deluded.

[422] Orders to desist.

[423] In conclusion.

[424] To attempt a military test of strength.

[425] Conditions for the country's safety, approved by Claudius.

[426] Pleases.

[427] When there is leisure to consider it well.

Answer, and think upon this business.
Meantime we thank you for your well-took labour.
Go to your rest; at night we'll feast together.
Most welcome home!

Exeunt Voltimand and Cornelius

Lord Polonius   This business is well ended.   85
  My liege and madam, to expostulate
  What majesty should be, what duty is,
  Why day is day, night night, and time is time,
  Were nothing but to waste night, day and time.
  Therefore, since brevity is the soul of wit,   90
  And tediousness the limbs and outward flourishes,[428]
  I will be brief. Your noble son is mad—
  Mad call I it, for, to define true madness,
  What is't but to be nothing else but mad?
  But let that go.
Queen Gertrude   More matter, with less art.   95
Lord Polonius
  Madam, I swear I use no art at all.
  That he is mad, 'tis true; 'tis true 'tis pity,
  And pity 'tis 'tis true—a foolish figure,[429]
  But farewell it, for I will use no art.
  Mad let us grant him, then. And now remains   100
  That we find out the cause of this effect,
  Or rather say the cause of this defect,
  For this effect defective comes by cause.[430]
  Thus it remains, and the remainder thus.
  Perpend.[431]   105

[428] Rhetorical embellishments.
[429] I.e., of speech.
[430] Has a reason, a cause.
[431] Consider.

I have a daughter, have while she is mine,
Who, in her duty and obedience, mark,
Hath given me this. Now gather and surmise.
(*Reads*) 'To the celestial and my soul's idol, the most beau-
tified Ophelia,'—That's an ill phrase, a vile phrase; 'beauti- 110
fied' is a vile phrase. But you shall hear.
(*Reads*) 'In her excellent white bosom,[432] these.[433]

Queen Gertrude

Came this from Hamlet to her?

Lord Polonius

Good madam, stay[434] awhile. I will be faithful.
> *'Doubt thou the stars are fire;*   115
>> *Doubt that the sun doth move;*
> *Doubt*[435] *truth to be a liar;*
>> *But never doubt I love.'*

'O dear Ophelia, I am ill at these numbers.[436] I have not
art to   reckon[437] my groans. But that I love thee best, O 120
most best, believe it. Adieu.

> Thine evermore, most dear lady, whilst
> this machine[438] is to him,

>> Hamlet.'

This, in obedience, hath my daughter shown me,   125
And more above[439] hath his solicitings,
As they fell out by time, by means, and place,
All given to mine ear.

---

[432] I.e., where one should keep a love letter.

[433] I.e., these lines.

[434] Wait.

[435] Suspect.

[436] I am bad at verse-making.

[437] Count.

[438] Body; see glossary.

[439] Moreover.

King Claudius

    But how hath she received his love?

Lord Polonius

    What do you think of me?   130

King Claudius

    As of a man faithful and honourable.

Lord Polonius

    I would fain[440] prove so. But what might you think,

    When I had seen this hot love on the wing,

    As I perceived it, I must tell you that,

    Before my daughter told me, what might you,   135

    Or my dear majesty your Queen here, think,

    If I had played the desk or table-book,[441]

    Or given my heart a winking,[442] mute and dumb,

    Or looked upon this love with idle sight,[443]

    What might you think? No, I went round[444] to work,   140

    And my young mistress thus I did bespeak:[445]

    'Lord Hamlet is a prince, out of thy star.[446]

    This must not be.' And then I precepts gave her,

    That she should lock herself from his resort,

    Admit no messengers, receive no tokens.   145

    Which done, she took the fruits of my advice,[447]

    And he, repulsed—a short tale to make—

    Fell into a sadness, then into a fast,

---

[440] Gladly.

[441] Both associated with writing, thus "been a means of communication" between the lovers.

[442] Had my heart close its eyes.

[443] Seen without acting.

[444] Without more ado.

[445] Address.

[446] Above your class/station as determined by birth.

[447] My advice bore fruit, i.e., she obeyed completely.

Thence to a watch,[448] thence into a weakness,
Thence to a lightness,[449] and, by this declension,[450]   150
Into the madness wherein now he raves,
And all we[451] mourn for.

King Claudius   Do you think 'tis this?

Queen Gertrude

    It may be, very likely.

Lord Polonius

    Hath there been such a time, I'd fain know that,
    That I have positively said, ''Tis so,'   155
    When it proved otherwise?

King Claudius   Not that I know.

Lord Polonius (*pointing to his head and shoulder*)

    Take this from this, if this be otherwise.
    If circumstances lead me, I will find
    Where truth is hid, though it were hid indeed
    Within the centre.[452]

King Claudius   How may we try[453] it further?   160

Lord Polonius

    You know, sometimes he walks four hours together
    Here in the lobby.

Queen Gertrude   So he does indeed.

Lord Polonius

    At such a time I'll loose[454] my daughter to him.
    Be you and I behind an arras[455] then,

---

[448] Sleeplessness.

[449] Lightheadedness.

[450] Decline.

[451] All of us.

[452] I.e., of the earth.

[453] Test.

[454] "Let loose" instead of cooping her up (l. 145); but also as one lets animals loose to mate.

[455] Wall hanging; tapestry.

Mark the encounter. If he love her not   165
And be not from his reason fallen thereon,[456]
Let me be no assistant for a state,
But keep a farm and carters.[457]
King Claudius   We will try it.

Enter Hamlet, reading a book

Queen Gertrude
But, look, where sadly the poor wretch comes reading.
Lord Polonius
Away, I do beseech you, both away!   170
I'll board him presently.[458] O, give me leave:
                    Exeunt King Claudius, Queen Gertrude, and Attendants
How does my good Lord Hamlet?
Hamlet
Well, God-a-mercy.[459]
Lord Polonius
Do you know me, my lord?
Hamlet
Excellent well; you are a fishmonger.[460]   175
Lord Polonius
Not I, my lord.
Hamlet
Then I would you were so honest a man.
Lord Polonius
Honest, my lord!
Hamlet
Ay, sir. To be honest, as this world goes, is to be one

---

[456] For that cause.
[457] Wagon drivers.
[458] Approach him immediately.
[459] "God have mercy," a polite greeting, especially to social inferiors.
[460] See glossary.

man picked out of ten thousand.   180

Lord Polonius

That's very true, my lord.

Hamlet

For if the sun breed maggots[461] in a dead dog, being a
good kissing carrion,[462]—have you a daughter?

Lord Polonius

I have, my lord.

Hamlet

Let her not walk i' the sun.[463] Conception is a blessing, but 185
as your daughter may conceive. Friend, look to't.[464]

Lord Polonius (*aside*)

How say you by that? Still harping on my daughter. Yet he
knew me not at first; he said I was a fishmonger. He is far
gone, far gone. And truly in my youth I suffered much
extremity for love, very near this. I'll speak to him again. 190
What do you read, my lord?

Hamlet

Words, words, words.

Lord Polonius

What is the matter,[465] my lord?

Hamlet

Between who?

Lord Polonius

I mean, the matter that you read, my lord.   195

Hamlet

Slanders, sir: for the satirical rogue says here that old men
have grey beards, that their faces are wrinkled, their eyes

---

[461] The sun was thought to be able to breed life out of dead matter.

[462] Carrion: 1) dead flesh; 2) "available flesh," prostitute.

[463] See notes 461 and 462.

[464] Take care.

[465] 1) The contents; 2) the problem, the cause of a quarrel.

purging[466] thick amber[467] and plum-tree gum, and that
they have a plentiful lack of wit,[468] together with most
weak hams. All which, sir, though I most powerfully and 200
potently believe, yet I hold it not honesty[469] to have it thus
set down, for yourself, sir, should be old as I am—if like
a crab you could go backward.

Lord Polonius (*aside*)

Though this be madness, yet there is method in't—
Will you walk out of the air,[470] my lord?   205

Hamlet

Into my grave.

Lord Polonius

Indeed, that is out o'the air.

(*Aside*) How pregnant[471] sometimes his replies are! A happiness that often madness hits on, which reason and sanity
could not so prosperously be delivered of. I will leave 210
him, and suddenly[472] contrive the means of meeting between him and my daughter—My honourable lord, I will
most humbly take my leave of you.

Hamlet

You cannot, sir, take from me any thing that I will more
willingly part withal[473]—except my life, except my life, 215
except my life.

Lord Polonius

Fare you well, my lord.

---

[466] Exuding.

[467] Resin.

[468] Native intelligence.

[469] Proper behavior.

[470] Fresh air was believed to be harmful to the afflicted.

[471] Full of meaning.

[472] Immediately.

[473] With.

Hamlet

> These tedious old fools!

Enter Rosencrantz and Guildenstern

Lord Polonius

> You go to seek the Lord Hamlet. There he is.

Rosencrantz

> God save you, sir!   *Exit Polonius*   220

Guildenstern

> My honoured lord!

Rosencrantz

> My most dear lord!

Hamlet

> My excellent good friends! How dost thou, Guildenstern?
> Ah, Rosencrantz! Good lads, how do ye both?

Rosencrantz

> As the indifferent[474] children of the earth.   225

Guildenstern

> Happy in that we are not over-happy;
> On Fortune's[475] cap we are not the very button.[476]

Hamlet

> Nor the soles of her shoe?

Rosencrantz

> Neither, my lord.

Hamlet

> Then you live about her waist, or in the middle of her   230
> favours?

Guildenstern

> 'Faith, her privates[477] we.

---

[474] Ordinary.
[475] See glossary.
[476] Highest point.
[477] 1) Ordinary citizen; 2) private parts of the body.

Hamlet

> In the secret parts of Fortune? O, most true; she is a strumpet.[478] What's the news?

Rosencrantz

> None, my lord, but that the world's grown honest.   235

Hamlet

> Then is doomsday near! But your news is not true. Let
> me question more in particular. What have you, my good
> friends, deserved at the hands of Fortune, that she sends
> you to prison hither?

Guildenstern

> Prison, my lord!   240

Hamlet

> Denmark's a prison.

Rosencrantz

> Then is the world one.

Hamlet

> A goodly[479] one, in which there are many confines,[480]
> wards,[481] and dungeons, Denmark being one o'the worst.

Rosencrantz

> We think not so, my lord.   245

Hamlet

> Why, then, 'tis none to you, for there is nothing either
> good or bad, but thinking makes it so. To me it is a prison.

Rosencrantz

> Why then, your ambition makes it one; 'tis too narrow
> for your mind.

Hamlet

> O God, I could be bounded in a nutshell and count myself 250

---

[478] Whore.
[479] Fine.
[480] Cells; enclosures.
[481] Cells.

a king of infinite space, were it not that I have bad dreams.

Guildenstern

Which dreams indeed are ambition, for the very substance
of the ambitious is merely the shadow of a dream.

Hamlet

A dream itself is but a shadow.

Rosencrantz

Truly, and I hold ambition of so airy and light a quality 255
that it is but a shadow's shadow.

Hamlet

Then are our beggars bodies, and our monarchs and out-
stretched heroes the beggars' shadows.[482] Shall we to the
court? For, by my fay,[483] I cannot reason.

Rosencrantz and Guildenstern

We'll wait upon[484] you.   260

Hamlet

No such matter. I will not sort[485] you with the rest of my
servants, for, to speak to you like an honest man, I am
most dreadfully attended. But, in the beaten way[486] of
friendship, what make you[487] at Elsinore?

Rosencrantz

To visit you, my lord, no other occasion.   265

Hamlet

Beggar that I am, I am even poor in thanks, but I thank
you. And sure, dear friends, my thanks are too dear a

---

[482] Beggars have no ambition; ergo, they have substance and can cast shadows. Ergo, also, monarchs and heroes, those with ambition and thus mere
shadows, must be the beggars' shadows.

[483] Faith.

[484] Attend.

[485] Classify.

[486] Clear path; plain words.

[487] What are you doing.

halfpenny.[488] Were you not sent for? Is it your own inclin-
ing? Is it a free visitation? Come, deal justly with me.
Come, come. Nay, speak.

Guildenstern

What should we say, my lord?   270

Hamlet

Why, any thing but to the purpose. You were sent for.
And there is a kind of confession in your looks which
your modesties[489] have not craft enough to colour.[490] I
know the good King and Queen have sent for you.

Rosencrantz

To what end, my lord?   275

Hamlet

That you must teach me. But let me conjure you,[491] by
the rights of our fellowship, by the consonancy[492] of
our youth, by the obligation of our ever-preserved love,
and by what more dear a better proposer could charge
you withal, be even[493] and direct with me, whether you 280
were sent for or no?

Rosencrantz (*aside to Guildenstern*)

What say you?

Hamlet (*aside*)

Nay, then, I have an eye of[494] you. If you love me, hold
not off.

Guildenstern

My lord, we were sent for.   285

---

[488] 1) Not worth a halfpenny; 2) a halfpenny's worth more than the two
deserve.

[489] Decency.

[490] Hide.

[491] Entreat of you.

[492] Friendship that keeps us in harmony.

[493] Straightforward.

[494] On.

Hamlet

> I will tell you why. So shall my anticipation prevent your
> discovery,[495] and your secrecy to the King and Queen moult
> no feather.[496] I have of late, but wherefore I know not,
> lost all my mirth, forgone all custom of exercises. And
> indeed it goes so heavily with my disposition[497] that this 290
> goodly frame,[498] the earth, seems to me a sterile promon-
> tory, this most excellent canopy, the air, look you, this
> brave[499] o'erhanging firmament,[500] this majestical roof fret-
> ted[501] with golden fire, why, it appears no other thing to
> me than a foul and pestilent congregation[502] of vapours. 295
> What a piece of work[503] is a man! How noble in reason!
> How infinite in faculty! In form and moving how ex-
> press[504] and admirable! In action how like an angel! In
> apprehension how like a god! The beauty of the world!
> The paragon of animals! And yet, to me, what is this quin- 300
> tessence[505] of dust? Man delights not me—no, nor woman
> neither, though by your smiling you seem to say so.

Rosencrantz

> My lord, there was no such stuff in my thoughts.

Hamlet

> Why did you laugh then, when I said 'Man delights not
> me'?   305

---

[495] Come before what you have to say; "betrayal."

[496] Stay intact.

[497] My mind is so burdened (with melancholia).

[498] Structure.

[499] Splendid.

[500] The heavens.

[501] Adorned.

[502] Mass.

[503] Excellently crafted, well executed piece.

[504] Precise.

[505] See glossary.

Rosencrantz

> To think, my lord, if you delight not in man, what lenten entertainment[506] the players shall receive from you. We coted[507] them on the way, and hither are they coming, to offer you service.

Hamlet

> He that plays the king shall be welcome, his majesty shall 310 have tribute of me. The adventurous knight shall use his foil and target.[508] The lover shall not sigh gratis.[509] The humourous man[510] shall end his part in peace.[511] The clown[512] shall make those laugh whose lungs are tickled o' the sere.[513] And the lady shall say her mind freely, or the 315 blank verse shall halt for't. What players are they?

Rosencrantz

> Even those you were wont to take delight in, the tragedians[514] of the city.

Hamlet

> How chances it they travel? Their residence,[515] both in reputation and profit, was better both ways.   320

Rosencrantz

> I think their inhibition comes by the means of the late innovation.[516]

---

[506] Meager welcome; during Lent no plays were performed in London.

[507] Overtook.

[508] Sword and shield.

[509] For free.

[510] One governed by "the humors," thus given to moodswings and eccentric behavior, a stock figure in drama.

[511] Unhindered.

[512] The comic character; the jester.

[513] Sere: the part of the gunlock which holds the trigger in place; thus: those whose prompt to laughter is on a hair trigger.

[514] Players; actors.

[515] The place where they usually performed, opposed to being on tour.

[516] Maybe a reference to Fortinbras' "rebellion"—London theaters were

Hamlet

> Do they hold the same estimation[517] they did when I was in
> the city? Are they so followed?

Rosencrantz

> No, indeed are they not.   325

Hamlet

> How comes it? Do they grow rusty?

Rosencrantz

> Nay, their endeavour keeps in the wonted pace.[518] But
> there is, sir, an eyrie of children, little eyases,[519] that cry out
> on the top of question,[520] and are most tyrannically[521]
> clapped for't. These are now the fashion, and so berattle 330
> the common stages,[522] so they call them, that many wear-
> ing rapiers are afraid of goose-quills and dare scarce come
> thither.[523]

Hamlet

> What, are they children? Who maintains'em? How are they
> escoted?[524] Will they pursue the quality[525] no longer than 335
> they can sing?[526] Will they not say afterwards, if they should
> grow themselves to common players, as it is most like,[527]

---

usually closed during periods of public unrest; or maybe a topical allusion
to the new craze for companies of boy actors (see introduction to *Hamlet*).
[517] High esteem.

[518] Their efforts are as great as before.

[519] Eyrie = nest of a bird of prey; eyas= a young hawk; topical allusion to
the Children of the Chapel, laying at Blackfriars Theatre 1600-1608.

[520] As contentiously as possible.

[521] Excessively.

[522] Noisily assault the public playhouses (such as The Globe).

[523] The pen is mightier than the sword! Gentlemen are afraid to come to public
playhouses and thus expose themselves to being speared on a poet's pen.

[524] Provided for.

[525] Profession.

[526] I.e, until their voices break.

[527] Likely.

if their means are no better,[528] their writers do them wrong,

to make them exclaim against their own succession?[529]

Rosencrantz

'Faith, there has been much to do on both sides, and the   340
nation[530] holds it no sin to tar[531] them to controversy. There
was, for a while, no money bid for argument, unless the
poet and the player went to cuffs in the question.[532]

Hamlet

Is't possible?

Guildenstern

O, there has been much throwing about of brains.[533]   345

Hamlet

Do the boys carry it away?[534]

Rosencrantz

Ay, that they do, my lord, Hercules and his load too.[535]

Hamlet

It is not very strange, for mine uncle is King of Denmark, and those that would make mows[536] at him while
my father lived, give twenty, forty, fifty, an hundred duc-   350
ats[537] a-piece for his picture in little.[538] 'Sblood,[539] there is
something in this more than natural, if philosophy could
find it out.

---

[528] If they have no better way of earning a living.

[529] Contend against the end they must come to.

[530] People.

[531] Incite, like dogs to a dog fight.

[532] No new drama written that did not add fuel to this fire was paid for.

[533] A great battle of wits.

[534] Win the day.

[535] Hercules bearing the world on his shoulders was the sign of The Globe
Theatre; one of Hercules' labors was to relieve Atlas for a while.

[536] Pull faces.

[537] Generic name for a gold coin in much of Europe.

[538] In miniature.

[539] By God's blood.

Flourish of trumpets[540]

Guildenstern

> There are the players.

Hamlet

> Gentlemen, you are welcome to Elsinore. Your hands, 355
> come then. The appurtenance[541] of welcome is fashion
> and ceremony. Let me comply with you in this garb,[542] lest
> my extent[543] to the players—which, I tell you, must show
> fairly[544] outward—should more appear like entertain-
> ment[545] than yours. You are welcome. But my uncle-fa- 360
> ther and aunt-mother are deceived.

Guildenstern

> In what, my dear lord?

Hamlet

> I am but mad north-north-west. When the wind is
> southerly, I know a hawk from a handsaw.[546]

Enter Polonius

Lord Polonius

> Well be with you, gentlemen!   365

Hamlet

> Hark you, Guildenstern; and you too—at each ear a
> hearer—that great baby you see there is not yet out of his
> swaddling-clouts.[547]

[540] Players usually announced performance by trumpet calls.

[541] Fitting companion.

[542] Fashion (of shaking hands).

[543] Offer of welcome.

[544] Mannerly.

[545] Kind welcome.

[546] "My madness fluctuates with the winds"; North-north-west = the compass point closest to true north; southerly = furthest away from north.

[547] Swaddling clothes.

Rosencrantz

>Happily[548] he's the second time come to them; for they
>say an old man is twice a child.   370

Hamlet

>I will prophesy he comes to tell me of the players. Mark
>it.—You say right, sir, a Monday morning, 'twas so in-
>deed.

Lord Polonius

>My lord, I have news to tell you.

Hamlet

>My lord, I have news to tell you.   375
>When Roscius[549] was an actor in Rome—

Lord Polonius

>The actors are come hither, my lord.

Hamlet

>Buzz,[550] buzz!

Lord Polonius

>Upon mine honour—

Hamlet

>Then came each actor on his ass.   380

Lord Polonius

>The best actors in the world, either for tragedy, comedy,
>history, pastoral, pastoral-comical, historical-pastoral, tragi-
>cal-historical, tragical-comical-historical-pastoral, scene
>individable,[551] or poem unlimited.[552] Seneca[553] cannot be
>too heavy, nor Plautus[554] too light. For the law of writ 385

---

[548] Perhaps; maybe.

[549] The most famous actor of antiquity.

[550] Exclamation of contempt.

[551] Possibly: play uninterrupted by breaks for scenes.

[552] Unrestricted (by classical rules).

[553] Famous writer of tragedies in ancient Rome.

[554] Famous writer of comedies in ancient Rome.

and the liberty,[555] these are the only men.

Hamlet

O Jephthah, judge of Israel,[556] what a treasure hadst thou!

Lord Polonius

What a treasure had he, my lord?

Hamlet

Why, 'One fair daughter and no more,

The which he loved passing[557] well.'   390

Lord Polonius (*aside*)

Still on my daughter.

Hamlet

Am I not i'the right, old Jephthah?

Lord Polonius

If you call me Jephthah, my lord, I have a daughter that I

love passing well.

Hamlet

Nay, that follows not.   395

Lord Polonius

What follows, then, my lord?

Hamlet

Why, 'As by lot, God wot,' and then, you know, 'It came

to pass, as most like[558] it was.' The first row[559] of the pi-

ous chanson[560] will show you more, for look, where my

abridgement[561] comes.   400

---

[555] For plays that either do or do not observe classical rules.

[556] Judges xi.30-40. Jephthah swore to sacrifice the first living thing he saw, should he be granted victory over the Ammonites; he saw his daughter. The subject of a contemporary ballad, from which Hamlet now quotes.

[557] Extremely.

[558] Likely.

[559] Stanza.

[560] Ballad with religious subject matter.

[561] 1) That which cuts me short; 2) my entertainment.

Enter four or five Players

You are welcome, masters, welcome all. I am glad to see
thee well. Welcome, good friends. O, my old friend! Thy
face is valanced[562] since I saw thee last. Comest thou to
beard[563] me in Denmark? What, my young lady and mistress! By'r lady, your ladyship is nearer to heaven than when 405
I saw you last by the altitude of a chopine.[564] Pray God,
your voice, like a piece of uncurrent gold, be not cracked
within the ring.[565] Masters, you are all welcome. We'll e'en
to't like French falconers,[566] fly at any thing we see. We'll
have a speech straight.[567] Come, give us a taste of your 410
quality.[568] Come, a passionate speech.

First Player

What speech, my lord?

Hamlet

I heard thee speak me a speech once, but it was never
acted, or, if it was, not above once, for the play, I remember, pleased not the million. 'Twas caviare to the 415
general.[569] But it was, as I received it, and others, whose
judgments in such matters cried in the top of mine,[570] an

---

[562] Fringed, draped (with a beard).

[563] Oppose.

[564] Lady's platform shoe.

[565] A bit was often snipped off gold coins if only a little value was needed;
if the cut broke the ring around the sovereign's head, the coin was no
longer legal tender.

[566] A falcon is trained to fly at one specific type of prey. It is no compliment
to the French falconers that they let loose their bird at anything the hunter
sees.

[567] At once.

[568] Professional skill.

[569] General population.

[570] Confirmed my opinion with better authority.

excellent play, well digested[571] in the scenes, set down with
as much modesty[572] as cunning. I remember, one said there
were no sallets[573] in the lines to make the matter savoury, 420
nor no matter in the phrase that might indict the author
of affection, but called it an honest method, as wholesome as sweet, and by very much more handsome than
fine.[574] One speech in it I chiefly loved; 'twas Aeneas' tale
to Dido, and thereabout of it especially where he speaks 425
of Priam's slaughter.[575] If it live in your memory, begin at
this line—let me see, let me see—
The rugged[576] *Pyrrhus*[577], *like the Hyrcanian beast,*[578]—
'T is not so. It begins with Pyrrhus—
The rugged Pyrrhus, he whose sable[579] *arms,*   430
Black as his purpose, did the night resemble
When he lay couched[580] *in the ominous horse,*
Hath now this dread and black complexion[581] *smeared*
With heraldry[582] *more dismal. Head to foot*
Now is he total gules,[583] *horridly tricked*[584]   435
With blood of fathers, mothers, daughters, sons,

---

[571] Shaped.

[572] Proper style.

[573] Tasty, sharp morsels, i.e. bawdy.

[574] With more natural grace than affected art.

[575] The part of *The Aeneid*, and apparently this play, where Aeneas, whose
ships are being repaired at Carthage, tells Queen Dido of the sack of Troy,
especially of King Priam's murder.

[576] Savage.

[577] One of the Greek warriors in the Trojan Horse.

[578] The tiger.

[579] Black.

[580] Concealed.

[581] Refers to the appearance of the entire warrior, not just the face.

[582] Heraldic colors.

[583] Heraldic red.

[584] Delineated.

Baked and impasted with the parching streets,[585]
That lend a tyrannous and damned light
To their lord's murder. Roasted in wrath and fire,
And thus o'er-sized[586] with coagulate gore,   440
With eyes like carbuncles,[587] the hellish Pyrrhus
Old grandsire Priam seeks.

So, proceed you.

Lord Polonius

'Fore God, my lord, well spoken, with good accent and
good discretion.

First Player   *Anon*[588] *he finds him*   445
Striking too short at Greeks. His antique sword,
Rebellious to his arm, lies where it falls,
Repugnant[589] to command. Unequal matched,
Pyrrhus at Priam drives, in rage strikes wide;
But with the whiff and wind of his fell[590] sword   450
The unnerved[591] father falls. Then senseless Ilium[592]
Seeming to feel this blow, with flaming top
Stoops to his base, and with a hideous crash
Takes prisoner Pyrrhus' ear. For, lo! His sword,
Which was declining[593] on the milky[594] head   455
Of reverend Priam, seemed i'the air to stick.
So, as a painted tyrant,[595] Pyrrhus stood,

---

[585] The heat of the burning town bakes the blood upon him into a crust.

[586] Smeared with size as when preparing a canvas.

[587] Red gemstones, supposed to glow from within with their own fire.

[588] Soon.

[589] Rebellious.

[590] Fierce.

[591] Feeble.

[592] The inanimate citadel of Troy.

[593] Falling.

[594] White.

[595] A tyrant in a painting, thus not capable of action.

And, like a neutral to his will and matter,[596]
Did nothing.
But, as we often see, against[597] *some storm,*   460
A silence in the heavens, the rack[598] *stand still,*
The bold winds speechless and the orb[599] *below*
As hush as death, anon the dreadful thunder
Doth rend the region, so, after Pyrrhus' pause,
Aroused vengeance sets him new a-work,   465
And never did the Cyclops'[600] *hammers fall*
On Mars's armour forged for proof eterne[601]
With less remorse[602] *than Pyrrhus' bleeding sword*
Now falls on Priam.
Out, out, thou strumpet Fortune! All you gods,   470
In general synod, take away her power,
Break all the spokes and fellies[603] *from her wheel,*
And bowl the round nave[604] *down the hill of heaven,*
As low as to the fiends!

Lord Polonius

This is too long.   475

Hamlet

It shall to the barber's, with your beard. Prithee, say on.
He's for a jig[605] or a tale of bawdry, or he sleeps. Say on,

---

[596] Suspended, seemingly indifferent to what he wanted and what he was at.

[597] Before.

[598] Mass of clouds.

[599] Earth.

[600] One-eyed servants of Vulcan, the god of metalworking.

[601] Everlasting impenetrable quality.

[602] Compassion.

[603] Sections of wheel rim.

[604] Hub.

[605] Farcical (song and) dance following a dramatic performance and not related to it in content.

come to Hecuba.[606]

First Player

But who, O, who had seen the mobbled[607] Queen—

Hamlet

'The mobbled Queen?'   480

Lord Polonius

That's good; 'mobbled Queen' is good.

First Player

Run barefoot up and down, threatening the flames
With bisson rheum,[608] a clout[609] upon that head
Where late the diadem stood, and for a robe,
About her lank and all o'er-teemed[610] loins,   485
A blanket, in the alarm of fear caught up—
Who this had seen, with tongue in venom steeped,
'Gainst Fortune's state would treason have pronounced.
But if the gods themselves did see her then,
When she saw Pyrrhus make malicious sport   490
In mincing with his sword her husband's limbs,
The instant burst of clamour that she made,
Unless things mortal move them not at all,
Would have made milch the burning eyes of heaven,[611]
And passion[612] in the gods.   495

Lord Polonius

Look, whether he has not turned his colour and has tears
in's eyes. Prithee, no more.

Hamlet

'Tis well. I'll have thee speak out the rest soon. Good my

---

[606] Priam's queen, an emblem of sorrowing womanhood.
[607] With face covered in a scarf.
[608] Blinding tears.
[609] Cloth; scarf.
[610] Worn out with childbearing.
[611] Would have moistened heaven's eye with the milk of tears.
[612] Compassion.

lord, will you see the players well bestowed?[613] Do you
hear, let them be well used,[614] for they are the abstract[615] 500
and brief chronicles of the time. After your death you
were better have a bad epitaph than their ill report while
you live.

Lord Polonius

My lord, I will use them according to their desert.

Hamlet

God's bodkin, man, much better! Use every man after his 505
desert,[616] and who should 'scape whipping? Use them after your own honour and dignity. The less they deserve,
the more merit is in your bounty. Take them in.

Lord Polonius

Come, sirs.

Hamlet

Follow him, friends. We'll hear a play tomorrow.   510
Dost thou hear me, old friend? Can you play *The
Murder of Gonzago*?

First Player

Ay, my lord.

Hamlet

We'll ha't[617] tomorrow night. You could, for a need,[618]
study a speech of some dozen or sixteen lines, which I 515
would set down and insert in't, could you not?

First Player

Ay, my lord.

Hamlet

Very well. Follow that lord; and look you mock him not.

---

[613] Lodged.

[614] Treated.

[615] Brief report.

[616] As he deserves.

[617] Have it.

[618] If needed.

Exit Polonius with all the Players

(*To Rosencrantz and Guildenstern*) My good friends, I'll leave
  you till night. You are welcome to Elsinore.   520
Rosencrantz
  Good my lord!
Hamlet
  Ay, so, God be wi'ye.

Exeunt Rosencrantz and Guildenstern

  Now I am alone.
O, what a rogue and peasant[619] slave am I!
Is it not monstrous that this player here,
But in a fiction, in a dream of passion,   525
Could force his soul so to his own conceit[620]
That from her[621] working all his visage wanned,[622]
Tears in his eyes, distraction in's aspect,
A broken voice, and his whole function suiting
With forms to his conceit? And all for nothing!   530
For Hecuba!
What's Hecuba to him, or he to Hecuba,
That he should weep for her? What would he do,
Had he the motive and the cue for passion
That I have? He would drown the stage with tears   535
And cleave the general ear[623] with horrid speech,
Make mad the guilty and appal the free,[624]
Confound the ignorant, and amaze[625] indeed
The very faculties of eyes and ears.
Yet I,   540

---

[619] Base.

[620] Play so well that what his mind conceived seemed to become reality.

[621] The soul is seen as female.

[622] Paled.

[623] Everybody's ear.

[624] Guiltless.

[625] Shock; confuse.

A dull and muddy-mettled[626] rascal, peak,[627]
Like John-a-dreams,[628] unpregnant of[629] my cause,
And can say nothing—no, not for a King,
Upon whose property[630] and most dear life
A damned defeat[631] was made. Am I a coward?   545
Who calls me villain, breaks my pate[632] across,
Plucks off my beard and blows it in my face,
Tweaks me by the nose, gives me the lie i'the throat,
As deep as to the lungs?[633] Who does me this?
Ha!   550
'Swounds,[634] I should take it, for it cannot be
But I am pigeon-livered and lack gall[635]
To make oppression bitter, or ere this
I should ha' fatted all the region kites[636]
With this slave's offal! Bloody, bawdy villain!   555
Remorseless,[637] treacherous, lecherous, kindless villain!
Why, what an ass am I! This is most brave,[638]
That I, the son of a dear father murdered,
Prompted to my revenge by heaven and hell,
Must, like a whore, unpack my heart with words,   560

[626] Dull-spirited.
[627] Languish.
[628] A day-dreaming fellow.
[629] Not awakened to action by.
[630] "Proper person" and all that goes with it such as, here, kingship.
[631] Destruction.
[632] Head.
[633] Accuses me of being an out-and-out liar.
[634] By God's wounds.
[635] Pigeons, the symbol of meekness, were thought not to secrete gall, which, within the liver, was thought the origin of anger and bitterness.
[636] A kite is a small bird of prey that also exists on carrion, and its region is the air: all the kites in the air.
[637] This word also means pitiless.
[638] Admirable.

And fall a-cursing, like a very drab,[639]
A scullion![640] Fie upon't! Foh! About, my brain!
I have heard that guilty creatures sitting at a play
Have by the very cunning[641] of the scene
Been struck so to the soul that presently[642]   565
They have proclaimed their malefactions.
For murder, though it have no tongue, will speak
With most miraculous organ. I'll have these players
Play something like the murder of my father
Before mine uncle. I'll observe his looks,   570
I'll tent[643] him to the quick. If he but blench,
I know my course. The spirit that I have seen
May be the devil, and the devil hath power
T'assume a pleasing shape; yea, and perhaps
Out of my weakness and my melancholy,   575
As he is very potent with such spirits,[644]
Abuses[645] me to damn me. I'll have grounds
More relative[646] than this. The play's the thing
Wherein I'll catch the conscience of the King.   *Exit*

---

[639] Whore.

[640] Servant in the kitchen.

[641] Art; ingenuity.

[642] At once.

[643] Probe; a tent is a medical instrument for cleansing wounds.

[644] The melancholiac was prone to hallucinations, therefore an easy target for the devil to tempt.

[645] Deludes.

[646] Relevant; material.

Act III, Scene i

Enter King Claudius, Queen Gertrude, Lord Polonius, Ophelia, Rosencrantz
and Guildenstern, and Lords

King Claudius

    And can you, by no drift of circumstance,[647]

    Get from him why he puts on this confusion,

    Grating so harshly all his days of quiet

    With turbulent and dangerous lunacy?

Rosencrantz

    He does confess he feels himself distracted,[648]   5

    But from what cause he will by no means speak.

Guildenstern

    Nor do we find him forward to be sounded,[649]

    But, with a crafty madness, keeps aloof,

    When we would bring him on to some confession

    Of his true state.

Queen Gertrude   Did he receive you well?   10

Rosencrantz

    Most like a gentleman.

Guildenstern

    But with much forcing of his disposition.[650]

Rosencrantz

    Niggard of question,[651] but of our demands,[652]

    Most free in his reply.

---

[647] Course of conversation.

[648] Confused in his wits.

[649] Eager to be examined.

[650] Inclination; mood.

[651] Reluctant to converse.

[652] When we asked him.

Queen Gertrude   Did you assay him[653]

    To any pastime?   15

Rosencrantz

    Madam, it so fell out, that certain players

    We o'er-raught[654] on the way. Of these we told him,

    And there did seem in him a kind of joy

    To hear of it. They are about the court,

    And, as I think, they have already order   20

    This night to play before him.

Lord Polonius   'Tis most true,

    And he beseeched me to entreat your majesties

    To hear and see the matter.

King Claudius

    With all my heart. And it doth much content me

    To hear him so inclined.   25

    Good gentlemen, give him a further edge,[655]

    And drive his purpose on to these delights.

Rosencrantz

    We shall, my lord.   *Exeunt Rosencrantz and Guildenstern*

King Claudius   Sweet Gertrude, leave us too,

    For we have closely[656] sent for Hamlet hither,

    That he, as 'twere by accident, may here   30

    Affront[657] Ophelia.

    Her father and myself, lawful espials,[658]

    Will so bestow ourselves that, seeing unseen,

    We may of their encounter frankly judge,

    And gather by him, as he is behaved,   35

    If't be th'affliction of his love or no

---

[653] Did he seem as if he were inclined.

[654] Overtook.

[655] Spur him on; egg him on.

[656] Privately; secretly.

[657] Come face to face with.

[658] Spies.

That thus he suffers for.

Queen Gertrude　　　　　　　　I shall obey you.
　And for your part, Ophelia, I do wish
　That your good beauties be the happy cause
　Of Hamlet's wildness; so shall I hope your virtues　　40
　Will bring him to his wonted[659] way again,
　To both your honours.

Ophelia　　　　　　　　Madam, I wish it may.

Exit Queen Gertrude

Lord Polonius
　Ophelia, walk you here. Gracious, so please you.
　We will bestow ourselves. (*To Ophelia*) Read on this book,
　That show of such an exercise may colour　　45
　Your loneliness.[660]—We are oft to blame in this,
　'Tis too much proved[661] that with devotion's visage
　And pious action we do sugar o'er
　The devil himself.

King Claudius (*aside*)　　O, 'tis too true!
　How smart[662] a lash that speech doth give my conscience 50
　The harlot's cheek, beautied with plastering[663] art,
　Is not more ugly to the thing that helps it[664]
　Than is my deed to my most painted word.
　O heavy burden!

Lord Polonius
　I hear him coming; let's withdraw, my lord.　　55

Exeunt King Claudius and Polonius

[659] Usual.

[660] A woman alone reading a book was an icon of devotion.

[661] Tested by experience.

[662] Stinging.

[663] Using make-up and other beauty aides to cover blemishes.

[664] In comparison with the artificial cover of make-up.

Enter Hamlet

Hamlet

    To be, or not to be, that is the question:
    Whether 'tis nobler in the mind to suffer
    The slings and arrows of outrageous[665] fortune,
    Or to take arms against a sea of troubles,
    And by opposing, end them? To die—to sleep,   60
    No more; and by a sleep to say we end
    The heartache and the thousand natural shocks
    That flesh is heir to. 'Tis a consummation[666]
    Devoutly to be wished. To die, to sleep.
    To sleep, perchance to dream. Ay, there's the rub;[667]   65
    For in that sleep of death what dreams may come
    When we have shuffled off[668] this mortal coil,[669]
    Must give us pause. There's the respect[670]
    That makes calamity of so long life.[671]
    For who would bear the whips and scorns of time,   70
    The oppressor's wrong, the proud man's contumely,[672]
    The pangs of disprized[673] love, the law's delay,
    The insolence of office,[674] and the spurns[675]
    That patient merit of the unworthy takes,

[665] Unprincipled; unruly.
[666] Final ending.
[667] Obstacle.
[668] Sloughed.
[669] Body; turmoil of life.
[670] Consideration.
[671] Makes adversity so long-lived/makes a long life "a calamity."
[672] Abuse.
[673] Unvalued.
[674] I.e., people who hold office; bureaucrats.
[675] Hurts.

When he himself might his quietus[676] make 75
With a bare bodkin?[677] Who would fardels[678] bear,
To grunt and sweat under a weary life,
But that the dread of something after death,
The undiscovered country from whose bourn[679]
No traveller returns, puzzles the will 80
And makes us rather bear those ills we have
Than fly to others that we know not of?
Thus conscience[680] does make cowards of us all,
And thus the native hue[681] of resolution
Is sicklied o'er with the pale cast[682] of thought, 85
And enterprises of great pith[683] and moment
With this regard[684] their currents turn awry,
And lose the name of action. Soft you now![685]
The fair Ophelia!—Nymph, in thy orisons[686]
Be all my sins remembered.

Ophelia   Good my lord, 90
How does your honour for this many a day?

Hamlet
I humbly thank you, well, well, well.

Ophelia
My lord, I have remembrances of yours,

---

[676] *Quietus est* (Latin: laid to rest), was marked when an account was paid in full.

[677] A short dagger.

[678] Burdens; "packs."

[679] Border.

[680] 1) Natural faculty of knowing and understanding; 2) moral conscience.

[681] True color; resolution is "sanguinary" (see glossary: Four Humours), therefore red.

[682] Coloration.

[683] I.e., the highest point of a falcon's flight; thus: great importance.

[684] When considered.

[685] How now! (exclamation of surprise).

[686] Prayers.

That I have longed long to redeliver.
I pray you, now receive them.

Hamlet   No, not I.   95

I never gave you aught.

Ophelia

My honoured lord, you know right well you did,
And with them, words of so sweet breath composed
As made the things more rich. Their perfume lost,
Take these again; for to the noble mind   100
Rich gifts wax[687] poor when givers prove unkind.
There, my lord.

Hamlet

Ha, ha! Are you honest?[688]

Ophelia

My lord?

Hamlet

Are you fair?   105

Ophelia

What means your lordship?

Hamlet

That if you be honest and fair, your honesty should admit
no discourse to your beauty.[689]

Ophelia

Could beauty, my lord, have better commerce[690] than with
honesty?   110

Hamlet

Ay, truly, for the power of beauty will sooner transform
honesty from what it is to a bawd than the force of hon-

---

[687] Grow.

[688] 1) Truthful; 2) chaste.

[689] 1) Your chastity should allow nobody access to your beauty; 2) your
chastity should permit no close association with your beauty, for in the
association of beauty and chastity, chastity will suffer.

[690] "Intercourse" in all meanings.

esty can translate beauty into his[691] likeness. This was some-
time a paradox, but now the time[692] gives it proof. I did
love you once. 115

Ophelia

Indeed, my lord, you made me believe so.

Hamlet

You should not have believed me; for virtue cannot so
inoculate[693] our old stock but we shall relish of it. I loved
you not.

Ophelia

I was the more deceived. 120

Hamlet

Get thee to a nunnery.[694] Why wouldst thou be a breeder
of sinners? I am myself indifferent honest.[695] But yet I
could accuse me of such things that it were better my
mother had not borne me. I am very proud, revengeful,
ambitious, with more offences at my beck[696] than I have 125
thoughts to put them in, imagination to give them shape,
or time to act them in. What should such fellows as I do
crawling between earth and heaven? We are arrant[697]
knaves, all. Believe none of us. Go thy ways to a nunnery.
Where's your father? 130

Ophelia

At home, my lord.

---

[691] I.e., honesty's.

[692] The present age.

[693] Graft (horticultural term). If you graft honesty onto our original, sinful
nature, we shall still "taste" of sin; relish = taste.

[694] 1) House of devotion where her chastity would be preserved; 2) house
of "unchastity," brothel.

[695] Somewhat virtuous.

[696] Command (beck and call).

[697] Complete.

Hamlet

> Let the doors be shut upon him, that he may play the fool
> nowhere but in's own house. Farewell.

Ophelia

> O, help him, you sweet heavens!

Hamlet

> If thou dost marry, I'll give thee this plague for thy dowry: 135
> be thou as chaste as ice, as pure as snow, thou shalt not
> escape calumny. Get thee to a nunnery, go, farewell. Or if
> thou wilt needs marry, marry a fool; for wise men know
> well enough what monsters[698] you make of them. To a
> nunnery, go, and quickly too. Farewell.   140

Ophelia

> O heavenly powers, restore him!

Hamlet

> I have heard of your paintings[699] too, well enough. God
> hath given you one face, and you make yourselves an-
> other. You jig and amble,[700] and you lisp,[701] and nickname
> God's creatures,[702] and make your wantonness your igno- 145
> rance.[703] Go to, I'll no more on't. It hath made me mad. I
> say, we will have no more marriages. Those that are mar-
> ried already—all but one—shall live. The rest shall keep as
> they are. To a nunnery, go.   *Exit*

Ophelia

> O, what a noble mind is here o'erthrown!   150

---

[698] Cuckolds were thought of as growing horns, a visible proof of their state.

[699] Use of cosmetic aides.

[700] Both are dancesteps, an unnatural way to walk.

[701] Speak artificially.

[702] Find new and fashionable names instead of natural ones.

[703] You pretend your affected actions, of which you are fully aware, are due to ignorance.

The courtier's, soldier's, scholar's, eye, tongue, sword,
The expectancy and rose of the fair state,
The glass[704] of fashion and the mould of form,[705]
The observed of all observers, quite, quite down!
And I, of ladies most deject and wretched,   155
That sucked the honey of his music vows,
Now see that noble and most sovereign reason,
Like sweet bells jangled, out of tune and harsh;
That unmatched form and feature of blown[706] youth
Blasted[707] with ecstasy.[708] O, woe is me,   160
T'have seen what I have seen, see what I see!

Re-enter King Claudius and Polonius

King Claudius
    Love? His affections do not that way tend,
    Nor what he spake, though it lacked form a little,
    Was not like madness. There's something in his soul,
    O'er which his melancholy sits on brood,   165
    And I do doubt[709] the hatch and the disclose[710]
    Will be some danger; which for to prevent,
    I have in quick determination
    Thus set it down:[711] he shall with speed to England
    For the demand of our neglected tribute.   170
    Haply the seas and countries different

---

[704] Mirror.

[705] Pattern of correct behavior.

[706] In full bloom.

[707] Withered; cursed.

[708] Madness.

[709] Fear.

[710] Hatch = disclose: what is revealed when the chick breaks through the eggshell (see "brood" l.168); i.e., "disclosure to be publicly seen."

[711] Decided.

With variable objects[712] shall expel
This something-settled[713] matter in his heart,
Whereon his brains still[714] beating puts him thus
From fashion of himself.[715] What think you on't?   175

Lord Polonius

It shall do well. But yet do I believe
The origin and commencement of his grief
Sprung from neglected[716] love. How now, Ophelia!
You need not tell us what Lord Hamlet said,
We heard it all. My lord, do as you please,   180
But, if you hold it fit, after the play
Let his Queen mother all alone entreat him
To show his grief. Let her be round[717] with him,
And I'll be placed, so please you, in the ear[718]
Of all their conference. If she find him not,[719]   185
To England send him, or confine him where
Your wisdom best shall think.

King Claudius   It shall be so.
Madness in great ones must not unwatched go.   *Exeunt*

Act III, Scene ii

Enter Hamlet and three of the Players

---

[712] Different things to see and do.

[713] Which has to some degree taken root.

[714] Constantly.

[715] His normal ways.

[716] Unrequited.

[717] Direct.

[718] Within hearing.

[719] If she cannot find out the truth about him.

Hamlet

> Speak the speech, I pray you, as I pronounced it to you,
> trippingly on the tongue. But if you mouth it,[720] as many
> of your players do, I had as lief[721] the town-crier spoke
> my lines. Nor do not saw the air too much with your
> hand, thus, but use all gently; for in the very torrent, tem-   5
> pest, and, as I may say, whirlwind of your passion, you
> must acquire and beget a temperance that may give it
> smoothness. O, it offends me to the soul to hear a
> robustious[722] periwig-pated[723] fellow tear a passion to tat-
> ters, to very rags, to split the ears of the groundlings,[724]   10
> who for the most part are capable of nothing but inex-
> plicable dumbshows[725] and noise. I would have such a
> fellow whipped for o'erdoing Termagant.[726] It out-Herods
> Herod.[727] Pray you, avoid it.

First Player

> I warrant[728] your honour.   15

Hamlet

> Be not too tame neither, but let your own discretion be
> your tutor. Suit the action to the word, the word to the
> action, with this special observance, that you o'erstep not
> the modesty[729] of nature. For any thing so overdone is from[730]

[720] Use exaggerated mannerisms.

[721] As well.

[722] Exaggeratedly bombastic.

[723] Wearing a wig; wigs were then a stage prop, not worn in society.

[724] Those standing at ground level, having the cheapest admission.

[725] See glossary.

[726] A noisy Mystery Play character.

[727] The Biblical Herod, another Mystery Play character, always ranted and raved.

[728] Promise.

[729] Moderation.

[730] At variance with.

the purpose of playing, whose end, both at the first and   20
now, was and is to hold, as 'twere, the mirror up to nature, to show virtue her own feature, scorn her own image, and the very age and body of the time his form and
pressure.[731] Now this overdone, or come tardy off,[732]
though it make the unskilful[733] laugh, cannot but make the   25
judicious grieve, the censure of the which one[734] must in
your allowance o'erweigh a whole theatre of others. O,
there be players that I have seen play, and heard others
praise, and that highly, not to speak it profanely,[735] that,
neither having the accent of Christians nor the gait of   30
Christian, pagan, nor man, have so strutted and bellowed
that I have thought some of nature's journeymen had
made men, and not made them well, they imitated hu-
manity so abominably.

First Player

I hope we have reformed that indifferently[736] with us, sir.   35

Hamlet

O, reform it altogether. And let those that play your clowns
speak no more than is set down for them; for there be of
them[737] that will themselves laugh, to set on[738] some quantity of barren[739] spectators to laugh too, though, in the
mean time, some necessary question of the play be then   40
to be considered. That's villanous, and shows a most piti-

---

[731] True picture, as seen in the seal or signet's impression in wax.

[732] Inadequately accomplished.

[733] The undiscriminating; "the groundlings."

[734] I.e., of the discriminating, the judicious.

[735] In blasphemy; he goes on to speak of players created not by God, but by craftsmen.

[736] Somewhat.

[737] Those among them.

[738] Urge.

[739] Ignorant.

ful ambition in the fool that uses it. Go, make you ready.

Exeunt Players

Enter Polonius, Rosencrantz, and Guildenstern

How now, my lord! Will the King hear this piece of work?
Lord Polonius

And the Queen too, and that presently.[740]
Hamlet

Bid the players make haste.   *Exit Polonius* 45

Will you two help to hasten them?
Rosencrantz and Guildenstern   We will, my lord.

Exeunt Rosencrantz and Guildenstern

Hamlet

What ho! Horatio!

Enter Horatio

Horatio   Here, sweet lord, at your service.
Hamlet

Horatio, thou art e'en as just[741] a man

As e'er my conversation[742] coped[743] withal.
Horatio

O, my dear lord,—
Hamlet   Nay, do not think I flatter,   50

For what advancement[744] may I hope from thee

That no revenue hast but thy good spirits

To feed and clothe thee? Why should the poor be flattered?

No, let the candied[745] tongue lick absurd pomp,

---

[740] At once.

[741] With all four humors in balance (see glossary: Four Humors).

[742] Dealings in general.

[743] Met with; encountered.

[744] Favors.

[745] Sugary, i.e., flattering.

And crook the pregnant hinges of the knee[746]   55
Where thrift may follow fawning.[747] Dost thou hear?
Since my dear soul was mistress of her choice[748]
And could of men distinguish,[749] her election
Hath sealed thee for herself;[750] for thou hast been
As one in suffering all that suffers nothing,[751]   60
A man that Fortune's buffets and rewards
Hast ta'en with equal thanks. And blest are those
Whose blood[752] and judgment are so well commingled,
That they are not a pipe for Fortune's finger
To sound what stop she please. Give me that man   65
That is not passion's slave, and I will wear him
In my heart's core, ay, in my heart of heart,
As I do thee. Something too much of this.
There is a play tonight before the King,
One scene of it comes near the circumstance   70
Which I have told thee of my father's death.
I prithee, when thou seest that act afoot,
Even with the very comment of thy soul[753]
Observe mine uncle. If his occulted[754] guilt
Do not itself unkennel in one speech,   75
It is a damned ghost that we have seen,
And my imaginations are as foul
As Vulcan's stithy.[755] Give him heedful note,

---

[746] Knees ready to kneel.

[747] Where gain comes from flattery.

[748] Could choose informedly and deliberately.

[749] And was a good judge of men.

[750] Has chosen you.

[751] Gone through suffering without being essentially affected by it.

[752] Passion (see glossary: Blood).

[753] Giving it your utmost critical attention.

[754] Hidden.

[755] Smithy; Vulcan is the god of blacksmiths.

  For I mine eyes will rivet to his face,
  And after we will both our judgments join   80
  In censure of his seeming.
Horatio   Well, my lord.
  If he steal aught the whilst this play is playing,
  And 'scape detecting, I will pay the theft.

Enter trumpets and ketle-drums; sound a flourish

Hamlet

  They are coming to the play; I must be idle.[756]
  Get you a place.   85

Danish march. Enter King Claudius, Queen Gertrude, Lord Polonius, Ophelia, Rosencrantz, Guildenstern, and other Lords attending, with the King's Guard carrying torches

King Claudius

  How fares our cousin[757] Hamlet?

Hamlet

  Excellent, i'faith, of the chameleon's dish.[758] I eat the air,
  promise-crammed. You cannot feed capons[759] so.

King Claudius

  I have nothing with this answer, Hamlet. These words are
  not mine.   90

Hamlet

  No, nor mine now. (*To Polonius*) My lord, you played once
  i'the university, you say?

---

[756] 1) Be unoccupied; 2) act foolish.

[757] Kinsman.

[758] The chameleon was thought to feed on air (here: pun on heir); fares, l. 88: 1) does; 2) eats.

[759] Castrated cockerels, who, indeed, are "crammed" with food to fatten them for the table.

Lord Polonius

That did I, my lord, and was accounted a good actor.

Hamlet

What did you enact?

Lord Polonius

I did enact Julius Caesar. I was killed i'the Capitol. Brutus   95
killed me.[760]

Hamlet

It was a brute part of him to kill so capital a calf there. Be
the players ready?

Rosencrantz

Ay, my lord; they stay[761] upon your patience.

Queen Gertrude

Come hither, my dear Hamlet, sit by me.   100

Hamlet

No, good mother, here's metal more attractive.[762]

Sits by Ophelia

Lord Polonius (*to King Claudius*)

O, ho! Do you mark that?

Hamlet

Lady, shall I lie in your lap?

Ophelia

No, my lord.

Hamlet

I mean, my head upon your lap?   105

Ophelia

Ay, my lord.

---

[760] It is likely that, in an earlier production, the actor playing Polonius had
played Caesar, while Hamlet's actor had played Brutus.
[761] Wait.
[762] Of greater magnetic power.

Hamlet

Do you think I meant country matters?[763]

Ophelia

I think nothing, my lord.

Hamlet

That's a fair thought to lie between maids' legs.

Ophelia

What is, my lord?   110

Hamlet

Nothing.

Ophelia

You are merry, my lord.

Hamlet

Who, I?

Ophelia

Ay, my lord.

Hamlet

O God, your only jig-maker![764] What should a man do 115
but be merry? For, look you, how cheerfully my mother
looks, and my father died within these two hours.

Ophelia

Nay, 'tis twice two months, my lord.

Hamlet

So long? Nay then, let the devil wear black, for I'll have a
suit of sables.[765] O heavens! Die two months ago, and not 120
forgotten yet? Then there's hope a great man's memory
may outlive his life half a year. But, by'r lady, he must

---

[763] "Rustic lovemaking" with a bawdy pun on cunt/country. Note also
"lie" in the previous lines, and "nothing" (0 = the shape of female genita-
lia)/"thing," slang for penis).

[764] Best ever comic actor. The company clown performed the jig after the
play proper

[765] 1) Expensive fur; 2) heraldic term for black, the color of mourning.

build churches then, or else shall he suffer not thinking
on,[766] with the hobby-horse, whose epitaph is 'For O, for
O, the hobby-horse is forgot.'[767]   125

*Hautboys play. The dumb-show enters. Enter a King and a Queen very
lovingly, the Queen embracing him, and he her. She kneels, and makes show of
protestation unto him. He takes her up, and declines[768] his head upon her
neck. He lays him down upon a bank of flowers. She, seeing him asleep, leaves
him. Anon comes in a fellow, takes off his crown, kisses it, and pours poison in
the King's ears, and exit. The Queen returns, finds the King dead, and makes
passionate action. The Poisoner, with some two or three Mutes,[769] comes in
again, seeming to lament with her. The dead body is carried away. The Poisoner wooes the Queen with gifts. She seems loath and unwilling a while, but in
the end accepts his love. Exeunt the dumb show.*

Ophelia

What means this, my lord?

Hamlet

Marry, this is miching mallecho.[770] It means mischief.

Ophelia

Belike this show imports the argument[771] of the play.

Enter Prologue

Hamlet

We shall know by this fellow. The players cannot keep
counsel,[772] they'll tell all.   130

---

[766] Settle for being forgotten.

[767] The hobby-horse is a figure in the morris dance and the May Day games,
at the time Hamlet was written under attack by religious reformers.

[768] Rests.

[769] Non-speaking actors.

[770] Stealthy evildoing.

[771] Subject.

[772] Keep a secret.

Ophelia

　　Will he tell us what this show meant?

Hamlet

　　Ay, or any show that you'll show him. Be not you ashamed

　　to show, he'll not shame to tell you what it means.

Ophelia

　　You are naught,[773] you are naught. I'll mark the play.

Prologue

　　For us, and for our tragedy,　　　　　　　　　　　　135

　　Here stooping to your clemency,

　　We beg your hearing patiently.　　　　　　　　　*Exit*

Hamlet

　　Is this a prologue, or the posy of a ring?[774]

Ophelia

　　'Tis brief, my lord.

Hamlet

　　As woman's love.　　　　　　　　　　　　　　　140

Enter two Players, King and Queen

Player King

　　Full thirty times hath Phoebus' cart[775] gone round

　　Neptune's salt wash[776] and Tellus' orbed ground,[777]

　　And thirty dozen moons with borrow'd sheen[778]

　　About the world have times twelve thirties been,

　　Since love our hearts and Hymen[779] did our hands　　145

　　Unite commutual in most sacred bands.

---

[773] Worthless; thus bad, improper.

[774] Short motto engraved in a ring.

[775] The sun's chariot.

[776] The sea.

[777] The earth.

[778] Reflected brightness.

[779] God of marriage.

Player Queen

    So many journeys may the sun and moon

    Make us again count o'er ere love be done!

    But, woe is me, you are so sick of late,

    So far from cheer and from your former state,   150

    That I distrust you.[780] Yet, though I distrust,

    Discomfort you, my lord, it nothing must,

    For women's fear and love holds quantity,[781]

    In neither aught, or in extremity.[782]

    Now, what my love is, proof[783] hath made you know,   155

    And as my love is sized,[784] my fear is so.

    Where love is great, the littlest doubts are fear.

    Where little fears grow great, great love grows there.

Player King

    Faith, I must leave thee, love, and shortly too.

    My operant powers[785] their functions leave[786] to do,   160

    And thou shalt live in this fair world behind,

    Honoured, beloved; and haply[787] one as kind

    For husband shalt thou—

Player Queen   O, confound the rest!

    Such love must needs be treason in my breast!

    In second husband let me be accurst!   165

    None wed the second but who kill'd the first.

Hamlet (*aside*)

    Wormwood,[788] wormwood.

---

[780] Worry about you.

[781] Are in proportion to each other.

[782] Either nothing or everything.

[783] Experience.

[784] The size/quantity of my love.

[785] Faculties.

[786] Cease.

[787] Perhaps.

[788] A bitter, medicinal herb = "a bitter pill to swallow."

Player Queen

> The instances[789] that second marriage move[790]
> Are base respects of thrift,[791] but none of love.
> A second time I kill my husband dead,   170
> When second husband kisses me in bed.

Player King

> I do believe you think what now you speak;
> But what we do determine oft we break.
> Purpose is but the slave to memory,
> Of violent birth, but poor validity,[792]   175
> Which now, like fruit unripe, sticks on the tree,
> But fall unshaken when they mellow be.
> Most necessary 'tis that we forget
> To pay ourselves what to ourselves is debt.[793]
> What to ourselves in passion we propose,   180
> The passion ending, doth the purpose lose.
> The violence of either grief or joy
> Their own enactures with themselves destroy.[794]
> Where joy most revels, grief doth most lament;
> Grief joys, joy grieves, on slender accident.[795]   185
> This world is not for aye,[796] nor 'tis not strange
> That even our loves should with our fortunes change.
> For 'tis a question left us yet to prove
> Whether love lead fortune, or else fortune love.

---

[789] Motives.

[790] Promote.

[791] Thoughts of advantages, monetary or social.

[792] Little strength.

[793] "For our well-being, it is necessary that we must forget such promises made to ourselves."

[794] "Extreme grief and joy are both self-destructive, and so they cannot motivate us to action."

[795] For a very little cause.

[796] Forever.

The great man down, you mark his favourite flies;   190
The poor advanced[797] makes friends of enemies.
And hitherto[798] doth love on fortune tend,[799]
For who not needs shall never lack a friend,
And who in want a hollow friend doth try
Directly seasons him[800] his enemy.   195
But, orderly to end where I begun,
Our wills and fates do so contrary[801] run
That our devices still are overthrown.
Our thoughts are ours, their ends[802] none of our own.
So think thou wilt no second husband wed,   200
But die thy thoughts when thy first lord is dead.

Player Queen

Nor earth to me give food, nor heaven light!
Sport and repose lock from me day and night!
To desperation turn my trust and hope!
An anchor's cheer[803] in prison be my scope![804]   205
Each opposite[805] that blanks[806] the face of joy
Meet what I would have well and it destroy!
Both here and hence pursue me lasting strife,
If, once a widow, ever I be wife!

Hamlet

If she should break it now!   210

---

[797] When socially advantaged.
[798] That far.
[799] Attend.
[800] Matures; hardens him into.
[801] Our wishes and our fate are often opposites.
[802] What results.
[803] The life of an anchorite.
[804] Expectation.
[805] Opposite force.
[806] Pales.

Player King

'Tis deeply sworn. Sweet, leave me here awhile.

My spirits grow dull, and fain[807] I would beguile

The tedious day with sleep.

Player Queen   Sleep rock thy brain,

And never come mischance between us twain!

Player King sleeps. Exit Player Queen

Hamlet

Madam, how like you this play?   215

Queen Gertrude

The lady protests too much, methinks.

Hamlet

O, but she'll keep her word.

King Claudius

Have you heard the argument?[808] Is there no offence in't?

Hamlet

No, no, they do but jest, poison in jest. No offence i'the

world.   220

King Claudius

What do you call the play?

Hamlet

The Mousetrap! Marry, how tropically![809] This play is the

image of a murder done in Vienna. Gonzago is the Duke's

name, his wife, Baptista. You shall see anon. 'Tis a knavish

piece of work, but what o' that? Your majesty and we 225

that have free[810] souls, it touches us not. Let the galled

jade[811] wince, our withers are unwrung.

---

[807] Happily.

[808] Plot.

[809] From "trope," rhetorical figure, hence: "what a metaphor!"

[810] Guiltless.

[811] The horse with raw saddle sores.

Enter Lucianus

    This is one Lucianus, nephew to the King.
Ophelia
    You are as good as a chorus,[812] my lord.
Hamlet
    I could interpret between you and your love, if I could 230
    see the puppets dallying.[813]
Ophelia
    You are keen,[814] my lord, you are keen.
Hamlet
    It would cost you a groaning to take off my edge.[815]
Ophelia
    Still better, and worse.[816]
Hamlet
    So you mis-take your husbands.[817] Begin, murderer!   235
    Pox, leave thy damnable faces, and begin. Come!
    'The croaking raven doth bellow for revenge.'
Lucianus
    Thoughts black, hands apt, drugs fit, and time agreeing,
    Confederate season,[818] else no creature seeing.
    Thou mixture rank,[819] of midnight weeds collected,   240

---

[812] Which interprets the action of the play.

[813] The "interpreter" in a puppet show is the one speaking as the puppets "act." Also go-between for lovers.

[814] Bitter; sharp.

[815] "Edge": 1) that on, e.g., a knife; 2) sexual appetite. A woman will "groan" as her maidenhead is ruptured.

[816] Keener and more obscene.

[817] A woman "takes" a man in marriage "for better, for worse," which often proves false as she cheats on him.

[818] Time my accomplice.

[819] Noisome.

With Hecate's[820] ban thrice blasted,[821] thrice infected,
Thy natural magic and dire property,[822]
On wholesome life usurp immediately.

Pours the poison into the sleeper's ears

Hamlet

He poisons him i'the garden for's estate. His name's
Gonzago. The story is extant, and writ in choice Italian. 245
You shall see anon how the murderer gets the love of
Gonzago's wife.

Ophelia

The King rises.

Hamlet

What, frighted with false fire![823]

Queen Gertrude

How fares my lord?   250

Lord Polonius

Give o'er the play.

King Claudius

Give me some light! Away!

All

Lights, lights, lights!

Exeunt all but Hamlet and Horatio

Hamlet

Why, let the stricken deer go weep,
        The hart ungalled[824] play;   255

---

[820] Goddess of witchcraft.
[821] Cursed.
[822] Inherent quality.
[823] A blank charge.
[824] Unhurt.

For some must watch,[825] while some must sleep,
So runs the world away.[826]
Would not this, sir, and a forest of feathers[827]—if the rest
of my fortunes turn Turk[828] with me—with two Provin-
cial roses[829] on my razed[830] shoes, get me a fellowship[831] in   260
a cry[832] of players, sir?

Horatio

Half a share.

Hamlet

A whole one, I!
For thou dost know, O Damon[833] dear,
This realm dismantled was   265
Of Jove himself; and now reigns here
A very, very—pajock.[834]

Horatio

You might have rhymed.

Hamlet

O good Horatio, I'll take the ghost's word for a thousand
pound. Didst perceive?   270

Horatio

Very well, my lord.

---

[825] Keep watch.

[826] Probably from a lost ballad. Deer were thought to weep when wounded.

[827] Flamboyant hats with feathers were often worn on stage.

[828] Play false (literally: become infidel).

[829] *Rose de Provençe*, the cabbage rose; here large rosettes to hide shoe fasten-
ings.

[830] Decorated with slashes.

[831] Membership (for profit).

[832] Troupe.

[833] Traditional, pastoral shepherd's name, associated with the golden age,
thus appropriate for Horatio who has golden-age qualities.

[834] 1) "Patchock," a low, rude, savage fellow; 2) peacock, the emblem of
pride. The rhyme, of course, would be "ass."

Hamlet

Upon the talk of the poisoning?

Horatio

I did very well note him.

Hamlet

Ah, ha! Come, some music! Come, the recorders!

For if the King like not the comedy,   275

Why then, belike, he likes it not, perdy.[835]

Come, some music!

Re-enter Rosencrantz and Guildenstern

Guildenstern

Good my lord, vouchsafe me a word with you.

Hamlet

Sir, a whole history.

Guildenstern

The King, sir—   280

Hamlet

Ay, sir, what of him?

Guildenstern

Is in his retirement marvellous distempered.[836]

Hamlet

With drink, sir?

Guildenstern

No, my lord, rather with choler.[837]

Hamlet

Your wisdom should show itself more richer[838] to signify 285

this to his doctor, for, for me to put him to his purga-

---

[835] *Pardieu* (French) = by God.

[836] Badly out of humor, temper. Hamlet interprets the term as "drunk."

[837] Anger; also, see glossary.

[838] More informed.

tion[839] would perhaps plunge him into far more choler.

Guildenstern

Good my lord, put your discourse into some frame[840]
and start[841] not so wildly from my affair.

Hamlet

I am tame, sir. Pronounce.   290

Guildenstern

The Queen, your mother, in most great affliction of spirit,
hath sent me to you.

Hamlet

You are welcome.

Guildenstern

Nay, good my lord, this courtesy is not of the right
breed.[842] If it shall please you to make me a wholesome[843] 295
answer, I will do your mother's commandment. If not,
your pardon[844] and my return shall be the end of my
business.

Hamlet

Sir, I cannot.

Guildenstern

What, my lord?   300

Hamlet

Make you a wholesome answer. My wit's diseased. But,
sir, such answer as I can make, you shall command, or
rather, as you say, my mother. Therefore no more, but to
the matter. My mother, you say?

---

[839] Cleansing; physically by bleeding him to remove the excess humor,
spiritually by hearing his confession.

[840] Order.

[841] Shy away.

[842] Kind.

[843] Sane.

[844] Permission to leave.

Rosencrantz

> Then thus she says: your behavior hath struck her into 305
> amzement and admiration.[845]

Hamlet

> O wonderful son, that can so astonish a mother! But is
> there no sequel at the heels of this mother's admiration?
> Impart.[846]

Rosencrantz

> She desires to speak with you in her closet[847] ere you go to 310
> bed.

Hamlet

> We shall obey, were she ten times our mother. Have you
> any further trade[848] with us?

Rosencrantz

> My lord, you once did love me.

Hamlet

> So I do still, by these pickers and stealers.[849]   315

Rosencrantz

> Good my lord, what is your cause of distemper? You do
> surely bar the door upon your own liberty if you deny
> your griefs to your friend.

Hamlet

> Sir, I lack advancement.

Rosencrantz

> How can that be, when you have the voice[850] of the King 320
> himself for your succession in Denmark?

---

[845] Astonishment.

[846] Do tell.

[847] Private room.

[848] Business.

[849] Hands. *The Book of Common Prayer*'s catechism: "To keep my hands from picking and stealing."

[850] Vote. Denmark is here an elective monarchy.

Hamlet

> Ay, but sir, 'While the grass grows[851]. . .'—the proverb is
> something musty.[852]

Enter Players with recorders

> O, the recorders! Let me see one.—To withdraw[853] with
> you, why do you go about to recover the wind of me,[854] 325
> as if you would drive me into a toil?

Guildenstern

> O, my lord, if my duty be too bold, my love is too un-
> mannerly.[855]

Hamlet

> I do not well understand that. Will you play upon this
> pipe?   330

Guildenstern

> My lord, I cannot.

Hamlet

> I pray you.

Guildenstern

> Believe me, I cannot.

Hamlet

> I do beseech you.

Guildenstern

> I know no touch of it, my lord.   335

---

[851] ". . . the horse starves."

[852] Somewhat stale, too stale to quote.

[853] Speak in private.

[854] Get on the windward side of me (your quarry), so you can drive me into
the net/snare (toil).

[855] "If I press on out of duty, it is only because my love makes me forget
my manners."

Hamlet

'Tis as easy as lying. Govern these ventages[856] with your fingers and thumb, give it breath with your mouth, and it will discourse most eloquent music. Look you, these are the stops.[857]

Guildenstern

But these cannot I command to any utterance of har- 340 mony. I have not the skill.

Hamlet

Why, look you now, how unworthy a thing you make of me! You would play upon me, you would seem to know my stops, you would pluck out the heart of my mystery, you would sound[858] me from my lowest note to the top 345 of my compass.[859] And there is much music, excellent voice, in this little organ,[860] yet cannot you make it speak. 'Sblood, do you think I am easier to be played on than a pipe? Call me what instrument you will, though you can fret[861] me, yet you cannot play upon me.   350

Enter Polonius

God bless you, sir!

Lord Polonius

My lord, the Queen would speak with you, and presently.

Hamlet

Do you see yonder cloud that's almost in shape of a camel?

---

[856] Finger holes.

[857] Finger holes.

[858] 1) Play on; 2) fathom, measure my depth.

[859] Range.

[860] Instrument.

[861] 1) Irritate; 2) punning on the "frets" on a stringed instrument to mark finger positions.

Lord Polonius

By the mass, and 'tis like a camel, indeed.

Hamlet

Methinks it is like a weasel.   355

Lord Polonius

It is backed like a weasel.

Hamlet

Or like a whale?

Lord Polonius

Very like a whale.

Hamlet

Then I will come to my mother by and by. (*Aside*) They
fool me to the top of my bent.[862] (*Aloud*) I will come by 360
and by.

Lord Polonius

I will say so.

Hamlet

By and by is easily said.   *Exit Polonius*
Leave me, friends.   *Exeunt all but Hamlet*
'Tis now the very witching time of night,   365
When churchyards yawn and hell itself breathes out
Contagion to this world. Now could I drink hot blood,
And do such bitter business as the day
Would quake to look on. Soft now to my mother.
O heart, lose not thy nature![863] Let not ever   370
The soul of Nero[864] enter this firm[865] bosom.
Let me be cruel, not unnatural.
I will speak daggers to her, but use none.
My tongue and soul in this be hypocrites[866] —

---

[862] As far as I can go.

[863] Natural, filial love.

[864] Roman emperor, who murdered his mother for poisoning his father.

[865] Resolved.

[866] I will appear to be violent.

How in my words somever she be shent,[867]   375
To give them seals[868] never my soul consent!   *Exit*

Act III, Scene iii

Enter King Claudius, Rosencrantz, and Guildenstern

King Claudius

    I like him not, nor stands it safe with us
    To let his madness range. Therefore prepare you.
    I your commission will forthwith dispatch,[869]
    And he to England shall along with you.
    The terms of our estate[870] may not endure   5
    Hazard so dangerous as doth hourly grow
    Out of his brows.[871]

Guildenstern   We will ourselves provide.
    Most holy and religious fear[872] it is
    To keep those many many bodies safe
    That live and feed upon your majesty.   10

Rosencrantz

    The single and peculiar[873] life is bound,
    With all the strength and armour of the mind,
    To keep itself from noyance;[874] but much more
    That spirit upon whose weal[875] depend and rest,

---

[867] Censured.

[868] A seal ratifies a document; Hamlet will not let his words become deeds.

[869] Deal with.

[870] Position.

[871] I.e., generated in the head; plots.

[872] Care.

[873] Individual and private.

[874] Harm.

[875] Welfare.

The lives of many. The cease[876] of majesty   15
Dies not alone, but, like a gulf,[877] doth draw
What's near it with it. It is a massy wheel,
Fixed on the summit of the highest mount,
To whose huge spokes ten thousand lesser things
Are mortised[878] and adjoined, which, when it falls,   20
Each small annexment, petty consequence,
Attends[879] the boisterous ruin. Never alone
Did the king sigh, but with a general groan.

King Claudius

Arm you,[880] I pray you, to this speedy voyage;
For we will fetters put upon this fear,   25
Which now goes too free-footed.

Rosencrantz and Guildenstern

We will haste us.   *Exeunt Rosencrantz and Guildenstern*

Enter Polonius

Lord Polonius

My lord, he's going to his mother's closet.
Behind the arras[881] I'll convey myself,
To hear the process[882] and warrant she'll tax him home.[883]   30
And, as you said, and wisely was it said,
'Tis meet[884] that some more audience than a mother,
Since nature makes them partial, should o'erhear

---

[876] Death.
[877] Whirlpool.
[878] Fixed.
[879] Follows.
[880] Make yourselves ready.
[881] Tapestry.
[882] Proceedings.
[883] Give him a talking-to.
[884] Fitting.

The speech of vantage.[885] Fare you well, my liege:
I'll call upon you ere you go to bed,   35
And tell you what I know.

King Claudius   Thanks, dear my lord.

Exit Polonius

O, my offence is rank! It smells to heaven!
It hath the primal eldest curse[886] upon't,
A brother's murder. Pray can I not,
Though inclination be as sharp as will,[887]   40
My stronger guilt defeats my strong intent,
And, like a man to double business bound,[888]
I stand in pause where I shall first begin,
And both neglect. What if this cursed hand
Were thicker than itself with brother's blood,   45
Is there not rain enough in the sweet heavens
To wash it white as snow?[889] Whereto serves mercy
But to confront the visage of offence?
And what's in prayer but this two-fold force,
To be forestalled[890] ere we come to fall,   50
Or pardoned being down? Then I'll look up.
My fault is past. But, O, what form of prayer
Can serve my turn? 'Forgive me my foul murder'?
That cannot be, since I am still possessed
Of those effects for which I did the murder,   55
My crown, mine own ambition, and my Queen.
May one be pardoned and retain th'offence?[891]

---

[885] In addition.

[886] A reference to Cain's killing his brother Abel (Genesis iv.10-12).

[887] "Both will (which may overcome nature) and inclination (a natural urge) prompt me."

[888] With obligations in two different directions.

[889] See Isaiah i.15-18.

[890] Prevented.

[891] The gain reaped from the sin.

In the corrupted currents of this world
Offence's gilded[892] hand may shove by[893] justice,
And oft 'tis seen the wicked prize itself   60
Buys out the law. But 'tis not so above.
There is no shuffling,[894] there the action lies
In his true nature,[895] and we ourselves compelled,
Even to the teeth and forehead of[896] our faults,
To give in evidence. What then? What rests?[897]   65
Try what repentance can. What can it not?
Yet what can it when one cannot repent?
O wretched state! O bosom black as death!
O limed soul, that, struggling to be free,
Art more engaged![898] Help, angels! Make assay![899]   70
Bow, stubborn knees, and heart with strings of steel,
Be soft as sinews of the newborn babe!
All may be well.   *Retires and kneels*

Enter Hamlet

Hamlet

Now might I do it pat,[900] now he is a-praying;
And now I'll do't.   *Draws his sword*
            And so he goes to heaven,   75
And so am I revenged? That would be scanned.[901]

---

[892] Bearing gold (with a hint to bribing, thus a pun on guilt).

[893] Push away.

[894] Getting off through trickery.

[895] True aspect; "action" = the legal term as well as deed.

[896] Confronted face-to-face with.

[897] What possibility is open.

[898] More securely caught; "limed" refers to catching birds with a sticky paste smeared on branches.

[899] Do your utmost.

[900] Neatly.

[901] That needs pondering.

A villain kills my father, and for that,
I, his sole son, do this same villain send
To heaven.
O, this is hire and salary, not revenge!   80
He took my father grossly, full of bread,[902]
With all his crimes broad blown,[903] as flush[904] as May,
And how his audit[905] stands, who knows save heaven?
But in our circumstance and course of thought,[906]
'Tis heavy with him. And am I then revenged,   85
To take him in the purging of his soul,
When he is fit and seasoned[907] for his passage?
No!   *He sheathes his sword*
Up, sword, and know thou a more horrid hent.[908]
When he is drunk asleep, or in his rage,   90
Or in th'incestuous pleasure of his bed,
At gaming, swearing, or about some act
That has no relish[909] of salvation in't.
Then trip him, that his heels may kick at heaven,
And that his soul may be as damned and black   95
As hell, whereto it goes. My mother stays.[910]
This physic[911] but prolongs thy sickly days.   *Exit*

King Claudius (*rising*)

My words fly up, my thoughts remain below:
Words without thoughts never to heaven go.   *Exit*

---

[902] Amidst indulgence, not fasting and so prepared for Heaven.

[903] His sins in full flower.

[904] Full of life.

[905] Account.

[906] As far as we can ascertain in our situation here on earth.

[907] Matured; well prepared.

[908] Opportunity.

[909] Taste.

[910] Is waiting.

[911] Medicine; i.e., prayer.

Act III, Scene iv

Enter Queen Gertrude and Polonius

Lord Polonius
    A[912] will come straight. Look you lay home to him.[913]
    Tell him his pranks[914] have been too broad[915] to bear with,
    And that your grace hath screened and stood between
    Much heat and him. I'll silence me even here.
    Pray you, be round[916] with him.   5
Hamlet (*within*)
    Mother, mother, mother!
Queen Gertrude   I'll warrant you, fear me not.
    Withdraw, I hear him coming.
                                        Polonius hides behind the arras

Enter Hamlet

Hamlet
    Now, mother, what's the matter?
Queen Gertrude
    Hamlet, thou hast thy father much offended.
Hamlet
    Mother, you have my father much offended.   10
Queen Gertrude
    Come, come, you answer with an idle tongue.
Hamlet
    Go, go, you question with a wicked tongue.

---

[912] He.
[913] Remonstrate with him.
[914] Outrageous, indecent acts.
[915] Gross; unrestrained.
[916] Plain; blunt.

Queen Gertrude

    Why, how now, Hamlet!

Hamlet   What's the matter now?

Queen Gertrude

    Have you forgot me?[917]

Hamlet   No, by the rood,[918] not so.

    You are the Queen, your husband's brother's wife[919]   15

    And, would it were not so, you are my mother.

Queen Gertrude

    Nay, then, I'll set those to you that can speak.[920]

Hamlet

    Come, come, and sit you down; you shall not budge.

    You go not till I set you up a glass[921]

    Where you may see the inmost part of you.   20

Queen Gertrude

    What wilt thou do? Thou wilt not murder me?

    Help, help, ho!

Lord Polonius (*behind the arras*)   What, ho! Help, help, help!

Hamlet (*drawing*)

    How now! A rat? Dead, for a ducat, dead![922]

                              Makes a pass through the arras

Lord Polonius (*behind*)

    O, I am slain!   *Falls and dies*

Queen Gertrude   O me, what hast thou done?

Hamlet

    Nay, I know not. Is it the King?   25

---

[917] Forgotten your duties to me as my son.

[918] The holy cross.

[919] Marrying one's husband's brother constituted incest according to *The Book of Common Prayer*.

[920] I.e., with someone as rude as you are.

[921] Mirror.

[922] I'll kill him for a ducat.

Queen Gertrude

    O, what a rash and bloody deed is this!

Hamlet

    A bloody deed! Almost as bad, good mother,

    As kill a king and marry with his brother.

Queen Gertrude

    As kill a king!

Hamlet (*lifts up the arras and discovers Polonius dead*)

                Ay, lady, 'twas my word.

    Thou wretched, rash, intruding fool, farewell!   30

    I took thee for thy better. Take thy fortune.

    Thou find'st to be too busy is some danger—

    Leave wringing of your hands. Peace, sit you down,

    And let me wring your heart, for so I shall

    If it be made of penetrable stuff,   35

    If damned custom[923] have not brassed[924] it so

    That it is proof and bulwark against sense.

Queen Gertrude

    What have I done, that thou dar'st wag thy tongue

    In noise so rude against me?

Hamlet   Such an act

    That blurs the grace and blush of modesty,   40

    Calls virtue hypocrite, takes off the rose[925]

    From the fair forehead of an innocent love

    And sets a blister[926] there, makes marriage-vows

    As false as dicers' oaths. O, such a deed

    As from the body of contraction plucks   45

    The very soul, and sweet religion makes

---

[923] Condemnable habit.

[924] Made hard as brass; brazed.

[925] Emblem of ideal love.

[926] Prostitutes were branded in the forehead as punishment.

A rhapsody[927] of words. Heaven's face doth glow,[928]
Yea, this solidity and compound mass,[929]
With tristful[930] visage, as against the doom,[931]
Is thought-sick[932] at the act.

Queen Gertrude   Ay me, what act,   50
That roars so loud, and thunders in the index?[933]

Hamlet

Look here, upon this picture, and on this,
The counterfeit presentment[934] of two brothers.
See, what a grace was seated on this brow,
Hyperion's[935] curls, the front[936] of Jove himself,   55
An eye like Mars,[937] to threaten and command,
A station[938] like the herald Mercury[939]
New-lighted[940] on a heaven-kissing hill;
A combination and a form indeed,
Where every god did seem to set his seal,   60
To give the world assurance of a man.[941]
This was your husband. Look you now what follows:
Here is your husband, like a mildewed ear,[942]

---

[927] Confused, senseless mass.

[928] Blush.

[929] The earth, made up of four elements.

[930] Sorrowful.

[931] The day of judgment.

[932] Mentally distressed.

[933] Table of contents; preface.

[934] Image; portrait.

[935] The sun god.

[936] Forehead.

[937] The god of war.

[938] Manner of standing.

[939] The gods' winged messenger, the epitome of grace and handsomeness.

[940] Newly landed.

[941] Present to the world the ideal man.

[942] Diseased ear of grain.

Blasting[943] his wholesome brother. Have you eyes?
Could you on this fair mountain leave[944] to feed,   65
And batten[945] on this moor? Ha! Have you eyes?
You cannot call it love, for at your age
The hey-day in the blood[946] is tame, it's humble,
And waits upon the judgment; and what judgment
Would step from this to this? Sense,[947] sure, you have,   70
Else could you not have motion;[948] but sure, that sense
Is apoplexed,[949] for madness would not err,
Nor sense to ecstasy was ne'er so thralled
But it reserved some quantity of choice,[950]
To serve in such a difference. What devil was't   75
That thus hath cozened you at hoodman-blind?[951]
Eyes without feeling, feeling without sight,
Ears without hands or eyes, smelling sans all[952]
Or but a sickly part of one true sense
Could not so mope.[953] O shame! Where is thy blush?   80
Rebellious hell,
If thou canst mutine[954] in a matron's bones,
To flaming youth let virtue be as wax,
And melt in her own fire! Proclaim no shame

[943] Infecting.
[944] Cease.
[945] Feed ravenously.
[946] The blood is the set of sexual passion.
[947] The five senses collectively, and also the ability to perceive through them.
[948] Aristotle sees the five senses as having to be present in any creature which possesses locomotion.
[949] Paralyzed.
[950] Some little power to choose.
[951] Blind man's buff.
[952] Without any other sense.
[953] Exist in a daze.
[954] Create mutiny.

When the compulsive ardour gives the charge,[955]   85
Since frost[956] itself as actively doth burn,
And reason panders will.[957]

Queen Gertrude   O Hamlet, speak no more!
Thou turn'st mine eyes into my very soul,
And there I see such black and grained[958] spots
As will not leave their tinct.[959]

Hamlet   Nay, but to live   90
In the rank sweat of an enseamed[960] bed,
Stewed[961] in corruption, honeying and making love
Over the nasty sty—

Queen Gertrude   O, speak to me no more!
These words like daggers enter in mine ears;
No more, sweet Hamlet!

Hamlet   A murderer and a villain!   95
A slave that is not twentieth part the tithe[962]
Of your precedent[963] lord, a vice[964] of kings;
A cutpurse[965] of the empire and the rule,
That from a shelf the precious diadem stole,
And put it in his pocket!   100

Queen Gertrude
No more!

---

[955] Sounds the attack.

[956] The subdued passions of a matron.

[957] Will = instinct to gratify passions, the opposite of reason.

[958] Dyed indelibly.

[959] Color.

[960] Seam = animal fat; this and other animal references combine to create a grossly repellent picture of sexuality.

[961] Steeped in; "stew" = slang for brothel.

[962] Tenth.

[963] Former.

[964] Model of sinful behavior; also, see glossary.

[965] Pickpocket.

Hamlet

> A king of shreds and patches![966]

Enter Ghost

> Save me, and hover o'er me with your wings,
> You heavenly guards! What would your gracious figure?

Queen Gertrude

> Alas, he's mad!   105

Hamlet

> Do you not come your tardy son to chide,
> That, lapsed in time and passion,[967] lets go by
> The important[968] acting of your dread command?
> O, say!

Ghost   Do not forget. This visitation

> Is but to whet thy almost blunted purpose.   110
> But look, amazement[969] on thy mother sits.
> O, step between her and her fighting soul!
> Conceit[970] in weakest bodies strongest works.
> Speak to her, Hamlet.

Hamlet

> How is it with you, lady?

Queen Gertrude   Alas, how is't with you,   115

> That you do bend your eye on vacancy
> And with the incorporal[971] air do hold discourse?
> Forth at your eyes your spirits wildly peep,
> And, as the sleeping soldiers in the alarm,[972]

---

[966] Reference to motley, the buffoon's costume.

[967] Who has let both time and passion for revenge slip.

[968] Urgent.

[969] Bewilderment.

[970] Imagination.

[971] Having no substance or body.

[972] Call to arms.

Your bedded[973] hair, like life in excrements,[974]   120
Start up, and stand on end. O gentle son,
Upon the heat and flame of thy distemper[975]
Sprinkle cool patience. Whereon do you look?

Hamlet

On him, on him! Look you, how pale he glares!
His form and cause conjoined,[976] preaching to stones,   125
Would make them capable.[977] Do not look upon me,
Lest with this piteous action you convert
My stern effects.[978] Then what I have to do
Will want true colour[979]—tears perchance for blood.

Queen Gertrude

To whom do you speak this?   130

Hamlet

Do you see nothing there?

Queen Gertrude

Nothing at all, yet all that is I see.

Hamlet

Nor did you nothing hear?

Queen Gertrude

No, nothing but ourselves.

Hamlet

Why, look you there! Look, how it steals away!   135
My father, in his habit as he lived![980]
Look, where he goes, even now, out at the portal!   *Exit Ghost*

---

[973] Laid flat.

[974] Lifeless growths such as hair, beard, and nails.

[975] Sick mind.

[976] The ghost's appearance and his cause united in one.

[977] Responsive.

[978] Deeds to be done.

[979] Not have its proper characteristics; tears are colorless, blood is red.

[980] Dressed and behaving as in life.

Queen Gertrude

 This is the very coinage of your brain:

 This bodiless creation ecstasy[981]

 Is very cunning in.

Hamlet   Ecstasy!   140

 My pulse, as yours, doth temperately keep time,

 And makes as healthful music. It is not madness

 That I have uttered. Bring me to the test,

 And I the matter will re-word, which madness

 Would gambol[982] from. Mother, for love of grace, 145

 Lay[983] not that flattering unction[984] to your soul,

 That not your trespass, but my madness speaks.

 It will but skin[985] and film the ulcerous place,

 Whilst rank corruption, mining[986] all within,

 Infects unseen. Confess yourself to heaven. 150

 Repent what's past, avoid what is to come;

 And do not spread the compost on the weeds

 To make them ranker. Forgive me this my virtue,[987]

 For in the fatness[988] of these pursy times

 Virtue itself of vice must pardon beg,   155

 Yea, curb[989] and woo for leave to do him good.

Queen Gertrude

 O Hamlet, thou hast cleft my heart in twain.

---

[981] Madness.

[982] Shy away.

[983] Apply.

[984] Ointment; a contrast to sacramental unction that blesses.

[985] Let skin grow over.

[986] Undermining.

[987] Virtuous pronouncements.

[988] Physical and moral grossness; "pursy," literally "flabby," has same meaning.

[989] Bow.

Hamlet

> O, throw away the worser part of it,
> And live the purer with the other half!
> Good night. But go not to mine uncle's bed.   160
> Assume[990] a virtue if you have it not.
> That monster, custom, who all sense doth eat,
> Of habits devil, is angel yet in this,
> That to the use of actions fair and good
> He likewise gives a frock or livery,   165
> That aptly[991] is put on.[992] Refrain to-night,
> And that shall lend a kind of easiness
> To the next abstinence, the next more easy;
> For use[993] almost can change the stamp of nature,
> And either in[994] the devil, or throw him out   170
> With wondrous potency. Once more, good night,
> And when you are desirous to be blessed,
> I'll blessing beg of you. For this same lord,
> I do repent. But heaven hath pleased it so,
> To punish me with this and this with me,   175
> That I must be their scourge and minister.[995]
> I will bestow[996] him, and will answer[997] well
> The death I gave him. So, again, good night.
> I must be cruel, only to be kind.
> Thus bad begins and worse remains behind.   180
> One word more, good lady.

---

[990] Pretend.

[991] Easily.

[992] Habit ("custom") erodes our perception of evil if repeated often enough, but we can turn to good habits by repetition.

[993] Habit.

[994] Let in.

[995] Both agents of divine punishment.

[996] Stow away.

[997] Answer for.

Queen Gertrude   What shall I do?

Hamlet

    Not this, by no means, that I bid you do:

    Let the bloat King tempt you again to bed,

    Pinch wanton[998] on your cheek, call you his mouse,[999]

    And let him, for a pair of reechy[1000] kisses,   185

    Or paddling[1001] in your neck with his damned fingers,

    Make you to ravel[1002] all this matter out,

    That I essentially am not in madness,

    But mad in craft.[1003] 'Twere good you let him know;

    For who, that's but[1004] a queen, fair, sober, wise,   190

    Would from a paddock,[1005] from a bat, a gib,[1006]

    Such dear concernings[1007] hide? Who would do so?

    No, in despite of sense and secrecy,

    Unpeg the basket on the house's top.

    Let the birds fly, and, like the famous ape,   195

    To try conclusions, in the basket creep,

    And break your own neck down.[1008]

Queen Gertrude

    Be thou assured, if words be made of breath,

    And breath of life, I have no life to breathe

    What thou hast said to me.   200

---

[998] Leave pinching marks.

[999] Term of endearment to a woman.

[1000] Filthy.

[1001] Fondle.

[1002] Unravel; clear up.

[1003] Slyness.

[1004] Only; just.

[1005] Toad or frog.

[1006] Tomcat.

[1007] Such important matters.

[1008] Probably a story involving an ape who let birds—difficult creatures to catch!—out of a basket on a rooftop, then tried to fly like they did.

Hamlet

I must to England. You know that?

Queen Gertrude   Alack,

I had forgot, 'tis so concluded on.[1009]

Hamlet

There's letters sealed, and my two schoolfellows,

Whom I will trust as I will adders fanged,

They bear the mandate, they must sweep my way   205

And marshal me to knavery.[1010] Let it work.

For 'tis the sport to have the engineer[1011]

Hoist with his own petard.[1012] And't shall go hard

But I will delve one yard below their mines,[1013]

And blow them at the moon. O, 'tis most sweet,   210

When in one line two crafts[1014] directly meet.

This man shall set me packing.

I'll lug the guts into the neighbour room.

Mother, good night indeed. This counsellor

Is now most still, most secret, and most grave,   215

Who was in life a foolish prating knave.

Come, sir, to draw toward an end[1015] with you.

Good night, mother.

Exit Hamlet dragging in Polonius. Manet Queen

[1009] Decided.

[1010] Lead me where I shall suffer from knavery.

[1011] Maker of war engines.

[1012] Blown up by his own bomb; "petard" = a then new military device to blast through walls or gates.

[1013] Tunnels.

[1014] Ingenious plots.

[1015] Finish the business.

Act IV, Scene i

Enter King Claudius to Queen Gertrude with Rosencrantz and Guildenstern

King Claudius

> There's matter in these sighs, these profound heaves,
> You must translate. 'Tis fit we understand them.
> Where is your son?

Queen Gertrude

> Bestow this place on us a little while.

> > > > *Exeunt Rosencrantz and Guildenstern*

> Ah, my good lord, what have I seen to-night!   5

King Claudius

> What, Gertrude? How does Hamlet?

Queen Gertrude

> Mad as the sea and wind, when both contend
> Which is the mightier. In his lawless fit,
> Behind the arras hearing something stir,
> Whips out his rapier, cries 'A rat, a rat!'   10
> And, in this brainish apprehension,[1016] kills
> The unseen good old man.

King Claudius   O heavy deed!

> It had been so with us,[1017] had we been there!
> His liberty is full of threats to all,
> To you yourself, to us, to everyone.   15
> Alas, how shall this bloody deed be answered?[1018]
> It will be laid to us,[1019] whose providence[1020]

[1016] Deluded perception.
[1017] The "royal we," often used by Claudius.
[1018] Explained.
[1019] Blamed on me.
[1020] Foresight.

Should have kept short,[1021] restrained, and out of haunt[1022]
This mad young man. But so much was our love,
We would not understand what was most fit,   20
But, like the owner[1023] of a foul disease,
To keep it from divulging,[1024] let it feed
Even on the pith[1025] of life. Where is he gone?

Queen Gertrude

To draw apart the body he hath killed,
O'er whom his very madness, like some ore[1026]   25
Among a mineral[1027] of metals base,
Shows itself pure. He weeps for what is done.

King Claudius

O Gertrude, come away!
The sun no sooner shall the mountains touch
But we will ship him hence. And this vile deed   30
We must, with all our majesty and skill,
Both countenance[1028] and excuse. Ho, Guildenstern!

Re-enter Rosencrantz and Guildenstern

Friends both, go join you with some further aid.
Hamlet in madness hath Polonius slain,
And from his mother's closet hath he dragged him.   35
Go seek him out, speak fair, and bring the body
Into the chapel. I pray you, haste in this.

Exeunt Rosencrantz and Guildenstern

[1021] On a short leash.
[1022] Away from public places.
[1023] Bearer.
[1024] Becoming publicly known.
[1025] Necessary substance.
[1026] Vein of gold.
[1027] Mine.
[1028] Condone.

Come, Gertrude, we'll call up our wisest friends
And let them know, both what we mean to do,
And what's untimely done. So envious slander,   40
Whose whisper o'er the world's diameter,[1029]
As level as the cannon to his blank,[1030]
Transports his poisoned shot, may miss our name
And hit the woundless[1031] air. O, come away!
My soul is full of discord and dismay.   *Exeunt* 45

Act IV, Scene ii

Enter Hamlet

Hamlet
    Safely stowed.
Rosencrantz and Guildenstern (*within*)
    Hamlet! Lord Hamlet!
Hamlet
    What noise? Who calls on Hamlet?
    O, here they come.

Enter Rosencrantz and Guildenstern

Rosencrantz
    What have you done, my lord, with the dead body?   5
Hamlet
    Compounded[1032] it with dust, whereto 'tis kin.

[1029] Entire width.
[1030] Blank = center of target; "as straight as the cannon to its target."
[1031] Invulnerable.
[1032] Mingled.

Rosencrantz

    Tell us where 'tis, that we may take it thence

    And bear it to the chapel.

Hamlet

    Do not believe it.

Rosencrantz

    Believe what?   10

Hamlet

    That I can keep your counsel and not mine own. Besides,
to be demanded of[1033] a sponge! What replication[1034] should
be made by the son of a king?

Rosencrantz

    Take you me for a sponge, my lord?

Hamlet

    Ay, sir, that soaks up the King's countenance,[1035] his rewards   15
his authorities. But such officers do the King best service
in the end. He keeps them, like an ape, in the corner of his
jaw— first mouthed to be last swallowed. When he needs
what you have gleaned, it is but squeezing you, and, sponge,
you shall be dry again.   20

Rosencrantz

    I understand you not, my lord.

Hamlet

    I am glad of it. A knavish speech sleeps in a foolish ear.[1036]

Rosencrantz

    My lord, you must tell us where the body is, and go with
us to the King.

Hamlet

    The body is with the King, but the King is not with the   25

[1033] Interrogated by.

[1034] Answer.

[1035] Tokens of goodwill.

[1036] Fools do not get an insult.

body.[1037] The King is a thing—
Guildenstern

A thing, my lord?
Hamlet

Of nothing. Bring me to him. Hide fox, and all after.[1038]

Exeunt

Act IV, Scene iii

Enter King Claudius, attended

King Claudius

I have sent to seek him, and to find the body.
How dangerous is it that this man goes loose!
Yet must not we put the strong law on him.
He's loved of[1039] the distracted[1040] multitude,
Who like not in their judgment, but their eyes,[1041]   5
And where 'tis so, the offender's scourge[1042] is weighed,
But never the offence. To bear all smooth and even,[1043]
This sudden sending him away must seem
Deliberate pause.[1044] Diseases desperate grown
By desperate appliance[1045] are relieved,   10

[1037] 1) A reference to the King's two bodies: the natural, mortal body and the immortal body of the state (see glossary); 2) Polonius' body is at the palace, but the King is not yet dead.

[1038] The game of fox-and-hounds, much like hide-and-seek.

[1039] By.

[1040] Irrational.

[1041] Who judge by appearance, not by substance.

[1042] Punishment.

[1043] To manage affairs without arousing opposition.

[1044] A result of careful deliberation.

[1045] Remedy.

Or not at all.

Enter Rosencrantz and others

> How now! What hath befallen?

Rosencrantz

Where the dead body is bestowed, my lord,

We cannot get from him.

King Claudius   But where is he?

Rosencrantz

Without, my lord, guarded, to know your pleasure.

King Claudius

Bring him before us.   15

Rosencrantz

Ho, Guildenstern! Bring in my lord.

Enter Hamlet and Guildenstern

King Claudius

Now, Hamlet, where's Polonius?

Hamlet

At supper.

King Claudius

At supper! Where?

Hamlet

Not where he eats, but where he is eaten. A certain con-   20
vocation of politic[1046] worms are e'en at him. Your worm
is your only emperor for diet.[1047] We fat all creatures else
to fat us, and we fat ourselves for maggots. Your fat king

[1046] Shrewd (in statescraft).

[1047] A worm eats better than a king—it can eat a king. Also wordplay on
"diet" = council, and so the Council of Worms, Germany, in 1521, pre-
sided over by Emperor Charles V, where Luther was banned after refusing
to retract his thesis that salvation is contingent on faith alone.

and your lean beggar is but variable service,[1048] two dishes,
but to one table. That's the end.   25

King Claudius

Alas, alas!

Hamlet

A man may fish with the worm that hath eat of a king,
and eat of the fish that hath fed of that worm.

King Claudius

What dost you mean by this?

Hamlet

Nothing but to show you how a king may go a progress[1049]   30
through the guts of a beggar.

King Claudius

Where is Polonius?

Hamlet

In heaven. Send thither to see. If your messenger find
him not there, seek him i'the other place yourself. But
indeed, if you find him not within this month, you shall   35
nose him as you go up the stairs into the lobby.

King Claudius (*to some Attendants*)

Go seek him there.

Hamlet

He will stay till ye come.

King Claudius

Hamlet, this deed, for thine especial safety,
Which we do tender[1050] as we dearly grieve   40
For that which thou hast done, must send thee hence
With fiery quickness. Therefore prepare thyself.
The bark is ready, and the wind at help,

[1048] Different courses.
[1049] Progress = a state journey, usually including the monarch. Elizabeth I was famous for the style and extravagance of hers.
[1050] Regard greatly.

Th'associates tend,[1051] and every thing is bent[1052]

For England.   45

Hamlet

For England?

King Claudius

Ay, Hamlet.

Hamlet

Good.

King Claudius

So is it, if thou knew'st our purposes.

Hamlet

I see a cherub[1053] that sees them. But come, for England!   50

Farewell, dear mother.

King Claudius

Thy loving father, Hamlet.

Hamlet

My mother. Father and mother is man and wife, man and
wife is one flesh,[1054] and so, my mother. Come, for En-
gland!   *Exit* 55

King Claudius

Follow him at foot.[1055] Tempt him with speed aboard.

Delay it not. I'll have him hence to-night.

Away! For everything is sealed and done

That else leans on the affair.[1056] Pray you, make haste.

                                            Exeunt all except the King

[1051] "Your attendants await you."

[1052] Ready.

[1053] The order of angels with the keenest sight.

[1054] As seen in *The Book of Common Prayer*'s marriage ritual.

[1055] Closely.

[1056] Belong to this matter.

And, England,[1057] if my love thou hold'st at aught,[1058]   60
As my great power thereof may give thee sense,[1059]
Since yet thy cicatrice[1060] looks raw and red
After the Danish sword, and thy free awe[1061]
Pays homage to us, thou mayst not coldly set
Our sovereign process,[1062] which imports at full,[1063]   65
By letters congruing to[1064] that effect,
The present[1065] death of Hamlet. Do it, England;
For like the hectic[1066] in my blood he rages,
And thou must cure me. Till I know 'tis done,
Howe'er my haps,[1067] my joys were ne'er begun.   *Exit* 70

Act IV, Scene iv

Enter Fortinbras with his army, marching over the stage

Prince Fortinbras

Go, captain, from me greet the Danish King.
Tell him that, by his licence,[1068] Fortinbras

[1057] King of England; the King was often identified with the country; see e.g., I.i.16.

[1058] Of any value.

[1059] Reason.

[1060] Scar.

[1061] Freely given respect, i.e., England is unoccupied by military.

[1062] "Value my royal decree lightly."

[1063] Gives directions in detail.

[1064] In accordance with.

[1065] Immediate.

[1066] Fever.

[1067] Fate.

[1068] Leave; permission.

Craves the conveyance of[1069] a promised march
Over his kingdom. You know the rendezvous.
If that his majesty would aught with us,   5
We shall express our duty in his eye,[1070]
And let him know so.

Captain   I will do't, my lord.

Prince Fortinbras
    Go softly on.   *Exeunt Fortinbras and Soldiers*

Enter Hamlet, Rosencrantz, Guildenstern, and others

Hamlet
    Good sir, whose powers[1071] are these?
Captain
    They are of Norway, sir.   10
Hamlet
    How purposed, sir, I pray you?
Captain
    Against some part of Poland.
Hamlet
    Who commands them, sir?
Captain
    The nephew to old Norway, Fortinbras.
Hamlet
    Goes it against the main of Poland, sir,   15
    Or for some frontier?
Captain
    Truly to speak, and with no addition,[1072]

[1069] Escort for.
[1070] Pay our respects face to face.
[1071] Army; forces.
[1072] Embellishment.

> We go to gain a little patch of ground
>
> That hath in it no profit but the name.
>
> To pay five ducats, five, I would not farm[1073] it,   20
>
> Nor will it yield to Norway or the Pole
>
> A ranker[1074] rate, should it be sold in fee.[1075]

Hamlet

> Why, then the Polack never will defend it.

Captain

> Yes, it is already garrisoned.

Hamlet

> Two thousand souls and twenty thousand ducats   25
>
> Will not debate the question of this straw![1076]
>
> This is th'imposthume[1077] of much wealth and peace,
>
> That inward breaks,[1078] and shows no cause without
>
> Why the man dies. I humbly thank you, sir.

Captain

> God buy you,[1079] sir.   *Exit*

Rosencrantz   Wilt please you go, my lord?   30

Hamlet

> I'll be with you straight. Go a little before.

> *Exeunt all except Hamlet*

> How all occasions do inform against me,[1080]
>
> And spur my dull revenge! What is a man,
>
> If his chief good and market[1081] of his time
>
> Be but to sleep and feed? A beast, no more.   35

[1073] Lease.

[1074] Greater.

[1075] With absolute possession; outright.

[1076] Insignificant thing.

[1077] Abscess.

[1078] Ruptures inside.

[1079] Be with you.

[1080] Declare me guilty.

[1081] Profit.

Sure, he that made us with such large discourse,[1082]
Looking before and after,[1083] gave us not
That capability and god-like reason
To fust[1084] in us unused. Now, whether it be
Bestial oblivion,[1085] or some craven scruple   40
Of thinking too precisely on th'event,
A thought which, quartered, hath but one part wisdom
And ever three parts coward, I do not know
Why yet I live to say 'This thing's to do,'
Sith[1086] I have cause, and will, and strength, and means   45
To do't. Examples gross as earth exhort me.
Witness this army of such mass and charge[1087]
Led by a delicate and tender[1088] prince,
Whose spirit with divine ambition puffed
Makes mouths at[1089] the invisible event,[1090]   50
Exposing what is mortal and unsure
To all that fortune, death, and danger dare,
Even for an eggshell. Rightly to be great
Is not to stir without great argument,[1091]
But greatly to find quarrel in a straw   55
When honour's at the stake.[1092] How stand I, then,
That have a father killed, a mother stained,

[1082] Reasoning powers.

[1083] Considering both past and future.

[1084] Grow moldy.

[1085] Animals, lacking reason, do not remember.

[1086] As.

[1087] Cost.

[1088] "Of tender age"; young.

[1089] Makes (scorning) faces.

[1090] Unforeseeable aftermath.

[1091] Cause.

[1092] "True greatness is found in noble action rather than in long, rational deliberation."

Excitements of my reason and my blood,
And let all sleep while, to my shame, I see
The imminent death of twenty thousand men,   60
That, for a fantasy[1093] and trick[1094] of fame,
Go to their graves like beds, fight for a plot
Whereon the numbers cannot try the cause,[1095]
Which is not tomb enough and continent[1096]
To hide the slain? O, from this time forth,   65
My thoughts be bloody, or be nothing worth!   *Exit*

Act IV, Scene v

Enter Queen Gertrude, Horatio, and Gentleman

Queen Gertrude
    I will not speak with her.
Gentleman   She is importunate,
    Indeed distract.[1097] Her mood will needs be pitied.
Queen Gertrude
    What would she have?
Gentleman
    She speaks much of her father, says she hears
    There's tricks i'the world, and hems, and beats her heart,   5
    Spurns enviously at straws,[1098] speaks things in doubt,[1099]
    That carry but half sense. Her speech is nothing,

[1093] Illusion.
[1094] Toy.
[1095] Not big enough to fight the battle on.
[1096] Container.
[1097] Mad; not in her right mind.
[1098] Is angered by trifles.
[1099] Unclearly.

Yet the unshaped use[1100] of it doth move
The hearers to collection.[1101] They aim[1102] at it,
And botch the words up fit to[1103] their own thoughts,   10
Which,[1104] as her winks, and nods, and gestures yield them,
Indeed would make one think there might be thought,
Though nothing sure, yet much unhappily.[1105]

Horatio

'Twere good she were spoken with, for she may strew
Dangerous conjectures in ill-breeding minds.   15

Queen Gertrude

Let her come in.   *Exit Horatio*
To my sick soul, as sin's true nature is,
Each toy[1106] seems prologue to some great amiss.[1107]
So full of artless jealousy[1108] is guilt,
It spills itself in fearing to be spilt.   20

Re-enter Horatio, with Ophelia

Ophelia

Where is the beauteous majesty of Denmark?

Queen Gertrude

How now,[1109] Ophelia!

Ophelia (*sings*)

How should I your true love know
From another one?

[1100] Jumbled matter.
[1101] Make inferences.
[1102] Make conjecture.
[1103] To fit.
[1104] I.e., her words.
[1105] "Much harmful, but nothing certain, could be supposed."
[1106] Trivial thing.
[1107] Ill fortune.
[1108] Fear of evil; suspicion.
[1109] What is this.

By his cockle hat and staff,   25
    And his sandal shoon.[1110]

Queen Gertrude

    Alas, sweet lady, what imports[1111] this song?

Ophelia

    Say you? Nay, pray you, mark.[1112]

(*Sings*) He is dead and gone, lady,
      He is dead and gone.   30
      At his head a grass-green turf,
      At his heels a stone.

Queen Gertrude

    Nay, but, Ophelia,—

Ophelia

    Pray you, mark.

(*Sings*) White his shroud as the mountain snow,—   35

Enter King Claudius

Queen Gertrude

    Alas, look here, my lord.

Ophelia (*sings*)

      Larded[1113] with sweet flowers,
      Which bewept to the grave did not[1114] go
      With true-love showers.[1115]

King Claudius

    How do you, pretty lady?   40

[1110] The garb of a pilgrim.
[1111] Means.
[1112] Listen well.
[1113] Strewn.
[1114] The "not" interrupts the meter and the meaning of the song, but, interpolated by Ophelia, it fits the matter on her mind, her father's death.
[1115] I.e., of tears.

Ophelia

>Well, God 'ield[1116] you! They say the owl was a baker's
>daughter.[1117] Lord, we know what we are, but know not
>what we may be. God be at your table!

King Claudius

>Conceit[1118] upon her father.

Ophelia

>Pray you, let's have no words of this, but when they ask   45
>you what it means, say you this:

>(*Sings*) To-morrow is Saint Valentine's day,
>>All in the morning betime,[1119]
>>And I a maid at your window,
>>To be your Valentine.[1120]   50

>>Then up he rose, and donned his clothes,
>>And dupped[1121] the chamber-door.
>>Let in the maid, that out a maid
>>Never departed more.

King Claudius

>Pretty Ophelia!   55

Ophelia

>Indeed, la, without an oath, I'll make an end on't.[1122]

>(*Sings*) By Gis[1123] and by Saint Charity,
>>Alack, and fie for shame!

[1116] Yield = reward.

[1117] In a folktale, Christ turned a baker's daughter into an owl because she stinted on the bread given him. Also, at the time, bakers' daughters were traditionally women of bad reputation.

[1118] Brooding thoughts.

[1119] Early.

[1120] Synonymous with sweetheart; the first person of the opposite sex one sees on Saint Valentine's Day was customarily regarded as such.

[1121] Opened; "dup" = do up.

[1122] Of it.

[1123] Jesus.

Young men will do't if they come to't;
   By Cock,[1124] they are to blame.   60
Quoth she, "Before you tumbled me,
   You promised me to wed."
  He answers,
    So would I ha' done, by yonder sun,
     An[1125] thou hadst not come to my bed.

King Claudius

How long hath she been thus?   65

Ophelia

I hope all will be well. We must be patient. But I cannot
choose but weep, to think they should lay him i'th'cold
ground. My brother shall know of it. And so I thank you
for your good counsel. Come, my coach! Good night,
ladies, good night, sweet ladies, good night, good night.   70

Exit

King Claudius (*to Horatio*)

Follow her close; give her good watch, I pray you.

Exit Horatio

O, this is the poison of deep grief! It springs
All from her father's death. O Gertrude, Gertrude,
When sorrows come, they come not single spies[1126]
But in battalions. First, her father slain.   75
Next, your son gone, and he most violent author
Of his own just remove. The people muddied,[1127]
Thick and unwholesome in their thoughts and whispers
For good Polonius' death; and we have done but greenly,[1128]

[1124] "Cock" is a corruption of God. "By Cock" is a mild oath, but certainly also wordplay on "penis."
[1125] If.
[1126] Reconnoitering soldiers.
[1127] Bewildered; confused.
[1128] Not maturely, hence foolishly.

In hugger-mugger[1129] to inter him. Poor Ophelia   80
Divided from herself and her fair judgment,
Without the which we are pictures, or mere beasts!
Last, and as much containing[1130] as all these,
Her brother is in secret come from France,
Feeds on his wonder, keeps himself in clouds,[1131]   85
And wants not buzzers[1132] to infect his ear
With pestilent speeches of his father's death,
Wherein necessity,[1133] of matter beggared,[1134]
Will nothing stick[1135] our person to arraign[1136]
In ear and ear.[1137] O my dear Gertrude, this,   90
Like to a murdering-piece,[1138] in many places
Gives me superfluous death.[1139]   *A noise within*

Queen Gertrude
Alack, what noise is this?

King Claudius
Where are my Switzers?[1140] Let them guard the door.

Enter another Gentleman

What is the matter?

Gentleman   Save yourself, my lord!   95

[1129] Furtively; in secrecy.

[1130] As significant.

[1131] In speculations (not facts).

[1132] Has no lack of scandal-mongers.

[1133] (. . . Which is the mother of invention!)

[1134] Which has nothing substantial to work with.

[1135] Will not balk at.

[1136] Accuse.

[1137] In one ear after another.

[1138] Small cannon that, firing grapeshot, could do much damage.

[1139] Death again and again.

[1140] Guard of Swiss mercenaries.

The ocean, overpeering[1141] of his list,[1142]
Eats not the flats with more impetuous haste
Than young Laertes, in a riotous head,[1143]
O'erbears your officers. The rabble call him lord,
And, as[1144] the world were now but[1145] to begin,   100
Antiquity forgot, custom not known,
The ratifiers and props of every word,[1146]
They cry 'Choose we! Laertes shall be King!'
Caps, hands, and tongues applaud it to the clouds:
'Laertes shall be King! Laertes King!'   105

Queen Gertrude

How cheerfully on the false trail they cry!
O, this is counter,[1147] you false Danish dogs!   *Noise within*

King Claudius

The doors are broke.

Enter Laertes, armed; Danes following

Laertes

Where is this King? Sirs, stand you all without.

Danes

No, let's come in.

Laertes   I pray you, give me leave.   110

Danes

We will, we will.

Laertes

I thank you. Keep the door.   *Exeunt Followers*

[1141] Rising above.

[1142] Barrier.

[1143] Insurrection.

[1144] As if.

[1145] Just now.

[1146] Maxim.

[1147] Like a hound running along the trail the wrong way, away from the prey.

O thou vile King,

>Give me my father!

Queen Gertrude   Calmly, good Laertes.

Laertes

>That drop of blood that's calm proclaims me bastard,
>Cries cuckold to my father, brands the harlot   115
>Even here, between the chaste unsmirched brow
>Of my true mother.

King Claudius   What is the cause, Laertes,

>That thy rebellion looks so giant-like?
>Let him go, Gertrude, do not fear our person,
>There's such divinity doth hedge a king,   120
>That treason can but peep to what it would,[1148]
>Acts little of his[1149] will. Tell me, Laertes,
>Why thou art thus incensed. Let him go, Gertrude.
>Speak, man.

Laertes   Where is my father?

King Claudius   Dead.

Queen Gertrude

>But not by him.

King Claudius   Let him demand his fill.   125

Laertes

>How came he dead? I'll not be juggled with![1150]
>To hell, allegiance! Vows, to the blackest devil!
>Conscience and grace, to the profoundest pit!
>I dare damnation. To this point I stand,
>That both the worlds I give to negligence,[1151]   130
>Let come what comes! Only I'll be revenged
>Most throughly[1152] for my father.

[1148] Treason can only glance at what it wants to do.

[1149] Its.

[1150] Toyed with.

[1151] "I care not about this world or the one to come."

[1152] Thoroughly.

King Claudius   Who shall stay[1153] you?

Laertes

    My will, not all the world!

    And for my means, I'll husband them so well,

    They shall go far with little.

King Claudius   Good Laertes,   135

    If you desire to know the certainty

    Of your dear father's death, is't writ in your revenge,

    That, swoopstake,[1154] you will draw both friend and foe,

    Winner and loser?

Laertes

    None but his enemies.

King Claudius   Will you know them then?   140

Laertes

    To his good friends thus wide I'll ope my arms;

    And like the kind life-rendering pelican,[1155]

    Repast[1156] them with my blood.

King Claudius   Why, now you speak

    Like a good child and a true gentleman.

    That I am guiltless of your father's death,   145

    And am most sensibly[1157] in grief for it,

    It shall as level[1158] to your judgment pierce

    As day does to your eye.

Danes (*within*)   Let her come in.

Laertes

    How now! What noise is that?

[1153] Stop.

[1154] Without discrimination.

[1155] In fable, the female pelican supposedly opens a wound in her own breast to feed or revive her young in need.

[1156] Feed.

[1157] Feelingly.

[1158] Straight.

Re-enter Ophelia

> O heat, dry up my brains! Tears seven times salt, 150
> Burn out the sense and virtue of mine eye!
> By heaven, thy madness shall be paid by weight,
> Till our scale turn the beam.[1159] O rose of May!
> Dear maid, kind sister, sweet Ophelia!
> O heavens! Is't possible a young maid's wits 155
> Should be as mortal as an old man's life?
> Nature is fine in love, and where 'tis fine,
> It sends some precious instance[1160] of itself
> After the thing it loves.

Ophelia (*sings*)

>> They bore him barefaced on the bier, 160
>>> Hey non nonny, nonny, hey nonny,
>> And in his grave rain'd many a tear—
> Fare you well, my dove!

Laertes

> Hadst thou thy wits, and didst persuade[1161] revenge,
> It could not move thus. 165

Ophelia

> You must sing *A-down, a-down*, and you *Call him a-down-a.*
> O, how the wheel[1162] becomes it! It is the false steward
> that stole his master's daughter.[1163]

Laertes

> This nothing's more than matter.[1164]

Ophelia

> There's rosemary, that's for remembrance. Pray, you love, 170

[1159] Tilt the balance in our favor.

[1160] Specimen; he implies that Ophelia's sanity followed her father in death.

[1161] Argue for.

[1162] Refrain.

[1163] We have no reference to this tale.

[1164] "Her seeming nonsense is most eloquent."

remember. And there is pansies, that's for thoughts.[1165]

Laertes

A document in madness, thoughts and remembrance fitted.

Ophelia

There's fennel for you, and columbines. There's rue for
you, and here's some for me. We may call it Herb-Grace
o' Sundays. You must wear your rue with a difference.[1166] 175
There's a daisy. I would give you some violets,[1167] but they
withered all when my father died. They say he made a
good end,—

(sings) For bonny sweet Robin is all my joy.

Laertes

Thought and affliction, passion,[1168] hell itself,   180
She turns to favour[1169] and to prettiness.

Ophelia *(sings)*

    And will a not come again?
    And will a not come again?
      No, no, he is dead,
      Go to thy death-bed,   185
    He never will come again.

    His beard was as white as snow,
    All flaxen[1170] was his poll.[1171]

[1165] Rosemary and pansies for Laertes; later fennel and columbine (both
signify marital infidelity) for Gertrude, and rue or herb of grace (repentance)
and daisies ((unhappy) love and/or seduction) for Claudius, rue for herself.

[1166] In a coat-of-arms there are minor variations to indicate a different
(younger) branch of the family; also Ophelia and the King feel differently.

[1167] Faithfulness.

[1168] Suffering.

[1169] Loveliness.

[1170] White blond.

[1171] Hair.

He is gone, he is gone,

And we cast away moan. 190

God ha' mercy on his soul!

And of all Christian souls, I pray God. God b'wi'ye. *Exit*

Laertes

Do you see this, O God?

King Claudius

Laertes, I must commune with your grief,

Or you deny me right. Go but apart, 195

Make choice of whom your wisest friends you will,

And they shall hear and judge 'twixt you and me.

If by direct or by collateral hand[1172]

They find us touched,[1173] we will our kingdom give,

Our crown, our life, and all that we call ours, 200

To you in satisfaction.[1174] But if not,

Be you content to lend your patience to us,

And we shall jointly labour with your soul

To give it due content.

Laertes   Let this be so.

His means of death, his obscure funeral— 205

No trophy, sword, nor hatchment o'er his bones,[1175]

No noble rite nor formal ostentation[1176]—

Cry to be heard, as 'twere from heaven to earth,

That[1177] I must call't in question.

King Claudius   So you shall.

And where the offence is let the great axe fall. 210

[1172] By mine or my agent's hand.

[1173] I.e., with guilt.

[1174] As recompense.

[1175] When a knight was buried properly, within the church, he would have his sword, shield, coat-of-arms, and helmet hung above his grave. "[H]atchment" = painted tablet of the coat-of-arms.

[1176] Ceremony.

[1177] So that.

I pray you, go with me.   *Exeunt*

Act IV, Scene vi

Enter Horatio and a Servant

Horatio

What are they that would speak with me?

Servant

Sailors, sir. They say they have letters for you.

Horatio

Let them come in.   *Exit Servant*

I do not know from what part of the world

I should be greeted if not from Lord Hamlet.   5

Enter Sailors

First Sailor

God bless you, sir.

Horatio

Let him bless thee too.

First Sailor

He shall, sir, an't please him. There's a letter for you, sir. It
comes from the ambassador that was bound for England—if your name be Horatio, as I am let to know it is.   10

Horatio (*reads*)

'Horatio, when thou shalt have overlooked[1178] this, give
these fellows some means[1179] to the King. They have letters for him. Ere we were two days old at sea, a pirate of

---

[1178] Read.
[1179] Way to get to.

very warlike appointment[1180] gave us chase. Finding ourselves too slow of sail, we put on a compelled valour, 15
and in the grapple I boarded them. On the instant they
got clear of our ship, so I alone became their prisoner.
They have dealt with me like thieves of mercy, but they
knew what they did.[1181] I am to do a good turn for them.
Let the King have the letters I have sent, and repair thou 20
to me[1182] with as much speed as thou wouldst fly death. I
have words to speak in thine ear will make thee dumb, yet
are they much too light for the bore[1183] of the matter.
These good fellows will bring thee where I am.
Rosencrantz and Guildenstern hold their course for En- 25
gland. Of them I have much to tell thee. Farewell.

> He that thou knowest thine,
> Hamlet.'

Come, I will make you way for[1184] these your letters,
And do't the speedier that you may direct me 30
To him from whom you brought them. *Exeunt*

Act IV, Scene vii

Enter King Claudius and Laertes

King Claudius

Now must your conscience my acquaintance seal,[1185]
And you must put me in your heart for friend,

[1180] Outfit.

[1181] They want something in return.

[1182] Come to me.

[1183] Caliber.

[1184] Give you a way, a means to deliver.

[1185] "Now you must agree I'm innocent."

Sith[1186] you have heard, and with a knowing ear,
That he which hath your noble father slain
Pursued my life.

Laertes   It well appears. But tell me   5
Why you proceeded not against these feats,[1187]
So crimeful and so capital[1188] in nature,
As by your safety, wisdom, all things else
You mainly[1189] were stirred up.

King Claudius   O, for two special reasons,
Which may to you, perhaps, seem much unsinewed,[1190]   10
But yet to me they're strong. The Queen his mother
Lives almost by his looks, and for myself—
My virtue or my plague, be it either which—
She's so conjunctive[1191] to my life and soul,
That, as the star moves not but in his sphere,[1192]   15
I could not but by her. The other motive,
Why to a public count[1193] I might not go,
Is the great love the general gender[1194] bear him,
Who, dipping all his faults in their affection,
Would, like the spring that turneth wood to stone,[1195]   20
Convert his gyves[1196] to graces, so that my arrows,

[1186] Since.

[1187] Acts.

[1188] So criminal and punishable by death.

[1189] Much.

[1190] Of little strength.

[1191] Closely bound.

[1192] According to Ptolemaeus, the spheres carried the planets in fixed orbit around the earth.

[1193] Reckoning; accounting.

[1194] The ordinary people; "the man in the street."

[1195] Much limestone dissolved in water will petrify wood. One such spring was to be found close to Shakespeare's birthplace.

[1196] Shackles, and so faults; what disables him.

Too slightly timbered[1197] for so loud a wind,
Would have reverted to my bow again,
And not where I had aimed them.

Laertes

And so have I a noble father lost,   25
A sister driven into desperate terms,
Whose worth, if praises may go back again,[1198]
Stood challenger on mount of all the age
For her perfections.[1199] But my revenge will come.

King Claudius

Break not your sleeps for that. You must not think   30
That we are made of stuff so flat and dull
That we can let our beard be shook with danger
And think it pastime. You shortly shall hear more.
I loved your father, and we love ourself.
And that, I hope, will teach you to imagine—   35

Enter a Messenger with letters

How now! What news?

Messenger   Letters, my lord, from Hamlet.
This to your majesty, this to the Queen.

King Claudius

From Hamlet! Who brought them?

Messenger

Sailors, my lord, they say. I saw them not.
They were given me by Claudio. He received them   40
Of him that brought them.

King Claudius   Laertes, you shall hear them.
Leave us.   *Exit Merssenger*

[1197] Made of too light wood.
[1198] I.e., to what she used to be.
[1199] I.e., she was an unrivaled paragon.

(*Reads*) 'High and mighty, you shall know I am set naked[1200] on your kingdom. To-morrow shall I beg leave
to see your kingly eyes, when I shall, first asking your par-   45
don,[1201] thereunto recount the occasion of my sudden and
more strange return.

                                     Hamlet.'

What should this mean? Are all the rest come back?
Or is it some abuse,[1202] and no such thing?

Laertes

Know you the hand?

King Claudius   'Tis Hamlet's character.   50
'Naked'! And in a postscript here he says
'Alone.' Can you advise me?

Laertes

I'm lost in it, my lord. But let him come.
It warms the very sickness in my heart
That I shall live and tell him to his teeth,   55
'Thus diest thou.'

King Claudius   If it be so, Laertes,
As how should it be so? How otherwise?[1203]
Will you be ruled by me?

Laertes   Ay, my lord,
So[1204] you will not o'errule me to a peace.

King Claudius

To thine own peace. If he be now returned,   60
As checking[1205] at his voyage, and that he means

[1200] Without belongings.

[1201] Permission.

[1202] Fraud.

[1203] The King is confused; Hamlet cannot have returned—and if not, from where come these letters?

[1204] If.

[1205] Shying from; stopping suddenly.

No more to undertake it, I will work him
To an exploit, now ripe in my device,[1206]
Under the which he shall not choose but fall;
And for his death no wind of blame shall breathe,   65
But even his mother shall uncharge[1207] the practise[1208]
And call it accident.

Laertes   My lord, I will be ruled,
The rather, if you could devise it so
That I might be the organ.[1209]

King Claudius   It falls right.
You have been talked of, since your travel, much,   70
And that in Hamlet's hearing, for a quality
Wherein, they say, you shine. Your sum of parts[1210]
Did not together pluck such envy from him
As did that one, and that, in my regard,
Of the unworthiest siege.[1211]

Laertes   What part is that, my lord?   75

King Claudius
A very ribbon[1212] in the cap of youth,
Yet needful too, for youth no less becomes[1213]
The light and careless livery that it wears
Than settled age his sables and his weeds,[1214]
Importing health and graveness.[1215] Two months since   80

[1206] Planning.

[1207] Not accuse.

[1208] Scheme.

[1209] Instrument.

[1210] Talents.

[1211] Status.

[1212] Just an adornment.

[1213] Is made to look to advantage by.

[1214] Black, richly trimmed garments.

[1215] Seriousness; fencing was regarded as part of a young, happy-go-lucky lifestyle.

Here was a gentleman of Normandy.
I've seen myself, and served against, the French,
And they can well[1216] on horseback; but this gallant
Had witchcraft in't. He grew unto his seat,
And to such wondrous doing brought his horse   85
As he had been incorpsed and demi-natured[1217]
With the brave beast. So far he topped my thought,
That I, in forgery[1218] of shapes and tricks,[1219]
Come short of what he did.

Laertes   A Norman was't?

King Claudius
A Norman.   90

Laertes
Upon my life, Lamord.

King Claudius   The very same.

Laertes
I know him well! He is the brooch[1220] indeed
And gem of all the nation.

King Claudius   He made confession of you,[1221]
And gave you such a masterly report
For art and exercise in your defence,[1222]   95
And for your rapier[1223] most especially,
That he cried out 'twould be a sight indeed
If one could match you. The scrimers[1224] of their nation,

[1216] Excel.

[1217] Shared the body and half the nature of the horse, i.e.. was a centaur.

[1218] Fabrication.

[1219] Skills needed by a war-horse and for exhibition.

[1220] Ornament.

[1221] He testified about you.

[1222] Swordsmanship.

[1223] At the time, the most fashionable weapon.

[1224] Fencers.

He swore, had neither motion, guard, nor eye,
If you opposed them. Sir, this report of his   100
Did Hamlet so envenom with his envy
That he could nothing do but wish and beg
Your sudden coming o'er to play with him.
Now, out of this—

Laertes   What out of this, my lord?

King Claudius

Laertes, was your father dear to you?   105
Or are you like the painting of a sorrow,
A face without a heart?

Laertes   Why ask you this?

King Claudius

Not that I think you did not love your father,
But that I know love is begun by time,[1225]
And that I see, in passages of proof,[1226]   110
Time qualifies[1227] the spark and fire of it.
There lives within the very flame of love
A kind of wick or snuff[1228] that will abate it;
And nothing is at a like[1229] goodness still,[1230]
For goodness, growing to a plurisy,[1231]   115
Dies in his own too much.[1232] That we would do
We should do when we would, for this 'would' changes
And hath abatements and delays as many
As there are tongues, are hands, are accidents;

[1225] Created by circumstance.

[1226] Time tested experience.

[1227] Tempers.

[1228] The burnt and smoking part of the wick.

[1229] Constant.

[1230] Always.

[1231] Inflammation of the chest, thought to be caused by an excess of humors; Latin *plus* = more.

[1232] Superfluity.

And then this 'should' is like a spendthrift[1233] sigh,   120
That hurts by easing. But, to the quick o' the ulcer[1234]—
Hamlet comes back. What would you undertake
To show yourself your father's son in deed
More than in words?

Laertes   To cut his throat i' the church.

King Claudius

No place, indeed, should murder sanctuarize.[1235]   125
Revenge should have no bounds. But, good Laertes,
Will you do this? Keep close within your chamber.
Hamlet returned shall know you are come home.
We'll put on[1236] those shall[1237] praise your excellence
And set a double varnish on the fame   130
The Frenchman gave you, bring you in fine[1238] together
And wager on your heads. He, being remiss,[1239]
Most generous[1240] and free from all contriving,
Will not peruse the foils, so that, with ease,
Or with a little shuffling, you may choose   135
A sword unbated,[1241] and, in a pass of practise[1242]
Requite him for your father.

Laertes   I will do't!
And, for that purpose, I'll anoint my sword.

[1233] Sighing was thought to use up blood from the heart; contemplated deed without action is a waste.

[1234] To the heart of the matter.

[1235] Give sanctuary to a murderer.

[1236] Appoint.

[1237] Who shall.

[1238] Finally.

[1239] Too trusting.

[1240] Magnanimous.

[1241] Not blunted; not a practice foil.

[1242] Trickery.

I bought an unction[1243] of a mountebank,[1244]
So mortal that, but dip a knife in it,   140
Where it draws blood no cataplasm[1245] so rare,
Collected from all simples[1246] that have virtue[1247]
Under the moon, can save the thing from death
That is but scratched withal. I'll touch my point
With this contagion, that, if I gall[1248] him slightly,   145
It may be death.

King Claudius   Let's further think of this;
Weigh what convenience both of time and means
May fit us to our shape.[1249] If this should fail,
And that our drift[1250] look through[1251] our bad performance,
'Twere better not essayed. Therefore this project   150
Should have a back or second,[1252] that might hold,
If this should blast in proof.[1253] Soft, let me see.
We'll make a solemn wager on your cunnings[1254]—
I ha't!
When in your motion[1255] you are hot and dry,   155
As make your bouts more violent to that end,
And that he calls for drink, I'll have prepared him
A chalice for the nonce,[1256] whereon but sipping,

[1243] Salve.
[1244] Wandering quack.
[1245] Plaster; poultice.
[1246] Healing herbs.
[1247] Healing power.
[1248] Scratch.
[1249] The role we are to act.
[1250] Trick.
[1251] Is visible in.
[1252] A back-up plan.
[1253] Backfire when tried.
[1254] Ability.
[1255] Exertion.
[1256] For the occasion.

If he by chance escape your venomed stuck,[1257]
Our purpose may hold there.

Enter Queen Gertrude

How now, sweet Queen!   160
Queen Gertrude
    One woe doth tread upon another's heel,
    So fast they follow. Your sister's drowned, Laertes.
Laertes
    Drowned! O, where?
Queen Gertrude
    There is a willow grows aslant a brook,
    That shows his hoar[1258] leaves in the glassy stream.   165
    Therewith fantastic garlands did she make
    Of crow-flowers, nettles, daisies, and long purples[1259]
    That liberal shepherds give a grosser name,[1260]
    But our cold[1261] maids do dead men's fingers call them.
    There, on the pendent boughs her coronet weeds   170
    Clambering to hang, an envious sliver[1262] broke,
    When down her weedy trophies and herself
    Fell in the weeping brook. Her clothes spread wide,
    And, mermaid-like, a while they bore her up,
    Which time she chanted snatches of old tunes   175

[1257] Lunge, thrust.
[1258] The willow was an emblem of mourning and unrequited love; "hoar" = the color of the grayish white leaves.
[1259] An orchis with a long, purple spur, said to have been called "dead-men's-fingers."
[1260] Probably a bawdy pun. The orchis has many names associated with penis and testicles.
[1261] Chaste.
[1262] A malicious twig.

As one incapable of[1263] her own distress,
Or like a creature native and indued
Unto that element.[1264] But long it could not be
Till that her garments, heavy with their drink,
Pulled the poor wretch from her melodious lay[1265]   180
To muddy death.

Laertes   Alas, then, she is drowned?

Queen Gertrude
    Drowned, drowned.

Laertes
    Too much of water hast thou, poor Ophelia,
    And therefore I forbid my tears. But yet
    It is our trick;[1266] nature her custom holds,   185
    Let shame say what it will. (*Weeps*) When these are gone,
    The woman will be out.[1267] Adieu, my lord.
    I have a speech of fire, that fain[1268] would blaze,
    But that this folly douts[1269] it.   *Exit*

King Claudius   Let's follow, Gertrude.
    How much I had to do to calm his rage!   190
    Now fear I this will give it start again;
    Therefore let's follow.   *Exeunt*

[1263] Not understanding.
[1264] Someone who was native to, belonged in the water.
[1265] Song.
[1266] The way we naturally act.
[1267] I will have lost all softness, my feminine traits.
[1268] Happily.
[1269] Douses.

Act V, Scene i

Enter two Clowns,[1270] *a Gravedigger and Another, with a spade and a pickaxe*

First Clown

> Is she to be buried in Christian burial that wilfully seeks
> her own salvation?[1271]

Second Clown

> I tell thee she is, and therefore make her grave straight.[1272]
> The crowner[1273] hath sat on her,[1274] and finds it Christian
> burial.   5

First Clown

> How can that be, unless she drowned herself in her own
> defence?

Second Clown

> Why, 'tis found so.

First Clown

> It must be *se offendendo,*[1275] it cannot be else. For here lies
> the point: if I drown myself wittingly,[1276] it argues an act, 10
> and an act hath three branches. It is to act, to do, to per-
> form.[1277] Argal,[1278] she drowned herself wittingly.

[1270] "Clown" is the Elizabethan term for the troupe's comedian, often
found in stage directions instead of a character's name.

[1271] Malapropism for "damnation," most probably; suicides were denied
Christian rites and not buried in consecrated ground.

[1272] Straight away; immediately.

[1273] Coroner.

[1274] Held her inquest.

[1275] Malapropism for Latin *se defendendo*, in self-defense; First Clown uses
one opposite for the other.

[1276] Voluntarily.

[1277] A famous 1554 suicide case lists "imagination, resolution, and perfection" of the act.

[1278] Ergo; therefore.

Second Clown

Nay, but hear you, Goodman Delver[1279]—

First Clown

Give me leave. Here lies the water—good. Here stands
the man—good. If the man go to this water, and drown 15
himself, it is, will he, nill he,[1280] he goes. Mark you that.
But if the water come to him and drown him, he drowns
not himself; argal, he that is not guilty of his own death
shortens not his own life.

Second Clown

But is this law? 20

First Clown

Ay, marry, is't, crowner's quest[1281] law.

Second Clown

Will you ha' the truth on't? If this had not been a gentlewoman, she should have been buried out o' Christian
burial.

First Clown

Why, there thou say'st,[1282] and the more pity that great folk 25
should have countenance in this world to drown or hang
themselves more than their even Christian.[1283] Come, my
spade. There is no ancient gentlemen but gardeners,
ditchers, and grave-makers—they hold up[1284] Adam's
profession. 30

Second Clown

Was he a gentleman?

[1279] "Goodman" is used as a term of address when followed by the man's
occupation, not name. Delver = gravedigger.

[1280] Willy-nilly.

[1281] Inquest.

[1282] "There you go"; "How right you are."

[1283] Fellow Christians.

[1284] Continue.

First Clown

He was the first that ever bore arms.[1285]

Second Clown

Why, he had none.

First Clown

What, art a heathen? How dost thou understand the Scripture? The Scripture says Adam digged. Could he dig with-   35
out arms? I'll put another question to thee. If thou
answerest me not to the purpose, confess thyself[128]—

Second Clown

Go to.[1287]

First Clown

What is he that builds stronger than either the mason, the
shipwright, or the carpenter?   40

Second Clown

The gallows-maker, for that frame[1288] outlives a thousand
tenants.

First Clown

I like thy wit well, in good faith. The gallows does[1289] well.
But how does it well? It does well to those that do ill.
Now thou dost ill to say the gallows is built stronger than   45
the church, argal, the gallows may do well to thee. To't
again, come.

Second Clown

'Who builds stronger than a mason, a shipwright, or a
carpenter?'

[1285] A coat-of-arms of a gentleman with a pun on "limbs" and "weapons";
also a suggestion that all were of the gentleman class in Adam's time, and
therefore equal.

[1286] "Confess thyself and be hanged" (proverb).

[1287] "Come on!"

[1288] Pun on 1) gallows; 2) lumber structure of a building.

[1289] Will do.

First Clown

    Ay, tell me that, and unyoke.[1290]   50

Second Clown

    Marry, now I can tell!

First Clown

    To't.

Second Clown

    Mass,[1291] I cannot tell.

First Clown

    Cudgel thy brains no more about it, for your dull ass will
    not mend his pace[1292] with beating, and, when you are 55
    asked this question next, say 'a grave-maker.' The houses
    that he makes lasts till doomsday. Go, get thee to
    Yaughan.[1293] Fetch me a stoup[1294] of liquor.

*Exit Second Clown. First Clown digs and sings. While he is singing, Enter
Hamlet and Horatio*

    In youth, when I did love, did love,
        Methought it was very sweet,   60
    To contract,[1295] O, the time, for, ah, my behove,[1296]
        O, methought, there was nothing meet.

Hamlet

    Has this fellow no feeling of his business, that a[1297] sings
    at grave-making?

[1290] Relax, like oxen do when their yoke is removed after work.

[1291] By the mass.

[1292] Speed up.

[1293] Probably close-by innkeeper.

[1294] Container; bottle of no specific size.

[1295] Shorten.

[1296] Advantage.

[1297] He.

Horatio

    Custom hath made it in him a property of easiness.[1298]   65

Hamlet

    'Tis e'en so. The hand of little employment hath the dain-
    tier sense.[1299]

First Clown (*sings*)

    But age with his stealing steps,

        Hath clawed me in his clutch,

    And hath shipped[1300] me intil[1301] the land,   70

        As if I had never been such.   *Throws up a skull*

Hamlet

    That skull had a tongue in it and could sing once. How
    the knave jowls[1302] it to the ground as if 'twere Cain's
    jawbone, that did the first murder![1303] This might be the
    pate of a politician, which this ass now o'er-offices,[1304]   75
    one that would circumvent God, might it not?

Horatio

    It might, my lord.

Hamlet

    Or of a courtier, which could say 'Good morrow, sweet
    lord! How dost thou, good lord?' This might be my Lord
    Such-a-one, that praised my Lord Such-a-one's horse   80
    when he meant to beg it, might it not?

Horatio

    Ay, my lord.

[1298] "Custom makes all things easy" (proverb).

[1299] Feels more delicately.

[1300] Conveyed.

[1301] To; "shipped . . . land" may be "sent me into the grave"; next line's
"such" may be = a young man.

[1302] Dashes.

[1303] Cain's murder of Abel, a fratricide, was committed with the jawbone of
an ass.

[1304] Lords it over.

Hamlet

> Why, e'en so, and now my Lady Worm's, chapless,[1305] and
> knocked about the mazzard[1306] with a sexton's spade.
> Here's fine revolution,[1307] an we had the trick to[1308] see't. 85
> Did these bones cost no more the breeding, but to play at
> loggats with 'em?[1309] Mine ache to think on't.

First Clown (*sings*)

> A pickaxe, and a spade, a spade,
>> For and[1310] a shrouding sheet.
> O, a pit of clay for to be made   90
>> For such a guest is meet.[1311]   *Throws up another skull*

Hamlet

> There's another! Why may not that be the skull of a law-
> yer? Where be his quiddities now, his quillities,[1312] his cases,
> his tenures,[1313] and his tricks? Why does he suffer this rude
> knave now to knock him about the sconce[1314] with a dirty 95
> shovel, and will not tell him of his action of battery?[1315]
> Hum! This fellow might be in's time a great buyer of
> land, with his statutes,[1316] his recognizances,[1317] his fines,[1318]

[1305] Without a jaw.

[1306] Head.

[1307] Rotation of Fortune's wheel (see glossary).

[1308] If only we could.

[1309] "Were these bones nurtured to become worthless enough to use as game pieces." "Loggats" = wooden shapes to be thrown as close as possible to a determined spot or stake.

[1310] And also.

[1311] Fitting.

[1312] Quibbles; "quiddities" has the same meaning.

[1313] Titles to property.

[1314] Head.

[1315] Liability to be taken to court for assault.

[1316] Mortgage on land.

[1317] A bond of obligation or debt.

[1318] Action leading to an agreement.

his double vouchers,[1319] his recoveries.[1320] Is this the fine[1321]
of his fines, and the recovery[1322] of his recoveries, to have 100
his fine[1323] pate full of fine[1324] dirt? Will his vouchers vouch[1325]
him no more of his purchases, and double ones too, than
the length and breadth of a pair of indentures?[1326] The
very conveyances[1327] of his lands will hardly lie in this box;[1328]
and must the inheritor[1329] himself have no more, ha?   105

Horatio

Not a jot more, my lord.

Hamlet

Is not parchment made of sheepskins?

Horatio

Ay, my lord, and of calf-skins too.

Hamlet

They are sheep and calves[1330] which seek out assurance[1331]
in that. I will speak to this fellow. Whose grave's this, 110
sirrah?[1332]

[1319] Two witnesses or second warrantor.

[1320] Suit to obtain ownership.

[1321] End result.

[1322] Sum total.

[1323] Refined and handsome.

[1324] Powdery fine.

[1325] Assure.

[1326] Deed with the wording duplicated on the same document, then separated on a zigzag line (the indent) so genuineness could be proven when both halves were present. The grave of this lawyer, his final land purchase, will hardly be larger that the elaborate document of purchase.

[1327] Deeds.

[1328] Deed box; coffin.

[1329] Proprietor.

[1330] Foolish people.

[1331] 1) Possession; 2) legal deed of possession.

[1332] Form of "sir" used to a social inferior.

First Clown

>   Mine, sir.

>   (*Sings*) O, a pit of clay for to be made

>>   For such a guest is meet.

Hamlet

>   I think it be thine indeed, for thou liest in't.   115

First Clown

>   You lie out on't, sir, and therefore it is not yours. For my

>   part, I do not lie in't, and yet it is mine.

Hamlet

>   Thou dost lie in't, to be in't and say it is thine. 'Tis for the

>   dead, not for the quick;[1333] therefore thou liest.

First Clown

>   'Tis a quick[1334] lie, sir, 'twill away again, from me to you. 120

Hamlet

>   What man dost thou dig it for?

First Clown

>   For no man, sir.

Hamlet

>   What woman, then?

First Clown

>   For none, neither.

Hamlet

>   Who is to be buried in't?   125

First Clown

>   One that was a woman, sir, but, rest her soul, she's dead.

Hamlet

>   How absolute[1335] the knave is! We must speak by the

>   card,[1336] or equivocation will undo us. By the Lord, Horatio,

---

[1333] Living.

[1334] Agile.

[1335] Pedantic.

[1336] With precision; "card" = a navigational chart.

these three years I have taken a note of it. The age is
grown so picked[1337] that the toe of the peasant comes so 130
near the heel of the courtier, he galls his kibe.[1338] How
long hast thou been a grave-maker?

First Clown

Of all the days i'the year, I came to't that day that our last
King Hamlet o'ercame Fortinbras.

Hamlet

How long is that since?   135

First Clown

Cannot you tell that? Every fool can tell that. It was the
very day that young Hamlet was born, he that is mad, and
sent into England.

Hamlet

Ay, marry, why was he sent into England?

First Clown

Why, because he was mad. He shall recover his wits there; 140
or, if he do not, it's no great matter there.

Hamlet

Why?

First Clown

'Twill not be seen in him there. There the men are as mad
as he.

Hamlet

How came he mad?   145

First Clown

Very strangely, they say.

Hamlet

How strangely?

First Clown

Faith, e'en with losing his wits.

[1337] Refined.

[1338] The peasant affects the manners of the court; "kibe" = sore on the heel.

Hamlet

Upon what ground?[1339]

First Clown

Why, here in Denmark. I have been sexton here, man and 150
boy, thirty years.

Hamlet

How long will a man lie i'the earth ere he rot?

First Clown

I'faith, if he be not rotten before he die—as we have
many pocky corses[1340] now-a-days, that will scarce hold
the laying in[1341]—a will last you some eight year or nine 155
year. A tanner will last you nine year.

Hamlet

Why he more than another?

First Clown

Why, sir, his hide is so tanned with his trade that he will
keep out water a great while, and your water is a sore
decayer of your whoreson[1342] dead body. Here's a skull 160
now. This skull has lain in the earth three and twenty years.

Hamlet

Whose was it?

First Clown

A whoreson mad fellow's it was. Whose do you think it
was?

Hamlet

Nay, I know not.   165

First Clown

A pestilence on him for a mad rogue! A poured a flagon

[1339] 1) For what reason; 2) in what place.
[1340] Bodies dead from venereal disease, therefore already decomposing before death.
[1341] Stay in one piece through the burial.
[1342] A contemptuous expression; "damned."

of Rhenish[1343] on my head once! This same skull, sir, was
Yorick's skull, the King's jester.

Hamlet

This?

First Clown

E'en that.   170

Hamlet

Let me see.   *Takes the skull*

Alas, poor Yorick! I knew him, Horatio, a fellow of infinite jest, of most excellent fancy. He hath borne me on his
back a thousand times—and now, how abhorred in my
imagination it is! My gorge rises at it. Here hung those lips 175
that I have kissed I know not how oft. Where be your
gibes now, your gambols, your songs, your flashes of
merriment, that were wont to set the table on a roar? Not
one now, to mock your own grinning? Quite chap-
fallen?[1344] Now get you to my lady's chamber and tell 180
her, let her paint an inch thick, to this favour[1345] she must
come. Make her laugh at that. Prithee, Horatio, tell me
one thing.

Horatio

What's that, my lord?

Hamlet

Dost thou think Alexander[1346] looked o' this fashion i' 185
t'earth?

Horatio

E'en so.

Hamlet

And smelt so? Pah!   *Puts down the skull*

[1343] Rhine wine.

[1344] Jaw-dropped; amazed and "down in the mouth."

[1345] Appearance.

[1346] Alexander the Great.

Horatio

> E'en so, my lord.

Hamlet

> To what base uses we may return, Horatio! Why may not 190
> imagination trace the noble dust of Alexander till a find it
> stopping a bung-hole?[1347]

Horatio

> 'Twere to consider too curiously[1348] to consider so.

Hamlet

> No, faith, not a jot, but to follow him thither with mod-
> esty enough,[1349] and likelihood to lead it, as thus: Alexander 195
> died, Alexander was buried, Alexander returneth into dust,
> the dust is earth, of earth we make loam,[1350] and why of
> that loam, whereto he was converted, might they not stop
> a beer-barrel?
>
> Imperious Caesar, dead and turned to clay,   200
> Might stop a hole to keep the wind away.
> O, that that earth, which kept the world in awe,
> Could patch a wall t'expel the winter's flaw![1351]
> But soft! But soft! Aside. Here comes the King,
> The Queen, the courtiers.

Enter Bearers with Ophelia's coffin, a Priest, King Claudius, Queen Gertrude, Laertes, and Attendants

> > Who is this they follow? 205
> And with such maimed[1352] rites? This doth betoken

[1347] Plugging a cask of ale or wine.

[1348] With too much imagination.

[1349] Moderately, reasonably enough.

[1350] Plastering material (clay and straw) used for building.

[1351] Squall of wind.

[1352] I.e., much less pomp than a court funeral should have.

The corse they follow did with desperate hand
Fordo[1353] its own life. 'Twas of some estate.[1354]
Couch we[1355] a while, and mark.   *Retiring with Horatio*

Laertes

What ceremony else?   210

Hamlet

That is Laertes, a very noble youth. Mark.

Laertes

What ceremony else?

First Priest

Her obsequies have been as far enlarged
As we have warrantise.[1356] Her death was doubtful,
And, but that great command o'ersways the order,[1357]   215
She should in ground unsanctified have lodged
Till the last trumpet. For[1358] charitable prayers,
Shards, flints, and pebbles should be thrown on her,
Yet here she is allowed her virgin crants,[1359]
Her maiden strewments,[1360] and the bringing home   220
Of bell and burial.[1361]

Laertes

Must there no more be done?

First Priest   No more be done.
We should profane the service of the dead
To sing sage[1362] requiem and such rest to her

[1353] Harm.

[1354] Social standing.

[1355] Let us hide.

[1356] Sanction for burial.

[1357] Usual practice.

[1358] Instead of.

[1359] Wreath or garland worn as a sign of virginity.

[1360] Flowers strewn over the grave.

[1361] The tolling of the bell and the rites of funeral.

[1362] Grave.

As to peace-parted souls.

Laertes   Lay her i'th' earth,   225

And from her fair and unpolluted flesh

May violets spring! I tell thee, churlish priest,

A ministering angel shall my sister be,

When thou liest howling.[1363]

Hamlet

What, the fair Ophelia!

Queen Gertrude (*scattering flowers*)

                                    Sweets to the sweet. Farewell!   230

I hoped thou shouldst have been my Hamlet's wife.

I thought thy bride-bed to have decked, sweet maid,

And not have strewed thy grave.

Laertes   O, treble woe

Fall ten times treble on that cursed head,

Whose wicked deed thy most ingenious sense[1364]   235

Deprived thee of! Hold off the earth a while,

Till I have caught her once more in mine arms.

                                        Leaps into the grave

Now pile your dust upon the quick and dead,

Till of this flat a mountain you have made

To o'ertop old Pelion,[1365] or the skyish head   240

Of blue Olympus.

Hamlet (*advancing*)   What is he whose grief

Bears such an emphasis?[1366] Whose phrase of sorrow

Conjures the wandering stars,[1367] and makes them stand

Like wonder-wounded hearers? This is I,

[1363] I.e., with the damned.

[1364] Capable intelligence.

[1365] In their war with the gods the Giants piled Mount Pelion on top of Mount Ossa to reach the top of Olympus according to Greek myth.

[1366] Excess.

[1367] Planets.

    Hamlet the Dane.[1368]   *Leaps into the grave* 245

Laertes (*grappling with him*)

    The devil take thy soul!

Hamlet   Thou pray'st not well.

    I prithee, take thy fingers from my throat,

    For, though I am not splenitive[1369] and rash,

    Yet have I something in me dangerous,

    Which let thy wiseness fear. Hold off thy hand.   250

King Claudius

    Pluck them asunder.

Queen Gertrude

    Hamlet, Hamlet!

All

    Gentlemen!

Horatio

    Good my lord, be quiet.

        The Attendants part them, and they come out of the grave

Hamlet

    Why I will fight with him upon this theme   255

    Until my eyelids will no longer wag.[1370]

Queen Gertrude

    O my son, what theme?

Hamlet

    I loved Ophelia. Forty thousand brothers

    Could not, with all their quantity of love,

    Make up my sum. What wilt thou do for her?   260

King Claudius

    O, he is mad, Laertes.

Queen Gertrude

    For love of God, forbear him.[1371]

[1368] Hamlet assumes the title of the King of Denmark.

[1369] Of a hot temper; see glossary, "Four Humors."

[1370] Blink; this is the tiniest sign that life remains.

[1371] Leave him be.

Hamlet

    'Swounds, show me what thou'lt do!

    Woo't[1372] weep? Woo't fight? Woo't fast? Woo't tear thyself?

    Woo't drink up eisel?[1373] Eat a crocodile?   265

    I'll do't. Dost thou come here to whine?

    To outface me with leaping in her grave?

    Be buried quick with her, and so will I.

    And, if thou prate of mountains, let them throw

    Millions of acres on us, till our ground,   270

    Singeing his pate[1374] against the burning zone,[1375]

    Make Ossa like a wart! Nay, an thou'lt mouth,[1376]

    I'll rant as well as thou.

Queen Gertrude   This is mere madness,

    And thus awhile the fit will work on him.

    Anon,[1377] as patient as the female dove,[1378]   275

    When that her golden couplets are disclosed,[1379]

    His silence will sit drooping.

Hamlet   Hear you, sir,

    What is the reason that you use me thus?

    I loved you ever. But it is no matter;

    Let Hercules himself do what he may,   280

    The cat will mew and dog will have his day.[1380]   *Exit*

King Claudius

    I pray you, good Horatio, wait upon him.   *Exit Horatio*

[1372] Wilt thou.

[1373] Vinegar.

[1374] Head.

[1375] The sun's sphere.

[1376] If you will speak exaggeratedly.

[1377] Soon.

[1378] A proverbially meek bird.

[1379] Her pair of young are hatched.

[1380] "Calming Laertes is more than even Hercules could manage; still my day will come."

(*To Laertes*) Strengthen your patience in[1381] our last night's speech.
We'll put the matter to the present push.[1382]
Good Gertrude, set some watch over your son.   285
This grave shall have a living monument.[1383]
An hour of quiet shortly shall we see;
Till then, in patience our proceeding be.   *Exeunt*

Act V, Scene ii

Enter Hamlet and Horatio

Hamlet

So much for this, sir. Now shall you see the other.[1384]
You do remember all the circumstance?

Horatio

Remember it, my lord?

Hamlet

Sir, in my heart there was a kind of fighting,
That would not let me sleep. Methought I lay   5
Worse than the mutines[1385] in the bilboes.[1386] Rashly,[1387]
And praised be rashness for it, let us know,[1388]
Our indiscretion[1389] sometimes serves us well

[1381] Thinking of.

[1382] Immediate action.

[1383] 1) A monument that will endure; 2) a possible reference to the plot against Hamlet's life.

[1384] Other matter.

[1385] Mutineers.

[1386] Shackles.

[1387] On impulse; without premeditation.

[1388] Let us mark and remember.

[1389] Impulsive action.

When our deep plots do pall,[1390] and that should teach us
There's a divinity that shapes our ends,   10
    Rough-hew them[1391] how we will—

Horatio   That is most certain.

Hamlet

    Up from my cabin,
    My sea-gown[1392] scarfed about[1393] me, in the dark
    Groped I to find out them, had my desire.
    Fingered[1394] their packet, and in fine[1395] withdrew   15
    To mine own room again, making so bold,
    My fears forgetting manners, to unseal
    Their grand commission, where I found, Horatio—
    O royal knavery!—an exact command,
    Larded[1396] with many several sorts of reasons   20
    Importing[1397] Denmark's health and England's too,
    With, ho! such bugs and goblins in my life,[1398]
    That, on the supervise,[1399] no leisure bated,[1400]
    No, not to stay[1401] the grinding of the axe,
    My head should be struck off.

Horatio   Is't possible?   25

Hamlet

    Here's the commission. Read it at more leisure.

[1390] Weaken.
[1391] Shape them roughly.
[1392] Sailor's costume.
[1393] Wrapped around in haste.
[1394] Snatched.
[1395] Finally.
[1396] Embellished.
[1397] Concerning.
[1398] Such horrors should I stay alive; "bugs" = bugbears.
[1399] Reading.
[1400] With no time to lose.
[1401] Wait for.

But wilt thou hear me how I did proceed?

Horatio

    I beseech you.

Hamlet

    Being thus benetted round with villainies—

    Ere I could make a prologue to my brains,   30

    They had begun the play[1402]—I sat me down,

    Devised a new commission, wrote it fair.[1403]

    I once did hold it, as our statists[1404] do,

    A baseness to write fair and laboured much

    How to forget that learning, but, sir, now   35

    It did me yeoman's service.[1405] Wilt thou know

    Th'effect of what I wrote?

Horatio   Ay, good my lord.

Hamlet

    An earnest conjuration[1406] from the King,

    As England was his faithful tributary,

    As love between them like the palm might flourish,   40

    As peace should still[1407] her wheaten garland[1408] wear

    And stand a comma[1409] 'tween their amities,

    And many such-like 'As'es' of great charge,[1410]

    That, on the view and knowing of these contents,

    Without debatement further, more or less,   45

    He should the bearers put to sudden death,

[1402] "Before I could begin to plan, my brain had started acting for me."

[1403] With a scribes handwriting.

[1404] Statesmen.

[1405] Served me bravely; "yeoman" = freeholder, fighting for his own country, not for pay.

[1406] Petition.

[1407] Always.

[1408] Both wheat and palms are symbolic of peace and plenty.

[1409] Smallest mark of punctuation; not very significant.

[1410] Burden; importance.

Not shriving-time[1411] allowed.

Horatio   How was this sealed?

Hamlet

Why, even in that was heaven ordinant.[1412]

I had my father's signet in my purse,

Which was the model of that Danish seal;   50

Folded the writ up in form of th'other,

Subscribed it,[1413] gave't the impression,[1414] placed it safely,

The changeling[1415] never known. Now, the next day

Was our sea-fight, and what to this was sequent[1416]

Thou know'st already.   55

Horatio

So Guildenstern and Rosencrantz go to't.

Hamlet

Why, man, they did make love to this employment,

They are not near my conscience. Their defeat[1417]

Does by their own insinuation[1418] grow.

'Tis dangerous when the baser nature[1419] comes   60

Between the pass[1420] and fell incensed[1421] points

Of mighty opposites.

Horatio   Why, what a king is this!

Hamlet

Does it not, think'st thee, stand me now upon[1422]—

[1411] Time for confession, a rite usually granted the condemned man.

[1412] The director of events.

[1413] Signed it.

[1414] Sealed it (with wax).

[1415] A fairy child substituted for a stolen mortal infant.

[1416] What followed this.

[1417] Downfall.

[1418] Sneaking in.

[1419] The lower sort.

[1420] Rapier thrust.

[1421] Fiercely furious.

[1422] "Does it not now seem to you to be my duty."

He that hath killed my King and whored my mother,
Popped in between the election[1423] and my hopes,   65
Thrown out his angle[1424] for my proper[1425] life,
And with such cozenage[1426]—is't not perfect conscience[1427]
To quit[1428] him with this arm? And is't not to be damned
To let this canker[1429] of our nature come
In further evil?   70

Horatio

It must be shortly known to him from England
What is the issue[1430] of the business there.

Hamlet

It will be short. The interim is mine;
And a man's life's no more than to say 'One.'[1431]
But I am very sorry, good Horatio,   75
That to Laertes I forgot myself,
For, by the image[1432] of my cause, I see
The portraiture of his. I'll court his favours.
But sure, the bravery[1433] of his grief did put me
Into a towering passion.

Horatio   Peace! Who comes here?   80

Enter Osric, a courtier

[1423] In this play, Denmark is an elective monarchy.
[1424] Fishing hook.
[1425] Own.
[1426] Underhandedness.
[1427] Perfectly reasonable; perfectly in accordance with what is right.
[1428] Requite.
[1429] A growth; a growing sore.
[1430] Outcome.
[1431] A very short span, only a single syllable can measure it.
[1432] Mirror image.
[1433] Flamboyance.

Osric

> Your lordship is right welcome back to Denmark.

Hamlet

> I humbly thank you, sir. (*Aside*) Dost know this water-fly?

Horatio

> No, my good lord.

Hamlet

> Thy state is the more gracious,[1434] for 'tis a vice to know
> him. He hath much land, and fertile. Let a beast be lord 85
> of beasts, and his crib shall stand at the king's mess.[1435] 'Tis
> a chuff.[1436] But, as I say, spacious in the possession of dirt.

Osric

> Sweet lord, if your lordship were at leisure, I should im-
> part a thing to you from his majesty.

Hamlet

> I will receive it, sir, with all diligence of spirit. Put your 90
> bonnet[1437] to his right use; 'tis for the head.

Osric

> I thank your lordship, it is very hot.

Hamlet

> No, believe me, 'tis very cold. The wind is northerly.

Osric

> It is indifferent cold,[1438] my lord, indeed.

Hamlet

> But yet methinks it is very sultry and hot for my complex- 95
> ion.[1439]

[1434] Blessed.

[1435] A rich enough animal might be accepted sitting at the king's table.

[1436] A well-off churl.

[1437] Hat.

[1438] Quite cold.

[1439] Constitution.

Osric

    Exceedingly, my lord, it is very sultry, as 'twere—I cannot
tell how. But, my lord, his majesty bade me signify to you
that a[1440] has laid a great wager on your head. Sir, this is
the matter—   100

Hamlet

    I beseech you, remember.   *Hamlet moves him to put on his hat*

Osric

    Nay, good my lord, for mine ease, in good faith.[1441] Sir,
here is newly come to court Laertes, believe me, an absolute gentleman, full of most excellent differences,[1442] of
very soft society[1443] and great showing.[1444] Indeed, to speak 105
feelingly[1445] of him, he is the card or calendar of gentry,[1446] for you shall find in him the continent of what
part[1447] a gentleman would see.

Hamlet

    Sir, his definement suffers no perdition[1448] in you, though,
I know, to divide him inventorially would dizzy the arith- 110
metic of memory,[1449] and yet but yaw[1450] neither, in respect of his quick sail. But, in the verity of extolment,[1451] I
take him to be a soul of great article;[1452] and his infu-

[1440] He.

[1441] Conventional way of saying "Thank you, no."

[1442] Qualities.

[1443] Gracious manners.

[1444] Looks.

[1445] Justly.

[1446] Model of gentility; "card" = chart; "calendar" = directory.

[1447] Whatever part.

[1448] Loss.

[1449] The list of his perfect qualities is so long the memory grows dizzy
reckoning them.

[1450] Steer in zigzag, like a ship not on a true course.

[1451] "As your praise is true."

[1452] Of a grand theme.

sion[1453] of such dearth[1454] and rareness, as, to make true
diction[1455] of him, his semblable is his mirror,[1456] and who 115
else would trace him, his umbrage,[1457] nothing more.

Osric

Your lordship speaks most infallibly of him.

Hamlet

The concernancy,[1458] sir? Why do we wrap the gentleman
in our more rawer breath?[1459]

Osric

Sir?   120

Horatio

Is't not possible to understand in another tongue?
You will to't, sir, really.

Hamlet

What imports the nomination[1460] of this gentleman?

Osric

Of Laertes?

Horatio

His purse is empty already; all's golden words are spent. 125

Hamlet

Of him, sir.

Osric

I know you are not ignorant—

Hamlet

I would you did, sir. Yet, in faith, if you did, it would not

---

[1453] What has been instilled in him.

[1454] Rarity.

[1455] Make a true pronouncement.

[1456] His like can only be found in his own reflection.

[1457] A shadow of him.

[1458] "How does this concern me?"

[1459] "Why do we discuss him in words that can only fall short of describing him?" i.e., "Why are we discussing him?"

[1460] Mention.

much approve[1461] me. Well, sir?

Osric

You are not ignorant of what excellence Laertes is—   130

Hamlet

I dare not confess that, lest I should compare with him in
excellence.[1462] But, to know a man well, were to know
himself.[1463]

Osric

I mean, sir, for his weapon. But in the imputation[1464] laid
on him, by them in his meed[1465] he's unfellowed.[1466]   135

Hamlet

What's his weapon?

Osric

Rapier and dagger.

Hamlet

That's two of his weapons. But well.

Osric

The King, sir, hath wagered with him six Barbary horses,[1467]
against the which he has impawned,[1468] as I take it, six French 140
rapiers and poniards, with their assigns[1469] as girdle,[1470]
hangers,[1471] and so. Three of the carriages, in faith, are

[1461] Speak well of.

[1462] "Only excellence can approach excellence, so how dare I?"

[1463] One must know oneself well in order to know another well.

[1464] Estimation.

[1465] In his service.

[1466] Unrivaled.

[1467] A swift and most sought after breed.

[1468] Staked.

[1469] Accessories.

[1470] Belt.

[1471] Shoulder straps, attached to the belt with a plate to attach the scabbard;
the sum total is "a carriage."

very dear to fancy,[1472] very responsive to the hilts,[1473] most delicate[1474] carriages, and of very liberal conceit.[1475]

Hamlet

What call you the carriages?   145

Horatio

I knew you must be edified by the margin[1476] ere you had done.

Osric

The carriages, sir, are the hangers.

Hamlet

The phrase would be more german to the matter, if we could carry cannon by our sides.[1477] I would it might be 150 hangers till then. But on. Six Barbary horses against six French swords, their assigns, and three liberal-conceited carriages; that's the French bet against the Danish. Why is this 'impawned,' as you call it?

Osric

The King, sir, hath laid,[1478] that in a dozen passes between 155 yourself and him, he shall not exceed you three hits.[1479] He[1480] hath laid on twelve for nine, and it would come to immediate trial if your lordship would vouchsafe the answer.[1481]

Hamlet

How if I answer 'no'?

[1472] Very fashionable.

[1473] With designs to match the sword hilts.

[1474] Finely made.

[1475] Created with lavish use of imagination.

[1476] Explanatory notes were found printed in the margins of books.

[1477] "Carriage" is the name for the frame on which a cannon is mounted.

[1478] Made a bet.

[1479] Out of twelve bouts, Laertes may score three more hits than Hamlet, no more, for Hamlet to win.

[1480] I.e., Laertes.

[1481] Acceptance of the challenge.

Osric

I mean, my lord, the opposition of your person in trial.   160

Hamlet

Sir, I will walk here in the hall. If it please his majesty, 'tis
the breathing time[1482] of day with me. Let the foils be
brought, the gentleman willing, and the King hold his
purpose, I will win for him and I can. If not, I will gain
nothing but my shame and the odd hits.   165

Osric

Shall I re-deliver you e'en so?

Hamlet

To this effect, sir; after what flourish your nature will.

Osric

I commend my duty[1483] to your lordship.

Hamlet

Yours, yours.   *Exit Osric*

He does well to commend it himself; there are no tongues 170
else for's turn.[1484]

Horatio

This lapwing runs away with the shell on his head.[1485]

Hamlet

A did comply with his dug[1486] before a sucked it. Thus
has he—and many more of the same bevy that I know
the drossy age[1487] dotes on—only got the tune of the time 175
and outward habit of encounter;[1488] a kind of yeasty col-

[1482] Time for exercise.

[1483] 1) Present to your regard; 2) praise.

[1484] To serve his purpose.

[1485] Lapwings, or plovers, will leave the nest very shortly after hatching; thus
they became the image of precocious youth.

[1486] He saluted his mother's breast.

[1487] These worthless times.

[1488] Know only the fashionable formulas, not true substance, of conversation ("encounter").

lection,[1489] which carries them through and through the most fanned and winnowed opinions,[1490] and[1491] do but blow them to their trial, the bubbles are out.[1492]

Enter a Lord

Lord

My lord, his majesty commended him to you by young 180
Osric, who brings back to him that you attend him in the hall. He sends to know if your pleasure hold to play with Laertes, or that you will take longer time.

Hamlet

I am constant to my purpose; they follow the King's pleasure. If his fitness speaks, mine is ready,[1493] now or when- 185
soever, provided I be so able as now.

Lord

The King and Queen and all are coming down.

Hamlet

In happy time.

Lord

The Queen desires you to use some gentle entertainment to Laertes[1494] before you fall to play.   190

Hamlet

She well instructs me.   *Exit Lord*

Horatio

You will lose this wager, my lord.

[1489] Frothiness; empty clichés.

[1490] Most carefully worded ("fan and winnow" = separate chaff and wheat) opinions.

[1491] But.

[1492] "If one tests them (like Hamlet just did), the bubbles burst."

[1493] "I am at his disposal."

[1494] Approach Laertes graciously.

Hamlet

    I do not think so. Since he went into France, I have been
    in continual practice. I shall win at the odds. But thou
    wouldst not think how ill all's here about my heart—but it 195
    is no matter.

Horatio

    Nay, good my lord—

Hamlet

    It is but foolery, but it is such a kind of gain-giving[1495] as
    would perhaps trouble a woman.

Horatio

    If your mind dislike any thing, obey it. I will forestall their 200
    repair[1496] hither, and say you are not fit.

Hamlet

    Not a whit, we defy augury. There's a special providence[1497]
    in the fall of a sparrow.[1498] If it be now, 'tis not to come.
    If it be not to come, it will be now. If it be not now, yet
    it will come. The readiness is all. Since no man has aught 205
    of what he leaves, what is't to leave betimes?[1499]

Enter King Claudius, Queen Gertrude, Laertes, Lords, Osric, and Atten-
dants with foils and gauntlets, a table and flagons of wine on it.

King Claudius

    Come, Hamlet, come, and take this hand from me.

               King Claudius puts Laertes' hand into Hamlet's

---

[1495] Misgiving.

[1496] Coming.

[1497] God-given direction.

[1498] See Matthew x.29.

[1499] "As worldly possessions cannot go along with one when one dies,
what does the time of leaving matter?"

Hamlet

> Give me your pardon, sir, I've done you wrong.
> But pardon't, as you are a gentleman.
> This presence knows,[1500]   210
> And you must needs have heard, how I am punished
> With sore distraction. What I have done,
> That might your nature, honour, and exception[1501]
> Roughly awake, I here proclaim was madness.
> Was't Hamlet wronged Laertes? Never Hamlet.   215
> If Hamlet from himself be ta'en away,
> And when he's not himself does wrong Laertes,
> Then Hamlet does it not, Hamlet denies it.
> Who does it, then? His madness. If't be so,
> Hamlet is of the faction that is wronged.   220
> His madness is poor Hamlet's enemy.
> Sir, in this audience,
> Let my disclaiming from a purposed evil[1502]
> Free me so far in your most generous thoughts
> That I have shot mine arrow o'er the house,   225
> And hurt my brother.

Laertes   I am satisfied in nature,

> Whose motive, in this case, should stir me most
> To my revenge. But in my terms of honour
> I stand aloof, and will no reconcilement,
> Till by some elder masters of known honour,   230
> I have a voice and precedent of peace,[1503]
> To keep my name ungored.[1504] But till that time,

[1500] Those here present know.

[1501] Disapproval.

[1502] My denial of evil intentions.

[1503] "I cannot be reconciled with you until men of sober judgment pronounce that I may."

[1504] Intact; unhurt.

I do receive your offered love like love,
And will not wrong it.

Hamlet   I embrace it freely;
And will this brother's wager frankly play.   235
Give us the foils. Come on.

Laertes   Come, one for me.

Hamlet

I'll be your foil,[1505] Laertes. In mine ignorance
Your skill shall, like a star i'th'darkest night,
Stick fiery off[1506] indeed.

Laertes   You mock me, sir.

Hamlet

No, by this hand.   240

King Claudius

Give them the foils, young Osric. Cousin Hamlet,
You know the wager?

Hamlet   Very well, my lord.
Your grace hath laid the odds o' the weaker side.[1507]

King Claudius

I do not fear it; I have seen you both.
But since he is bettered,[1508] we have therefore odds.   245

Laertes

This is too heavy, let me see another.

Hamlet

This likes me well. These foils have all a length?

Osric

Ay, my good lord.   *They prepare to play*

King Claudius

Set me the stoups of wine upon that table.

[1505] Contrasting background against which a jewel shone more brightly.
[1506] Stand clearly out.
[1507] Backed the underdog.
[1508] Said to be better.

If Hamlet give the first or second hit,   250
Or quit in answer of the third exchange,[1509]
Let all the battlements their ordnance fire!
The King shall drink to Hamlet's better breath.[1510]
And in the cup an union[1511] shall he throw,
Richer than that which four successive kings   255
In Denmark's crown have worn. Give me the cups,
And let the kettle[1512] to the trumpet speak,
The trumpet to the cannoneer without,
The cannons to the heavens, the heaven to earth,
'Now the King drinks to Hamlet.' Come, begin!   260
And you, the judges, bear a wary eye.

Hamlet

Come on, sir.

Laertes

Come, my lord.   *They play*

Hamlet

One.

Laertes

No.   265

Hamlet

Judgment.

Osric

A hit, a very palpable hit.

Laertes

Well, again.

King Claudius

Stay, give me drink. Hamlet, this pearl is thine.
Here's to thy health.

[1509] The third bout is a draw.
[1510] Energy.
[1511] A pearl of great perfection.
[1512] Kettledrum.

Drums and trumpets sound, and cannon shot off within
                    Give him the cup.   270
Hamlet
    I'll play this bout first; set it by awhile.
    Come.
                    Another hit! What say you?
Laertes   *They play again*
    A touch, a touch, I do confess.
King Claudius
    Our son shall win.
Queen Gertrude   He's fat,[1513] and scant of breath.
    Here, Hamlet, take my napkin,[1514] rub thy brows.   275
    The Queen carouses to thy fortune, Hamlet.
Hamlet
    Good madam!
King Claudius   Gertrude, do not drink.
Queen Gertrude
    I will, my lord. I pray you, pardon me.
                    She drinks and offers the cup to Hamlet
King Claudius (*aside*)
    It is the poisoned cup. It is too late.
Hamlet
    I dare not drink yet, madam—by and by.[1515]   280
Queen Gertrude
    Come, let me wipe thy face.
Laertes
    My lord, I'll hit him now.
King Claudius   I do not think't.
Laertes (*aside*)
    And yet 'tis almost 'gainst my conscience.

[1513] Sweaty.
[1514] Handkerchief.
[1515] In a little while.

Hamlet

> Come, for the third, Laertes, you but dally.
> I pray you, pass[1516] with your best violence.   285
> I am afeard you make a wanton of me.[1517]

Laertes

> Say you so? Come on.   *They play*

Osric   Nothing neither way.

Laertes

> Have at you now!   *Laertes wounds Hamlet; then in scuffling,*
>   *they change rapiers, and Hamlet wounds Laertes*

King Claudius   Part them! They are incensed!

Hamlet

> Nay, come, again!   *Queen Gertrude falls*

Osric   Look to the Queen there, ho!

Horatio

> They bleed on both sides. How is it, my lord?   290

Osric

> How is't, Laertes?

Laertes

> Why, as a woodcock to mine own springe,[1518] Osric.
> I am justly killed with mine own treachery.

Hamlet

> How does the Queen?

King Claudius   She swoons to see them bleed.

Queen Gertrude

> No, no, the drink, the drink! O my dear Hamlet,   295
> The drink, the drink! I am poisoned.   *Dies*

Hamlet

> O villainy! Ho! Let the door be locked!   *Exit Osric*

[1516] Thrust.

[1517] Toy with me; "wanton" = overindulged child.

[1518] Woodcocks were proverbially seen as stupid—as was the man caught in his own trap; "spring" = trap.

Treachery! Seek it out.

Laertes

It is here, Hamlet. Hamlet, thou art slain.

No medicine in the world can do thee good.   300

In thee there is not half an hour of life.

The treacherous instrument is in thy hand,

Unbated[1519] and envenomed. The foul practice

Hath turned itself on me. Lo, here I lie,

Never to rise again. Thy mother's poisoned.   305

I can no more. The King, the King's to blame.

Hamlet

The point! Envenomed too!

Then, venom, to thy work.   *Stabs King Claudius*

All

Treason! Treason!

King Claudius

O, yet defend me, friends! I am but hurt.   310

Hamlet

Here, thou incestuous, murderous, damned Dane,

Drink off this potion. Is thy union[1520] here?

Follow my mother.   *King Claudius dies*

Laertes   He is justly served.

It is a poison tempered[1521] by himself.

Exchange forgiveness with me, noble Hamlet.   315

Mine and my father's death come not upon thee,[1522]

Nor thine on me.   *Dies*

Hamlet

Heaven make thee free of it! I follow thee.

[1519] Unblunted.

[1520] 1) The pearl; 2) the marriage to Gertrude.

[1521] Concocted.

[1522] "May your soul will be free of my father's and my death on the Day of Judgment."

I am dead, Horatio. Wretched Queen, adieu!
You that look pale and tremble at this chance,   320
That are but mutes[1523] or audience to this act,
Had I but time—as this fell sergeant,[1524] Death,
Is strict in his arrest—O, I could tell you—
But let it be. Horatio, I am dead,
Thou livest. Report me and my cause aright
To the unsatisfied.   325

Horatio   Never believe it!
I am more an antique Roman than a Dane.[1525]
Here's yet some liquor left.

Hamlet   As thou'rt a man,
Give me the cup. Let go! By heaven, I'll have't!
O God, Horatio, what a wounded name,   330
Things standing thus unknown, shall live behind me!
If thou didst ever hold me in thy heart
Absent thee from felicity awhile,
And in this harsh world draw thy breath in pain
To tell my story.   *March afar off, and shot within*
                          What warlike noise is this?   335

Enter Osric

Osric
Young Fortinbras, with conquest come from Poland,
To the ambassadors of England gives
This warlike volley.

Hamlet   O, I die, Horatio!
The potent poison quite o'ercrows[1526] my spirit.

[1523] Non-speaking actors; non-participants.
[1524] Officer of the courts with the power to arrest.
[1525] I.e., Horatio prefers suicide to a dishonorable life.
[1526] Exults over, like the winning rooster in a cock fight.

I cannot live to hear the news from England,   340
But I do prophesy the election lights
On Fortinbras. He has my dying voice.[1527]
So tell him, with the occurrents,[1528] more and less,   *Dies*
Which have solicited.[1529] The rest is silence.

Horatio

Now cracks a noble heart. Good night sweet prince,   345
And flights of angels sing thee to thy rest!
Why does the drum come hither?   *March within*

Enter Fortinbras and Soldiers with drum and colours, the English Ambassadors, and others

Prince Fortinbras

Where is this sight?

Horatio   What is it ye would see?

If aught of woe or wonder, cease your search.

Prince Fortinbras

This quarry[1530] cries on havoc.[1531] O proud death,   350
What feast is toward[1532] in thine eternal cell
That thou so many princes at a shot
So bloodily hast struck?

First Ambassador   The sight is dismal,

And our affairs from England come too late.
The ears are senseless that should give us hearing   355
To tell him[1533] his commandment is fulfilled,

[1527] Vote. Denmark is here presented as an elective monarchy. Fortinbras gets greater claim to the throne through the vote of the dying monarch.
[1528] Events.
[1529] Prompted me (to vote for him).
[1530] Heap of hunted deer.
[1531] Outright slaughter.
[1532] Being prepared.
[1533] I.e., Claudius.

That Rosencrantz and Guildenstern are dead.
Where should we have our thanks?

Horatio   Not from his mouth,
Had it th'ability of life to thank you.
He never gave commandment for their death.   360
But since, so jump upon this bloody question,[1534]
You from the Polack wars, and you from England,
Are here arrived, give order that these bodies
High on a stage[1535] be placed to the view;
And let me speak to th'yet unknowing world   365
How these things came about. So shall you hear
Of carnal, bloody, and unnatural acts,
Of accidental judgments,[1536] casual[1537] slaughters,
Of deaths put on[1538] by cunning and forced cause,
And, in this upshot, purposes mistook   370
Fallen on the inventors' heads. All this can I
Truly deliver.

Prince Fortinbras   Let us haste to hear it,
And call the noblest to the audience.
For me, with sorrow I embrace my fortune.
I have some rights of memory[1539] in this kingdom,   375
Which now to claim my vantage[1540] doth invite me.

Horatio
Of that I shall have also cause to speak,
And from his mouth whose voice will draw on more.[1541]

[1534] So quickly succeeding this bloody matter.

[1535] Platform.

[1536] God's judgment, seemingly accidentally presented.

[1537] Chance-driven.

[1538] Instigated.

[1539] Still remembered rights.

[1540] Opportunity.

[1541] Whose vote will inspire more votes (for Fortinbras).

But let this same be presently performed,
Even while men's minds are wild, lest more mischance   380
On[1542] plots and errors happen.
Prince Fortinbras   Let four captains
Bear Hamlet, like a soldier, to the stage,
For he was likely, had he been put on,[1543]
To have proved[1544] most royally; and for his passage,
The soldiers' music and the rites of war   385
Speak loudly for him.
Take up the bodies. Such a sight as this
Becomes the field,[1545] but here shows much amiss.
Go, bid the soldiers shoot.

A dead march. Exeunt, bearing off the dead bodies; after which a peal of ordnance is shot off

[1542] On top of.
[1543] Tested.
[1544] Borne himself.
[1545] Is becoming to the battlefield.

THE REVENGER'S TRAGEDY

by

CYRIL TOURNEUR

Introductory Remarks

Cyril Tourneur

The Revenger's Tragedy was entered in The Stationers' Register in October 1607, and was probably written in 1606-07. There is considerable critical debate surrounding the issue of authorship for *The Revenger's Tragedy*. Tourneur's name does not appear on the play's contemporary title page, and its style is very different from that of *The Atheist's Tragedy*, which is known to be penned by Tourneur. The present editor finds the evidence for other authorship unconvincing.[1] The question of style arises because Renaissance dramatists often collaborated with each other, writing the scenes considered their *forte* as their contribution to the final product. Shakespeare, for instance, collaborated with Fletcher on *The Two Noble Kinsmen*, and the present volume's *Maid's Tragedy* is a result of the very fertile collaboration between Beaumont and Fletcher. Dramatists were exposed to one another's style, played with it, and imitated it frequently. We must remember that in the Renaissance the very close use of sources often was considered to be a compliment to a fellow writer rather than an issue of plagiarism.

We know very little of Tourneur's life.[2] We assume a birthdate for him some time between 1570 and 1580. We know nothing of his educational background, and often can only conjecture what poems and plays, more or less loosely ascribed to him, are really his work. *The Revenger's Tragedy* was in existence in 1607, and we know that he was connected with the Cecil and the Vere families and fought abroad in service with them, probably in the Netherlands between 1600 and 1610. A funeral poem to Francis Vere (1609) is ascribed to him. *The Atheist's Tragedy* was entered in the Stationers' Register in 1611. In 1613 he received 40 shillings for

[1] See McAlindon, *English Renaissance Tragedy*.
[2] See Nicoll, *The Works of Cyril Tourneur*.

carrying letters to Belgium, and in 1617 the Cecil family rescued him from problems with the Privy Council.[3] He then went on the Cadiz expedition with Sir Edward Cecil in 1625, fell gravely ill, and was set ashore in Kinsdale where he died in February of 1626.

The Play

Setting and Characters

The Renaissance period was taken with spectacle, the display of rank and wealth, and everything colorful and remarkable, but also with the common end to which we all come: death and decay. How can moral corruption better be portrayed than by juxtaposing a gorgeous exterior with the presence of putrefaction and the bone beneath? The splendid surface, like our flesh, is, after all, only clothing or disguise for the reality of the skeleton. Tourneur achieves this effect splendidly in this play.

The Revenger's Tragedy takes place in an amoral universe; in Renaissance England, such a universe was best represented by choosing Italy as the scene. Throughout the period, the English image of what becomes a symbolic Italy develops into an image of sophisticated decadence, political, religious, and moral corruption, vengefulness, sexual abandon, and wanton violence. Once the action is removed to a symbolic place like this, the playwright can comment on contemporary moral and political shortcomings in his own world with greater ease. The only way to stay morally intact in Tourneur's society is to isolate oneself from the corruption, but isolation breeds discontent and brooding, a different erosion of the moral self, but still an erosion.

Tourneur blends his image of Italy with elements of the Mediaeval morality play to further make his characters transcend from the specific to the general. The characters' names are rarely proper names *per se*, but a description of the person's moral state or social standing. Vindice, for example, is "The Avenger," his sister Castiza is "The Chaste One," her pursuer Lussurioso "The Lecherous

[3] See glossary.

One."[4] The ruling couple are known only as "The Duke" and "The Duchess." The characters are all static and allegorical and do not develop; all in all they are best seen as embodied passions or states. Also like the Mediaeval moralities, warnings are made against deadly sins such as pride, lechery, and covetousness; the looseness of women, the chancy administration of the law, and the corrupting influence of money are viewed with condemnation. The comic spirit of the Mediaeval Vice, his glee and tendency to become "director" of the action, is definitely present in Vindice. But though Tourneur makes use of Mediaeval satire and scorn, there is no Mediaeval religious haven to be had in *The Revenger's Tragedy*, and no moral security.

The central symbol of this play is presented to us immediately. Vindice carries with him the skull of his beloved Gloriana, who was as beautiful as she was chaste, and whom the Duke poisoned because she refused to submit to his lust (I.i.1-49). Gloriana's fate, use and abuse by the court, is one that threatens all women in the play, physically as well as morally. The Duchess, who is of the court, is female corruption personified; she happily commits incest with her husband's bastard son to get back at her husband for his treatment of her own son. Gratiana is persuaded to become Lussurioso's pander and "sell" her daughter to his lust, and is saved from this sin only because Castiza is adamantly chaste and has her brother's support. No such good fortune saves Antonio's lady, who commits suicide after having been raped by the Duchess' Younger Son, who gloats over his prowess. When Gloriana's skull is employed by Vindice to avenge herself and all womankind, it is dressed up as a coy country lady; the Duke meets his end in the process of seducing what should under normal circumstances have been easy prey, but turns out to represent his ultimate fate. Still, in the process of being used, Gloriana awakens disgust in Vindice; all women have become repulsive to him:

---

[4] See notes to the list of *dramatis personae* also.

> And now methinks I could e'en chide myself
> For doting on her beauty . . .
> Does the silkworm expend her yellow labours
> For thee? For thee does she undo herself?
>   . . . It were fine methinks
> To have thee seen at revels, forgetful feasts
> And unclean brothels . . .
>   . . . see, ladies, with false forms
> You may deceive men but cannot deceive worms.
>   (III.V.68-97)

The chaste and lovely Gloriana is turned into a temptress and murderess by Vindice; the theme of female corruption permeates the play.

  Vindice, son to a father dead from discontent (I.i.127), sets out originally to revenge the death of his beloved, but his quest soon becomes directed at the moral and sexual corruption of the court itself. He moves from the observer railing at the court from a distance to active participation in various disguises. He acts the villain in disguise with such *verve* that it becomes obvious to both the audience and himself that he has natural talent for evil. His schemes become increasingly wilder, his deeds increasingly heinous; he is the revenger who turns into what he sets out to eradicate. Both he and his brother Hippolito become moral degenerates.

> Vindice exults. . . that with the game nearly over, Lussurioso has "lost." He does not see that Lussurioso has in his own way triumphed as well. Lussurioso sought to hire a villain and he succeeded. He sought to hire a cunning pander, and he succeeded in that too. Finally he hired Vindice to kill himself and Vindice does so, because he comes to love the game of evil for its own sake and to relish the murder rather than its "moral"

> purpose. . . Vindice, who hated the revels of the
> court, becomes in the end one of the court
> masquers.
>
> (Ornstein, *The Moral Vision of Jacobean Tragedy*,
> p. 114-115)

Vindice's disguises increase in intensity. His Piato disguise serves mainly to test his mother and sister. But when he chastises Gratiana for the unmotherly role she has played, the audience wonders at his own unbrotherly and unfilial attitude earlier; who is more sinful, accuser or accused? When he sheds Piato's disguise to become himself again, this "self" has changed drastically from the Vindice that opened the play, and when he is hired to "kill his Piato-self," the "new Vindice-self" seems like another disguise; he is playacting himself. Finally, disguised in the Masque of Revengers, he has become what he detested, part of the corrupt court. Unlike Hieronimo and Hamlet, Vindice has no time with his audience to show what manner of man he was before Gloriana's death, nor anybody to paint us such a picture. He has waited nine years for his revenge, and when we meet him he is already affected by the changes revenge plans work on the revenger. Also unlike Hieronimo and Hamlet, he has no compunction about acting, and he displays no moral suffering; he actually revels in the gruesome murder of the Duke and goes to his death decidedly without repentance, betrayed by his own nimble tongue.

The Duke and Duchess are addressed as "your grace," ironically, for there is nothing gracious about them or their brood of sons and stepson, legitimate and illegitimate. This court is a brilliant illustration of the fact that a splendid exterior may serve to hide putrefaction and moral decay. There is no marital fidelity and no respect for one's subjects; brother turns against brother, ambition is stronger than family ties, and incest presents no real moral problem if it furthers one's own ends. Even the law is seen as less important than princely inclinations; the Duchess asks mercy after her son has committed rape, implying that princes are above the law. The Duke brings her son to court only because not doing so would stain the name he leaves behind him (I.ii).

The name of Gratiana, Vindice's mother, implies grace, and in many ways she is indeed the Duchess' opposite. In the face of temptation, the Duchess always succumbs. Ironically, Gratiana gives in, too, and promises to persuade her daughter to become Lussurioso's whore, though she later claims that only her silver-tongued son Vindice could have tempted her (IV.iv.34). She does repent, however, and regains the respect of her children and her state of grace. Her falling off is the more blatant because Castiza is so adamantly and insistently chaste, even to the point of tormenting her mother with her pretended plans to give herself to Lussurioso's lust only to punish her mother mentally, much like her brothers have punished her physically. The same fate that threatens the "country ladies" coming to court is close to reaching Vindice's sister, and probably only her isolation from the corrupting influences of the court environment preserves her.

Another character that functions as a contrast is Antonio, who stands opposite Lussurioso. In Lussurioso's short time as reigning Duke, we see that he is likely to continue in his father's footsteps, and that he is susceptible to flattery to a high degree. Once Antonio is invested with power, he dismisses Vindice and Hippolito's flattery when they claim that they have murdered for him; if that act is possible, he might well be next on their list of victims, and so they are better executed. His, and the play's, last line, "Pray Heaven their blood may wash away all treason," expresses the hope present at the close of all tragedies, that order may be restored after the reign of chaos that has been the body of the play. In this case, however, this hope may be vain. The moral fiber of the society depicted is permeated with corruption, and though Antonio is morally upright, he is without another strong and supporting character, old, unmarried, and without an heir. We get the sense that at best a breathing space has been achieved.

The Moral Universe

Tourneur's *The Revenger's Tragedy* differs from *The Spanish Tragedy* and *Hamlet* in the presentation of its revenge plot. Kyd and Shakespeare follow the same pattern: a wrong is committed, a supernatural entity reveals the wrong, a revenger is found, and revenge is finally executed at the expense of the revenger and whomever he may draw into his vortex, suffering death or madness. Tourneur uses no ghost to reveal its wishes to the audience or Vindice; the impetus that drives Vindice into his revenge frenzy comes from a tangible relic of his beloved, the

> . . . sallow picture of my poisoned love,
> My studies' ornament, thou shell of death,
> Once the bright face of my betrothed lady. . .
>
> (I.i.14-16)

> . . . the form that living shone so bright. . .
>
> (III.v.66)

her skull. Since her death, Gloriana's skull has been with him, a visible *memento mori*, and also a reminder of the frailty and vanity of life as well as an inducement to revenge.

Vindice's obsession with death and decay is commonly found in the Renaissance, and it reminds one of the Mediaeval *danse macabre*, the dance of death, which as drama and as concept was in vogue into the Renaissance. Probably inspired by the repeated outbreaks of the Black Death, the *danse macabre* presents Death, not as "the destroyer," but as God's messenger who summons all people of all walks of life to their reckoning without warning. Ultimately, Death comes for every man and woman, and it behooves us all to be prepared. Death emerges in the form of a series of skeletons; the first one approaches the pinnacle of society, King or Pope, who does not want to submit to the summons, but who is ultimately persuaded and led off stage by the messenger; another skeleton leads off another victim, one step down on the social ladder, and thus the play progresses through, usually, twenty-four victims, representing society as a whole. At beginning and end a sermon is read to reinforce the lesson of the play: all that lives must die and face the Creator; we are all equal before death, and we would all do well to be prepared for this journey at any time. Pictorial representations of the dance of death as murals and engravings[5] are many, but despite Death's grinning skull and obvious dancing movements, he is still often clad in rotting grave clothes teeming with worms, and the effect is frightening; queen or whore, adult or child, we do not know the ultimate destination of our final journey. Gloriana's skull is just one such *memento mori.*

Vindice's message is that the times are corrupt and evil, there is no true concept of glory and honor, and all are subject to abuse from the court, man and woman alike. His own father died in the court's disfavor, as does Vindice himself along with his brother. The play alternates between manic action and long, meditative passages dominated by Vindice. His language centers on imagery uniting sexuality, putrefying flesh, meat-become-food, and the indifference to the fate of one's land if it can be sold or pawned to obtain the gratification of the flesh. No longer is it enough to have enough to be satisfied and live a good life; surfeit is the goal. "Stirring meats" (I.ii.180ff; II.i.196ff), already themselves in the beginning stages of putrefaction, entice women to lechery; sexuality and decay are closely linked in the speeches of both The Bastard and Vindice. What could be desirable and sweet leads to moral corruption through overindulgence.

The result of overindulgence is death in a state of moral decay; Vindice is often the one to mock death in this form. Making use of the beloved's skeleton, changing his mind about her in the process, is itself a kind of mockery, but when the Duke finally succumbs to the poison on the lips of the skull, he is not left alone. He is stomped upon, dressed in Vindice's disguise, and repeatedly

[5] Hans Holbein has left us a glorious series of woodcuts of the *Totentanz.*

stabbed[6] before he is finally abandoned. Lussurioso is also mocked in death. After the stabbing, Vindice speaks aside to him:

> Vindice
>> How fares my lord the Duke?
>
> Lussurioso   Farewell to all.
>> He that climbs highest has the greatest fall.
>> My tongue is out of office.
>
> Vindice
>> . . . Now thou'lt not prate on't, 'twas Vindice
>> murdered thee!
>
> Lussurioso
>> O!
>
> Vindice
>> Murdered thy father!
>
> Lussurioso   O!
>
> Vindice   And I am he!
>> Tell nobody.
>
>   (V.iii.73-78)

Ironically, Vindice himself goes to his death at the hands of a friend for his own moral corruption.

The play's language, most often from the lips of Vindice, is intense, ironic, highly poetic, and often beautiful, but also able to impress the audience with the seductive qualities of moral decay and the difficulty one has in avoiding it. Even Vindice himself, the play's avenger and moral critic, falls prey. The play has been popular with college and university theater departments for quite some time, but only in 1966, directed by Trevor Nunn, did it regain popularity on the public stage.[7] He staged the double masque at the end as a *danse macabre*, Death on his unavoidable mission, waiting to bring justice to us all.

---

[6] Vindice yells, "Sa, sa, sa, thump!"(V.i.57) as he stabs the Duke.
[7] See Styan, *The English Stage*, pp. 218-221.

THE
REVENGERS
TRAGÆDIE.

As it hath beene sundry times Acted,
by the Kings Maiesties
Seruants.

AT LONDON
Printed by G. E I D, and are to be sold at his
house in Fleete-lane at the signe of the
Printers-Presse.
1 6 o 8.

Figure 6. STC 24150, the 1608 title page for *The Revenger's Tragedy.*
By permission of the Folger Shakespeare Library.

Dramatis Personae

The Duke
Lussurioso,[8] the Duke's son
Spurio,[9] the Duke's bastard son
The Duchess
Ambitioso,[10] the Duchess' eldest son
Supervacuo,[11] the Duchess' second son
The Youngest Son of the Duchess

Gratiana,[12] a widow
Vindice,[13] also disguised as Piato,[14] Gratiana's son
Hippolito, also known as Carlo, Gratiana's son
Castiza,[15] Gratiana's daughter
Dondolo,[16] Castiza's servant

Antonio, an old lord
Piero, a lord

Judges, Nobles, Lords, Gentlemen, Officers, Keeper, Guards, and Servants
Nencio[17] and Sordido[18]

Scene: a city in Italy

[8] The Lecherous One.
[9] The Bastard One.
[10] The Ambitious One.
[11] The Useless One.
[12] She of Grace.
[13] The Revenger.
[14] The Controversial One.
[15] The Chaste One.
[16] The Gullible One.
[17] The Foolish One.
[18] The Unclean One.

Act I, Scene i

Enter Vindice with a skull in his hand. The Duke, Duchess, Lussurioso, Spurio with a train,[19] *pass over the stage with torchlight*

Vindice
    Duke! Royal lecher! Go, grey-haired adultery![20]
    And thou his son, as impious steeped as he,
    And thou his bastard true-begot in evil,
    And thou his Duchess that will do with[21] devil,
    Four excellent characters! O, that marrowless age   5
    Should stuff the hollow bones with damned desires,
    And, 'stead of heat kindle infernal fires
    Within the spendthrift veins of a dry Duke,
    A parched and juiceless luxur?[22] O God! One
    That has scarce blood enough to live upon,   10
    And he to riot it like a son and heir!
    O the thought of that
    Turns my abused heartstrings into fret.
    (*To the skull*) Thou sallow picture of my poisoned love,
    My studies' ornament, thou shell of death,   15
    Once the bright face of my betrothed lady,
    When life and beauty naturally filled out
    These ragged imperfections,
    When two heaven-pointed diamonds were set
    In those unsightly rings—then 'twas a face   20
    So far beyond the artificial shine
    Of any woman's bought complexion
    That the uprightest man (if such there be,

---

[19] A group of attendants.

[20] The Duke is seen by Vindice as his sin personified.

[21] Have sexual relations with.

[22] Lecher; incontinent one.

That sins but seven times a day) broke custom
And made up eight with looking after her.   25
O she was able to ha' made a usurer's son
Melt all his patrimony in a kiss;
And what his father fifty years[23] told[24]
To have consumed, and yet his suit been cold.
But O, accursed palace!   30
Thee, when thou wert apparelled in thy flesh,
The old Duke poisoned,
Because thy purer part would not consent
Unto his palsied lust. For old men lustful
Do show like young men angry, eager, violent,   35
Outbidden like their limited performances.
O, 'ware[25] an old man hot and vicious.
"Age, as in gold, in lust is covetous."[26]
Vengeance, thou murder's quit-rent,[27] and whereby
Thou show'st thyself tenant[28] to tragedy,   40
O keep thy day, hour, minute, I beseech,
For those thou hast determined. Hum! Whoe'er knew
Murder unpaid? Faith, give Revenge her due,
She has kept touch hitherto. Be merry, merry,
Advance thee, O thou terror to fat folks,   45
To have their costly, three-piled[29] flesh worn off
As bare as this. For banquets, ease, and laughter

---

[23] Here, as often, pronounced as two syllables, as is, e.g., "Duke's," in order to fit the metre.

[24] Counted.

[25] Beware.

[26] Phrases set in quotation marks are proverbial; they are also so marked in the original text.

[27] You who can make up for murder.

[28] A tenant pays rent; see "quit-rent" in line 39.

[29] Three-piled velvet was the best and most expensive quality, soft and luscious.

Can make great men, as greatness goes by clay,[30]
But wise men little are more great than they.

Enter his brother Hippolito

Hippolito
    Still sighing o'er death's vizard?[31]
Vindice   Brother, welcome!   50
    What comfort bring'st thou? How go things at court?
Hippolito
    In silk and silver, brother, never braver.
Vindice
    Pooh!
    Thou play'st upon my meaning. Prithee, say
    Has that bald madam, Opportunity,[32]   55
    Yet thought upon's? Speak, are we happy yet?
    Thy wrongs and mine are for one scabbard fit.
Hippolito
    It may prove happiness.
Vindice   What is't may prove?
    Give me to taste.
Hippolito   Give me your hearing, then.
    You know my place at court.
Vindice   Ay, the Duke's Chamber.   60
    But 'tis a marvel thou'rt not turned out yet!
Hippolito
    Faith, I've been shoved at, but 'twas still my hap
    To hold by th'Duchess' skirt. You guess at that;
    Whom such a coat[33] keeps up can ne'er fall flat.

---

[30] As greatness is counted here on earth by men.
[31] Mask; face.
[32] Opportunity or Occasion was shown as a nude, winged female, bald, but with a forelock which had to be caught in time.
[33] Here, skirt.

But to the purpose— 65
Last evening, predecessor unto this,
The Duke's son warily inquired for me,
Whose pleasure I attended. He began
By policy to open and unhusk me
About the time and common rumour. 70
But I had so much wit to keep my thoughts
Up in their built houses,[34] yet afforded him
An idle satisfaction without danger.
But the whole aim and scope of his intent
Ended in this: conjuring me in private 75
To seek some strange-digested fellow[35] forth
Of ill-contented nature, either disgraced
In former times, or by new grooms displaced
Since his stepmother's nuptials. Such a blood,[36]
A man that were for evil only good; 80
To give you the true word, some base-coined[37] pander.[38]

Vindice

I reach you, for I know his heat is such,
Were there as many concubines as ladies,
He would not be contained, he must fly out.
I wonder how ill-featured, vild[39]-proportioned 85
That one should be, if she were made for woman,
Whom at the insurrection of his lust
He would refuse for once. Heart! I think none,
Next to a skull, though more unsound than one.
Each face he meets he strongly dotes upon. 90

---

[34] Unuttered; within myself.

[35] A man of a very strange disposition.

[36] Fellow.

[37] Lowborn.

[38] Procurer; prostitute's go-between.

[39] Vile.

Hippolito

    Brother, y'have truly spoke him.

    He knows not you, but I'll swear you know him.

Vindice

    And therefore I'll put on[40] that knave for once,

    And be a right man, then, a man o'the time,

    For to be honest is not to be i'the world.   95

    Brother, I'll be that strange-composed fellow.

Hippolito

    And I'll prefer you,[41] brother.

Vindice   Go to, then.

    The smallest advantage fattens wronged men.

    It may point out Occasion. If I meet her,

    I'll hold her by the foretop[42] fast enough,   100

    Or, like the French mole,[43] heave up hair and all.

    I have a habit[44] that will fit it quaintly.[45]

Enter Gratiana and Castiza

    Here comes our mother.

Hippolito   And sister.

Vindice   We must coin.[46]

    Women are apt, you know, to take false money.

    But I dare stake my soul for these two creatures,   105

    Only excuse excepted, that they'll swallow

    Because their sex is easy in belief.[47]

---

[40] Pretend to be.

[41] Promote you.

[42] See note 32.

[43] A skin condition, the eruption of which resembles a molehill; there may be a reference to syphilis.

[44] A costume.

[45] Uncommonly well.

[46] Make up something false.

[47] The two women are credulous because they are women, but morally sound.

Gratiana

    What news from court, son Carlo?

Hippolito   Faith, mother,

    'Tis whispered there the Duchess' younger son

    Has played a rape on Lord Antonio's wife.   110

Gratiana

    On that religious lady!

Castiza

    Royal blood! Monster! He deserves to die,

    If Italy had no more hopes but he.[48]

Vindice

    Sister, y'have sentenced most direct and true.

    The law's a woman,[49] and would she were you.   115

    Mother, I must take leave of you.

Gratiana

    Leave for what?

Vindice   I intend speedy travail.[50]

Hippolito

    That he does, madam.

Gratiana   Speedy indeed!

Vindice

    For since my worthy father's funeral

    My life's unnaturally to me, e'en compelled,   120

    As if I lived now when I should be dead.

Gratiana

    Indeed, he was a worthy gentleman,

    Had his estate been fellow to his mind.

Vindice

    The Duke did much deject him.

Gratiana   Much!

---

[48] Even if he were the sole heir.

[49] Iustitia, justice personified, was female.

[50] Both travel and work.

Vindice   Too much.

    And, though disgrace oft smothered in his spirit   125

    When it would mount, surely I think he died

    Of discontent, the nobleman's consumption.

Gratiana

    Most sure he did.

Vindice   Did he, 'lack? You know all,

    You were his midnight secretary.

Gratiana   No.

    He was too wise to trust me with his thoughts.   130

Vindice

    I'faith then, father, thou wast wise indeed.

    "Wives are but made to go to bed and feed."

    Come, mother, sister; you'll bring me onward, brother?

Hippolito

    I will.

Vindice (*aside*)   I'll quickly turn into another.   *Exeunt*

Act I, Scene ii

Enter the old Duke, Lussurioso his son, the Duchess, Spurio the bastard, the Duchess' two sons Ambitioso and Supervacuo; the third, her Youngest Son, brought out by Officers for the rape. Two Judges.

Duke

    Duchess, it is your youngest son, we're sorry

    His violent act has e'en drawn blood of honour

    And stained our honours;

    Thrown ink upon the forehead[51] of our state

    Which envious spirits will dip their pens into   5

    After our death, and blot us in our tombs.

[51] See glossary.

For that which would seem treason in our lives
Is laughter when we're dead. Who dares now whisper
That dares not then speak out, and e'en proclaim
With loud words and broad pens our closest shame.   10

First Judge

Your grace hath spoke like to your silver years,
Full of confirmed gravity. For what is it to have
A flattering false insculption[52] on a tomb,
And in men's hearts reproach? The bowelled[53] corpse
May be cered in, but, with free tongue I speak,   15
"The faults of great men through their cerecloths[54] break."

Duke

They do, we're sorry for't. It is our fate
To live in fear and die to live in hate.
I leave him to your sentence; doom him, lords—
The fact[55] is great—whilst I sit by and sigh.   20

Duchess

My gracious lord, I pray be merciful,
Although his trespass far exceed his years.
Think him to be your own, as I am yours;
Call him not son-in-law: the law I fear
Will fall too soon upon his name and him.   25
Temper his fault with pity.

Lussurioso   Good my lord,

Then 'twill not taste so bitter and unpleasant
Upon the judges' palate; for offences
Gilt o'er[56] with mercy show like fairest women,
Good only for their beauties, which, washed off,   30

---

[52] Inscription in stone.

[53] Disemboweled for preservation.

[54] Waxed sheets to wrap the body in (see "cered," l. 15).

[55] Offense.

[56] Covered up with a coat of gilding.

No sin is uglier.

Ambitioso   I beseech your grace,
    Be soft and mild. Let not relentless law
    Look with an iron forehead on our brother.

Spurio (*aside*)
    He yields small comfort yet, hope he shall die.
    And if a bastard's wish might stand in force,   35
    Would all the court were turned into a corse![57]

Duchess
    No pity yet? Must I rise fruitless, then?
    A wonder in a woman! Are my knees
    Of such low metal,[58] that without respect—

First Judge
    Let the offender stand forth: 40
    'Tis the Duke's pleasure that impartial doom
    Shall take fast hold of his unclean[59] attempt.
    A rape! Why 'tis the very core of lust,
    Double adultery.

Youngest Son   So, sir.

Second Judge   And which was worse,
    Committed on the Lord Antonio's wife,   45
    That general honest[60] lady. Confess, my lord,
    What moved you to't?

Youngest Son   Why, flesh and blood, my lord.
    What should move men unto a woman else?

Lussurioso
    O do not jest thy doom! Trust not an ax
    Or sword too far. The law is a wise serpent   50
    And quickly can beguile thee of thy life.

---

[57] Corpse.

[58] Material.

[59] Not chaste; morally reprehensible.

[60] Always chaste and without moral fault.

Though marriage only has made thee my brother,
I love thee so far: play not with thy death.

Youngest Son

I thank you, troth; good admonitions, faith,
If I'd the grace now to make use of them.   55

First Judge

That lady's name has spread such a fair wing
Over all Italy, that if our tongues
Were sparing toward the fact, judgment itself
Would be condemned and suffer in men's thoughts.

Youngest Son

Well then, 'tis done, and it would please me well   60
Were it to do again. Sure she's a goddess,
For I'd no power to see her, and to live.
It falls out true in this, for I must die;
Her beauty was ordained to be my scaffold.
And yet, methinks, I might be easier 'sessed.[61]   65
My fault being sport,[62] let me but die in jest.

First Judge

This be thy sentence—

Duchess

O, keep't upon your tongue, let it not slip!
Death too soon steals out of a lawyer's lip.
Be not so cruel-wise!

First Judge   Your grace must pardon us,   70
'Tis but the justice of the law.

Duchess   The law
Is grown more subtle than a woman should be.

Spurio (*aside*)

Now, now he dies! Rid'em away.

Duchess (*aside*)

O what it is to have an old-cool Duke,

---

[61] Assessed.

[62] A pastime only; dalliance.

To be as slack in tongue as in performance.   75

First Judge

Confirmed, this be the doom irrevocable.

Duchess

O!

First Judge

Tomorrow early—

Duchess   Pray be abed, my lord.

First Judge

Your grace much wrongs yourself.

Ambitioso   No, 'tis that tongue;

Your too much right does do us too much wrong.

First Judge

Let that offender—

Duchess   Live, and be in health.   80

First Judge

—Be on a scaffold—

Duke   Hold, hold my lord!

Spurio (*aside*)   Pox on't,

What makes my dad speak now?

Duke

We will defer the judgment till next sitting;

In the meantime, let him be kept close prisoner.

Guard, bear him hence.

Ambitioso (*aside*)   Brother, this makes for thee.[63]   85

Fear not, we'll have a trick to set thee free.

Youngest Son (*aside*)

Brother, I will expect it from you both,

And in that hope I rest.   *Exit with a Guard*

Supervacuo   Brother, be merry.

Spurio (*aside*)

Delayed! Deferred! Nay then, if judgment have

---

[63] Works for you.

Cold blood, flattery and bribes will kill it.   90

Duke

About it, then, my lords, with your best powers.

More serious business calls upon our hours.

Exeunt; manet[64] *Duchess*

Duchess

Was't ever known step-duchess was so mild

And calm as I? Some now would plot his death

With easy doctors, those loose-living men,   95

And make his withered grace[65] fall to his grave,

And keep church better.[66]

Some second wife would do this, and dispatch

Her double-loathed lord at meat and sleep.

Indeed 'tis true an old man's twice a child,   100

Mine cannot speak. One of his single words

Would quite have freed my youngest dearest son

From death or durance, and have made him walk

With a bold foot upon the thorny law,

Whose prickles should bow under him. But 'tis not,   105

And therefore wedlock faith shall be forgot.

I'll kill him in his forehead![67] Hate, there feed!

That wound is deepest though it never bleed.

And here comes he whom my heart points unto   *Enter Spurio*

His bastard son, but my love's true-begot.   110

Many a wealthy letter have I sent him,

Swelled up with jewels, and the timorous man

Is yet but coldly kind.

That jewel's mine that quivers in his ear,

[64] Stays; remains.

[65] A duke is addressed as "your grace."

[66] Because of the Duke's privilege to be buried within the church, he will never miss a service.

[67] Give him the horns of a cuckold.

    Mocking his master's chilliness and vain fear.   115
    He has spied me[68] now.

Spurio   Madam, your grace so private?
    My duty on your hand.

Duchess
    Upon my hand, sir. Troth, I think you'd fear
    To kiss my hand too, if my lip stood there.

Spurio
    Witness I would not, madam.   *Kisses her*

Duchess   'Tis a wonder,   120
    For ceremony has made many fools.
    It is as easy way unto a duchess
    As to a hatted dame,[69] if her love answer.
    But that by timerous honours, pale respects,
    Idle degrees of fear, men make their ways   125
    Hard of themselves. What have you thought of me?

Spurio
    Madam, I ever think of you in duty,
    Regard, and—

Duchess   Pooh! upon my love, I mean.

Spurio
    I would 'twere love, but 'tis a fouler name
    Than lust. You are my father's wife,   130
    Your grace may guess now what I could call it.

Duchess
    Why, th'art his son but falsely.
    'Tis a hard question whether he begot thee.

Spurio
    I'faith, 'tis true too. I'm an uncertain man
    Of more uncertain woman. May be his groom   135

---

[68] Seen me.

[69] Hats were worn by lower class women only, not by noble ladies. The Duchess comments on the availability of her entire sex.

O'the stable begot me, you know I know not.
He could ride a horse well. A shrewd suspicion, marry!
He was wondrous tall. He had his length, i'faith,
For peeping over half-shut holyday windows.
Men would desire him light.[70] When he was afoot   140
He made a goodly show under a pent-house,[71]
And when he rid, his hat would check[72] the signs
And clatter barbers' basins.[73]

Duchess   Nay, set you a-horseback once,[74]
You'll ne'er light off.

Spurio   Indeed, I am a beggar.[75]

Duchess
That's more the sign thou'rt great. But to our love.   145
Let it stand firm, both in thought and mind,
That the Duke was thy father, as no doubt then
He bid fair for't—thy injury is the more,
For had he cut thee a right diamond,
Thou hadst been next set in the dukedom's ring,   150
When his worn self, like age's easy slave,
Had dropped out of the collet[76] into th'grave.
What wrong can equal this? Canst thou be tame
And think upon't?

Spurio   No, mad and think upon't.

Duchess
Who would not be revenged of such a father,   155
E'en in the worst way? I would thank that sin

---

[70] Dismounted. Otherwise he might see to what use people could put their time on a holy day.

[71] The eaves.

[72] Hit.

[73] The sign of a barber's shop.

[74] With a bawdy reference.

[75] "If wishes were horses, beggars would ride," with a bawdy reference.

[76] The place for the stone in a ring.

That could most injure him, and be in league with it.
O what a grief 'tis that a man should live
But once i'the world, and then to live a bastard,
The curse o'the womb, the thief of nature,   160
Begot against the seventh commandment,
Half damned in the conception by the justice
Of that unbribed everlasting law.

Spurio

O, I'd a hot-backed devil to my father.

Duchess

Would not this mad e'en patience, make blood rough?   165
Who but an eunuch would not sin? His bed,
By one false minute disinherited.

Spurio

Ay, there's the vengeance that my birth was wrapped in!
I'll be revenged for all. Now, hate, begin!
I'll call foul incest but a venial sin.   170

Duchess

Cold still! In vain then must a duchess woo?

Spurio

Madam, I blush to say what I will do.

Duchess

Thence flew sweet comfort. Earnest,[77] and farewell.

Kisses him

Spurio

O, one incestuous kiss picks open hell.

Duchess

Faith, now, old Duke, my vengeance shall reach high,   175
I'll arm thy brow with woman's heraldry.[78]   *Exit*

Spurio

Duke, thou didst do me wrong, and by thy act

[77] A pledge.
[78] Give you the horns of a cuckold.

Adultery is my nature.
Faith, if the truth were known, I was begot
After some gluttonous dinner. Some stirring[79] dish   180
Was my first father, when deep healths went round,
And ladies' cheeks were painted red with wine,
Their tongues, as short and nimble as their heels,
Uttering words sweet and thick. And when they rose
Were merrily disposed to fall again.   185
In such a whispering and withdrawing hour,
When base male-bawds kept sentinel at stair-head,
Was I stolen[80] softly. O, damnation met!
The sin of feasts, drunken adultery,
I feel it swell me! My revenge is just,   190
I was begot in impudent wine and lust.
Stepmother, I consent to thy desires.
I love thy mischief well, but I hate thee,
And those three cubs, thy sons, wishing confusion,
Death, and disgrace may be their epitaphs.   195
As for my brother, the Duke's only son,
Whose birth is more beholding to report[81]
Than mine, and yet perhaps as falsely sown
(Women must not be trusted with their own),
I'll loose my days[82] upon him, hate-all I.   200
Duke, on thy brow I'll draw my bastardy.
For indeed a bastard by nature should make cuckolds,
Because he is the son of a cuckold-maker.   *Exit*

---

[79] Sexually arousing.
[80] Conceived immorally.
[81] With reputation intact.
[82] Spend my time.

Act I, Scene iii

Enter Vindice and Hippolito, Vindice in disguise to attend Lord Lussurioso,
the Duke's son.

Vindice

    What, brother, am I far enough from myself?

Hippolito

    As if another man had been sent whole

    Into the world, and none wist[83] how he came.

Vindice

    It will confirm me bold, the child o'the court,

    Let blushes dwell i'the country. Impudence!   5

    Thou goddess of the palace, mistress of mistresses,

    To whom the costly perfumed people pray,

    Strike thou my forehead into dauntless marble,

    Mine eyes to steady sapphires. Turn my visage,

    And if I must needs glow, let me blush inward,   10

    That this immodest season may not spy

    That scholar in my cheeks, fool bashfulness,

    That maid in the old time, whose flush of grace

    Would never suffer her to get good clothes.

    Our maids are wiser, and are less ashamed;   15

    Save[84] Grace the bawd, I seldom hear grace named.

Hippolito

    Nay, brother, you reach out o'the verge[85] now—

    'Sfoot,[86] the Duke's son, settle your looks.

                              Enter Lussurioso with servants

---

[83] Knew.
[84] Except for.
[85] Limits.
[86] By God's foot.

Vindice

    Pray let me not be doubted.

Hippolito

    My lord—

Lussurioso   Hippolito! Be absent, leave us.   20

Hippolito

    My lord, after long search, wary inquiries,

    And politic siftings, I made choice of yon fellow,

    Whom I guess rare for many deep employments.

    This our age swims within him; and if Time[87]

    Had so much hair, I should take him for Time,   25

    He is so near kin to this present minute.

Lussurioso

    'Tis enough,

    We thank thee; yet words are but great men's blanks;[88]

    Gold, though it be dumb, does utter the best thanks.

                                 Gives him money

Hippolito

    Your plenteous honour. An excellent fellow, my lord.   30

Lussurioso

    So, give us leave. (*Exit Hippolito*) Welcome, be not far off,

    We must be better acquainted. Push,[89] be bold

    With us, thy hand.

Vindice   With all my heart, i'faith.

    How dost, sweet muskcat?[90] When shall we lie together?

Lussurioso

    Wondrous knave,   35

    Gather him into boldness![91] 'Sfoot, the slave's

---

[87] The emblematic figure of Occasion; the time to be seized.

[88] Blank bonds, not signed.

[89] An exclamation, much like "Come on."

[90] The musk-deer; its musk was used as an ingredient in perfume.

[91] "Give him an inch, he'll take it all."

Already as familiar as an ague,[92]
And shakes me at his pleasure. Friend, I can
Forget myself in private, but elsewhere
I pray do you remember me.

Vindice   O, very well, sir,   40
I conster myself saucy.[93]

Lussurioso   What hast been?
Of what profession?

Vindice   A bone-setter.

Lussurioso   A bone-setter?

Vindice
A bawd, my lord.
One that sets bones together.

Lussurioso   Notable bluntness!
(*Aside*) Fit, fit for me, e'en trained up to my hand,   45
Thou hast been a scrivener[94] to much knavery, then?

Vindice
Fool to abundance, sir. I have been witness
To the surrenders of a thousand virgins,
And not so little.
I have seen patrimonies washed a-pieces,   50
Fruit fields turned into bastards,
And in a world of acres,
Not so much dust due to the heir 'twas left to
As would well gravel a petition.[95]

Lussurioso (*aside*)
Fine villain, troth! I like him wonderously.   55
He's e'en shaped for my purpose. (*Aloud*) Then thou know'st
I'the world strange lust?

---

[92] A fever with accompanying chills.
[93] "I see I was too forward."
[94] One who writes contracts out.
[95] Sand the wet ink on the document to dry it quickly.

Vindice   O Dutch lust! Fulsome lust!
    Drunken procreation, which begets so many drunkards.
    Some father dreads not, gone to bed in wine, to slide
    From the mother and cling[96] the daughter-in-law.   60
    Some uncles are adulterous with their nieces,
    Brothers with brothers' wives. O hour of incest!
    Any kin now, next to the rim[97] o'the sister,
    Is man's meat in these days; and in the morning,
    When they are up and dressed, and their mask on,   65
    Who can perceive this, save that eternal eye
    That sees through flesh and all? Well, if any thing
    Be damned it will be twelve o'clock at night,
    That twelve will never 'scape;
    It is the Judas of the hours,[98] wherein   70
    Honest salvation is betrayed to sin.

Lussurioso
    In troth, it is, too. But let this talk glide.
    It is our blood to err, though hell gaped loud.
    Ladies know Lucifer fell, yet still are proud.
    Now, sir, were thou as secret as thou'rt subtle   75
    And deeply fathomed into all estates,
    I would embrace thee for a near employment,
    And thou shouldst swell in money, and be able
    To make lame beggars crouch to thee.

Vindice   My lord!
    Secret? I ne'er had that disease o'the mother,[99]   80
    I praise my father. Why are men made close
    But to keep thoughts in best? I grant you this,
    Tell but some woman a secret over night,

---

[96] Cling to, sexually; embrace.
[97] Chink.
[98] The hour of betrayal.
[99] Hysteria; and a tendency to babble.

Your doctor may find it in the urinal i'the morning.

But, my lord—

Lussurioso   So thou'rt confirmed in me.   85

And thus I enter thee.[100]   *Gives money*

Vindice   This Indian devil[101]

Will quickly enter any man, but a usurer;

He prevents that by entering the devil first.

Lussurioso

Attend me.[102] I am past my depth in lust,

And I must swim or drown. All my desires   90

Are levelled[103] at a virgin not far from court,

To whom I have conveyed by messenger

Many waxed lines,[104] full of my neatest spirit,[105]

And jewels that were able to ravish her

Without the help of man; all which and more   95

She, foolish-chaste, sent back, the messengers

Receiving frowns for answers.

Vindice   Possible?

'Tis a rare Phoenix,[106] whoe'er she be.

If your desires be such, she so repugnant,

In troth, my lord, I'd be revenged and marry her.   100

Lussurioso

Push! The dowry of her blood and of her fortunes

Are both too mean—good enough to be bad withal.

I'm one of that number can defend

Marriage is good, yet rather keep a friend.[107]

---

[100] Hire you.

[101] India is the land of riches.

[102] Listen well.

[103] Aimed like a weapon.

[104] Letters sealed with wax.

[105] Elegantly phrased.

[106] Only one Phoenix exists at any given time.

[107] Lover.

Give me my bed by stealth—there's true delight;   105
What breeds a loathing in't but night by night?

Vindice

A very fine religion.

Lussurioso   Therefore thus:
I'll trust thee in the business of my heart
Because I see thee well experienced
In this luxurious day wherein we breathe.   110
Go thou, and with a smooth, enchanting tongue
Bewitch her ears, and cozen[108] her of all grace.
Enter upon the portion[109] of her soul,
Her honour, which she calls her chastity,
And bring it into expense,[110] for honesty   115
Is like a stock of money laid to sleep,
Which, ne'er so little broke, does never keep.

Vindice

You have gi'en't the tang,[111] i'faith, my lord.
Make known the lady to me, and my brain
Shall swell with strange invention. I will move it   120
Till I expire with speaking, and drop down
Without a word to save me, but I'll work—

Lussurioso

We thank thee, and will raise thee. Receive her name:
It is the only daughter to Madame Gratiana, the late widow.

Vindice (*aside*)

O, my sister, my sister!

Lussurioso   Why dost thou walk aside?   125

Vindice

My lord, I was thinking how I might begin,

---

[108] Swindle.
[109] Birthright.
[110] Make her spend her birthright.
[111] "Hit the nail right on the head."

As thus: 'O lady"—or twenty hundred devices.
Her very bodkin[112] will put a man in.[113]

Lussurioso

Ay, or the wagging of her hair.

Vindice

No, that shall put you in, my lord.   130

Lussurioso

Shall't? Why, content. Dost know the daughter, then?

Vindice

O, excellent well by sight.

Lussurioso   That was her brother
That did prefer thee to us.

Vindice   My lord, I think so;
I knew I had seen him somewhere—

Lussurioso

And therefore, prithee, let thy heart to him   135
Be as a virgin, close.

Vindice   O my good my lord.

Lussurioso

We may laugh at that simple age within him.

Vindice

Ha, ha, ha!

Lussurioso

Himself being made the subtle instrument,
To wind up a good fellow.[114]

Vindice   That's I, my lord.   140

Lussurioso

That's thou,
To entice and work his sister.

Vindice   A pure novice!

---

[112] Hair pin.
[113] Give one a subject for beginning.
[114] Set a thief on the track.

Lussurioso

    'Twas finely managed!

Vindice   Gallantly carried!

    A pretty, perfumed villain!

Lussurioso   I've bethought me,

    If she prove chaste still and immovable,   145

    Venture upon the mother, and with gifts

    As I will furnish thee, begin with her.

Vindice

    O fie, fie, that's the wrong end, my lord! 'Tis mere impos-

    sible that a mother by any gifts should become a bawd to

    her own daughter!   150

Lussurioso

    Nay, then, I see thou'rt but a puny[115]

    In the subtle mystery of a woman.

    Why, 'tis held now no dainty dish: the name

    Is so in league with age,[116] that nowadays

    It does eclipse three quarters of a mother.   155

Vindice

    Does't so, my lord?

    Let me alone[117] then to eclipse the fourth.

Lussurioso

    Why, well said! Come, I'll furnish thee, but first

    Swear to be true in all.

Vindice   True!

Lussurioso   Nay, but swear!

Vindice

    Swear?—I hope your honour little doubts my faith.   160

Lussurioso

    Yet, for my humour's sake, 'cause I love swearing.

---

[115] Inexperienced fellow.

[116] Our times.

[117] Leave it to me.

Vindice

    'Cause you love swearing, 'slud,[118] I will.

Lussurioso   Why, enough.

    Ere long, look to be made of better stuff.

Vindice

    That will do well indeed, my lord.

Lussurioso   Attend me!   *Exit*

Vindice

    O!   165

    Now let me burst, I've eaten noble poison;

    We are made strange fellows, brother, innocent villains.

    Wilt not be angry when thou hear'st on't, think'st thou?

    I'faith, thou shalt. Swear me to foul my sister!

    Sword, I durst make a promise of him to thee.   170

    Thou shalt disheir him, it shall be thine honour.

    And yet, now angry froth[119] is down in me,

    It would not prove the meanest policy

    In this disguise to try the faith of both.

    Another might have had the selfsame office,   175

    Some slave, that would have wrought effectually,

    Ay, and perhaps o'erwrought 'em; therefore I,

    Being thought travelled,[120] will apply myself

    Unto the selfsame form, forget my nature,

    As if no part about me were kin to 'em.   180

    So touch'em,[121] though I durst almost for good

    Venture my lands in heaven upon their blood.[122]   *Exit*

---

[118] Contraction of "by God's blood."

[119] Wrath.

[120] Whom they think has have left on a journey.

[121] Test them.

[122] Honesty, truth.

Act I, Scene iv

Enter the discontented Lord Antonio, whose wife the Duchess' Youngest Son ravished; he discovering[123] *the body of her, dead, to certain Lords, among them Piero and Hippolito*

Antonio
    Draw nearer, lords, and be sad witnesses
    Of a fair comely building newly fallen,
    Being falsely undermined. Violent rape
    Has played a glorious act. Behold, my lords,
    A sight that strikes man out of me.   5
Piero
    That virtuous lady!
Antonio   Precedent for wives!
Hippolito
    The blush of many women, whose chaste presence
    Would e'en call shame up to their cheeks, and make
    Pale wanton sinners have good colour.
Antonio   Dead!
    Her honour first drunk poison, and her life   10
    Being fellows in one house, did pledge[124] her honour.
Piero
    O, grief of many!
Antonio   I marked not this before,
    A prayer book the pillow to her cheek;
    This was her rich confection.[125] And another
    Placed in her right hand, with a leaf tucked up,   15
    Pointing to these words:

---

[123] Reveals, probably in the discovery space behind a curtain.
[124] Drank to.
[125] The best thing she knew.

Melius virtute mori, quam per dedecus vivere .[126]
True and effectual[127] it is indeed.

Hippolito

My lord, since you invite us to your sorrows,
Let's truly taste'em, that with equal comfort,   20
As to ourselves, we may relieve your wrongs.
We have grief too, that yet walks without tongue;
Curae leves loquuntur, majores stupent.[128]

Antonio

You deal with truth, my lord.
Lend me but your attentions, and I'll cut   25
Long grief into short words. Last reveling night,
When torchlight made an artificial noon
About the court, some courtiers in the masque,
Putting on better faces than their own,
Being full of fraud and flattery, amongst whom   30
The Duchess' youngest son—that moth to honour—
Fill'ed up a room,[129] and with long lust to eat
Into my wearing,[130] amongst all the ladies
Singled out that dear form, who ever lived
As cold in lust as she is now in death   35
—Which that step-duchess' monster knew too well—
And therefore in the height of all the revels,
When music was heard loudest, courtiers busiest,
And ladies great with laughter—O vicious minute,
Unfit but for relation to be spoke of!—   40
Then with a face more impudent than his vizard[131]

---

[126] "Better to die honorably than live with dishonor."

[127] Relevant, "to the point."

[128] "Little sorrows can be talked about, large sorrows make silent."

[129] Was one of the company.

[130] Moths' larvae eat into cloth.

[131] Mask.

He harried[132] her amidst a throng of panders,[133]
That live upon damnation[134] of both kinds,
And fed the ravenous vulture of his lust.
O death to think on't! She, her honour forced,   45
Deemed it a nobler dowry for her name
To die with poison than to live with shame.

Hippolito

A wondrous lady, of rare fire compact.
She has made her name an empress by that act.

Piero

My lord, what judgment follows the offender?   50

Antonio

Faith, none, my lord; it cools and is deferred.

Piero

Delay the doom for rape!

Antonio

O, you must note who 'tis should die,
The Duchess' son! She'll look to be a saver.
"Judgment in this age is near kin to favor."   55

Hippolito

Nay then, step forth, thou bribeless officer

Draws his sword[135]

I bind you all in steel to bind you surely.
Here let your oaths meet, to be kept and paid,
Which else will stick like rust, and shame the blade.
Strengthen my vow, that if at the next sitting   60
Judgment speak all in gold and spare the blood
Of such a serpent, e'en before their seats

---

[132] Raped.

[133] Procurers.

[134] Mortal sin.

[135] A sword hilt is cruciform, so often used *in lieu* of a cross to swear a binding oath on.

To let his soul out, which long since was found
Guilty in heaven.

All   We swear it, and will act it.

They swear on his sword

Antonio

Kind gentlemen, I thank you in mine ire.   65

Hippolito

'Twere pity
The ruins of so fair a monument
Should not be dipped in the defacer's blood.

Piero

Her funeral shall be wealthy, for her name
Merits a tomb of pearl. My Lord Antonio,   70
For this time wipe your lady from your eyes;
No doubt our grief and yours may one day court it,
When we are more familiar with revenge.

Antonio

That is my comfort, gentlemen, and I joy
In this one happiness above the rest,   75
Which will be called a miracle at last,
That, being an old man, I'd a wife so chaste.   *Exeunt*

Act II, Scene i

Enter Castiza, the sister of Vindice

Castiza

    How hardly[136] shall that maiden be beset
    Whose only fortune are her constant thoughts,
    That has no other child's part[137] but her honour,
    That keeps her low and empty in estate.
    Maids and their honours are like poor beginners.   5
    Were not sin rich, there would be fewer sinners.
    Why had not virtue a revenue? Well,
    I know the cause, 'twould have impoverished hell.

Enter Dondolo

    How now, Dondolo?
Dondolo

    Madonna, there is one, as they say, a thing of flesh and   10
    blood, a man I take him by his beard, that would very
    desirously mouth to mouth with you.
Castiza

    What's that?
Dondolo

    Show his teeth in your company.
Castiza

    I understand thee not.   15
Dondolo

    Why, speak with you, madonna.[138]

---

[136] Violently.
[137] Inheritance.
[138] Term of respectful address.

Castiza

> Why, say so, madman, and cut off a great deal of dirty
> way. Had it not been better spoke in ordinary words,
> that one would speak with me?

Dondolo

> Ha, ha, that's as ordinary as two shillings. I would strive a   20
> little to show myself in my place. A gentleman-usher
> scorns to use the phrase and fancy of a servingman.

Castiza

> Yours be your own, sir. Go, direct him hither.   *Exit Dondolo*
> I hope some happy tidings from my brother
> That lately travelled, whom my soul affects.[139]   25
> Here he comes.

Enter Vindice, her brother, disguised.

Vindice

> Lady, the best of wishes to your sex,
> Fair skins and new gowns.

Castiza   O, they shall thank you, sir.

> Whence this?

Vindice   O, from a dear and worthy friend,

> Mighty.

Castiza   From whom?

Vindice   The Duke's son!

Castiza   Receive that!   30

> *Castiza administers a box o'th' ear to her brother*

> I swore I'd put anger in my hand,
> And pass the virgin limits of my sex
> To him that next appeared in that base office,
> To be his sin's attorney. Bear to him

---

[139] Cares deeply about.

That figure[140] of my hate upon thy cheek   35
Whilst 'tis yet hot, and I'll reward thee for't.
Tell him my honour shall have a rich name
When several harlots shall share his with shame.
Farewell, commend me to him in my hate.   *Exit*
Vindice
It is the sweetest box that e'er my nose came nigh,   40
The finest drawn-work[141] cuff[142] that e'er was worn!
I'll love this blow forever, and this cheek
Shall still henceforward take the wall[143] of this.
O, I'm above my tongue. Most constant sister,
In this thou hast right honourable shown;   45
Many are called by their honour[144] that have none.
Thou art approved forever in my thoughts.
It is not in the power of words to taint thee.
And yet for the salvation of my oath,[145]
As my resolve[146] in that point, I will lay   50
Hard siege unto my mother, though I know
A siren's[147] tongue could not bewitch her so.   *Enter Gratiana*
Mass,[148] fitly, here she comes! Thanks, my disguise.
Madam, good afternoon.
Gratiana   Y'are welcome, sir.

---

[140] Shape; handprint.
[141] Ornamental embroidery involving the pulling-out of threads in the fabric.
[142] Both "the cuff of a sleeve" and "the cuff on the cheek."
[143] Have the privilege of walking on the part of the street nearest to the wall, where there was less chance of being soiled—both from the street and from above; here, i.e., the smarting cheek gets best treatment.
[144] Addressed "honourable."
[145] To keep my word.
[146] Determination.
[147] Singing enchantress.
[148] By the mass.

Vindice

    The next of Italy[149] commends him to you,   55

    Our mighty expectation, the Duke's son.

Gratiana

    I think myself much honoured that he pleases

    To rank me in his thoughts.

Vindice   So may you, lady,

    One that is like to be our sudden Duke.

    The crown gapes for him every tide,[150] and then   60

    Commander o'er us all. Do but think on him,

    How blessed were they now that could pleasure him,

    E'en with anything almost.

Gratiana   Ay, save their honour.

Vindice

    Tut, one would let a little of that go too,

    And ne'er be seen in't, ne'er be seen in't, mark you.   65

    I'd wink and let it go.

Gratiana   Marry, but I would not.

Vindice

    Marry, but I would, I hope. I know you would too,

    If you'd that blood[151] now which you gave your daughter.

    To her indeed 'tis this wheel[152] comes about.

    That man that must be all this, perhaps ere morning,   70

    For his white[153] father does but mold away,

    Has long desired your daughter.

Gratiana   Desired?

Vindice

    Nay, but hear me!

---

[149] The prince next in line for the throne.

[150] Constantly; all the time.

[151] See glossary.

[152] I.e., of Fortune.

[153] White-haired with age.

He desires now that will command hereafter,
Therefore be wise. I speak as more a friend   75
To you than him. Madam, I know you're poor
And, 'lack the day,
There are too many poor ladies already.
Why should you wax[154] the number? 'Tis despised.
Live wealthy, rightly understand the world,   80
And chide away that foolish country girl
Keeps company with your daughter, Chastity.

Gratiana

O fie, fie! The riches of this world cannot hire
A mother to such a most unnatural task.

Vindice

No, but a thousand angels[155] can.   85
Men have no power, angels must work you to't.
The world descends into such baseborn evils
That forty angels can make fourscore devils.
There will be fools still, I perceive, still fools.
Would I be poor, dejected, scorned of greatness,   90
Swept from the palace, and see other daughters
Spring with the dew o'the court, having mine own
So much desired and loved by the Duke's son?
No, I would raise my state upon her breast,
And call her eyes my tenants. I would count   95
My yearly maintenance[156] upon her cheeks,
Take coach upon her lip, and all her parts
Should keep men after men, and I would ride
In pleasure upon pleasure.
You took great pains for her, once when it was,   100
Let her requite it now, though it be but some.

---

[154] Make larger.
[155] An angel is also a coin worth ten shillings.
[156] Livelihood.

You brought her forth,[157] she may well bring you home.[158]

Gratiana

    O heavens! This overcomes me!

Vindice (*aside*)

    Not, I hope, already?

Gratiana (*aside*)

    It is too strong for me. Men know that know us   105
    We are so weak their words can overthrow us.
    He touched me nearly,[159] made my virtues bate,[160]
    When his tongue struck upon my poor estate.

Vindice (*aside*)

    I e'en quake to proceed, my spirit turns edge.
    I fear me she's unmothered, yet I'll venture.   110
    "That woman is all male, whom none can enter."
    What think you now, lady? Speak, are you wiser?
    What said advancement to you? Thus it said,
    "The daughter's fall lifts up the mother's head."
    Did it not, madam? But I'll swear it does   115
    In many places. Tut, this age fears no man.
    "'Tis no shame to be bad, because 'tis common."

Gratiana

    Ay, that's the comfort on't.

Vindice   The comfort on't!
    I keep the best for last. Can these persuade you
    To forget heaven, and—   *Gives her money*

Gratiana   Ay, these are they—   120

Vindice (*aside*)

    O!

Gratiana —That enchant our sex, these are the means

---

[157] Gave birth to her.

[158] Be your financial salvation.

[159] He has the measure of my condition.

[160] Abate; shrink.

That govern our affections. That woman
Will not be troubled with the mother[161] long,
That sees the comfortable shine of you!
I blush to think what for your sakes I'll do!   125
Vindice (*aside*)
    O suffering[162] heavens, with thy invisible finger
    E'en at this instant turn the precious side
    Of both mine eyeballs inward, not to see myself.
Gratiana
    Look you, sir.
Vindice   Holla.
Gratiana   Let this thank your pains.   *Gives money*
Vindice
    O, you're kind, madam.   130
Gratiana
    I'll see how I can move.
Vindice (*aside*)   Your words will sting.
Gratiana
    If she be still chaste, I'll ne'er call her mine.
Vindice (*aside*)
    Spoke truer than thou meant it.
Gratiana
    Daughter Castiza!

Enter Castiza

Castiza   Madam.
Vindice   O, she's yonder,
    Meet her.   135
    Troops of celestial soldiers guard her heart.
    Yon dam has devils enough to take her part.

[161] Hysteria.
[162] Long-suffering.

Castiza

    Madam, what makes yon evil-officed man

    In presence of you?

Gratiana   Why?

Castiza   He lately brought

    Immodest writing sent from the Duke's son   140

    To tempt me to dishonourable act.

Gratiana

    Dishonourable act! Good honourable fool,

    That wouldst be honest 'cause thou wouldst be so,

    Producing no one reason but thy will.

    And't[163] has a good report, prettily commended,   145

    But pray, by whom? Mean[164] people, ignorant people!

    The better sort, I'm sure, cannot abide it.

    And by what rule should we square out our lives

    But by our betters' actions? O, if thou knew'st

    What 'twere to lose it, thou wouldst never keep it.   150

    But there's a cold curse laid upon all maids,

    Whilst others clip[165] the sun, they clasp the shades.

    Virginity is paradise locked up.

    You cannot come by yourselves without fee,

    And 'twas decreed that man should keep the key!   155

    Deny advancement, treasure, the Duke's son!

Castiza

    I cry you mercy, lady, I mistook you.

    Pray, did you see my mother? Which way went you?

    Pray God I have not lost her.

Vindice (*aside*)   Prettily put by.

---

[163] "And it." "It" is often used addressing a child, but the use here is to demean Castiza.

[164] Of low class.

[165] Embrace.

Gratiana

Are you as proud to me as coy to him?   160

Do you not know me now?

Castiza   Why, are you she?

The world's so changed, one shape into another,

It is a wise child now that knows her mother.

Vindice (*aside*)

Most right i'faith.

Gratiana   I owe your cheek my hand

For that presumption now, but I'll forget it.   165

Come, you shall leave those childish 'haviours,[166]

And understand your time. Fortunes flow to you,

What, will you be a girl?

If all feared drowning that spy waves ashore,

Gold would grow rich, and all the merchants poor.   170

Castiza

It is a pretty saying of a wicked one,

But methinks now it does not show so well

Out of your mouth. Better in his.

Vindice

Faith, bad enough in both,

Were I in earnest, as I'll seem no less.   175

I wonder, lady, your own mother's words

Cannot be taken, nor stand in full force.

'Tis honesty you urge, what's honesty?

'Tis but heaven's beggar!

And what woman is so foolish to keep honesty   180

And be not able to keep herself? No,

Times are grown wiser and will keep less charge.[167]

A maid that has small portion now intends

To break up house, and live upon her friends.

---

[166] Behavior.

[167] Expenditure.

How blessed are you! You have happiness alone,   185
Others must fall to thousands, you to one,
Sufficient in himself to make your forehead[168]
Dazzle the world with jewels, and petitionary people
Start at your presence.

Gratiana   O, if I were young,
I should be ravished.

Castiza   Ay, to lose your honour!   190

Vindice

'Slid,[169] how can you lose your honour
To deal with my lord's grace?
He'll add more honour to it by his title.
Your mother will tell you how.

Gratiana   That I will.

Vindice

O, think upon the pleasure of the palace!   195
Secured ease and state! The stirring[170] meats
Ready to move out of the dishes,
That e'en now quicken[171] when they're eaten!
Banquets abroad by torchlight! Music! Sports!
Bareheaded vassals, that had ne'er the fortune   200
To keep their own hats, but let horns wear'em![172]
Nine coaches waiting! Hurry, hurry, hurry!

Castiza

Ay, to the devil.

Vindice

Ay, to the devil! To the Duke, by my faith.

[168] See glossary.
[169] By God's eyelid.
[170] With aphrodisiac effect.
[171] Come alive; rouse.
[172] "Bareheaded," because their hats were off in the presence of their betters. But also wordplay on cuckoldom, because stags' horns were used as hatracks.

Gratiana

 Ay, to the Duke! Daughter, you'd scorn to think   205
 O'the devil, and you were there once.

Vindice (*aside*)   True, for most

 There are as proud as he for his heart, i'faith.
 (*Aloud*) Who'd sit at home in a neglected room,
 Dealing her short-lived beauty to the pictures
 That are as useless as old men, when those   210
 Poorer in face and fortune than herself
 Walk with a hundred acres on their backs,[173]
 Fair meadows cut into green foreparts? O,
 It was the greatest blessing ever happened to woman,
 When farmers' sons agreed and met again,   215
 To wash their hands, and come up gentlemen.[174]
 The commonwealth has flourished ever since!
 Lands that were mete[175] by the rod,[176] that labour spared,
 Tailors ride down and measure'em by the yard.
 Fair trees, those comely foretops[177] of the field,   220
 Are cut to maintain head-tires[178]—much untold.
 All thrives but Chastity, she lies a-cold.
 Nay, shall I come nearer to you? Mark but this: Why are
 there so few honest women, but because 'tis the poorer
 profession? That's accounted best that's best followed. Least 225
 in trade, least in fashion, and that's not honesty, believe it.

---

[173] The price obtained for a hundred acres of land would pay for a court wardrobe.

[174] When farmers were in agreement and worked to better their social position.

[175] Measured.

[176] Measuring stick.

[177] Platform for outlook on a ship's foremast (timber was often profitably sold for building ships); but also archaic term for crown of the head.

[178] Headdresses.

And do but note the love and dejected price of it!
Lose but a pearl, we search and cannot brook[179] it,
But that[180] once gone, who is so mad to look it?

Gratiana

Troth, he says true.

Castiza   False! I defy you both.   230
I have endured you with an ear of fire,
Your tongues have struck hot irons on my face!
Mother, come from that poisonous woman there!

Gratiana

Where?

Castiza   Do you not see her? She's too inward, then.
Slave, perish in thine office! You heavens, please   235
Henceforth to make the mother a disease,
Which first begins with me; yet I've outgone[181] you.   *Exit*

Vindice (*aside*)

O, angels, clap your wings upon the skies
And give this virgin crystal[182] plaudities!

Gratiana

Peevish,[183] coy, foolish! But return this answer: 240
My lord shall be most welcome when his pleasure
Conducts him this way. I will sway mine own.
Women with women can work best alone.   *Exit*

Vindice

Indeed, I'll tell him so.
O, more uncivil, more unnatural,   245
Than those base-titled creatures that look downward.[184]
Why does not heaven turn black, or with a frown

---

[179] Endure.
[180] I.e., honesty.
[181] Outdistanced.
[182] Crystal is pure and clear.
[183] Contrary.
[184] Animals. Man, endowed with reason, is closer to God.

Undo the world? Why does not earth start up
And strike the sins that tread upon't? O!   249
Were't not for gold and women, there would be no damnation.
Hell would look like a lord's great kitchen without fire in't.
But 'twas decreed before the world began
That they should be the hook to catch a man.   *Exit*

Act II, Scene ii

Enter Lussurioso with Hippolito, Vindice's brother

Lussurioso

    I much applaud thy judgment.

    Thou art well read in a fellow,

    And 'tis the deepest art to study man.

    I know this, which I never learned in schools,

    The world's divided into knaves and fools.

Hippolito (*aside*)   5

    Knave in your face, my lord—behind your back[185]—

Lussurioso

    And I much thank thee that thou hast preferred

    A fellow of discourse,[186] well mingled,

    And whose brain time hath seasoned.

Hippolito   True, my lord.

    (*Aside*) We shall find seasons once, I hope. O, villain!   10

    To make such an unnatural slave of me, but—

Enter Vindice, disguised

---

[185] There's a knave here, my lord, but you cannot see him!

[186] Interesting conversation.

Lussurioso

    Mass, here he comes.

Hippolito (*aside*)

    And now shall I have free leave to depart.

Lussurioso

    Your absence, leave us.

Hippolito (*aside*)   Are not my thoughts true?

    (*To Vindice*) I must remove, but brother, you may stay.   15

    Heart,[187] we are both made bawds a new-found way!   *Exit*

Lussurioso

    Now we're an even number. A third man's dangerous,

    Especially her brother. Say, be free,

    Have I a pleasure toward?

Vindice   O, my lord!

Lussurioso

    Ravish me in thine answer! Art thou rare?   20

    Hast thou beguiled her of salvation.

    And rubbed hell o'er with honey? Is she a woman?

Vindice

    In all but in desire.

Lussurioso   Then she's in nothing.

    I bate[188] in courage now.

Vindice   The words I brought

    Might well have made indifferent honest naught.   25

    A right good woman in these days is changed

    Into white money[189] with less labour far.

    Many a maid has turned to Mahomet[190]

    With easier working; I durst undertake,

    Upon the pawn and forfeit of my life,   30

[187] By God's heart.

[188] Decline.

[189] Silver. The implication is that women are cheaply bought.

[190] Become infidel; i.e., become a prostitute.

With half those words to flat[191] a Puritan's wife.
But she is close and good, yet 'tis a doubt
By this time.——O, the mother, the mother!

Lussurioso

I never thought their sex had been a wonder
Until this minute. What fruit from the mother?   35

Vindice (*aside*)

Now must I blister my soul, be forsworn,
Or shame the woman that received me first.
I will be true, thou[192] liv'st not to proclaim.
Spoke to a dying man, shame has no shame.
My lord.

Lussurioso   Who's that?

Vindice   Here's none but I, my lord.   40

Lussurioso

What would thy haste utter?

Vindice   Comfort.

Lussurioso   Welcome.

Vindice

The maid being dull, having no mind to travel
Into unknown lands, what did I straight
But set spurs to the mother? Golden spurs
Will put her to a false gallop in a trice.   45

Lussurioso

Is't possible that in this
The mother should be damned before the daughter?

Vindice

O, that's good manners, my lord. The mother, for her
age, must go foremost, you know.   49

Lussurioso

Thou'st spoke that true, but where comes in this comfort?

---

[191] Get her on her back.
[192] Thou = Lussurioso.

Vindice

    In a fine place, my lord. The unnatural mother

    Did with her tongue so hard beset her honour,

    That the poor fool was struck to silent wonder.

    Yet still the maid, like an unlighted taper,

    Was cold and chaste, save that her mother's breath   55

    Did blow fire on her cheeks. The girl departed,

    But the good ancient madam, half mad, threw me

    These promising words, which I took deeply note of:

    "My lord shall be most welcome—"

Lussurioso   Faith, I thank her!

Vindice

    "—When his pleasure conducts him this way—"   60

Lussurioso

    That shall be soon, i'faith.

Vindice   "—I will sway mine own—"

Lussurioso

    She does the wiser. I commend her for't.

Vindice

    "—Women with women can work best alone."

Lussurioso

    By this light, and so they can, give'em their due. Men are

    not comparable to'em.   65

Vindice

    No, that's true, for you shall have one woman knit more

    in an hour than any man can ravel again in seven and twenty

    year.

Lussurioso

    Now my desires are happy, I'll make'em freemen[193] now.

    Thou art a precious fellow, faith, I love thee.   70

[193] Unfetter them.

Be wise and make it thy revenue: beg, leg![194]

What office couldst thou be ambitious for?

Vindice

Office, my lord! Marry, if I might have my wish, I would
have one that was never begged yet.

Lussurioso

Nay, then thou canst have none.   75

Vindice

Yes, my lord, I could pick out another office yet, nay, and
keep a horse and drab[195] upon't.

Lussurioso

Prithee, good bluntness, tell me.

Vindice

Why, I would desire but this, my lord: to have all the fees
behind the arras,[196] and all the farthingales[197] that fall plump   80
about twelve o'clock at night upon the rushes.[198]

Lussurioso

Thou'rt a mad apprehensive[199] knave. Dost think to make
any great purchase[200] of that?

Vindice

O, 'tis an unknown thing, my lord. I wonder't has been
missed so long.   85

Lussurioso

Well, this night I'll visit her, and 'tis till then
A year in my desires. Farewell. Attend!
Trust me with thy preferment.   *Exit*

Vindice   My loved lord.

---

[194] "Make a leg," bow.

[195] Woman.

[196] Tapestry.

[197] Hooped skirts.

[198] Rushes were used for strewing floors.

[199] Smart.

[200] Gains.

O, shall I kill him o'th'wrong side now? No!
Sword, thou wast never a backbiter yet.   90
I'll pierce him to his face, he shall die looking on me.
Thy veins are swelled with lust, this shall unfill'em.
Great men were gods if beggars could not kill'em.
Forgive me, heaven to call my mother wicked,
O, lessen not my days upon the earth.   95
I cannot honour her! By this, I fear me,
Her tongue has turned my sister into use.
I was a villain not to be forsworn
To this our lecherous hope, the Duke's son;
For lawyers, merchants, some divines, and all   100
Count beneficial perjury[201] a sin small.
It shall go hard yet, but I'll guard her honour,
And keep the ports sure.

Enter Hippolito

Hippolito   Brother, how goes the world?
   I would know news of you, but I have news
   To tell you.
Vindice   What, in the name of knavery?   105
Hippolito
   Knavery, faith!
   This vicious old Duke's worthily abused,
   The pen[202] of his bastard writes him cuckold!
Vindice
   His bastard?
Hippolito   Pray, believe it! He and the Duchess
   By night meet in their linen, they have been seen   110
   By stair-foot panders.

---

[201] Lying under oath for a good cause.
[202] Also "penis."

Vindice   O, sin foul and deep.
    Great faults are winked at when the Duke's asleep.
    See, see, here comes the Spurio.

Enter Spurio and Servants

Hippolito   Monstrous luxur!
Vindice
    Unbraced,[203] two of his valiant bawds with him.
    O, there's a wicked whisper, hell's in his ear.   115
    Stay, let's observe his passage.
Spurio
    O, but are you sure on't?
Servant
    My lord, most sure on't, for 'twas spoke by one
    That is most inward with the Duke's son's lust,
    That he intends within this hour to steal   120
    Unto Hippolito's sister, whose chaste life
    The mother has corrupted for his use.
Spurio
    Sweet words, sweet occasion! Faith then, brother,
    I'll disinherit you in as short time
    As I was when I was begot in haste.   125
    I'll damn you at your pleasure, precious deed!
    After your lust, O, 'twill be fine to bleed.
    Come, let our passing out be soft[204] and wary.
                                  Exeunt Spurio and Servants
Vindice
    Mark there! There! That step, now to the Duchess.
    This their second meeting writes the Duke cuckold   130
    With new additions, his horns newly revived.

---

[203] With loosened clothes.
[204] Soundless.

Night, thou that look'st like funeral herald's fees
Torn down betimes in the morning,[205] thou hangst fitly
To grace those sins that have no grace at all.
Now 'tis full sea abed over the world,   135
There's juggling of all sides. Some that were maids
E'en at sunset are now perhaps i'the toll-book.
This woman in immodest thin apparel
Lets in her friend[206] by water. Here a dame
Cunning nails leather hinges to a door   140
To avoid proclamation.[207] Now cuckolds are
A-coining, apace, apace, apace, apace!
And careful sisters spin that thread i'the night
That does maintain them and their bawds i'the day.

Hippolito

You flow well, brother.

Vindice   Pooh, I'm shallow yet,   145
Too sparing and too modest. Shall I tell thee?
If every trick were told that's dealt by night,
There are few here that would not blush outright.

Hippolito

I am of that belief, too.

Vindice   Who's this comes?

Enter Lussurioso

The Duke's son up so late? Brother, fall back,   150
And you shall learn some mischief.—My good lord.

Lussurioso

Piato! Why, the man I wished for! Come,

---

[205] Fees: here black wall hangings for a funeral, "pheese."

[206] I.e., lover.

[207] The squeaking of ordinary hinges.

I do embrace this season for the fittest
To taste of that young lady.

Vindice (*aside*)   Heart and all.

Hippolito (*aside*)

Damned villain.

Vindice (*aside*)   I have no way now to cross it,   155
But to kill him.

Lussurioso   Come, only thou and I.

Vindice

My lord, my lord!

Lussurioso   Why dost thou start us?

Vindice

I'd almost forgot. The bastard!

Lussurioso   What of him?

Vindice

This night, this hour, this minute, now—

Lussurioso   What? What?

Vindice

—Shadows the Duchess—

Lussurioso   Horrible word!   160

Vindice

—And like strong poison eats
Into the Duke your father's forehead.

Lussurioso   O!

Vindice

He makes horn royal.

Lussurioso   Most ignoble slave!

Vindice

This is the fruit of two beds.

Lussurioso   I am mad.

Vindice

That passage he trod warily—

Lussurioso   He did!   165

Vindice

 —And hushed his villains every step he took.

Lussurioso

 His villains! I'll confound them!

Vindice

 Take'em finely, finely now.[208]

Lussurioso

 The Duchess' chamber door shall not confound me.

Exeunt Lussurioso and Vindice

Hippolito

 Good, happy, swift! There's gunpowder i'the court, 170

 Wildfire at midnight. In this heedless fury

 He may show violence to cross himself.

 I'll follow the event.   *Exit*

Act II, Scene iii

The Duke and Duchess in bed.[209] *Enter Lussurioso and Vindice, disguised*

Lussurioso

 Where is that villain?

Vindice

 Softly, my lord, and you may take'em twisted.

Lussurioso

 I care not how!

Vindice   O, 'twill be glorious

 To kill'em doubled, when they're heaped. Be soft, my lord.

[208] With precision.

[209] Probably behind a curtain in the discovery space.

Lussurioso

 Away, my spleen[210] is not so lazy. Thus and thus   5
 I'll shake their eyelids ope, and with my sword
 Shut'em again forever! Villain! Strumpet!

Duke

 You upper guard, defend us!

Duchess   Treason! Treason!

Duke

 O, take me not in sleep.
 I have great sins, I must have days,   10
 Nay, months, dear son, with penitential heaves,[211]
 To lift'em out, and not to die unclear.[212]
 O, thou wilt kill me both in heaven and here.

Lussurioso

 I am amazed to death.

Duke   Nay, villain traitor,
 Worse than the foulest epithet, now I'll gripe thee   15
 E'en with the nerves of wrath, and throw thy head
 Amongst the lawyers! Guard!

Enter Nobles and sons Ambitioso and Supervacuo, with Hippolito.

First Noble

 How comes the quiet of your grace disturbed?

Duke

 This boy, that should be my self after me,
 Would be my self before me, and in heat   20
 Of that ambition bloodily rushed in,
 Intending to depose me in my bed!

[210] See glossary.
[211] Sighs.
[212] Clouded with sin.

Second Noble

 Duty and natural loyalty forfend!

Duchess

 He called his father villain, and me strumpet,

 A word that I abhor to file[213] my lips with.   25

Ambitioso

 That was not so well done, brother.

Lussurioso (*aside*)

 I am abused!

 I know there's no excuse can do me good.

Vindice (*to Hippolito*)

 'Tis now good policy to be from sight.

 His vicious purpose to our sister's honour   30

 Is crossed beyond our thought.

Hippolito   You little dreamt

 His father slept here.

Vindice   O, 'twas far beyond me.

 But since it fell so—without frightful words,

 Would he have killed him, 'twould have eased our swords.

            Exeunt Vindice and Hippolito

Duke

 Be comforted, our Duchess, he shall die.   35

Lussurioso

 Where's this slave-pander now? Out of mine eye,

 Guilty of this abuse.[214]

Enter Spurio with his servants at one door; exit Duchess at the other[215]

---

[213] Defile.

[214] Vilification.

[215] The Duchess' exit is the editor's stage direction. No original exit exists, and this seemed the best point to achieve a meaningful exit.

Spurio	Y'are villains, fablers![216]

    You have knaves' chins and harlots' tongues, you lie,

    And I will damn you with one meal a day.

First Servant

    O good my lord!

Spurio   'Sblood, you shall never sup.   40

Second Servant

    O, I beseech you, sir!

Spurio   To let my sword

    Catch cold so long and miss him.

First Servant   Troth, my lord

    'Twas his intent to meet there.

Spurio   Heart, he's yonder.

    Ha, what news here? Is the day out o'the socket.

    That it is noon at midnight? The court up?   45

    How comes the guard so saucy with his elbows?

Lussurioso

    The bastard here?

    Nay, then the truth of my intent shall out!

    My lord and father, hear me.

Duke   Bear him hence.

Lussurioso

    I can with loyalty excuse—   50

Duke

    Excuse? To prison with the villain!

    Death shall not long lag after him.

Spurio

    Good, i'faith, then 'tis not much amiss.

Lussurioso

    Brothers, my best release lies in your tongues.

    I pray, persuade for me.   55

---

[216] Liars.

Ambitioso

It is our duties. Make yourself sure of us.

Supervacuo

We'll sweat in pleading.

Lussurioso   And I may live to thank you.

Exeunt Lussurioso and Guards

Ambitioso (*aside*)

No, thy death shall thank me better.

Spurio (*aside*)

He's gone. I'll after him

And know his trespass, seem to bear a part   60

In all his ills, but with a Puritan[217] heart.

Exit Spurio and his servants

Ambitioso

Now, brother, let our hate and love be woven

So subtly together, that in speaking

One word for his life, we may make three for his death.

The craftiest pleader gets most gold for breath.   65

Supervacuo

Set on. I'll not be far behind you, brother.

Duke

Is't possible a son should be disobedient as far as the sword?

It is the highest. He can go no farther.

Ambitioso

My gracious lord, take pity—

Duke   Pity, boys?

Ambitioso

Nay, we'd be loath to move[218] your grace too much,   70

We know the trespass is unpardonable,

Black, wicked, and unnatural.

---

[217] Hypocritical; also, see glossary.
[218] Stir to strong passion; persuade.

Supervacuo

In a son, O, monstrous!

Ambitioso   Yet, my lord

A duke's soft hand strokes the rough head of law,

And makes it lie smooth.

Duke   But my hand shall ne'er do't.   75

Ambitioso

That as you please, my lord.

Supervacuo   We must needs confess

Some father would have entered into hate

So deadly pointed, that before his eyes

He would ha' seen the execution sound[219]

Without corrupted favour.

Ambitioso   But, my lord,   80

Your grace may live the wonder of all times,

In pardoning that offense, which never yet

Had face to beg a pardon.

Duke   Honey, how's this?

Ambitioso

Forgive him, good my lord. He is your son,

And I must needs say 'twas the viler done.   85

Supervacuo

He's the next heir, yet this true reason gathers,

None can possess that dispossess their fathers.

Be merciful—

Duke (*aside*)   Here's no stepmother's wit.

I'll try 'em both upon their love and hate.

Ambitioso

Be merciful, although—

Duke   You have prevailed.   90

My wrath, like flaming wax, hath spent itself.

---

[219] Well performed.

I know 'twas but some peevish moon[220] in him.

Go, let him be released.

Supervacuo   'Sfoot, how now, brother?

Ambitioso

Your grace doth please to speak beside your spleen,[221]

I would it were so happy.

Duke   Why go, release him.   95

Supervacuo

O, my good lord, I know the fault's too weighty

And full of general loathing, too inhumane,

Rather by all men's voices worthy death.

Duke

'Tis true too.

Here then, receive this signet.[222] Doom shall pass.   100

Direct it to the judges. He shall die

Ere many days. Make haste.

Ambitioso   All speed that may be.

We could have wished his burden not so sore,

We knew your grace did but delay before.

Exeunt Ambitioso and Supervacuo

Duke

Here's envy with a poor, thin cover o'er't,   105

Like scarlet hid in lawn,[223] easily spied through.

This their ambition by their mother's side

Is dangerous, and for safety must be purged.

I will prevent their envies. Sure it was

But some mistaken fury in our son,   110

Which these aspiring boys would climb upon.

---

[220] Instability; changeable like the moon.

[221] See glossary.

[222] A seal, usually in a ring, to give proof that e.g. an order stems from the authority figure.

[223] Fine linen.

He shall be released suddenly.[224]

Enter Nobles

First Noble
    Good morning to your grace.
Duke   Welcome, my lords.
Second Noble
    Our knees shall take away
    The office of our feet forever,   115
    Unless your grace bestow a father's eye
    Upon the clouded fortunes of your son,
    And in compassionate virtue grant him that
    Which makes e'en mean men happy, liberty.
Duke
    How seriously their loves and honours woo   120
    For that which I'm about to pray them do,
    Which—rise, my lords—your knees sign his release.
    We freely pardon him.
First Noble
    We owe your grace much thanks, and he much duty.
                            Exeunt Nobles
Duke
    It well becomes that judge to nod at crimes   125
    That does commit greater himself, and lives.
    I may forgive a disobedient error,
    That expect pardon for adultery,
    And in my old days am a youth in lust.
    Many a beauty have I turned to poison   130
    In the denial,[225] covetous of all.
    Age hot is like a monster to be seen.
    My hairs are white, and yet my sins are green.   *Exit*

---

[224] At once.
[225] When she denied me.

Act III, Scene i

Enter Ambitioso and Supervacuo

Supervacuo

    Brother, let my opinion sway you once.

    I speak it for the best to have him die

    Surest and soonest. If the signet come

    Unto the judges' hands, why then his doom

    Will be deferred till sittings and court-days,   5

    Juries and further. Faiths are bought and sold,

    Oaths in these days are but the skin of gold.

Ambitioso

    In troth, 'tis true too.

Supervacuo   Then let's set by[226] the judges

    And fall to[227] the officers. 'Tis but mistaking

    The Duke our father's meaning; and where he named   10

    "Ere many days," 'tis but forgetting that,

    And have him die i'the morning.

Ambitioso   Excellent!

    Then I am heir, Duke in a minute.

Supervacuo (*aside*)   Nay,

    And he were once puffed out, here is a pin[228]

    Should quickly prick your bladder.

Ambitioso   Blessed occasion!

    He being packed, we have some trick and wile   15

    To wind our youngest brother out of prison

    That lies in for the rape. The lady's dead,

    And people's thoughts will soon be buried.

---

[226] Set aside.

[227] Rely upon.

[228] His sword or dagger.

Supervacuo

 We may with safety do't, and live and feed.   20

 The Duchess' sons are too proud to bleed.

Ambitioso

 We are, i'faith, to say true. Come, let's not linger.

 I'll to the officers, go you before,

 And set an edge upon[229] the executioner.

Supervacuo

 Let me alone to grind him!   *Exit*

Ambitioso   Meet. Farewell.   25

 I am next now. I rise just in that place

 Where thou'rt cut off, upon thy neck, kind brother.

 The falling of one head lifts up another.   *Exit*

Act III, Scene ii

Enter with Nobles Lussurioso from prison

Lussurioso

 My lords, I'm so much indebted to your loves

 For this, O, this delivery —

First Noble   But our duties,[230]

 My lord, unto the hopes that grow in you.

Lussurioso

 If e'er I live to be myself, I'll thank you.

 O liberty, thou sweet and heavenly dame!   5

 But hell for prison is too mild a name.   *Exeunt*

---

[229] Make sharp and keen.
[230] That is only our duty.

Act III, Scene iii

Enter Ambitioso and Supervacuo with Officers

Ambitioso

    Officers, here's the Duke's signet, your firm warrant,

    Brings the command of present death along with it

    Unto our brother, the Duke's son. We are sorry

    That we are so unnaturally employed

    In such an unkind office, fitter far   5

    For enemies than brothers.

Supervacuo   But you know,

    The Duke's commands must be obeyed.

First Officer

    It must and shall, my lord. This morning then,

    So suddenly?

Ambitioso   Ay, alas, poor good soul!

    He must breakfast betimes; the executioner   10

    Stands ready to put forth his cowardly valour.

Second Officer

    Already?

Supervacuo

    Already, i'faith. O sir, destruction hies,

    And that is least imprudent,[231] soonest dies.

First Officer

    Troth, you say true, my lord. We take our leaves,   15

    Our office shall be sound. We'll not delay

    The third part of a minute.

Ambitioso   Therein you show

    Yourselves good men and upright officers.

    Pray, let him die as private as he may.

    Do him that favour, for the gaping people   20

---

[231] The least imprudent is the most farsighted.

Will but trouble him at his prayers,
And make him curse and swear, and so die black.[232]
Will you be so far kind?

First Officer   It shall be done, my lord.

Ambitioso

Why, we do thank you. If we live to be,
You shall have better office.

Second Officer   Your good lordship.   25

Supervacuo

Commend us to the scaffold in our tears.

First Officer

We'll weep, and do your commendations.   *Exeunt Officers*

Ambitioso

Fine fools in office!

Supervacuo   Things fall out so fit!

Ambitioso

So happily! Come, brother, ere next clock
His head will be made serve a bigger block.[233]   *Exeunt* 30

Act III, Scene iv

Enter in prison the Duchess' Youngest Son and his Keeper

Youngest Son

Keeper!

Keeper   My lord?

Youngest Son   No news lately from our brothers?
Are they unmindful of us?

Keeper

My lord, a messenger came newly in

---

[232] Tainted by sin.
[233] The executioner's block, of course, but the word also means "hat."

| | And brought this from'em. | *Gives him a letter* |

Youngest Son   Nothing but paper comforts?

I looked for my delivery before this,   5
Had they been worth their oaths. Prithee, be from us!

Exit Keeper

Now, what say you, forsooth? Speak out, I pray.
(*He reads*) "Brother, be of good cheer."
'Slud, it begins like a whore with good cheer.
"Thou shalt not be long a prisoner."   10
Not five and thirty year like a bankrout[234]—I think so!
"We have thought upon a device to get thee out by a
trick." By a trick? Pox o'your trick and it be so long a-
playing. "And so rest comforted, be merry, and expect it
suddenly."   *He tears the letter* 15
Be merry! Hang merry, draw and quarter merry![235] I'll be
mad. Is't not strange that a man should lie in a whole
month for a woman? Well, we shall see how sudden our
brothers will be in their promise. I must expect still[236] a
trick! I shall not be long a prisoner.   *Re-enter Keeper* 20
How now, what news?

Keeper

Bad news, my lord, I am discharged of you.

Youngest Son

Slave, call'st thou that bad news! (*Aside*) I thank you, brothers!

Keeper

My lord, 'twill prove so. Here come the officers
Into whose hands I must commit you.

Enter Officers

---

[234] Bankrupt.
[235] A reference to the traitor's punishment; see glossary.
[236] Always.

Youngest Son	Ha!	25

    Officers! What? Why?

First Officer   You must pardon us, my lord,

    Our office must be sound.[237] Here is our warrant,

    The signet from the Duke. You must straight suffer,

Youngest Son

    Suffer? I'll suffer you to be gone! I'll suffer you

    To come no more! What would you have me suffer?   30

Second Officer

    My lord, those words were better changed to prayers,

    The time's but brief with you. Prepare to die.

Youngest Son

    Sure 'tis not so.

Third Officer   It is too true, my lord.

Youngest Son

    I tell you 'tis not, for the Duke my father

    Deferred me till next sitting, and I look   35

    E'en every minute threescore times an hour

    For a release, a trick wrought by my brothers.

First Officer

    A trick, my lord? If you expect such comfort,

    Your hope's as fruitless as a barren woman,

    Your brothers were the unhappy messengers   40

    That brought this powerful token for your death.

Youngest Son

    My brothers? No, no!

Second Officer   'Tis most true, my lord.

Youngest Son

    My brothers to bring a warrant for my death?

    How strange this shows!

Third Officer   There's no delaying time.

---

[237] Well performed.

Youngest Son

> Desire'em hither, call'em up, my brothers!   45
> They shall deny it to your faces.

First Officer   My lord,

> They're far enough by this, at least at court,
> And this most strict command they left behind'em.
> When grief swum in their eyes, they showed like brothers,
> Brimful of heavy sorrow, but the Duke   50
> Must have his pleasure.

Youngest Son   His pleasure!

First Officer

> These were their last words which my memory bears:
> "Commend us to the scaffold in our tears."

Youngest Son

> Pox dry their tears! What should I do with tears?
> I hate'em worse than any citizen's son   55
> Can hate salt water. Here came a letter now,
> New-bleeding from their pens, scarce stinted yet.
> Would I'd been torn in pieces when I tore it!

> > *He reassembles the pieces of the letter*

> Look, you officious whoresons, words of comfort,
> "Not long a prisoner."   60

First Officer

> It says true in that, sir, for you must suffer presently.

Youngest Son

> A villainous Duns[238] upon the letter, knavish exposition!
> Look you here then, sir! "We'll get you out by a trick,"
> says he.

Second Officer

> That may hold too, sir, for you know a trick is commonly   65
> four cards, which was meant by us four officers.

---

[238] Interpretation; the allusion is to Dons Scotus, philosopher and theologian.

Youngest Son
    Worse and worse dealing.
First Officer   The hour beckons us,
    The headsman waits. Lift up your eyes to heaven.
Youngest Son
    I thank you, faith, good pretty wholesome counsel!
    I should look up to heaven as you said,   70
    Whilst he behind me cozens me of my head.
    Ay, that's the trick.
Third Officer   You delay too long, my lord.
Youngest Son
    Stay, good Authority's bastard, since I must
    Through brothers' perjury die, O let me venom
    Their souls with curses.
First Officer   Come, 'tis no time to curse.   75
Youngest Son
    Must I bleed[239] then without respect of sign?[240] Well!
    My fault was sweet sport, which the world approves.
    I die for that which every woman loves.   *Exeunt*

Act III, Scene v

Enter Vindice in disguise with Hippolito, his brother

Vindice
    O sweet, delectable, rare, happy, ravishing!
Hippolito
    Why, what's the matter, brother?
Vindice   O, 'tis able

---

[239] Be bled for medicinal purposes.
[240] Astrological condition; astrology plays a great part in mediaeval medicine.

To make a man spring up and knock his forehead
Against yon silver ceiling.[241]

Hippolito   Prithee, tell me
Why may not I partake with you? You vowed once   5
To give me share to every tragic thought.

Vindice
By the mass, I think I did too.
Then I'll divide it to thee.[242] The old Duke
Thinking my outward shape and inward heart
Are cut out of one piece (for he that prates his secrets,   10
His heart stands o'the outside), hires me by price
To greet him with a lady
In some fit place, veiled from the eyes o'the court,
Some darkened blushless angle, that is guilty
Of his forefathers' lust and great folks' riots.[243]   15
To which I easily, to maintain my shape,
Consented, and did wish his impudent grace
To meet her here in this unsunned lodge,
Wherein 'tis night at noon; and here the rather
Because, unto the torturing of his soul,   20
The bastard and the Duchess have appointed
Their meeting too in this luxurious[244] circle,
Which most afflicting sight will kill his eyes
Before we kill the rest of him.

Hippolito
'Twill, i'faith! Most dreadfully digested![245]   25
I see not how you could have missed me,[246] brother.

[241] The heavens.
[242] Share with you.
[243] Lewd behavior.
[244] Lewd.
[245] Ordered.
[246] Not informed me.

Vindice

    True, but the violence of my joy forgot it.

Hippolito

    Ay, but where's that lady now?

Vindice   O, at that word

    I'm lost again. You cannot find me yet.

    I'm in a throng of happy apprehensions.[247]   30

    He's suited for a lady, I have took care

    For a delicious lip, a sparkling eye—

    You shall be witness, brother.

    Be ready, stand with your hat off.   *Exit*

Hippolito

    Troth, I wonder what lady it should be?   35

    Yet, 'tis no wonder, now I think again,

    To have a lady stoop to a Duke, that stoops unto his men.

    'Tis common to be common through the world,

    And there's more private common shadowing vices

    Than those who are known both by their names and prices.

    'Tis part of my allegiance to stand bare   41

    To the Duke's concubine. And here she comes!

Re-enter Vindice with the skull of his beloved dressed up in tires [248]

Vindice

    Madam, his grace will not be absent long.

    Secret? Ne'er doubt us, madam. 'Twill be worth

    Three velvet gowns to your ladyship. Known?   45

    Few ladies respect that disgrace, a poor thin shell!

    'Tis the best grace you have to do it well.

    I'll save your hand that labour, I'll unmask you.

[247] Thoughts.
[248] Headdresses.

Hippolito

 Why brother, brother!

Vindice

 Art thou beguiled[249] now? Tut, a lady can,   50

 At such all hid, beguile a wiser man.

 Have I not fitted the old surfeiter

 With a quaint piece[250] of beauty? Age and bare bone

 Are e'er allied in action. Here's an eye

 Able to tempt a great man—to serve God!   55

 A pretty hanging lip, that has forgot now to dissemble;

 Methinks this mouth should make a swearer tremble,

 A drunkard clasp his teeth and not undo'em

 To suffer wet damnation to run through'em.

 Here's a cheek keeps her colour, let the wind go whistle! 60

 Spout rain, we fear thee not, be hot or cold,

 All's one with us. And is not he absurd,

 Whose fortunes are upon their faces set[251]

 That fear no other god but wind and wet?

Hippolito

 Brother, you've spoke that right.   65

 Is this the form that, living, shone so bright?

Vindice

 The very same.

 And now, methinks, I could e'en chide myself

 For doting on her beauty, though her death

 Shall be revenged after no common action.   70

 Does the silkworm expend her yellow labours

 For thee? For thee does she undo[252] herself?

---

[249] Double meaning: cheated and diverted.

[250] Cleverly made; both "quaint" and "piece" carry sexual innuendo.

[251] Staked.

[252] Use (up).

Are lordships[253] sold to maintain ladyships[254]
For the poor benefit of a bewitching minute?
Why does yon fellow falsify highways,[255]   75
And put his life between the judge's lips,
To refine such a thing?[256] Keeps horse and men
To beat[257] their valours for her?
Surely we're all mad people, and they
Whom we think are, are not, we mistake those.   80
'Tis we are mad in sense, they but in clothes.[258]

Hippolito

Faith, and in clothes too we, give us our due.

Vindice

Does every proud and self-affecting dame
Camphire[259] her face for this, and grieve her Maker
In sinful baths of milk, when many an infant starves,   85
For her superfluous[260] outside? All for this?
Who now bids twenty pounds a night, prepares
Music, perfumes, and sweetmeats? All are hushed.
Thou may'st lie chaste now! It were fine, methinks,
To have thee seen at revels, forgetful feasts,   90
And unclean brothels. Sure, 'twould fright the sinner
And make him a good coward, put a reveler
Out of his antic amble,
And cloy an epicure[261] with empty dishes.

[253] Both the dignity of the lord and his lands.

[254] Ironic; these "ladyships" are whores.

[255] Be the highwayman.

[256] A mistress.

[257] Bring down, degrade.

[258] Madmen only look mad, but real folly is love of a mistress and the spending that entails.

[259] Improve the complexion with camphor washes.

[260] Unnecessary (for salvation).

[261] One sensually inclined; gourmand.

Here might a scornful and ambitious woman   95
Look through and through herself! See, ladies, with false forms
You deceive men, but cannot deceive worms.
Now to my tragic business. Look you, brother,
I have not fashioned this only for show
And useless property,[262] no, it shall bear a part   100
E'en in its own revenge. This very skull,
Whose mistress the Duke poisoned, with this drug,
The mortal curse of the earth, shall be revenged
In the like strain, and kiss his lips to death.
As much as the dumb thing can, he shall feel.   105
What fails in poison, we'll supply in steel.

Hippolito

Brother, I do applaud thy constant vengeance,
The quaintness[263] of thy malice, above thought.

> *Vindice poisons the mouth of the skull*

Vindice

So, 'tis laid on! Now come and welcome, Duke,
I have her for thee. I protest it, brother,   110
Methinks she makes almost as fair a fine[264]
As some old gentlewoman in a periwig.
Hide thy face now for shame! Thou hadst need have a mask now.
'Tis vain when beauty flows, but when it fleets,
This would become graves better than the streets.   115

Hippolito

You have my voice in that. Hark, the Duke's come!

Vindice

Peace, let's observe what company he brings,
And how he doth absent'em,[265] for you know

---

[262] A (theater) prop.
[263] Intricacy.
[264] Fine lady.
[265] Send them away.

He'll wish all private. Brother, fall you back a little
With the bony lady.

Hippolito   That I will.   *He retires*

Vindice   So, so.   120

Now nine years' vengeance crowd into a minute!

Enter the Duke and Gentlemen

Duke

You shall have leave to leave us, with this charge,
Upon your lives, if we be missed by the Duchess
Or any of the nobles, to give out
We're privately rid forth.[266]

Vindice (*aside*)   O happiness!   125

Duke

With some few honourable gentlemen, you may say.
You may name those that are away from court.

First Gentleman

Your will and pleasure shall be done, my lord.

Exeunt Gentlemen

Vindice (*aside*)

"Privately rid forth!"   129

He strives to make sure work on't. (*Advances*) Your good grace!

Duke

Piato, well done, hast brought her! What lady is't?

Vindice

Faith, my lord, a country lady, a little bashful at first, as
most of them are, but after the first kiss, my lord, the
worst is past with them. Your grace knows what you have
to do. She has somewhat of a grave look with her, but— 135

Duke

I love that best. Conduct her.

---

[266] Double meaning: ridden out; violently removed.

Vindice (*aside*)   Have at[267] all.

Duke

    In gravest looks the greatest faults seem less.

    Give me that sin that's robed in holiness.

Vindice (*to Hippolito*)

    Back with the torch, brother, raise the perfumes!

Duke

    How sweet can a Duke breathe! Age has no fault,   140

    Pleasure should meet in a perfumed mist.

    Lady, sweetly encountered. I came from court,

    I must be bold with you. (*Kisses her skull*) O! What's this! O!

Vindice

    Royal villain! White devil![268]

Duke   O !

Vindice   Brother,

    Place the torch here, that his affrighted eyeballs   145

    May start into those hollows. Duke, dost know

    Yon dreadful vizard? View it well! 'Tis the skull

    Of Gloriana, whom thou poisoned'st last.

Duke

    O! 'T has poisoned me.

Vindice

    Didst not know that till now?

Duke   What are you two?   150

Vindice

    Villains all three! The very ragged bone

    Has been sufficiently revenged.

Duke

    O, Hippolito, call treason!

Hippolito

    Yes, my good lord! Treason, treason, treason!

---

[267] Attack.

[268] The white devil is worse than the black because it looks innocent; also refers to the Duke's white hair.

Stamping on him

Duke

    Then I'm betrayed.   155

Vindice

    Alas, poor lecher, in the hands of knaves

    The slavish Duke is baser than his slaves.

Duke

    My teeth are eaten out.

Vindice   Hadst any left?

Hippolito

    I think but few

Vindice

    Then those that did eat are eaten.

Duke   O, my tongue!   160

Vindice

    Your tongue? 'Twill teach you to kiss closer,

    Not like a slobbering Dutchman. You have eyes still.

    Look monster, what a lady hast thou made me

    My once-betrothed wife.   *Removes disguise*

Duke   Is it thou, villain?

    Nay then—

Vindice   'Tis I, 'tis Vindice, 'tis I!   165

Hippolito

    And let this comfort thee: Our lord and father

    Fell sick upon the infection of thy frowns,

    And died in sadness. Be that thy hope of life.

Duke

    O !

Vindice

    He had his tongue, yet grief made him die speechless.   170

    Pooh! 'Tis but early yet. Now I'll begin

    To stick thy soul with ulcers. I will make

    Thy spirit grievous sore. It shall not rest,

    But like some pestilent man toss in thy breast.

Mark me, Duke! 175

 Thou art a renowned, high, and mighty cuckold.

Duke

 O!

Vindice

 Thy bastard, thy bastard rides a-hunting in thy brow.

Duke

 Millions of deaths!

Vindice   Nay, to afflict thee more,

 Here in this lodge they meet for damned clips![269] 180

 Those eyes shall see the incest of their lips.

Duke

 Is there a hell besides this, villains?

Vindice   Villain?

 Nay, heaven is just, scorns[270] are the hires[271] of scorns.

 I ne'er knew yet adulterer without horns.

Hippolito

 Once ere they die 'tis quitted.

Vindice   Hark the music. 185

 Their banquet is prepared, they're coming—

Duke   O !

 Kill me not with that sight.

Vindice   Thou shalt not lose

 That sight for all thy dukedom.

Duke   Traitors! Murderers!

Vindice

 What! Is not thy tongue eaten out yet?

 Then we'll invent a silence. Brother, stifle the torch! 190

Duke

 Treason! Murder!

[269] Embraces.

[270] Contempts.

[271] Rewards.

Vindice

>Nay, faith, we'll have you hushed. Now, with thy dagger
>Nail down his tongue, and mine shall keep possession
>About his heart; if he but gasp, he dies.
>We dread not death to quittance[272] injuries. Brother,   195
>If he but wink, not brooking[273] the foul object,
>Let our two other hands tear up his lids
>And make his eyes like comets shine through blood.
>When the bad bleeds, then is the tragedy good.

Hippolito

>Whist, brother! Music's at our ear! They come!   200

Enter Spurio the Bastard meeting the Duchess

Spurio

>Had not that kiss a taste of sin, 'twere sweet.

Duchess

>Why, there's no pleasure sweet but it is sinful.

Spurio

>True! Such a bitter sweetness fate hath given,
>Best side to us is the worst side to Heaven.

Duchess

>Push,[274] come. 'Tis the old Duke, thy doubtful father,   205
>The thought of him rubs Heaven in thy way.
>But I protest, by yonder waxen fire,
>Forget him, or I'll poison him.

Spurio

>Madam, you urge a thought which ne'er had life.
>So deadly do I loathe him for my birth,   210

---

[272] Requite.
[273] Bearing to see.
[274] Exclamation like "Come on!"

That if he took me hasped[275] within his bed,
I would add murder to adultery,
And with my sword give up his years to death.
Duchess
Why, now thou'rt sociable! Let's in and feast.
Loud music sound! Pleasure is banquet's guest.   215
Exeunt Spurio and Duchess
Duke
I cannot brook—   *Dies*
Vindice   The brook is turned to blood.
Hippolito
Thanks to loud music.
Vindice   'Twas our friend indeed.
'Tis state in music for a duke to bleed.
The dukedom wants a head, though yet unknown,
As fast as they peep up, let's cut'em down.   *Exeunt* 220

Act III, Scene vi

Enter the Duchess' two sons, Ambitioso and Supervacuo

Ambitioso
Was not his execution rarely plotted?
We are the Duke's sons now.
Supervacuo
Ay, you may thank my policy[276] for that.
Ambitioso
Your policy for what?
Supervacuo
Why, was't not my invention, brother,   5

[275] Sexually engaged in incest.
[276] Subversive plans.

To slip the judges? And in lesser compass
Did not I draw the model of his death,
Advising you to sudden officers,
And e'en extemporal execution?

Ambitioso

Heart, 'twas a thing I thought on too.   10

Supervacuo

You thought on't too! 'Sfoot, slander not your thoughts
With glorious untruth. I know 'twas from you![277]

Ambitioso

Sir, I say, 'twas in my head!

Supervacuo   Ay, like your brains, then,
Ne'er to come out as long as you lived.

Ambitioso

You'd have the honour on't, forsooth, that your wit   15
Led him to the scaffold.

Supervacuo   Since it is my due,
I'll publish't, but I'll ha't in spite of you.

Ambitioso

Methinks y'are much too bold. You should a little
Remember us, brother, next to be honest Duke.

Supervacuo (*aside*)

Ay, it shall be as easy for you to be duke   20
As to be honest, and that's never, i'faith!

Ambitioso

Well, cold he is by this time, and because
We're both ambitious, be it our amity,
And let the glory be shared equally.

Supervacuo

I am content to that.   25

Ambitioso

This night our younger brother shall out of prison.

---

[277] "You couldn't have conceived of it."

    I have a trick.

Supervacuo   A trick. Prithee, what is't?

Ambitioso

    We'll get him out by a wile.

Supervacuo   Prithee, what wile?

Ambitioso

    No sir, you shall not know it till't be done,

    For then you swear 'twere yours.   30

Enter an Officer with a head

Supervacuo

    How now, what's he?

Ambitioso   One of the officers.

Supervacuo

    Desired news.

Ambitioso   How now, my friend?

Officer

    My lords, under your pardon, I am allotted

    To that desertless office to present you

    With the yet bleeding head.

Supervacuo *(aside)*   Ha, ha, excellent!   35

Ambitioso *(to Supervacuo)*

    All's sure our own, brother. Canst weep, think'st thou?

    'Twould grace our flattery much. Think of some dame,

    'Twill teach thee to dissemble.

Supervacuo *(to Ambitioso)*   I have thought.

    Now for yourself.

Ambitioso   Our sorrows are so fluent,

    Our eyes o'erflow our tongues. Words spoke in tears   40

    Are like the murmurs of the waters, the sound

    Is loudly heard, but cannot be distinguished.

Supervacuo

    How died he, pray?

Officer   O, full of rage and spleen.
Supervacuo
     He died most valiantly, then. We're glad to hear it.
Officer
     We could not woo him once to pray.   45
Ambitioso
     He showed himself a gentleman in that
     Give him his due.
Officer   But in the stead of prayer
     He drew forth oaths.
Supervacuo   Then did he pray, dear heart.
     Although you understood him not.
Officer   My lords,
     E'en at his last, with pardon be it spoke,   50
     He cursed you both.
Supervacuo   He cursed us? 'Las good soul.
Ambitioso
     It was not in our powers, but the Duke's pleasure.
     (*aside*) Finely dissembled o' both sides, sweet fate.
     O happy opportunity!

Enter Lussurioso

Lussurioso
     Now, my lords—
Both   O!
Lussurioso   Why do you shun me, brothers?
     You may come nearer now.   56
     The savour[278] of the prison has forsook me,
     I thank such kind lords as yourselves, I'm free.
Ambitioso
     Alive!

[278] 1) Sign of the experience; 2) smell.

Supervacuo   In health!

Ambitioso   Released!

    We were both e'en amazed with joy to see it.   60

Lussurioso

    I am much to thank you.

Supervacuo

    Faith, we spared no tongue unto my lord the Duke.

Ambitioso

    I know your delivery, brother,

    Had not been half so sudden but for us.

Supervacuo

    O, how we pleaded!

Lussurioso   Most deserving brothers   65

    In my best studies I will think of it.   *Exit Lussurioso*

Ambitioso

    O death and vengeance!

Supervacuo   Hell and torments!

Ambitioso

    Slave, cam'st thou to delude us?

Officer   Delude you, my lords?

Supervacuo

    Ay, villain! Where's this head now?

Officer   Why here, my lord.

    Just after his delivery you both came   70

    With warrant from the Duke to behead your brother,

Ambitioso

    Ay, our brother, the Duke's son.

Officer   The Duke's son,

    My lord, had his release before you came.

Ambitioso

    Whose head's that, then?

Officer   His whom you left command for,

    Your own brother's.

Ambitioso	Our brother's? O, furies![279]		75

Supervacuo

    Plagues!

Ambitioso   Confusions!

Supervacuo   Darkness!

Ambitioso   Devils!

Supervacuo

    Fell it out so accursedly?

Ambitioso   So damnedly?

Supervacuo

    Villain, I'll brain thee with it!

Officer   My good lord!

Supervacuo

    The devil overtake thee!   *Exit Officer*

Ambitioso   O, fatal!

Supervacuo

    O prodigious to our bloods.

Ambitioso	Did we dissemble?	80

Supervacuo

    Did we make our tears women for thee?

Ambitioso

    Laugh and rejoice for thee?

Supervacuo

    Bring warrant for thy death?

Ambitioso   Mock off thy head?

Supervacuo

    You had a trick, you had a wile, forsooth.

Ambitioso

    A murrain meet'em![280] There's none of these wiles that ever   85
    come to good. I see now, there's nothing sure in mortality,
    but mortality.

---

[279] The furies are avenging spirits.
[280] May the plague get them!

Well, no more words. Shalt be revenged, i'faith.
Come, throw off clouds now, brother, think of vengeance
And deeper-settled hate. Sirrah, sit fast!   90
We'll pull down all, but thou shalt down at last.   *Exeunt*

Act IV, Scene i

Enter Lussurioso with Hippolito

Lussurioso
    Hippolito!
Hippolito   My lord? Has your good lordship
    Aught to command me in?
Lussurioso   I prithee, leave us.
Hippolito
    How's this? Come and leave us?
Lussurioso   Hippolito.
Hippolito
    Your honour.
    I stand ready for any duteous employment.   5
Lussurioso
    Heart, what mak'st thou here?
Hippolito *(aside)*   A pretty lordly humour!
    He bids me to be present to depart. Something
    Has stung his honour.
Lussurioso   Be nearer, draw nearer.
    You're not so good, methinks, I'm angry with you.
Hippolito
    With me, my lord? I'm angry with myself for't.   10
Lussurioso
    You did prefer a goodly fellow to me.
    'Twas wittily elected, 'twas. I thought
    He had been a villain, and he proves a knave,
    To me a knave.
Hippolito   I chose him for the best, my lord.
    'Tis much my sorrow, if neglect in him   15
    Breed discontent in you.

Lussurioso

    Neglect! 'Twas will![281] Judge of it.

    Firmly to tell of an incredible act,

    Not to be thought, less to be spoken of,

    'Twixt my stepmother and the bastard, O,   20

    Incestuous sweets between'em.

Hippolito   Fie, my lord!

Lussurioso

    I in kind loyalty to my father's forehead

    Made this a desperate arm, and in that fury

    Committed treason on the lawful bed,

    And with my sword e'en raced[282] my father's bosom   25

    For which I was within a stroke of death.

Hippolito

    Alack, I'm sorry!   *Enter Vindice*

            (*Aside*) 'Sfoot, just upon the stroke

    Jars in my brother. 'Twill be villainous music.

Vindice

    My honoured lord.

Lussurioso   Away!

    Prithee, forsake us, hereafter we'll not know thee.   30

Vindice

    Not know me, my lord? Your lordship cannot choose.

Lussurioso

    Begone, I say! Thou art a false knave.

Vindice

    Why, the easier to be known, my lord.

Lussurioso

    Push, I shall prove too bitter with a word,

    Make thee a perpetual prisoner,   35

[281] Done willfully, an intended act.

[282] Wounded superficially.

And lay this iron-age[283] upon thee.

Vindice (*aside*)   Mum,

> For there's a doom would make a woman dumb.
> Missing the bastard, next him, the wind's come about.
> Now 'tis my brother's turn to stay, mine to go out.

Exit Vindice

Lussurioso

> He has greatly moved me.

Hippolito   Much to blame, i'faith.   40

Lussurioso

> But I'll recover, to his ruin. 'Twas told me lately, I know
> not whether falsely, that you'd a brother.

Hippolito

> Who, I? Yes, my good lord, I have a brother.

Lussurioso

> How chance the court ne'er saw him? Of what nature?
> How does he apply his hours?

Hippolito   Faith, to curse fates,   45

> Who, as he thinks, ordained him to be poor,
> Keeps at home, full of want and discontent.

Lussurioso (*aside*)

> There's hope in him, for discontent and want
> Is the best clay to mold a villain of.—
> Hippolito, wish him repair to us.   50
> If there be aught in him to please our blood,
> For thy sake we'll advance him, and build fair
> His meanest fortunes, for it is in us
> To rear up towers from cottages.

Hippolito

> It is so my lord. He will attend your honour.   55
> But he's a man in whom much melancholy dwells.

---

[283] Here: collection of iron, probably both his sword and manacles and chains are included. Also, see glossary.

Lussurioso

    Why, the better! Bring him to court.

Hippolito

    With willingness and speed. —

    (*aside*) Whom he cast off e'en now, must now succeed.

    Brother, disguise must off,   60

    In thine own shape now I'll prefer thee to him.

    How strangely does himself work to undo him.   *Exit*

Lussurioso

    This fellow will come fitly, he shall kill

    That other slave, that did abuse my spleen

    And made it swell to treason. I have put   65

    Much of my heart into him; he must die.

    He that knows great men's secrets, and proves slight,

    That man ne'er lives to see his beard turn white.

    Ay, he shall speed him. I'll employ thee, brother,

    Slaves are but nails to drive out one another.   70

    He being of black condition,[284] suitable

    To want and ill content, hope of preferment

    Will grind him to an edge.

The Nobles enter

First Noble

    Good days unto your honour.

Lussurioso

    My kind lords, I do return the like.   75

Second Noble

    Saw you my lord the Duke?

Lussurioso   My lord and father—

    Is he from court?

---

[284] Melancholy; see glossary under "Four humors" and "Four temperaments."

First Noble   He's sure from court,
    But where, which way his pleasure took, we know not,
    Nor can we hear on't.

The Duke's Gentlemen enter

Lussurioso   Here comes those should tell.
    Saw you my lord and father?   80
First Gentleman
    Not since two hours before noon, my lord.
    And then he privately rid forth.
Lussurioso
    O, he's rode forth.
First Noble   'Twas wondrous privately.
Second Noble
    There's none i'th'court had any knowledge on't.
Lussurioso
    His grace is old and sudden. 'Tis no treason   85
    To say the Duke my father has a humour[285]
    Or such a toy[286] about him. What in us
    Would appear light,[287] in him seems virtuous.
First Gentleman
    'Tis oracle, my lord.   *Exeunt*

---

[285] Acts on a whim.
[286] Fancy.
[287] Frivolous.

Act IV, Scene ii

Enter Vindice, out of his disguise, and Hippolito

Hippolito

So, so, all's as it should be, y'are yourself.

Vindice

How that great villain puts me to my shifts.[288]

Hippolito

He that did lately in disguise reject thee

Shall, now thou art thyself, as much respect thee.

Vindice

'Twill be the quainter[289] fallacy. But brother,   5

'Sfoot, what use will he put me to now, think'st thou?

Hippolito

Nay, you must pardon me in that, I know not.

He has some employment for you, but what 'tis

He and his secretary, the Devil, knows best.

Vindice

Well, I must suit my tongue to his desires,   10

What colour soe'er they be, hoping at last

To pile up all my wishes on his breast.[290]

Hippolito

Faith, brother, he himself shows the way.

Vindice

Now the Duke is dead, the realm is clad in clay.[291]

His death being not yet known, under his name   15

The people still are governed. Well, thou his son

---

[288] Changes of clothing and stratagems both.

[289] More intricate.

[290] Pressing with weights is a form of torture; see glossary.

[291] The use of the term "clay" for the transitory nature of human flesh suggests that the dukedom is now in dire straits.

Art not long-lived, thou shalt not joy his death.
To kill thee, then, I should most honour thee,
For 'twould stand firm in every man's belief,
Thou'st a kind child, and only died'st with grief.   20

Hippolito

You fetch about[292] well, but let's talk in present.
How will you appear in fashion different,
As well as in apparel, to make all things possible?
If you be but once tripped, we fall forever.
It is not the least policy to be doubtful.[293]   25
You must change tongue,[294] familiar[295] was your first.

Vindice

Why, I'll bear me in some strain[296] of melancholy,
And string myself with heavy-sounding wire,
Like such an instrument that speaks merry things sadly.

Hippolito

Then 'tis as I meant.   30
I gave you out at first in discontent.

Vindice

I'll turn[297] myself, and then—

Enter Lussurioso

Hippolito   'Sfoot, here he comes.
Hast thought upon't?

Vindice   Salute him, fear not me.[298]

---

[292] Make turns; change course.

[293] It is clever to be cautious.

[294] Alter your speech.

[295] "Known"; but also suggesting intimacy, chumminess.

[296] Tune.

[297] "Turning" an instrument = tuning it.

[298] Don't worry about me.

Lussurioso

    Hippolito!

Hippolito   Your lordship.

Lussurioso   What's he yonder?

Hippolito

    'Tis Vindice, my discontented brother,   35

    Whom, 'cording to your will, I've brought to court.

Lussurioso

    Is that thy brother? Beshrew me, a good presence.

    I wonder he has been from the court so long.

    Come nearer.

Hippolito

    Brother, Lord Lussurioso, the Duke's son.   40

Lussurioso

    Be more near to us, welcome. Nearer yet.

Vindice snatches off his hat and makes a leg[299] to him

Vindice

    How don you?[300] God you good den.[301]

Lussurioso   We thank thee.

    How strangely such a coarse homely salute

    Shows in the palace, where we greet in fire,

    Nimble and desperate tongues. Should we name   45

    God in a salutation, 'twould ne'er be stood on. Heaven!

    Tell me, what has made thee so melancholy?

Vindice

    Why, going to law.

Lussurioso

    Why, will that make a man melancholy?

---

[299] Bows.

[300] How do you do?

[301] God give you a good evening.

Vindice

>Yes, to look long upon ink and black buckram.[302] I went me   50
>to law in *anno quadragesimo secundo,*[303] and I waded out of
>it in *anno sextagesimo tertio.*[304]

Lussurioso

>What, three and twenty years in law?

Vindice

>I have known those that have been five and fifty, and all
>about pullen[305] and pigs.   55

Lussurioso

>May it be possible such men should breathe,
>To vex the terms[306] so much?

Vindice   'Tis food to some, my lord.

>There are old men at the present that are so poisoned
>with the affectation of law-words (having had many suits
>canvassed), that their common talk is nothing but Barbary   60
>Latin. They cannot so much as pray but in law, that their
>sins may be removed with a writ of error,[307] and their
>souls fetched up to heaven with sasarara.[308]

Lussurioso

>It seems most strange to me.
>Yet all the world meets round in the same bent,   65
>Where the heart's set, there goes the tongue's consent.
>How dost apply thy studies, fellow?

Vindice

>Study? Why to think how a great rich man lies a-dying,

---

[302] The black material an attorney's bag was made from.

[303] The 42nd year of the reign.

[304] The 63rd year.

[305] Chicks, young animals.

[306] The times when court is in session.

[307] Writ to reverse a judgment when an error has been found.

[308] A corruption of *certiorari*, a writ obtainable from a superior court, if an inferior court, according to the defendant, has not dealt justly with him.

and a poor cobbler tolls the bell for him. How he cannot
depart the world and see the great chest stand before 70
him. When he lies speechless, how he will point you readily
to all the boxes. And when he is past all memory, as the
gossips guess, then thinks he of forfeitures[309] and obligations.[310] Nay, when to all men's hearings he whurls and
rottles[311] in the throat, he's busy threatening his poor ten- 75
ants. And this would last me now some seven years' thinking or thereabouts. But, I have a conceit a-coming in picture[312] upon this. I draw it myself, which i'faith, la, I'll present
to your honour. You shall not choose but like it, for your
lordship shall give me nothing for it. 80

Lussurioso

Nay, you mistake me then,

For I am published[313] bountiful enough.

Let's taste of your conceit.

Vindice

In picture, my lord?

Lussurioso   Ay, in picture.

Vindice

Marry, this it is: "A usuring father, to be boiling in hell, and 85
his son and heir with a whore dancing over him."

Hippolito (*aside*)

He has pared him to the quick.

Lussurioso

The conceit's pretty, i'faith

But take't upon my life, 'twill ne'er be liked.

---

[309] Becoming liable to lose life, goods, position, or the like in consequence
of a crime.

[310] Being legally bound by agreement to pay a certain sum or render a certain
service.

[311] Words chosen to mimic deathrattles.

[312] I am composing a wittily artful illustration.

[313] Known publicly.

Vindice

No? Why I'm sure the whore will be liked well enough.   90

Hippolito (*aside*)

Ay, if she were out o'the picture, he'd like her then himself.

Vindice

And as for the son and heir, he shall be an eyesore to no
young revelers, for he shall be drawn in cloth of gold
breeches.

Lussurioso

And thou hast put my meaning in the pockets,   95
And canst not draw that out? My thought was this:
To see the picture of a usuring father
Boiling in hell, our rich men would ne'er like it.

Vindice

O, true, I cry you heartily mercy.[314] I know the reason, for
some of 'em had rather be damned indeed than damned 100
in colours.[315]

Lussurioso (*aside*)

A parlous[316] melancholy! He has wit enough
To murder any man, and I'll give him means.—
I think thou art ill-monied?

Vindice   Money! Ho, ho!
'Tas been my want so long, 'tis now my scoff,[317]   105
I've e'en forgot what colour silver's of.

Lussurioso (*aside*)

It hits as I could wish.

Vindice   I get good clothes
Of those that dread my humour, and for table-room
I feed on those that cannot be rid of me.   109

---

[314] I beg your pardon.
[315] In a picture.
[316] Dangerous.
[317] Scorn.

Lussurioso

    Somewhat to set thee up withal.   *He gives him gold*

Vindice

    O, mine eyes!

Lussurioso   How now, man?

Vindice   Almost struck blind!

    This bright unusual shine to me seems proud,

    I dare not look till the sun be in a cloud.

Lussurioso (*aside*)

    I think I shall affect[318] his melancholy.—

    How are they now?

Vindice   The better for your asking.

Lussurioso

    You shall be better yet if you but fasten   115

    Truly on my intent. Now y'are both present,

    I will unbrace[319] such a close private villain

    Unto your vengeful swords, the like ne'er heard of,

    Who hath disgraced you much and injured us.

Hippolito

    Disgraced us, my lord?

Lussurioso   Ay, Hippolito.   120

    I kept it here[320] till now, that both your angers

    Might meet him at once.

Vindice   I'm covetous

    To know the villain.

Lussurioso (*to Hippolito*)   You know him, the slave pander

    Piato, whom we threatened last

    With irons in perpetual 'prisonment.   125

Vindice (*aside*)

    All this is I!

---

[318] Like.

[319] Literally: unclothe; here also disclose.

[320] Probably "in my breast," " my heart."

Hippolito   Is't he, my lord?

Lussurioso   I'll tell you,
    You first preferred him to me.

Vindice   Did you, brother?

Hippolito
    I did indeed.

Lussurioso   And the ungrateful villain,
    To quit that kindness, strongly wrought with me,
    Being as you see a likely man for pleasure,   130
    With jewels to corrupt your virgin sister.

Hippolito
    O villain!

Vindice   He shall surely die that did it.

Lussurioso
    I, far from thinking any virgin harm,
    Especially knowing her to be as chaste
    As that part which scarce suffers to be touched,   135
    The eye, would not endure him.

Vindice   Would you not, my lord?
    'Twas wondrous honorably done.

Lussurioso
    But with some fine frowns kept him out.

Vindice
    Out, slave!

Lussurioso
    What did me he but, in revenge of that,   140
    Went of his own free will to make infirm
    Your sister's honour, whom I honour with my soul
    For chaste respect; and not prevailing there,
    As 'twas but desperate folly to attempt it,
    In mere spleen,[321] by the way, waylays your mother,   145
    Whose honour being a coward as it seems,

---

[321] (Here) impulse.

    Yielded by little force.

Vindice   Coward indeed.

Lussurioso

    He, proud of their[322] advantage, as he thought,

    Brought me these news for happy, but I, heaven

    Forgive me for it—

Vindice   What did your honour?   150

Lussurioso

    —In rage pushed him from me,

    Trampled beneath his throat, spurned him, and bruised!

    Indeed I was too cruel, to say troth.

Hippolito

    Most nobly managed!

Vindice (*aside*)

    Has not heaven an ear? Is all the lightning wasted?   155

Lussurioso

    If I now were so impatient in a modest cause,

    What should you be?

Vindice   Full mad! He shall not live

    To see the moon change.

Lussurioso   He's about the palace.

    Hippolito, entice him this way, that thy brother

    May take full mark of him.   160

Hippolito

    Heart! That shall not need, my lord!

    I can direct him so far.

Lussurioso   Yet for my hate's sake,

    Go, wind[323] him this way, I'll see him bleed myself.

Hippolito (*to Vindice*)

    What now, brother?

---

[322] Probably "the news" is referred to by "their."

[323] Drive.

Vindice (*to Hippolito*)

    Nay, e'en what you will. Y'are put to it, brother.   165

Hippolito (*aside*)

    An impossible task, I'll swear,

    To bring him hither that's already here.   *Exit Hippolito*

Lussurioso

    Thy name? I have forgot it.

Vindice   Vindice, my lord.

Lussurioso

    'Tis a good name, that.

Vindice   Ay, a revenger.

Lussurioso

    It doth betoken courage. Thou shouldst be valiant   170

    And kill thine enemies.

Vindice   That's my hope, my lord.

Lussurioso

    This slave is one.

Vindice   I'll doom him.

Lussurioso   Then I'll praise thee.

    Do thou observe[324] me best, and I'll best raise thee.

Enter Hippolito

Vindice

    Indeed, I thank you.

Lussurioso

    Now, Hippolito, where's the slave pander?   175

Hippolito

    Your good lordship would have

    A loathsome sight of him, much offensive,

    He's not in case[325] now to be seen, my lord.

[324] Please and obey.
[325] In condition.

The worst of all the deadly sins is in him,

That beggarly damnation, drunkenness.   180

Lussurioso

Then he's a double slave.

Vindice (*aside*)   'Twas well conveyed[326]

Upon a sudden wit.

Lussurioso   What, are you both

Firmly resolved? I'll see him dead myself.

Vindice

Or else, let not us live.

Lussurioso   You may direct

Your brother to take note of him.

Hippolito   I shall.   185

Lussurioso

Rise but in this, and you shall never fall.

Vindice

Your honour's vassals.

Lussurioso(*aside*)   This was wisely carried.

Deep policy in us makes fools of such,

Then must a slave die when he knows too much.

Exit Lussurioso

Vindice

O, thou almighty patience! 'Tis my wonder   190

That such a fellow, impudent and wicked,

Should not be cloven as he stood,

Or with a secret wind burst open!

Is there no thunder left, or is't kept up

In stock for heavier vengeance? (*Thunder*) There it goes! 195

Hippolito

Brother, we lose ourselves.

Vindice   But I have found it.

'Twill hold, 'tis sure. Thanks, thanks to any spirit

That mingled it 'mongst my inventions.

[326] Managed.

Hippolito
    What is't?
Vindice   'Tis sound and good. Thou shalt partake it.
    I'm hired to kill myself.
Hippolito   True.
Vindice   Prithee, mark it.   200
    And the old Duke being dead, but not conveyed[327]
    For he's already missed too, and you know
    Murder will peep out of the closest husk[328]—
Hippolito
    Most true!
Vindice   What say you then to this device?
    If we dressed up the body of the Duke—   205
Hippolito
    In that disguise of yours.
Vindice   Y'are quick, y'have reached it.
Hippolito
    I like it wondrously.
Vindice
    And bring in drink, as you have published him,
    To lean him on his elbow, as if sleep had caught him,
    Which claims most interest in such sluggy men.   210
Hippolito
    Good yet, but here's a doubt:
    We, thought by th'Duke's son to kill that pander,
    Shall, when he is known, be thought to kill the Duke.
Vindice
    Neither, O thanks! It is substantial.[329]
    For that disguise being on him which I wore, it will be 215
    thought I, which he calls the pander, did kill the Duke and

---

[327] Removed.
[328] The outer skin or shell of an animal.
[329] "Of substance," thus it will hold up.

fled away in his apparel, leaving him so disguised to avoid
swift pursuit.

Hippolito

Firmer and firmer.

Vindice   Nay, doubt not 'tis in grain,[330]

I warrant it hold colour.

Hippolito   Let's about it.   220

Vindice

But by the way too, now I think on't brother,

Let's conjure that base devil out of our mother.   *Exeunt*

Act IV, Scene iii

*Enter the Duchess, arm in arm with Spurio the Bastard; He seemeth[331]
lasciviously to her. After them, enter Supervacuo, running with a rapier. His
brother Ambitioso stops him.*

Spurio

Madam, unlock yourself.[332] Should it be seen,

Your arm would be suspected

Duchess

Who is't that dare suspect or this or these?[333]

May not we deal our favours where we please?

Spurio

I'm confident you may.   *Exeunt Spurio and Duchess*

Ambitioso   'Sfoot, brother, hold!   5

[330] It is well dyed.

[331] Behaves.

[332] Remove yourself from me.

[333] Either this or these (said as she bestows affection, such as embraces and
kisses maybe, upon him).

Supervacuo

Would't let the bastard shame us?

Ambitioso   Hold, hold brother!

There's fitter time than now.

Supervacuo   Now, when I see it.

Ambitioso

'Tis too much seen already.

Supervacuo   Seen and known.

The nobler she's, the baser she is grown.

Ambitioso

If she were bent lasciviously, the fault   10

Of mighty women that sleep soft, O death!

Must she needs choose such an unequal sinner

To make all worse?

Supervacuo   A bastard, the Duke's bastard!

Shame heaped on shame.

Ambitioso   O our disgrace!

Most women have small waists the world throughout,   15

But their desires are thousand miles about.

Supervacuo

Come, stay not here. Let's after and prevent,

Or else they'll sin faster than we'll repent.   *Exeunt*

Act IV, Scene iv

Enter Vindice and Hippolito bringing out Gratiana, their mother, by the shoulders with daggers in their hands

Vindice

O thou, for whom no name is bad enough!

Gratiana

What means my sons? What, will you murder me?

Vindice
    Wicked, unnatural parent!

Hippolito   Fiend of women!

Gratiana
    O! Are sons turned monsters? Help!

Vindice   In vain.

Gratiana
    Are you so barbarous to set iron nipples   5
    Upon the breast that gave you suck?

Vindice   That breast
    Is turned to quarled[334] poison.

Gratiana
    Cut not your days for't! Am not I your mother?[335]

Vindice
    Thou dost usurp that title now by fraud,
    For in that shell of mother breeds a bawd.   10

Gratiana
    A bawd? O name far loathsomer than hell.

Hippolito
    It should be so, knew'st thou thy office well.

Gratiana
    I hate it.

Vindice
    Ah, is't possible, Thou only Powers on high,
    That women should dissemble when they die?   15

Gratiana
    Dissemble?

Vindice   Did not the Duke's son direct
    A fellow of the world's condition hither,
    That did corrupt all that was good in thee?

---

[334] Meaning uncertain; the sound of the word suggests "curdled."
[335] The allusion is both to the fourth and fifth commandments, and to Exodus 20:12.

Made thee uncivilly forget thyself
And work our sister to his lust?

Gratiana   Who, I?   20
That had been monstrous! I defy that man
For any such intent. None lives so pure,
But shall be soiled with slander
Good son, believe it not.

Vindice (*aside*)   O, I'm in doubt
Whether I'm myself or no—   25
Stay, let me look again upon this face.
Who shall be saved when mothers have no grace?

Hippolito
'Twould make one half despair.

Vindice   I was the man.
Defy me now, let's see. Do't modestly!

Gratiana
O hell unto my soul.   30

Vindice
In that disguise, I, sent from the Duke's son,
Tried you and found you base metal,[336]
As any villain might have done.

Gratiana   O no,
No tongue but yours could have bewitched me so.

Vindice
O, nimble in damnation, quick in tune.   35
There is no devil could strike fire so soon.
I am confuted in a word.

Gratiana
O sons, forgive me! To myself I'll prove more true.
You that should honour me, I kneel to you.

                          She kneels and weeps

---

[336] Metal not strong enough to withstand the test.

Vindice

    A mother to give aim[337] to her own daughter!   40

Hippolito

    True, brother. How far beyond nature 'tis,

    Though many mothers do't.

Vindice

    Nay, and you draw tears once, go you to bed,

    Wet will make iron blush and change to red.

    Brother, it rains, 'twill spoil your dagger. House it.   45

Hippolito

    'Tis done.

Vindice

    I'faith, 'tis a sweet shower, it does much good.

    The fruitful grounds and meadows of her soul

    Has been long dry. Pour down, thou blessed dew!

    Rise, mother. Troth, this shower has made you higher.   50

Gratiana

    O you heavens!

    Take this infectious spot out of my soul,

    I'll rinse it in seven waters of mine eyes!

    Make my tears salt enough to taste of grace.

    To weep is to our sex naturally given,   55

    But to weep truly, that's a gift from heaven.

Vindice

    Nay, I'll kiss you now. Kiss her, brother,

    Let's marry her to our souls, wherein's no lust,

    And honourably love her.

Hippolito   Let it be.

Vindice

    For honest women are so seld[338] and rare,   60

    'Tis good to cherish those poor few that are.

---

[337] Give direction to; incite (sexually).

[338] Unusual.

O you of easy wax,[339] do but imagine,
Now the disease has left you, how leprously
That office would have clinged unto your forehead.
All mothers that had any graceful hue[340]   65
Would have worn masks to hide their face at you.
It would have grown to this: at your foul name
Green-coloured[341] maids would have turned red with shame.

Hippolito

And then our sister, full of hire[342] and baseness.

Vindice

There had been boiling lead again.   70
The Duke's son's great concubine!
A drab[343] of state, a cloth o'silver slut,
To have her train borne up, and her soul trail i'the dirt.

Hippolito

Great, to be miserably great, rich, to be eternally wretched.

Vindice

O common madness.   75
Ask but the thrivingest harlot in cold blood,
She'd give the world to make her honour good.
Perhaps you'll say, but only to th'Duke's son,
In private. Why, she first begins with one,
Who afterwards to thousand proves a whore: 80
"Break ice in one place, it will crack in more."

Gratiana

Most certainly applied.

Hippolito

O brother, you forget our business.

---

[339] One who, like wax, takes impressions easily.
[340] Complexion.
[341] Immature, young; see also glossary under "green sickness."
[342] Hire as a prostitute.
[343] Whore.

Vindice

    And well remembered. Joy's a subtle elf.

    I think man's happiest when he forgets himself.   85

    Farewell, once dried, now holy-watered mead,[344]

    Our hearts wear feathers that before wore lead.

Gratiana

    I'll give you this, that one I never knew[345]

    Plead better for and 'gainst the devil than you.

Vindice

    You make me proud on't.   90

Hippolito

    Commend us in all virtue to our sister.

Vindice

    Ay, for the love of heaven, to that true maid.

Gratiana

    With my best words.

Vindice   Why, that was motherly said.

                          Exeunt Vindice and Hippolito

Gratiana

    I wonder now what fury did transport me?

    I feel good thoughts begin to settle in me.   95

    O, with what forehead can I look on her,

    Whose honour I've so impiously beset?

Enter Castiza

    And here she comes.

Castiza

    Now, mother, you have wrought with me so strongly,

    That what for my advancement, as to calm   100

    The trouble of your tongue, I am content.

[344] Meadow.

[345] "I never knew anyone who could . . ."

Gratiana

    Content to what?

Castiza   To do as you have wished me,

    To prostitute my breast to the Duke's son,

    And put myself to common[346] usury.

Gratiana

    I hope you will not so.

Castiza   Hope you I will not?   105

    That's not the hope you look to be saved in.

Gratiana

    Truth, but it is.

Castiza   Do not deceive yourself.

    I am, as you, e'en out of marble wrought.

    What would you now? Are ye not pleased yet with me?

    You shall not wish me to be more lascivious   110

    Than I intend to be.

Gratiana   Strike not me cold.

Castiza

    How often have you charged me on your blessing

    To be a cursed woman? When you knew

    Your blessing had no force to make me lewd,

    You laid your curse upon me; that did more.   115

    The mother's curse is heavy, where that fights

    Sons set in storm, and daughters lose their lights.

Gratiana

    Good child, dear maid, if there be any spark

    Of heavenly intellectual fire within thee,

    O let my breath revive it to a flame!   120

    Put not all out with woman's willful follies.

    I am recovered of that foul disease

    That haunts too many mothers. Kind,[347] forgive me,

---

[346] a) for use by all and sundry; b) she herself will become common, lower.
[347] "Kind one"; also child, a creature of one's own kind. Also, see glossary.

Make me not sick in health. If then
My words prevailed when they were wickedness,   125
How much more now when they are just and good?

Castiza

I wonder what you mean? Are you not she
For whose infect persuasions I could scarce
Kneel out my prayers, and had much ado
In three hours' reading to untwist so much   130
Of the black serpent as you wound about me?

Gratiana

'Tis unfruitful, held tedious, to repeat what's past.
I'm now your present mother.

Castiza   Push, now 'tis too late.

Gratiana

Bethink again, thou know'st not what thou say'st!

Castiza

No? "Deny advancement? Treasure the Duke's son!"   135

Gratiana

O see, I spoke those words, and now they poison me.
What will the deed do then?
Advancement? True. As high as shame can pitch.
For treasure? Whoe'er knew a harlot rich?
Or could build by the purchase of her sin   140
A hospital to keep their bastards in?
The Duke's son? O, when women are young
Courtiers, they are sure to be old beggars.
To know the miseries most harlots taste,
Thou'dst wish thyself unborn, when thou art unchaste.   145

Castiza

O mother, let me twine about your neck,
And kiss you till my soul melt on your lips.
I did but this to try you.

Gratiana   O, speak truth!

Castiza

    Indeed, I did not,[348] for no tongue has force

    To alter me from honest.   150

    If maidens would, men's words could have no power;

    A virgin honour is a crystal tower,

    Which, being weak, is guarded with good spirits.

    Until she basely yields, no ill inherits.

Gratiana

    O happy child! Faith and thy birth hath saved me.   155

    'Mongst thousand daughters, happiest of all others,

    Be thou a glass for maids, and I for mothers.   *Exeunt*

---

[348] I did not speak the truth.

Act V, Scene i

Enter Vindice and Hippolito with the Duke's corpse dressed in Vindice's disguise. They place him.

Vindice

So, so, he leans well. Take heed you wake him not, brother.

Hippolito

I warrant you, my life for yours.

Vindice

That's a good lay,[349] for I must kill myself.

Brother, that's I, that sits for me, do you mark it. And I
must stand ready here to make away my self yonder. I   5
must sit to be killed, and stand to kill myself. I could vary
it not so little as thrice over again. 'Tas some eight returns,[350] like Michaelmass[351] Term.

Hippolito

That's enow,[352] o'conscience.

Vindice

But, sirrah, does the Duke's son come single?   10

Hippolito

No, there's the hell on't. His faith's too feeble to go alone,
he brings flesh-flies after him that will buzz against
suppertime and hum for his coming out.

Vindice

Ah, the fly-flop[353] of vengeance beat'em to pieces! Here
was the sweetest occasion, the fittest hour, to have made   15

---

[349] Bet.

[350] A sheriff's report to the court on the status of its issued writs; legal
term.

[351] September 29, a quarterday in England.

[352] Enough.

[353] Fly swatter.

my revenge familiar with him. Show him the body of the
Duke his father, and how quaintly[354] he died like a politician, in hugger-mugger,[355] made no man acquainted with
it; and in catastrophe, slain him over his father's breast,
and . . . O, I'm mad to lose such a sweet opportunity.   20

Hippolito

Nay, push, prithee be content, There's no remedy present.
May not hereafter times open in as fair faces as this?

Vindice

They may, if they can paint so well.

Hippolito

Come now, to avoid all suspicion, let's forsake this room
and be going to meet the Duke's son.   25

Vindice

Content. I'm for any weather. Heart, step close, here he
comes.

Enter Lussurioso

Hippolito

My honoured lord.

Lussurioso   O me! You both present?

Vindice

E'en newly, my lord, just as your lordship entered now.
About this place we had notice given he should be, but in   30
some loathsome plight or other.

Hippolito

Came your honour private?

Lussurioso

Private enough for this. Only a few
Attend my coming out.

---

[354] Cunningly.
[355] In secret.

Vindice (*aside*)   Death rot those few!

Lussurioso

    Stay, yonder's the slave.   35

Vindice

    Mass, there's the slave indeed, my lord.—

    (*aside*) 'Tis a good child, he calls his father slave.

Lussurioso

    Ay, that's the villain, the damned villain. Softly,

    Tread easy.

Vindice   Pooh, I warrant you, my lord,

    We'll stifle in our breaths.

Lussurioso   That will do well   40

    Base rogue, thou sleepest thy last. (*aside*) 'Tis policy

    To have him killed in's sleep, for if he waked

    He would betray all to them.

Vindice   But, my lord—

Lussurioso

    Ha, what say'st?

Vindice   Shall we kill him now he's drunk?

Lussurioso

    Ay, best of all.

Vindice   Why, then he will ne'er live   45

    To be sober.

Lussurioso   No matter, let him reel to hell.

Vindice

    But being so full of liquor, I fear he will

    Put out all the fire—

Lussurioso   Thou art a mad beast.

Vindice (*aside*)

    And leave none to warm your lordship's golls[356] withal.

    (*Aloud*) For he that dies drunk, falls into hell-fire   50

    Like a bucket of water—qush, qush!

[356] Hands.

Lussurioso   Come,

    Be ready, nake[357] your swords, think of your wrongs,

    This slave has injured you.

Vindice   Troth, so he has—

    (*aside*) And he has paid well for't.

Lussurioso

    Meet with him now!

Vindice   You'll bear us out,[358] my lord?   55

Lussurioso

    Pooh, am I a lord for nothing, think you?

    Quickly, now.

Vindice   Sa, sa, sa, thump!   *Stabs the Duke's corpse*

                          There he lies.

Lussurioso

    Nimbly done!—Ha! O, villains, murderers,

    'Tis the old Duke, my father!

Vindice   That's a jest.

Lussurioso

    What! Stiff and cold already?   60

    O pardon me to call you from your names,[359]

    'Tis none of your deed. That villain Piato,

    Whom you thought now to kill, has murdered him

    And left him thus disguised.

Hippolito   And not unlikely.

Vindice

    O rascal! Was he not ashamed   65

    To put the Duke into a greasy doublet?

Lussurioso

    He has been cold and stiff, who knows how long?

Vindice (*aside*)

    Marry, that do I.

[357] Bare.

[358] Support our story.

[359] Accuse you by name-calling.

Lussurioso

 No words, I pray, of anything intended.

Vindice   O my lord

Hippolito

 I would fain have your lordship think that we have small   70

 reason to prate.

Lussurioso

 Faith, thou say'st true. I'll forthwith send to court,

 For all the nobles, bastard, Duchess, all,

 How here by miracle we found him dead,

 And in his raiment that foul villain fled.   75

Vindice

 That will be the best way, my lord, to clear us all. Let's cast

 about[360] to be clear.

Lussurioso

 Ho, Nencio, Sordido, and the rest!

Enter all his company

First Servant

 My lord.

Second Servant   My lord.

Lussurioso

 Be witnesses of a strange spectacle.   80

 Choosing for private conference that sad room,

 We found the Duke my father 'gealed[361] in blood.

First Servant

 My lord the Duke! Run, hie thee, Nencio,

 Startle the court by signifying so much!   *Exit Nencio*

Vindice (*aside*)

 Thus much by wit a deep revenger can,   85

---

[360] Make an effort.

[361] Congealed.

When murder's known, to be the clearest man.
We're farthest off, and with as bold an eye
Survey his body, as the standers-by.

Lussurioso

My royal father, too basely let blood
By a malevolent slave.

Hippolito (*to Vindice*)   Hark,   90
He calls thee slave again.

Vindice(*to Hippolito*)   He has lost. He may.

Lussurioso

O sight! Look hither, see, his lips are gnawn
With poison!

Vindice   How? His lips? By th'mass, they be.
O villain! O rogue! O slave! O rascal!

Hippolito (*aside*)

O good deceit! He quits him with like terms.   95

Ambitioso (*within*)

Where?

Supervacuo (*within*) Which way?

Enter Ambitioso and Supervacuo with Nobles and Gentlemen.

Ambitioso

Over what roof hangs this prodigious comet[362]
In deadly fire?

Lussurioso   Behold, behold my lords!
The Duke my father's murdered by a vassal that owes[363]
this habit, and here left disguised.   100

Enter Duchess and Spurio

---

[362] Comets were portends of coming evils, usually warnings to Kings and Princes.
[363] Owns.

Duchess

> My lord and husband!

Second Noble   Reverend majesty!

First Noble

> I have seen these clothes often attending on him.

Vindice (*aside*)

> That nobleman has been i'th'country, for he does not lie!

Supervacuo (*to Ambitioso*)

> Learn of our mother! Let's dissemble too.

> I'm glad he's vanished, so I hope are you.   105

Ambitioso (*to Supervacuo*)

> Ay, you may take my word for't.

Spurio   Old dad, dead?

> (*Aside*) I, one of his cast[364] sins, will send the Fates

> Most hearty commendations by his own son.

> I'll tug in the new stream[365] till strength be done.

Lussurioso

> Where be those two that did affirm to us   110

> My lord the Duke was privately rid forth?

First Gentleman

> O, pardon us, my lords, he gave that charge

> Upon our lives, if he were missed at court,

> To answer so. He rode not anywhere,

> We left him private with that fellow here.   115

Vindice (*aside*)

> Confirmed.

Lussurioso   O heavens, that false charge was his death.

> Impudent beggars! Durst you to our face

> Maintain such a false answer? Bear him straight

> To execution!

First Gentleman   My lord!

[364] Discarded.

[365] Hold my own in the new current.

Lussurioso   Urge me no more

   In this, th'excuse may be called half the murder.   120

Vindice (*aside*)

   You've sentenced well.

Lussurioso   Away, see it be done.

                              Exeunt Gentlemen and guard

Vindice (*aside*)

   Could you not stick?[366] See what confession doth?

   Who would not lie when men are hanged for truth?

Hippolito (*to Vindice*)

   Brother, how happy is our vengeance!

Vindice (*to Hippolito*)   Why, it hits

   Past the apprehension of indifferent wits.   125

Lussurioso

   My lord, let post horse be sent into all

   Places to entrap the villain.

Vindice (*aside*)   Post horse! Ha, ha!

First Noble

   My lord, we're something bold to know our duty.

   Your father's accidentally departed,

   The titles that were due to him meet you.   130

Lussurioso

   Meet me? I'm not at leisure, good my lord,

   I've many griefs to dispatch out o'th'way.—

   (*Aside*) Welcome, sweet titles.—Talk to me, my lords,

   Of sepulchers and mighty emperors' bones,

   That's thought for me.

Vindice (*aside*)   So one may see by this   135

   How foreign markets go.

   Courtiers have feet o'th'nines, and tongues o'th'twelves,[367]

   They flatter dukes, and dukes flatter themselves.

---

[366] Keep silent.

[367] Size nine feet and size twelve tongues.

Second Noble

 My lord, it is your shine must comfort us.

Lussurioso

 Alas, I shine in tears, like the sun in April.   140

First Noble

 You're now my lord's grace.

Lussurioso   My lord's grace!

 I perceive you'll have it so.

First Noble   'Tis but your own.

Lussurioso

 Then, heavens, give me grace to be so!

Vindice (*aside*)

 He prays well for himself.

Second Noble (*to Duchess*) Madam, all sorrows

 Must run their circles into joys. No doubt but time 145

 Will make the murderer bring forth himself.

Vindice (*aside*)

 He were an ass then, i'faith.

First Noble   In the mean season,

 Let us bethink the latest funeral honours

 Due to the Duke's cold body, and withal,

 Calling to memory our new happiness,   150

 Spread in his royal son.[368] Lords, gentlemen,

 Prepare for revels!

Vindice (*aside*)   Revels!

Second Noble   Time hath several falls.[369]

 Grief lifts up joys, feasts put down funerals.

Lussurioso

 Come then, my lords, my favours to you all.—

 (*Aside*) The Duchess is suspected foully bent. 155

 I'll begin dukedom with her banishment.

---

[368] Spread = grow; for son/sun pun, see glossary.
[369] Time clothes itself in various ways; fall = veil.

Exeunt Lussurioso, Nobles, and Duchess

Hippolito (*to Vindice*)

    Revels!

Vindice (*to Hippolito*) Ay, that's the word. We are firm yet.

    Strike one strain more,[370] and then we crown our wit.

Exeunt Vindice and Hippolito

Spurio (*aside*)

    Well, have at[371] the fairest mark!   160

    So said the Duke when he begot me,

    And if I miss his heart or thereabout,

    Then have at any! A bastard scorns to be out.[372]   *Exit Spurio*

Supervacuo

    Notest thou that Spurio, brother?

Ambitioso

    Yes, I note him to our shame.   165

Supervacuo

    He shall not live, his hair shall not grow much longer. In

    this time of revels tricks may be set afoot. Seest thou yon

    new moon? It shall outlive the new Duke by much. This

    hand shall disposses him, then we're mighty.

    A mask is treason's license, that built upon.   170

    'Tis murder's best face when a vizard's on.   *Exit Supervacuo*

Ambitioso

    Is't so? 'Tis very good.

    And do you think to be Duke than, kind brother?

    I'll see fair play: drop one, and there lies t'other.   *Exit*

---

[370] Play the next bit of music.

[371] Shoot for; target.

[372] To be out of the game; out of contention.

Act V, Scene ii

Enter Vindice and Hippolito with Piero and other Lords.

Vindice

    My lords, be all of music.

    Strike old griefs into other countries

    That flow in too much milk[373] and have faint livers,[374]

    Not daring to stab home their discontents.

    Let our hid flames break out as fire, as lightning,   5

    To blast this villainous dukedom vexed with sin.

    Wind up[375] your souls to their full heights again.

Piero

    How?

First Lord   Which way?

Second Lord   Any way. Our wrongs are such,

    We cannot justly be revenged too much.

Vindice

    You shall have all enough. Revels are toward,   10

    And those few nobles that have long suppressed you

    Are busied to the furnishing of a masque,[376]

    And do affect[377] to make a pleasant tale on't.

    The masquing suits are fashioning; now comes in

    That which must glad us all; we to take pattern   15

    Of all those suits, the colour, trimming, fashion,

    E'en to an undistinguished hair, almost.

    Then, entering first, observing the true form,

    Within a strain[378] or two we shall find leisure

---

[373] The milk of human kindness; gentleness.

[374] Violent passions are generated in the liver.

[375] Draw up.

[376] See glossary.

[377] Hope.

[378] Melody.

    To steal our swords out handsomely,   20
    And when they think their pleasure sweet and good,
    In midst of all their joys, they shall sigh blood.

Piero

    Weightily, effectually![379]

Third Lord

    Before the other masquers come—

Vindice

    We're gone, all done and past.   25

Piero

    But how for the Duke's guard?

Vindice   Let that alone.

    By one and one their strengths shall be drunk down.[380]

Hippolito

    There are five hundred gentlemen in the action,
    That will apply themselves and not stand idle.

Piero

    O, let us hug your bosoms!

Vindice   Come, my lords,   30
    Prepare for deeds! Let other times have words!   *Exeunt*

Act V, Scene iii

In a dumb show, the possessing[381] of the young Duke, with all his Nobles. Then sounding[382] music. A furnished table[383] is brought forth. Then enters the Duke Lussurioso and his Nobles to the banquet. A blazing star[384] appeareth

---

[379] Workable.

[380] "They will be weakened with drink, every one."

[381] The installation; coronation.

[382] Loud.

[383] A table with the banquet on it.

[384] A comet.

First Noble

    Many harmonious hours and choicest pleasures

    Fill up the royal numbers of your years.

Lussurioso

    My lords, we're pleased to thank you, though we know

    'Tis but your duty now to wish it so.

Second Noble

    That shine makes us all happy.

Third Noble (*aside*)   His grace frowns.   5

Second Noble (*aside*)

    Yet we must say he smiles.

First Noble (*aside*)   I think we must.

Lussurioso (*aside*)

    That foul-incontinent Duchess we have banished.

    The bastard shall not live. After these revels

    I'll begin strange ones. He and the stepsons

    Shall pay their lives for the first subsidies.[385]   10

    We must not frown so soon, else't had been now.

First Noble

    My gracious lord, please you prepare for pleasure.

    The masque is not far off.

Lussurioso   We are for pleasure—

(*To the star*) Beshrew thee! What art thou? Madest me start?

Thou hast committed treason! A blazing star!   15

First Noble

    A blazing star? O where, my lord?

Lussurioso   Spy out.

Second Noble

    See, see, my lords, a wondrous dreadful one!

Lussurioso

    I am not pleased at that ill-knotted fire,

---

[385] Subsidies are monies granted to the King or Queen of England in a time of special need, such as war.

That bushing,[386] flaring star. Am not I Duke?
It should not quake me now. Had it appeared   20
Before it,[387] I might then have justly feared.
But yet they say, whom art and learning weds,
When stars wear locks, they threaten great men's heads.
Is it so? You are read,[388] my lords.

First Noble   May it please your grace,
It shows great anger.

Lussurioso   That does not please our grace.   25

Second Noble
Yet here's the comfort, my lord: many times
When it seems most,[389] it threatens farthest off.

Lussurioso
Faith, and I think so too.

First Noble   Beside, my lord,
You're gracefully established with the loves
Of all your subjects, and for natural death,   30
I hope it will be threescore years a-coming.

Lussurioso
True, no more but threescore years?

First Noble
Fourscore, I hope, my lord.

Second Noble   And fivescore, I.

Third Noble
But 'tis my hope, my lord, you shall ne'er die.

Lussurioso
Give me thy hand. These others I rebuke.   35
He that hopes so is fittest for a Duke.

---

[386] The comet resembles a burning bush.
[387] I.e., before Lussurioso becoming Duke.
[388] Learned; well-read.
[389] When the comet seems to be closest.

Thou shalt sit next me. Take your places, lords,
We're ready now for sports, let'em set on!—
(*To star*) You thing! We shall forget you quite anon!
Third Noble
    I hear'em coming, my lord.

Enter the Masque of Revengers: the brothers Vindice and Hippolito and two
Lords more

Lussurioso   Ah, 'tis well.—   40
    (*Aside*) Brothers, and bastard, you dance next in hell.

The Revengers dance; at the end, they steal out their swords, and these four kill
the four at the table in their chairs. It thunders.

Vindice
    Mark, thunder!
    Dost know thy cue, thou big-voiced crier?
    Dukes' groans are thunder's watchwords.[390]
Hippolito
    So, my lords, you have enough.   45
Vindice
    Come, let's away, no lingering.
Hippolito   Follow! (*to the Lords*) Go!
                        Exeunt Revengers except Vindice
Vindice
    No power is angry when the lustful die.
    When thunder claps, heaven likes the tragedy.   *Exit Vindice*

Enter the other masque of intended murderers: Ambitioso and Supervacuo,
Spurio, and a Lord, coming in dancing. Lussurioso recovers a little in voice,

---

[390] Signals to attack.

groans, and calls, "A guard! Treason!" At which they all start out of their measure,[391] *and turning toward the table, they find them all to be murdered.*

Lussurioso
    O, O!
Spurio   Whose groan was that?
Lussurioso   Treason! A guard!
Ambitioso
    How now? All murdered?
Supervacuo   Murdered!   50
Lord with the Intended Murderers
    And those his nobles!
Ambitioso   Here's a labour saved.
    I thought to have sped him. 'Sblood, how came this?
Supervacuo
    Then I proclaim myself! Now I am Duke!
Ambitioso
    Thou Duke! Brother, thou!   *Kills Supervacuo*
Spurio   Slave, so dost thou.
                                            Kills Ambitioso
Lord with the Intended Murderers
    Base villain, hast thou slain my lord and master?   55
                                            Kills Spurio

Enter the first masquers, Vindice, Hippolito, and the two Lords

Vindice
    Pistols! Treason! Murder! Help! Guard my lord
    The Duke!

Enter Antonio and the Guard

[391] Dance.

Hippolito   Lay hold upon this traitor!

They seize the Lord with the Intended Murderers

Lussurioso

O!

Vindice

Alas, the Duke is murdered!

Hippolito   And the nobles.

Vindice

Surgeons! Surgeons! (*aside*) Heart! Does he breathe so long?

Antonio

A piteous tragedy! Able to wake   60

An old man's eye bloodshot.

Lussurioso   O !

Vindice   Look to my lord

The Duke! (*aside*) A vengeance throttle him.—

(*To the Lord with the Intended Murderers*)

Confess, thou murderous and unhallowed man,

Didst thou kill all these?

Lord with the Intended Murderers   None but the bastard, I.

Vindice

How came the Duke slain, then?

Lord with the Intended Murderers   We found him so.   65

Lussurioso

O villain.

Vindice   Hark.

Lussurioso   Those in the masque did murder us.

Vindice

Law you now,[392] sir!

O marble impudence! Will you confess now?

Lord with the Intended Murderers

'Slud, 'tis all false!

Antonio   Away with that foul monster,

---

[392] Expression to add emphasis; "You *see*!"

    Dipped in a prince's blood.

Lord with the Intended Murderers   Heart, 'tis a lie!   70
Antonio

    Let him have bitter execution.

                 Exit Lord with the Intended Murderers under guard

Vindice *(aside)*

    New marrow![393] No, I cannot be expressed.—

    How fares my lord, the Duke?

Lussurioso   Farewell to all.

    He that climbs highest has the greatest fall.

    My tongue is out of office.

Vindice   Air, gentlemen, air!—   75

                     The others give room

    (Whispers to Lussurioso)

    Now thou'lt not prate on't, 'twas Vindice murdered thee.—

Lussurioso

    O!

Vindice *(whispers)* Murdered thy father—

Lussurioso   O!

Vindice   And I am he!

    Tell nobody.—*(Lussurioso dies)* So, so, the Duke's departed.

Antonio

    It was a deadly hand that wounded him.

    The rest, ambitious who should rule and sway   80

    After his death, were so made all away.

Vindice

    My lord was unlikely.[394]

Hippolito *(to Antonio)*   Now the hope

    Of Italy lies in your reverend years.

Vindice

    Your hair will make the silver age again.

---

[393] Marrow was considered a delicacy.
[394] Not likely to be a good ruler.

When there was fewer but more honest men.   85
Antonio
    The burden's weighty and will press age down.
    May I so rule that heaven may keep the crown.
Vindice
    The rape of your good lady has been quitted.
    With death on death.
Antonio   Just is the law above.
    But of all things it puts me most to wonder   90
    How the old Duke came murdered.
Vindice   O, my lord.
Antonio
    It was the strangeliest carried. I've not heard
    Of the like.
Hippolito   'Twas all done for the best, my lord.
Vindice
    All for your grace's good.
    We may be bold to speak it now.   95
    'Twas somewhat wittily carried though we say it,
    'Twas we two murdered him.
Antonio   You two?
Vindice
    None else, i'faith, my lord, nay 'twas well managed.
Antonio
    Lay hands upon those villains!
Vindice   How? On us?
Antonio
    Bear'em to speedy execution.   100
Vindice
    Heart! Was't not for your good, my lord?
Antonio
    My good! Away with'em! Such an old man as he!
    You, that would murder him, would murder me!

Vindice

    Is't come about?

Hippolito   'Sfoot, brother, you begun.

Vindice

    May not we set[395] as well as the Duke's son?   105

    Thou hast no conscience.[396] Are we not revenged?

    Is there one enemy left alive amongst those?

    'Tis time to die when we're ourselves our foes.

    When murderers shut deeds close, this curse does seal'em:

    If none disclose'em, they themselves reveal'em!   110

    This murder might have slept in tongueless brass

    But for ourselves, and the world died an ass.

    Now I remember too, here was Piato

    Brought forth a knavish sentence once.

    No doubt, said he, but time   115

    Will make the murderer bring forth himself.

    'Tis well he died, he was a witch!

    And now, my lord, since we are in forever,

    This work was ours, which else might have been slipped.

    And if we list, we could have nobles[397] clipped[398]   120

    And go for less than beggars, but we hate

    To bleed so cowardly. We have enough,

    I'faith, we're well. Our mother turned,[399] our sister true,

    We die after a nest of Dukes. Adieu.

                   Exeunt Vindice and Hippolito under guard

---

[395] Die (as the sun sets).

[396] Concept of right and wrong.

[397] Nobleman; a coin worth 8 shillings, sixpence.

[398] Coins can be clipped to bits when the price is less than their whole value (cp. American usage of "bits"); clip, from OE, "to call; name."

[399] Converted.

Antonio

How subtly was that murder 'closed![400] Bear up   125
Those tragic bodies. 'Tis a heavy season.
Pray heaven their blood may wash away all treason.   *Exeunt*

[400] Disclosed.

THE MAID'S TRAGEDY

by

FRANCIS BEAUMONT & JOHN FLETCHER

Introductory Remarks

Francis Beaumont and John Fletcher

Beaumont and Fletcher's collaboration became legendary in their own time. We do not, unfortunately, have much knowledge, either of the details of their lives or about the collaboration itself; many years after the deaths of the playwrights, Aubrey wrote about them in his *Brief Lives*:

> They lived together on the Banke side[1], not far from the Play-house, both batchelors; lay together—from Sir John Hales, etc.; had one wench in the house between them, which they did so admire; the same cloathes and cloake, &c., betweene them.
>
> (I, 96)

This is probably a report of some of the gossip from which the Beaumont and Fletcher legend was created. Whatever their private relationship may have been, the fact remains that their plays were most popular, and that they, along with Shakespeare and Jonson, were the only playwrights to have Folio editions of their collected works published.

Francis Beaumont was born 1584 or 85, the third son of a Justice of Common Pleas, a judge. As a younger son, he could not expect any inheritance of substance, and apparently turned to writing as a means to earn a living. He entered Oxford University in 1597, but transferred to the Inner Temple in 1600, probably to study law, but maybe also because the law students were notoriously interested in the theater and frequently sponsored plays, of-

---

[1] I.e., in Southwark where many theaters were situated.

ten of a controversial nature.[2]

There are indications that Beaumont had a theatrical flop or two before he entered into the collaboration with Fletcher. Though both were gentlemen, and therefore part of the mainstream of tastes, inclinations, and preferences of the indoor theater's coterie audience—*The Maid's Tragedy* was written for the Blackfriars stage[3]—Beaumont apparently was of slightly higher social standing than Fletcher.

John Fletcher, too, was a younger son, born 1579 as one of nine children. He may be the "John Fletcher" who entered Cambridge University in 1591, but there is no record of his graduation. His father was a clergyman, who became Bishop of London in 1595, only to die the following year, in debt and in disfavor with Queen Elizabeth, which may explain the lack of records for his son. Like Beaumont, Fletcher may have taken up playwriting to make a living, and he, too, had a few unsuccessful plays performed before he joined with Beaumont. He, however, was a favorite of playwright Ben Jonson's, and when the Beaumont-Fletcher collaboration began, both dramatists moved in Jonson's circles; an indication of the closeness of their relationship are the introductory poems they wrote for each other's printed plays.

Between 1591 and 1607 or 08, the years that mark the beginning of the two playwrights' fruitful relationship, there is no record of Fletcher's life. He surfaces again with *Cupid's Revenge,* the first joint venture, written for a boys' company, but in 1609 Beaumont and Fletcher created *Philaster* for the King's Men, Shakespeare's company. With few exceptions, this was the company they continued writing for while the collaboration lasted.

In 1613, Beaumont married the heiress Ursula Isley and re-

---

[2] Shakespeare's *Troilus and Cressida* is thought to have been written with law students as its target audience.

[3] It should be noted that the act divisions in this play are original to the text, not imposed on it by a later editor.

tired almost completely from writing. He died in 1616, the same year as Shakespeare. Fletcher continued, however, collaborating with several people, one of them Shakespeare himself.[4] At the end of his career in 1625, when he died of the plague, he had his name associated with more than fifty plays.

It is uncertain which collaborator contributed exactly what to the joint effort; a close collaboration can produce completely "seamless" text. It seems, though, that Beaumont excelled at dramatic conception, at generating an idea for a plot, and Fletcher excelled at creating the dramatic effect that gives key scenes in for example *The Maid's Tragedy* such force. Finally Beaumont would revise, polish, and unify.

Beaumont and Fletcher, short though their collaboration was, created many immensely popular plays. *The Maid's Tragedy* was performed regularly into the 18th century and has enjoyed several modern revivals. As gentlemen, both playwrights were somewhat above their fellow playwrights' social station and attuned to the tastes of their audience; they were able to explore *risqué* topics that challenged the spectators, as well as cater to the changes of playgoing fashion. Tastes became increasingly more sophisticated with an interest in the decadent, and the coterie audience was intrigued mainly with watching people like themselves, other aristocrats. The King in *The Maid's Tragedy* is not the main protagonist as he would have been earlier in the period, but only the catalyst for the play's moral message; the truly interesting characters are the nobility.

Beaumont and Fletcher produced tragedy and comedy, but were also instrumental in creating the new hybrid genre of tragicomedy, an immensely popular, fashionable trend on the stage that remained in vogue till the closing of the theaters in 1642.

---

[4] *The Two Noble Kinsmen*, a tragicomedy, is the noteworthy result of this collaboration.

The Play

Setting and Characters

The Maid's Tragedy takes place on Rhodes, an island in the Aegean sea with a somewhat turbulent political history. It played a role as a supply port during the Crusades, and was occupied by the Saracens twice. Beginning 1309, The Knights of St. John of Jerusalem made Rhodes into "an almost impregnable fortress"[5] and equipped it with a fleet for protection against the Turks. In 1523, the island was yielded to the Turks, who were in power when *The Maid's Tragedy* was written. However, it is the status of Rhodes as an island fortress that makes it a wonderful choice of setting for a play that debates the rights of a ruler. The very location points at the similarities between the play's Rhodes and the audience's England.

James I had very firm ideas of the ruler's divine right to absolute power,[6] which made him responsible to God alone, not to his people. In *Basilikon Doron,* James I claims that the king as the maker of the law is also above the law, and that while a good king will abide by the laws he has set down, he is by no means obliged to do so. But

> . . . [o]pponents of royal absolutism also used divine law to deny the king's right to intervene in the government of the family, constructed as an autonomous little state. . .
>
> The more James asserted his unlimited and irrevocable authority, the more voluble became the voices for restricting and putting conditions on his rule. He

---

[5] *The New Encyclopædia Britannica* 15th ed., vol. 10, p. 25.
[6] See his *The True Law of Free Monarchies* (1603), which refutes ideas that the king should be elected by and responsible to the people, and *Basilikon Doron* (1599), written for his infant son as a handbook in the art of government.

had, in fact, created and empowered an opposing set
of rights based on authorities his assertion of divinity
had usurped.

(Allman, *Jacobean Revenge Tragedy
and the Politics of Virtue*,   40)

Tyranny and the fear of tyranny was a topic under debate at the
time, and *The Maid's Tragedy* is clearly part of this debate. It describes the chaos resulting from the monarch's taking his divine
right into the family, the building block at the core of society, and
willfully blurring the lines drawn between the public and the private sphere, domestic and political matters.

The King of Rhodes is clearly a tyrant, who flouts the sanctity
of marriage, disregards his subjects' well-being, and firmly believes
that what he wants he has every right to take and, once done with it,
every right to discard. He supercedes an existing marriage contract
in order to marry his mistress off to a loyal subject who will be
obedient to him, thus providing the King with physical access to
her for as long as he should want her, a convenient "cover" for
eventual children, and a home to discard her in after she is no longer
desirable to him. Any audience member would quail at the thought
of such infringements upon the family's autonomy. In revenge tragedy, we expect the character provoking the revenge to suffer a
punishment equal to the pain and suffering he has inflicted upon
others. Aptly enough, the King is bound and stabbed to death on
his bed of lechery. His brother, Lysippus, learns from his bad example and vows not to follow in his footsteps at play's end.

Amintor, the nobleman selected for a husband to the King's
mistress, is a young, upright, honorable man, able to inspire love
and friendship, but also somewhat naïve. Once his wife tells him
the King is her lover, and that she has no inclination to give up her
relationship or share a bed with her husband, his natural impulse
to revenge his honor evaporates; Amintor is emasculated by the
power with which the monarch is invested. Moreover, he is haunted

by guilt over discarding his first love at the King's mere bidding. Though not a revenger, his death is a natural consequence of his failure to act, to do what he knows is right and honorable. Like his discarded betrothed, Aspatia, he dies a virgin.

The King's mistress, Evadne, is an interesting Renaissance woman. She is headstrong and willful, determined to have her own way at any cost. The relationship with the King gives her a feeling of power no ordinary wife or woman has. She does not clearly see the precariousness of her situation, but she sees its possibilities:

> Evadne
>> I swore indeed that I would never love
>> A man of lower place, but if your fortune
>> Should throw you from this height, I bade you trust
>> I would forsake you and would bend to him
>> That won your throne. I love with my ambition,
>> Not with my eyes.
>
> (III.i.175-180)

Like Bel-imperia of *The Spanish Tragedy*, Evadne is a far cry from the chaste, silent, and obedient female ideal of her day. It takes her brother's forceful persuasion to convince her of her guilt, but though the hand that stabs the King is Evadne's, she is only a tool used for revenge; Melantius is the true revenger. Through killing the King, Evadne desperately seeks to exculpate herself in Amintor's eyes and be accepted by him as his wife, but he has been too deeply offended by her. Seeing herself as an unnatural and abominable being, unable to be cleansed and return as a man's "possession," suicide is her only option.

Melantius, honorable and courageous soldier, is close friends with Amintor. His loyalty to his friend surpasses all loyalty to the King, and even to his own family. Once convinced of Amintor's plight, Melantius orchestrates his revenge brilliantly, even succeeding in getting the keys to the impregnable fort from his enemy Calianax through political maneuverings. Melantius is admired for his martial skills, and it seems that his military experience has given him a new and different view that allows him to see through the double standards of the court and act upon what is moral and honorable. Still, however justifiable his acts may seem, the revenger is not safe at play's end. Melantius vows never to "eat/Or drink or sleep, or have to do with that/That may preserve life" (V.iii.291-293) in order to follow his close friend in death; however, Lysippus, the new King, in the same breath acknowledges his own lesson and the necessity of not showing mercy to the killer of a divinely appointed ruler:

> Lysippus
>> May this a fair example be to me
>> To rule with temper, for on lustful kings
>> Unlooked-for, sudden deaths from God are sent.
>> But cursed is he that is their instrument.
>>> (V.iii.295-298)

Melantius is a traitor to the throne, however just his case may seem.

Aspatia, the epitome of the chaste and obedient Renaissance woman, is the play's title character. Her tragedy lies in following the rules of society as they have been dictated to her. However, no success is possible when other, more influential people elect not to follow these same rules. She is morbid in her grief, sometimes reminding one of Shakespeare's Ophelia's powerlessness in a similar situation. She finally decides to break the mold; as she cannot obtain consummation in marriage from Amintor, she can make him the instrument of her death.

Evadne and Aspatia are diametrical opposites of each other, one being a forward, willful, sexual being, the other a meek, obedient soul, passive even when forcing her own murder. Both are created by a King who tyrannically transgresses the social institution of honorable marriage, and who ultimately is responsible for their deaths.

Major Themes

The convenience of our shared belief in social convention is a major theme in *The Maid's Tragedy*. The play opens with wedding preparations, a glowing picture of normalcy. The court is even preparing an elaborate masque in the honor of Amintor's marriage to Evadne. The celebration continues through the masque (I.ii), which presents Night, the favorite time for eager lovers, but also a time with ominous undertones, in conversation with Cynthia, the Moon, emblem of instability, mutability, and inconstancy.[7] Though the court does not bring the happy couple to bed, a custom the King is happy to break in this case, normalcy continues in II.i with the ladies' undressing of Evadne, sprinkled with spicy comments about the night to come. Aspatia's grief is a damper on the proceedings; still, despite three subtle foreshadowings, the audience does not suspect that anything is amiss. Our complacent belief in the sanctity of accepted social rituals is rudely shattered later in II.i, when the bride impertinently tells the groom that she is no virgin, and that she will never share his bed. Amintor, eager for sexual consummation but painfully loyal to his King, is rendered unable to act, and, emasculated, agrees to go along with the deception. In this play, the King believes that he can use the sacrament of marriage as cover for his own lust, and that he can do so with equanimity. This intrusion of the King's "right" into the family unit, prostituting the institution of marriage, is an offense no audience wants him to escape punishment for. After all, at this time the eldest son inherited according to the rules of primogeni-

---

[7] Compare Bel-imperia and Horatio's tryst in II.iv of *The Spanish Tragedy*. The invocation of night, associated as it is with the powers of evil, provides strong foreshadowing.

ture, and what father would wish his lands and goods to be passed on to another man's child?[8] Love, honor, and marriage are expected to go hand-in-hand, but not in this play. Here love and honor have become perverted and polluted, and can be manipulated to act against each other with destructive result.

The divine right of kings and its limitations is another major theme.[9] When a king behaves tyrannically in the microcosm that is the family, how far does he exceed his authority? Should a tyrant be severely punished, when laying violent hands on God's anointed constitutes capital treason? Amintor's love of his King and belief in his divine right prevents him, a subject, from defending his own honor and what is rightfully his. The mere name of "King" has the power to reduce him to a powerless, almost feminine state. Evadne's love for the King and the power that follows along with being his mistress prevents her from forming an honorable bond with her husband in marriage. She fully intends to foist her eventual children onto Amintor and pass them off as his. Aspatia's love of Amintor, whom she cannot have because the King has canceled their marriage contract, sends her into death, and Melantius' love of Amintor makes him the avenger of Amintor's and his own family's honor with fateful results for himself. Marriage and the family are the accepted and honorable sphere for love and sexuality, and the King's logical step should have been making Evadne his queen. However, marriage is a bond transcending fleeting sexual passion; sex is for now, marriage is forever. He who asks sexual favors from a woman not his wife may well corrupt that woman, as society's definition of a "good woman" at the time is one who is, above all, chaste. When bloodlines and inheritance are important enough to base alliances on, promiscuity in a wife must be regarded as abominable; still, who dares refuse a

---

[8] See also Shakespeare's *King John*, where inheritance and royal fornication is a main issue.

[9] See above under "Setting and Characters."

king? The conflict between love and honor sends all of the major characters into a consummation, not in love, but in death; what initiates this destructive process is the King's belief that he has the absolute right to do as he pleases. The audience is invited to pass its own judgment.

The theme of male friendship and its power is also of great importance in *The Maid's Tragedy*. Amintor and Melantius share a bond of uncommon strength.[10] Close friendship between two males was, at the time, seen as the purest bond that could exist between two human beings. The bond of married love between a husband and wife, while strong and holy, still has the element of sexuality and therefore irrationality to possibly taint it. As we so clearly see in *The Maid's Tragedy*, when lust enters, reason leaves, when sexuality is allowed free reign, the ability to use clear, unbiased judgment melts away. Friendship between two men of equal background and similar temperament and interests allows them to share intellectual pleasures and pure, untainted love. Modern readers often balk at the language used between two such friends, but the language of love is the only one capable of expressing such feelings.[11] Renaissance close male friends will risk anything for one another, even, as in this case, being the friend's avenger. Hamlet and Horatio share a similar bond, which is also being tested to an extreme point at the end of the play when Hamlet convinces Horatio not to follow him in death, but to remain as the only witness to events who can present Hamlet's point of view. Melantius immediately sees through to Amintor's grief despite the jolly appearance he puts on, and is the only one who can get a confession from him. Even though his own sister is branded as a whore by Amintor's tale, Melantius eventually believes Amintor and decides

[10] See also glossary: Male Friendship.
[11] Much modern criticism reads homoerotic, if not homosexual, relationships into male friendship. However, contemporary texts that discuss the quality of friendship between two men leave the present editor unconvinced.

to avenge him without endangering him in the process. When this plan is thwarted by Aspatia's "suicide-by-duel," and Amintor's stabbing himself by her body in grief, Melantius sees no reason to live on without his friend, who is more important to him than family; he ignores his sister's corpse to mourn by his friend's, and is determined to end his own life.

Revenge, of course, is at the center of this play. As a late revenge play, *The Maid's Tragedy* differs significantly from *The Spanish Tragedy*, but then Thomas Kyd's society differs significantly from Beaumont and Fletcher's. Kyd experimented with the genre, and gave it all the ingredients that make revenge tragedy so popular: fights, blood and gore, illicit love, ghosts returned from beyond the grave, madness, and the ultimate, spectacular revenge bloodbath. His intended audience was not homogenous, and so there is something for everyone in his play. Beaumont and Fletcher wrote *The Maid's Tragedy* for the Blackfriars stage, for an intended audience of some sophistication, taste and education, whose preferences they knew well. We have no ghosts in this play, and no swordplay, but we do indeed have illicit love that turns people into beasts and makes them irrational, a degree of madness. The revenge bloodbath is certainly present, but its even bloodier aftermath clearly demonstrates the irrationality of private revenge. Evadne does indeed kill the King in spectacular fashion, but she herself commits suicide along with Aspatia and Amintor. Even after death, the King's evil has dire effects.

In Elizabeth's time, when Kyd wrote *The Spanish Tragedy*, revenge tragedy tested the human spirit; both Hieronimo and Hamlet are noble creatures sorely tested. During the time of King James, revenge tragedy had become a vehicle for social criticism.

Figure 7. STC 1680, the 1638 title page for *The Maid's Tragedy*, depicting the self-sacrifice of the title character. By permission of the Folger Shakespeare Library.

Dramatis Personae

King of Rhodes
Lysippus, brother to the King
Gentlemen of the King's bedchamber

Amintor, a noble gentleman
Evadne, his wife
Dula, lady-in-waiting to Evadne
Servant to Amintor

Aspatia, betrothed to Amintor and rejected
Calianax, her father, a humorous[12] lord
Diagoras, his servant
Antiphila, servant to Aspatia
Olympias, servant to Aspatia

Melantius, Evadne's brother and a soldier
Diphilus, his brother
A Lady, wooed by Melantius

Cleon, a gentleman
Strato, a gentleman

CHARACTERS IN THE MASQUE

Night	Favonius
Cynthia	The Winds
Neptune	Proteus
Aeolus	Sea Gods

Lords and Ladies, Guards, Servants

---

[12] Dominated by one of the four humors, in this case that of choler.

Act I, Scene i

Enter Cleon, Strato, Lysippus, and Diphilus

Cleon
    The rest are making ready, sir.

Lysippus   So let them,
    There's time enough.

Diphilus
    You are the brother to the King, my lord,
    We'll take your word.

Lysippus
    Strato, thou hast some skill in poetry,   5
    What think'st thou of a masque?[13] Will it be well?

Strato
    As well as masques can be.

Lysippus   As masques can be?

Strato
    Yes, they must commend their king, and speak
    In praise of the assembly, bless the bride and groom
    In person of some god. They're tied to rules   10
    Of flattery.

Cleon
    See, good my lord, who is returned!

Enter Melantius

Lysippus
    Noble Melantius!
    The land by me welcomes[14] thy virtues home to Rhodes,

---

[13] See glossary.

[14] Lysippus, heir to the throne after his brother, extends the greeting of the country as a whole to praise Melantius.

Thou that with blood abroad buyest us our peace.   15
The breath of kings is like the breath of gods.
My brother wished thee here, and thou art here.
He will be too kind and weary thee
With often welcomes, but the time doth give thee
A welcome above his or all the world's.   20

Melantius

My lord, my thanks, but these scratched limbs of mine
Have spoke my love and truth unto my friends
More than my tongue e'er could. My mind's the same
It ever was to you; where I find worth
I love the keeper[15] till he let it go,   25
And then I follow it.

Diphilus   Hail, worthy brother!
He that rejoices not at your return
In safety is mine enemy forever.

Melantius

I thank thee, Diphilus, but thou art faulty.
I sent for thee to exercise thine arms
With me at Patria.[16] Thou cam'st not, Diphilus.   30
'Twas ill!

Diphilus   My noble brother, my excuse
Is my King's strict command, which you, my lord,
Can witness with me.

Lysippus   'Tis most true, Melantius.
He might not come till the solemnities   35
Of this great match were past.

Diphilus   Have you heard of it?

Melantius

Yes, and have given cause to those that here

---

[15] He who possesses it.
[16] Patras, a fortified city on the western coast of Greece.

Envy my deeds abroad to call me gamesome.[17]
I have no other business here at Rhodes.

Lysippus

We have a masque tonight,   40
And you must tread a soldier's measure.[18]

Melantius

These soft and silken wars are not for me.
The music must be shrill and all confused
That stirs my blood, and then I dance with arms.
But is Amintor wed?

Diphilus   This day.   45

Melantius

All joys upon him, for he is my friend.
Wonder not that I call a man so young my friend.
His worth is great. Valiant he is and temperate,
And one that never thinks his life his own
If his friend need it. When he was a boy,   50
As oft as I returned (as, without boast
I brought home conquest), he would gaze upon me
And view me round to find in what one limb
The virtue[19] lay to do those things he heard.
Then would he wish to see my sword and feel   55
The quickness[20] of the edge, and in his hand
Weigh it. He oft would make me smile at this.
His youth did promise much, and his ripe years
Will see it all performed.

Enter Aspatia, passing by, attended.

[17] Eager for entertainment, sport.
[18] Dance, slow and serious.
[19] Power; physical strength.
[20] Sharpness.

                            Hail, maid and wife!

Thou fair Aspatia, may the holy knot[21]   60
That thou hast tied today last till the hand
Of age undo't. Mayst thou bring a race[22]
Unto Amintor that may fill the world
Successively[23] with soldiers.

Aspatia   My hard fortunes

Deserve not scorn, for I was never proud   65
When they[24] were good.   *Exit Aspatia, attended*

Melantius   How's this?

Lysippus

You are mistaken, for she is not married.

Melantius

You said Amintor was.

Diphilus

'Tis true, but—

Melantius   Pardon me, I did receive

Letters at Patria from my Amintor   70
That he should marry her.

Diphilus   And so it stood

In all opinion long, but your arrival
Made me imagine you had heard the change.

Melantius

Who has he taken then?

Lysippus   A lady, sir,

That bears the light above her,[25] and strikes dead   75

---

[21] Holy wedlock.

[22] I.e., of children.

[23] One after the other.

[24] I.e., her fortunes.

[25] "Her" can be referring to Aspatia, and so Evadne is more shiningly lovely than she.

With flashes of her eye,[26] the fair Evadne,

Your virtuous sister.

Melantius   Peace of heart betwixt them!

But this is strange.

Lysippus   The King, my brother, did it

To honour you, and these solemnities[27]

Are at his charge.[28]   80

Melantius

'Tis royal like himself, but I am sad

My speech bears so infortunate a sound

To beautiful Aspatia. There is rage

Hid in her father's breast, Calianax,

Bent long against me, and he should not think,   85

If I could call it back,[29] that I would take

So base revenges as to scorn the state

Of his neglected daughter. Holds he still

His greatness[30] with the King?

Lysippus   Yes, but this lady

Walks discontented with her watery eyes   90

Bent on the earth. The unfrequented woods

Are her delight, and when she sees a bank

Stuck full of[31] flowers, she with a sigh

Will tell her servants what a pretty place

It were to bury lovers in, and make her maids   95

Pluck 'em and strew her over like a corpse.[32]

[26] Evadne's "killing eyes" remind one of the basilisk; a mythological reptile, hatched from a cock's egg, it could kill with its very breath or gaze.

[27] Celebrations.

[28] Are ordered by him.

[29] If I could make good my offense to Aspatia.

[30] High position.

[31] Teeming with.

[32] Scattering flowers over the body, as is the case with *Hamlet*'s Ophelia, is usually done for a virgin.

She carries with her an infectious grief
That strikes[33] all her beholders. She will sing
The mournful'st things that ever ear hath heard,
And sigh, and sing again, and when the rest   100
Of our young ladies in their wanton[34] blood
Tell mirthful tales in course[35] that fill the room
With laughter, she will with so sad a look
Bring forth a story of the silent death
Of some forsaken virgin, which her grief   105
Will put in such a phrase that, ere she end,
She'll send them weeping one by one away.

Melantius

She has a brother under my command
Like her,[36] a face as womanish as hers,
But with a spirit that hath much outgrown   110
The number of his years.

Enter Amintor

Cleon   My lord the bridegroom!

Melantius

I might run fiercely, not more hastily
Upon my foe. I love thee well, Amintor
My mouth is much too narrow for my heart[37]
I joy to look upon those eyes of thine.   115
Thou art my friend, but my disordered speech
Cuts off my love.

---

[33] Infects.

[34] Unrestrained and merry.

[35] "Round robin," taking turns one by one. Group storytelling was a popular pastime in the Renaissance.

[36] A fact Aspatia makes use of in V.iii.

[37] My heart is so full I cannot utter my feelings in words.

Amintor   Thou art Melantius

    All love is spoke in that. A sacrifice

    To thank the gods Melantius is returned

    In safety! Victory sits on his sword   120

    As she was wont;[38] may she build there and dwell[39]

    And may thy armour be as it hath been

    Only thy valour and thine innocence.[40]

    What endless treasures would our enemies give

    That I might hold the still thus![41]

Melantius   I am poor   125

    In words, but credit me, young man, thy mother

    Could do no more but weep for joy to see thee

    After long absence. All the wounds I have

    Fetched not so much away,[42] nor all the cries

    Of widowed mothers. But this is a peace,   130

    And that was war.

Amintor   Pardon thou holy god

    Of marriage bed,[43] and frown not, I am forced

    In answer of such noble tears as those,

    To weep upon my wedding day.

Melantius

    I fear thou art grown too fickle,[44] for I hear   135

    A lady mourns for thee, men say to death,

    Forsaken of thee, on what terms I know not.

Amintor

    She had my promise, but the King forbade it

---

[38] Used to.

[39] May she find a home there always.

[40] Moral purity.

[41] I.e., in an embrace of friendship.

[42] Were not occasion for that many tears.

[43] Hymen, the god of marriage.

[44] Unreliable.

And made me make this worthy change,[45] thy sister,
Accompanied with graces[46] about her   140
With whom I long to lose my lusty youth[47]
And grow old in her arms.

Melantius   Be prosperous!

Enter a Messenger

Messenger
My lord, the masquers rage[48] for you.

Lysippus   We are gone.
Cleon, Strato, Diphilus![49]

Amintor
We'll all attend you.

                    Exeunt Lysippus, Cleon, Strato, and Diphilus
                    We shall trouble you   145
With our solemnities.

Melantius   Not so, Amintor
But if you laugh at my rude carriage[50]
In peace, I'll do as much for you in war
When you come thither. But I have a mistress[51]
To bring to your delights. Rough though I am,   150
I have a mistress and she has a heart,
She says, but trust me, it is stone, no better.

[45] Exchange.
[46] Goddesses personifying charm, grace, and beauty.
[47] Amintor is a virgin; "grow old" in the next line may refer to the belief that semen, created from the blood, ages one whenever expended.
[48] Are wildly impatient.
[49] The four lords are probably actors in the masque.
[50] Unrefined behavior.
[51] Love and war were thought to be irreconcilable. Melantius claims to not be totally devoted to warlike activities.

There is no place[52] that I can challenge.[53]
But you stand still, and here my way lies.   *Exeunt*

Act I, Scene ii

Enter Calianax and Diagoras

Calianax

Diagoras, look to the doors better, for shame. You let in
all the world, and anon[54] the King will rail at[55] me. Why,
very well said![56] By Jove, the King will have the show
i'th'court.[57]

Diagoras

Why do you swear so, my lord? You know he'll have it   5
here.

Calianax

By this light, if he be wise, he will not.

Diagoras

And if he will not be wise, you are forsworn.[58]

Calianax

One may sweat his heart out with swearing, and get thanks
on no side. I'll be gone. Look to't who will.

Diagoras

My lord, I shall never keep them out. Pray stay, your looks[59]   10

---

[52] In her heart, that is.

[53] Penetrate, militarily and sexually.

[54] Presently.

[55] Scold.

[56] Well done.

[57] Apparently the court presents a problem with controlling who is in the
audience to the masque.

[58] You have committed perjury.

[59] Calianax' "looks" carry authority.

will terrify them.

Calianax

My looks terrify them![60] You coxcombly[61] ass, you! I'll be judged by all the company whether thou hast not a worse face than I.

Diagoras

I mean because they know you and your office.   15

Calianax

Office! I would I could put it off![62] I am sure I sweat right through my office! I might have made room[63] at my daughter's wedding; they ha' near killed her amongst them. And now I must do service for him that hath forsaken her. Serve that will![64]   *Exit Calianax* 20

Diagoras

He is so humorous[65] since his daughter was forsaken!

                                        Knock within

Hark, hark! There, there! So, so! Codes,[66] codes! What now!

Melantius (*within*)

Open the door!

Diagoras

Who's there?   25

Melantius (*within*)

Melantius.

Diagoras (*opening the door*)

I hope your lordship brings no troop[67] with you, for if you

---

[60] Calianax thinks he is being called "ugly."

[61] The coxcomb or jester's hat was part of the "court fool's" uniform.

[62] Calianax sees his "office" as an uncomfortably warm garment.

[63] Kept the door to keep out the uninvited.

[64] "Let somebody who wants this job have it!"

[65] So unbalanced; see glossary under "four humors."

[66] Corruption of "gods."

[67] (Military) group of people.

do, I must return them.

Enter Melantius and a Lady

Melantius

None but this lady, sir.

Diagoras

The ladies are all placed above,[68] save those that come in   30
the King's troop. The best of Rhodes sit there, and there's
room.

Melantius

I thank you, sir. When I have seen you placed, madam, I
must attend the King. But the masque done, I'll wait on[69]
you again.   *Exit Melantius with the Lady at another door*   35

Diagoras

Stand back there! Room for my lord Melantius! Pray bear[70]
back! This is no place for such youths and their trulls.[71] Let
the doors shut again. Ay, do your heads itch?[72] I'll scratch
them, for you! (*Shuts the door*) So, now thrust and hang![73]
(*Knocking within*) Again! Who is't now? I cannot blame my   40
lord Calianax for going away. Would he were here. He
would run raging amongst them, and break a dozen wiser
heads than his own in the twinkling of an eye. What's the
news now?

---

[68] This can mean on the balcony or maybe off stage altogether; we do not
see the lady again in this scene.

[69] Attend.

[70] Stand.

[71] Loose women.

[72] I.e., itch for a beating, but also for a chance to enter with a sexual pun
continued in "thrust," l. 37.

[73] Hang yourselves.

Voice Within

    I pray you, can you help me to the speech[74] of the   45
    master cook?

Diagoras

    If I open the door, I'll cook some of your calves' heads.[75]

    Peace, rogues! (*Knocking within*) Again! Who is't?

Melantius (*within*)

    Melantius.

Enter Calianax

Calianax

    Let him not in.   50

Diagoras

    O my lord, a[76] must. Make room there for my lord!

Enter Melantius

    Is your lady placed?

Melantius

    Yes, sir, I thank you. My lord Calianax, well met!

    Your causeless hate to me I hope is buried?

Calianax

    Yes, I do service for your sister here,   55

    That brings mine own poor child to timeless[77] death.

    She loves your friend Amintor, such another

    False-hearted lord as you.

Melantius   You do me wrong

    A most unmanly one, and I am slow

---

[74] To speak with.

[75] 1) Foolish heads; 2) calf's brain was a delicacy.

[76] He.

[77] Untimely.

> In taking vengeance, but be well advised. 60

Calianax

> It may be so. Who placed the lady there
> So near the presence of the King?[78]

Melantius   I did.

Calianax

> My lord, she must not sit there.

Melantius   Why?

Calianax

> The place is kept for women of more worth.

Melantius

> More worth than she? It misbecomes your age 65
> And place to be thus womanish. Forbear!
> What you have spoke I am content to think
> The palsy[79] shook your tongue to.[80]

Calianax   Why, 'tis well

> If I stand here to place men's wenches.

Melantius   I

> Shall quite forget this place, thy age, my safety, 70
> And through all cut that poor sickly week
> Thou hast to live away from thee!

Calianax

> Nay, I know you can fight for your whore.

Melantius

> Bate me the King,[81] and be he flesh and blood
> A lies that says it! Thy mother at fifteen 75
> Was black and sinful to her.

---

[78] A person's social standing determined how close to the King that person was placed during entertainment at King James I's court.

[79] A condition that makes the whole body or parts thereof shake.

[80] "I will take it that your old age spoke (and offended my lady), not truly Calianax."

[81] The King excepted.

Diagoras   Good my lord—
Melantius
    Some god pluck threescore[82] years from that fond[83] man
    That I may kill him and not stain mine honour!
    It is the curse of soldiers that in peace
    They shall be braved by[84] such ignoble men   80
    As, if the land were troubled,[85] would with tears
    And knees beg succor from'em. Would that blood
    That sea of blood that I have lost in fight
    Were running in thy veins, that I might make thee
    Apt to say less, or able to maintain,[86]   85
    Shouldst thou say more! This Rhodes, I see, is nought
    But a place privileged to do men wrong.
Calianax
    Ay, you may say your pleasure.[87]

Enter Amintor

Amintor   What vile injury
    Has stirred my worthy friend, who is as slow
    To fight with words as he is quick of hand?   90
Melantius
    That heap of age, which I should reverence
    If it were temperate, but testy years[88]
    Are most contemptible.
Amintor   Good sir, forbear.

[82] Sixty.
[83] Foolish.
[84] Treated cavalierly by.
[85] I.e., with war.
[86] Support with action.
[87] "You are one to talk like that!"
[88] An angry old man.

Calianax

There is just such another as yourself.

Amintor

He will wrong you, or me, or any man,   95
And talk as if he had no life to lose,
Since this our match. The King is coming in.
I would not for more wealth than I enjoy
He should perceive you raging. He did hear
You were at difference now, which hastened him.   100

Calianax

Make room there!

Hautboys[89] play within. Enter the King, Evadne, Aspatia, Lords, and Ladies

King

Melantius, thou art welcome, and my love
Is with thee still. But this is not a place
To brabble[90] in. Calianax, join hands.

Calianax

He shall not have my hand.

King   This is no time   105
To force you to't. I do love you both.
Calianax, you look well to your office,[91]
And you, Melantius, are welcome home.
Begin the masque.

Melantius

Sister, I joy to see you and your choice.   110
You looked with my eyes when you took that man;
Be happy in him.   *Recorders play[92]*

---

[89] Oboes.

[90] Quarrel.

[91] "Go do your job well."

[92] The recorder, a wind instrument, was often used to create a solemn mood.

Evadne   O, my dearest brother,
    Your presence is more joyful than this day
    Can be unto me.

The Masque

Night rises[93] *in mists*

Night
    Our reign is come, for in the raging sea   115
    The sun is drowned, and with him fell the day.
    Bright Cynthia,[94] hear my voice. I am the Night
    For whom thou bear'st about thy borrowed light,[95]
    Appear! No longer thy pale visage shroud,
    But strike thy silver horns[96] quite through a cloud,   120
    And send a beam upon my swarthy face,
    By which I may discover all the place
    And persons, and how many longing eyes
    Are come to wait on our solemnities.

Enter Cynthia

    How dull and black am I! I could not find   125
    This beauty[97] without thee, I am so blind.
    Methinks they show like to those eastern streaks
    That warn us hence before the morning breaks.
    Back, my pale servant, for these eyes know how
    To shoot far more and quicker rays than thou.   130

---

[93] Probably from the trapdoor in the stage floor.

[94] The goddess of the moon and chastity.

[95] The moon's light is a reflection from the sun, not its own.

[96] I.e., this is the crescent moon.

[97] I.e., the beauty of the assembled ladies in the on-stage audience to the masque.

Cynthia

> Great Queen, they be a troop for whom alone
> One of my clearest moons I have put on,
> A troop that looks as if thyself and I
> Had plucked our reins in and our whips laid by[98]
> To gaze upon these mortals that appear   135
> Brighter than we.

Night   Then let us keep 'em here,

> And never more our chariots drive away,
> But hold our places and outshine the Day.

Cynthia

> Great Queen of shadows, you are pleased to speak
> Of more than may be done. We may not break   140
> The gods' decrees, but when our time is come,
> Must drive away and give the Day our room.
> Yet whilst our reign lasts, let us stretch our power
> To give our servants one contented hour,
> With such unwonted[99] solemn grace and state   145
> As may forever after force them hate
> Our brother's glorious beams, and wish the night
> Crowned with a thousand stars and our cold light.
> For almost all the world their service bend
> To Phoebus,[100] and in vain my light I lend,   150
> Gazed on unto my setting from my rise
> Almost of none but of unquiet eyes.

Night

> Then shine at full, fair Queen, and by thy power
> Produce a birth, to crown this happy hour,
> Of nymphs and shepherds; let their songs discover,   155
> Easy and sweet, who is a happy lover.

[98] I.e., they have stopped Night's chariot, frozen time.
[99] Unusual.
[100] "The radiant one," a name for Apollo, the god of the sun.

Or, if thou wilt, then call thine own Endymion[101]
From the sweet, flow'ry bed he lies upon,
On Latmos' top,[102] thy pale beams drawn away,
And of his long night let him make this day.   160
Cynthia
Thou dream'st, dark Queen; that fair boy was not mine,
Nor went I down to kiss him. Ease and wine
Have bred these bold tales. Poets, when they rage[103]
Turn gods to men and make an hour an age.
But I will give a greater state and glory   165
And raise to time a nobler memory
Of what these lovers are. Rise, rise, I say,
Thou power of deeps, thy surges laid away,
Neptune,[104] great King of waters, and by me
Be proud to be commanded.[105]

Neptune rises[106]

Neptune   Cynthia, see,   170
Thy word has fetched me hither. Let me know
Why I ascend.
Cynthia   Doth this majestic show
Give thee no knowledge yet?
Neptune   Yes, now I see
Something intended, Cynthia, worthy thee.

---

[101] A handsome youth, beloved by the moon-goddess Selene, who sleeps
eternally in a cave, being visited by his love, probably during the dark of the
moon.
[102] Mt. Latmos stands in Asia Minor.
[103] Are in an inspired frenzy.
[104] The god of the sea; one of his daughters is named Evadne, like the day's
bride.
[105] The moon governs the tides.
[106] Again, probably through the trapdoor.

Go on, I'll be a helper.

Cynthia   Hie thee,[107] then,   175

And charge the Wind[108] go from his rocky den,

Let loose his subjects; only Boreas,[109]

Too foul for our intentions as he was,

Still keep him fast chained. We must have none here

But vernal[110] blasts and gentle winds appear,   180

Such as blow[111] flowers, and through the glad boughs sing

Many soft welcomes to the lusty spring.

These are our music. Next, thy wat'ry race[112]

Bring on in couples. We are pleased to grace

This noble night each in their richest things[113]   185

Your own deeps or the broken vessel[114] brings.

Be prodigal, and I shall be as kind,

And shine at full upon you.

Enter Aeolus out of a rock[115]

Neptune   O, the wind-

Commanding Aeolus!

Aeolus   Great Neptune!

Neptune   He.

Aeolus

What is thy will?

Neptune   We do command thee free   190

---

[107] Hurry up.

[108] Aeolus, ruler of the winds, keeps them closed in a cave when not needed.

[109] The north wind, a rough and unruly wind.

[110] Of the spring.

[111] Make to bloom.

[112] Minor sea-gods.

[113] I.e., they should come dressed in all their finery.

[114] Sunken ship.

[115] "The rock" is a stage prop representing the cave of the winds.

Favonius[116] and thy milder winds to wait
Upon our Cynthia, but tie Boreas straight,[117]
He's too rebellious.

Aeolus   I shall do it.

Neptune   Do,   *Exit Aeolus*

Great mistress of the flood and all below,
Thy full command has taken—

Enter Aeolus with the Winds

Aeolus   O! The Main![118]   195

    Neptune!

Neptune   Here.

Aelous   Boreas has broke his chain,

And struggling with the rest has got away.

Neptune

Let him alone, I'll take him up at sea;
He will not long be thence. Go once again
And call out of the bottoms of the Main   200
Blue Proteus[119] and the rest. Charge them put on
Their greatest pearls and the most sparkling stone
The beaten[120] rock breeds, till this night is done
By me a solemn honour to the Moon.
Fly like a full sail!

Aeolus   I am gone.   *Exit Areolus*

Cynthia   Dark Night,   205

Strike a full silence, do a thorough right
To this great chorus, that our music may

[116] The west wind.
[117] At once.
[118] The high sea.
[119] A shape-changing sea-god.
[120] Beaten by the waves.

Touch high as heaven, and make the East break day
At midnight.   *Music plays*

Enter Proteus and other sea-deities.

Sea-Gods (*sing*)
    Cynthia, to thy power and thee.   210
        We obey,
    Joy to this great company!
        And no day
    Come to steal this night away
    Till the rites of love are ended,   215
    And the lusty Bridegroom say,
    "Welcome light, of all befriended!"

    Pace out, you watery powers below!
        Let your feet,
    Like the galleys[121] when they row,   220
        Even beat.[122]
    Let your unknown measures, set
    To the still winds, tell to all
    That gods are come, immortal, great,
    To honour this great nuptial.   225

The sea-deities and the Winds dance

Sea-Gods (*sing*)
    Hold back thy hours, dark Night, till we have done;
        The day will come too soon.
    Young maids will curse thee if thou steal'st away

---

[121] The slaves rowing the galley.

[122] A drumbeat kept time for the galley's oarsmen.

And leav'st their blushes open to the day.
                    Stay, stay, and hide   230
                    The blushes of the bride.

Stay, gentle Night, and with thy darkness cover
                    The kisses of her lover
Stay and confound her tears and her shrill cryings,
Her weak denials, vows and often-dyings.[123]   235
                    Stay and hide all,
                    But help not[124] though she call.

Neptune

Great Queen of us and heaven, hear what I bring
To make this hour a full one, if not her measure.[125]

Cynthia

Speak, sea's King.   240

Neptune

The tune my Amphitrite[126] joys to have,
When she will dance upon the rising wave,
And court me as she sails. My Tritons,[127] play
Music to lay a storm! I'll lead the way.

                              They dance, Neptune leading

Sea-Gods (*sing*)

                    To bed, to bed! Come, Hymen,[128] lead the bride,   245
                    And lay her by her husband's side.
                    Bring in virgins every one
                    That grieve to lie alone,
                    That they may kiss while they may say a maid.

[123] "To die" is a Renaissance allusion to sexual orgasm.

[124] Do not interfere.

[125] 1) Adequate portion; 2) pun on the "measure" of a dance.

[126] A sea-nymph, his wife.

[127] Minor sea-gods.

[128] God of marriage.

Tomorrow t'will be other, kiss'd and said   250
Hesperus,[129] be long a-shining,
Whilst these lovers are a-twining!

Enter Aeolus

Aeolus

  Ho, Neptune!

Neptune   Aeolus!

Aeolus   The sea goes high!

  Boreas hath raised a storm. Go and apply
  Thy trident;[130] else I prophesy ere day   255
  Many a tall ship will be cast away.
  Descend with all the gods and all their power
  To strike a calm.   *Exit*

Cynthia

  A thanks to everyone, and to gratulate
  So great a service done at my desire,   260
  Ye shall have many floods, fuller and higher
  Than you have wished for, and no ebb shall dare
  To let the day see where your dwellings are.
  Now back unto your government[131] in haste
  Lest your proud charge should swell above the waste[132] 265
  And win upon[133] the island.

Neptune   We obey.

    Neptune and the Sea-Gods descend. Aeolus and Winds exeunt.

---

[129] The evening star.
[130] Neptune's scepter is trident-shaped.
[131] Domain.
[132] The beach; usually "uncultivated land."
[133] Flood.

Cynthia

> Hold up thy head, dead Night. See'st thou not Day?
>
> The East begins to lighten. I must down
>
> And give my brother[134] place.

Night   O, I could frown

> To see the Day, the Day that flings his light   270
>
> Upon my kingdom and contemns[135] old Night!
>
> Let him go on and flame! I hope to see
>
> Another wild fire in his axle-tree,[136]
>
> And all fall drenched! But I forget. Speak, Queen,
>
> The day grows on; I must no more be seen.   275

Cynthia

> Heave up thy drowsy head again and see
>
> A greater light, a greater majesty[137]
>
> Between our sect[138] and us. Whip up thy team.
>
> The day breaks here, and yon sun-flaring stream[139]
>
> Shot from the south.[140] Say, whither wilt thou go?   280

Night

> I'll vanish into mists.

Cynthia   I into day.   *Exeunt Night and Cynthia*
>   *The Masque ends*

---

[134] The sun.

[135] Spites.

[136] A fixed bar with bearings at the end to mount (chariot) wheels. Phaeton, son of Apollo the sun god, was promised anything he wanted when he found his father. He chose to drive the sun's chariot for a day but could not manage the horses. The chariot caught fire, and Phaeton was killed by Zeus before he could do more than scorch the earth.

[137] I.e., the King's in the on-stage audience.

[138] Group of gods and goddesses.

[139] The blinding rays of the rising sun; see glossary under "sun."

[140] The king is usually seated at the south of the hall—another compliment!

King

> Take lights there! Ladies, get the bride to bed!
> We will not see you laid.[141] Good night, Amintor,
> We'll ease you of that tedious ceremony.
> Were it my case I should think time run slow.   285
> If thou be'st noble, youth, get me a boy
> That may defend my kingdom from my foes.

Amintor

> All happiness to you.

King   Goodnight, Melantius.   *Exeunt*

---

[141] Customarily, the newlyweds were taken to the bedchamber by the guests, enduring many bawdy remarks.

Act II, Scene i

Enter Evadne, Aspatia, Dula, and Ladies.

Dula

    Madam, shall we undress you for this fight?

    The wars are nak'd that you must make tonight.

Evadne

    You are very merry, Dula.

Dula   I should be

    Far merrier, madam, if it were with me

    As it is with you.

Evadne   How's that?

Dula   That I might go   5

    To bed with him with credit that you do.[142]

Evadne

    Why, how now, wench?

Dula   Come, ladies, will you help?

Evadne

    I am soon undone.[143]

Dula   And soon done.[144]

    Good store of clothes will trouble you at both.[145]

Evadne

    Art thou drunk, Dula?

Dula   Why, here's none but we.   10

Evadne

    Thou think'st belike there is no modesty

    When we're alone.

---

[142] Dula wishes that, with honor, she could share Amintor's bed.

[143] Unbuttoned and unlaced.

[144] Deflowered.

[145] Many clothes hinder both activities.

Dula

   Ay, by my troth, you hit my thoughts aright.

 Evadne

   You prick me, lady.

Dula   'Tis against my will.

   Anon you must endure more[146] and lie still,   15

   You're best to practice.

Evadne   Sure this wench is mad.

Dula

   No, faith, this is a trick[147] that I have had

   Since I was fourteen.

Evadne   'Tis high time to leave it.

Dula

   Nay, now I'll keep it till the trick leave me.

   A dozen wanton words put in your head   20

   Will make you livelier in your husband's bed.

Evadne

   Nay, faith, then take it.

Dula   Take it[148] madam! Where?

   We all I hope, will take it that are here.

Evadne

   Nay then, I'll give you o'er.[149]

Dula   So will I make

   The ablest[150] man in Rhodes, or his heart ache.   25

Evadne

   Wilt take my place tonight?

---

[146] With sexual innuendo.

[147] "A trick of madness," but also "a trick at cards" (the cardgame is used playfully for the sexual act in the following lines).

[148] Evadne's "take it (or leave it, whatever you want)" is turned into Dula's idea of having sex.

[149] "I'll dismiss you."

[150] Most sexually potent.

Dula   I'll hold your cards

 Against any two I know.

Evadne   What wilt thou do?

Dula

 Madam, we'll do't, and make'em leave play too.

Evadne

 Aspatia, take her part.

Dula   I will refuse it.

 She will pluck down a side,[151] she does not use it.[152] 30

Evadne

 Why, do, I prithee.

Dula   You will find the play

 Quickly, because your head lies well that way.[153]

Evadne

 I thank thee, Dula. Would thou couldst instill

 Some of thy mirth into Aspatia.

 Nothing but sad thoughts in her breast do dwell 35

 Methinks a mean betwixt you would do well.

Dula

 She is in love. Hang me if I were so,

 But I could run my country.[154] I love too

 To do those things that people in love do.

Aspatia

 It were a timeless[155] smile should prove my cheek. 40

 It were a fitter hour for me to laugh

 When at the altar the religious priest

 Were pacifying the offended powers

 With sacrifice, than now. This should have been

---

[151] Lose at cards.

[152] She is inexperienced at both cards and sex.

[153] "You have a head for the game/aptitude for sex."

[154] Govern my space/myself, but also with a play on country/cunt.

[155] Untimely.

My night,[156] and all your hands have been employed   45
In giving me, a spotless offering,
To young Amintor's bed, as we are now
For you. Pardon, Evadne, would my worth
Were great as yours, or that the king, or he,
Or both thought so. Perhaps he found me worthless,   50
But till he did so, in these ears of mine,
These credulous ears he poured the sweetest words
That art or love could frame. If he were false,
Pardon it, heaven; and if I did want
Virtue, you safely may forgive that too,   55
For I have lost none that I had from you.

Evadne

Nay, leave this sad talk, madam.

Aspatia   Would I could,
Then should I leave the cause.

Evadne

See if you have not spoiled all Dula's mirth!

Aspatia

Thou think'st thy heart hard, but if thou be'st caught,   60
Remember me. Thou shalt perceive a fire
Shot suddenly into thee.

Dula   That's not so good.
Let'em shoot anything but fire, and I
Fear'em not.

Aspatia   Well, wench, thou may'st be taken.

Evadne

Ladies, good night, I'll do the rest myself.   65

Dula

Nay, let your lord do some.

Aspatia (*singing*)
     Lay a garland on my hearse of the dismal yew—

---

[156] Wedding night.

Evadne

    That's one of your sad songs, madam.

Aspatia

    Believe me, 'tis a very pretty one.

Evadne

    How is it, madam?   70

Aspatia (*sings*)

        Lay a garland on my hearse of the dismal yew[157]
        Maidens, willow branches[158] *bear, say I died true.*
        My love was false, but I was firm, from my hour of birth.
        Upon my buried body lie lightly, gentle earth.

Evadne

    Fie on't madam! The words are so strange, they are able   75
    to make one dream of hobgoblins.[159] *I could never have the*
    power—sing that, Dula.

Dula (*sings*)

        I could never have the power
        To love one above an hour,
        But my heart would prompt mine eye   80
        On some other man to fly.
        Venus, fix mine eyes fast,
        Or if not, give me all that I shall see at last.

Evadne

    So, leave me now.

Dula   Nay, we must see you laid.

Aspatia

    Madam, good night. May all the marriage joys   85
    That longing maids imagine in their beds
    Prove so unto you! May no discontent
    Grow twixt your love and you. But if there do,

---

[157] Emblem of death.

[158] Emblem of slighted love, especially in forsaken women.

[159] Mischievous spirits.

Inquire of me and I will guide your moan,
And teach you an artificial[160] way to grieve,   90
To keep your sorrow waking. Love your lord
No worse than I, but if you love so well,
Alas, you may displease him. So did I.
This is the last time you shall look on me.
Ladies, farewell. As soon as I am dead,   95
Come all and watch one night about my hearse.
Bring each a mournful story and a tear
To offer at it when I go to earth;
With flattering ivy clasp my coffin round,
Write on my brow my fortune,[161] let my bier   100
Be borne by virgins that shall sing by course[162]
The truth of maids and perjuries of men.

Evadne

Alas, I pity thee.   *Exit Evadne*

All   Madam, good night.

First Lady

Come, we'll let in the bridegroom.

Dula   Where's my lord?

Enter Amintor

First Lady

Here, take this light.

Dula   You'll find her in the dark.   105

First Lady

Your lady's scarce abed yet; you must help her.

---

[160] Artful; skilled.

[161] A woman, especially, was thought to carry the signs of her wrongdoing written on her forehead (see later in IV.i); she, however, is sinned against, not sinning.

[162] In turn.

Aspatia

    Go, and be happy in your lady's love.

    May all the wrongs that you have done to me

    Be utterly forgotten in my death!

    I'll trouble you no more, yet will I take   110

    A parting kiss, and will not be denied.   *Kisses Amintor*

    You'll come, my lord, and see the virgins weep

    When I am laid in earth, though you yourself

    Can know no pity. Thus I wind myself

    Into this willow garland, and am prouder   115

    That I was once your love, though now refused,

    Than to have had another true to me.

    So with prayers I leave you, and must try

    Some yet unpracticed way to grieve and die.   *Exit Aspatia*

Dula

    Come, ladies, will you go?

All   Good night, my lord.   120

Amintor

    Much happiness unto you all!   *Exeunt Ladies*

    I did that lady wrong. Methinks I feel

    Her grief shoot suddenly through all my veins.

    Mine eyes run; this is strange at such a time.

    It was the King first moved me to't, but he   125

    Has not my will in keeping. Why do I

    Perplex myself thus? Something whispers me,

    "Go not to bed." My guilt is not so great

    As mine own conscience, too sensible,[163]

    Would make me think. I only brake[164] a promise,   130

    And 'twas the King that forced me. Timorous flesh,

    Why shak'st thou so? Away, my idle fears!

---

[163] Sensitive.

[164] Broke.

Enter Evadne

    Yonder she is, the luster of whose eye
    Can blot away the sad remembrance
    Of all these things. O, my Evadne, spare   135
    That tender body! Let it not take cold!
    The vapors of the night shall not fall here.
    To bed, my love, Hymen will punish us
    For being slack performers of his rites.
    Cam'st thou to call me?

Evadne   No.

Amintor   Come, come, my love,   140
    And let us loose ourselves to one another.
    Why art thou up so long?

Evadne   I am not well.

Amintor
    To bed, then. Let me wind you in these arms
    Till I have banished sickness.

Evadne   Good my lord,
    I cannot sleep.

Amintor   Evadne, we'll watch,   145
    I mean no sleeping.[165]

Evadne   I'll not go to bed.

Amintor
    I prithee, do.

Evadne   I will not for the world.

Amintor
    Why, my dear love?

Evadne   Why? I have sworn I will not.

Amintor
    Sworn?

---

[165] Keep watch; Amintor does not expect to sleep on his wedding night.

Evadne   Ay.

Amintor   How? Sworn, Evadne!

Evadne

 Yes, sworn, Amintor, and will swear again   150

 If you will wish to hear me.

Amintor

 To whom have you sworn this?

Evadne

 If I should name him the matter were not great.[166]

Amintor

 Come, this is but the coyness of a bride.

Evadne

 The coyness of a bride!

Amintor   How prettily   155

 That frown becomes thee.

Evadne   Do you like it so?

Amintor

 Thou canst not dress thy face in such a look

 But I shall like it.

Evadne   What look likes you best?

Amintor

 Why do you ask?

Evadne

 That I may show you one less pleasing to you.   160

Amintor

 How's that?

Evadne

 That I may show you one less pleasing to you.

Amintor

 I prithee, put thy jests in milder looks,

 It shows as thou wert angry.

Evadne   So perhaps

---

[166] "My oath would not mean anything if I told you."

I am indeed.

Amintor   Why, who has done thee wrong? 165
    Name me the man, and by thyself I swear,
    Thy yet unconquered[167] self, I will revenge thee.

Evadne
    Now shall I try thy truth. If thou dost love me,
    Thou weigh'st not anything compared with me.
    Life, honour, joys eternal, all delights 170
    This world can yield, or hopeful people fain,[168]
    Or in the life to come, are light as air
    To a true lover when his lady frowns
    And bids him to do this. Wilt thou kill this man?
    Swear, my Amintor, and I'll kiss the sin 175
    Off from thy lips.

Amintor   I wonnot[169] swear, sweet love,
    Till I do know the cause.

Evadne   I would thou would'st.
    Why, it is thou that wrong'st me. I hate thee!
    Thou shouldst have killed thyself.

Amintor
    If I should know that, I should quickly kill 180
    The man you hated.

Evadne   Know it, then, and do't!

Amintor
    O no! What look soe'er thou shalt put on
    To try my faith, I shall not think thee false.
    I cannot find one blemish in thy face
    Where falsehood should abide. Leave, and to bed. 185
    If you have sworn to any of the virgins
    That were your old companions to preserve

---

[167] Virginal.
[168] Desire.
[169] Will not.

Your maidenhead a night, it may be done
Without this means.

Evadne

A maidenhead, Amintor, at my years?   190

Amintor

Sure she raves.—This cannot be
Thy natural temper.[170] Shall I call thy maids?
Either thy healthful sleep hath left thee long,
Or else some fever rages in thy blood.

Evadne

Neither, Amintor. Think you I am mad   195
Because I speak the truth?

Amintor   Is this the truth?
Will you not lie with me tonight?

Evadne   Tonight!
You talk as if you thought I would hereafter.

Amintor

Hereafter? Yes, I do.

Evadne   You are deceived.[171]
Put off amazement, and with patience mark   200
What I shall utter, for the oracle[172]
Knows nothing truer. 'Tis not for a night
Or two that I forbear thy bed, but ever.

Amintor

I dream! Awake, Amintor!

Evadne   You hear right.
I sooner will find out the beds of snakes,   205
And with my youthful blood warm their cold flesh,

---

[170] Temperament.
[171] Mistaken.
[172] I.e., Apollo's oracle at Delphi.

Letting them curl themselves about my limbs,
Than sleep one night with thee. This is not feigned,
Nor sounds it like the coyness of a bride.

Amintor

    Is flesh so earthly to endure all this?   210
    Are these the joys of marriage? Hymen, keep
    This story, that will make succeeding youth
    Neglect thy ceremonies,[173] from all ears!
    Let it not rise up for thy shame and mine
    To after ages. We will scorn thy laws   215
    If thou no better bless them. Touch the heart
    Of her that thou hast sent me, or the world
    Shall know there's not an altar that will smoke
    In praise of thee. We will adopt our sons;
    Then virtue shall inherit, and not blood.   220
    If we do lust, we'll take the next we meet,
    Serving ourselves as other creatures do,
    And never take note of the female more,
    Nor of her issue.[174] I do rage in vain.
    She can but jest. O, pardon me my love!   225
    So dear the thoughts are that I hold of thee
    That I must break forth.[175] Satisfy my fear.
    It is a pain beyond the hand of death
    To be in doubt. Confirm it with an oath
    If this be true.

Evadne   Do you invent the form.[176]   230
    Let there be in it all the binding words
    Devils and conjures can put together,

---

[173] Refrain from marrying.
[174] Amintor implies that without marriage, a social ceremony, mankind would be no better than beasts.
[175] Speak out.
[176] "You dictate what that oath shall be."

And I will take it. I have sworn before,
And here by all things holy do again,
Never to be acquainted with thy bed!   235
Is your doubt over now?

Amintor

I know too much! Would I had doubted still!
Was ever such a marriage night as this?
You powers above, if you did ever mean
Man should be used thus, you have thought a way   240
How he may bear himself and save his honour.
Instruct me in it, for to my dull eyes
There is no mean, no moderate course to run.
I must live scorned or be a murderer.
Is there a third? Why is this night so calm?   245
Why does not heaven speak in thunder to us
And drown her voice?

Evadne   This rage will do no good.

Amintor

Evadne, hear me. Thou hast ta'en an oath,
But such a rash one that, to keep it, were
Worse than to swear it. Call it back to thee.   250
Such vows as those never ascend to heaven;[177]
A tear or two will wash it quite away.
Have mercy on my youth, my hopeful youth,
If thou be pitiful, for, without boast,
This land was proud of me. What lady was there   255
That men called fair and virtuous in this isle
That would have shunned my love? It is in thee
To make me hold this worth.[178] O, we vain men
That trust all our reputation
To rest upon the weak and yielding hand   260

---

[177] This is an "unholy" oath, so breaking it is no sin.
[178] It is in Evadne's power to uphold his reputation.

Of feeble woman! But thou art not stone.
Thy flesh is soft, and in thine eyes doth dwell
The spirit of love. Thy heart cannot be hard.
Come, lead me from the bottom of despair
To all the joys thou hast—I know thou wilt—   265
And make me careful lest the sudden change
O'ercome my spirits.

Evadne   When I call back this oath
The pains of hell environ[179] me!

Amintor

I sleep and am too temperate. Come to bed,
Or by those hairs, which, if thou hast a soul   270
Like to thy locks, were threads for kings to wear
About their arms—

Evadne   Why, so perhaps they are.

Amintor

I'll drag thee to my bed, and make thy tongue
Undo this wicked oath, or on thy flesh
I'll print a thousand wounds to let out life!   275

Evadne

I fear thee not. Do what thou dar'st to me!
Every ill-sounding word or threat'ning look
Thou showest to me will be revenged at full.

Amintor

It will not sure, Evadne.

Evadne

Do not you hazard[180] that.   280

Amintor

Ha' ye your champions?

Evadne

Alas, Amintor, think'st thou I forbear

---

[179] Surround.
[180] Run the risk of.

To sleep with thee because I have put on
A maiden's strictness? Look upon these cheeks,
And thou shalt find the hot and rising blood   285
Unapt for such a vow. No, in this heart
There dwells as much desire and as much will
To put that wished act in practice as ever yet
Was known to woman,[181] and they have been shown
Both. But it was the folly of thy youth   290
To think this beauty, to what hand soe'er
It shall be called, shall stoop to any second.[182]
I do enjoy the best, and in that height
Have sworn to stand or die! You guess the man.

Amintor

No, let me know the man that wrongs me so,   295
That I may cut his body into motes[183]
And scatter it before the northern wind.

Evadne

You dare not strike him!

Amintor   Do not wrong me so.
Yes, if his body were a poisonous plant
That it were death to touch, I have a soul   300
Will throw me on him.

Evadne   Why, 'tis the King.

Amintor

The King!

Evadne   What will you do now?

Amintor   'Tis not the King!

---

[181] "I both desire and am resolved to engage in intercourse, as much as any woman ever was."

[182] The falcon, when called, will "stoop" to land on its master's glove. "Second" may refer to both a second master/lover and a second best one.

[183] Little bits.

Evadne
>What did he make this match for, dull Amintor?

Amintor
>Oh, thou hast named a word that wipes away
>All thoughts revengeful. In that sacred name,   305
>The King, there lies a terror. What frail man
>Dares lift his hand against it? Let the gods
>Speak to him when they please, till when let us
>Suffer and wait.[184]

Evadne
>Why should you fill yourself so full of heat[185]   310
>And haste so to my bed? I am no virgin.

Amintor
>What devil hath put it in thy fancy, then,
>To marry me?

Evadne   Alas, I must have one
>To father children,[186] and to bear the name
>Of husband to me, that my sins may be   315
>More honourable.

Amintor   What strange thing am I?

Evadne
>A miserable one, one that myself
>Am sorry for.

Amintor   Why, show it then in this:
>If thou hast pity, though thy love be none,
>Kill me, and all true lovers that shall live   320
>In after ages, crossed in their desires,
>Shall bless thy memory and call thee good,
>Because such mercy in thy heart was found

---

[184] The person of the absolute monarch was seen as inviolate, and only God, his immediate "superior," could strike him down with impunity.
[185] Lustful passion.
[186] To be my children's legal father.

To rid a lingering wretch.[187]

Evadne   I must have one

    To fill thy room again if thou wert dead,   325

    Else, by this night, I would! I pity thee.

Amintor

    These strange and sudden injuries have fallen

    So thick upon me that I lose all sense

    Of what they are. Methinks I am not wronged,

    Nor is it aught, if from the censuring world   330

    I can but hide it. Reputation,

    Thou art a word, no more! But thou hast shown

    An impudence so high that to the world

    I fear thou wilt betray or shame thyself.

Evadne

    To cover shame I took thee. Never fear   335

    That I would blaze myself.[188]

Amintor   Nor let the King

    Know I conceive he wrongs me; then mine honour

    Will thrust me into action. That my flesh[189]

    Could bear with patience, and it is some ease

    To me in these extremes that I know this   340

    Before I touched thee. Else, had all the sins

    Of mankind stood betwixt me and the King,

    I had gone through'em to his heart and thine.

    I have left one desire, 'tis not his crown

    Shall buy me to thy bed, now I resolve   345

    He has dishonoured thee. Give me thy hand.

    Be careful of thy credit, and sin close.[190]

    'Tis all I wish. Upon thy chamber floor

---

[187] "To kill me quickly and spare me much suffering."

[188] Expose myself.

[189] My human frailty.

[190] In great secrecy.

I'll rest tonight, that morning visitors
May think we did as married people use.[191]   350
And prithee, smile upon me when they come
And seem to toy as if thou hadst been pleased
With what we did.

Evadne   Fear not, I will do this.

Amintor

Come, let us practice,[192] and as wantonly
As ever loving bride and bridegroom met,   355
Let's laugh and enter here.

Evadne   I am content.

Amintor

Down all the swellings of my troubled heart!
When we walk thus entwined, let all eyes see
If ever lovers better did agree.   *Exeunt*

Act II, Scene ii

Enter Aspatia, Antiphila, Olympias with a sewing box

Aspatia

Away, you are not sad! Force it no further
Good gods, how well you look! Such a full colour
Young bashful brides put on. Sure you are new-married.

Antiphila

Yes, madam, to your grief.

Aspatia   Alas, poor wenches,
Go learn to love first, learn to lose yourselves,   5
Learn to be flattered, and believe and bless

[191] Usually do.
[192] Carry it out.

The double tongue that did it. Make a faith
Out of the miracles of ancient lovers,
Such as speak truth and died in't.[193] And, like me,
Believe all faithful, and be miserable.   10
Did you ne'er love yet, wenches? Speak, Olympias,
Thou hast an easy temper, fit for stamp.[194]

Olympias
     Never.

Aspatia   Nor you, Antiphila?

Antiphila   Nor I.

Aspatia

Then, my good girls, be more than women wise.
At least, be more than I was, and be sure   15
You credit anything the light gives life to
Before a man.[195] Rather believe the sea
Weeps for the ruined merchant when he roars,
Rather the wind courts but the pregnant[196] sails
When the strong cordage[197] cracks; rather the sun   20
Comes but to kiss the fruit in wealthy autumn
When all falls blasted.[198] If you needs must love,
Forced by ill fate, take to your maiden bosoms
Two dead-cold aspics,[199] and of them make lovers.
They cannot flatter or forswear; one kiss   25
Makes a long peace for all. But man—
O, that beast man! Come, let's be sad, my girls.

[193] Miracles, because in myth and tale these lovers remained true to each other, so unlike Aspatia's contemporary lover.
[194] That easily takes an impression.
[195] Any living being can be trusted more than a man.
[196] Full with wind.
[197] Ropes of the rigging.
[198] Spoiled.
[199] Poisonous snakes.

That downcast of thine eye, Olympias,
Shows a fine sorrow. Mark, Antiphila,
Just such another was the nymph Oenone's,[200]   30
When Paris brought home Helen. Now a tear,
And then thou art a piece[201] expressing fully
The Carthage Queen[202] when from the cold sea rock,
Full with her sorrow, she tied fast her eyes
To the fair Trojan ships, and, having lost them,   35
Just as thine does, down stole a tear. Antiphila,
What would this wench do if she were Aspatia?
Here she would stand, till some more pitying god
Turned her to marble.[203] 'Tis enough, my wench.
Show me the piece of needlework you wrought.   40

Antiphila
    Of Ariadne,[204] madam?

Aspatia   Yes, that piece.
    This should be Theseus. He's[205] a cozening[206] face.
    You meant him for a man?

Antiphila   He was so, madam.

Aspatia
    Why, then 'tis well enough. Never look back.
    You have a full wind and a false heart, Theseus!   45
    Does not the story say his keel was split

---

[200] A nymph married to Paris of Troy, who deserted her for Helen; she committed suicide

[201] A piece of artwork; a representation.

[202] Dido, Queen of Carthage, who was deserted by Aeneas and committed suicide.

[203] Probably Niobe, who was turned to stone after the loss of all her children.

[204] A princess of Crete, who helped Theseus escape from the Labyrinth. She was later abandoned by him.

[205] He has.

[206] Deceiving.

Or his masts spent,[207] or some kind rock or other
Met with his vessel?

Antiphila   Not as I remember.

Aspatia
It should ha' been so. Could the gods know this
And none of all their number raise a storm?   50
But they are all as ill.[208] This false smile
Was well expressed. Just such another caught me.
You shall not go so![209]
Antiphila, in this place work a quicksand,
And over it a shallow smiling water,   55
And his ship plowing it, and then a Fear.[210]
Do that Fear to the life,[211] wench.

Antiphila   'Twill wrong the story.

Aspatia
'Twill make the story, wronged[212] by wanton[213] poets,
Live long and be believed. But where's the lady?

Antiphila
There, madam.

Aspatia   Fie, you have missed it here,   60
Antiphila, you are much mistaken, wench.
These colours are not dull and pale enough
To show a soul so full of misery
As this sad lady was. Do it by me,[214]
Do it again, by me, the lost Aspatia,   65

---

[207] Broken.
[208] The Greek and Roman gods abandoned their share of women.
[209] Follow the legend.
[210] A personification of fear itself.
[211] Realistically.
[212] Told wrongly.
[213] Morally loose (male) poets.
[214] Copy me; make me your model.

And you shall find all true but the wild island.[215]
Suppose I stand upon the sea breach[216] now,
Mine arms thus, and mine hair blown with the wind,
Wild as that desert, and let all about me[217]
Tell that I am forsaken. Do my face,   70
If thou hadst ever feeling of a sorrow,
Thus, thus, Antiphila. Strive to make me look
Like sorrow's monument.[218] And the trees about me,
Let them be dry and leafless; let the rocks
Groan with continual surges; and behind me   75
Make all a desolation. Look, look, wenches,
A miserable life[219] of this poor picture.

Olympias

Dear madam!

Aspatia   I have done. Sit down[220] and let us
Upon that point fix all our eyes, that point there.
Make a dumb silence till you feel a sudden sadness   80
Give us new souls.

Enter Calianax

Calianax

The King may do this, and he may not do it.
My child is wronged, disgraced. Well, how now, hussies,[221]
What, at your ease? Is this a time to sit still?

[215] Deserted, uncivilized island; Aspatia herself is on civilized Rhodes.
[216] Beach; where the waves break.
[217] Everything pertaining to me such as posture, hair, and clothes.
[218] Statue.
[219] Living representation.
[220] "Sitting on the ground" is a posture of extreme mourning.
[221] Forward women; worthless women.

Up, you young lazy whores, up, or I'll swinge[222] you!   85

Olympias

Nay, good my lord—

Calianax

You'll lie down shortly. Get you in and work!

What, are you grown so resty[223] you want heats?[224]

We shall have some of the court boys do that office,

Antiphila

My lord, we do no more than we are charged.[225]   90

It is the lady's pleasure we be thus

In grief; she is forsaken.

Calianax   There's a rogue[226] too,

A young, dissembling slave. Well, get you in!

I'll have a bout with that boy! 'Tis high time

Now to be valiant. I confess my youth   95

Was never prone that way. What, made an ass!

A court-stale![227] Well, I will be valiant

And beat some dozen of these whelps, I will. And there's

Another of 'em, a trim, cheating soldier![228]

I'll maul that rascal! He's out-braved[229] twice!   100

But now, I thank the gods, I'm valiant.

Go, get you in! I'll take a course withall.[230]   *Exeunt*

---

[222] Beat.

[223] Passive.

[224] Heating up (with the beating).

[225] Ordered.

[226] I.e., Amintor.

[227] A worthless courtier, no longer of use.

[228] I.e., Melantius.

[229] Defied. We know from I.i that there is enmity between the two before the play opens.

[230] "I'll make sure things are set right."

Act III, Scene i

Enter Cleon, Strato, Diphilus

Cleon

Your sister is not up yet.

Diphilus

O, brides must take their morning's rest; the night is troublesome.

Strato

But not tedious.

Diphilus

What odds he has not my sister's maidenhead tonight?   5

Strato

None. It's odds against any bridegroom living.[231] He ne'er gets it while he lives.

Diphilus

You're merry with my sister. You'll please to allow me the same freedom with your mother.

Strato

She's at your service.[232]   10

Diphilus

Then she's merry enough of herself, she needs no tickling. Knock at the door.

Strato

We shall interrupt them.

Diphilus

No matter, they have the year before them. Good morrow, sister! Spare yourself today. The night will come again.   15

---

[231] Implying that no brides are virgins.
[232] With a sexual pun.

Enter Amintor

Amintor

    Who's there? My brother?[233] I am no readier yet. Your
    sister is but up now.

Diphilus

    You look as you had lost your eyes[234] tonight. I think you
    ha' not slept.

Amintor

    I'faith, I have not.   20

Diphilus

    You have done better, then.

Amintor

    We ventured for a boy. When he is twelve
    'A[235] shall command against the foes of Rhodes.
    Shall we be merry?

Strato

    You cannot. You want sleep.

Amintor (*aside*)   'Tis true, but she   25

    As if she had drunk Lethe[236] or had made
    Even with heaven[237] did fetch so still a sleep,
    So sweet and sound—

Diphilus   What's that?

Amintor   Your sister frets

    This morning, and doth turn her eyes upon me
    As people on their headsman.[238] She does chafe   30
    And kiss and chafe again and clap[239] my cheeks.

---

[233] Brother-in-law.

[234] They are half closed with lack of sleep.

[235] He.

[236] The river of oblivion in the Underworld.

[237] "Paid her mortal debt"; had died.

[238] Hangman, with a pun on maidenhead.

[239] Slap (gently).

　　　She's in another world.

Diphilus

　　　Then I had lost. I was about to lay

　　　You had not got her maidenhead tonight.

Amintor (*aside*)

　　　Ha! Does he mock me?—(*Aloud*) You'd lost indeed!　　35

　　　I do not use[240] to bungle!

Cleon　　　　　　　　　　　　You do deserve her.

Amintor (*aside*)

　　　I laid my lips to hers, and that wild breath

　　　That was so rude and rough to me last night

　　　Was sweet as April. I'll be guilty too

　　　If these be the effects.[241]　　　　　　　　　　　　40

Enter Melantius

Melantius

　　　Good day, Amintor, for to me the name

　　　Of brother is too distant. We are friends,

　　　And that is nearer.

Amintor　　　　　　　Dear Melantius,

　　　Let me behold thee! Is it possible?　　　　*Embraces him*

Melantius

　　　What sudden gaze[242] is this?

Amintor　　　　　　　　　　'Tis wondrous strange　　45

Melantius

　　　Why does thine eye desire so strict[243] a view

　　　Of that it knows so well? There's nothing here

　　　That is not thine.

[240] I usually do not.

[241] The effects of a guilty conscience is usually sleeplessness.

[242] Studying look.

[243] Penetrating.

Amintor   I wonder much, Melantius,
    To see those noble looks that make me think
    How virtuous thou art, and on the sudden   50
    'Tis strange to me thou shouldst have worth and honour,
    Or not be base and false and treacherous,
    And every ill. But—
Melantius   Stay, stay, my friend.
    I fear this sound will not become our loves.
    No more embrace me.
Amintor   O, mistake me not!   55
    I know thee to be full of all those deeds
    That we frail men call good, but by the course
    Of nature thou shouldst be as quickly changed
    As the winds, dissembling as the sea
    That now wears brows as smooth as virgins' be,   60
    Tempting the merchant to invade his face,
    And in an hour calls his billows up
    And shoots'em at the sun, destroying all
    'A carries on him. (*Aside*) O, how near am I
    To utter my sick thoughts!   65
Melantius
    But why, my friend, should I be so by nature?
Amintor
    I have wed thy sister, who hath virtuous thoughts
    Enough for one whole family, and it is strange
    That you should feel no want.
Melantius   Believe me,
    This is compliment too cunning[244] for me.   70
Diphilus
    What should I be then by the course of nature,
    They having both robbed me of so much virtue?

[244] Too subtly put.

Strato

> O, call the bride, my lord Amintor,
>
> That we may see her blush and turn her eyes down;
>
> It is the prettiest sport.   75

Amintor

> Evadne!

Evadne (*within*)   My lord?

Amintor   Come forth, my love,

> Your brothers do attend to wish you joy.

Evadne (*within*)

> I am not ready yet.

Amintor   Enough, enough.

Evadne (*within*)

> They'll mock me.

Amintor   Faith, thou shalt come in.

Enter Evadne

Melantius

> Good morrow, sister. He that understands   80
>
> Whom you have wed need not to wish you joy;
>
> You have enough. Take heed you be not proud.

Diphilus

> O, sister, what have you done?

Evadne

> I, done? Why, what have I done?

Strato

> My lord Amintor swears you are no maid now.   85

Evadne

> Push![245]

---

[245] An exclamation of contempt.

Strato

    I'faith he does.

Evadne   I knew I should be mocked.

Diphilus

    With a truth.

Evadne   If 'twere to do again,

    In faith, I would not marry.

Amintor (*aside*)   Nor I, by heaven!

Diphilus

    Sister Dula swears she heard you cry two rooms off.   90

Evadne

    Fie, how you talk!

Diphilus

    Let's see you walk, Evadne. By my troth, you're spoiled![246]

Melantius

    Amintor—

Amintor

    Ha?

Melantius

    Thou art sad.   95

Amintor

    Who, I? I thank you for that. Shall Diphilus, thou, and I
    sing a catch?[247]

Melantius

    How?

Amintor

    Prithee, let's.

Melantius

    Nay, that's too much the other way.   100

Amintor

    I am so lightened with my happiness!

---

[246] Ruined; "used hard."

[247] A round for three or more voices.

How dost thou, love? Kiss me.

Evadne

    I cannot love you, you tell tales of me.

Amintor

    Nothing but what becomes us. Gentlemen

    Would you had all such wives, and all the world,   105

    That I might be no wonder. You're all sad.

    What, do you envy me? I walk, methinks,

    On water and ne'er sink, I am so light.

Melantius

    'Tis well you are so.

Amintor

    Well? How can I be other when she looks thus?   110

    Is there no music there? Let's dance.

Melantius

    Why, this is strange, Amintor!

Amintor

    I do not know myself. (*Aside*) Yet I could wish my joy
    were less.

Diphilus

    I'll marry too, if it will make one thus.[248]   115

Evadne (*aside*)

    Amintor, hark!

Amintor

    What says my love? I must obey.

Evadne (*aside*)

    You do it scurvily.[249] 'Twill be perceived.

Cleon

    My lord the King is here!

Enter King and Lysippus

---

[248] I.e., thus happy.
[249] Vilely; contemptibly.

Amintor   Where?

Strato   And his brother.

King

    Good morrow, all!   120

    Amintor, joy on joy fall thick upon thee!

    And madam, you are altered since I saw you,

    I must salute you.[250] You are now another's.

    How liked you your night's rest?

Evadne   Ill, sir.

Amintor

    Indeed she took but little.   125

Lysippus

    You'll let her take more, and thank her too, shortly.[251]

King

    Amintor, wert thou truly honest[252] till thou wert married?

Amintor

    Yes, sir.

King

    Tell me then, how shows the sport unto thee?[253]

Amintor

    Why, well.   130

King

    What did you do?

Amintor

    No more nor less than other couples use.[254]

    You know what 'tis. It has but a coarse name.[255]

[250] Greet, often with a formal kiss.

[251] A husband's interest in sex supposedly waned faster than that of his wife.

[252] Chaste.

[253] How do you like the exercise?

[254] Usually do.

[255] There is no polite way of putting it.

King

> But prithee, I should think by her black eye
> And her red cheek she should be quick and stirring   135
> In this same business, ha?

Amintor   I cannot tell,

> I ne'er tried other, sir. But I perceive
> She is as quick as you delivered.[256]

King

> Well, you'll trust me then, Amintor,
> To choose a wife for you again?

Amintor   No, never, sir.   140

King

> Why? Like you this so ill?

Amintor   So well I like her!

> For this I bow my knee in thanks to you,
> And unto heaven will pay my grateful tribute
> Hourly, and do hope we shall draw out
> A long, contented life together here   145
> And die both full of grey hairs in one day,
> For which the thanks is yours. But if the powers
> That rule us please to call her first away,
> Without pride spoke,[257] this world holds not a wife
> Worthy to take her room.

King (*aside*)   I do not like this!   150

> (*Aloud*) All forbear[258] the room but you, Amintor,
> And your lady. I have some speech with you
> That may concern your after-living well.

> > > > > *Exeunt all but King, Amintor, and Evadne*

Amintor (*aside*)

> 'A will not tell me that he lies with her!

---

[256] As quick a study; as actively engaged.
[257] Stated humbly.
[258] Leave.

If he do, something heavenly stay[259] my heart,   155
For I shall be apt to thrust this arm of mine
To acts unlawful!

King   You will suffer me
To talk with her, Amintor, and not have
A jealous pang?

Amintor   Sir, I dare trust my wife
With whom she dares to talk, and not be jealous.   *Steps aside*

King
How do you like Amintor?

Evadne   As I did, sir.   161

King
How's that?

Evadne
As one that to fulfill your will and pleasure
I have given leave to call me wife and love.

King
I see there is no lasting faith in sin.   165
They that break word[260] with heaven will break again
With all the world, and so dost thou with me.

Evadne
How, sir?

King   This subtle woman's ignorance
Will not excuse you. Thou hast taken oaths,
So great that methought they did misbecome   170
A woman's mouth, that thou wouldst ne'er enjoy
A man but me.

Evadne   I never did swear so,
You do me wrong.

King   Day and night have heard it.

---

[259] Control; support.
[260] A vow.

Evadne

    I swore indeed that I would never love

    A man of lower place, but if your fortune   175

    Should throw you from this height, I bade you trust

    I would forsake you and would bend to him

    That won your throne. I love with my ambition,

    Not with my eyes. But if I ever yet

    Touched any other, leprosy[261] light here   180

    Upon my face, which for your royalty

    I would not stain.

King

    Why, thou dissemblest, and it is in me

    To punish thee.

Evadne   Why, it is in me, then,

    Not to love you, which will more afflict   185

    Your body than your punishment can mine.

King

    But thou hast let Amintor lie with thee.

Evadne

    I ha' not.

King   Impudence! He says himself so.

Evadne

    'A lies.

King   'A does not.

Evadne   By this light, he does

    Strangely and basely, and I'll prove it so!   190

    I did not only shun him for a night,

    But told him I would never close with[262] him.

King

    Speak lower! 'Tis false.

---

[261] Then an incurable disease that eats away at the skin; often used metaphorically about moral corruption.

[262] 1) make love to; 2) (legally) close a contract; consummate.

Evadne   I am no man
    To answer with a blow, or if I were,
    You are the King.[263] But urge[264] not, 'tis most true.   195
King
    Do not I know the uncontrolled thoughts
    That youth brings with him when his blood is high
    With expectation and desire of that
    He long hath waited for? Is not his spirit
    Though he be temperate, of a valiant strain[265]   200
    As this our age hath known? What could he do
    If such a sudden[266] speech had met his blood,
    But ruin thee forever, if he had not killed thee?
    He could not bear it thus. He is as we
    Or any other wronged man.
Evadne   It is dissembling.   205
King
    Take him! Farewell. Henceforth I am thy foe,
    And what disgraces I can blot[267] thee with, look for!
Evadne
    Stay sir! Amintor! You shall hear Amintor.
Amintor (*coming up to them*)
    What, my love?
Evadne
    Amintor, thou hast an ingenious[268] look,   210
    And shouldst be virtuous. It amazeth me
    That thou canst make such base, malicious lies.

---

[263] A subject cannot lay hand upon the Monarch unpunished.
[264] Press.
[265] So valiantly capable of controlling himself.
[266] Surprising.
[267] Stain.
[268] Honest; straightforward.

Amintor

What, my dear wife?

Evadne   Dear wife! I do despise thee.

Why, nothing can be baser than to sow

Dissension amongst lovers.

Amintor   Lovers! Who?   215

Evadne

The King and me—

Amintor   O, God!

Evadne

Who should live long and love without distaste

Were it not for such pickthanks[269] as thyself.

Did you lie with me? Swear now, and be punished

In hell for this!

Amintor   The faithless sin I made   220

To fair Aspatia is not yet revenged,

It follows me. I will not loose a word

To this vile woman, but to you, my King,

The anguish of my soul thrusts out this truth:

You're a tyrant! And not so much to wrong   225

An honest man thus, as to take a pride

In talking with him of it.

Evadne

Now sir, see how loud this fellow lied!

Amintor

You, that can know to wrong, should know how men

Must right themselves. What punishment is due   230

From me to him that shall abuse my bed?

It is not death, nor can that satisfy,

Unless I send your lives[270] through all the land

---

[269] Flattering self-seekers.

[270] Your "biographies," telling of your sinful living.

To show how nobly I have freed myself.[271]

King

    Draw not thy sword, thou know'st I cannot fear   235

    A subject's hand, but thou shalt feel the weight

    Of this[272] if thou doth rage.

Amintor   The weight of that!

    If you have any worth, for heaven's sake think

    I fear not swords, for, as you are mere man,

    I dare as easily kill you for this deed   240

    As you dare think to do it. But there is

    Divinity about you[273] that strikes dead

    My rising passions. As you are my King,

    I fall before you and present my sword

    To cut mine own flesh, if it be your will.   245

    Alas, I am nothing but a multitude

    Of walking griefs! Yet, should I murder you,

    I might before the world take the excuse

    Of madness; for compare my injuries,

    And they will well appear too sad[274] a weight   250

    For reason to endure. But fall I first[275]

    Amongst my sorrows, ere my treacherous hand

    Touch holy things. But why? I know not what

    I have to say. Why did you choose out me

    To make thus wretched? There were thousands, fools   255

    Easy to work on and of state enough

    Within the island.

---

[271] Amintor states that killing such a rival would not be enough to salvage his reputation; defamation must follow. On stage, he would begin to draw his sword.

[272] His sword. The King's sword is the symbol of justice, ironically enough.

[273] Reference to the King's two bodies; see glossary.

[274] Heavy.

[275] May I first fall.

Evadne   I would not have a fool.
    It were no credit for me.
Amintor   Worse and worse!
    Thou, that dar'st talk unto thy husband thus,
    Profess thyself a whore and more than so,   260
    Resolve to be so still! It is my fate
    To bear and bow beneath a thousand griefs
    To keep that little credit with the world.
    But there were wise ones too; you might have ta'en
    Another.
King   No, for I believe thee honest,[276]   265
    As thou wert valiant.
Amintor   All the happiness
    Bestowed upon me turns into disgrace.
    Gods, take your honesty again, for I
    Am loaden[277] with it! Good my lord the King,
    Be private[278] in it.
Amintor   Thou may'st live, Amintor,   270
    Free as thy King, if thou wilt wink at[279] this
    And be a means that we may meet in secret.
Amintor
    A bawd! Hold, hold my breast! A bitter curse
    Seize me, if I forget not all respects
    That are religious, on another word   275
    Sounded like that, and through a sea of sins
    Will wade to my revenge, though I should call
    Pains here, and after life, upon my soul.

[276] Loyal and trustworthy.
[277] Too heavily burdened.
[278] Secretive; discreet.
[279] Close your eyes to.

King

    Well, I am resolute[280] you lay not with her,

    And so I leave you.   *Exit King*

Evadne   You must needs be prating,[281]   280

    And see what follows!

Amintor   Prithee, vex me not,

    Leave me. I am afraid some sudden start[282]

    Will pull a murder on me.

Evadne   I am gone,

    I love my life well.   *Exit Evadne*

Amintor   I hate mine as much.

    This 'tis to break a troth![283] I should be glad   285

    If all this tide of grief would make me mad.   *Exit*

Act III, Scene ii

Enter Melantius

Melantius

    I'll know the cause of all Amintor's griefs.

    Or friendship shall be idle.[284]

Enter Calianax

Calianax   O, Melantius,

    My daughter will die.

---

[280] Convinced.

[281] Babbling.

[282] Irresistible fit of passion.

[283] Marriage contract.

[284] Inactive; worth nothing.

Melantius   Trust me, I am sorry.
    Would thou hadst ta'en her room.[285]
Calianax   Thou art a slave,[286]
    A cut-throat slave, a bloody, treacherous slave!   5
Melantius
    Take heed, old man, thou wilt be heard to rave
    And lose thine office.
Calianax   I am valiant grown
    At all these years, and thou art but a slave.
Melantius
    Leave! Some company will come, and I respect
    Thy years, not thee, so much that I could wish   10
    To laugh at thee alone.
Calianax   I'll spoil your mirth!
    I mean to fight with thee. There lie, my cloak,
    This was my father's sword, and he durst fight.
    Are you prepared?
Melantius   Why? Wilt thou dote thyself
    Out of thy life?[287] Hence, get thee to bed,   15
    Have careful looking to,[288] and eat warm things,
    And trouble not me. My head is full of thoughts
    More weighty than thy life or death can be.
Calianax
    You have a name[289] in war, where you stand safe
    Amongst a multitude, but I will try   20
    What you dare do unto a weak old man
    In single fight. You'll give ground, I fear.
    Come, draw!

[285] Place.

[286] Lowly fellow.

[287] Let your senile behavior kill you.

[288] See that good care is taken of you.

[289] Reputation.

Melantius

> I will not draw, unless thou pull'st thy death
> Upon thee with a stroke. There's no one blow   25
> That thou canst give hath strength enough to kill me.
> Tempt me not so far, then; the power of earth
> Shall not redeem thee.

Calianax (*aside*)   I must let him alone.

> He's stout[290] and able, and, to say the truth,
> However I may set a face[291] and talk,   30
> I am not valiant. When I was a youth
> I kept my credit with a testy[292] trick
> I had 'mongst cowards, but durst never fight.

Melantius

> I will not promise to preserve your life
> If you do stay.

Calianax (*aside*)   I would give half my land   35

> That I durst fight with that proud man a little.
> If I had men to hold him, I would beat him
> Till he asked me mercy.

Melantius   Sir, will you be gone?

Calianax (*aside*)

> I dare not stay, but I will go home and beat
> My servants all over for this.   *Exit Calianax* 40

Melantius

> This old fellow haunts me,
> But the distracted carriage[293] of mine Amintor
> Takes deeply on me.[294] I will find the cause.
> I fear his conscience cries he wronged Aspatia.

[290] Strong.

[291] Put on a brave and fierce face.

[292] Hot-tempered.

[293] Behavior.

[294] Touches me deeply.

Enter Amintor

Amintor (*aside*)

 Men's eyes are not so subtle to perceive   45
 My inward misery. I bear my grief
 Hid from the world. How art thou wretched, then?
 For aught I know, all husbands are like me,
 And everyone I talk with of his wife
 Is but a well dissembler[295] of his woes   50
 As I am. Would I knew it, for the rareness[296]
 Afflicts me now.

Melantius   Amintor, we have not enjoyed
 Our friendship of late, for we were wont to charge[297]
 Our souls in talk.

Amintor

 Melantius, I can tell thee a good jest of Strato and a lady   55
 the last day.

Melantius

 How was't?

Amintor

 Why, such an odd one.

Melantius   I have longed to speak
 With you, not of an idle jest that's forced,[298]
 But of matter you are bound to utter to me.   60

Amintor

 What is that, my friend?

Melantius

 I have observed your words fall from your tongue
 Wildly, and all your carriage

---

[295] A clever disguiser.

[296] The feeling of being alone, the only one in this situation.

[297] Fill to the brim; "load."

[298] Told uncalled for, as a cover-up.

Like one that strove to show his merry mood,
When he were ill disposed. You were not wont   65
To put such scorn into your speech, or wear
Upon your face ridiculous jollity.
Some sadness sits here, which your cunning would
Cover o'er with smiles, and 'twill not be.
What is it?

Amintor   A sadness here? What cause   70
Can Fate provide for me to make me so?
Am I not loved through all this isle? The King
Rains greatness on me. Have I not received
A lady to my bed, that in her eye
Keeps mounting fire, and on her tender cheeks   75
Inevitable[299] colour, in her heart
A prison for all virtue? Are not you
Which is above all joys, my constant friend?
What sadness can I have? No, I am light,[300]
And feel the courses of my blood more warm   80
And stirring than they were. Faith, marry too,
And you will feel so unexpressed[301] a joy
In chaste embraces[302] that you will indeed
Appear another.[303]

Melantius   You may shape, Amintor,
Causes[304] to cozen[305] the whole world withal,   85
And yourself too, but 'tis not like a friend
To hide your soul from me. 'Tis not your nature

---

[299] Constant.

[300] I.e., light of heart.

[301] Impossible to put in to words, inexpressible.

[302] Sexual intercourse without sin, because sanctified by marriage.

[303] Seem to be a different man.

[304] Reasons.

[305] Deceive.

To be thus idle.[306] I have seen you stand
As you were blasted[307] 'midst of all your mirth,
Call thrice aloud, and then start, feigning joy   90
So coldly. World, what do I here? A friend
Is nothing. Heaven! I would have told that man[308]
My secret sins! I'll search an unknown land
And there plant friendship; all is withered here.
Come with a compliment! I would have fought   95
Or told my friend 'a lied ere soothed him so.
Out of my bosom!

Amintor

But there is nothing.

Melantius   Worse and worse! Farewell!
From this time have acquaintance, but no friend.

Amintor

Melantius, stay, you shall know what that is.   100

Melantius

See how you played with[309] friendship! Be advised
How you give cause unto yourself to say
You've lost a friend.

Amintor   Forgive what I have done,
For I am so o'ergone[310] with injuries
Unheard of, that I lose consideration[311]   105
Of what I ought to do. O! O!

Melantius

Do not weep. What is't? May I once but know the man
Hath turned my friend thus.

---

[306] Playful; without purpose.

[307] Struck by lightning.

[308] The Amintor that was.

[309] 1) Treated lightly; 2) gambled.

[310] Overwhelmed.

[311] My judgment; my power of reasoning.

Amintor   I had spoke at first
     But that—
Melantius   But what?
Amintor   I held it most unfit
     For you to know. Faith, do not know it yet.   110
Melantius

     Thou seest my love, that will keep company
     With thee in tears. Hide nothing then from me,
     For when I know the cause of thy distemper,
     With mine old armour I'll adorn myself,
     My resolution, and cut through thy foes   115
     Unto thy quiet,[312] till I place thy heart
     As peaceable as spotless innocence.
     What is it?
Amintor   Why, 'tis this—It is too big
     To get out. Let my tears make way[313] awhile.
Melantius

     Punish me strangely, heaven, if he 'scape   120
     Of life or fame[314] that brought this youth to this!
Amintor

     Your sister—
Melantius   Well said.
Amintor   You'll wish't unknown
     When you have heard it.
Melantius   No.
Amintor   Is much to blame,
     And to the King has given her honour up,
     And lives in whoredom with him.
Melantius   How's this?   125
     Thou art run mad with injury indeed,

---

[312] For your peace of mind.
[313] I.e., make a way for the confession to come forth.
[314] If he gets away with life or reputation intact.

Thou couldst not utter this else. Speak again,
For I forgive it freely. Tell thy griefs.

Amintor

She's wanton. I am loath to say a whore,
Though it be true.   130

Melantius

Speak yet again, before mine anger grow
Up beyond throwing down. What are thy griefs?

Amintor

By all our friendship, these.

Melantius   What, am I tame?
After mine actions[315] shall the name of friend
Blot[316] all our family and strike the brand[317]   135
Of whore upon my sister unrevenged?
My shaking flesh, be thou a witness for me
With what unwillingness I go to scourge
This railer, whom my folly hath called friend!
I will not take thee basely[318] (*he draws his sword*).   140
                                    Thy sword
Hangs near thy hand. Draw it, that I may whip
Thy rashness to repentance. Draw thy sword!

Amintor

Not on thee, did thine anger go as high
As troubled waters. Thou shouldst do me ease
Here and eternally,[319] if thy noble hand   145
Would cut me from my sorrows.

Melantius   This is base

---

[315] My heroic acts in battle.

[316] Stain.

[317] Mark from a branding iron.

[318] Like a coward.

[319] Being killed by Melantius is better than the suicide that will damn Amintor to hell.

And fearful. They that use to utter lies
Provide not blows but words to qualify[320]
The men they wronged. Thou hast a guilty cause.

Amintor

 Thou pleasest me, for so much more like this[321]   150
 Will raise my anger up above my griefs,
 Which is a passion easier to be borne,
 And I shall then be happy.

Melantius   Take, then, more
 To raise thine anger. 'Tis mere cowardice
 Makes thee not draw, and I will leave thee dead   155
 However. But if thou art so much pressed
 With guilt and fear as not to dare to fight,
 I'll make thy memory loathed and fix a scandal
 Upon thy name forever.

Amintor (*drawing his sword*) Then I draw,
 As justly as our magistrates their swords   160
 To cut offenders off.[322] I knew before
 'Twould grate your ears, but it was base in you
 To urge a weighty secret from your friend
 And then rage at it. I shall be at ease
 If I be killed, and if you fall by me,   165
 I shall not long outlive you.

Melantius   Stay awhile!
 The name of friend is more than family,
 Or all the world besides. I was a fool,
 Thou searching[323] human nature, that didst wake
 To do me wrong, thou art inquisitive,   170
 And thrusts me upon questions that will take

[320] Make peace with.
[321] Of this kind of talk.
[322] Sentence to execution.
[323] Curious.

My sleep away. Would I had died ere known
This sad dishonour! Pardon me, my friend. *Sheathes his sword*
If thou wilt strike, here is a faithful heart;
Pierce it, for I will never heave my hand   175
To thine. Behold the power thou hast in me.
I do believe my sister is a whore,
A leprous one. Put up thy sword, young man.

Amintor

How should I bear it then, she being so?
I fear, my friend, that you will lose me shortly   180
And I shall do a foul act on myself
Through these disgraces.

Melantius   Better half the land
Were buried quick[324] together. No, Amintor,
Thou shalt have ease. O, this adulterous King
That drew her to't! Where got he the spirit   185
To wrong me so?

Amintor   What is it then to me,
If it be wrong to you?

Melantius   Why, not so much.
The credit of our house[325] is thrown away.
But from his iron den I'll waken Death
And hurl him on this King. My honesty   190
Shall steel my sword, and on my horrid[326] point
I'll wear my cause, that shall amaze the eyes
Of this proud man and be too glittering
For him to look on.

Amintor   I have quite undone my fame.

Melantius

Dry up thy watery eyes   195

---

[324] Alive.
[325] Our family honor.
[326] Horrible.

And cast a manly look upon my face,
For nothing is so wild as I thy friend
Till I have freed thee. Still this swelling breast![327]
I go thus from thee, and will never cease
My vengeance till I find thy heart at peace.   200

Amintor

It must not be so. Stay. Mine eyes would tell
How loath I am to this, but love and tears
Leave me awhile, for I have hazarded
All that this world calls happy. Thou hast wrought
A secret from me under name of friend,   205
Which art could ne'er have found, nor torture wrung
From out my bosom. Give it me again,
For I will find it wheresoe'er it lies,
Hid in the mortal'st part. Invent a way
To give it back.

Melantius   Why would you have it back?   210
I will to death pursue him with revenge.

Amintor

Therefore I call it back from thee, for I know
Thy blood[328] so high that thou wilt stir[329] in this
And shame me to posterity. Take thy weapon.

Melantius

Hear thy friend that bears more years than thou.   215

Amintor

I will not hear, but draw, or I—

Melantius   Amintor!

Amintor

Draw then, for I am full as resolute
As fame and honour can enforce me be.

---

[327] Amintor's chest is still heaving with weeping.
[328] Temper.
[329] Act.

I cannot linger. Draw!

Melantius (*drawing*)   I do. But is not

 My share of credit equal with thine   220

 If I do stir?

Amintor   No, for it will be called

 Honour in thee to spill thy sister's blood

 If she her birth[330] abuse, and on the King

 A brave revenge; but on me that have walked

 With patience in it, it will fix the name   225

 Of fearful cuckold. O, that word! Be quick.

Melantius

 Then join with me.

Amintor

 I dare not do a sin, or else I would be speedy.

Melantius

 Then dare not fight with me, for that's a sin.   229

 (*Aside*) His grief distracts him. (*Aloud*) Call thy thoughts again,

 And to thyself pronounce the name of friend

 And see what that will work. I will not fight.

Amintor

 You must!

Melantius   I will be killed first. Though my passions

 Offered the like to you, 'tis not this earth

 Shall buy my reason to it. Think awhile,   235

 For you are—I must weep when I speak it—

 Almost besides yourself.

Amintor   O, my soft temper!

 So many sweet words from thy sister's mouth

 I am afraid would make me take her

 To embrace and pardon her. I am mad indeed,   240

 And know not what I do. Yet have a care

 Of me in what thou dost.

[330] Her birth-given status, thus her family's honor.

Melantius   Why, thinks my friend

    I will forget his honour, or to save

    The bravery[331] of our house will lose his fame[332]

    And fear to touch the throne of majesty?   245

Amintor

    A curse will follow that; but rather live

    And suffer with me.

Melantius   I will do what worth[333]

    Shall bid me, and no more.

Amintor   Faith, I am sick,

    And desperately, I hope. Yet, leaning thus,

    I feel a kind of ease.

Melantius   Come, take again   250

    Your mirth[334] about you.

Amintor   I shall never do't.

Melantius

    I warrant you. Look up! We'll walk together.

    Put thine arm here. All shall be well again.

Amintor

    Thy love—O wretched!—Ay, thy love, Melantius,

    Why, I have nothing else.

Melantius   Be merry then. *Exeunt*[335] 255

Enter Melantius again

---

[331] Splendid honor.

[332] Reputation.

[333] What is worthy and honorable.

[334] The organ associated with both mirth and anger is the spleen. See glossary under "the four humors."

[335] There are no stage directions for sheathing and unsheathing swords. If the friends exit with a drawn sword in the hand not embracing, they present a picture of united revenge to come.

Melantius

>This worthy young man may do violence
>Upon himself, but I have cherished[336] him
>As well as I could, and sent him smiling from me
>To counterfeit again. Sword, hold thine edge!
>My heart will never fail me!

Enter Diphilus

>   Diphilus!   260
>Thou com'st as sent!

Diphilus   Yonder has been such laughing,

Melantius

>Betwixt whom?

Diphilus   Why, our sister and the King.

>I thought their spleens[337] would break, they laughed us all
>Out of the room.

Melantius   They must weep, Diphilus.

Diphilus

>Must they?

Melantius   They must!   265

>Thou art my brother, and if I did believe
>Thou hadst a base thought, I would rip it out,
>Lie where it durst.

Diphilus   You should not; I would first

>Mangle myself and find it.

Melantius   That was spoke

>According to our strain.[338] Come, join thy hands to mine, 270
>And swear a firmness to what project I
>Shall lay before thee.

---

[336] Comforted.

[337] See note 334 above.

[338] As our family would behave.

Diphilus   You do wrong us both.

    People hereafter shall not say there passed

    A bond more than our loves to tie our lives

    And deaths together.   275

Melantius

    It is as nobly said as I would wish.

    Anon I'll tell you wonders. We are wronged.

Diphilus

    But I will tell you now, we'll right ourselves!

Melantius

    Stay not. Prepare the armour in my house,

    And what friends you can draw unto our side,   280

    Not knowing of the cause, make ready too.

    Haste, Diphilus, the time requires it. Haste!   *Exit Diphilus*

    I hope my cause is just. I know my blood

    Tells me it is, and I will credit it.

    To take revenge and lose myself withal   285

    Were idle,[339] and to 'scape impossible

    Without I had the fort,[340] which—misery!—

    Remaining in the hands of my old enemy,

    Calianax. But I must have it.

Enter Calianax

                    See

    Where he comes shaking[341] by me. Good my lord,   290

    Forget your spleen[342] to me. I never wronged you,

    But would have peace with every man.

Calianax   'Tis well.

---

[339] Foolish.

[340] Fortified building; castle.

[341] Moving like a very old man.

[342] See note 334 above.

  If I durst fight, your tongue would lie at quiet.

Melantius

  You're touchy without all cause.

Calianax   Do! Mock me!

Melantius

  By mine honour, I speak truth.

Calianax   Honour? Where is't? 295

Melantius

  See what starts[343] you make into your idle

  Hatred to my love and freedom[344] to you.

  I come with resolution to obtain

  A suit of you.

Calianax   A suit of me?

  'T'is very like it should be granted, sir!   300

Melantius

  Nay, go not hence!

  'Tis this: you have the keeping of the fort,

  And I would wish you, by the love you ought

  To bear unto me, to deliver it

  Into my hands.

Calianax   I am in hope thou art mad 305

  To talk to me thus.

Melantius   But there is a reason

  To move you to it. I would kill the King

  That wronged you and your daughter.

Calianax

  Out, traitor!

Melantius   Nay, but stay!

  I cannot 'scape the deed once done, without 310

  I have this fort.

Calianax   And should I help thee?

---

[343] Fits.

[344] Openness.

Now thy treacherous mind betrays itself.

Melantius

    Come, delay me not!

    Give me a sudden answer, or already

    Thy last is spoke! Refuse not offered love   315

    When it comes clad in secrets.

Calianax (*aside*)   If I say

    I will not, he will kill me, I do see't

    Writ in his looks. And should I say I will,

    He'll run and tell the King. (*Aloud*) I do not shun

    Your friendship, dear Melantius, but this cause   320

    Is weighty. Give me but an hour to think.

Melantius

    Take it. (*Aside*) I know this goes unto the King,

    But I am armed.   *Exit Melantius*

Calianax   Methinks I feel myself

    But twenty now again. This fighting fool

    Wants policy.[345] I shall revenge my girl   325

    And make her red[346] again. I pray my legs

    Will last that pace that I will carry them.

    I shall want breath before I find the King.   *Exit*

---

[345] Lacks statecraft.

[346] Give her her color back; make her look healthy.

Act IV, Scene i

Enter Melantius, Evadne, and Ladies

Melantius

　　God save you!

Evadne　　　　　　Save you, sweet brother!

Melantius

　　In my blunt eye, methinks, you look[347] Evadne—

Evadne

　　Come, you would make me blush.

Melantius　　　　　　　　　　I would, Evadne,

　　I shall displease my ends else.

Evadne

　　You shall if you commend me. I am bashful.　　　　　5

　　Come, sir, how do I look?

Melantius

　　I would not have your women hear me break

　　Into commendations of you; 'tis not seemly.

Evadne

　　Go wait me[348] in the gallery.[349]　　　　　*Exeunt Ladies*

　　　　　　　　　Now speak.

Melantius

　　I'll lock the door first.

Evadne　　　　　　Why?

Melantius　　　　　　　　　I will not have　　　　　10

　　Your gilded things,[350] that dance in visitation

　　With their Milan skins[351] choke up my business.

---

[347] Look like (but, as he knows, she is not what she seems).

[348] Wait for me.

[349] Hallway-like room with chamber doors opening into it along its length.

[350] Dressed-up women-in-waiting and/or courtiers; frivolous creatures.

[351] Gloves. Milan was famous for the quality of its leather goods.

Evadne

    You are strangely disposed, sir.

Melantius

    Good madam, not to make you merry.

Evadne

    No, if you praise me 'twill make me sad.   15

Melantius

    Such a sad commendation I have for you.

Evadne

    Brother, the court has made you witty

    And learn to riddle.[352]

Melantius

    I praise the court for't. Has it learned you nothing?

Evadne

    Me?   20

Melantius

    Ay, Evadne. Thou art young and handsome,

    A lady of a sweet complexion

    And such a flowing carriage[353] that it cannot

    Choose but inflame a kingdom.

Evadne   Gentle brother—

Melantius

    'Tis yet in thy repentance, foolish woman,   25

    To make me gentle.

Evadne   How is this?

Melantius   'Tis base,

    And I could blush at these years,[354] through all

    My honoured scars, to come to such a parley.[355]

---

[352] To speak in riddles; to circumlocute.

[353] Graceful way of carrying yourself.

[354] "At my age."

[355] Melantius sees the confrontation with Evadne in military terms.

Evadne

 I understand ye not.

Melantius   You dare not, fool!

 They that commit thy faults fly the remembrance.   30

Evadne

 My faults, sir? I would have you know I care not

 If they were written here, here in my forehead.[356]

Melantius

 Thy body is too little for the story,

 The lusts of which would fill another woman,

 Though she had twins within her.[357]

Evadne   This is saucy.   35

 Look you intrude no more. There lies your way.

Melantius

 Thou art my way, and I will tread upon thee

 Till I find truth out.

Evadne   What truth is that you look for?

Melantius

 Thy long-lost honour. Would the gods had set me

 Rather to grapple with the plague, or stand   40

 One of their loudest bolts![358] Come, tell me quickly.

 Do it without enforcement,[359] and take heed

 You swell me not above my temper.

Evadne   How, sir!

 Where got you this report?

Melantius   Where there was people,

 In every place.

---

[356] See glossary.

[357] Her forehead, according to Melantius, would be much to small too describe her crime. There is need for a surface as large as that of the belly of a woman carrying twins.

[358] Stand up against a loud thunderbolt.

[359] Without my forcing you.

Evadne　　　　　　　　They and the seconds of it [360]　　　　45
　　Are base people. Believe them not! They lied!
Melantius (*seizes her*)
　　Do not play with mine anger, do not, wretch!
　　I come to know that desperate fool that drew thee
　　From thy fair[361] life. Be wise and lay him open![362]
Evadne
　　Unhand me, and learn manners! Such another　　　　50
　　Forgetfulness[363] forfeits your life.
Melantius
　　Quench me this mighty humour,[364] and then tell me
　　Whose whore you are, for you are one, I know it.
　　Let all mine honours perish but I'll find him,
　　Though he lie locked up in thy blood.[365] Be sudden!　　55
　　There is no facing[366] it. And be not flattered.
　　The burnt air when the Dog[367] reigns is not fouler
　　Than thy contagious name, till thy repentance,
　　If the gods grant thee any, purge thy sickness.
Evadne
　　Be gone! You are my brother, that's your safety.　　60
Melantius
　　I'll be a wolf[368] first. 'Tis, to be thy brother,
　　An infamy below the sin of coward.

---

[360] Those who repeat.

[361] Clean; honorable.

[362] Expose him.

[363] Disrespect

[364] 1) Help me govern my temper; 2) an exhortation for Evadne to govern her pride.

[365] "Even though I have to wound you to make you tell."

[366] Outfacing.

[367] Sirius, the Dog Star, reigns over the dog-days, July and August, the hottest part of the year.

[368] Banished outlaw.

I am as far from being part of thee
As thou art from thy virtue. Seek a kindred
'Mongst sensual beasts,[369] and make a goat[370] thy brother,
A goat is cooler.[371] Will you tell me yet?   66

Evadne

If you stay here and rail thus, I shall tell you
I'll ha' you whipped. Get you to your command
And there preach to your sentinels, and tell them
What a brave man you are. I shall laugh at you.   70

Melantius

You're grown a glorious whore! Where be your fighters?[372]
What mortal fool durst raise thee to this daring,
And I alive? By my just sword, he'd safer
Bestrid a billow when the angry North[373]
Plows up the sea, or make heaven's fire[374] his foe!   75
Work me no higher.[375] Will you discover yet?

Evadne

The fellow's mad. Sleep, and speak sense.

Melantius

Force my swollen heart no further. I would save thee.
Your great maintainers[376] are not here, they dare not.
Would they were all, and armed, I would speak loud!   80
Here's one should thunder to'em! Will you tell me?
Thou hast no hope to 'scape? He that dares most,

---

[369] Animals, not having the human power of reason, were seen as governed by their senses.

[370] Goats were used as symbols of lechery.

[371] I.e., less sexually "hot" than Evadne.

[372] Men hired to protect a prostitute.

[373] The north wind.

[374] 1) Lightning; or 2) the sun.

[375] "Provoke my anger no further."

[376] Those who support her in her sinful life.

And damns away his soul to do thee service,[377]
Will sooner snatch meat from a hungry lion
Than come to rescue thee. Thou hast death about thee.   85
He's undone thine honour, poisoned thy virtue,
And of a lovely rose left thee a canker.[378]

Evadne

Let me consider.

Melantius   Do, whose child thou wert.
Whose honour thou hast murdered, whose grave opened,
And so pulled on[379] the gods, that in their justice   90
They must restore him flesh again, and life,
And raise his dry bones to revenge this scandal.

Evadne

The gods are not of my mind. They had better
Let'em lie sweet still in the earth; they'll stink here.

Melantius

Do you raise mirth out of my easiness?[380]   95
Forsake me then, all weaknesses of nature,
That make men women!   *He draws his sword*
                              Speak, you whore, speak truth,
Or by the dear soul of thy sleeping father
This sword shall be thy lover! Tell or I'll kill thee!
And when thou hast told all, thou wilt deserve it!   100

Evadne

You will not murder me!

Melantius

No, 'tis a justice, and a noble one,
To put the light[381] out of such base offenders.

---

[377] Sexual attentions.
[378] Growth, like a cancer.
[379] Provoked.
[380] "Do you think you can joke, just because I am gentle?"
[381] Spark of life.

Evadne

   Help!

Melantius

   By thy foul self, no human help shall help thee   105

   If thou criest. When I have killed thee, as I

   Have vowed to do if thou confess not, naked

   As thou hast left thine honour will I leave thee,

   That on thy branded flesh the world may read

   Thy black shame and my justice. Wilt thou bend yet?   110

Evadne

   Yes.   *She kneels*

Melantius   Up, and begin your story.

Evadne   O, I

   Am miserable.

Melantius   'Tis true thou art. Speak truth still.

Evadne

   I have offended. Noble sir, forgive me.

Melantius

   With what secure[382] slave?

Evadne   Do not ask me, sir.

   Mine own remembrance is a misery   115

   Too mighty for me.

Melantius   Do not fall back again,

   My sword's unsheathed yet.

Evadne   What shall I do?

Melantius

   Be true, and make your fault less.

Evadne   I dare not tell.

Melantius

   Tell, or I'll be this day a-killing thee.

Evadne

   Will you forgive me then?   120

---

[382] Self-assured.

Melantius

> Stay. I must ask mine honour first.
> I have too much foolish nature[383] in me. Speak.

>> *He sheathes his sword*

Evadne

> Is there none else here?

Melantius

> None but a fearful conscience; that's too many.
> Who is't?

Evadne   O, hear me gently. It was the King.   125

Melantius

> No more. My worthy father's and my services
> Are liberally rewarded! King, I thank thee!
> For all my dangers and my wounds thou hast paid me
> In my own metal. These are soldiers' thanks!
> How long have you lived thus, Evadne?

Evadne   Too long.   130

Melantius

> Too late you find it. Can you be sorry?

Evadne

> Would I were half as blameless.

Melantius

Evadne,

> Thou wilt to thy trade again.

Evadne   First to my grave.

Melantius

> Would gods thou hadst been so blest!
> Dost thou not hate this King now? Prithee, hate him.   135
> Couldst thou not curse him? I command thee, curse him!
> Curse till the gods hear and deliver him
> To thy just wishes. Yet I fear, Evadne,

---

[383] Natural, brotherly love, which makes him imprudent, wanting to forgive her.

You had rather play your game out.[384]

Evadne   No, I feel

Too many sad confusions here to let in   140

Any loose flame hereafter.

Melantius   Dost thou

Not feel, amongst all those, one brave anger

That breaks out nobly and directs thine arm

To kill this base King?

Evadne   All the gods forbid it!

Melantius

No, all the gods require it. They are   145

Dishonoured in him.

Evadne   'Tis too fearful.

Melantius

You're valiant in his bed, and bold enough

To be a stale whore, and have your madam's name

Discourse for grooms and pages, and hereafter,

When his cool majesty[385] hath laid you by   150

To be at pension with some needy sir

For meat and coarser clothes. Thus far you knew

No fear. Come, you shall kill him.

Evadne   Good sir!

Melantius

And 'twere to kiss him dead,[386] thou'dst[387] smother him.

Be wise and kill him. Canst thou live and know   155

What noble minds shall make thee see thyself,

Found out with every finger,[388] made the shame

Of all successions,[389] and in this great ruin

---

[384] Continue till the game is done; continue in her old ways.

[385] When the King's passion is cooled, is sated.

[386] Kill him with kisses.

[387] = Thou wouldst.

[388] Pointed at by all.

[389] Coming generations.

Thy brother and thy noble husband broken?
Thou shalt not live thus. Kneel and swear to help me   160
When I shall call thee to it, or by all
Holy in heaven and earth, thou shalt not live
To breathe a full hour longer, not a thought!
Come, 'tis a righteous oath. Give me thy hand,
And, both to heaven held up, swear by that wealth[390]   165
This lustful thief stole from thee, when I say it
To let his foul soul out.

Evadne   Here I swear it,
And all you spirits of abused ladies
Help me in this performance!

Melantius
Enough. This must be known to none   170
But you and I, Evadne, not to your lord,
Though he be wise and noble, and a fellow
Dares step as far into a worthy action
As the most daring, ay, as far as justice.
Ask me not why. Farewell.   *Exit Melantius* 175

Evadne
Would I could say so to my black disgrace.
Gods, where have I been all this time? How friended,
That I should lose myself thus desperately,
And none for pity show me how I wandered?[391]
There is not in the compass of the light   180
A more unhappy creature. Sure I am monstrous,
For I have done those follies, those mad mischiefs,
Would dare[392] a woman. O, my loaden soul,

Enter Amintor

[390] The jewel of her virginity.
[391] Strayed from the path of morality.
[392] Frighten.

Be not so cruel to me, choke not up
The way to my repentance. O, my lord.   185

Amintor

How now?

Evadne   My much abused lord.

Amintor   This cannot be!

Evadne   *She kneels*

I do not kneel to live. I dare not hope it,
The wrongs I did are greater. Look upon me,
Though I appear with all my faults.

Amintor   Stand up.

This is a new way to beget more sorrows,   190
Heaven knows I have too many. Do not mock me.
Though I am tame and bred up with my wrongs,
Which are my foster brothers, I may leap
Like the hand-wolf[393] into my natural wildness
And do an outrage. Prithee, do not mock me.   195

Evadne

My whole life is so leprous it infects
All my repentance. I would buy your pardon
Though at the highest set,[394] even with my life.
That slight contrition, that's no sacrifice
For what I have committed.

Amintor   Sure, I dazzle.[395]   200

There cannot be a faith in that foul woman
That knows no god more mighty than her mischiefs.
Thou dost still worse, still number on[396] thy faults,
To press my poor heart thus. Can I believe
There's any seed of virtue in that woman   205

---

[393] Tamed wolf.
[394] Though the price is set as high as possible.
[395] "I am confused."
[396] Add to.

Left to shoot up, that dares go on in sin
Known, and so known as thine is? O, Evadne,
Would there were any safety in [397] thy sex,
That I might put a thousand sorrows off
And credit thy repentance. But I must not.   210
Thou hast brought me to that dull calamity,
To that strange misbelief of all the world
And all things that are in it, that I fear
I shall fall like a tree and find my grave,
Only remembering that I grieve.

Evadne   My lord,   215
Give me your griefs. You are an innocent,
A soul as white as heaven. Let not my sins
Perish your noble youth. I do not fall here
To shadow[398] by dissembling with my tears,
As all say women can, or to make less   220
What my hot will[399] hath done, which heaven and you
Knows to be tougher than the hand of time
Can cut from man's remembrance. No, I do not.
I do appear the same, the same Evadne,
Dressed in the shames I lived in, the same monster.   225
But these are names of honour to what I am.
I do present myself the foulest creature,
Most poisonous, dangerous, and despised of men
Lerna[400] e'er bred or Nilus.[401] I am hell,
Till you, my dear lord, shoot your light into me   230

---

[397] Trusting.

[398] Hide.

[399] Obstinate lust.

[400] A Lake in Greece that bred the Lernean Hydra, a many-headed monster slain by Hercules as one of his labors.

[401] God of the River Nile, on the banks of which crocodiles were thought to spontaneously generate out of the mud.

The beams of your forgiveness. I am soul-sick,
And wither with the fear of one condemned,
Till I have got your pardon.

Amintor   Rise, Evadne.

Those heavenly powers that put this good into thee
Grant a continuance of it. I forgive thee.   235
Make thyself worthy of it, and take heed,
Take heed, Evadne, this be serious.
Mock not the powers above that can, and dare,
Give thee a great example of their justice
To all ensuing eyes, if thou play'st   240
With thy repentance, the best sacrifice.

Evadne

I have done nothing good to win belief,
My life hath been so faithless. All the creatures
Made for heaven's honours have their ends, and good ones,
All but the cozening crocodiles,[402] false women.   245
They reign here like those plagues, those killing sores
Men pray against, and when they die, like tales
Ill told and unbelieved, they pass away
And go to dust forgotten. But, my lord,
Those short days I shall number to my rest,[403]   250
As many[404] must not see me, shall, though too late,
Though in my evening, yet perceive a will,
Since I can do no good because a woman,
Reach constantly at something that is near it.
I will redeem one minute of my age   255
Or like another Niobe[405] I'll weep

---

[402] Deceiving crocodiles, which supposedly can weep on demand to pretend grief. Evadne likens false women to crocodiles.

[403] Death.

[404] I.e., many days.

[405] The emblem of grief. Her pride offended the gods, who killed her children as punishment; even when changed to stone she was still weeping.

       Till I am water.

Amintor   I am now dissolved,

    My frozen soul melts. May each sin thou hast

    Find a new mercy. Rise, I am at peace.

    Hadst thou been thus, thus excellently good   260

    Before that devil King tempted thy frailty,

    Sure thou hadst made a star.[406] Give me thy hand.

    From this time I will know thee, and as far

    As honour gives me leave, be thy Amintor.

    When we meet next, I will salute[407] thee fairly,   265

    And pray the gods to give thee happy days.

    My charity shall go along with thee,

    Though my embraces must be far from thee.

    I should ha' killed thee, but this sweet repentance

    Locks up my vengeance, for which, thus I kiss thee,   270

    The last kiss we must take; and would to heaven

    The holy priest that gave our hands together

    Had given us equal virtues! Go, Evadne,

    The gods thus part our bodies. Have a care

    My honour falls no further. I am well then.   275

Evadne

    All the dear joys here, and above hereafter,

    Crown thy fair soul! Thus I take leave, my lord,

    And never shall you see the foul Evadne

    Till she have tried all honoured means that may

    Set her in rest and wash her stains away.   *Exeunt* 280

---

[406] Been taken into heaven as a star like heroes and heroines before her.
[407] Greet with a kiss.

Act IV, Scene ii

Hautboys play within. A banquet is set out. Enter the King and Calianax

King

 I cannot tell how I should credit this

 From you that are his enemy.

Calianax   I am sure

 He said it to me, and I'll justify it

 What way he dares oppose, but with my sword.

King

 But did he break[408] without all circumstance   5

 To you, his foe, that he would have the fort

 To kill me, and then 'scape?

Calianax   If he deny it

 I'll make him blush.

King   It sounds incredibly.

Calianax

 Ay, so does everything I say of late.

King

 Not so, Calianax.

Calianax   Yes, I should sit   10

 Mute whilst a rogue with strong arms cuts your throat.

King

 Well, I will try him, and if this be true,

 I'll pawn[409] my life I'll find it. If't be false,

 And that you clothe your hate in such a lie,

 You shall hereafter dote in your own house,   15

 Not in the court.

Calianax   Why, if it be a lie

---

[408] Disclose.
[409] Bet.

Mine ears are false, for I'll be sworn I heard it.
Old men are good for nothing; you were best
Put me to death for hearing, and free him
For meaning it. You would ha' trusted me   20
Once, but the time is altered.

King   And will still
Where I may do with justice to the world.
You have no witness.

Calianax   Yes, myself.

King   No more,
I mean, there were that heard it.

Calianax   How no more?
Would you have more? Why, am not I enough   25
To hang a thousand rogues?

King   But so you may
Hang honest men too, if you please.

Calianax   I may.
'Tis like I will do so. There are a hundred
Will swear it for a need too, if I say it.

King
Such witnesses we need not.

Calianax   And 'tis hard   30
If my word cannot hang a boisterous knave.

King
Enough. Where's Strato?

Enter Strato

Strato
Sir?

King
Why, where's all the company? Call Amintor in,
Evadne. Where's my brother and Melantius?   35
Bid him come too, and Diphilus. Call all

That are without there. *Exit Strato*

      If he should desire

The combat of you,[410] 'tis not in the power

Of all our laws to hinder it, unless

We mean to quit'em.[411]

Calianax   Why, if you do think   40

 'Tis fit an old man, and a councilor,

 To fight for what he says, then you may grant it.

Enter Amintor, Evadne, Melantius, Diphilus, Lysippus, Cleon, Strato, and Diagoras

King

 Come, sirs. Amintor, thou art yet a bridegroom,

 And I will use thee so; thou shalt sit down.

 Evadne, sit, and you, Amintor, too.   45

 This banquet is for you, sir. Who has brought

 A merry tale about him to raise laughter

 Amongst our wine? Why, Strato, where art thou?

 Thou wilt chop out[412] with them unseasonably

 When I desire'em not.   50

Strato

 'Tis my ill luck, sir, so to spend them, then.

King

 Reach me a bowl of wine, Melantius.

        (To Amintor) Thou art sad.

Amintor

 I should be, sir, the merriest here,

 But I ha' ne'er a story of mine own

 Worth telling at this time.

[410] Should challenge you to a duel.

[411] Abandon them.

[412] Blurt out.

King   Give me the wine.   55
    Melantius, I am now considering
    How easy 'twere for any man we trust
    To poison one of us in such a bowl.

Melantius
    I think it were not hard, sir, for a knave.

Calianax
    Such as you are.   60

King
    I'faith, 'twere easy. It becomes us well
    To get plain-dealing men about ourselves,
    Such as you all are here. Amintor, to thee
    And to thy fair Evadne.   *Drinks*

Melantius (*aside*)   Have you thought
    Of this, Calianax?

Calianax   Yes, marry,[413] have I.   65

Melantius
    And what's your resolution?

Calianax   Ye shall have it
    Soundly, I warrant you.

King
    Reach[414] to Amintor, Strato.

Amintor (*drinks and passes the cup to Evadne*)
                      Here, my love.
    This wine will do thee wrong, for it will set
    Blushes upon thy cheeks, and till thou dost   70
    A fault, 'twere pity.

King   Yet I wonder much
    Of the strange desperation of these men
    That dare attempt such acts here in our state.
    He could not 'scape that did it.

---

[413] (Oath) By the Virgin Mary.
[414] Pass the cup.

Melantius   Were he known
> Unpossible.

King   It would be known, Melantius.   75

Melantius
> It ought to be. If he got then away,
> He must wear all our lives upon his sword.[415]
> He need not fly the island, he must leave
> No one alive.

King   No, I should think no man
> Could kill me and 'scape clear, but that old man.   80

Calianax
> But I! Heaven bless me! Should I, my liege?

King
> I do not think thou wouldst, but yet thou mightst,
> For thou hast in thy hands the means to 'scape
> By keeping of the fort. He has, Melantius,
> And he has kept it well.

Melantius   From cobwebs, sir.   85
> 'Tis clean swept. I can find no other art
> In keeping of it now; 'twas ne'er besieged
> Since he commanded.

Calianax   I shall be sure
> Of your good word, but I have kept it safe
> From such as you.

Melantius   Keep your ill temper in.   90
> I speak no malice; had my brother kept it
> I should ha' said as much.

King   You are not merry.
> Brother, drink wine. Sit you all still. Calianax!

The King draws Calianax apart

> I cannot trust this. I have thrown out words
> That would have fetched warm blood upon the cheeks   95

---

[415] He must kill us all.

Of guilty men, and he is never moved.

He knows no such thing.

Calianax   Impudence may 'scape

When feeble virtue is accused.

King   'A must,

If he were guilty, feel an alteration

At this our whisper, whilst we point at him.   100

You see he does not.

Calianax   Let him hang himself.

What care I what he does. This he did say.

King

Melantius, you can easily conceive

What I have meant, for men that are in fault

Can subtly apprehend when others aim   105

At what they do amiss; but I forgive

Freely before this man. Heaven do so too.

I will not touch thee so much as with shame

Of telling it. Let it be so no more.

Calianax

Why, this is very fine!

Melantius   I cannot tell   110

What 'tis you mean, but I am apt enough

Rudely to thrust into ignorant fault.

But let me know it; happily[416] 'tis nought

But misconstruction, and where I am clear

I will not take forgiveness of the gods   115

Much less of you.

King   Nay, if you stand so stiff

I shall call back my mercy.

Melantius   I want smoothness[417]

To thank a man for pardoning a crime

---

[416] Perhaps.

[417] I lack ingratiating ways.

I never knew.

King

    Not to instruct your knowledge, but to show you   120

    My ears[418] are everywhere, you meant to kill me

    And get the fort to 'scape.

Melantius   Pardon me, sir,

    My bluntness will be pardoned. You preserve

    A race of idle people here about you,

    Facers[419] and talkers to defame the worth   125

    Of those that do things worthy. The man that uttered this

    Had perished without food, be't who it will,

    But for this arm had fenced him[420] from the foe.

    And if I thought you gave a faith to[421] this,

    The plainness of my nature would speak more,   130

    Give me a pardon,[422] for you ought to do't,

    To kill him that spake this.

Calianax (*aside*)   Ay, that will be

    The end of all. Then I am fairly paid

    For all my care and service.

Melantius   That old man

    Who calls me enemy, and of whom I,   135

    Though I will never match my hate so low,

    Have no good thought, would yet, I think, excuse me

    And swear he thought me wronged in this.

Calianax   Who, I?

    Thou shameless fellow, didst thou not speak to me

    Of it thyself?

Melantius   O, then it came from him?   140

[418] My spies.

[419] Boastful people.

[420] Defended him.

[421] Believed.

[422] Give me permission.

Calianax

    From me! Who should it come from but from me?

Melantius

    Nay, I believe your malice is enough,

    But I ha' lost my anger. Sir, I hope

    You are well satisfied.

King   Lysippus, cheer

    Amintor and his lady; there's no sound   145

    Comes from you. I will come and do't myself.

Amintor

    You have done already, sir, for me, I thank you.

King

    Melantius, I do credit this from him,

    How slight soe'er you make it.

Melantius   'Tis strange you should.

Calianax

    'Tis strange 'a should believe an old man's word   150

    That never lied in's life.

Melantius   I talk not to thee.

    Shall the wild words of this distempered man,

    Frantic with age and sorrow, make a breach

    Betwixt your majesty and me? 'Twas wrong

    To harken to him, but to credit him   155

    As much, at least, as I have power to bear.

    But pardon me, whilst I speak only truth,

    I may commend myself. I have bestowed

    My careless blood with you,[423] and should be loath

    To think[424] an action that would make me lose   160

    That, and my thanks too. When I was a boy

    I thrust myself into my country's cause

---

[423] I have freely, with no thought for my own safety, given of my blood to you, i.e., Melantius has bled much in battle.

[424] To even imagine.

And did a deed that plucked five years from time
And styled me man[425] then, and for you, my King.
Your subjects all have fed by virtue of   165
My arm. This sword of mine hath plowed the ground
And reaped the fruit in peace,
And you yourself have lived at home in ease.
So terrible I grew that without swords
My name[426] hath fetched you conquest, and my heart   170
And limbs are still the same, my will as great
To do you service. Let me not be paid
With such a strange distrust.

King   Melantius,
I held it great injustice to believe
Thine enemy, and did not. If I did,   175
I do not; let that satisfy. (*To the others*) What, struck
With sadness all? More wine!

Calianax   A few fine words
Have overthrown my truth. Ah, thou'rt a villain!

Melantius (*to Calianax*)
Why, thou wert better let me have the fort.
Dotard,[427] I will disgrace thee thus forever;   180
There shall no credit lie upon thy words.
Think better, and deliver it.

Calianax   My liege,
He's at me now again to do it! Speak,
Deny it if thou canst! Examine him
Whilst he is hot, for if he cool again   185
He will forswear it.

King   This is lunacy,
I hope, Melantius.

---

[425] Made me a man.
[426] Reputation.
[427] Senile, old man.

Melantius   He hath lost himself
    Much since his daughter missed the happiness
    My sister gained, and though he call me foe,
    I pity him.
Calianax   'A pity! A pox upon you!   190
Melantius
    Mark his disordered words, and at the masque
    Diagoras knows he raged and railed at me,
    And called a lady 'whore' so innocent
    She understood him not. But it becomes
    Both you and me to forgive distraction.   195
    Pardon him as I do.
Calianax   I'll not speak for thee
    For all thy cunning! If you will be safe,
    Chop off his head, for there was never known
    So impudent a rascal.
King   Some that love him,
    Get him to bed. Why, pity should not let   200
    Age make itself contemptible; we must be
    All old. Have him away.
Melantius   Calianax,
    The King believes you. Come, you shall go home
    And rest. You ha' done well. (*Aside*) You'll give it up
    When I have used you thus a month, I hope.   205
Calianax
    Now, now, 'tis plain, sir, he doth move me still.
    He says he knows I'll give him up the fort
    When he has used me thus a month. I am mad,
    Am I not, still?
Omnes[428]   Ha, ha, ha!
Calianax
    I shall be mad indeed if you do thus.   210

---

[428] All.

Why should you trust a sturdy fellow there
That has no virtue in him, all's in his sword,
Before me? Do but take his weapons from him
And he's an ass, and I am a very fool
Both with him and without him, as you use me.   215

Omnes

Ha, ha, ha!

King

'Tis well, Calianax; but if you use[429]
This once again, I shall entreat some other
To see your offices be well discharged.
Be merry, gentlemen. It grows somewhat late.   220
Amintor, thou wouldst be abed again.

Amintor

Yes, sir.

King   And you, Evadne. Let me take
Thee in my arms, Melantius, and believe thou art,
As thou deservest to be, my friend,
Still and forever. Good Calianax,   225
Sleep soundly, it will bring thee to thyself.

                Exeunt all but Melantius and Calianax

Calianax

Sleep soundly! I sleep soundly now, I hope![430]
I could not be thus else. How dar'st thou stay
Alone with me, knowing how thou hast used me?

Melantius

You cannot blast me with your tongue, and that's   230
The strongest part you have about you.

Calianax   I
Do look for some great punishment for this,

---

[429] Do.

[430] = This must be a dream!

For I begin to forget all my hate
And take't unkindly that mine enemy
Should use me so extraordinarily scurvily.[431]   235

Melantius

I shall melt too, if you begin to take
Unkindness. I never meant you hurt.

Calianax

Thou'lt anger me again. Thou wretched rogue,
Meant me no hurt! Disgrace me with the King,
Lose all my offices! This is no hurt,   240
Is it? I prithee, what dost thou call hurt?

Melantius

To poison men because they love me not,
To call the credit of men's wives in question,
To murder children betwixt me and land,[432]
This I call hurt.

Calianax   And this, thou think'st, is sport,   245
For mine is worse. But use thy will with me,
For betwixt grief and anger I could cry.

Melantius

Be wise then, and be safe. Thou may'st revenge.

Calianax

Ay, o'th'King. I would revenge of thee!

Melantius

That you must plot yourself.

Calianax   I am a fine plotter.   250

Melantius

The short is, I will hold thee with the King
In this perplexity till peevishness
And thy disgrace have laid thee in thy grave.

---

[431] Basely; contemptibly.
[432] Murder children, who otherwise would inherit land. All three are serious crimes indeed.

But if thou wilt deliver up the fort,

I'll take thy trembling body in my arms   255

And bear thee over dangers. Thou shalt hold

Thy wonted state.[433]

Calianax   If I should tell the King,

Canst thou deny't again?

Melantius   Try, and believe.

Calianax

Nay, then thou canst bring anything about.

Melantius, thou shalt have the fort.

Melantius   Why, well.   260

Here let our hate be buried, and this hand

Shall right us both. Give me thy aged breast

To compass.[434]

Calianax   Nay, I do not love thee yet.

I cannot well endure to look on thee,

And if I thought it were a courtesy,   265

Thou shouldst not have it. But I am disgraced,

My offices are to be ta'en away,

And if I did but hold this fort a day,

I do believe the King would take it from me

And give it thee, things are so strangely carried.[435]   270

Ne'er thank me for't, but yet the King shall know

There was some such thing in't I told him of,

And that I was an honest man.

Melantius   He'll buy

That knowledge very dearly.

Enter Diphilus

---

[433] You shall stay in your former position.

[434] Let me embrace you closely.

[435] Things have taken such a strange turn.

Diphilus,

    What news with thee?   275

Diphilus   This were a night indeed
    To do it in. The King hath sent for her.

Melantius
    She shall perform it then. Go, Diphilus,
    And take from this good man, my worthy friend,
    The fort. He'll give it thee.

Diphilus   Ha' you got that?

Calianax   280
    Art thou of the same breed? Canst thou deny
    This to the King too?

Diphilus   With a confidence
    As great as his.

Calianax   Faith, like enough.

Melantius
    Away, and use him kindly.

Calianax   Touch not me,
    I hate the whole strain.[436] If thou follow   285
    Me a great way off, I'll give thee up the fort,
    And hang yourselves.

Melantius   Be gone.

Diphilus   He's finely wrought.[437]

Exeunt Calianax and Diphilus

Melantius
    This is a night, spite of astronomers,[438]
    To do the deed in. I will wash the stain
    That rests upon our house off with his blood.

Enter Amintor

---

[436] Clan; family.
[437] 1) He is worked up; 2) "He's a piece of work."
[438] People who take omens from the stars; astrologers.

Amintor

    Melantius, now assist me, if thou be'st   290

    That which thou say'st. Assist me! I have lost

    All my distempers,[439] and have found a rage

    So pleasing. Help me!

Melantius (*aside*)   Who can see him thus

    And not swear vengeance?—What's the matter, friend?

Amintor

    Out with thy sword, and hand in hand with me   295

    Rush to the chamber of this hated King,

    And sink him with the weight of all his sins

    To hell forever.

Melantius   'Twere a rash attempt,

    Not to be done with safety. Let your reason

    Plot your revenge, and not your passion.   300

Amintor

    If thou refusest me in these extremes

    Thou art no friend. He sent for her to me,

    By heaven, to me, myself! And I must tell ye

    I love her as a stranger. There is worth

    In that vile woman, worthy things, Melantius,   305

    And she repents. I'll do't myself, alone,

    Though I be slain. Farewell.

Melantius (*aside*)   He'll overthrow

    My whole design with madness.—Amintor,

    Think what thou dost. I dare as much as valour,[440]

    But 'tis the King, the King, the King, Amintor,   310

    With whom thou fightest! (*Aside*) I know he's honest[441]

    And this will work with him.

Amintor   I cannot tell

---

[439] Confusion.

[440] As a valiant man dares.

[441] Earlier in the play as well, the King's status has subdued Amintor. Honest = honorable.

What thou hast said, but thou hast charmed my sword
Out of my hand, and left me shaking here,
Defenceless.

Melantius   I will take it up for thee.   315

Amintor

What a wild beast is uncollected man![442]
The thing that we call honour bears us all
Headlong unto sin, and yet itself is nothing.

Melantius

Alas, how variable are thy thoughts.

Amintor

Just like my fortunes. I was run[443] to that   320
I purposed to have chid thee for. Some plot
I did distrust thou hadst against the King
By that old fellow's carriage. But take heed!
There's not the least limb growing to a king
But carries thunder in't.[444]

Melantius   I have none   325
Against him.

Amintor   Why come then, and still remember
We may not think revenge.

Melantius   I will remember.   *Exeunt*

---

[442] The human being who disregards reason.

[443] Driven.

[444] A king, divinely appointed, is here thought to have the power of the thunderbolt within his grasp.

Act V, Scene i

Enter Evadne and a Gentleman

Evadne

    Sir, is the King abed?

Gentleman

    Madam, an hour ago.

Evadne

    Give me the key, then, and let none be near.

    'Tis the King's pleasure.

Gentleman

    I understand you, madam, would 'twere mine!   5

    I must not wish good rest unto your ladyship.

Evadne

    You talk, you talk.

Gentleman

    'Tis all I dare do, madam, but the King

    Will wake, and then methinks . . .

Evadne

    Saving your imagination, pray, good night, sir.   10

Gentleman

    A good night be it then, and a long one, madam.

    I am gone.   *Exit*

Evadne

    The night grows horrible, and all about me

    Like my black purpose. O, the conscience

    Of a lost virgin, wither wilt thou pull me?   15

    To what things dismal as the depths of hell

    Wilt thou provoke me? Let no woman dare

    From this hour be disloyal, if her heart

    Be flesh, if she have blood and can fear. 'Tis a madness

    Above that desperate fool that left his peace   20

And went to sea to fight.[445] 'Tis so many sins
An age cannot repent 'em, and so great
The Gods want mercy for.[446] Yet I must through 'em.
I have begun a slaughter on my honour,
And I must end it there.   *Discovers the King in his bed asleep*[447]
                              'A sleeps. O God,   25
Why give you peace to this untemperate beast
That has so long transgressed you? I must kill him,
And I will do't bravely. The mere joy
Tells me I merit in it. Yet I must not
Thus tamely do it as he sleeps, that were   30
To rock him to another world. My vengeance
Shall take him waking, and then lay before him
The number of his wrongs and punishments.
I'll shape his sins like Furies[448] till I waken
His evil angel, his sick conscience,   35
And then I'll strike him dead.   *She ties his arms to the bed*
                              King, by your leave,
I dare not trust your strength. Your grace and I
Must grapple upon even terms no more.
So. If he rail me not from my resolution,
I shall be strong enough.   40
My lord the King! My lord! 'A sleeps
As if he meant to wake no more. My lord!
Is he not dead already? Sir! My lord!

---

[445] The sea, as well as the wars, are ruled by chance and fortune, so there is no peace to be found in the constant change they present.

[446] Sins so great even the gods do not have sufficient mercy to forgive them.

[447] The bed is probably situated behind a curtain hung before the discovery space; Evadne only has to pull the curtain aside.

[448] Avenging powers of retribution and bloodguilt, especially within the family; they often ensure the natural order of things.

King
>   Who's that?

Evadne   O, you sleep soundly, sir.

King   My dear Evadne,
>   I have been dreaming of thee. Come to bed.   45

Evadne
>   I am come at length, sir, but how welcome?

King
>   What pretty new device is this, Evadne?
>   What, do you tie me to you by my love?
>   This is a quaint one. Come, my dear, and kiss me.
>   I'll be thy Mars![449] To bed, my queen of love!   50
>   Let us be caught together, that the gods may see
>   And envy our embraces.

Evadne   Stay, sir, stay!
>   You are too hot,[450] and I have brought you physic
>   To temper your high veins.

King
>   Prithee, to bed then, let me take it warm.   55
>   There thou shalt know the state of my body better.

Evadne
>   I know you have a surfeited foul body,
>   And you must bleed.

King   Bleed!   *She draws a knife*

Evadne
>   Ay, you shall bleed. Lie still, and if the devil,
>   Your lust, will give you leave, repent. This steel   60
>   Comes to redeem the honour that you stole,

---

[449] The god of war. He was caught with Venus, his lover, when her husband Vulcan threw a net over them.

[450] 1) Too sexually charged; 2) in a fever and therefore in need of bleeding (see glossary).

King, my fair name, which nothing but thy death
Can answer to the world.

King   How's this, Evadne?

Evadne

I am not she,[451] nor bear I in this breast
So much cold spirit to be called a woman   65
I am a tiger! I am anything
That knows not pity. Stir not. If thou dost,
I'll take thee unprepared,[452] thy fears upon thee,
That make thy sins look double, and so send thee,
By my revenge I will, to look[453] those torments   70
Prepared for such black souls.

King

Thou dost not mean this! 'Tis impossible!
Thou art too sweet and gentle.

Evadne   No, I am not.

I am as foul as thou art, and can number
As many such hells here. I was once fair,[454]   75
Once I was lovely, not a blowing[455] rose
More chastely sweet, till thou, thou, thou foul canker—
Stir not!—didst poison me. I was a world of virtue
Till your cursed court and you—hell bless you for't—
With your temptations on temptations   80
Made me give up mine honour, for which, King,
I am come to kill thee.

King   No!

Evadne   I am!

King   Thou art not!

---

[451] I am not the Evadne you are calling to.

[452] Without the benefit of repentance or last rites.

[453] See.

[454] 1) Beautiful; 2) free of sin.

[455] Blooming.

I prithee speak not these things! Thou art gentle,
And wert not meant thus rugged.

Evadne   Peace, and hear me.
   Stir nothing but your tongue, and that for mercy   85
   To those above us, by whose lights I vow,
   Those blessed fires[456] that shot to see our sin,
   If thy hot soul had substance with thy blood,
   I would kill that too, which, being past my steel,
   My tongue shall reach. Thou art a shameless villain,   90
   A thing out of the overcharge[457] of nature,
   Sent like a thick cloud to disperse a plague
   Upon weak catching[458] women, such a tyrant
   That for his lust would sell away his subjects,
   Ay, all his heaven hereafter.

King   Hear, Evadne,   95
   Thou soul of sweetness, hear! I am thy King!

Evadne
   Thou art my shame. Lie still! There's none about you
   Within your cries;[459] all promises of safety
   Are but deluding dreams. Thus, thus, thou foul man,
   Thus I begin my vengeance!   *She stabs him*

King   Hold, Evadne!   100
   I do command thee, hold!

Evadne   I do not mean, sir,
   To part so fairly with you. We must change[460]
   More of these love-tricks yet.

King   What bloody villain
   Provoked thee to this murder?

---

[456] Shooting stars; comets or meteors.

[457] Excess.

[458] Susceptible to catch that plague.

[459] Within earshot.

[460] Exchange.

Evadne   Thou, thou monster!

                                                    She stabs him

King

    O!   105

Evadne

    Thou kept'st me brave[461] at court, and whored me, King,

    Then married me to a young noble gentleman

    And whored me still.

King   Evadne, pity me!

Evadne

    Hell take me then! (*Stabs*) This, for my lord Amintor!

    This for my noble brother! And this stroke   110

    For the most wronged of women!   *Kills him*

King   O, I die!

Evadne

    Die all our faults together! I forgive thee.   *Exit*

Enter two Gentlemen of the Bedchamber

First Gentleman

    Come, now she's gone. Let's enter. The King expects it

    and will be angry.

Second Gentleman

    'Tis a fine wench. We'll have a snap at her one of these 115

    nights as she goes from him.

First Gentleman

    Content. How quickly he had done with her! I see kings

    can do no more that way than other mortal people.

Second Gentleman

    How fast[462] he is! I cannot hear him breathe.

[461] 1) In splendor; 2) publicly.
[462] I.e., fast asleep.

First Gentleman

Either the tapers give a feeble light,   120

Or he looks very pale.

Second Gentleman   And so he does.

Pray heaven he be well! Let's look. Alas!

He's stiff, wounded, and dead! Treason! Treason!

First Gentleman

Run forth and call!

Second Gentleman

Treason! Treason!   *Exit Second Gentleman*   125

First Gentleman

This will be laid on us. Who can believe

A woman could do this?

Enter Cleon and Lysippus

Cleon   How now! Where's the traitor?

First Gentleman

Fled, fled away, but there her woeful act

Lies still.

Cleon   Her act? A woman!

Lysippus   Where's the body?

First Gentleman

There.   130

Lysippus

Farewell, thou worthy man. There were two bonds

That tied our loves, a brother and a king,

The least of which might fetch a flood of tears.

But such the misery of greatness is,

They have no time to mourn. Then pardon me.   135

Enter Strato

Sirs, which way went she?

Strato   Never follow her,
    For she, alas, was but the instrument.
    News is now brought in that Melantius
    Has got the fort, and stands upon the wall,
    And with a loud voice calls those few that pass   140
    At this dead time of night, delivering
    The innocence of this act.
Lysippus   Gentlemen,
    I am your King.
Strato   We do acknowledge it.
Lysippus
    I would I were not. Follow all, for this
    Must have a sudden stop.[463]   *Exeunt* 145

Act V, Scene ii

Enter Melantius, Diphilus, Calianax on the wall[464]

Melantius
    If the dull people can believe I'm armed —
    Be constant, Diphilus. Now we have time
    Either to bring our banished honours home[465]
    Or to create new ones in our ends.[466]
Diphilus   I fear not.
    My spirit lies not that way. Courage, Calianax!   5
Calianax
    Would I had any, you should quickly know it.

[463] Must be terminated immediately.
[464] Located on the balcony stage.
[465] Restore our lost honors.
[466] Our deaths.

Melantius

    Speak to the people, thou art eloquent.

Calianax

    'Tis a fine eloquence to come to the gallows.

    You were born to be my end, the devil take you!

    Now must I hang for company.[467] 'Tis strange   10

    I should be old and neither wise nor valiant.

Enter Lysippus, Diagoras, Cleon, Strato, and Guard

Lysippus

    See where he stands as boldly confident

    As if he had his full command[468] about him.

Strato

    He looks as if he had the better cause, sir.

    Under your gracious pardon let me speak it.   15

    Though he be mighty-spirited and forward[469]

    To all great things, to all things of that danger

    Worse men shake at the telling of, yet certain

    I do believe him noble, and this action

    Rather pulled on[470] than sought. His mind was ever   20

    As worthy as his hand.

Lysippus   'Tis my fear too.

    Heaven forgive all! Summon him, Lord Cleon.

Cleon

    Ho! From the walls there!

Melantius   Worthy Cleon, welcome.

    We could ha' wished you here, lord, you are honest.   24

---

[467] "Because I am in these people's company." Calianax sees himself as innocent of treason.

[468] All his soldiers.

[469] First in line.

[470] Forced upon him.

Calianax (*aside*)

> Well, thou art as flattering a knave, though I dare not tell
> thee so.

Lysippus

> Melantius.

Melantius

> Sir?

Lysippus

> I am sorry that we meet thus. Our old love
> Never required such distance. Pray to heaven   30
> You have not left yourself[471] and sought this safety
> More out of fear than honour. You have lost
> A noble master, which your faith, Melantius,
> Some think might have preserved. Yet you know best.

Calianax (*aside*)

> When time was, I was mad. Some that dares fight   35
> I hope will pay this rascal.

Melantius

> Royal young man, those tears look lovely on thee.
> Had they been shed for a deserving one,
> They had been lasting monuments. Thy brother,
> Whilst he was good, I called him King and served him   40
> With that strong faith, that most unwearied valour,
> Pulled people from the farthest sun to seek him
> And buy his friendship. I was then his soldier,
> But since his hot pride drew him to disgrace me,
> And brand my noble actions with his lust,   45
> (That never-cured dishonour of my sister,
> Base stain of whore, and which is worse,
> The joy to make it still so), like myself
> Thus I have flung him off with my allegiance

[471] Abandoned your old self/nature.

And stand here, mine own justice,[472] to revenge   50
What I have suffered in him, and this old man
Wronged almost to lunacy.

Calianax   Who? I!
You would draw me in! I have had no wrong.
I do disclaim you all.

Melantius   The short is this:
'Tis no ambition to lift up myself   55
Urgeth me thus. I do desire again
To be a subject, so[473] I may be free.
If not, I know my strength and will unbuild
This goodly town. Be speedy, and be wise
In a reply.

Strato   Be sudden, sir, to tie   60
All up again. What's done is past recall.
And past you to revenge, and there are thousands
That wait for such a troubled hour as this.
Throw him the blank.[474]

Lysippus   Melantius, write in that
Thy choice. My seal is at it.   65

Melantius
It was our honours drew us to this act,
No gain, and we will only work[475] our pardons.

Calianax
Put my name in too.

Diphilus   You disclaimed us all
But now, Calianax.

Calianax   That's all one.

---

[472] Creating my own justice.

[473] If only.

[474] Document with spaces to be filled in above the seal. It seems Melantius can dictate his own terms.

[475] Write in; ask.

I'll not be hanged hereafter by a trick,   70
    I'll have it in.

Melantius   You shall, you shall.
    Come to the back gate and we'll call you King
    And give you up the fort.

Lysippus   Away, away!   *Exeunt*

Act V, Scene iii

Enter Aspatia in man's apparel

Aspatia
    This is my fatal hour. Heaven may forgive
    My rash attempt that causelessly hath laid
    Griefs on me that will never let me rest,
    And put a woman's heart into my breast.
    It is more honour for you[476] that I die,   5
    For she that can endure the misery
    That I have on me, and be patient too,
    May live and laugh at all that you can do.

Enter Servant

    God save you, sir.

Servant   And you, sir. What's your business?

Aspatia
    With you, sir, now, to do me the fair office   10
    To help me to your lord.

Servant   What, would you serve him?

Aspatia
    I'll do him any service. But to haste,

---

[476] You = heaven

For my affairs are earnest,[477] I desire
To speak with him.

Servant

    Sir, because you are in such a haste, I would   15
Be loath to delay you longer. You cannot.

Aspatia

    It shall become you, though, to tell your lord.

Servant

    Sir, he will speak with nobody,
But in particular, I have in charge,[478]
About no weighty matters.

Aspatia   This is most strange.   20
    Art thou gold-proof? (*She gives him money*)
                  There's for thee. Help me to him.

Servant

    Pray, be not angry, sir, I'll do my best.   *Exit*

Aspatia

    How stubbornly this fellow answered me!
There is a vile dishonest trick in man,
More than in woman. All the men I meet   25
Appear thus to me, are harsh and rude,
And have a subtlety in everything,
Which love could never know. But we fond[479] women
Harbour the easiest and the smoothest thoughts,
And think all shall go so.[480] It is unjust   30
That men and women should be matched together.

Enter Amintor and his Servant

---

[477] Serious
[478] I am under orders.
[479] Indulgent; "silly."
[480] Think everybody will behave the same way (as we).

Amintor
    Where is he?

Servant   There, my lord.

Amintor   What would you, sir?

Aspatia
    Please it your lordship to command your man
    Out of the room. I shall deliver things
    Worthy your hearing.

Amintor   Leave us.   *Exit Servant*

Aspatia (*aside*)   O, that that shape   35
    Should bury falsehood in it.

Amintor   Now your will, sir.

Aspatia
    When you know me, my lord, you needs must guess
    My business, and I am not hard to know.
    For till the chance of war marked this smooth face
    With these few blemishes, people would call me   40
    My sister's picture, and her mine. In short,
    I am the brother to the wronged Aspatia.

Amintor
    The wronged Aspatia! Would thou wert so[481] too
    Unto the wronged Amintor! Let me kiss
    That hand of thine, in honour that I bear   45
    Unto the wronged Aspatia. Here I stand
    That did it. Would he[482] could not. Gentle youth,
    Leave me, for there is something in thy looks
    That calls my sins in a most hideous form
    Into my mind, and I have grief enough   50
    Without thy help.

Aspatia   I would I could with credit.

---

[481] I wish that you were my brother(-in-law).
[482] He = Amintor himself.

Since I was twelve years old I have not seen
My sister till this hour I now arrived.
She sent for me to see her marriage,
A woeful one, but they that are above   55
Have ends in everything. She used few words,
But yet enough to make me understand
The baseness of the injuries you did her.
That little training I have had is war.
I may behave myself rudely in peace;   60
I would not, though. I shall not need to tell you
I am but young, and would be loath to lose
Honour that is not easily gained again.
Fairly I mean to deal. The age is strict
For[483] single combats, and we shall be stopped   65
If it be published. If you like your sword,
Use it. If mine appear a better to you,
Change, for the ground is this, and this the time
To end our difference.   *She draws*

Amintor   Charitable youth,
If thou be'st such, think not I will maintain   70
So strange[484] a wrong, and for thy sister's sake,
Know that I could not think that desperate thing
I durst not do. Yet to enjoy this world[485]
I would not see her, for beholding thee,
I am I know not what. If I have aught   75
That may content thee, take it, and be gone,
For death is not so terrible as thou.

---

[483] In regards to. Duels were often resorted to to resolve disputes, but their
ethics were under much debate. James I was violently opposed to duels.
Also, see glossary.

[484] Unnatural.

[485] If I could have the whole world for it. The sight of the "brother"
profoundly stirs Amintor's guilty conscience.

Thine eyes shoot guilt into me.

Aspatia   Thus she swore
    Thou wouldst behave thyself, and give me words
    That would fetch tears into my eyes, and so   80
    Thou dost indeed. But yet she bade me watch
    Lest I were cozened,[486] and be sure to fight
    Ere I returned.

Amintor   That must not be with me.
    For her I'll die directly, but against her
    Will never hazard[487] it.

Aspatia   You must be urged.   85
    I do not deal uncivilly with those
    That dare to fight, but such a one as you
    Must be used thus.   *She strikes him*

Amintor   I prithee, youth, take heed!
    Thy sister is a thing to me so much
    Above mine honour, that I can endure   90
    All this. Good gods! A blow I can endure!
    But stay not, lest thou draw a timeless[488] death
    Upon thyself.

Aspatia   Thou art some prating[489] fellow
    One that has studied out a trick to talk   94
    And move soft-hearted people, to be kicked,   *She kicks him*
    Thus to be kicked! (*Aside*) Why should he be so slow
    In giving me my death?

Amintor   A man can bear
    No more and keep his flesh.[490] Forgive me then,
    I would endure yet if I could. Now show   *He draws*

---

[486] Tricked.
[487] Risk.
[488] 1) Untimely; 2) everlasting.
[489] Tongue wagging.
[490] Manhood.

The spirit thou pretendest, and understand   100
Thou hast no hour to live!   *They fight. Aspatia is wounded*
                      What dost thou mean?
Thou canst not fight! The blows thou mak'st at me
Are quite besides,[491] and those I offer at thee
Thou spread'st thine arms and tak'st upon thy breast,
Alas, defenseless!

Aspatia   I have got enough,   105
And my desire. There is no place so fit
For me to die as here.

Enter Evadne, her hands bloody, with a knife

Evadne

Amintor, I am loaden[492] with events
That fly to make thee happy. I have joys
That in a moment can call back thy wrongs   110
And settle thee in thy free state again.
It is Evadne still that follows thee,
But not her mischiefs.[493]

Amintor

Thou canst not fool me to believe again!
But thou hast looks and things so full of news   115
That I am stayed.[494]

Evadne

Noble Amintor, put off thy amaze,[495]
Let thine eyes loose, and speak. Am I not fair?
Looks not Evadne beauteous with these rites now?

[491] Off the mark.
[492] Weighed down.
[493] Wrongdoings.
[494] Made to wait.
[495] Amazement.

Were those hours half so lovely in thine eyes   120
When our hands met before the holy man?
I was too foul within to look fair then;
Since I knew ill[496] I was not free till now.

Amintor

There is presage of some important thing
About thee, which it seems thy tongue hath lost.   125
Thy hands are bloody, and thou hast a knife.

Evadne

In this consists thy happiness and mine.
Joy to Amintor, for the King is dead!

Amintor

Those most have power to hurt us that we love.
We lay our sleeping lives within their arms.   130
Why, thou hast raised up mischief to his height,
And found one to out-name thy other faults.
Thou hast no intermission of thy sins,
But all thy life is a continued ill.
Black is thy colour now, disease thy nature.   135
Joy to Amintor! Thou hast touched a life
The very name of which had power to chain
Up all my rage, and calm my wildest wrongs.

Evadne

'Tis done, and since I could not find a way
To meet thy love so clear as through his life,   140
I cannot now repent it.

Amintor

Couldst thou procure the gods to speak to me
To bid me love this woman and forgive,
I think I should fall out with them. Behold,
Here lies a youth whose wounds bleed in my breast,   145
Sent by his violent fate to fetch his death

---

[496] Since I began sinning.

From my slow[497] hand, and to augment my woe
You now are present, stained with a king's blood
Violently shed. This keeps night here
And throws an unknown wilderness about me.   150

Aspatia

    O! O! O!

Amintor

    No more! Pursue me not.

Evadne   Forgive me, then,

    And take me to thy bed. We may not part.   *Kneels*

Amintor

    Forbear, be wise, and let my rage go this way.

Evadne

    'Tis you that I would stay,[498] not it.

Amintor   Take heed!   155

    It will return with me.

Evadne   If it must be,

    I shall not fear to meet it. Take me home.

Amintor

    Thou monster of cruelty, forbear!

Evadne

    For heaven's sake, look more calm! Thine eyes are sharper
    Than thou canst make thy sword.

Amintor   Away! Away!   160

    Thy knees are more to me than violence.
    I am worse than sick to see knees follow me
    For that I must not grant. For God's sake, stand!

Evadne

    Receive me then.

Amintor   I dare not stay thy language.[499]

---

[497] Unwilling.

[498] Make remain.

[499] I cannot remain and listen to you.

In midst of all my anger and my grief,   165
Thou dost awake something that troubles me
And says I loved thee once. I dare not stay.
There is no end of woman's reasoning.   *He leaves her*

Evadne

Amintor, thou shalt love me now again.
Go, I am calm. Farewell, and peace forever.   170
Evadne, whom thou hat'st, will die for thee.   *Stabs herself*

Amintor

I have a little human nature yet
That's left for thee, that bids me stay thy hand.   *Returns*

Evadne

Thy hand was welcome, but it came too late.
O, I am lost! The heavy sleep makes haste.   *She dies* 175

Aspatia

O! O! O!

Amintor

This earth of mine doth tremble, and I feel
A stark affrighted motion in my blood.
My soul grows weary of her house,[500] and I
All over am a trouble to myself.   180
There is some hidden power in these dead things
That calls my flesh unto 'em. I am cold.
Be resolute and bear 'em company.
There's something yet which I am loath to leave.
There's man enough in me to meet the fears   185
That death can bring, and yet, would it were done.
I can find nothing in the whole discourse
Of death I durst not meet the boldest way,
Yet still betwixt the reason and the act
The wrong I to Aspatia did stands up.   190
I have not such another fault to answer;

---

[500] His body, the temple of the soul.

Though she may justly arm herself with scorn
And hate of me, my soul will part less troubled
When I have paid to her in tears my sorrow.
I will not leave this act unsatisfied,[501]   195
If all that's left in me can answer it.

Aspatia

Was it a dream? There stands Amintor still,
Or I dream still?

Amintor

How dost thou? Speak! Receive my love and help.
Thy blood climbs up to his old place again,[502]   200
There's hope of thy recovery.

Aspatia

Did you not name Aspatia?

Amintor   I did.

Aspatia

And talked of tears and sorrow unto her?

Amintor

'Tis true, and till these happy signs in thee
Stayed my course, it was thither I was going.   205

Aspatia

Thou art there already, and these wounds are hers.
Those threats I brought with me sought no revenge,
But came to fetch this blessing from thy hand.
I am Aspatia yet.

Amintor

Dare my soul ever look abroad[503] again?   210

Aspatia

I shall sure live, Amintor, I am well.
A kind of healthful joy wanders within me.

---

[501] Undone.
[502] She is blushing.
[503] Look at anybody else.

Amintor

>The world wants lives to excuse thy loss.

>Come, let me bear thee to some place of help.

Aspatia

>Amintor, thou must stay. I must rest here. 215

>My strength begins to disobey my will.

>How dost thou, my best soul? I would fain live

>Now, if I could. Wouldst thou have loved me then?

Amintor

>Alas, all that I am's not worth a hair

>From thee! 220

Aspatia

>Give me thine hand. Mine hands grope up and down

>And cannot find thee. I am wondrous sick.

>Have I thy hand, Amintor?

Amintor

>Thou greatest blessing of the world, thou hast.

Aspatia

>I do believe thee better than my sense. 225

>O, I must go. Farewell. *She dies*

Amintor

>She swoons! Aspatia! Help! For God's sake, water,

>Such as may chain life ever to this frame!

>Aspatia! Speak! What, no help? Yet I fool.[504]

>I'll chafe her temples. Yet there nothing stirs. 230

>Some hidden power, tell her Amintor calls,

>And let her answer me. Aspatia, speak!

>I have heard, if there be any life, but bow

>The body thus,[505] and it will show itself.

>O, she is gone! I will not leave her yet. 235

---

[504] I behave like a fool.

[505] Bend the body to bring blood to the head.

Since out of justice we must challenge nothing,[506]
I'll call it mercy if you'll pity me,
You heavenly powers, and lend forth some few years
The blessed soul to this fair seat again.
No comfort comes. The gods deny me too.   240
I'll bow the body once again. Aspatia!
The soul is fled forever, and I wrong
Myself so long to lose her company.
Must I talk now? Here's to be with thee, love.

He stabs himself

Enter Servant

Servant

This is a great grace to my lord to have the new King   245
come to him. I must tell him he is entering.—O God!
Help! Help!

Enter Lysippus, Melantius, Calianax, Cleon, Diphilus, and Strato

Lysippus
Where's Amintor?
Strato
O, there! There!
Lysippus
How strange is this!   250
Calianax
What should we do here?
Melantius
These deaths are such acquainted things with me,
That yet my heart dissolves not. May I stand
Stiff here forever! Eyes, call up your tears.

[506] As we humans can only ask, not demand, from the gods.

This is Amintor! Heart, he was my friend.   255
Melt! Now it flows. Amintor, give a word
To call me to thee.

Amintor

O!

Melantius

Melantius calls his friend Amintor. O!
Thy arms are kinder to me than thy tongue.   260
Speak! Speak!

Amintor

What?

Melantius

That little word was worth all the sounds
That ever I shall hear again.

Diphilus   O, brother,
Here lies your sister slain! You lose yourself   265
In sorrow there.

Melantius   Why, Diphilus, it is
A thing to laugh at in respect of this.[507]
Here was my sister, father, brother, son,
All that I had! Speak once again.
What youth lies slain here by thee?   270

Amintor   'Tis Aspatia.
My last is said. Let me give up my soul
Into thy bosom.

Calianax   *He dies*
What's that? What's that? Aspatia!

Melantius   I never did
Repent the greatness of my heart till now.
It will not burst at need.   275

Calianax

My daughter dead here too! And you have all fine new

[507] Again, male friendship is stronger than kinship bonds.

tricks to grieve, but I ne'er knew any but direct crying.

Melantius.

I am a prattler, but no more!   *He makes to stab himself*

Diphilus   Hold, brother!

Lysippus

Stop him!   280

Diphilus

Fie, how unmanly was this offer in you!

Does this become our strain?[508]

Calianax

I know not what the matter is, but I am grown very kind,

and am friends with you all now. You have given me that

among you will kill me quickly, but I'll go home and live 285

as long as I can.   *Exit*

Melantius

His spirit is but poor that can be kept

From death for want of weapons.

Is not my hands a weapon sharp enough

To stop my breath? Or if you tie down those,   290

I vow, Amintor, I will never eat,

Or drink or sleep, or have to do with that

That may preserve life. This I swear to keep!

Lysippus

Look to him, though, and bear those bodies in.

May this a fair example be to me   295

To rule with temper,[509] for on lustful kings

Unlooked-for, sudden deaths from God are sent.

But cursed is he that is their instrument.

Exeunt with the bodies

---

[508] Family.

[509] Without tyranny; moderately.

Texts in Context

There is much and clear evidence that, though readers and audiences respond with sympathy and understanding to the urge to revenge, private revenge was not morally acceptable in the Renaissance. The following short quotations from contemporary texts, printed here to whet the reader's appetite and as an encouragement to go to the texts themselves for more material, illustrate this. Spelling and punctuation have been modernized. I am indebted to Eleanor Prosser for pointing me to many of the texts below in her *Hamlet and Revenge*.

King James I was violently opposed to dueling. He is quoted by Bacon as having said:

> I come forth and see myself nobly attended, but I know not whether any of them shall live four and twenty hours: For it is but the mistaking of a word in heat, and that brings the lie, and that brings a challenge, and then comes the loss of their lives.
>
> (qtd. in the introduction to
Discourse of Warre and Single Combat
(see below))

Ballads and broadsides were popular in the Renaissance; besides relating exciting events such as describing executions in detail, they were often used to send a political or moral message like the one below from "The Bellman's Goodmorrow," *Old English Ballads 1553-1625*, p. 234-35.

> 3.
> From all the rage of wickedness
> look that you strip you quite;

In garments of true godliness
   see that your selves be decked.
Shake off all shame and sorrow
   which doth your souls destroy,—
God give you all good morrow
and send you happy day.

4.

And rise not to revenge thee
   of any trespass past;
Thou knowst not of a certainty
   how long thy life will last.
Seek not thy neighbours sorrow
   in any kind of way.
God give you all good morrow
and send you happy day.

5.

Forgive thy brother friendly
   For *Christ* doth will it so;
And let not spite and envy
   within thy stomack grow,
Lest God shoot forth his arrow
   thy malice to destroy.
God give you all good morrow
and send you happy day.

Francis Bacon, jurist, courtier, writer, and philosopher, wrote essays on almost any thinkable topic current in the Renaissance in order to aid and edify his fellow man. His essays were widely read during his lifetime. His style includes presenting both sides of a problem without committing himself, but still bringing the reader to draw a sound conclusion.

OF REVENGE

Revenge is a kind of wild justice, which the more man's nature runs to, the more ought law to weed it out. For as for the first wrong, it doth but offend the law, but the revenge of that wrong putteth the law out of office. Certainly in taking revenge, a man is but even with his enemy, but in passing it over, he is superior, for it is a prince's part to pardon ... The most tolerable sort of revenge is for those wrongs which there is no law to remedy, but then let a man take heed the revenge be such that there is no law to punish; else a man's enemy is still beforehand [has the advantage], and it is two for one ... This is certain that a man that studieth revenge keeps his own wounds green, which otherwise would heal and do well. Public revenges are for the most part fortunate ... But in private revenge it is not so. Nay rather, vindictive persons live the lives of witches, who, as they are mischievous, so end they infortunate.

Sir Thomas Elyot wrote *The Book named The Governor* to assist those gentleman "magistrates" a king needs to support his government. He discusses the need for training leaders, starting early with education in classical languages, literature, and history, but also training the body through sports, dancing, and hunting. Once so trained, the young gentleman is ready to absorb moral and political philosophy and recognize the value of gentlemanly virtues. One such virtue is patience. From *The Book named The Governor* (1531), pp. 191-192:

Unto him that is valiant of courage it is a great pain and difficulty to sustain injury, and not to be forthwith revenged. And yet often times is accounted more valiantness in the sufferance than in hasty revenging ...

Julius Caesar, when Catullus the poet wrote against him contumelious or reproachable verses, he not only forgave him, but to make him his friend caused him oftentimes to sup with him ... Some men will not praise this manner of patience, but account it for foolishness; but if they behold on the other side what incommodity cometh of impatience, how a man is therewith abstract from reason and turned into a monstrous figure, and do confer all that with the stable countenance and pleasant regard of him that is patient, and with the commodity that doth ensue thereof, they shall affirm that that simplicity is an excellent wisdom. Moreover the best way to be avenged is so to condemn injury and rebuke, and live with such honesty that the doer shall at the last be thereof ashamed, or at the least, lose the fruit of his malice, that is to say, shall not rejoice and have glory of thy hindrance or damage.

From Timothy Bright's *A Treatise of Melancholie*, p. 228 (It should be understood that a melancholic disposition is particularly susceptible to satanic influences, as Hamlet is so clearly aware of):

[The Devil's] temptations are properly such as neither our natures seem to incline unto, but in generality to all kind of wickedness ... Of this kind are certain blasphemies suggested of the Devil, [such as] laying violent hands on themselves or upon others, neither moved thereto by hate or malice, or any occasion of revenge. Of the same sort is the despair and distrust of God's mercy and grace, besides many others [such] as taking away the seed of the word out of the heart of the negligent hearers, [and] the suggesting of errors and such like without our nature's special inclination that way, but rather contrarily affected.

From the Protestant Pastor Bertrand de Loque's *Discourses of Warre and Single Combat* (pp. 51-55). The first part of his book justifies warfare on a national scale, while the second part speaks eloquently against dueling because it goes against both secular justice and religious morals. The aristocracy both in France, where de Loque wrote, and in England increasingly relied on duels to settle "matters of honor." Between 1606 and 1609, an estimated 2,000 French noblemen were killed dueling.

Chapter III
Of the Combat undertaken by private authority.

... it is manifest that all private revenge is forbidden and condemned, as contrary to the vocation and devoir of Christians: see here the reasons.

1. Firstly God doth forbid it: *Thou shalt not kill*, so saith his law: and as Paul saith: *Avenge not your selves, but rather give place unto wrath:* for God hath said: *Vengeance is mine, and I will repay.*

2. That we cannot be admitted to be judges in our own cause. For that we be blindfolded ... that is to say with the love of our selves, we should be partial in judgment, and judge the right still on our selves and the wrong to our neighbour.

3. That the impatience which is in us, and the choler which both dominate and bear rule in us, doth let [hinder] and distemper us, that we cannot keep a mean [moderation] in the vengeance, that we would take on him that wrongeth us ... we can stir other weapons, but this [i.e., choler, here seen as a weapon] stirreth us. Our hands handle other weapons, but this handleth our hands We possess other weapons, but this possesseth us ...

4.   ... [W]hoever doth revenge himself, committeth sacrilege, appropriating unto himself that which belongeth by right unto God himself.

... [I]f it be not lawful for the civil magistrate, to put to death the transgressor, without giving him before some time and leisure to repent himself, for fear that he destroy the soul with the body, how shall it be lawful for a private man to revenge himself on his neighbour, by endangering on a sudden both his body and soul ...

... Now these which die in combat, having their mind purposed and bent to revenge, to kill and slay, having their death's blow on a sudden, so far are they from having any leisure to premeditate of their death, as contrariwise they are eager to cast themselves headlong into the nets of death, even as a man should run blindfolded into the sea.

... How miserable is the thirst for revenge? How hurtful is the achieving thereof? She maketh thee take no quiet rest in thine house, and thou hast no assurance to be in the fields; she tosseth thee with continual cares, she tormenteth thee with a thousand fears, she carrieth thy judgment and reason clean out of their proper seats, and playeth the tyrant over them. When thou thinketh thyself safest, then she threateneth thee most: she is importunate with thee, she gnaweth thee to the heart, she devoureth thee ...

Honour is a thing too precious, and virtue is a thing too noble of itself, to depend on a superfluous humour, so base and villainous, as the desire of vengeance is.

Sir William Segar, a trained scrivener, worked his way to his title through the College of Arms. He studied heraldry and chivalric law and wrote about military and chivalric traditions. His *The Book of Honor and Armes* is interesting because it is one of the very few texts that defend private revenge, though still admitting that Christianity demands patient suffering. The quotations here are from the introduction, fol. A2, and p. 20.

> To the Reader.
> The cause of all Quarrel is Injury and reproach, but the matter of content, is Justice and Honor. For love whereof, we shun no care of mind, loss of wealth, nor adventure [risking] of life ... True it is, that the Christian law willeth men to be of so perfect patience, as not only to endure injurious words, but also quietly to suffer every force and violence. Notwithstanding, forsomuch as none (or very few men) have attained such perfection, the laws of all Nations, for avoiding further inconveniences, and the manifestation of truth, have (among many other trials) permitted, that such questions as could not be civilly proved by confession, witnesses, or other circumstances, should receive judgment by fight and Combat, supposing that GOD (who only knoweth the secret thoughts of all men) would give victory to him that justly adventured his life, for Truth, Honor, and Justice.

> [from Book 2, chapter 1]
> An injurie ... [offered] in such evil sort, as the fact appeareth to be done contrary to honor and reason, in that case, to what purpose should the injured challenge the injurer? seeing the matter to be plain and apparent. But haply it may be said by him that is injured, *Shall I rest without revenge?* ... [I]n mine opinion, whosoever receiveth an Injurie in deeds dishonorably

offered, is thereby neither dishonored nor burdened: and for revenge of such cowardly and beastly offenses, it is allowable to use any advantage or subtlety, according to the Italian proverb ... which is that one advantage requireth another, and one treason may be with another acquitted.

From *The Book of Homilies*, "A Homily Against Contention and Brawling" (pp. 93-94). Thomas Cranmer, Protestant Archbishop of Canterbury, had this collection of twelve sermons published. They were meant to be read in churches throughout England in a repeated cycle in order to discourage undesirable behavior. The contents are not solely religious, but have a healthy portion of politics interspersed as well.

Forgive ... a light trespass to thy neighbour that Christ may forgive thee many thousands of trespasses, which art every day an offender. For if thou forgive thy brother, being to thee a trespasser, then hast thou a sure sign and token that GOD will forgive thee, to whom all men be debtors and trespassers. How wouldst thou have GOD merciful to thee, if thou wilt be cruel onto thy brother? Canst thou not find in thine heart to do that towards another that is thy fellow, which God hath done to thee, that art but his servant? Ought not one sinner to forgive another, seeing that Christ which was no sinner, did pray to his father to them that without mercy and despitefully put him to death? Who, when he was reviled, he did not use reviling words again, and when he suffered wrongfully, he did not threaten, but gave all vengeance to the judgment of his father which judgeth rightfully.

From Thomas Becon's *Prayers and Other Pieces*, "A Prayer for Our Enemies," p. 38. Becon was Chaplain to the Protestant Archbishop Thomas Cranmer, who collected the material for and oversaw the publication of *The Book of Homilies*.

> O Lord ... [t]hou hast commanded us to love not only our friends, but also our very enemies; to forgive them that offend us, to bless them that curse us, to do good to them that hate us, to pray for them that do us wrong and persecute us ... but our corrupt nature, which ever striveth against thy blessed will, seeketh all means possible to be revenged, to requite tooth for tooth and eye for eye, to render evil for evil when vengeance is thine and thou wilt reward ...

And from his *The Catechism*, p. 179:

> Whomsoever will obtain at the hand of God grace, favour, and remission of his sins, he must also forgive them that have offended him ... according to this commandment of our Savior Christ: "Be ye merciful, as your heavenly Father is merciful." ... After this manner ought all Christians to be affected, not to revenge, but ready to forgive; not to curse, but to bless; not to render evil for evil, but to overcome evil with goodness, leaving all vengeance to God which saith: "Vengeance is mine: I will reward." Whosoever is otherwise minded, let him look for no favour at the hand of God.

From Archbishop Edwin Sandy's *Sermons*, "A Sermon Preached at an Assizes," p. 228, and "A Sermon Made at the Spittle[1]

---

[1] I.e., hospital.

in London," p. 289.

> *Nolite judicare* : "judge not." Mercy will not be hasty to judge. There be judgments civil, and judgments ecclesiastical; judgments public, and private judgments. Christ neither forbiddeth the magistrate, neither the public minister, to judge according to the law; neither the parent or master, to judge and correct their offending children or servants. It is uncharitable private judgment which God forbiddeth, when men unadvisedly take upon them to give sentence of others, as if God had resigned his own right into their hands ... Verily this merciless judging of others is the cause why we fall into many perils and secret temptations. Love mercy, therefore; and judge not. He that judgeth with the Pharisee with the Pharisee shall be judged.

> Nothing is hid from [God's] eyes, he seeth the secrets of all hearts: he will not be corrupted, but give unto everyone according to his works. Christ is judge. Wherefore we are taught to leave revenge unto him ... For private men to revenge wrongs is to usurp Christ's office, to take judgment out of his hands whom God the Father hath appointed judge of the quick and the dead ... he died to be a sacrifice for us: he rose again to justify us: he is made our judge, and doth judge justly.

Glossary

Angel—Many puns can be found playing on the heavenly angel and the coin; an angel, a gold coin current in the 15th, 16th, and 17th centuries, was worth approximately ten shillings. Its name comes from its obverse side, which bore an image of the Archangel Michael killing a dragon.

Bleeding or Bloodletting—This was a much used cure for many ills, and that most commonly resorted to, as too much "blood" in a person made him or her too lively and amorous. The person performing the "operation" was most often the local barber; a wonderful example of amorousness and bloodletting can be found in act three, lines 366 ff. of Beaumont and Fletcher's *The Knight of the Burning Pestle.* By bleeding a person, an attempt was made to re-create the ideal balance of the four humors. Other frequently used purgatives were enemas, laxatives, emetics, and diuretics; these means of purging could be quite hard on the poor patient!

Blood—Blood, generated in the heart but sometimes referred to in connection with the liver, was corresponding to the element of water and associated with erotic passion. Out of blood semen was thought to be generated, demanding much blood as raw material in order to create a small amount. With each ejaculation essential blood would be expended, and so life might be shortened. This was an excellent argument for continence.

Body Politic, The—Shakespeare's *The Tragedy of Coriolanus*, I.i.114-118, examines the idea that the king is the "head" of his country:

> The Kingly crown'd head, the vigilant eye,
> The counsellor heart, the arm our soldier,

> Our steed the leg, our tongue the trumpeter,
> With other muniments[2] and petty helps
> In this our fabric[3] ...

Traditionally, there was a correspondence seen between the human body with its interdependent limbs and organs and "the body politic." As head of his country, and father of his country, the king is obliged to govern wisely, uphold the laws, and provide for his people. Claudius plays on this concept in *Hamlet* I.ii.47-49: "The head is not more native[4] to the heart,/ The hand more instrumental to the mouth,/Than is the throne of Denmark to thy father." The "body politic" is the public body of the ruler, not the individual, mortal body of the king.

Cloth of Gold—Fabric woven completely or partially of gold thread to create garments for ceremonial use.

Clown—This is the term for the acting company's comedian. It is theorized that much of his part was not written down, and that he would extemporize much as the audience encouraged him. Will Kemp, for a time the clown in Shakespeare's company, was celebrated for his ability to extemporize. In many speech headings the term "clown" is used instead of the actual name of the character; and indeed these comic characters can be seen as metadramatic, as stage-audience catalysts.[5]

Commedia dell'Arte—An Italian theater form, existing in *scenario* form, i.e. no fixed script. The players portrayed "stock" characters such as Pantalone, the old man, Zanni, the clown, and other well-known types such as the father, the maiden in love, the

---

[2] Fortifications.

[3] Body.

[4] Naturally joined to.

[5] See Videbæk, *The Stage Clown In Shakespeare's Theatre.*

lover, etc. Slapstick was widely used. Renaissance drama often presents such easily labeled types.

Court Masque, The—see "Masque."

Die—This verb refers not only to actual death, but also the "loss of the senses" during sexual orgasm. Ornstein defines (in *The Moral Vision of Jacobean Tragedy*, p. 176): "the consummation of the flesh in orgiastic pleasure or in the rot of the grave."

Dowry—The marriage portion given from a father or guardian to his daughter's husband upon her marriage. This could be in the form of money, goods, or estate. The groom's family provided the couple with the means to live on until the son inherited, if he were first in line. (See also Marriage.)

Duel—The duel as seen in the Renaissance originated in the earlier "trial by combat," the judicial duel, where issues were decided by which combatant won. See Shakespeare's *Richard II* for an example of this. However, dueling became fashionable and moved from the arena of public revenge into that of private. Dueling was easy to engage in, as fashion dictated wearing a sword or rapier as part of everyday dress, and became so easily provoked that in 1566 Charles IX of France decreed the death penalty for dueling. Examples of provocation can be seen in *The Maid's Tragedy* v.iii, where a slap is considered ample provocation. England did not go quite that far, but during the Jacobean period the ethics of dueling were hotly debated; James I was adamantly opposed to duels and had made dueling a capital offense in Scotland in 1600.

Dumb Show—This device seems to a modern spectator or reader to be one of the more artificial tricks of the Renaissance stage, as actors wordlessly demonstrate action. However, it is a very economical device that allows much action and meaning to be compressed into a very short timespan. In *Hamlet*, for instance, Claudius may be occupied with Polonius or his wife as the "Mousetrap" Dumb Show unfolds, but the audience are prepared by these two or three minutes of action; not only is the outcome of the playlet proper clear to the spectator and thus comes as no surprise, but we know not to watch the "Mousetrap" only, but also the spectators-on-stage, especially the King. Dumb Shows are one of the many stage devices that, in a desirable way, distance the audience from emotional involvement and invites us to analyze the action intellectually rather than emotionally. Also, a dumb show can be an excellent vehicle for spectacle.

Fishmonger—References to "fishmongers" at the time *Hamlet* was written suggest that fishmongers were more than usually sexually active. Also, they were connected with salt from the sea, and salt was thought to induce both lust and fertility; thus fishmongers' wives and daughters, through close proximity, were not only of dubious virtue but also excessively fertile. Many a joke on fishmongers and their female relatives can be found in Renaissance plays.

Folio—Renaissance printing started with a "sheet" of handmade paper some eighteen by fourteen inches in size. Folded once to make four pages, the size became "folio." The sheet was printed all at once, then folded, cut, and bound. *The First Folio* of Shakespeare's works, unbound, sold for about £1.

Fool—Much punning is possible on this word: 1) a "natural fool," an idiot; 2) a court fool, a jester; 3) a baby, because it is not yet educated; and 4) a husband, who can be hoodwinked.

Forehead—A very visible part of the face, expected to be smooth and clear. The forehead is the place of male shame when a wife cuckolds her husband and gives him "horns." Female shame in association with the forehead can be "blushing" for shame, visible, or "unblushing impertinence" in accusations. In Renaissance times offenders were often branded as part of their punishment; from this practice arose the metaphor of the inscribed forehead, especially female, where supposedly all sins could be read (see especially Evadne and Aspatia's references *The Maid's Tragedy*). By even further extension, the Duke in *The Revenger's Tragedy* refers to "the forehead of our state" (I.ii.4) as soiled. Moreover, the forehead is a place to display jewels dangling from hair ornaments.

Fortune—Fortune is usually seen as female because it is fickle. She has a wheel that turns unpredictably; one minute we find ourselves on top of the world, the next we are in the dust beneath the wheel. Nobody is safe from changes wrought by fortune, a theme often explored in tragedy.

Four Elements, The—The planet earth and all natural things and beings upon it were thought to be composed of four elements, earth, air, fire, and water, which were present in various proportions to make up each entity. A person's psychological make-up was determined by which element predominated within him or her. (See also Four qualities and Four humors.)

Four Humors, The—The Greeks were the first to theorize that a person's health depends on a balance of four humors within the body; these are blood, black bile, phlegm, and choler. Mediaeval medicine embraced this theory, which is still very much in evidence in the Renaissance. Each humor was linked to an organ of the body, had its corresponding element, and possessed two of the four qualities. Blood was created in the heart, was hot and moist, and corresponded to water; black bile was created in the spleen, was cold and dry, and corresponded to earth; phlegm was created in the brain, was cold and moist, and corresponded to air; and choler was created in the liver, was hot and dry, and corresponded to fire. Illness was attributed to an imbalance of humors, and could often be observed in a change of complexion or personality. (See also Four elements, Four qualities, and Four temperaments)

Four Qualities, The—Hippocrates thought, and Aristotle demonstrated, that all natural entities are possessed of four qualities, hot, cold, dry, and moist. In a person, these qualities were believed to determine secondary qualities, and were used to effect a cure in medicine. If one was deemed "excessively moist," one could be cured by ingesting something predominantly "dry."(See also Four elements and Four humors.)

Four Seasons, The—Spring, childhood, was associated with blood/water; summer, young adulthood, with choler/fire; fall, adulthood, with black bile/earth; and winter, old age, with phlegm/air.

Four Temperaments, The—One's personality was determined by the humor that held sway in one's composition. Blood, water, ruled the "sanguinary temperament," the person who was an extrovert, generally happy and generous, and given to amorousness. "The phlegmatic" was dominated by phlegm, air, and tended towards calmness, laziness, cowardice, and a certain toughness of personality. The violent "choleric" personality that exploded out of the starting gate once convinced that the cause was right, the revenger, the highly energetic, possessed too much choler, fire. Finally, the "melancholic," the one dominated by black bile, earth, tended to be brooding, gloomy, worrying, but also slow to kindle, leaning towards gluttony, and quite sentimental. It is an interesting exercise to match temperaments to protagonists in Renaissance plays; sometimes one gets interesting insights.

Gentleman—"Gentle," as in a Renaissance gentleman, can be translated into our "noble" and does not refer to a gentle and mild disposition necessarily. A gentleman was well educated in classical languages, mathematics, astronomy, and rhetoric, he mastered horsemanship and swordsmanship, and he was also expected to be righteous and just as well as merciful. For an indepth discussion of this, see Castiglione's *The Book of the Courtier*, Book One; see also Ophelia's description of Hamlet before his "antic disposition" is put on, *Hamlet* III.i.153-164.

Golden Age, The—An imaginary period in early human history, when humans lived a life of ease and grace, free from sin and suffering, a period that knew no work, strife, or war. It was brought to an end through a variety of inventions that made work and war possible, such as the first sword, the first ship, the first plough, the first fortified wall. In Renaissance times this "age" is often referred to as an unobtainable ideal.

Great Chain of Being, The—From the Middle Ages to the late eighteenth century, the structure of the universe was accepted as "a great chain" consisting of an infinite number of links in strict order. The chain's origin was the Creator, followed by the nine orders of angels; the human soul formed the connection between immortals and mortals. The earth's contents were then listed, beginning with the king, the highest ranking of men, and ending with the least significant form of existence. Minerals and other inanimates can be similarly listed. The removal of one link or disturbance of the order could result in dissolution of the cosmic order.

Green-sickness—Chlorosis, an anemic condition in young girls which gives a greenish tint to the skin and has irritability and faintness among its symptoms, generally associated with immaturity. The word is used figuratively to mean "morbid appetites" such as eating chalk and charcoal. The remedy most often suggested, jokingly, is marriage; many sexually charged jokes center around green sickness and "green girls." A 1681 broadside, *Canto on Miracle Wrought by the Duke of M* runs: "But O, the greensick girls may boast/The Duke hath cured them to his cost" (OED).

Groundlings—The spectators in a public playhouse who had standing room around the stage platform, the cheapest place in the house.

Hobby-horse—A character in the May Day games and the Morris Dance. Its costume was a horse body with a foot cloth concealing the legs of the man inside. The hobby-horse often portrayed ritual death and resurrection, but also included many bawdy tricks in its performance, and so was particularly abhorred by the Puritans. Why the hobby-horse should be "forgot" (*Hamlet* III.ii.127-128) remains a mystery. See also "Morris Dance."

Horns—(see also "Forehead") A cheating wife furnishes her cuckolded husband with "horns," dreaded emblem of his state. The image of the fearful, jealous husband with his hands to his head to check for budding horns is used in both comedy and tragedy, as are the puns on deer/dear and heart/hart.

Incest—In Clerke's *The Triall of Bastardie* (London, 1594) can be found a list of prohibited marriage partners. Thus a man may not marry his mother, stepmother, or wife's mother; his son's daughter, his daughter's daughter, his wife's son's daughter, or his wife's daughter's daughter; his daughter, wife's daughter, or son's wife; his sister, wife's sister, or brother's wife; his father's sister, mother's sister, or father's brother's wife. Incest had a much wider definition then than now, and with that in mind it is easy to understand why Hamlet is so profoundly disturbed by his mother's marriage to his uncle.

Kind—The word is often used as near-synonym for "kin," but also with overtones of community and mutually benevolent feelings. The adjective "kind" has our modern meaning, but also the meaning of "natural" (e.g., natural feelings among one's kind/kin); "unkind" = unnatural. The proverb "The nearer in kin, the less in kindness" provides a sarcastic comment.

King's Two Bodies, The—The King embodied in himself "the body natural," which was his own, mortal body, and "the body politic," which was his connection with his country, and which was passed on from ruler to ruler. The King was God's anointed, God's chosen ruler and His representative on earth. This "body" represents the law of the land in God's name; this is the "body" that endures from father to son in — preferably — a direct, hereditary line. King James I[6] was deeply interested in and wrote about the necessity of absolute monarchy, sanctioned by God; but contemporary writers began examining what happens to the country and "the body politic" when "the body natural" acts in ways unbecoming to a King. This debate is clearly seen in *The Revenger's Tragedy*, *Hamlet*, and *The Maid's Tragedy*.

Law—Law was seen as existing on three levels. There was divine law, which was perfect; natural law, which rested in itself with-

[6] See his *The Trew Law of Free Monarchies*.

out needing representatives of authority to uphold it; and the law of nations, which was needed to impose restrictions on sinful man in order to keep him under control. The law of nations manifests itself in, for example, the king, God's representative on earth, as absolute authority, because his "body politic" embodied the law.

> Now that law which, as it is laid up in the bosom of God, they call eternal, receiveth according unto the different kinds of things which are subject unto it different and sundry kinds of names. That part of it which ordereth natural agents we call usually nature's law; that which angels do clearly behold and without any swerving observe is law celestial and heavenly; the law of reason, that which bindeth creatures reasonable in this world, and with which by reason they may most plainly perceive themselves bound; That which bindeth them, and is not known but by special revelation from God, divine law; human law, that which out of the law either of reason or of God men probably gather to be expedient, they make it law.
>
> (Richard Hooker, *Of the Laws of Ecclesiastical Polity*, 1593, qtd. in McDonald's *The Bedford Companion*, 350)

Liver—This is the seat of the humor choler, associated with the element of fire; violent passions stem from the liver.

Machiavel—Machiavelli's book *The Prince*, the ultimate ruler's how-to manual (should the ruler wish to obtain and retain power), was more widely known of than translated and read. In Renaissance plays "The Machiavel" is most often the stage villain, the one who schemes and plots for personal gain; the end justifies the means, and people and ideals are easily sacrificed in the process. "Political" / "politician" were negatively loaded words in Renaissance England, as it was associated with Machiavellian traits. He is an enemy of moral order rather than completely politically subversive. Ornstien[7] theorizes that the Machiavel is a personification of ruthless economic and political opportunism. Good examples of stage Machiavels would be *The Spanish Tragedy*'s Lorenzo, *The Revenger's Tragedy*'s Vindice, *Hamlet*'s Claudius, late in the play Hamlet himself, and *The Maid's Tragedy*'s King.

Machine—Equals an elaborate and admirable structure composed of many individual parts. The Elizabethans saw nature as a complicated "machine." It came also to refer to the human body, an intricate machine indeed, which is made truly alive by the presence of the soul.

Male friendship—This is the ideal relationship between two people. Men were seen as endowed with reason to a higher degree than emotion-driven women, and a close relationship between a man and a woman would include a sexual, passionate, and therefore less than reasonable element. Male friendship is ideally so close, all-inclusive, and perfect that the two friends seem to be seamlessly one; such a friendship is valued higher than family or a love-interest. Much Renaissance literature portrays male friendship; both Sidney and Spenser[8] praise it in their writings. But drama often complicates and jeopardizes such friendships when they are complicated by love of a woman. Sir Thomas Elyot describes such a relationship well in *The Book named The Governor:*

[7] See Ornstein, *The Moral Vision of Jacobean Tragedy*, p. 24 ff.
[8] See especially Book Four of *The Faerie Queene.*

> [Of a]ll things that cometh from God, nothing is of
> more great estimation than love, called in Latin *amor*,
> whereof *amicitia* cometh, named in English friend-
> ship or amity; the which taken away from the life of
> man, no house shall abide standing, no field shall be
> in culture ... But now resort to speak of them in whom
> friendship is most frequent, and they also thereto be
> most aptly disposed. Undoubtedly it be specially they
> which be wise and of nature inclined to beneficence,
> liberality, and constance... Now, let us try out what is
> that friendship that we suppose to be in good men.
> Verily it is a blessed and stable connection of sundry
> wills, making of two persons one in having and suf-
> fering. And therefore a friend is properly named of
> philosophers the other I. For that in them is but one
> mind and one possession and that which more is, a
> man more rejoiceth at his friend's good fortune than
> at his own.
>
> (Book II, Ch. XI, 133-134)

Hamlet celebrates Hamlet and Horatio's friendship; the relationship between the brothers Hippolito and Vindice in *The
Revenger's Tragedy* share the same characteristics; *The Maid's Tragedy*
illustrates male friendship beautifully in the relationship between Melantius and Amintor. Only in *The Spanish Tragedy*,
fraught with irony as so many other aspects, do we see the
dark side of male friendship. Lorenzo uses Balthazar's friendship to reach his own goals.

Marriage—In our western culture, marriage ought, supposedly, to
be based on mutual attraction or love — if not it seems
"wrong," even "immoral," especially if money or estate is the
grounds; on the assumption that no marriage is happy unless
it is based on love and mutual attraction; on the right of the

individual to choose a marriage partner freely, even overriding family interest. This was not so in Renaissance England. Among people of property, marriage was a family-based decision, but people lower on the social scale tended to emulate their "betters" when able. The upper class married young, and their marriages were often arranged long before the wedding; the state of the estate was more important than the feelings of the couple. Generally, the more money and land at stake, the less say the couple would have in the arrangement. *The Book of Common Prayer* lists the reasons for marriage as follows: For propagation; for mutual aid and comfort; to avoid the sin of fornication. Love and sexual passion are low on the list of grounds for marriage. Of course such feelings existed, and those are the ones examined in most tragedies, where the outcome is never happy.

Masque, or The Court Masque—This is not truly a dramatic art form, though some acting is involved, as there is no true plot development. A masque was created for aristocratic entertainment, usually for a specific social, private occasion such as a wedding. Masques generally have three parts, made up of three dances and three songs. Performers would include some professional singers, dancers, and musicians, but also men and women, sometimes children, of the court. We must remember that on the public stage all Renaissance performers were male; only in the court masque did women perform. Costumes were as lavish and expensive as possible; often they were symbolic, such as Night, Cynthia, and others in the wedding masque in *The Maid's Tragedy*. The stage machinery was elaborate, scene changes frequent, and setting richly and lavishly presented. Each masque unites the talent of a set designer and a poet, who cooperate on a theme befitting the occasion for the masque. King James' court especially was notorious for its lavish masques, which never omitted praise of the monarch himself, and Queen Anne and her ladies were frequent actresses in masques. The most extravagantly expensive masques were created by the playwright Ben Jonson (script) and the architect Inigo Jones (scenery and machinery).

Melancholia (see also "four temperaments)—The melancholic's symptoms include bad dreams and troubled sleep as well as a persistent feeling of imprisonment. Gluttony, laziness, and sentimentality could also be present. It is interesting to look at Hamlet in this light.

Memento mori—Usually, as in *Hamlet* and *The Revenger's Tragedy*, a skull, but also e. g. the representation of a skeleton; this is an emblem teaching us that whatever our social status or position, we will all be reduced to bare bones in the end. This is, among other things, a warning against pride, the deadliest of the seven deadly sins.

Miracle Play—Also known as Mystery Plays, these are the first examples of "public performances" seen in England. They are stage representations of Biblical scenes or scenes from saints' lives, many of them found in cycles performed in connection with a church festival where people would congregate. Despite the serious, religious subject matter, much comedy is interspersed.

Morality Plays—These plays developed alongside the Miracle Plays, but here we find allegorical characters or personified abstractions such as vices and virtues. The main purpose is not to teach religious matter but to teach moral values. *Everyman*, for example, could be seen as a "how-to" manual on how to save one's almost-lost soul for heaven, and *Respublica*, performed during the reign of Bloody Mary, attacks those who have gotten rich from church property during Henry VIII's reformation. The plots are simple, the meaning and message clear, and humor is often an element as a teaching tool.

Morris Dance—This is "dance drama," a performance without a text. It includes several grotesque characters such as the hobby-horse and the fool (in Shakespeare and Fletcher's *The Two Noble Kinsmen* there is a baboon character), but also characters from the Robin Hood legends such as Friar Tuck and Maid Marian. The dance, rich with variations, often incorporated "death and resurrection" ritual (the fool and the hobby-horse), and was often connected with the May Day celebrations; spring is the season of rebirth.

Natural—The word carries the meaning "of nature," "in the way of nature." "Unnatural" means a breach with the rules of nature, a "natural fool" was born foolish, and a "natural son" did not have the benefit of legitimacy.

Occasion—also known as Opportunity, can be seized. Therefore Occasion is depicted, originally, as a nude, youthful male with a shaven head, apart from the "forelock" which is long and graspable. After the eleventh century, Occasion merged some-what with Fortune (see Fortune). It is now depicted as a nude female with a forelock, balanced on a sphere or a wheel. In this form, Occasion, unlike Fortune in her pure form, allows man some influence, but the fickleness is still present, as is the unpredictable rolling of the sphere or wheel.

Patrimony—An estate inherited from one's father or other ances-tor, but also property held by ancient right or inheritance.

Playhouse, Private or Indoor—These playhouses were smaller than the public theaters (6-700 seats), and admission was more ex-pensive. The stage area was smaller (about 400 square feet), and made even more so by the possibility of expensive seating on the stage itself. Along the walls were tiers of galleries, and the floor space in front of the stage had benches. Lighting was probably achieved from a combination of natural light from windows and artificial light from tallow candles. The possibility to regulate the light and achieve relative darkness made it possible to perform more elaborate and mysterious "tricks" on stage; these theaters had somewhat elaborate stage machinery as well. Indoor theaters catered to a coterie audience, often people who both wanted to see and be seen, and plays written mainly for these stages tend to be more complicated in contents; however, the same plays were often performed at both public and private theaters. Admission went from sixpence for the cheapest seats furthest from the stage to one shilling sixpence in the front row; more had to be paid for a seat on the stage itself.

Playhouse, Public or Outdoor—London was home to several of these theaters during the Renaissance, one of them Shakespeare's Globe. We know something of their construction from a contemporary drawing, but also from archeological excavations, and directions within the plays themselves. The structure itself[9] was either square or polygon so many-sided as to approach a circle, open to the sky, with an elevated stage projection into the arena, surrounded by standing-room for spectators; seating was found in galleries. The stage (about 1200 square feet) was covered by "the heavens," supported by columns. Above was the "balcony" and probably a room for musicians. To the rear of the stage itself were doors for

---

[9] A wonderful book is Mulryne and Shewring's *Shakespeare's Globe Rebuilt*, Cambridge U.P., 1997. See also the Globe website: www.shakespeares-globe.org for the Globe Theatre project, a wonderful tour of the "real" theatre structure and the thoughts of those who recreated it.

entrances and exits, and a curtained "discovery space" where people or objects could be kept until needed for display. In the middle of the stage floor was a trapdoor, the entrance to "hell," a convenient and convincing place to take the damned soul or furnish entrance for ghosts. Props were minimal, and often only consisted of what the actors could conveniently carry themselves, "hand props," which, because relatively scarce, take on great significance. Costumes were lavish, and we have evidence of huge and spectacular wardrobes for the actors. The Globe could house about 3,000 spectators. There is much debate about the composition of the audience, but generally it is accepted that all walks of life would attend plays in public playhouses.[10] Entrance to stand: one penny; for an additional penny a seat could be obtained.

Play-within—A playlet or dumbshow inserted into the play proper; its function is to illuminate the main action or to further it economically.

Pressing (torture)—Also known as *peine forte et dure* (strong and hard pain), this method was used to "press to plead" when the accused refused to plead either guilty or not guilty. The prisoner was laid on the ground, his/her arms and legs fastened so the body formed an "X"; weights were then placed upon his/her body in increasing number until he/she either confessed or died. This torture could be stretched over several days or ended quickly if a kindly executioner placed a sharp stone under the spine to end the suffering quickly. The confession rate reportedly was excellent. This is not a punishment as no case has been established or tried; also it is not torture technically, as torture was prohibited under English law.

[10] For a thorough discussion, see McDonald, *The Bedford Companion to Shakespeare*, pp. 109-144.

Primogeniture—"Exclusive right of inheritance ... under English law, belonging to the eldest son or, failing lineal descendants, the eldest male in the next degree of consanguinity ("of the same blood," ed.), to take all the real estate of which an ancestor died seized ("in possession of," ed.) and intestate to the exclusion of all female and younger male descendants of equal degree" (*Webster's Third International Dictionary*, 1986). An estate was held together, not broken up, following this system, but the arrangement could be disastrous for both the "trapped" older son and for those left without inheritance, should the father not be able to provide for them adequately. Many children died young, and so it was desirable to have more than one son in case the first son died, but often the younger sons had only the clergy, the military, or the sea as an option to subsist, often unmarried. Women had no such options for work. The larger the estate, the smaller the child's option to successfully plead with parents to let the heart rule.

Prince—A term used for "ruler," whatever his more precise title may be.

Privy Council, The—This body originated as the *curia regis*, a body made up of any prominent persons the king chose. It was the British king's private group of advisors, functioning splendidly as long as the king was able to choose his advisors well. Its charge was performing all the functions of government, which rendered the group extremely powerful.

Progress—A journey of state, be it the monarch's travels through the realm, accompanied by great display of power and wealth as Elizabeth I was a master performer of; a church dignitary's visitation; or a judge on circuit. All instances had elements of theatricality and display in the Renaissance.

Puritan—The word has many connotations in Renaissance England. A Puritan is a Protestant, but towards the end of Elizabeth I's reign it came to stand for those Church of England members who strove to purify the English church of any residue of Roman practices such as elaborate vestments and music, kneeling, and the like. Puritans became increasingly opposed to plays and actors because of the cross-dressing (no female actors on stage; Puritans were also vehemently vocal in their anti-homosexual stance), rich and colorful costumes (Puritans were highly critical of fashionable clothing and the changes brought about by fashion), and the general immorality they saw in plays. On stage, a "Puritan" often came to mean a too-strict, straightlaced, comical character such as Malvolio in Shakespeare's *Twelfth Night*. The word is also a synonym for "hypocrisy."

Quarto—Renaissance printing started with a "sheet" of handmade paper some eighteen by fourteen inches in size. Folded once to make four pages, the size became "folio;" folded twice to make four leaves/ eight pages, the size became "quarto." The entire sheet was printed at once, then folded, cut, and bound. A quarto would sell for about sixpence.

Quintessence—The fifth essence or element, the other four being earth, air, fire, and water, was thought to be superior to the four but could be extracted from them. It could be found in the heavenly bodies as well as the purest extract of things earthly.

Royal We—The King or ruler often refers to himself in the first person plural (we, our) when he speaks as head of his country rather than as his personal self. *Hamlet*'s Claudius is a masterful wielder of the royal we.

Senecan Tragedy—Lucius Annaeus Seneca, who died 65 AD, wrote works of moral philosophy in the Stoic tradition, but also nine tragedies. His revenge tragedies include such ingredients as a high, rhetorical style; restless ghosts; speculations on sin, vice, despair, and violent death; graphic violence; and lengthy set speeches reminiscent of narrative poetry. His style was popular in the early Renaissance, and can be clearly seen in a more workable, stageable dramatic form in Kyd's *The Spanish Tragedy*, and is further developed in the three other plays in this collection. *Thyestes* is Seneca's most famous revenge tragedy.

Service, to serve—A lover would often term himself his lady's "servant," a word which could also imply a sexual relationship.

Sirrah—A form of address, like sir, but used to an underling.

Spleen, the—The organ associated with black bile and melancholy, it is the origin of impulsive behavior such as passionate anger, but it is also often seen as the seat of mirth.

Sport—Besides referring to idle time that could be filled by "playing sport," "pastime," the word is often a pun on "amorous dalliance" and is frequently used with a heavy sexual charge.

Stichomythia—line-by-line dialogue, making a rapid exchange, often ironic or of opposing viewpoint possible. An example is *The Spanish Tragedy* I.iii.77 ff., where stichomythia serves to characterize Bel-imperia. This dramatic convention originated with Seneca.

Sumptuary Law—a law regulating expenditure, especially with view to restraining excess in food, dress, equipage, etc. (OED).

Sun/Son—The sun is an emblem for the King, as only one can be found. Also, the King as father of his country, is responsible for its health and well-being, much as the sun sustains life on earth. Especially in *Hamlet* I.ii, being "too much in the sun/son" has significance. Hamlet is too much in the King's presence for comfort, and treated too much like a son in the sunshine of the King's favor for comfort.

Sword—The sword is the traditional emblem of justice. As the hilt is cruciform, a sword is an excellent "cross" on which to swear.

Tender (sb., vb., adj.)—Much punning is possible on this word. 1) To offer in connection with feelings (to tender sympathy; to tender love); 2) Money tendered in payment (in the same sense as the fact that money is legal tender (sb.)); 3) to feel tender towards somebody ("my tender (adj.) love"); 4) to put (commercial) value upon something. Polonius' "Tender yourself more dearly/Or . . . /You'll tender me a fool" (I.iii.107-109) makes use of all four meanings, managing at the same time to commercialize Ophelia's feelings as well as Ophelia herself.

Traitor's Punishment, the—High treason was considered the most heinous of crimes, directed as it was against the King or Queen, God's representative on earth. The Traitor's Punishment, also known as hanging, drawing, and quartering, was, in the hands of a skilled executioner, a most hideous way to die. Executions were public spectacle, and the aim of this excessive suffering was to impress upon the eager group of spectators what not to do, presumably an effective crime deterrent. Having been pulled to the place of execution tied to a hurdle, the victim was first hanged by the neck, almost to the point of suffocation. Then he was taken down, placed on a table, and revived, so he could fully appreciate the pain of having his abdomen slit open and his entrails pulled out and burned on an adjacent fire. Preferably at this point the victim would still be alive as his still beating heart was removed. After death the head was removed and the body divided into quarters and parboiled to last longer. The segments were then displayed at various points throughout the Kingdom as a warning against treason. An added horror was the belief that the soul would be unable to find the body it needed for eternal afterlife if the earthly body were dismembered.

> The traitor stands at an uncertain threshold of Renaissance society, athwart a line that sets off the human from the demonic, the natural from the unnatural, and the rational from the enigmatic and obscure realm of unreason.
>
> (Mullaney, *The Place of the Stage*, 116)

Vice, the—This character has his roots in the Morality Plays, which presented specific human vices on stage. Gradually, all vices were combined into one stock character, "The Vice," a rogue and troublemaker, very often taking on the job of a director who shares the delights of the plot to come with the audience. He is not the Devil incarnate, though they are on the same side. The Vice is always a comic character, a "clown," whose popularity as a type resounds throughout secular Renaissance drama. One example is the Gravedigging Clown in *Hamlet*.

Will—This word is a source of much punning. The most elaborate use can be found in Shakespeare's Sonnet 135, where "will" means: 1) conscious volition; 2) wishes; 3) sexual desire; 4) (last will and) testament; 5) male and female sexual organs; 6) William abbreviated to "Will."

Bibliography

Entries marked with • are particularly recommended for further study.

Allman, Eileen. *Jacobean Revenge Tragedy and the Politics of Virtue.* Newark: University of Delaware Press, 1999.

Aubrey, John. *Brief Lives*, ed. Andrew Clark. Oxford, 1898.

Babb, Lawrence. "The Physiological Concept of Love in the Elizabethan and Early Stewart Drama." *PMLA, LVI,* 1941.

Barroll, Leeds. *Politics, Plague, and Shakespeare's Theater: The Stuart Years.* Ithaca and London: Cornell U. P., 1991.

Boas, ed. *Works of Thomas Kyd.* Oxford, 1901.

Bonnefoy, Yves. *Greek and Egyptian Mythologies.* University of Chicago Press, 1991, 1992.

—. *Roman and European Mythologies.* University of Chicago Press, 1991, 1992.

Buckness, Peter. *Entertainment and Ritual, 600-1600.* London: Stainer and Bell, 1979.

Castiglione, Baldesar. *The Book of the Courtier.* New York: Norton Critical Edition, 2002.

Chambers, E.K., *The Elizabethan Stage.* Vol. 1-4. Oxford: Clarendon Press, 1923.

Cotterel, Arthur and Rachel Storm. *The Ultimate Encyclopedia of Mythology.* Hermes House, 1999.

• Dover Wilson, J. *What Happens in Hamlet?* Cambridge University Press, 1935.

—. *Life in Shakespeare's England: A Book of Elizabethan Prose.* Cambridge University Press, 1926.

Elizabethan and Stuart Plays, ed. Charles Read Baskerville. New York: Henry Holt and Co., 1934.

Elliott, G. R. *Scourge and Minister: A Study of Hamlet as Tragedy of Revengefulness and Justice.* Durham, N. C.: Duke University Press, 1951.

Elyott, Sir Thomas. *The Book named The Governor*, ed. S. E. Lehmberg. London: Everyman's Library, 1962.

Fenton, Doris. *The Extra-Dramatic Moment in Elizabethan Plays Before 1616*. 1930. Folcroft, Pennsylvania: Folcroft Press, 1970.

Freeman, Arthur. *Thomas Kyd: Facts and Problems*. Oxford, 1967.

• Greenblatt, Stephen. *Hamlet in Purgatory*. Princeton University Press, 2001.

Gurr, Andrew. *Playgoing in Shakespeare's London*, 2nd ed. Cambridge, Cambridge U.P., 1987, 1996.

—. *The Shakespearean Stage 1574-1642*. Cambridge, Cambridge U.P., 1992.

• Gurr, Andrew and Mariko Ichikawa. *Staging in Shakespeare's Theatres*. Oxford: Oxford U. P., 2000.

Harbage, Alfred (revised by S. Schoenbaum). *Annals of English Drama 975-1700*. London: Methuen & Co., 1964.

Henslowe's Diaries, ed. R. A. Foakes and R. T. Rickert. Cambridge U. P., 1961.

Honan, Park. *Shakespeare: A Life*. Oxford: Oxford U.P., 1998.

• Kerrigan, John. *Revenge Tragedy: Aeschylus to Armageddon*. Oxford: Clarendon Press, 1996.

Kerrigan, Michael. *The Instruments of Torture*. New York: The Lyons Press, 2001.

Lovejoy, Arthur O. *The Great Chain of Being*. Cambridge, Mass: Harvard U.P., 1936, 1964.

Machiavelli, Niccolo. *The Prince*. New York: Norton Critical Edition, 1992.

McAlindon, T. *English Renaissance Tragedy*. Vancouver: The University of British Columbia Press, 1986.

• McDonald, Russ. *The Bedford Companion to Shakespeare: An Introduction with Documents*. Boston: Bedford/St. Martin's, 2001.

Mercer, Peter. *Hamlet and the Acting of Revenge*. Iowa City: Iowa University Press, 1987.

Mullaney, Steven. *The Place of the Stage: License, Play. and Power in Renaissance England*. Ann Arbor: Michigan U.P., 1988.

• Mulryne, J.R., and Margaret Shewring, Eds. *Shakespeare's Globe Rebuilt.* Cambridge University Press, 1997.

Murray, Peter B. *A Study of Cyril Tourneur.* Philadelphia, 1964.

Nagler, A.M. *Shakespeare's Stage.* 1917. New Haven and London: Yale University Press, 1981.

Nicoll, Allardyce. *The Works of Cyril Tourneur.* New York, 1963.

Norton Shakespeare, The, ed. Stephen Greenblatt. New York: W. W. Norton & Co., 1997.

• Ornstein, Robert. *The Moral Vision of Jacobean Tragedy.* Madison: University of Wisconsin Press, 1960.

Oxford English Dictionary, The; online.

Panofsky, Erwin. *Studies in Iconology: Humanistic Themes in the Art of the Renaissance.* 1939. New York: Harper & Row, 1972.

Prosser, Eleanor. *Hamlet and Revenge.* 1967. Stanford, California: Stanford University Press, 1971.

Rosenbaum, Ron. "Shakespeare in Rewrite." *The New Yorker*, May 2002.

Salingar, L. G. *"The Revenger's Tragedy* and the Morality Tradition." *Scrutiny* VI (March 1938), 402-22.

Saxo Grammaticus. *Danmarks Krønike.* København, 1911.

Seneca, The Tragedies, Vol. 1 and 2 ed. and trans. David R. Slavitt. Baltimore: The Johns Hopkins University Press, 1992.

Shurgot, Michael W. *Stages of Play: Shakespeare's Theatrical Energies in Elizabethan Performance.* Newark: University of Delaware Press, 1998.

Simpson, Percy. *The Theme of Revenge in Elizabethan Literature.* Annual Shakespeare Lecture, 1935.

—. *Studies in Elizabethan Drama.* Oxford: Clarendon Press,1955.

Stone, Lawrence. *The Crisis of the Aristocracy, 1558-1641.* Oxford: Oxford U.P., 1965.

—. *The Family, Sex, and Marriage in England, 1500-1800.* New York: Harper, 1977.

Styan, J.L. *Drama, Stage, and Audience.* Cambridge University Press, 1975.

— . *Perspectives on Shakespeare in Performance.* New York : Peter Lang Publishing, Inc., 2000.

• — . *Shakespeare's Stagecraft,* Cambridge University Press, 1967.

— . *The English Stage: A History of Drama and Performance.* Cambridge University Press, 1996.

— . *The Shakespeare Revolution.* Cambridge University Press, 1977.

Thomasen, Anne-Liese. Interviews on Medical History with Bente Videbæk 1982-1984.

—. *Kvinders Rosengård.* Nordisk Tidskrift for Bok- och Biblioteksvaesen, Årgang 86, 1981.

Tillyard, E.M.W. *The Elizabethan World Picture.* London: Pelican Books, 1943.

Tomlinson, T.B. *A Study of Elizabethan and Jacobean Tragedy.* Cambridge University Press, 1964.

Videbaek, Bente A. *The Stage Clown in Shakespeare's Theatre.* Westport, Connecticut: Greenwood Presses, 1996.

Weimann, Robert. *Shakespeare and the Popular Tradition in the Theatre: Studies in the Social Dimension of Dramatic Form and Function.* Edited and translated by Robert Schwartz. Baltimore and London: Johns Hopkins University Press, 1978.

• Wickham, Glynne. *A History of the Theatre.* Cambridge: Cambridge University Press, 1985.

— . *The Medieval Theatre.* Cambridge: Cambridge University Press, 1987.

— . *Shakespeare's Dramatic Heritage: Collected Studies in Medieval, Tudor, and Shakespearean Drama.* New York: Barnes and Noble, 1969.

Supporting Texts

Bacon, Francis. *A Selection of His Works.* Ed. Sidney Warhaft. New York: The Odyssey Press, 1965.

Bright, Timothy. *A Treatise of Melancholie* (1586). Amsterdam: Da Capo Press, 1969.

Becon, Thomas. *Prayers and Other Pieces.* Cambridge: Cambridge U.P., 1844.

—— . *The Catechism.* Cambridge: Cambridge U.P., 1844.

de Loque, Bertrand. *Discourses of Warre and Single Combat.* Trans. John Eliot, 1591. London : H. A. Humphrey Ltd., 1968.

Elyott, Sir Thomas. *The Book named The Governor,* ed. S. E. Lehmberg. London: Everyman's Library, 1962.

Rollins, Hyder E, ed. *Old English Ballads 1553-1625 : Chiefly from Manuscripts.* Cambridge: Cambridge U.P., 1920

Sandys, Edwin. *Sermons and Miscellaneous Pieces.* Cambridge: Cambridge U.P., 1844

Segar, Sir William. *The Book of Honor and Armes (1590) and Honor Military and Civil (1602).* New York: Scholars' Facsimiles & Reprints, 1975.

A Few Useful Websites

Unfortunately, only Shakespeare is well represented on the Internet. Below, please find a list of sites that have been useful in my teaching, and to some degree in research. Suggestions for additions, especially websites for the three non-Shakespearean authors in this book will be most welcome, so if you stumble over one, please contact me.

"Mr. William Shakespeare and the Internet,"
    shakespeare.palomar.edu/ for a comprehensive, annotated guide to resources on the Web.

www.rdg.ac.uk/globe for theatre and Shakespeare information.

www.shakespeares-globe.org for the Globe Theatre project, a wonderful tour of a "real" theatre structure and the thoughts of those who recreated it.

www.ulen.com/Shakespeare for student and teacher guides to the plays.

A comprehensive list of web sites can be found in Russ McDonald, *The Bedford Companion to Shakespeare: An introduction with Documents.*